ANDREW J. DUBRIN

COLLEGE OF BUSINESS, ROCHESTER INSTITUTE OF TECHNOLOGY

TERRI GEERINCK

SIR SANDFORD FLEMING COLLEGE

Third Canadian Edition

HUMAN RELATIONS
Interpersonal, Job-Oriented Skills

PEARSON

Prentice
Hall

Toronto

Once again, to Melanie.
—*Andrew J. DuBrin*

This book is dedicated to my family and my friends who keep me smiling.
—*Terri Geerinck*

Library and Archives Canada Cataloguing in Publication

DuBrin, Andrew J.
  Human relations : interpersonal, job-oriented skills / Andrew J. DuBrin, Terri Geerinck. —3rd Canadian ed.

Includes bibliographical references and index.
ISBN 978-0-13-230915-8

  1. Interpersonal relations—Textbooks.   2. Success in business—Textbooks.   3. Personnel management—Textbooks.
4. Interpersonal communication—Textbooks.   5. Self-management (Psychology—Textbooks.   I. Geerinck, Terri, 1958-
II. Title.

HD6955.D823 2009   650.1'3   C2007-905983-X

ISBN-13: 978-0-13-230915-8
ISBN-10:   0-13-230915-7

Vice President, Editorial Director: Gary Bennett
Acquisitions Editor: Chris Helsby
Marketing Manager: Toivo Pajo
Associate Editor: Brian Simons
Production Editor: Amanda Wesson
Copy Editor: Shirley Rennie
Proofreader: Susan McNish
Production Coordinator: Avinash Chandra
Composition: Integra
Art Director: Julia Hall
Cover and Interior Design: Geoff Agnew
Cover Image: Veer Incorporated

1 2 3 4 5   12 11 10 09 08

Printed and bound in the United States of America.

Contents

Preface

Welcome to the third Canadian edition of *Human Relations: Interpersonal, Job-Oriented Skills.* Success in any position involving interaction with people requires two broad sets of competencies: functional skills and generic skills. The term *functional skills* refers to knowledge of one's discipline (or organizational function), technical skills, specialty skills, or simply details of the job. *Generic skills* refers to competencies important in a variety of jobs. Among these generic skills are good work habits and time management, computer skills, high ethical standards, and interpersonal skills.

Our purpose in writing this book is to help readers improve their interpersonal skills in the workplace. By improving interpersonal skills, a person has a better chance of capitalizing upon his or her other skills. Two primary approaches are used in this text to achieve this lofty goal. First, basic concepts are introduced to enhance understanding of key topics in interpersonal relations in organizations. Second, skill-building suggestions, exercises, and cases are designed to improve interpersonal skills related to the topic. Chapter 4, for example, presents general information about the nature of teamwork, followed by suggestions for improving teamwork. The chapter also includes several exercises or experiential activities and two case problems—all designed to improve teamwork skills.

Third, examples and box inserts provide insight into how a particular skill is applied on the job. For example, in Chapter 15, we describe a successful entrepreneur who relies heavily on networking and mentoring to advance his career and help others.

AUDIENCE

The primary audience for this book is people taking courses that emphasize the development of interpersonal skills. Such courses typically include the term *human relations.* Because interpersonal relations contribute so heavily to effective leadership, the text is suited to participants in leadership and supervisory training courses that emphasize interpersonal skills rather than leadership theory and research.

FRAMEWORK

The book is a blend of current and traditional topics dealing with interpersonal relations in organizations, with a heavy component of skill development and self-assessment. The information is organized into chapters, all emphasizing interpersonal relations between two or more people. Chapter 1, "A Framework for Interpersonal Skill Development," sets the stage for improving one's interpersonal skills on the job. Chapter 2, "Understanding Individual Differences," presents information that is the foundation of effective interpersonal relations. Chapter 3, "Interpersonal Communication," deals with skills necessary for sending and receiving messages.

Chapter 4, "Developing Teamwork Skills," sensitizes the reader to a vital set of skills required in the workplace. Chapter 5, "Group Problem-Solving and Decision-Making," provides additional information about skills relevant to collaborative effort. Chapter 6, "Cross-Cultural Relations and Diversity," is about developing cross-cultural skills in a diverse workforce and includes statistics from the latest Canadian census. Chapter 7, "Resolving Conflicts with Others," helps the reader develop skills necessary for finding constructive solutions to differences of opinion and disputes with others.

Four consecutive chapters deal with exerting influence over others: Chapter 8, "Becoming an Effective Leader," presents information relevant to exercising leadership in the workplace; Chapter 9, "Motivating Others," emphasizes skills required in encouraging others to work hard to achieve goals; Chapter 10, "Helping Others Develop and Grow," is about coaching, counselling, and teaching others; and Chapter 11, "Positive Political Skills," describes how to use power and influence for constructive purposes.

Chapter 12, "Customer Satisfaction Skills," describes several approaches to enhancing skills required for satisfying customers—skills that lie at the heart of the quality revolution. Chapter 13, "Enhancing Ethical Behaviour," translates ethical principles into usable skills. The rationale here is that an ethical base is important for achieving career-long effectiveness in interpersonal relations. Chapter 14, "Personal Productivity and Stress Management," supports the development of interpersonal skills by showing that productive people who have stress under control can relate more effectively to others. Chapter 15, "Job Search and Career Management Skills," includes information about the application of interpersonal skills (such as networking) in advancing one's career.

CHANGES IN THE NEW EDITION

The new edition of *Human Relations* adds several new features in response to reviewer suggestions.

- Many new opening case anecdotes

- Boxed inserts, providing an application of a key concept or concepts, appear in most chapters

- A second case has been added to each chapter, and several of the cases from the previous edition have been replaced. More of the cases now have role-plays linked to them.

- New *Job-Oriented Interpersonal Skills in Action* boxes highlight real company situations pertinent to each chapter's coverage.

- New information, research findings, and examples appear throughout the text. Several new self-quizzes and skill-development exercises have also been added. Material that may have lost some of its relevance has been selectively pruned.

The new topics in the text are as follows:

- Chart on sources of learning on the job (Chapter 1)
- Optimism–pessimism as a key personality trait (Chapter 2)
- Complete overhaul of presentation of Myers-Briggs cognitive styles (Chapter 2)
- The relationship-building aspects of interpersonal communication (Chapter 3)
- Crews as a type of work group (Chapter 4)
- New presentation of group roles, using the role theory of Belbin (Chapter 4)
- New scavenger hunt exercise for team building (Chapter 4)
- Organizational citizenship behaviour as a team player skill (Chapter 4)
- More information about the nominal group technique (Chapter 5)
- More information about stand-up meetings including their application at the Jet Propulsion Laboratory (Chapter 5)
- *Cultural intelligence,* a new concept about fitting in with people from other cultures (Chapter 6)
- *Cultural intelligence training,* a program based on the principles of cultural intelligence (Chapter 6)
- Role-play about cross-cultural relations based on a call centre in India (Chapter 6)
- More information about dealing with bullies in the workplace and the extent of workplace bullying in Canada (Chapter 7)
- Incivility and rudeness as a source of interpersonal conflict (Chapter 7)
- More coverage about morality in leadership (Chapter 8)
- Instructions for developing a personal leadership journal (Chapter 8)
- The influence of moods on motivation (Chapter 9)
- Information about taking into account the trainee's learning style during training (Chapter 10)
- Brief explanation of the problems created by high-maintenance employees (Chapter 10)
- Role-playing exercise for dealing with a difficult person (Chapter 10)
- Boxed information about dealing with bossophobia (Chapter 11)
- Minimizing microinequities (small, unintentional slights) in dealing with other people (Chapter 11)
- How emotional support from co-workers can lead to better customer service (Chapter 12)
- Use of customer relationship management (CRM) software to improve customer service (Chapter 12)
- How hostility by customer contact workers creates problems in customer service (Chapter 12)

- Results of a survey on the extent of employee lying (Chapter 13)

- Addition to skill-building exercise about ethics (stretching the truth on a résumé) (Chapter 13)

- Sampling of ethical guidelines and regulations for several Canadian professions and companies (Chapter 13)

- Role-play about confronting an ethically-deviant manager (Chapter 13)

- Importance of a healthy diet for stress management, including reference to the new Canada's Guide to Healthy Eating (Chapter 14)

- Updated statistics on work-life stress for Canadians (Chapter 14)

- Research on the importance of building relationships to ward off stress (Chapter 14)

- Description of the freeze-frame technique for dealing with stress (Chapter 14)

- Use of time log to help manage time wasters (Chapter 14)

- Quiz on perfectionism as it relates to time wasting (Chapter 14)

- New suggestions for cover letters in terms of comparing requirements to qualifications (Chapter 15)

- Exercise on goal setting and developing action plans for career (Chapter 15)

- Exercise on understanding what constitutes a professional image (Chapter 15)

- Importance of establishing relationships as part of job to help avoid being outsourced (Chapter 15)

- Role-playing exercise about helping a job seeker prepare his résumé (Chapter 15)

This third Canadian edition features an increased presence of Canadian examples, research, and statistics. As well, whenever possible, Canadian businesses and organizations, or those with Canadian locations, were used to provide better examples of practices in Canada. Many companies are international with global locations, so not all were replaced. This edition also features more notable Canadians, and almost half of the Canadian Scene boxed features have been updated or replaced.

SUPPLEMENTAL MATERIALS

INSTRUCTOR'S MANUAL

The Instructor's Manual for this edition contains chapter outlines, lecture notes, answers to discussion questions and case problems, and comments about the exercises in each chapter of the text.

TEST ITEM FILE

The Test Item File for this edition contains 25 multiple-choice and 25 true/false test questions for every chapter in the text.

POWERPOINT PRESENTATIONS

A set of PowerPoint slides offers additional lecture aids for each chapter in the text.

ACKNOWLEDGMENTS

My appreciation goes to the many people who contributed to the development and production of this book. Appreciation is also expressed to the outside reviewers who made suggestions for shaping this and previous editions of the text: H. Frederick Holmes, Ogeechee Technical Institute; Judy Bowie, DeVry Institute of Technology; Gary W. Piggrem, Ph.D., DeVry Institute of Technology; James E. Wetz, Central Florida Community College; Ruth V. Kellar, Ivy Tech State College; Lou Jean Peace, Valdosta Technical Institute; Patricia Lynn Anderson, Valdosta State University; and John Adamski II, Ivy Tech State College.

My family members give me an additional reason for writing, so I extend my appreciation to Drew, Douglas, Melanie, Gizella, Rosie, Clare, and Camila.

Andrew J. DuBrin
Rochester, New York

My sincere appreciation goes to the many people who contributed to the development and production of this book. My primary thanks are extended to the editorial and production team at Pearson Education Canada, including Chris Helsby, Acquisitions Editor, Toivo Pajo, Marketing Manager, Brian Simons, Associate Editor, Amanda Wesson, Production Editor, and Geoff Agnew and Julia Hall, designers.

I would also like to thank my co-workers and friends for their support and encouragement. And last, but never least, thanks to my wonderful family, who tolerate my writing binges and continue to be my best inspiration.

Terri Geerinck
Peterborough, Ontario

Chapter 1

A Framework for Interpersonal Skill Development

Learning Outcomes

After reading and studying this chapter and doing the exercises, you should be able to

- Explain how interpersonal skills are learned.
- Explain the model for interpersonal skill improvement.
- Pinpoint your needs for improvement in interpersonal relations.
- Describe potential opportunities for developing interpersonal skills on the job.

Dominique was one of several receptionists at a large hotel located not far from the airport in Vancouver BC. Two of the hotel executives were discussing which receptionist should be promoted to assistant hotel manager, a vacancy created because the present assistant manager was being promoted to manager of one of the company's suburban hotels.

One manager said to the other, "I think that Dominique is the strongest candidate for the assistant manager position. She has a little less experience than the other three receptionists, but I think she would make a wonderful assistant manager."

The other manager replied, "But take Todd, for example; he has a much better knowledge of hotel operations and our computer system than Dominique does. So maybe Todd should get the promotion this time." The first manager pointed out that Dominique's superior skills with people make her the best candidate for the assistant manager position. "I think that in time Dominique can learn more about our operations, including the new computer system. We can't forget that hotels are a people business, and Dominique gets along great with people. I've seen her resolve tough problems with both guests and other members of the hotel staff. And what a warm smile she has."

After thinking for a few moments, the second manager said, "You've got a good point. Let's offer the promotion to Dominique, with Todd as a strong second choice. We'll also coach Todd on his people skills so he can be promoted in the future. At that time we would offer him the promotion, assuming he were interested."

1

Scenes like this one are common in the workplace. Many people are promoted to a supervisory position because they have good human relations skills combined with adequate technical skills. As the Dale Carnegie organization states, "To achieve success in today's work world—with its emphasis on collaboration, teamwork, motivation, and leadership—you need to perfect your interpersonal skills."[1]

Effective **interpersonal relations** must be combined with technical knowledge and good work habits to achieve success in any job involving interaction with people. Workers at all levels are expected not only to solve problems and improve processes (how work is performed), but also to interact effectively with other employees.[2] Furthermore, the lack of good interpersonal skills can adversely affect a person's career. A study found that 90 percent of firings result from poor attitudes, inappropriate behaviour, and problems in interpersonal relationships.[3]

This chapter explains how people develop interpersonal skills and how the workplace can be a natural setting for that development. This chapter also presents a model that can serve as a foundation for improving your interpersonal skills.

PLAN OF THE BOOK

This entire book is devoted to the many different ways of improving interpersonal relations in organizations. A three-part strategy is presented for achieving the high level of effectiveness in interpersonal relations required in today's workplace. First, each chapter presents key concepts required for understanding a particular aspect of interpersonal relations, such as resolving conflict. Second, the chapter provides specific suggestions or behavioural guidelines for improvement in that aspect of interpersonal relations. Third, a variety of exercises gives you the opportunity to work on and improve your skills. Among these exercises are self-assessment quizzes, skill-building exercises, and cases for analysis. In addition, the questions at the end of each chapter give you an opportunity to think through and apply that chapter's key ideas. Weblinks are provided at the end of each chapter to enable you to explore areas of interest in more depth.

Much of this book is concerned with **interpersonal skills training**, the teaching of skills in dealing with others, so those skills can be put into practice. Interpersonal skills training is referred to as *soft-skill* training to differentiate it from technical training. (Technical skills are referred to as *hard skills*.) Soft-skill training builds interpersonal skills, including communication, listening, group problem-solving, cross-cultural relations, and customer service. Several specific competencies related to soft skills are as follows:

- Effectively translating and conveying information

- Being able to accurately interpret other people's emotions

- Being sensitive to other people's feelings

- Calmly arriving at resolutions to conflicts

- Avoiding negative gossip

- Being polite[4]

Soft-skill training is more important than ever as organizations realize that a combination of human effort and technology is needed to produce results. For example, assume that a company establishes an elaborate intranet system to enable employees to exchange work-related information with each other. The system will not achieve its potential unless employees are motivated to use it properly and develop a spirit of cooperation. The employees must also be willing to share some of their best ideas with each other. Recent findings from the Conference Board of Canada illustrate the increased need for soft skills. (See the Canadian Scene box for a summary of these findings.)

The Canadian Scene

SKILLS FOR A GLOBAL ECONOMY

What soft skills will Canadians need to work in a global economy? In other words, what skills, abilities, and knowledge will employers be seeking as they hire new workers over the next several years? A document developed by the Corporate Council of Education, a program of the National Business and Education Centre of The Conference Board of Canada, outlines the foundation skills for employability. The Corporate Council includes representation from numerous Canadian companies, including Air Canada, Bell Canada, General Motors of Canada Limited, IBM Canada, Nortel, Shell Canada Limited, and Xerox Canada Limited, to name a few. A summary of these skills follows in Exhibit 1. Note the emphasis on interpersonal skills and the ability to communicate effectively.

Exhibit 1

EMPLOYABILITY SKILLS PROFILE: CRITICAL SKILLS REQUIRED FOR THE CANADIAN WORKPLACE

Academic Skills	Personal Management Skills	Teamwork Skills
Those skills that provide the basic foundation to get, keep, and progress on a job and to achieve the best results	The combination of skills, attitudes, and behaviours required to get, keep, and progress on a job and to achieve the best results	Those skills needed to work with others on a job and to achieve the best results
Canadian employers need a person who can	Canadian employers need a person who can demonstrate	Canadian employers need a person who can
Communicate • Understand and speak the languages in which business is conducted • Listen to understand, and learn • Read, comprehend, and use written materials including graphs, charts, and displays • Write effectively in the languages in which business is conducted	**Positive Attitudes and Behaviours** • Self-esteem and confidence • Honesty, integrity, and personal ethics • A positive attitude toward learning, growth, and personal health • Initiative, energy, and persistence to get the job done	**Work with Others** • Understand and contribute to the organization's goals • Understand and work within the culture of the group • Plan and make decisions with others and support the outcomes

(Continued)

Think
- Think critically and act logically to evaluate situations, solve problems, and make decisions
- Understand and solve problems involving mathematics and use the results
- Use technology, instruments, tools, and information systems effectively
- Access and apply specialized knowledge from various fields (e.g., skilled trades, technology, physical sciences, arts, and social services)

Learn
- Continue to learn for life

Responsibility
- The ability to set goals and priorities in work and personal life
- The ability to plan and manage time, money, and other resources to achieve goals
- Accountability for actions taken

Adaptability
- A positive attitude toward change
- Recognition of and respect for people's diversity and individual differences
- The ability to identify and suggest new ideas to get the job done creatively

- Respect the thoughts and opinions of others in the group
- Exercise "give and take" to achieve group results
- Seek a team approach as appropriate
- Lead when appropriate, mobilizing the group for high performance

Source: **Employability Skills 2000+** Brochure 2000 E/F (Ottawa: The Conference Board of Canada, 2000)

A MODEL FOR IMPROVING INTERPERSONAL SKILLS

Following a basic model of learning as it applies to changing your behaviour causes you to acquire and improve interpersonal skills. Learning is a complex subject, yet its fundamentals follow a five-part sequence, as shown in Figure 1-1. To change your behaviour, and therefore improve, you need a goal and a way to measure your current reality (behaviours or actions) against this goal. You also need a way to assess your reality, and a way to obtain feedback on the impact of your new actions.[5]

Goal or Desired State of Affairs

Changing your behaviour, including improving your interpersonal relations, requires a clear goal or desired state of affairs. Your goal can also be regarded as what you want to accomplish as a result of your effort. A major reason why a goal is important is that having a specific goal improves performance. With a goal in mind, a person will usually not be satisfied until the goal is attained. So he or she keeps plugging away until the goal is attained, thereby increasing both personal satisfaction and performance on the task. Goals are also important because where people perceive that they have not attained their goal, they typically increase their effort or modify their strategy to reach the goal.[6]

As a concrete example, let us take the common problem of a person who nibbles his fingernails during tense situations, such as being called on in a meeting. The nibbler might say, "My hope (a goal) is to be able to sit in a meeting and not bite my nails, even though I know I might be called upon." This man's desired state of affairs (his goal) is to avoid putting his nails in his mouth so that he can appear calm and professional.

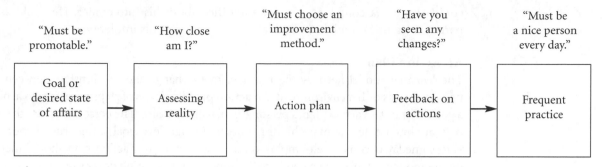

Figure 1-1   A Model for Improving Interpersonal Skills

Having a goal helps provide motivation and makes it possible to exercise the self-discipline necessary to follow through on your plans. In short, the goal focuses your effort on making the behavioural improvements you seek.

Here we turn to Sean, a credit analyst who is being blocked from promotion because his manager perceives him as having poor interpersonal skills. After a discussion with his manager, Sean recognizes that he must improve his interpersonal relations if he wants to become a team leader.

Sean's goal is to be considered promotable to a leadership position. To achieve his goal, he will have to achieve the general goal of improving his interpersonal relations. By conferring with the human resources director, Sean learns that his broad goal of "improving my interpersonal relations" will have to be supported by more specific goals. Having poor interpersonal relations or "rubbing people the wrong way" includes many different behaviours. To begin, Sean selects one counterproductive behaviour to improve: He is exceptionally intolerant of others and does not hide his intolerance. Sean's goal is to become less intolerant and more patient in his dealings with others on the job.

Assessment of Current Reality

The second major requirement for changing behaviour is to assess the current reality. Sean needs a way to estimate how far he is from his goal of being eligible for promotion, and how intolerant he is perceived as being. Sean has already heard from his manager, Alison, that he is not currently eligible for promotion. Sean might want to dig for more information by finding answers to the following questions:

"If I were more tolerant, would I be promoted now?"

"How bad are my interpersonal relations in the office?"

"How many people in the office think I rub them the wrong way?"

"How many deficiencies do my manager and co-workers perceive me to have?"

One starting point in answering these questions might be for Sean to confer with Alison about his behaviour. To be more thorough, however, Sean might ask a friend in the office to help him answer the questions. Sometimes a co-worker is in an excellent position to provide feedback on how one is perceived by others in the office. Sean could also ask a confidante outside the office about his intolerance. He could ask a parent, a significant other, or both about the extent of his intolerance.

An Action Plan

The learning model needs some mechanism to change the relationship between the person and his or her environment. An **action plan** is a series of steps necessary to achieve a goal. Without an action plan, a personal goal will be elusive. The person who sets the goal may not initiate steps to make his or her dream (a high-level goal) come true. If your goal is to someday become a self-employed business owner, your action plan should include saving money, establishing a good credit rating, and developing dozens of contacts.

Sean has to take action to improve his interpersonal relations, especially his intolerance. The changes should ultimately lead to the promotion he desires. Sean's action plan for becoming more tolerant includes the following:

- Pausing to attempt to understand why a person is acting the way he or she is. An example would be trying to understand why a sales representative wants to extend credit to a customer with a poor credit rating.

- Learning to control his own behaviour so he does not make intolerant statements simply because he is experiencing pressure.

- Taking a course in interpersonal or human relations.

- Asking Alison to give him a quick reminder whenever she directly observes or hears of him being intolerant toward customers or workmates.

In addition to formulating these action plans, Sean must have the self-discipline to implement them. For example, he should keep a log of situations in which he was intolerant and those in which he was tolerant. He might also make a mental note to attempt to be cooperative and flexible in most of his dealings at work. When a customer does not provide all the information he needs to assess his or her creditworthiness, Sean should remind himself to say, "I want to process your credit application as quickly as possible. To do this, I need some important additional information." Sean's habitual reflex in the same situation had been to snap: "I can't read your mind. If you want to do business with us, you've got to stop hiding the truth."

Feedback on Actions

The fourth step in the learning model is to measure the effects of one's actions against reality—you obtain feedback on the consequences of your actions. When your skill-improvement goal is complex, such as becoming more effective at resolving conflict, you will usually need to measure your progress in several different ways. You will also need both short- and long-term measures of the effectiveness of your actions. Long-term measures are important because skill-development activities of major consequence have long-range implications.

To obtain short-range feedback, Sean can consult with Alison to see whether she has observed any changes in his tolerance levels. Alison can also collect any feedback she hears from others in the office. Sean will also profit from feedback over a prolonged period of time, perhaps one or two years. He will be looking to see if he has become more tolerant by being polite in his interactions instead of snapping at others or being impatient.

Frequent Practice

The final step in the learning model makes true skill development possible. Implementing the new behaviour and using feedback for fine-tuning is an excellent start in acquiring a new interpersonal skill. For the skill to be long-lasting, however, it must be integrated into your usual way of conducting yourself. In Sean's case, he will have to practise being tolerant regularly until it becomes habitual.

Once a skill has been programmed into your repertoire, it becomes a habit. This is important because a skill involves many habits. For example, good customer service skills include the habits of smiling and listening carefully. After you attempt the new interpersonal skills described in this book, you will need to practise them frequently to make a noticeable difference in your behaviour.

A sports analogy is appropriate here. Assume that Marty, a tennis player, takes a lesson to learn how to hit the ball with greater force. The instructor points out that the reason Marty is not hitting with much force is that he is relying on his arm too much and not enough on his leg and body strength. To hit the ball with more force, Marty is told that he must put one foot out in front of him when he strikes the ball.

Under the watchful eye of the coach, Marty does indeed put a foot out in front of him when he strikes the ball. Marty is excited about the good results. But if Marty fails to make the same manoeuvre with his feet during matches, he will persist in hitting weakly. If Marty makes the effort to make better use of his legs on almost every shot, he will soon integrate the new movement into his game.

In summary, a model for learning skills comprises five steps: (1) choosing a goal, (2) assessing the current reality, (3) deciding on an action plan, (4) gathering feedback on actions, (5) frequently practising the new behaviour.

IDENTIFICATION OF DEVELOPMENTAL NEEDS

An important concept in skill development is that people are most likely to develop new skills when they feel the need for change. The importance of the perceived need for change is reflected in a variation of an old joke:

Question: How many psychologists does it take to change a light bulb?

Answer: None, if the light bulb wants to change.

As you read this book and do the experiential exercises, you will probably be more highly motivated to follow through with skill development in areas in which you think you need improvement. A specific area in which a person needs to change is referred to as a **developmental need**. For instance, some people are too shy or too abrasive. Some do not give others the encouragement they need.

To improve interpersonal skills, we must first be aware of how we are perceived by other people who interact with us.[7] Developmental needs related to interpersonal skills can be identified in several ways. First, if you are candid with yourself, you can probably point to areas in which change is needed. You might reflect on your experiences and realize that you have repeatedly encountered problems in resolving conflict. A second, related approach is to think of feedback you have received. If you have been consistently asked to improve in a particular area, you could assume that the feedback has merit. If five different people have told you that you are not a good team player, you should probably list "becoming a better team player" as one of your developmental needs.

A third approach to assessing developmental needs is to solicit feedback. Ask the people who know you well to help you identify areas for improvement with respect to interpersonal skills. Present and previous managers are a valuable source of this type of feedback.

A fourth approach to pinpointing developmental needs is closely related to the previous three: feedback from performance appraisals or evaluations. If you have worked for a firm that conducts performance appraisals, you may have already received constructive suggestions that you can revisit now.

For example, one manager advised his assistant: "You need to project more self-confidence when you talk on the telephone. You tend to sound unsure and vague. I have noticed this, and several customers have joked about it." The recipient of this feedback was prompted to participate in assertiveness training, where she learned how to express herself more positively.

Self-Assessment Quiz 1-1 provides you with an opportunity to identify your developmental needs. The same exercise is a first step in improving your interpersonal relations on the job, because identification of a problem is the first—and most important—step toward change. For example, if you cite improving your relations with people from cultures different than your own, you have planted the seeds for change. You are then more likely to seek out people from other cultures in the workplace or at school and cultivate their friendship.

Now that you (and perhaps another person) have identified specific behaviours that may require change, you need to draw up an action plan. Proceed with your action plan even though you have just begun studying this text, but peek ahead to relevant chapters if you wish. For each checked statement, briefly describe a plan of attack for bringing about the change you hope to achieve. Ideas for your action plan can come from information presented anywhere in this text, from outside reading, or from talking to a person experienced in dealing with people. A basic example: if you check "I feel awkward dealing with a customer," you could study materials about customer service or observe an effective model.

Self-Assessment Quiz 1-1

WHAT ARE YOUR DEVELOPMENTAL NEEDS?

This exercise is designed to heighten your awareness of areas in which you could profit from personal improvement. It is not a test and there is no scoring, yet your answers to the checklist may prove helpful to you in mapping out a program to improve your interpersonal relations.

Directions: Below are a number of statements reflecting specific problems in interpersonal relations. Check each statement that is generally true for you. To get a more accurate picture of your developmental needs, consider asking one or two other people who know you well to select the statements they think describe you, and compare their answers with yours.

(Continued)

	Place check in this column
1. I'm too shy.	_____
2. I'm overbearing and obnoxious.	_____
3. I intimidate too many people.	_____
4. I have trouble expressing my feelings.	_____
5. I make negative comments about people too readily.	_____
6. I have a difficult time solving problems when working in a group.	_____
7. I'm a poor team player.	_____
8. Very few people listen to me.	_____
9. My temper is too often out of control.	_____
10. I am a poor listener.	_____
11. When I'm in conflict with another person, I usually lose.	_____
12. I hog too much time in meetings or in class.	_____
13. I'm very poor at office politics.	_____
14. People find me boring.	_____
15. It is difficult for me to criticize others.	_____
16. I'm too serious most of the time.	_____
17. I feel awkward working with a person from a culture quite different from mine.	_____
18. I avoid controversy in dealing with others.	_____
19. It is difficult for me to find things to talk about with others.	_____
20. I don't get my point across well.	_____
21. I feel awkward dealing with a customer.	_____
22. I don't get the point of the importance of ethics in business.	_____
23. My attempts to lead others have failed.	_____
24. I rarely smile when I am with other people.	_____
25. (Fill in your own statement.)	_____

UNIVERSAL NEEDS FOR IMPROVING INTERPERSONAL RELATIONS

We have just described how understanding your unique developmental needs makes improving your interpersonal skills possible. There are also areas for skill improvement in interpersonal relations that are shared by most managerial, professional, technical, and sales personnel. We refer to these common areas as **universal training needs**. Almost any professional person, for example, could profit from improving his or her negotiating and listening skills.

This book provides opportunities for skill development in a number of these common areas. In working through these universal training needs, be aware that many will also fit your specific developmental needs; a given universal training need can be an individual's developmental need at the same time. It is reasonable to expect that you will be more strongly motivated to improve skills that relate closely to your developmental needs.

The following major universal training needs are covered in this text:

1. *Understanding individual differences.* To deal effectively with others in the workplace, it is necessary to recognize that people have different capabilities, needs, and interests.

2. *Interpersonal communication.* Effective communication with people is essential for carrying out more than 50 percent of the work conducted by most professional and managerial staff.

3. *Developing teamwork skills.* The most sweeping change in the organization of work in recent years has been a shift to teams and away from conventional departments. Knowing how to be an effective team player therefore increases your chances for success in the modern organization.

4. *Group problem-solving.* As part of the same movement that emphasizes work teams, organizations now rely heavily on group problem-solving. As a consequence, being an above-average contributor to group problem-solving is a key component of effective interpersonal relations on the job.

5. *Cross-cultural relations.* The modern workplace has greater cultural diversity than ever before. Being able to deal effectively with people from different cultures, from both within and outside Canada, is therefore an important requirement for success.

6. *Resolving conflicts with others.* Conflict in the workplace is almost inevitable as people compete for limited resources. Effective interpersonal relations therefore depend on knowing how to resolve conflict successfully.

7. *Becoming an effective leader.* In today's organizations, a large number of people have the opportunity to practise leadership, even if only through temporary assignments. Improving one's leadership skills is therefore almost a universal requirement.

8. *Motivating others.* Whether you have the title of manager or leader or are working alone, you need to know how to motivate people on whom you depend to get your work accomplished. Given that few people are gifted motivators, most people can profit from skill development in motivation.

9. *Helping others develop.* As power is shared in organizations among managers and individual contributors (non-managers) alike, more people are required to help each other grow and develop. To carry out this role, most of us need skill development in coaching and mentoring.

10. *Positive political skills.* Whether you work in a small firm or a large one, part of having effective interpersonal relations is being able to influence others so your interests are satisfied. Positive political skills help you satisfy your interests without being unethical or devious.

11. *Customer service skills.* The current emphasis on customer satisfaction dictates that every worker should know how to provide good service to customers. Most people can benefit from strengthening their skills in serving both external and

internal customers. (**Internal customers** are the people within your company for whom you perform a service as a part of your job.)

12. *Emphasizing ethical behaviour.* Although in their hearts most workers know right from wrong, we can all sharpen our ability to make ethical decisions. By consistently making highly ethical decisions, people can improve their interpersonal relations.

13. *Personal productivity and stress management.* Even though they are not interpersonal skills themselves, having good work habits and time-management skills contributes to relating well to others. By being efficient and productive and having your stress under control, you are in a better position to relate comfortably to others. Co-workers enjoy relating to a person who does not procrastinate and who is not visibly stressed.

14. *Job search and career-management skills.* Finding an outstanding job for yourself, holding onto it, and moving ahead are not specifically interpersonal skills. However, both finding the right job and managing your career rely heavily on good interpersonal skills. Two basic examples are conducting yourself well in an interview and developing a network of contacts through which you can advance.

DEVELOPING INTERPERSONAL SKILLS ON THE JOB

The primary thrust of this book is to teach interpersonal skills that can be applied to the job. As part of your effort to enhance these skills, you should be aware that learning opportunities exist both inside and outside the workplace. This dual environment for learning soft skills mirrors the way hard skills are learned. For example, studying a text and doing laboratory exercises for an information technology (IT) course will help you learn useful information technology skills. On the job one day you might be asked to insert a digital photograph on a website. Never having performed this task before, you search a computer manual, ask questions of co-workers, telephone a help desk, and use trial and error. Within an hour you have acquired a valuable new skill. The information technology skills you learned in the course facilitated learning new computer tasks. Yet the actual learning of how to insert the photograph was done on the job.

We now look at two related aspects of learning interpersonal skills on the job—informal learning and specific developmental experiences.

INFORMAL LEARNING

Business firms, as well as nonprofit organizations, invest an enormous amount of money and time in teaching interpersonal skills. Teaching methods include sending employees to courses, conducting training on company premises, video-conferencing, courses on CD or DVD, computer-assisted learning programs, or reimbursing employees for taking courses over the internet. Workers also develop interpersonal skills by interacting with work associates and observing how others confront interpersonal challenges. Figure 1-2 presents a summary of how people learn on the job. Observe that the

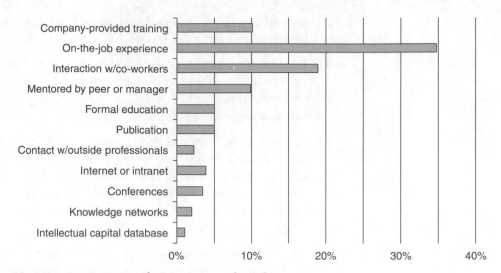

Figure 1-2   Sources of Learning on the Job

Source: Reprinted with permission. Capital Works, LLC, *http://agelesslearner.com/intros/informal.html.*

learning experiences are a mixture of formal learning, such as company-provided training, and informal learning, such as interaction with co-workers. Much of the learning shown in Figure 1-2 refers to technical skills and knowledge, but learning about interpersonal skills is also included.

Informal learning is the acquisition of knowledge and skills that takes place naturally outside a structured learning environment. In the context of the workplace, informal learning occurs without direct supervision by the organization. A study of more than 1000 employees at seven companies found that up to 70 percent of learning takes place informally. Another researcher reported about the same figure more recently.[8] The director of the first study emphasizes that formal training includes both a goal stated by the organization and a defined method or process. Informal learning can take place whether or not a goal is stated or the method defined.

Employees can learn interpersonal skills informally through such means as observing a co-worker, manager, or team leader deal with a situation. A newly hired assistant store manager could not help seeing and overhearing a customer screaming at the store manager about a defective space heater. The manager said calmly, "I can see you are pretty upset that your heater caused a short-circuit in your house. What can I do to help you?" The customer's anger was released like air from a balloon. The assistant store manager thought to herself, "Now I know how to handle a customer who has gone ballistic. I'll state what the customer is probably feeling and then offer to help."

Informal learning can also occur when another person shows you how to handle a situation. The store manager might have said to the new assistant manager, "Let me tell you what to do when you encounter customers who lose their temper. Summarize in a few words what they are probably feeling and then offer to help. The effect can be remarkable." (This incident is classified as informal learning because it takes place outside a classroom.)

Formal and informal learning of interpersonal skills supplement each other naturally. If you are formally studying interpersonal skills, your level of awareness about them will increase. You are therefore more likely to pick up new ideas about dealing effectively with people at work. You may have noticed that if you are taking lessons in a sport, you become much more observant of the techniques of outstanding athletes you watch in person or on television.

SPECIFIC DEVELOPMENTAL EXPERIENCES

Another perspective on developing interpersonal skills in the workplace is that certain experiences are particularly suited to such development. Coping with a difficult customer, as suggested above, would be one such experience. Morgan W. McCall Jr., an industrial psychologist, has for many years studied ways in which leaders develop on the job. Contending with certain challenges is at the heart of these key learning experiences. Several of the powerful learning experiences McCall has identified are particularly geared to developing better interpersonal skills:[9]

- *Unfamiliar responsibilities.* The person has to handle responsibilities that are new, very different, or much broader than previous ones. Dealing with these unfamiliar responsibilities necessitates asking others for help and gaining their cooperation. For example, being assigned to supervise a group doing work unfamiliar to you would put you in the position of needing to gain the cooperation of group members who know more about the work than you do.

- *Proving yourself.* If you feel added pressure to show others that you can deal effectively with responsibilities, you are likely to develop skills in projecting self-confidence and persuading others.

- *Problems with employees.* If you supervise employees or have co-workers who lack adequate experience, competence, or motivation, you need to practise such skills as effective listening and conflict resolution to be able to work smoothly with them.

- *Influencing without authority.* An excellent opportunity for practising influence skills is being forced to influence co-workers, higher management, company outsiders, and other key people over whom you have no control. Team leaders typically face the challenge of needing to influence workers whom they lack the authority to discipline or grant raises to. (A team leader usually does not have as much formal authority as a traditional manager.)

- *Difficult manager.* If you and your manager have different opinions on how to approach problems, or if your manager has serious shortcomings, you will need to use your best human relations skills to survive. You will need to develop such subtle skills as using diplomacy to explain to your manager that his or her suggestion is completely unworkable.

The general point to be derived from these scenarios is that certain on-the-job challenges require a high level of interpersonal skills. Faced with such challenges, you will be prompted to use the best interpersonal skills you have. Formal training can be a big help at these times because you might remember a skill that could be effective. Assume, for instance, that you are faced with an overbearing manager who belittles you in front of others. You might be prompted to try a conflict-resolution technique you acquired in class. Thus the formal training you have experienced will assist you in using a new technique to confront this person.

SUMMARY

Effective interpersonal relations must be combined with technical knowledge to achieve success in any job involving interaction with people. This book presents a three-part strategy for achieving a high level of interpersonal skills. Each chapter presents concepts related to an area of interpersonal skills, as well as behavioural guidelines and experiential exercises. Interpersonal skills training is also referred to as *soft-skill training* to differentiate it from technical training.

A five-part model of learning can be applied to improving interpersonal skills. First, state a goal or desired state of affairs. Second, assess the reality of how far you are from your goal. Third, develop an action plan to change the relationship between yourself and your environment, remembering that self-discipline is required to implement the action plan. Fourth, solicit feedback to measure the effects of your actions against reality. Fifth, continue to practise your newly learned skill.

People are most likely to develop new skills when they feel the need for change. A developmental need is the specific area a person needs to change. Identifying your developmental needs in relation to interpersonal relations can be achieved through self-analysis and feedback from others. You can also solicit feedback and make use of the feedback you have received in performance appraisals.

Universal training needs are those areas for improvement that are common to most people. The major topics in this text reflect universal training needs because addressing these needs is necessary for success in most positions involving interaction with people.

Opportunities exist in the workplace to develop interpersonal skills. A general approach to developing these skills is informal learning, whereby you acquire skills naturally outside a structured work environment. Informal learning often takes place through such means as observing a co-worker, manager, or team leader cope with a situation. Certain workplace experiences are particularly well-suited to developing interpersonal skills. These include facing unfamiliar responsibilities, proving yourself to others, having problems with employees, influencing without authority, and having a difficult manager.

An Interpersonal Relations Case Problem

CAN CLAIMS EXAMINER CARRIE BE HELPED?

Carrie Donahoe is one of five claims examiners in a regional office of a large casualty and property insurance company. The branch is still thriving despite the insurer's success at selling many policies online. A centralized office conducts billing. The sales group sells not only policies but also services to already existing businesses (for example, consulting with managers and business owners about

(Continued)

upgrading their policies). The sales representatives also answer questions about policies, such as whether the policy owner is covered against a terrorist attack.

Carrie works with four other examiners, as well as her supervisor, Michelle Pettigrew. The essential job of the claims examiner is to visit the site of a client with a demand for reimbursement for damages, such as from a fire, flood, or industrial accident. The claims examiner then files a report with a recommendation for payment that is reviewed by the examiner's supervisor. In addition, the home office reviews estimated payments beyond $15 000. Carrie has held her position for five years. She has received satisfactory performance evaluations, particularly for the accuracy and promptness of her insurance claim reports.

Carrie has frequent negative interactions with her co-workers, who resent many of her suggestions and criticisms. Jim, a senior claims analyst, says his nickname for Carrie is "Ms. Pit Bull," although he has not shared this nickname with her. Asked why he refers to Carrie as a pit bull, he replied, "It's not that Carrie physically attacks people. It's that she's so negative about so many things. I'll give you two recent examples.

"Carrie asked me to show her a sample claims report for mud damage. I emailed her a report. Two days later she sent me back the report, underlining six words or phrases she said were wrong. She didn't even thank me for the report.

"Then, on another occasion, I had a two-day trip to inspect a building damaged by a runaway truck. When I returned to the office, Carrie asked me why it took me two days to investigate a simple claim."

Sharon, a junior claims examiner, says that at her best Carrie is a charming co-worker. Yet at her worst she grates on people's nerves. "Here's what I'm talking about. Last week I came to work wearing a blue skirt and a red blouse. The vice-president of claims was coming to visit our office that day, and Carrie tells me that a person should never wear a red-and-blue combination for a special event. Not only is Carrie critical, her criticisms are sometimes way off base.

"Another time she told me that I should not waste my time studying for advanced certification in claims. She said that no manager in the company really cares about certification. Either you can do your job or you can't."

A human resource specialist from the home office asked Michelle Pettigrew how she was handling Carrie's personality clashes with co-workers, as well as her own personal interactions with her. Michelle said that she was mildly concerned about Carrie's personality problems but that Carrie was still getting her work done. Yet Michelle did mention that several clients indicated that Carrie surprised them with some of her criticisms of their operation. She told one tool-and-die shop owner that a well-managed firm never has a serious accident. That was the company's first claim in 50 years of being insured by us.

"When she's snippy with me, I just shrug it off unless it gets too personal. Then I tell Carrie that she's gone too far. Like a week ago she told me that I don't do a good job of getting enough resources for our branch, and that if I were a strong branch manager, we would have our offices refurbished by now. I told Carrie that our conversation was now over."

The human resources director said to Michelle, "I think you and I should talk about effective ways of dealing with Carrie and her problems."

Case Questions

1. What are Carrie's developmental needs?
2. What are Carrie's universal training needs?
3. What do you recommend that Michelle Pettigrew do to improve Carrie's interpersonal relationships in the office?
4. What is your evaluation of Michelle's approach to dealing with Carrie so far?

An Interpersonal Relations Case Problem

HOW DO YOU SAY NO TO GIRL SCOUT COOKIES?

Bok Lei Goodman finds it hard to say no to a colleague selling Girl Scout cookies. "I know it's a good cause, but it can make you feel uncomfortable," said Goodman, of Greenville, Delaware, who is a real estate agent.

Goodman is not the only one who sometimes resents being put on the spot at work by fundraising co-workers or folks pushing cosmetics, vitamins, or cleaning products. According to Jen Jorgensen, spokesperson for the Society for Human Resource Management, because of what many see as an increase in at-work solicitations, several employers now ban selling in the office with explicit written anti-solicitation policies to eliminate the sale or distribution of materials on behalf of another organization.

The society's sample "no solicitations" policy states, in part, that solicitations for money, products, services, and memberships are not permitted on company property except in non-work areas during non-work time.

"I do think that more companies are putting in place policies to limit it," said John A. Challenger, chief executive of the Challenger, Gray & Christmas outplacement firm. "The solicitations at work seem to be getting more prevalent. Each office has one or two people who seem to inflict their charities on their co-workers."

"Some people are less able to stand up for themselves than others," said Devona E. G. Williams, president of an organizational performance firm.

Case Questions

1. What developmental needs might workers such as Bok Lei Goodman have in relation to their dealing with charity appeals at the office?
2. What developmental needs might the workers have who sell products for charity at the office?
3. Why might this case about soliciting for charity be considered a human relations problem?

Interpersonal Skills Role Play

One student plays the role of Kristina, who sells wellness products such as vitamins and food supplements for a direct sales company. (Direct sales are from person to person and not distributed through stores.) Kristina is working hard to reach her goal for the month, and she just needs to sell $75 more of products to attain her goal. Another student plays the role of Ricardo, who enjoys working with Kristina but thinks that wellness products are overrated. During lunch in the company cafeteria, Kristina approaches Ricardo and begins her sales pitch about her wonderful life-enhancing products.

Run the role play for about six minutes, while other class members observe the interactions and later provide feedback about the interpersonal skills displayed by Kristina and Ricardo.

QUESTIONS FOR DISCUSSION AND REVIEW

Research
Navigator.com

Research Navigator: Explore our research resources at www.researchnavigator.com. Consult your instructor for log-in information.

1. One of the most prestigious US business schools, the Wharton School, now places much more emphasis on "people skills" than previously. What do you suspect are the reasons for this change?
2. In your opinion, do high-ranking business executives rely more on soft skills or hard skills to accomplish their work?
3. Why do people need soft skills in an era of high technology?

4. When asked "What are your strengths?" during a job interview, the vast majority of candidates respond "Getting along with people." Why do you think so many job candidates make this claim?

5. How does a person know whether or not the feedback he or she receives from another person is accurate?

6. How could doing a thorough job with Self-Assessment Quiz 1-1 have a major impact on a person's career?

7. Identify two developmental needs related to interpersonal relations that you think are particularly relevant for (formerly Canadian) entrepreneur Conrad Black. Present whatever evidence you have for your conclusions.

8. Based on what you have learned so far in this book, and your own intuition, how would you respond to the statement "You can't learn how to get along with people from reading a book"?

9. Give an example of a skill you might have learned informally at any point in your life.

10. Using your Research Navigator, find one article about improving interpersonal skills. Often business magazines are excellent sources for such material. Share your findings with a classmate or in small teams.

WEBLINKS

www.conferenceboard.ca
The Conference Board of Canada site. This site is packed with information about job skills and includes links to related sites.

www.selfgrowth.com
A site devoted to self-knowledge, self-growth, and self-help. Sign up for a free monthly newsletter and read articles about various aspects of the "self." A great place to start identifying developmental needs.

Chapter 2

Understanding Individual Differences

Kaled Abedi and Mary Lou Gold graduated from the Simcoe Institute in the same year, both majoring in business administration. The two met three years later at a class reunion. After they exchanged hugs, Kaled said, "Mary Lou, it's time we caught up with each other. What kind of work have you been doing?"

Mary Lou responded that she had combined her interests in business and technical writing. Her job consisted of preparing technical manuals for electronic consumer products such as DVD players and TVs. She said she worked at her computer about 35 hours per week, preparing copy and diagrams. Kaled explained that he sold office furniture and lighting fixtures to business firms.

"How boring that must be, preparing manuals all day long," said Kaled. "You must get sick of such a grind."

Mary Lou responded: "Quite the opposite, Kaled, I love work that requires concentration and produces tangible results. What I'd have a hard time doing is what you do—knocking on doors and trying to convince strangers they should buy your products."

This exchange illustrates one of the most important factors influencing the behaviour of people in the workplace. People show substantial **individual differences**, or variations, in how they respond to the same situation, based on personal characteristics.

Kaled, an extrovert, is at his best away from the office, winning people over to his way of thinking. Mary Lou, in contrast, is introverted and analytical. She enjoys working on tasks that require prolonged concentration and attention to detail. In general, individual differences exert a profound effect on job performance and behaviour.[1] Such differences refer to variations in how people respond to the same situation based on personal characteristics. One of hundreds of possible examples is that some people can concentrate longer and harder on their work, thereby producing more and higher quality work, than others.

This chapter describes several of the major sources of individual differences on the job. It also gives you the opportunity to measure your standing on several key dimensions of behaviour and helps you develop skill in responding to individual differences. Knowing how to respond to such differences is the cornerstone of effective interpersonal relations.

PERSONALITY

"We're not going to promote you to department head," said the vice-president to the analyst. "Although you are a great troubleshooter, you've alienated too many people in the company. You're too blunt and insensitive." As this implies, successes and failures in people-contact jobs are largely attributable to interpersonal, or human relations, skills. Among the most important contributors to these skills are personality traits. The subject of individual differences in personality must therefore be given consideration in any serious study of interpersonal relations in the workplace.

Personality refers to those persistent and enduring behaviour patterns that tend to be expressed in a wide variety of situations. A person who is brash and insensitive in one situation is likely to behave similarly in many other situations. Your personality is what makes you unique. Your walk, your talk, your appearance, your speech, and your inner values and conflicts all contribute to your personality. Have you ever noticed that when you know a person well you can identify them by their footsteps? This is true because many people have a distinctive gait.

We will illustrate the importance of personality to interpersonal relations in organizations by describing eight key personality traits and psychological types related to cognitive styles. In addition, you will be given guidelines for dealing effectively with individuals with different personality types.

EIGHT MAJOR PERSONALITY FACTORS AND TRAITS

Many psychologists believe that the basic structure of human personality is represented by five broad factors, known as the Five Factor Model (or Big Five): extraversion (the scientific spelling of *extroversion*), emotional stability, agreeableness, conscientiousness, and openness to experience. Three other factors, self-monitoring of behaviour, risk-taking and thrill-seeking, and optimism, have received much recent attention and are also included here. Recent evidence has emphasized the contribution of genes, and strips of DNA in particular, in forming personality. Genes do not influence personality traits directly. Instead, they subtly bias the mind so that different individuals react to similar experiences in different ways. Another key speculation is that genes affect the operation of brain chemicals that influence our mood, such as dopamine and serotonin. For example, seeing a person you perceive as physically attractive, and eating chocolate, are two experiences that release dopamine. As a consequence of either ingesting chocolate or sighting the right person—or a combination of the two—you get a temporary high.

Genes appear to have their biggest impact on temperament traits such as impulsiveness, openness, conservatism, and hostility. However, genes alone do not control the chemistry of the brain. Environment heavily influences how genes will express themselves. For example, one impulsive person might become a day trader on the internet and another a shoplifter. Character helps control our personality traits.[2] A person of good moral character, for example, might channel his or her aggressiveness into being competitive rather than attacking other people verbally or physically.

All eight personality factors have a substantial impact on interpersonal relations and job performance. The interpretation and meaning of these factors provides useful information, enabling you to pinpoint important areas for personal development. Although these factors are partially inherited, most people can improve upon them, providing they exert much conscious effort over a period of time. For example, it usually takes a minimum of three months of effort before a person is perceived to be more agreeable. The eight personality factors, also shown in Figure 2-1, are described in detail in the following list.

1. *Extraversion.* Traits associated with the extraversion factor include being social, gregarious, assertive, talkative, and active. An outgoing person is often described as extraverted, while a shy person is described as being introverted.

2. *Emotional stability (or Neuroticism).* A person with a high degree of emotional stability or low neuroticism is calm, confident, and usually in control. Traits associated with low emotional stability or higher neuroticism include being anxious, depressed, angry, embarrassed, emotional, and worried. Thus, a person with low emotional stability is often referred to as neurotic or emotionally unstable.

3. *Agreeableness.* An agreeable person is friendly and cooperative. Traits associated with the agreeableness factor include being courteous, flexible, trusting, good-natured, cooperative, forgiving, soft-hearted, and tolerant.

4. *Conscientiousness.* A variety of meanings have been attached to the conscientiousness factor, but it generally signifies dependability. Traits associated with conscientiousness include being careful, thorough, responsible, organized, and purposeful. Honesty is also closely related to conscientiousness. Other related traits include being hard-working, achievement-oriented, and persevering. The person low in conscientiousness is lazy, disorganized, and unreliable.

5. *Openness to experience.* People who score high on the openness-to-experience factor have well-developed intellects. Traits commonly associated with this factor include being imaginative, cultured, curious, original, broad-minded, intelligent, and artistically sensitive. People low on this personality factor are practical, with narrow interests.

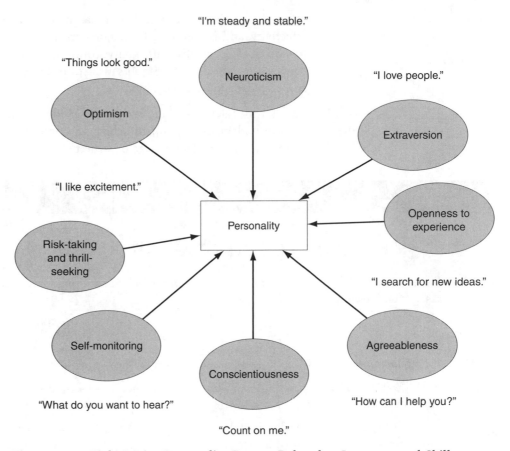

"I'm steady and stable."

"Things look good."

"I love people."

"I like excitement."

"I search for new ideas."

"What do you want to hear?"

"How can I help you?"

"Count on me."

Figure 2-1   Eight Major Personality Factors Related to Interpersonal Skills

6. *Self-monitoring of behaviour.* The self-monitoring trait refers to the process of observing and controlling how we are perceived by others. High self-monitors are pragmatic and even chameleon-like actors in social groups. They often say what others want to hear. Low self-monitors avoid situations that require them to adopt different outer images. In this way, their outer behaviour adheres to their inner values. Low self-monitoring can often lead to inflexibility.

7. *Risk-taking and thrill-seeking.* People with high risk-taking and thrill-seeking propensities tend to be sensation-seekers who pursue novel, intense, and complex sensations. They are willing to take risks for the sake of such experiences. The search for giant payoffs and daily thrills motivates people with an intense need for risk-taking and thrill-seeking.[3] Take Self-Assessment Quiz 2-1 to measure your propensity for risk-taking and thrill-seeking.

8. *Optimism* refers to a tendency to experience positive emotional states, and to typically believe that positive outcomes will be forthcoming from most activities. The other end of the scale is *pessimism*—a tendency to experience negative emotional states, and to typically believe that negative outcomes will be forthcoming from most activities. Optimism versus pessimism is also

referred to in more technical terms as positive affectivity versus negative affectivity, and is considered a major personality trait. A person's tendency toward having positive affectivity (optimism) versus negative affectivity (pessimism) also influences job satisfaction. Being optimistic, as you would suspect, tends to enhance job satisfaction.[4]

Evidence for the relevance of the Five Factor Model (traits one through five of the previous list) in understanding human behaviour comes from a cross-cultural study involving 7134 individuals. The five-factor structure of the American personality was

Self-Assessment Quiz 2-1

THE RISK-TAKING SCALE

Directions: Answer true or false to the following questions to obtain an approximate idea of your tendency to take risks, or your desire to do so:

	True	False
1. I eat sushi or other raw fish.	☐	☐
2. I think that amusement park roller coasters should be abolished.	☐	☐
3. I don't like trying foods from other cultures.	☐	☐
4. I would choose bonds over growth stocks.	☐	☐
5. I like to challenge people in positions of power.	☐	☐
6. I don't always wear a seat belt while driving.	☐	☐
7. I sometimes talk on my cell phone while driving at highway speeds.	☐	☐
8. I would love to be an entrepreneur (or I love being one).	☐	☐
9. I would like helping out in a crisis such as a product recall.	☐	☐
10. I would like to go cave exploring (or already have done so).	☐	☐
11. I would be willing to have at least one-third of my compensation based on a bonus for good performance.	☐	☐
12. I would be willing to visit a maximum security prison on a job assignment.	☐	☐

Scoring and Interpretation: Give yourself one point each time your answer agrees with the key. If you score 10–12, you are probably a high risk taker; 6–9, you are a moderate risk taker; 3–5, you are cautious; 0–2, you are a very low risk taker.

1. T	5. T	9. T
2. F	6. T	10. T
3. F	7. T	11. T
4. F	8. T	12. T

Source: The idea of a test about risk-taking comfort, as well as several of the statements on the quiz, comes from psychologist Frank Farley.

also found to hold true for German, Portuguese, Hebrew, Chinese, Korean, and Japanese samples when the personality test questions were translated into each of these languages. Based on this extensive study, it was concluded that personality structure is universal,[5] much like the structure of the brain or the body. This study also found that extraversion, agreeableness, and conscientiousness are major personality factors in most cultures. Neuroticism and openness are more dependent on the culture and are particularly relevant in the United States.[6]

THE EIGHT FACTORS AND TRAITS AND JOB PERFORMANCE

Depending on the job, any one of the preceding personality factors can be important for success. One explanation for personality being tied to performance is that a particular personality trait gives a **bias** or positive spin to certain actions.[7] A person high in conscientiousness, for example, believes that if people are diligent they will accomplish more work and receive just rewards. Conscientiousness relates to job performance for many different occupations, and has proven to be the personality trait most consistently related to success. However, there are a few instances in which being highly conscientious can interfere with job success. If the job requires considerable spontaneity and imagination, a highly conscientious person might perform poorly because he or she dislikes breaking the rules or straying from conventional thinking.[8] For example, a conscientious advertising worker might hesitate to develop a television advertisement that depicted a woman jumping out of a building onto a delivery truck.

Another important research finding is that extraversion is associated with success for managers and sales representatives. The explanation is that managers and salespeople are required to interact extensively with other people.[9]

For people who want to advance in their careers, being a high self-monitor is important. An analysis was made of the self-monitoring personality by combining 136 studies involving 23 101 people. A major finding was that high self-monitors tend to receive better performance ratings than low self-monitors. High self-monitors were also more likely to emerge as leaders and work their way into top management positions.[10] Another advantage to being a high self-monitor is that the individual is more likely to help out other workers, even when not required to.[11] An example would be helping a worker outside your department with a currency exchange problem, even though this is not your responsibility. The willingness to go beyond one's job description is referred to as **organizational citizenship behaviour**. Good organizational citizens are highly valued by employers.

A combination of **personality** factors will sometimes be more closely associated with job success than one factor alone. A study about personality and job performance ratings was conducted with diverse occupations including clerical workers and wholesale appliance sales representatives. A key finding was that conscientious workers who also scored high on agreeableness performed better than conscientious workers who were less agreeable.[12] (Being agreeable toward your manager helps elevate performance evaluations!) A study with experienced pharmaceutical sales representatives found that the combination of extraversion and conscientiousness was associated with higher sales. However, being conscientious was the personality factor most closely associated with growth in sales over several years for the experienced sales representatives.[13]

The extent to which a person has a high standing on agreeableness influences whether or not the supervisor perceives him or her as requiring high maintenance (needing a lot of attention). A study with 338 clerical workers in a manufacturing setting found that among employees who had a high standing on conscientiousness, being disagreeable prompted supervisors to rate them as engaging in high-maintenance behaviour.[14]

Optimism and pessimism also can be linked to job performance. Optimism can be quite helpful when attempting such tasks as selling a product or service or motivating a group of people. Yet psychologist Julie Normen has gathered considerable evidence that pessimism can sometimes enhance job performance. Pessimists usually assume that something will go wrong, and will carefully prepare to prevent botches and bad luck. A pessimist, for example, will carefully back up computer files or plan for emergencies that might shut down operations.[15]

COGNITIVE STYLES AND PERSONALITY TYPES

COGNITIVE STYLES

People go about solving problems in various ways. You may have observed, for example, that some people are more analytical and systematic, while others are more intuitive. The most widely used method of classifying problem-solving styles is the Myers-Briggs Type Indicator (MBTI).[16] Many readers of this book will have already taken the MBTI. Modes of problem solving are referred to as **cognitive styles.** According to this method of understanding problem-solving styles, your personality traits influence strongly how you approach problems, such as being introverted pointing you toward dealing with ideas. Knowledge of these cognitive styles can help you relate better to people because you can better appreciate how they make decisions.

According to the famous psychiatrist Carl Jung, how people gather and evaluate information determines their cognitive style. Jung's analysis became the basis for the Myers-Briggs Type Indicator. Jung reasoned that there are four dimensions of psychological functioning:

1. *Introverted versus Extraverted.* Introverts are oriented toward the inner world of ideas and feelings, whereas extraverts are oriented toward the outer world of people and objects.

2. *Thinking versus Feeling.* Thinkers prefer to make decisions logically based on facts and figures, whereas feelers base decisions on subjective information.

3. *Sensing versus Intuiting.* Sensing individuals prefer to concentrate on details, whereas intuitive individuals prefer to focus on broad issues (the "big picture").

4. *Judging versus Perceiving.* Judging types seek to resolve issues, whereas perceiving types are relatively flexible and search for additional information.

Combining the four types with each other results in 16 personality types, as shown in Figure 2-2. Research evidence for the MBTI is generally positive with respect to the 16 types, and the fact that people with different cognitive styles prefer different

ENTP (Conceptualizer)	ISTJ (Traditionalist)	INTJ (Visionary)	ESTJ (Organizer)
Quick, ingenious, will argue either side of issue for fun, may neglect routine assignments. (Good for creative work where deadlines are not crucial.)	Serious, quiet, practical, logical, dependable. (Good for work requiring careful attention to detail such as accountant or auditor.)	Skeptical, critical, independent, determined, original. (Good for major leadership role such as CEO.)	Practical, realistic, has a natural mind for business or mechanics, likes to organize and run activities. (Good for manufacturing supervisor.)

Figure 2-2   Four Cognitive Styles of the Myers-Briggs Typology

Note: I = Introvert, E = Extrovert, T = Thinking, F = Feeling, S = Sensing, N = Intuitive, J = Judging, and P = Perceiving.

Source: The personality descriptions are based on information from *Meyers-Briggs Type Indicator* by Katharine C. Briggs and Isabel Briggs Myers. Copyright 1983 by Consulting Psychologists Press, Inc. All rights reserved.

occupations.[17] For example, the ENTP cognitive type is labelled the "conceptualizer." He or she is passionate about new opportunities and dislikes routine, and is more likely to be an entrepreneur than a corporate manager. The ISTJ cognitive type is labelled the "traditionalist," and will often become an accountant or financial analyst. The INTJ type is labelled the "visionary." Although a small proportion of the population, these individuals are often chief executives of business firms. One of the most common types among people in general, as well as among managers, is the ESTJ, labelled the "organizer."

Many people who use the Myers-Briggs are unaware that it is an approximate measure, and not a definitive scale such as a measure of physical weight. The most reliable dimension appears to be thinking versus feeling, which is similar to reflecting about details versus jumping to a quick decision based on feel and experience, or being reflective versus impulsive.

If you take the Myers-Briggs Type Indicator, often available in career centres, you will discover your type. You can also study these four types and make a tentative judgment as to whether one of them fits your problem-solving style. Recognizing your problem-solving style can help you identify work that you are likely to perform well, as detailed in Figure 2-2.

GUIDELINES FOR DEALING WITH DIFFERENT PERSONALITY TYPES

A key purpose in presenting information about a sampling of various personality types is to provide guidelines for individualizing your approach to people. As a basic example, if you wanted to score points with an introvert, you would approach that person in a restrained, laid-back fashion. In contrast, a more gregarious, lighthearted approach might be more effective with an extravert. The purpose of individualizing your approach is to build a better working relationship or establish rapport with the other person. To match your approach to dealing with a person of a given personality type, you must first arrive at an approximate idea of the individual's personality. The following suggestions are therefore restricted to readily observable aspects of personality:

1. When relating to a person who appears to be neurotic, based on symptoms of worry and tension, be laid back and reassuring. Attempt not to project your own anxiety and fears. Be a good listener. If possible, minimize the emphasis on deadlines and the dire consequences of a project's failing. Show concern and interest in the person's welfare.

2. When relating to an *extraverted* individual, emphasize friendliness and warmth, and maintain a stream of chatter. Talk about people more than ideas, things, or data. Express an interest in a continuing working relationship.

3. When relating to an *introverted* individual, move slowly in forming a working relationship. Do not confuse quietness with a lack of interest. Tolerate moments of silence. Emphasize ideas, things, and data more heavily than people.

4. When relating to a person who is open to experience, emphasize information sharing, idea generation, and creative approaches to problems. Appeal to his or her intellect by discussing topics of substance rather than ordinary chatter and gossip.

5. When relating to a person who is *closed to experience*, stick closely to the facts of the situation at hand. Recognize that the person prefers to think small and deal with the here and now.

6. When relating to an *agreeable* person, just relax and be yourself. Reciprocate with kindness to sustain a potentially excellent working relationship.

7. When relating to a *disagreeable* person, be patient and tolerant. At the same time, set limits on how much mistreatment you will take. Disagreeable people sometimes secretly want others to put brakes on their anti-social behaviour.

8. When relating to a *conscientious* person, give him or her freedom and do not nag. The person will probably honour commitments without prompting. Conscientious people are often taken for granted, so remember to acknowledge the person's dependability.

9. When relating to a person who lacks *conscientiousness,* keep close tabs on him or her, especially if you need that person's output to do your job. Do not assume that the person's honest face and pleasing smile mean he or she will deliver as promised. Frequently follow up on your requests, and impose deadlines if you have the authority. Express deep appreciation when the person does follow through.

10. When dealing with a person you suspect is a *high self-monitor,* be cautious in thinking that the person genuinely supports your position. The person could just be following his or her natural tendency to appear to please others, without really being supportive.

11. When relating to a person with a *high propensity for risk-taking and thrill-seeking,* emphasize the risky and daring aspects of activities familiar to you. Talk about a new product introduction in a highly competitive market, stock options, investing in high technology start-up firms, bungee jumping, and race car driving.

Skill-Building Exercise 2-1

PERSONALITY ROLE PLAYS

The Extravert: One student assumes the role of a successful outside sales representative who has just signed a $3 million order for the company. The sales rep comes back to the office elated. The other student assumes the role of a member of the office support staff. He or she decides this is a splendid opportunity to build a good relationship with the triumphant sales rep. Run the role play for about 10 minutes. The people not involved in the role play will observe and then provide feedback when the role play is completed. (These directions regarding time, observation, and feedback also apply to the two other role plays in this exercise and throughout the book.)

The Open-to-Experience Type: One student plays the role of an experienced worker in the department who is told to spend some time orienting a new co-op student. Another student plays the role of the co-op student, who is open to experience and eager to be successful in this new position.

The Sensing and Intuiting Types: One student plays the role of a sensing-type individual who is responsible for reviewing the company expense accounts. The other student plays the role of a manager in whose department many expense account abuses (such as lack of documentation and high expenses) have been uncovered. This manager is an intuitive type. The person in charge of the accounts is visiting the manager in the latter's office to discuss this problem.

12. When relating to a person with a *low propensity for risk-taking and thrill-seeking,* emphasize the safe and secure aspects of activities familiar to you. Talk about the success of an established product in a stable market (like pencils and paperclips), talk about investing in government bonds, buying life insurance, camping, and gardening.

13. When dealing with a *sensing-type* person, emphasize facts, figures, and conventional thinking without sacrificing your own values. To convince the sensation type, emphasize logic more than emotional appeal. Focus on details more than on the big picture.

14. When dealing with an *intuiting-type* individual, emphasize feelings, judgments, playing with ideas, imagination, and creativity. Focus more on the big picture than on details.

To start putting these guidelines into practice, do the role plays in Skill-Building Exercise 2-1. Remember that a role player is an extemporaneous actor. Put yourself in the shoes of the character you play and visualize how he or she would act. Because you are given only the general idea of a script, use your imagination to fill in the details.

MENTAL ABILITY

Mental ability, or intelligence, is one of the major sources of individual differences affecting job performance and behaviour. **Intelligence** is the capacity to acquire and apply knowledge, including solving problems. Intelligent workers best solve abstract problems. In a very simple or rote job, such as packing shoes into boxes, having below-average intelligence is not a problem, as the employee can master the components of the job without difficulty.

Understanding the nature of intelligence contributes to effective interpersonal relations in organizations. Your evaluation of a person's intelligence can influence how you relate to that person. For example, if you think a person is intelligent, you will tend to seek his or her input on a difficult problem. If you realize that different types of intelligence exist, you are more likely to appreciate people's strengths regardless of their level of intelligence. You are thus less likely to judge others as being either good or poor problem-solvers.

Here we describe four important aspects of mental ability: (1) the components of traditional intelligence; (2) practical intelligence; (3) multiple intelligences; and (4) emotional intelligence. Knowledge of these four aspects will enrich your understanding of other workers and yourself.

COMPONENTS OF TRADITIONAL INTELLIGENCE

Intelligence consists of more than one component. A component of intelligence is much like a separate mental aptitude. Evidence suggests that intelligence consists of a **g (general) factor** and **s (special) factors** that contribute to problem-solving ability. Scores of tests of almost any type (such as math, aptitude for computer programming, or reading skill) are somewhat influenced by the g factor. The g factor helps explain why some people perform well in so many different mental tasks. Substantial evidence has accumulated over the years that workers with high intelligence tend to perform better. The relationship between g and job performance is likely to be strongest for those aspects of jobs involving thinking and knowledge, such as problem solving and technical expertise.[18]

Over the years, various investigators have arrived at different special factors contributing to overall mental aptitude. The following seven factors have been consistently identified:

1. *Verbal comprehension.* The ability to understand the meaning of words and their relationship to each other and to comprehend written and spoken information.

2. *Word fluency.* The ability to use words quickly and easily, without an emphasis on verbal comprehension.

3. *Numerical acuity.* The ability to handle numbers, engage in mathematical analysis, and do arithmetic calculations.

4. *Spatial perception.* The ability to visualize forms in space and manipulate objects mentally, particularly in three dimensions.

5. *Memory.* Having a good rote memory for symbols, words, and lists of numbers, along with other associations.

6. *Perceptual speed.* The ability to perceive visual details, to pick out similarities and differences, and to perform tasks requiring visual perception.

7. *Inductive reasoning.* The ability to discover a rule or principle and apply it in solving a problem and to make judgments and decisions that are logically sound.

Being strong in any of the preceding mental aptitudes often leads to an enjoyment of work associated with that aptitude. The reverse can also be true: enjoying a type of mental activity might lead to the development of an aptitude for the activity. Self-Assessment Quiz 2-2 gives you the opportunity to measure your preferences for numerical information.

Self-Assessment Quiz 2-2

ATTITUDES TOWARD NUMERICAL INFORMATION

Directions: Describe how much you agree with each of the following statements, using the following scale: disagree strongly (DS); disagree (D); neutral (N); agree (A); agree strongly (AS). Circle the number in the appropriate column.

	DS	D	N	A	AS
1. I enjoy work that requires the use of numbers.	1	2	3	4	5
2. I think quantitative information is difficult to understand.	5	4	3	2	1
3. I find it satisfying to solve day-to-day problems involving numbers.	1	2	3	4	5
4. Numerical information is very useful in everyday life.	1	2	3	4	5
5. I prefer not to pay attention to information involving numbers.	5	4	3	2	1
6. I think more information should be available in numerical form.	1	2	3	4	5
7. I don't like to think about issues involving numbers.	5	4	3	2	1
8. Numbers are not necessary for most situations.	5	4	3	2	1
9. Thinking is more enjoyable when it does not involve quantitative information.	5	4	3	2	1
10. I like to make calculations involving numerical information.	1	2	3	4	5
11. Quantitative information is vital for accurate decisions.	1	2	3	4	5
12. I enjoy thinking about issues that involve numerical information.	1	2	3	4	5
13. Understanding numbers is as important in daily life as reading or writing.	1	2	3	4	5
14. I easily lose interest in graphs, percentages, and other quantitative information.	5	4	3	2	1
15. I find numerical information to be relevant to most situations.	1	2	3	4	5
16. I think it is important to learn and use numerical information to make well-informed decisions.	1	2	3	4	5
17. Numbers are redundant for most situations.	5	4	3	2	1
18. It is a waste of time to learn information containing a lot of numbers.	5	4	3	2	1
19. I like to go over numbers in my mind.	1	2	3	4	5
20. It helps me think if I put down information as numbers.	1	2	3	4	5

Total Score _____

(Continued)

Scoring and Interpretation: Add the numbers you circled to obtain your total score.

85–100   You have strong positive attitudes toward numerical information and working with quantitative data.
55–84   You have moderately favourable attitudes toward numerical information and working with quantitative data.
20–54   You have very negative attitudes toward numerical information and working with quantitative data. Your dislike for quantitative solutions to problems is so strong that you are quick to distrust statistical analysis.

Source: Adapted with permission from Madhubalan Viswanathan, "Measurement of Individual Differences in Preference for Numerical Information," *Journal of Applied Psychology*, October 1993, p. 745.

PRACTICAL INTELLIGENCE

Many people, including psychologists, are concerned that the traditional way of understanding intelligence inadequately describes mental ability. An unfortunate implication of intelligence testing is that intelligence as traditionally calculated is based largely upon the ability to perform tasks related to scholastic work. Thus a person who scores very high on an intelligence test could follow a complicated instruction manual but might not be street smart.

To overcome the limited idea that intelligence mostly involves the ability to solve abstract problems, the **triarchic theory of intelligence** has been proposed. The theory holds that intelligence is composed of three different subtypes: analytical, creative, and practical. The *analytical* subtype is the traditional intelligence needed for solving difficult problems. Analytical intelligence is required to perform well in most school subjects. The *creative* subtype is the type of intelligence required for imagination and combining things in novel ways. The *practical* subtype is the type of intelligence required for adapting your environment to suit your needs.[19]

The idea of practical intelligence helps explain why a person who has a difficult time getting through school can still be a successful business person, politician, or athlete. Practical intelligence incorporates the ideas of common sense, wisdom, and street smarts.

A person with high practical intelligence would also have good **intuition**, an experience-based way of knowing or reasoning in which the weighing and balancing of evidence are done automatically. Examples of good intuition include a merchandiser who develops a hunch that a particular style will be hot next season, a basketball coach who sees the possibilities in a gangly youngster, and a supervisor who has a hunch that a neighbour would be a great fit for her department. Intuition is also required for creative intelligence.

One major reservation some have about practical intelligence is the implication that people who are highly intelligent in the traditional sense are not practical thinkers. In truth, most executives and other high-level workers score quite well on tests of mental ability. These tests usually measure analytical intelligence.

MULTIPLE INTELLIGENCES

Another approach to understanding the diverse nature of mental ability is the theory of **multiple intelligences**. According to Howard Gardner, people know and understand the world in distinctly different ways and learn in different ways. Individuals possess the following eight intelligences, or faculties, in varying degrees:

1. *Linguistic.* Enables people to communicate through language, including reading, writing, and speaking.

2. *Logical-mathematical.* Enables individuals to see relationships between objects and solve problems, as in calculus and statistics.

3. *Musical.* Gives people the capacity to create and understand meanings conveyed through sounds and to enjoy different types of music.

4. *Spatial.* Enables people to perceive and manipulate images in the brain and to recreate them from memory, as is required in making graphic designs.

5. *Bodily/kinesthetic.* Enables people to use their body and perceptual and motor systems in skilled ways such as in dancing, playing sports, and expressing emotion through facial expressions.

6. *Intrapersonal.* Enables people to perceive their own feelings and acquire accurate self-knowledge.

7. *Interpersonal.* Enables people to discern and respond appropriately to the moods, temperaments, motivations, needs, and desires of other people.

8. *Naturalist.* Enables individuals to differentiate among, classify, and utilize various features of the physical external environment.

Thus, according to this theory of "multiple intelligences," people are not intelligent or unintelligent, but are weak or strong in various areas of intelligence. The question for you to ask yourself, then, is not "How smart am I?" but rather "In what ways am I smart?" Your profile of intelligences influences how you learn best and to which types of jobs you are best suited. Gardner believes that it is possible to develop these separate intelligences through concentrated effort. However, any of these intelligences might fade if not used.[20] These separate types of intelligence might also be perceived as different talents or abilities. Having high general problem-solving ability *(g)* would contribute to high standing on each of the eight intelligences.

EMOTIONAL INTELLIGENCE

Later research has updated and expanded the idea of practical intelligence, suggesting that the effectiveness with which people use their emotions has a major impact on their success. **Emotional intelligence** refers to qualities such as understanding one's own feelings, having empathy for others, and regulating one's emotions to one's own benefit. A person with high emotional intelligence would be able to engage in such behaviours as assessing people, pleasing others, and influencing them. In recent years, several different versions of emotional intelligence have been proposed. Five key factors included in a well-accepted analysis of emotional intelligence are as follows:[21]

1. *Self-awareness.* The ability to understand your moods, emotions, and needs, as well as their impact on others. (A person with good self-awareness knows whether he or she is pushing other people too far.)

2. *Self-regulation.* The ability to control impulsiveness, to calm down anxiety and to react with appropriate anger to situations. (A person with low self-regulation would suddenly decide to drop a project because the work was frustrating.)

3. *Motivation.* A passion to work for reasons in addition to money or status. Also, drive, persistence, and optimism when faced with setbacks. (A person with this type of motivation would make the decision to keep trying when faced with a serious obstacle such as having lost a major account.)

4. *Empathy.* The ability to respond to the unspoken feelings of others. Also, the skill of responding to people according to their emotional reactions. (A manager with empathy would take into account the most likely reaction of group members before making a decision affecting them.)

5. *Social skill.* Competency in managing relationships and building networks of support and in having positive relationships with people. (A worker with social skill would use a method of persuasion that is likely to work well with a particular group or individual.)

Emotional intelligence thus incorporates many of the skills and attitudes necessary to achieve effective interpersonal relations in organizations. The Canadian Scene on the following page examines more closely the relationship of emotional intelligence and personality factors. Most of the human relations tasks dealt with in this book, such as resolving conflict, helping others develop, and deploying positive political skills, require emotional intelligence. Self-Assessment Quiz 2-3 gives you an opportunity to measure your emotional intelligence, but you will need persistence to derive the information. Such a measure is referred to as your **EQ**, or emotional intelligence quotient. Weblinks at the end of the chapter include additional websites for assessing your emotional intelligence.

Self-Assessment Quiz 2-3

WHAT IS YOUR EMOTIONAL INTELLIGENCE QUOTIENT (EQ)?

Psychologists have developed various measures of emotional intelligence. The internet is an excellent place to access various personality tests, including those that measure your emotional intelligence quotient (EQ). Below we suggest two excellent sources for tests that can be found on the web.

The first test can be done online at **www.queendom.com.** Because the web pages on this site move as new tests are added, use this address and then search under intelligence tests. One emotional IQ test takes 35 to 40 minutes to complete. It is scored online, and you will get your results immediately. Once you have your results, you can read further about emotional intelligence.

The EIQ test found by visiting **www.myskillsprofile.com** deals with 16 emotional competencies. The feedback report provides a chart of your emotional competencies, together with a detailed description of your profile. An advantage of this quiz is that it is based on the work of two of the original researchers in emotional intelligence, not the later popularizers of the concept.

The Canadian Scene

EMOTIONAL INTELLIGENCE AND PERSONALITY

Intelligence, including emotional intelligence, has been the topic of research interest for many years in the field of psychology. One Canadian study examined the relationship of emotional intelligence with several personality factors including the Big Five Personality Traits (Five Factor Model from earlier pages) and Type A behaviour.

The results demonstrated that EQ is related to the Five Factor Model. Individuals with a higher emotional intelligence tended to be more extraverted and conscientious. Also, individuals with higher EQs also reported lower scores in Neuroticism.

The Type A behaviour pattern (refer to page 338 in Chapter 14 for a full discussion of Type A) is also related to emotional intelligence. People who are high in Type A characteristics are often demanding, impatient, strive hard for success, and can be hostile and angry. Individuals with a higher EQ tended to be more hardworking and achievement-oriented like Type As, but without the irritability and lack of patience. A major conclusion of the study was that Emotional Intelligence is related to some aspects of personality as well as to the Type A behaviour pattern. Further research may continue to discover and develop more relationships between Emotional Intelligence and other aspects of personality.

Source: Day et. al, Predicting Psychological Health: Assessing the Incremental Validity of Emotional Intelligence Beyond Personality, Type A Behaviour, and Daily Hassles, *European Journal of Personality*, (19), pp. 519–536, Jan 2005.

GUIDELINES FOR RELATING TO PEOPLE OF DIFFERENT LEVELS AND TYPES OF INTELLIGENCE

Certainly, you cannot expect to administer mental ability and emotional intelligence tests to all of your work associates, gather their scores, and then relate to associates differently based on their scores. Yet it is possible to intuitively develop a sense for the mental quickness of people and the types of mental tasks they perform best. For example, managers must make judgments about mental ability in selecting people for jobs and assigning them to tasks. Following are several guidelines worth considering to improve your working relationships with others:

1. If you perceive another worker (your manager included) to be mentally quick in a specific area, present your ideas in depth. Incorporate difficult words into your conversation and reports. Ask the person challenging questions.

2. If you perceive another worker to be not as mentally proficient in a specific area, present your ideas with a minimum of technical depth. Use a basic vocabulary, without being patronizing. Ask for frequent feedback about having been clear.

3. If you perceive a workmate to relish crunching numbers, use quantitative information when attempting to persuade that person. Instead of using phrases such as "most people," say "about 65 percent."

Skill-Building Exercise 2-2

ADAPTING TO PEOPLE OF DIFFERENT MENTAL ABILITY

The Mentally Sharp Co-worker: One person plays the role of a worker who needs to load a new software package onto the hard drive of his or her computer. He or she wants to approach a particular co-worker known for having a sharp mind but wonders whether this highly intelligent person will be interested in the problem. The other person plays the role of the computer whiz who ordinarily does not like to solve problems for people that they should be able to solve themselves. The first worker meets with the second to discuss loading the software.

The Mentally Average Team Member: One student plays the role of a supervisor who needs to explain to a team member how to calculate discounts for customers. To the supervisor's knowledge, the team member does not know how to calculate discounts, although it will be an important part of the team member's new job. The supervisor and the team member get together for a session on calculating discounts.

4. If you perceive a work associate to have high creative intelligence, solicit his or her input on problems requiring a creative solution. Use statements such as "Here's a problem that requires a sharp, creative mind, so I've come to you."

5. If you perceive a work associate to have a lower emotional intelligence, explain your feelings and attitudes clearly. The person may not catch hints and indirect expressions.

To start putting these guidelines into practice, do the role play in Skill-Building Exercise 2-2.

VALUES AS A SOURCE OF INDIVIDUAL DIFFERENCES

Another group of factors influencing how a person behaves on the job is that person's values and beliefs. A **value** refers to the importance a person attaches to something. Values are also tied to the enduring belief that some modes of conduct are better than others. If you believe that good interpersonal relations are the most important part of your life, your humanistic values are strong. Similarly, you may think that people who are not highly concerned about interpersonal relations have poor values.

Values are closely related to **ethics**, or the moral choices a person makes. A person's values influence which kinds of behaviours he or she believes are ethical. An executive who strongly values profits might not find it unethical to raise prices higher than needed to cover additional costs. Another executive who strongly values family life might suggest that the company invest money in an on-premises daycare centre. Ethics is such an important topic in interpersonal relations in organizations that it receives separate attention in Chapter 13.

Differences in values among people often stem from age, or generational, differences. Workers over the age of 50, in general, may have values that are quite different from those of people much younger. These differences in values based on age have often been seen as a clash between Baby Boomers and members of Generation X and Generation Y. According

Table 2-1 Value Stereotypes for Several Generations of Workers

Baby Boomers (1946–1964)	Generation X (1965–1977)	Generation Y (1978–1984)
Uses technology as a necessary tool	Techno-savvy	Techno-savvy
Tolerates teams but values independent work	Teamwork very important	Teamwork very important Culturally diverse
Appreciates hierarchy	Dislikes hierarchy	Dislikes hierarchy
Strong career orientation	Strives for work/life balance but will work long hours for now	Strives for work/family balance but will work long hours for now
More loyalty to organization	Loyalty to own career and profession	Belief in informality Wants to strike it rich quickly Highly regards start-up companies
Favours diplomacy	Candid in conversation	Candid in conversation
Favours old economy	Appreciates old and new economy	Prefers the new economy
Expects a bonus based on performance	Would appreciate a signing bonus	Expects a signing bonus

Sources: Several of the ideas in this table are from Robert McGarvey, "The Coming of Gen X Bosses," *Entrepreneur,* November 1999, pp. 60–64; Joanne M. Glenn, "Teaching the Net Generation," *Business Education Forum,* February 2000, pp. 6–14; Charlene Marmer Solomon, "Ready or Not: Here Come the Kids," *Workforce,* February 2000, pp. 62–68; and Chris Penttila, "Generational Gyrations," *Entrepreneur,* April 2001, pp. 102–103.

to the stereotype, Boomers see Generation X and Generation Y as being disrespectful of rules, unwilling to pay their dues, and disloyal to employers. Generation X and Generation Y see Boomers as worshipping hierarchy (layers of authority), being overcautious, and wanting to preserve the status quo. Table 2-1 summarizes these stereotypes with the understanding that massive group stereotypes like this are only partially accurate, because there are literally millions of exceptions. For example, many Baby Boomers are fascinated with technology, and many members of Generation Y like hierarchy.

HOW VALUES ARE LEARNED

People acquire values in the process of growing up, and many values are learned by the age of four. One important way we acquire values is through observing others, or modelling. Models can be parents, teachers, friends, siblings, and even public figures. If we identify with a particular person, the probability is high that we will develop some of his or her major values, as the following scenario illustrates:

> Derek, a restaurant owner, was known for his willingness to offer employment to troubled teenagers and then help them get back on their feet. Asked why he put so much effort into helping youths in trouble, he explained, "I was greatly influenced as a boy by my Uncle Clarence. I was going through troubled times—stealing from Zellers and getting drunk on beer.
>
> "Uncle Clarence took me under his wing and spent hours listening to my problems. He would take me fishing and ask if there was anything he could do to help me.

Finally, I straightened out. I decided that I would be like Uncle Clarence if someday I had a chance to help young people."

Another major way values are learned is through the communication of attitudes. The attitudes that we hear expressed directly or indirectly help shape our values. For instance, if using credit to purchase goods and services were considered an evil practice among your family and friends, you might therefore hold negative values about instalment purchases.

Unstated but implied attitudes may also shape values. If key people in your life showed no enthusiasm when you talked about work accomplishments, you might not place such a high value on achieving outstanding results. If, on the other hand, your family and friends centred their lives on their careers, you might develop similar values. (Or you might rebel against such a value because it interfered with a more relaxed lifestyle.) Many key values are also learned through religion, and thus become the basis for society's morals. For example, most religions emphasize treating other people fairly and kindly. To "knife somebody in the back" is considered immoral both on and off the job.

CLARIFYING YOUR VALUES

The values that you develop early in life are directly related to the kind of person you are and to the quality of the relationships you form.[22] A recognition of this fact has led to exercises designed to help people clarify and understand some of their own values. Almost all of these values-clarification exercises ask you, in one way or another, to compare the relative importance you attach to different objects and activities. Self-Assessment Quiz 2-4 provides you with an opportunity to clarify your values.

THE MESH BETWEEN INDIVIDUAL AND JOB VALUES

Under the best of circumstances, the values of employees mesh with those required by the job. When this state of congruence exists, job performance is likely to be higher. A national survey of managers investigated the fit between the values of managers and those of their organizations. (One such mesh would be a highly ethical person working for a highly ethical firm.) A major finding was that managers who experienced a good fit were more successful and more likely to believe they could reach their career goals. They were also more confident about remaining with their present firm and more willing to work long hours.[23]

When the demands made by the organization or a superior clash with the basic values of the individual, that person suffers from **person–role conflict**. The individual wants to obey orders but does not want to perform an act that seems inconsistent with his or her values. A situation such as this might occur when an employee is asked to produce a product that he or she feels is unsafe or of no value to society. Consider the following scenario:

A manager of a commercial weight-reduction centre resigned after two years of service. The owners pleaded with her to stay, based on her excellent performance. The manager replied, "Sorry, I think my job is immoral. We sign up all these people with great expectations of losing weight permanently. Most of them do achieve short-term weight reduction. My conflict is that over 90 percent of our clientele regain the weight they lost once they go back to eating normal food. I think we are deceiving them by not telling them upfront that they will most likely gain back the weight they lose."

Self-Assessment Quiz 2-4

CLARIFYING YOUR VALUES

Directions: Examine the list of 17 values below. If there is another value that you would like to add, do so under the heading of Other. Now rank them from 1 to 17 (or 1 to 18 if you filled out the extra one) according to the importance of these values to you as a person. The most important value on the list receives a rank of 1.

_____   Having my own place to live

_____   Having one or more children

_____   Having an interesting job and career

_____   Owning a car

_____   Having a good relationship with co-workers

_____   Having good health

_____   Watching my favourite television shows

_____   Participating in sports or other pastimes

_____   Following a sports team, athlete, music group, or other entertainer

_____   Being a religious person

_____   Helping people less fortunate than myself

_____   Loving and being loved by another person

_____   Having physical intimacy with another person

_____   Making an above-average income

_____   Being in good physical condition

_____   Being a knowledgeable, informed person

_____   Completing my formal education

_____   Other

1. Discuss and compare your ranking of these values with the person next to you.

2. Perhaps your class, assisted by your instructor, can arrive at a class average on each of these values. How does your ranking compare with the class ranking?

3. Look back at your own ranking. Does it surprise you?

4. Any surprises in the class ranking? Which values did you think would be highest and lowest?

GUIDELINES FOR USING VALUES TO IMPROVE INTERPERSONAL RELATIONS

Values are intangible and abstract, and thus not easy to manipulate to help improve your interpersonal relations on the job. Despite their vagueness, values are an important driver of interpersonal effectiveness. Consider the following guidelines:

1. Establish the values you will use in your relationships with others on the job, and then use those values as firm guidelines in working with others. For example, following the Golden Rule, you might establish the value of treating others as you want to be treated. You would not then lie to others to gain personal advantage and would not backstab your rivals.

2. Establish the values that will guide you as an employee. When you believe that your values are being compromised, express your concern to your manager in a tactful and constructive manner. You might say to your manager, "Sorry, I choose not to tell our customers that our competitor's product is inferior just to make a sale. I choose not to say this because our competitor makes a fine product. But what I will say is that our service is exceptional." Remember, however, that being skilled at using your values requires day-by-day monitoring. If you believe that your values are right, and anybody who disagrees is wrong, you will have frequent conflict. For example, you may believe that the most important value top managers should have is to bring shareholders a high return on their investment. Another worker believes that profits are important, but providing jobs for as many people as possible is an equally important value. Both of you have a good point, but neither is right or wrong. So it is better to discuss these differences rather than hold grudges because of them.

To help you put the above guidelines into practice, do Skill-Building Exercise 2-3.

Skill-Building Exercise 2-3

THE VALUE-CONFLICT ROLE PLAY

One student plays the role of a company president who is announcing to the group that the company must soon lay off 10 percent of the workforce to remain profitable. The president also points out that the company has a policy against laying off good performers. He or she then asks four of the company managers to purposely give below-average performance ratings to 10 percent of employees. In this way, laying them off will fit company policy.

Four other students play the role of the company managers who receive this directive. If such manipulation of performance evaluations clashes with your values, engage in a dialogue with your manager expressing your conflict. Remember, however, that you may not want to jeopardize your job.

Conduct this group role play for about 10 minutes, with other class members observing and preparing to offer feedback.

SUMMARY

Individual differences are among the most important factors influencing the behaviour of people in the workplace. Knowing how to respond to such differences is the cornerstone of effective interpersonal relations.

Personality is one of the major sources of individual differences. The eight major personality factors described in this chapter are extraversion, emotional stability, agreeableness, conscientiousness, openness to experience, self-monitoring of behaviour, risk-taking and thrill-seeking, and optimism. Depending on the job, any one of these personality factors can be important for success, and they also affect interpersonal relations.

Personality also influences a person's cognitive style, or the mental processes used to perceive and make judgments from information. According to the Myers-Briggs Type Indicator (MBTI), four dimensions of psychological functioning are as follows: introverted versus extraverted; thinking versus feeling; sensing versus intuiting; and judging versus perceiving. Combining the four types with each other results in 16 personality types, such as a person being a conceptualizer, traditionalist, visionary, or organizer. For example, the organizer (ESTJ) scores high on extraversion, sensing, thinking, and judging.

Mental ability, or intelligence, is one of the major sources of individual differences affecting job performance and behaviour. Understanding the nature of intelligence contributes to effective interpersonal relations in organizations. For example, understanding that different types of intelligence exist will help a person appreciate the strengths of people.

Intelligence consists of many components. The traditional perspective is that intelligence includes a general factor along with special factors that contribute to problem-solving ability. A related perspective is that intelligence consists of seven components: verbal comprehension, word fluency, numerical acuity, spatial perception, memory, perceptual speed, and inductive reasoning.

To overcome the idea that intelligence involves mostly the ability to solve abstract problems, the triarchic theory of intelligence has been proposed. According to this theory, intelligence has three subtypes: analytical, creative, and practical (street smarts included). Another approach to understanding mental ability contends that people have multiple intelligences, or faculties, including linguistic, logical-mathematical, musical, spatial, bodily/kinesthetic, intrapersonal, interpersonal, and naturalist.

Emotional intelligence refers to factors other than traditional mental ability that govern a person's success. The five components of emotional intelligence are (1) self-awareness; (2) self-regulation; (3) motivation relating to task enjoyment and resiliency; (4) empathy; and (5) social skill.

Values and beliefs are another set of factors that influence behaviour on the job, including interpersonal relations. Values are closely related to ethics, the moral choices a person makes. People acquire values in the process of growing up and modelling their behaviour on that of others. The values a person develops early in life are directly related to the kind of adult he or she becomes and to the quality of relationships formed. Values-clarification exercises help people identify their values. Person–role conflict occurs when the demands made by an organization or a superior clash with the basic values of an individual.

An Interpersonal Relations Case Problem

MULTIPLE INTELLIGENCES IN THE OFFICE

Liz Russo is the general manager of the student loan division of a major bank. She prides herself on being a modern manager who searches continuously for new ways to manage the student loan business and to manage people. Recently she attended a talk by Harvard University psychologist Howard Gardner, given to the management group at the bank. Russo and the other managers listened intently as Gardner explained his theories of intelligence.

The psychologist emphasized that managers must discard the notion that there is only one kind of intelligence. Most of the managers nodded in agreement. Gardner explained that he wants people in charge of managing human resources to recognize that there are at least eight different kinds of intelligence. People with linguistic intelligence are really good at communicating with words. If you have logical-mathematical intelligence, you can deal with abstract relationships like formulating new ideas for products. People with musical intelligence can do wonders with sounds. Those who have spatial intelligence can work well with images and designs.

People who have bodily/kinesthetic intelligence can move their bodies easily, like dancers and athletes. Individuals gifted with intrapersonal intelligence can understand their own feelings well. People with interpersonal intelligence can read other people well. And finally, people with naturalist intelligence can understand and make good use of the environment.

During a lunch following the talk, Russo said to one of the other managers, "What a liberating bunch of thoughts. The way I interpret Dr. Gardner's theories, people who are talented athletes or dancers are just as intelligent as computer whizzes. It's just that they have a different kind of intelligence."

"Why stop there?" responded the other manager. "One of my kids is a great banjo player, but we're wondering if he'll ever make it through high school. His mom and I used to think he was mentally challenged. Now we know his intelligence is the musical type, not the logical type."

Gardner's ideas kept spinning through Russo's mind. She bought a copy of one of his books for each of her managers and asked them all to study the book carefully. Later she scheduled a half-day meeting in a hotel to discuss how to apply the idea of eight human intelligences to the student loan division. Russo said to her management team, "You all seem to agree with the idea that there are eight human intelligences. Now I want us to figure out how to apply Dr. Gardner's theories to make us a more productive business."

Molly Gerbrach, the head of information systems, said with a smirk on her face, "I have a suggestion. If I hire a programmer who proves to be poor at programming, I'll just ask him or her to be the department's official musician!"

"I appreciate the humour, Molly," said Russo, "but now let's get down to business. Let's figure out how to implement these great ideas about different human intelligences."

Case Questions

1. Is Liz Russo being realistic about applying the concept of eight human intelligences to the office setting?

2. Suggest at least two ways in which the theory of eight human intelligences could be applied to improving productivity in Russo's student loan division.

An Interpersonal Relations Case Problem

"WE'VE GOT TO MAKE OUR NUMBERS"

Bruce Malone works as an account manager for an office-supply company with branches in most major cities in Canada. The company has two lines of business, retail and commercial. Among the many products the company sells are computers and related equipment, office furniture, copy paper, and other basic office supplies.

The retail trade is served by customers walking directly into the store or ordering online. Many of the customers are small business owners or corporate employees who work at home for part of their work week. The commercial trade also does some walk-in purchasing and online ordering. However, each large customer is also assigned an account manager who calls on them periodically to discuss their needs for larger purchases such as office furniture and multiple copiers and desktop computers.

Malone is meeting his sales targets for the year despite a flat economy in the city where the office supplier is located. Shortly before Thanksgiving, Malone was analyzing his sales to estimate his performance for the year. According to his projections, his total sales would be 1 percent beyond his quota, giving him a satisfactory year. Making his quota would qualify him for a year-end bonus.

The Friday after Thanksgiving, Malone received an email message from his boss Lucille Whitman, requesting that the two meet Monday morning before Bruce began working with his customers. At the start of the meeting, Whitman told Malone that she had something very important to discuss with him. "Bruce, we are getting a lot of heat from corporate headquarters," Whitman began. "If we don't make our numbers [attaining the sales goals] the stock price could dip big time, and the home office executives will be in trouble. Even their bonuses will be at risk"

"I've done what I can," responded Malone. "I'm going to make my quota for the year plus a little extra margin. So I guess I'm covered. There isn't much I can do about the company as a whole."

"Let me be a little more specific," replied Whitman. "The company is in trouble, so we all have to pitch in and show better numbers for the year. What we need our account managers to do is to pump up the sales figures a little. Maybe you could count as December sales a few of the purchases your customers have planned for early January. Or maybe you could ship extra-large orders at a discount, and tell your customers they can pay as late as February or March.

"You're smart, Bruce. Beef up your sales figures for the year a little because we have got to make our numbers."

"Lucille, maybe I could work extra hard to pull in a few more sales in the next eight weeks. But I would feel rotten faking my sales figures for December. I'm a professional."

With an angry tone, Whitman responded, "I don't care what you call yourself; we have got to make our numbers. Get back to me soon with your plan for increasing your numbers before the end of December."

Case Questions

1. What is the nature of the conflict Bruce Malone is facing?
2. What type of values is Lucille Whitman demonstrating?
3. What do you recommend Bruce should have done to work his way out of the problem he was facing?
4. Is Bruce too naïve for a career in business?

Interpersonal Skills Role Play

Here is an opportunity to practise dealing with the type of conflict facing Bruce Malone. One person plays Bruce, who has a follow-up conversation with Lucille Whitman about improving his sales figures by less than straightforward means. Another student plays the role of Lucille Whitman, who is focused on the corporate demands of "making the numbers." Bruce wants to communicate clearly how uncomfortable he feels about fudging the facts, while Lucille feels enormous pressure to meet the demands of the executive group. Ideally, the two role-players will reach a solution acceptable to both sides.

QUESTIONS FOR DISCUSSION AND REVIEW

1. Why is responding to individual differences considered to be the cornerstone of effective interpersonal relations?

2. How can knowledge of major personality factors help a person form better interpersonal relations on the job?

3. In what way might the personality trait of optimism versus pessimism be relevant for job performance?

4. Suppose a highly self-monitoring person is attending a company-sponsored social event and that person dislikes such events. How is he or she likely to behave?

5. Identify two business occupations for which a high propensity for risk-taking and thrill-seeking would be an asset.

6. What kinds of problems would a sensing-type individual prefer to tackle?

7. Which of the seven components of intelligence represents your best mental aptitude? What is your evidence?

8. How could you use the concept of multiple intelligences to raise the self-esteem of people who do not consider themselves to be very smart?

9. Why is emotional intelligence so important for success in business?

10. How can you use information about a person's values to help you relate more effectively to him or her?

11. Open your Research Navigator. Intelligence is a well-researched area of study in the field of psychology. Under content selection, choose Psychology and using the keyword search, type in "intelligence research" or "intelligence tests." Choose a research article that is a PDF file so that you can download the entire article. Summarize the article, noting the main research findings. Note if there are any relationships between this chapter and those findings. Share your information with another class member or in a group.

Research
Navigator.com

WEBLINKS

www.queendom.com/tests
This site contains literally hundreds of tests, quizzes, and assessments, including locus-of-control tests, a conflict-management styles test, intelligence tests, and other personality assessments.

www.helpself.com/iq-test.htm
This is an emotional intelligence test. From here, you can also access additional information on emotional intelligence.

http://www.6seconds.org
This is another site devoted to emotional intelligence and includes an EQ Quote Library, links to other sites about EQ, and an area for parents and teachers.

Interpersonal Communication

"Why isn't this project ready for shipment today?" barked the manager. "I told you to get it done as soon as you could get to it."

"That's why it isn't done," replied the group member. "I was too busy to get to it."

This communication problem took place because the phrase "as soon as you can get to it" was interpreted differently by the two people involved. Communication breakdowns like this one are more common than you might think. In fact, they are responsible for many problems in the workplace.

Communication is the sending, receiving, and understanding of messages. It is also the basic process by which managers, customer-contact workers, and professionals accomplish their work. For example, a customer service representative cannot resolve a thorny customer problem without carefully receiving and sending information. Communication skills are a success factor for workers in a wide variety of jobs.

The information in this chapter is aimed at reducing communication problems and helping you communicate more effectively. The chapter explains the nature of key facets of interpersonal communication and presents guidelines for improving your effectiveness, along with skill-building exercises.

STEPS IN THE COMMUNICATION PROCESS

One way to understand how people communicate is to examine the steps involved in transmitting and receiving a message, illustrated in Figure 3-1. For effective communication to take place, six components must be present: a sender, a message, a channel, a receiver, feedback, and the environment. In addition, the entire communication process is affected by a seventh component—noise.

To help understand the communication process, assume that a production manager in a bicycle factory wants to inform a team leader that quality in her department slipped last month.

1. *Sender (or source).* The sender in a communication event is usually a person (in this case the production manager) attempting to send a spoken, written, sign-language, or nonverbal message to another person or persons. The perceived authority and credibility of the sender are important factors in influencing how much attention the message will receive.

2. *Message.* The heart of the communication event is the **message**, a purpose or idea to be conveyed. Many factors influence how a message is received. Among them are clarity, the alertness of the receiver, the complexity and length of the message, and how the information is organized. The production manager's message will most likely get across if he says directly, "I need to talk to you about last month's below-average quality figures."

3. *Channel (medium).* Several communication channels, or media, are usually available for sending messages in organizations. Typically, messages are written (usually electronically), spoken, or communicated as a combination of the two. Some kind of nonverbal signal such as a smile or hand gesture accompanies most spoken messages. In the production manager's case, he has chosen to drop by the team leader's office and deliver his message in a serious tone.

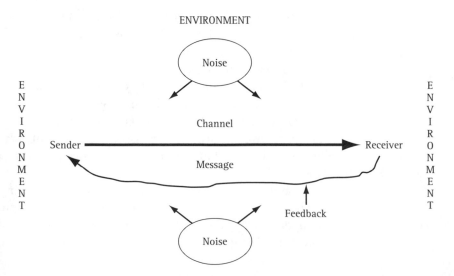

Figure 3-1   A Basic Model of the Communication Process

4. *Receiver.* A communication event can be complete only when another party receives the message and understands it properly. In the present example, the team leader is the receiver. Perceptual distortions of various types act as filters that can prevent a message from being received as intended by the sender. If the team leader is worried that her job is at stake, she might get defensive when she hears the production manager's message.

5. *Feedback.* Messages sent back from the receiver to the sender are referred to as **feedback**. Without feedback it is difficult to know whether a message has been received and understood. Feedback includes the *reactions* of the receiver. If the receiver takes action as intended by the sender, the message has been received satisfactorily. The production manager will know his message got across if the team leader says, "OK, when would you like to review last month's quality reports?" Effective interpersonal communication therefore involves an exchange of messages between two people. The two communicators take turns being receivers and senders.

6. *Environment.* A full understanding of communication requires knowledge of the environment in which messages are transmitted and received. The organizational culture (attitudes and atmosphere) is a key environmental factor influencing communication. It is easier to transmit controversial messages when trust and respect are high than when they are low.

7. *Noise.* Distractions have a pervasive influence on the components of the communication process. In this context, **noise** is anything that disrupts communication, including the attitudes and emotions of the receiver. Noise includes such factors as stress, fear, negative attitudes, and low motivation.

RELATIONSHIP BUILDING AND INTERPERSONAL COMMUNICATION

Another way of understanding the process of interpersonal communication is to examine how communication is a vehicle for building relationships. According to Ritch Sorenson, Grace DeBord, and Ida Ramirez, we establish relationships along two primary dimensions: dominate–subordinate, and cold–warm. In the process of communicating we attempt to dominate or subordinate. When we dominate, we attempt to control communication. When we subordinate we attempt to yield control, or think first of the wishes and needs of the other person. Dominators expect the receiver of messages to be submit to them; subordinate people send a signal that they expect the other person to dominate.[1]

We indicate whether we want to dominate or subordinate by the way we speak, write, or by the nonverbal signals we send. The dominator might speak loudly or enthusiastically, write forceful messages filled with exclamation points, or gesture with exaggerated, rapid hand movements. He or she might write a harsh email message such as, "It's about time you started taking your job seriously, and put in some real effort."

In the subordinate mode, we might speak quietly and hesitantly, in a meek tone, and being apologetic. A subordinate person might ask, "I know you have better things on your mind than to worry about me, but I was wondering when I can expect my reimbursement for travel expenses?" In a work setting we ordinarily expect people with more formal authority to have the dominant role in conversations. However, in more democratic, informal companies, workers with more authority are less likely to feel the need to dominate conversations.

The cold–warm dimension also shapes communication because we invite the same behaviour that we send. Cold, impersonal, negative messages evoke similar messages from others. In contrast, warm verbal and nonverbal messages evoke similar behaviour in others. Getting back to the inquiry about the travel-expense cheque, here is a colder versus warmer response by the manager:

> **Colder:** Travel vouchers really aren't my responsibility. You'll just have to wait like everybody else.
>
> **Warmer:** I understand your problem. Not getting reimbursed on time is a bummer. I'll follow up on the status of your expense cheque sometime today or tomorrow.

The combination of dominant and cold communication sends the signal that the sender of the message wants to control and to limit, or even withdraw from a personal relationship. A team leader might say that she cannot attend a Saturday morning meeting because she has to go out of town for her brother's wedding. A dominant and cold manager might say, "I don't want to hear about your personal life. Everyone in this department has to attend our Saturday meeting."

Subordinate actions combined with warm communication signal a desire to maintain or build the relationship while yielding to the other person. A manager communicating in a warm and subordinate manner in relation to the wedding request

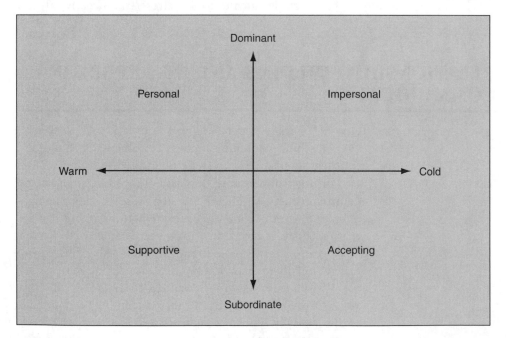

Figure 3-2   Communication Dimensions of Establishing a Relationship

Source: Sorenson, Ritch; Debord, Grace; Ramirez, Ida, *Business and Management Communication: A Guide Book*, 4th Edition, © 2001. Adapted by permission of Pearson Education, Inc. Upper Saddle River, NJ.

might say, "We'll miss you on Saturday morning because you are a key player in our department. However, I recognize that major events in personal life sometimes take priority over a business meeting."

Figure 3-2 summarizes how the dual dimensions of dominate–subordinate and cold–warm influence the relationship-building aspects of communication. Rather than regarding these four quadrants of relationships as good or bad, think of your purposes. In some situations you might want to dominate and be cold, yet in most situations you might want to submit a little and be warm in order to build a relationship. For example, being dominant and cold might be necessary for a security officer who is trying to control an unruly crowd at a sporting event.

Observe that the person in the quadrant *dominant–cold* has an impersonal relationship with the receiver, and the person in the *subordinate–warm* quadrant has a supportive relationship with the receiver. Being *dominant and warm* leads to a personal relationship, whereas being *submissive and cold* leads to an accepting relationship. The combinations of *dominant–cold* and *subordinate–warm* are more likely to produce the results indicated.

NONVERBAL COMMUNICATION IN ORGANIZATIONS

Our discussion so far has emphasized the use of words, or verbal communication. A substantial amount of communication between people, however, takes place at the nonverbal level. **Nonverbal communication** refers to the transmission of messages through means other than words. These messages accompany verbal messages, or sometimes stand alone. The general purpose of nonverbal communication is to communicate the feeling behind a message. For instance, you can say no with either a clenched fist or a smile, to communicate the intensity of your negative or positive feelings.

A classic study by Albert Mehrabian dramatizes the relevance of nonverbal communication. He calculated the relative weights of three elements of communication with respect to conveying emotion. The words we choose account for only about 7 percent of our emotional impact on others. Our tone of voice accounts for 38 percent of the impact, and our facial expressions for 55 percent. Nonverbal behaviour therefore accounts for 93 percent of the emotional impact of a message.[2] Mehrabian's study is often interpreted to mean that 93 percent of communication is nonverbal. In truth, the study deals only with the emotional impact of a message, not what we usually regard as the message's content.

The following paragraphs summarize the major modes of transmission of nonverbal communication and provide guidelines for improving it. Cultural differences in nonverbal communication are discussed in Chapter 6.

TRANSMISSION OF NONVERBAL COMMUNICATION

Nonverbal communication can be transmitted in many modes. You may be surprised that certain factors, such as dress and appearance, are considered part of nonverbal communication.

ENVIRONMENT

The environment, or setting, in which you send a message can influence how that message is received. Assume that your manager invites you out to lunch at a fine restaurant to discuss a problem. You will think it is a more important topic under these circumstances than you would if the manager had lunch with you in the company cafeteria.

Other important silent environmental messages include room colour, temperature, lighting, and furniture arrangement. A person who sits behind a large, uncluttered desk, for example, appears more powerful than a person who sits behind a small, messy desk.

INTERPERSONAL DISTANCE

The positioning of one's body in relation to someone else (*proxemics*) is widely used to transmit messages (see Figure 3-3). In general, getting physically close to another person conveys a positive attitude toward that person. Putting your arm around someone is generally interpreted as a friendly act. (Some people, however, recoil when touched by someone other than a close friend. Touching others on the job can also be interpreted as sexual harassment.) Also be aware that different cultures may have rules that govern touching and personal distance that may be very different from your own.

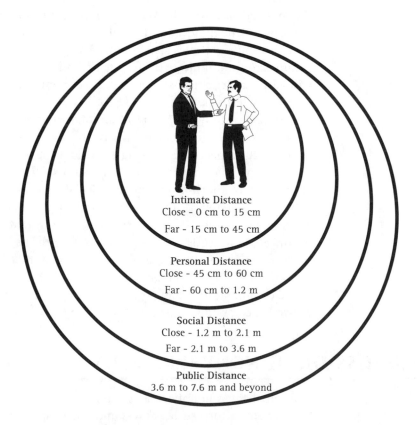

Intimate Distance
Close - 0 cm to 15 cm

Far - 15 cm to 45 cm

Personal Distance
Close - 45 cm to 60 cm

Far - 60 cm to 1.2 m

Social Distance
Close - 1.2 m to 2.1 m

Far - 2.1 m to 3.6 m

Public Distance
3.6 m to 7.6 m and beyond

Figure 3-3   Four Circles of Intimacy

Closely related to interpersonal distance is where and how you sit in relation to another person during a meeting. Sitting across the table from a person during a negotiation session creates a defensive, competitive atmosphere, often leading each party to take a firm stand on his or her point of view. The table becomes a tangible and psychological barrier between both parties. Recognition of this observation leads many managers and salespeople to sit down with another person with either no table or a coffee table between them. Even when seated on separate chairs instead of a sofa, removal of a large table or desk separating the two parties leads to a friendlier, more open negotiation or sales discussion.[3]

POSTURE

Posture communicates a variety of messages. Standing erect usually conveys the message that the person is self-confident and experiencing positive emotion. Slumping makes a person appear to be lacking in self-confidence or feeling down. Another interpersonal message conveyed by posture involves the direction of leaning. Leaning toward the sender suggests that you are favourably disposed toward his or her message; leaning backward communicates the opposite. Openness of the arms or legs serves as an indicator of liking or caring. In general, people establish closed postures (arms folded and legs crossed) when speaking to people they dislike. Can you think of an aspect of your posture that conveys a specific message?

GESTURES

Positive attitudes toward another person are shown by frequent hand movements. In contrast, dislike or lack of interest usually produces few gestures. An important exception is that some people wave their hands furiously while arguing. Gestures are also said to provide clues to a person's levels of dominance and submission. The gestures of dominant people are typically directed outward toward the other person. Examples include a steady, unwavering gaze and touching one's conversational partner. Submissive gestures are usually protective, such as touching oneself or shrugging one's shoulders.

FACIAL EXPRESSIONS

Using your head, face, and eyes in combination provides the clearest indications of interpersonal attitudes. Looking at the ceiling (without tilting your head), combined with a serious expression, almost always communicates the message "I doubt what you're saying is true." Maintaining eye contact with another person improves communication. To maintain eye contact, it is usually necessary to move your face and eyes *with* the other person. Moving your face and eyes *away* from the other person is often interpreted as defensiveness or a lack of self-confidence.

Facial expressions are also important, because many people interpret them as indicators of whether or not a person is telling the truth. In general, fabrication is suggested by facial tics and nervous mannerisms that reveal how uncomfortable the sender is with telling something false. Looking away from a person is often interpreted as covering up a lie. However, err on the side of caution. Recent research indicates that people have a variety of nervous mannerisms even when not lying.[4]

VOICE QUALITY

Often more significance is attached to the *way* something is said than to *what* is said. A forceful voice, which includes a consistent tone without vocalized pauses (like *uh* and *um*), connotes power and control. Closely related to voice tone are volume, pitch, and rate of speaking. Anger, boredom, and joy can often be interpreted from voice quality. Anger is noted when the person speaks loudly, with a high pitch and at a fast rate. Boredom is indicated by a monotone. Joy is indicated by loud volume. Avoiding an annoying voice quality can make a positive impact on others. The research of voice coach Jeffrey Jacobi provides some useful suggestions. He surveyed a sample of 1000 men and women and asked, "Which irritating or unpleasant voice annoys you the most?" The most irritating was a whining, complaining, or nagging tone.

Jacobi notes that we are judged by the way we sound. He also notes that careers can be damaged by voice problems such as those indicated in the survey. "We think about how we look and dress," says Jacobi, "and that gets most of the attention. But people judge our intelligence much more by how we sound than how we dress.[5] Do Self-Assessment Quiz 3-1 below to see how Jacobi's findings might apply to your development.

PERSONAL APPEARANCE

Your external image plays an important role in communicating messages to others. A current analysis confirms what has been known for a long time: a favourable personal appearance enhances a person's ability to persuade others, whether you are dealing with an individual receiver or an audience.[6] Job seekers show recognition of the personal appearance aspect of nonverbal communication when they carefully groom themselves for a job interview. People pay more respect and grant more privileges to those they perceive as being well-dressed and neatly groomed. The meaning of being well-dressed depends heavily on the situation. In an information technology firm, neatly pressed jeans, a stylish T-shirt, and clean sport shoes might qualify as being well-dressed. The same attire worn in a financial service firm would qualify as being poorly dressed.

Self-Assessment Quiz 3-1

VOICE-QUALITY CHECKUP

The voice-quality study cited in the text ranked voice quality in decreasing order of annoyance, as follows:

- Whining, complaining, or nagging tone—44.0%
- High-pitched, squeaky voice—15.9%
- Mumbling—11.1%
- Very fast talking—4.9%
- Weak and wimpy voice—3.6%

(Continued)

- Flat, monotonous tone—3.5%
- Thick accent—2.4%

Directions: Ask yourself and two other people familiar with your voice whether you have one or more of the preceding voice-quality problems. If your self-analysis and feedback from others does indicate a serious problem, get started on self-improvement. Record your voice on tape and attempt to modify the biggest problem. Another avenue of improvement is to consult with a speech coach or therapist.

A recent tendency is a return to more formal business attire, to suggest that a person is ambitious and successful. A recent analysis concluded that formal dress frequently makes a better impression than casual wear on customers and bosses.[7] The best advice for using appearance to communicate nonverbal messages is to size up the environment to figure out what type of appearance and dress connotes the image you want to project.

GUIDELINES FOR IMPROVING NONVERBAL COMMUNICATION

Nonverbal communication, like verbal communication, can be improved. Here are six suggestions to consider:

1. *Obtain feedback on your body language by asking others to comment on the gestures and facial expressions you use in conversations.* Have yourself video-taped conferring with another individual. After studying your body language, attempt to eliminate those mannerisms and gestures you think detract from your effectiveness. Common examples include nervous gestures such as moving knees from side to side, cracking knuckles, rubbing the eyes or nose, head scratching, and jingling coins.

2. *Learn to relax when communicating with others.* Take a deep breath and consciously allow your body muscles to loosen. Tension-reducing techniques should be helpful here. It is easier for other people to relax around a relaxed person. You are likely to elicit more useful information from other people when you are relaxed.

3. *Use facial, hand, and body gestures to supplement your speech, but don't overdo it.* A good starting point is to use hand gestures to express enthusiasm. You can increase the potency of enthusiastic comments by shaking the other person's hand, nodding approval, or smiling.

4. *Avoid using the same nonverbal gesture indiscriminately.* If you want to use nodding to convey approval, do not nod with approval when you dislike what somebody else is saying. Also, do not pat everybody on the back. Nonverbal gestures used indiscriminately lose their effectiveness.

5. *Use role-playing to practise various forms of nonverbal communication.* A good starting point would be to practise selling your ideas about an important project or concept to another person. During your interchange, supplement your spoken messages with appropriate nonverbal cues such as posture, voice intonation, gestures, and so on. Later, inquire about the other person's perception of the effectiveness of your nonverbal communication.

6. *Use mirroring to establish rapport.* Nonverbal communication can be improved through **mirroring**, or subtly imitating someone. The most successful mirroring technique is to imitate the breathing pattern of another person. If you adjust your own breathing rate to match someone else's, you will soon establish a rapport with that individual. Another effective mirroring technique is to adapt the voice speed of the person with whom you are communicating. If the other person speaks more slowly than you typically do, slow down to mirror him or her.

   You can also use mirroring to win favour by imitating a manager. Many group members have a relentless tendency to copy the boss's mannerisms, gestures, way of speaking, and dress. As a consequence, without realizing why, your manager may think more favourably of you.

   Caution: Do not use mirroring to the extent that you appear to be mocking another person, thereby adversely affecting rapport. One way to avoid mocking someone is to imitate the person after a slight pause. For example, if the person crosses his or her legs, do so after a brief pause. To get started in developing your mirroring skills, do Skill-Building Exercise 3-1 below.

Skill-Building Exercise 3-1

THE MIRRORING TECHNIQUE

To practise mirroring, during the next 10 days each class member schedules one mirroring session with an unsuspecting subject. An ideal opportunity would be an upcoming meeting at work. Another possibility would be to ask a friend if you could practise your interviewing techniques with him or her—but do not mention the mirroring technique. A third possibility would be to sit down with a friend and engage in a social conversation. Imitate the person's breathing pattern, rate of speech, hand movements, eye movements, leg movements, or any other noticeable aspect of behaviour.

Afterward, hold a class discussion about the results, focusing on these questions:

1. Did the other person notice the mirroring and comment on the behaviour of the person doing the mirroring?

2. Was rapport improved (or hindered) by the mirroring?

3. How many of the students intend to repeat the mirroring technique in the future?

GUIDELINES FOR OVERCOMING COMMUNICATION PROBLEMS AND BARRIERS

Communication problems are ever-present in organizations. Some interference usually takes place between idea formation and action, as suggested earlier by the noise factor in Figure 3-2. The type of message influences the amount of interference. Routine or neutral messages are the easiest to communicate. Interference is most likely to occur when a message is complex, emotionally arousing, or clashes with a receiver's mental set.

An emotionally arousing message deals with topics such as money or a relationship between two people. A message that clashes with a receiver's mental set requires the person to change his or her typical pattern of receiving messages. Try this experiment. The next time you visit a restaurant, order dessert first and the entrée second. The server probably will not receive your dessert order, because it deviates from the normal sequence.

We will now describe strategies and tactics for overcoming some of the more frequently observed communication problems in organizations (see Figure 3-4).

UNDERSTAND THE RECEIVER

Understanding the person you are trying to reach is fundamental to overcoming communication barriers. The more you know about your receiver, the more effectively you can deliver your message. Three important aspects of understanding the receiver are (1) developing empathy, (2) recognizing his or her motivational state, and (3) understanding the other person's frame of reference.

Developing **empathy** requires placing yourself in the receiver's shoes. To accomplish this, you need to imagine yourself in the other person's role and assume the viewpoints and emotions of that individual. For example, if a supervisor were trying to communicate the importance of customer service to her sales associates, she might ask herself, "If I were a part-time employee being paid close to the minimum wage, how receptive would I be to messages about high-quality customer service?" To empathize, you need to understand another person. (To *sympathize,* in contrast, means to understand and agree.)

1. Understand the receiver.
2. Minimize defensive communication.
3. Use multiple channels.
4. Use verbal and nonverbal feedback.
5. Display a positive attitude.
6. Use persuasive communication.
7. Engage in active listening.
8. Prepare for stressful conversations.
9. Recognize gender differences in communication styles.
10. Engage in metacommunications.

Figure 3-4   Overcoming Communication Problems and Barriers

The receiver's **motivational state** could include any active needs and interests operating at the time. People tend to listen attentively to messages that show promise of satisfying an active need. Management usually listens attentively to a suggestion framed in terms of cost savings or increased profits.

People perceive words and concepts differently because their vantage points and perspectives differ. Such differences in **frames of reference** create barriers to communication. A frame of reference can also be considered a lens through which we view the world. A manager attempted to chastise a team member by saying, "If you keep up your present level of performance, you'll be a repair technician all your life." The technician replied, "That's good news," because he was proud of being the first person in his family to hold a skilled job. Understanding another person's frame of reference requires empathy.

MINIMIZE DEFENSIVE COMMUNICATION

Defensive communication—the tendency to receive messages in such a way that our self-esteem is protected—is an important general communication barrier. Defensive communication also accounts for people sending messages to make themselves look good. For example, when being criticized for low production, an investment banker might blame the advertising agency used by his firm.

Overcoming the barrier of defensive communication requires two steps. First, people need to recognize the existence of defensive communication. Second, they need to try not to be defensive when questioned or criticized. Such behaviour is not easy because of the unconscious or semi-conscious process of **denial**—the suppression of information we find uncomfortable. For example, the investment banker just cited would find it uncomfortable to think of himself as being responsible for below-average performance.

USE MULTIPLE CHANNELS

Repetition improves communication, particularly when different channels are used to convey the same message. Effective communicators at many job levels follow spoken agreements with written documentation. Since most communication is subject to at least some distortion, the chances of a message being received as intended increase when two or more channels are used.

Many firms have a policy of using a multiple-channel approach to communicate the results of a performance appraisal. The group member receives an oral explanation from the manager of the results of the review. The group member is also required to read the form and indicate by signature that he or she has read and understands the meaning of the review. Another good use of multiple channels is following up a telephone call or in-person conversation with an email message summarizing key facts or agreements.

USE VERBAL AND NONVERBAL FEEDBACK

Ask for feedback to determine whether your message has been received as intended. A frequent managerial practice is to conclude a meeting with a question such as, "OK, what have we agreed upon?" Unless feedback of this nature is obtained, you will not know whether your message has been received until the receiver carries out your request. If the request is carried out improperly, or if no action is taken, you will know that the message was received poorly.

Obtaining feedback is important because it results in two-way communication in which people take turns being sender and receiver, thereby having a dialogue. Dialogues take time because they require people to speak more slowly and listen more carefully. The results of having employees engage in dialogue are said to include a deeper sense of community (a feeling of belongingness) and greater trust among employees.[8] You might relate this finding to your own experiences. Do you trust another person more when the two of you exchange ideas and listen to each other?

Feedback is also important because it provides reinforcement to the sender, and few people will continue to communicate without any reinforcement. The sender is reinforced when the receiver indicates understanding of the message. When the original receiver indicates that he or she understands the message, that person becomes the sender. A nod of approval would be an appropriate type of nonverbal reinforcement for the sender to receive.

Lastly, feedback is important to ensure that your words, including your terms, are appropriate. It can be easy to offend someone without meaning to and there are times when you may wish to obtain feedback about certain words, terms, or phrases. You will usually receive immediate feedback if the language is seen as offensive; other times it will be less obvious. If you say something, and you are unsure of its appropriateness or correct usage, obtain feedback by asking politely about the term or phrase. The Canadian Scene below illustrates how a term that most Canadians are not offended by was misunderstood.

The Canadian Scene

CANUCK OR NOT CANUCK?

Several years ago, a writer for a campus newspaper in the US used the word *Canucks* when referring to the large number of Canadians in the American entertainment field. The newspaper, *The Statesman*, is circulated at Indiana State University. Because of this incident and other prior incidents, the writer was fired. However, the writer was rehired after the editor received many letters from Canadians saying that they were not offended by the term. What's most interesting is that Merv Hendricks, the university's director of student publications at the time, had complained that the term was a derogatory label for French Canadians.[i]

There appears to have been some confusion at the university as to what the term *Canuck* means and whether or not it is offensive. As mentioned in the article, the Vancouver Canucks are a Canadian NHL hockey team. The term has been around for well over a century. Johnny Canuck was a cartoon character that appeared in newspapers in the 1860s. During World War II, he became a cartoon hero in comic books, protecting Canadians from the Nazi threat.[ii] If you are looking for Canadian content on the internet, many sites have *Canuck* in the address or the title. There is even a Canuck site of the day! It would appear that many Canadians use this term to refer to themselves. So what do you think? Is the Canuck label offensive, or is it OK to call ourselves Canucks?

Sources:

i. "'Canuck' No Slur, Editor Rehired," *Peterborough Examiner*, Sunday, February 28, 1999, pp. 40–42. Adapted with permission from the Associated Press.

ii. Andrew Phillips, "Fear and Hope at Home: Social Changes Caused by WW II," *Maclean's*, June 6, 1994.

DISPLAY A POSITIVE ATTITUDE

Being perceived as having a positive attitude helps melt communication barriers. Most people prefer to communicate with a positive person. According to Sharon Lund O'Neil, you must establish credibility and trustworthiness if you expect others to listen, let alone get them to react positively to your communication.[9] Being positive helps make you appear more credible and trustworthy, whereas being consistently negative makes you seem less so. As one co-worker said about a chronic complainer in his office, "Why take Margot seriously? She finds something wrong with everybody and everything."

USE PERSUASIVE COMMUNICATION

A powerful tactic for overcoming communication barriers is to communicate so persuasively, so convincingly, that obstacles disappear and the receiver "buys" the message. Persuasion thus involves selling messages. Hundreds of articles, books, and tapes have been developed to help people learn to be more persuasive. The following are representative suggestions for becoming a more persuasive communicator:[10]

1. *Know exactly what you want.* Your chances of selling an idea increase to the extent that you have clarified the idea in your own mind. The clearer and more committed you are at the outset of a selling or negotiating session, the stronger you are as a persuader.

2. *Never suggest an action without specifying its end benefit.* In asking for a raise, you might say, "If I get this raise, I'll be able to afford to stay in this job as long as the company likes."

3. *Get a "yes response" early on.* It is helpful to give the selling session a positive tone by establishing a "yes pattern" at the outset. Assume that an employee wanted to convince the boss to allow him or her to perform some work at home during normal working hours. The employee might begin the idea-selling questions with, "Is it important for the company to obtain maximum productivity from all its employees?"

4. *Use power words.* An expert tactic for being persuasive is to sprinkle your speech with power (meaning *powerful*) words. Power words stir emotion and bring forth images of exciting events. Examples of power words include *decimating* the competition, *bonding* with customers, *surpassing* previous profits, *capturing* customer loyalty, and *rebounding* from a downturn.

5. *Minimize raising your pitch at the end of sentences.* Part of being persuasive is to not sound unsure and apologetic. In English and several other languages, a convenient way to ask a question or express doubt is to raise the pitch of your voice at the end of a sentence or phrase. As a test, use the sentence "You like my ideas." First say *ideas* using approximately the same pitch and tone as with every other word. Then say the same sentence by pronouncing *ideas* with a higher pitch and louder tone. By saying *ideas* in this way, you sound much less certain and are less persuasive.

6. *Talk to your audience, not the screen.* Computer graphic presentations have become standard practice even in small-group meetings. Many presenters rely so heavily on computer-generated slides and transparencies that they essentially read the slides and transparencies to the audience. Jean Mausehund and R. Neil Dortch remind us that in an oral presentation, the predominant means of connection between sender and receiver should be eye contact. When your audience is frequently distracted by movement on the screen, computer sounds, garish colours, or your looking at the screen, eye contact suffers. As a result, the message is weakened and you are less persuasive.[11]

7. *Back up conclusions with data.* You will be more persuasive if you support your spoken and written presentations with solid data. You can collect the data yourself or quote from a printed or electronic source. Relying too much on research has a potential disadvantage, however. Being too dependent on data could suggest that you have little faith in your intuition. For example, you might convey a weak impression if, when asked your opinion, you respond, "I can't answer until I collect some data."

8. *Minimize "wimp" phrases.* Persuasive communicators minimize statements that make them appear weak and indecisive. Such phrases convey the impression that they are not in control of their actions. Wimp phrases include: "It's one of those days," "I'm not sure about that," "Don't quote me on that," and "I'll try my best to get it done." (It is better to commit yourself forcibly by saying, "I'll get it done.")

9. *Avoid or minimize common language errors.* You will be more persuasive if you minimize common language errors, because you will appear more articulate and informed. Here are several common language errors:

   a. "Just between you and I" is wrong. "Just between you and me" is correct.
   b. *Irregardless* is not a word; *regardless* is correct.
   c. Avoid double negatives (despite their increasing popularity). Common examples are "I didn't get *nothing* from my best customer this week" and "We don't have *no money* in the budget for travel." Double negatives make the sender appear so ill-informed that they fail to persuade.
   d. "We are customer-oriented" is correct. "We are customer-orientated" is wrong.

10. *Avoid overuse of jargon and clichés.* To feel "in" and hip, many workers rely heavily on jargon and clichés, such as referring to their "fave" (for *favourite*) product, or saying that "At the end of the day" something counts, or that software is "scalable" (meaning it can get bigger). Add to the list "a seamless company" to mean various departments cooperate with one another. The caution is that if a person uses jargon and hip phrases too frequently, the person appears to be too contrived, and lacking in imagination.[12]

If you can learn to implement most of the preceding 10 suggestions, you are on your way to becoming a persuasive communicator. In addition, you will need solid facts behind you, and you will need to make skillful use of nonverbal communication.

ENGAGE IN ACTIVE LISTENING

Persuasion deals primarily with sending messages. Improving one's ability to receive messages is also part of developing better communication skills. Unless you receive messages as they are intended, you cannot perform your job properly or be a good companion. Listening has even been described as our primary communication activity when we are engaged in face-to-face communication. Listening is a particularly important skill for anybody whose job involves troubleshooting, since one needs to gather information to solve problems.

Another reason that improving the listening skills of employees is important is that inadequate listening is extraordinarily costly. Listening mistakes lead to reprocessing letters, rescheduling appointments, reshipping orders, and the need to recall defective products. Effective listening also improves interpersonal relations, because the people listened to feel understood and respected.

A major component of effective listening is to be an **active listener**. The active listener listens intently, with the goal of empathizing with the speaker. As a result of listening actively, the listener can feed back to the speaker what he or she thinks the speaker meant. Feedback of this type relies on both verbal and nonverbal communication. Active listening also involves **summarization**. When you summarize, you pull together, condense, and thereby clarify the main points communicated by the other person. Here are three examples of summarization statements:

"What I heard you say during our meeting is that . . . "

"As I understand it, your position is that . . . "

"Your major objection then is that . . . "

Another component to active listening is to indicate by your body language that you are listening intently. When a co-worker comes to you with a question or concern, focus on that person and exclude all else. If you tap your fingers on the desk or glance around the room, you send the message that the other person and his or her concerns do not warrant your full attention. Listening intently through nonverbal communication also facilitates active listening because it demonstrates respect for the speaker.

Specific suggestions for improving active listening skills are summarized in Figure 3-5 on page 60. These suggestions relate to good listening in general, as well as to active listening. As with any other suggestions for developing a new skill, considerable practice (with some supervision) is required to bring about actual changes in behaviour.

One of the problems a poor listener will likely encounter is the difficulty of breaking old habits. Self-Assessment Quiz 3-2 gives you an opportunity to think about bad listening habits you may have acquired. To practise your listening skills, do Skill-Building Exercise 3-2 on page 60.

PREPARE FOR STRESSFUL CONVERSATIONS

Communication barriers will frequently surface when two or more people are engaged in a conversation fraught with emotion, such as a highly negative performance review,

Self-Assessment Quiz 3-2

LISTENING TRAPS

Communication specialists at Purdue University in the US have identified certain behaviour patterns that interfere with effective hearing and listening. After thinking carefully about each trap, note whether it is "Not a problem" for you or whether you "Need improvement." To respond to the statements accurately, visualize how you acted when you were recently in a situation calling for listening.

	Not a problem	Need improvement
Mind reader. You will receive limited information if you constantly think "What is this person really thinking or feeling?"	☐	☐
Rehearser. Your mental rehearsals for "Here's what I'll say next" tune out the sender.	☐	☐
Filterer. You engage in selective listening by hearing only what you want to hear. (Could be difficult to judge because the process is often unconscious.)	☐	☐
Dreamer. You drift off during a face-to-face conversation, which often leads you to an embarrassing "What did you say?" or "Could you repeat that?"	☐	☐
Identifier. If you refer everything you hear to your experience, you probably did not really listen to what was said.	☐	☐
Comparer. When you get sidetracked sizing up the sender, you are sure to miss the message.	☐	☐
Derailer. You change the subject too quickly, giving the impression that you are not interested in anything the sender has to say.	☐	☐
Sparrer. You hear what is said, but quickly belittle or discount it, putting you in the same class as the derailer.	☐	☐
Placater. You agree with everything you hear just to be nice or to avoid conflict. By behaving this way you miss out on the opportunity for authentic dialogue.	☐	☐

Interpretation: If you checked "Need improvement" for five or more of the above statements, you are correct—your listening needs improvement! If you checked only two or fewer of the above traps, you are probably an effective listener and a supportive person.

Source: Reprinted with permission from *Messages: The Communication Skills Book* (Oakland, California: New Harbinger Publications, 1983).

a rejection of a person for membership in a team, or the firing of an employee. Giving praise is another exchange that can make both or either parties uncomfortable. The sender might feel that he or she is patronizing the receiver, and the receiver might feel unworthy of the praise. One technique for reducing the stress in potentially stressful conversations is to prepare for them in advance.

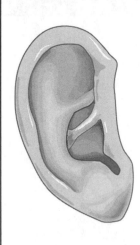

- *While your target is talking, look at him or her intently.* At the same time, maintain a steady eye contact.
- *Be patient about your turn to speak.* A common barrier to effective listening is to mentally prepare an answer while another person is speaking.
- *Nod your head in agreement from time to time.*
- *Mutter "mmh" or "uh-huh" periodically but not incessantly.*
- *Ask open-ended questions to encourage the other person to talk.* For example, you encourage more conversation by saying "What do you think of . . ." rather than asking "Do you agree that . . . ."
- *Reflect your target's content or meaning.* Rephrase and summarize concisely what the other person is saying.
- *Reflect the other person's feelings.* Reflection-of-feeling responses typically begin with "You feel that . . ."
- *Keep your ratio of talking to listening down to about 1 to 5.* In other words, spend 20 percent of your time talking, and 80 percent listening to be perceived as a great listener.
- *Ask yourself whether anything the other person is saying could benefit you.* Maintaining this perspective will enable you to benefit from most listening episodes and will motivate you to listen intently.

Figure 3-5   Suggestions for Active Listening

Skill-Building Exercise 3-2

LISTENING TO A CO-WORKER

Before conducting the following role plays, review the nine keys to effective listening presented in Figure 3-5. The sixth suggestion, about restating what you hear (summarization), is particularly important when listening to a person who is talking about an emotional topic.

The Elated Co-worker: One student plays the role of a worker who has just been offered a promotion to supervisor of another department. He or she will receive a 10 percent raise in pay and travel overseas twice a year for the company. This first worker is eager to describe full details of his or her good fortune to a co-worker, who is played by another student. The second worker decides to listen intently to the first worker. Other class members will rate the second student on his or her listening ability.

The Discouraged Co-worker: One student plays the role of an employee who has just been placed on probation for poor job performance. The employee's boss thinks that his or her performance is below standard and that his or her attendance and punctuality are poor. The worker is afraid that telling his or her spouse will end their relationship. The person is eager to tell this tale of woe to a co-worker, played by another student. The second worker decides to listen intently but is pressed for time. Other class members will rate the second student on listening ability.

A starting point in preparing for a stressful conversation is self-awareness about how you react to certain uncomfortable exchanges. For example, how do you feel when the receiver of the negative feedback reacts with hostility? Do you clam up, or do you become hostile yourself? If you anticipate a hostile reception to an upcoming conversation, rehearse the scenario with a neutral friend. Deliver the controversial content that you will be delivering during the real event. Practise the body language you will use when you deliver a message such as, "As team leader, I must tell you that you have contributed almost nothing of value to our current project." Another part of the rehearsal is to practise delivering clear content—be explicit about what you mean. "You've contributed almost nothing of value to our current project" is much more explicit than "Your contribution has much room for improvement."

Also, practise *temperate phrasing*, or being tactful while delivering negative feedback. Communications specialist Holly Weeks suggests, for instance, that instead of snapping at someone by saying "Stop interrupting me," you could try this: "Can you hold on a minute? I want to finish before I lose my train of thought." Temperate phrasing will take some of the sting out of a stressful conversation.[13]

RECOGNIZE GENDER DIFFERENCES IN COMMUNICATION STYLE

A trend in organizations for many years has been to move toward equality of the sexes. Despite this trend, substantial interest has arisen in identifying differences in communication styles between men and women. A book by linguist Deborah Tannen, *Talking from 9 to 5*, focuses especially on male–female differences in conversational style in the workplace. A book by John Gray, *Men Are from Mars, Women Are from Venus*, also explores this topic.

People who are aware of these differences face fewer communication barriers between themselves and members of the opposite sex. As we describe these differences, recognize that they are group stereotypes. Individual differences in communication style usually are more important than group (men versus women) differences. Here we will describe the major findings of gender differences in communication patterns.[14]

1. *Women prefer to use conversation for building rapport.* For most women, the intent of conversation is to build rapport and connections with people. Women are therefore more likely to emphasize similarities, to listen intently, and to be supportive.

2. *Men prefer to use talk as a means of preserving independence and status by displaying knowledge and skill.* When most men talk, they want to receive positive evaluation from others and maintain their hierarchical status within the group. Men are therefore more oriented to giving a *report* while women are more interested in establishing *rapport*.

3. *Women want empathy, not solutions.* When women share feelings of being stressed out, they seek empathy and understanding. If they feel they have been listened to carefully, they begin to relax. When listening to the woman, the man may feel blamed for her problems or that he has failed the woman in some way. To feel useful, the man might offer solutions to the woman's problems.

4. *Men prefer to work out their problems by themselves, whereas women prefer to talk out solutions with another person.* Women look upon having and sharing problems as an opportunity to build and deepen relationships. Men are more likely to look upon problems as challenges they must meet on their own.

The communication consequence of these differences is that men may become uncommunicative when they have a problem.

5. *Women are more likely to compliment the work of a co-worker, whereas men are more likely to be critical.* A communication problem may occur when a woman compliments the work of a male co-worker and expects reciprocal praise.

6. *Men tend to be more directive in their conversation, whereas women emphasize politeness.* Women are therefore more likely to frequently use the phrases "I'm sorry" and "Thank you," even when there is no need to express apology or gratitude. For example, a supermarket manager notices that the store has suddenly become busy. She might say to a store clerk unpacking boxes, "I'm sorry, Jason, but we've become busy all of a sudden. Could you please open up a new lane up front? Thank you." A manager who is a stereotypical male might say, "Jason, we need you to open a line up front, pronto. Put down the boxes and get up there."

7. *Women tend to be more conciliatory when facing differences, whereas men become more intimidating.* Again, women are more interested in building relationships, whereas men are more concerned about coming out ahead.

8. Men are more interested than women in calling *attention to their accomplishments or in monopolizing recognition.* In one instance, a sales representative who had already made her sales quota for the month turned over an excellent prospect to a co-worker. She reasoned, "It's somebody else's turn. I've received more than my fair share of bonuses for the month."

9. *Men tend to dominate discussions during meetings.* One study of college faculty meetings found that women's longest turns at speaking were, on average, of shorter duration than men's shortest turns. A possible explanation is that women are still less assertive than men in the workplace.

How can the information just presented help overcome communication problems on the job? As a starting point, remember that these gender differences often exist. Understanding these differences will help you interpret the communication behaviour of people. For example, if a male co-worker is not as effusive with praise as you would like, remember that he is simply engaging in gender-typical behaviour; do not take it personally.

A woman can remind herself to speak up more in meetings because her natural tendency might be toward diffidence. A man might remind himself to be more complimentary and supportive toward co-workers, even though his natural tendency might be to skip the praise.

A woman should not take it personally when a male co-worker or subordinate is tight-lipped when faced with a problem. She should recognize that he needs more encouragement to talk about his problems than would a woman. If the man persists in not wanting to talk about the problem, the woman might say, "It looks like you want to work out this problem on your own. Go ahead. I'm available if you want to talk about the problem."

Men and women should recognize that when women talk over problems, they might not be seeking hard-hitting advice. Instead, they might simply be searching for a sympathetic ear so they can deal with the emotional aspect of the problem.

A general suggestion for overcoming gender-related communication barriers is for men to improve communication by becoming more empathetic listeners. Women can improve communication by becoming more direct.

Ruth Sherman, a speech and communications consultant, advises you to be more aware of how you talk at work. If you feel that you are not being listened to in meetings or that you have trouble persuading managers of your ability or accomplishments, get feedback from others. Ask a colleague you trust to watch you during a meeting and provide analysis.[15]

ENGAGE IN METACOMMUNICATIONS

When confronted with a communication problem, one response is to attempt to work around the barrier, perhaps by using one of the methods already described. A more typical response is to ignore the barrier by making no special effort to deal with the problem—a "take it or leave it" approach to communication. Another possibility is to **metacommunicate**, or communicate about your communication, to help overcome barriers or resolve a problem.[16] If you as a team leader were facing heavy deadline pressures, you might say to a team member, "I might appear brusque today and tomorrow. Please don't take it personally. It's just that I have to make heavy demands on you because the team is facing a gruelling deadline."

SUMMARY

Communication is the basic process by which managers, customer-contact workers, and professionals accomplish their work, yet many communication problems exist in organizations. Communication among people is a complex process that can be divided into six components: sender or source, message, channel (or medium), receiver, feedback, and environment. Noise, or interference, can disrupt communication within any of these components.

Nonverbal communication plays an important part in sending and receiving messages and is especially important for imparting the emotional aspects of a message. Modes of nonverbal communication include the environment in which the message is sent, interpersonal distance, posture, gestures, facial expressions, voice quality, and personal appearance.

Nonverbal communication can be improved through such means as obtaining feedback, learning to relax, using gestures more discriminately, role-playing, and mirroring (which refers to subtly imitating someone).

Methods of overcoming communication barriers include the following: (1) understand the receiver; (2) minimize defensive communication; (3) use multiple channels; (4) use verbal and nonverbal feedback; (5) display a positive attitude; (6) use persuasive communication; (7) engage in active listening; (8) prepare for stressful conversations; (9) recognize gender differences in communication styles; and (10) engage in metacommunication (communicate about your communication).

An Interpersonal Relations Case Problem

THE SCRUTINIZED TEAM MEMBER CANDIDATE

HRmanager.com is a human-resources management firm that provides services such as payroll, benefits administration, affirmative action programs, and technical training to other firms. Teams perform most of the work, led by a rotating team leader. CEO and founder Jerry Clune regards the four-person new ventures team as vital for the future of the company. In addition to developing ideas for new services, the team members are responsible for obtaining clients for any new service they propose that Clune approves. The new ventures team thus develops and sells new services. After the service is launched and working well, the sales group is responsible for developing more clients.

As with other teams at HRmanager.com, the members of the new ventures team have a say in who is hired to join their team. In conjunction with Clune, the new ventures team decided it should expand to five members. The team posted the job opening for a new member on an internet recruiting service, ran classified ads in the local newspaper, and also asked present employees for referrals. One of the finalists for the position was Gina Cleveland, a 27-year-old business graduate. In addition to interviewing with Clune and the two company vice-presidents, Cleveland spent half a day with the new ventures team, breakfast and lunch included. About two-and-one-half hours of the time was spent in a team interview in which Gina sat in a conference room with the four team members.

The team members agreed that Cleveland appeared to be a strong candidate on paper. Her education and experience were satisfactory, her résumé was impressive, and she presented herself well during a telephone-screening interview. After Cleveland completed her time with the new ventures team, Lauren Nielsen, the team leader, suggested that the group hold a debriefing session to share ideas about Cleveland's suitability for the team.

Lauren commented, "It seems like we think that Gina is a strong candidate based on her credentials and what she said. But I'm a big believer in nonverbal communication. Studying Gina's body language can give us a lot of valuable information. Let's each share our observations about what Gina's body language tells us she is *really* like. I'll go first.

"I liked the way Gina looked so cool and polished when she joined us for breakfast. She's got all the superficial movements right to project self-confidence. But did anybody else notice how she looked concerned when she had to make a choice from the menu? She finally did choose a ham-and-cheese omelette, but she raised her voice at the end of the sentence when she ordered it. I got the hint that Gina is not very self-confident.

"I also noticed Gina biting her lips a little when we asked her how creative she thought she was. I know that Gina said she was creative and gave us an example of a creative project she completed. Yet nibbling at her lips like that suggests she's not a creative dynamo."

Michael chipped in: "I didn't make any direct observations about Gina's being self-confident or not, but I did notice something that could be related. I think Gina is on a power trip, and this could indicate high or low self-confidence. Did anybody notice how Gina put her hands on her hips when she was standing up? That's a pure and clear signal of somebody who wants to be in control. Her hair is almost the same length and style as that of most women who've made it to the top in Fortune 500 companies. I think she cloned her hairstyle from Carly Fiorina, the HP honcho.

"Another hint I get of Gina's power trip is the way she eyed the cheque in the restaurant at lunch. I could see it in her eyes that she really wanted to pay for the entire team. That could mean a desire to control and show us that she is very important. Do we want someone on the team with such a strong desire to control?"

Brenda then took the floor: "I observed a different picture of Gina based on her nonverbal communication. She dressed just right for the occasion; not too conservatively, not too business-casual. This tells me she can fit into our environment. Did you notice how well-groomed her shoes were? That says she is well-organized and good at details. Her attaché case was a soft, inviting leather. If she were really into

(Continued)

power and control she would carry a hard vinyl or aluminum attaché case. I see Gina as a sensitive and well-organized person who could blend right into our team."

"I hope that because I'm last, I'm not too influenced by the observations that you three have shared so far," said Larry. "My take is that Gina looks great on paper, but that she may have a problem in being a good team player. She's too laid back and distant. Did you notice her handshake? It was so insincere. She gave me the impression of wanting to have the least possible physical contact with me.

"I also couldn't help noticing that Gina did not lean much toward us during the team interview. Do you remember how she would pull her chair back ever so slightly when we got into a heavy discussion? I interpreted that as a sign that Gina does not want to be part of a close-knit group."

"As you've probably noticed," Lauren said, "I've been typing as fast as I can on my laptop, taking notes on your comments. We have some mixed observations here, and I want to summarize and integrate them before we make a decision. I'll send you an email with my summary observations by tomorrow morning. Make any changes you see fit and get back to me. After we have finished evaluating Gina carefully, we'll be able to make our recommendations to Jerry Clune."

Case Questions

1. To what extent are the team members making an appropriate use of nonverbal communication to size up Gina Cleveland?

2. Which team member do you think made the most realistic interpretation of nonverbal behaviour? Why?

3. Should Lauren, the team leader, have told Gina in advance that the team would be scrutinizing her nonverbal behaviour? Justify your answer.

An Interpersonal Relations Case Problem

THE DENTAL FLOSS COMMUNICATION CHALLENGE

Claudia Telfair has worked as a dental hygienist for five years in the same large dental practice in suburban Montreal, Quebec. She treats patients about 25 hours per week. In her words, "If I work too much more than 25 hours per week I'm liable to get tendonitis and carpal tunnel syndrome. All that precision scraping takes a toll on my right hand, and to some extent on my left hand. Hovering over patients can also give me back pains, if I do it for too long each week.

"I feel that my work is so important that I am willing to put up with a little physical pain to help my patients have healthy teeth and gums."

"You would then say that the biggest frustration in your work is its physical demands?" asked the case researcher.

"I never said that. You said that," replied Telfair. "The part of my job with the biggest impact on the health of patients is getting across my message about healthy habits to prevent tooth decay and gum disease. I lecture my patients. I demonstrate how they should be brushing and flossing, and how they should use soft wood plaque removers [such as Stim-u-Dents]. I give out samples.

"I do everything I can think of to convince my patients to take good care of their teeth and gums between cleaning appointments."

"What is so frustrating about what you have just described?"

"The frustration is that my patients don't seem to listen. They smile, they nod in agreement, and they pack the samples. Yet four months later when the patients return, it appears that most of them are engaging in the same old sloppy dental

(Continued)

habits. They continue with superficial brushing with an old toothbrush instead of using a battery-powered or electric one. It looks like they forgot my message about using wooden plaque removers. Yet flossing is the least used preventive treatment of them all."

"When you ask patients why they neglect flossing between their cleaning appointments, what do they say?" asked the case researcher.

"I hear more excuses than you get from violators in traffic court," said Telfair. Some of the typical excuses are that the patients forget, that they are too busy, and that flossing is too painful. A patient told me the other day that he dislikes flossing because the ritual is so ugly and weird."

"What do you tell the patients when you observe that they are not following your advice?"

"I usually just tell them that are doing a poor job of taking care of their teeth and gums. Also, I will usually give them more samples of floss and plaque remover so they will be reminded to do better. Sometimes I give them another brochure about a battery-powered toothbrush.

"I guess you could say that I'm doing a much better job treating tooth and gum problems than preventing them."

Case Questions

1. What communication problems is Claudia Telfair facing in her role as a dental hygienist?

2. What communication errors might Telfair be making?

3. Offer Telfair a couple of suggestions to help her accomplish her goal of being more effective at preventing dental and gum problems, based on your knowledge of interpersonal communication.

Interpersonal Skills Role Play

One student sits on a chair pretending to be a dental patient who does a sloppy job of dental care, such as brushing regularly and flossing. Another student plays the role of a dental hygienist. (A pencil or pen can be used to simulate a metal gum scraper.) With the patient in the chair, engage in a dialogue about the importance of using dental floss. The dental hygienist wants this patient to practise much better dental hygiene, whereas the patient is somewhat sceptical about that advice. Perhaps two or three different pairs can conduct the role play in front of the class. Other class members will observe the effectiveness of the communication episode in terms of the dental hygienist getting his or her message across.

QUESTIONS FOR DISCUSSION AND REVIEW

1. What are the reasons so many workers need improvement in communication skills?

2. How can knowing the steps in the communication process help a person become a more effective communicator?

3. How can people use their automobiles to send nonverbal messages?

4. What type of voice quality do you think would be effective in most work situations?

5. How could watching television provide some useful ideas for improving your job-oriented communication skills?

6. Should a person use power words when he or she is not in a powerful job? Explain.

7. Why is summarization such a powerful communication technique?

8. Identify three scenarios in the workplace that are likely to result in stressful conversations.

9. What are the implications of gender differences in communication for conducting meetings? Using your Research Navigator, find and examine one study regarding

Research Navigator.com

gender differences in communication. What were the results and how do they relate to the material in this chapter?

10. Describe an example from your work experience or personal life in which it would have been a good idea to metacommunicate.

WEBLINKS

www.members.aol.com/nonverbal2/probe.htm
This site is devoted to nonverbal communication, especially facial expressions and gestures. Literally hundreds of gestures and other nonverbal communication signals and their meanings can be found here.

www.listen.org
From the International Listening Association, a site for all about listening, featuring tests, articles, and other information.

http://www.optimalthinking.com/quiz-communication-skills.asp
Rate your level of communication.

Chapter 4

Developing Teamwork Skills

Learning Outcomes

After reading and studying this chapter and doing the exercises, you should be able to

- Identify several types of teams in organizations.
- Explain the strengths and weaknesses of teams.
- Identify various team member roles.
- Be ready to apply people-related tactics for effective team play.
- Be ready to apply task-related tactics for effective team play.

A few years ago, complaints of slow room service were plaguing a Ritz-Carlton hotel, a chain known for its superior service. To solve the problem, president Horst Schulze dispatched an investigative team composed of a room-service order taker, a waiter, and a cook. Everything seemed fine to the team, except that the service elevator took a long time. Next, the group consulted with the engineers in charge of the elevator. Neither the engineers nor the elevator company representative could find a technical problem with the elevator.

Next, team members took turns riding the elevators at all hours for a week. Finally, one of them observed that every time an elevator made its trip from the first floor to the twenty-fourth, it stopped four or five times. At each stop, housemen (who assisted the housekeepers) got on. The housemen were taking towels from other floors to bring them to housekeepers on their own floors who were short of towels. Foraging for towels was slowing down the elevators.

The team discovered that the Ritz-Carlton didn't really have a room-service problem or an elevator problem; it had a towel shortage. As the hotel bought more towels, room-service complaints dropped 50 percent.[1]

The problem-solving episode at the Ritz-Carlton underscores a major shift in the way in which work is accomplished in organizations. Many organizations rely more on teams than on individuals to accomplish work. To be successful in the modern organization, it is necessary to be an effective team player. You have to work smoothly with other members of the team to accomplish your goals. Teamwork is more important as people work their way up through the organization. Executives, such as CEOs, preach teamwork but tend to dominate meetings and make more decisions by themselves.[2]

The challenges a team member faces come to light when the true nature of a team is recognized. Two experts on the subject define a **team** as "a small number of people with complementary skills who are committed to a common purpose, set of performance goals, and approach for which they hold themselves mutually accountable."[3] In other words, members of a team work together smoothly and all pull in the same direction. A workplace team should be more like an effective athletic team than a group of people out for individual glory.

This chapter provides the information, insights, and preliminary practice necessary to develop effective teamwork skills. Self-Assessment Quiz 4-1 will help you assess your current mental readiness to be a contributing team member.

Self-Assessment Quiz 4-1

TEAM PLAYER ATTITUDES

Directions: Describe how well you agree with each of the following statements, using the following scale: Disagree strongly (DS); Disagree (D); Neutral (N); Agree (A); Agree strongly (AS).

	DS	D	N	A	AS
1. I am at my best when working alone.	5	4	3	2	1
2. I have belonged to clubs and teams ever since I was a child.	1	2	3	4	5
3. It takes far too long to get work accomplished within a group.	5	4	3	2	1
4. I like the friendship of working in a group.	1	2	3	4	5
5. I would prefer to run a one-person business than to be a member of a large firm.	5	4	3	2	1
6. It's difficult to trust others in the group on key assignments.	5	4	3	2	1
7. Encouraging others comes to me naturally.	1	2	3	4	5
8. I like the give-and-take of ideas that is possible in a group.	1	2	3	4	5
9. It is fun for me to share responsibility with other group members.	1	2	3	4	5
10. Much more can be accomplished by a team than by the same number of people working alone.	1	2	3	4	5

Total Score _____

Scoring and Interpretation: Add the numbers you circled to obtain your total score.

41–50 You have strong positive attitudes toward being a team member and working cooperatively with other members.

30–40 You have moderately favourable attitudes toward being a team member and working cooperatively with other members.

10–29 You much prefer working by yourself to being a team member. To work effectively in a company that emphasizes teamwork, you may need to develop more positive attitudes toward working jointly with others.

TYPES OF TEAMS

All teams in the workplace apply their members' various skills to cooperative work. Nevertheless, many specific types of work teams can be identified. Successful people will usually have the opportunity to be a member of several different types of teams.

Four basic types of team are self-managing work teams, cross-functional teams, virtual teams, and crews. Project teams, task forces, and committees are similar in design to cross-functional teams, so they do not receive separate mention here. No matter what label the team carries, its broad purpose is to contribute to a *collaborative workplace* in which people help each other achieve constructive goals. The idea is for workers to collaborate (a high level of cooperation) rather than compete with others or prevent them from getting their work done.

As teams have become more common in the workplace, much effort has been directed at specifying the skills and knowledge a person needs to function effectively on a team, particularly a self-managing work team. Self-Assessment Quiz 4-2 on page 71 lists representative team skills perceived by employers as necessary.

SELF-MANAGING WORK TEAMS

The best-known type of work team is a group of workers who take over much of the responsibility for managing their own work. This kind of team is referred to as a self-managing work team, a production work team, a work team, or just a team. A **self-managing work team** is a small group of employees responsible for managing and performing technical tasks to deliver a product or service to an external or internal customer.[4] The vast majority of large and medium-sized firms make some use of self-managing work teams. Work teams are used in a wide variety of activities, including the production of motorcycles, telephone directories, and major components for large computers.

Members of self-managing work teams typically work together on an ongoing, day-by-day basis. This is what differentiates them from task forces or committees. The work team is often given total responsibility for or "ownership" of an entire product or service, such as producing a telephone directory or designing a corporate web site. At other times, the team is given responsibility for a major component of a job, such as building an airplane engine (but not the entire airplane).

A major behavioural hurdle to overcome in forming self-managing teams is the attitude reflected in the statement "I'm not paid to think." Work teams rely less on supervisors and more on the workers assuming more responsibilities for managing their own activities. For example, work team members may be required to discipline other team members who have attendance, performance, or behavioural problems.[5]

As with all teams, mutual trust among members contributes to team effectiveness. A study conducted with business students, however, showed that if the members trust each other too much, they may not monitor (check up on) each other's work enough. As a result, group performance will suffer. This problem of too much trust surfaces primarily when the team members have individual assignments that do not bring them into frequent contact with each other.[6] An example of an individual, or autonomous, project would be preparing a statistical report that would later be given to the group.

CROSS-FUNCTIONAL TEAMS

It is common practice for teams to be composed of workers from different areas of an organization. A **cross-functional team** is a work group consisting of workers from different specialties at about the same organizational level who come together to accomplish a task. The purpose of the cross-functional team is to get workers from different specialties to blend their talents in accomplishing a task requiring such a mix. A typical application of a cross-functional team would be the development or major revision of a corporate web site. The team would include web site development staff, managers from various areas of the organization, members from the IT Department, marketing representatives, and any others in the organization that would be required for input into the development of the site. A major advantage of cross-functional teams for product development, including web sites, is that they enhance communication across groups, thereby saving time. In addition to product development, cross-functional teams are used for such purposes as improving quality, reducing costs, and running a company (in the form of a top management team).

Self-Assessment Quiz 4-2

TEAM SKILLS

A variety of skills are required to be an effective member of various types of teams. Several different business firms use the skill inventory below to help guide employees toward the competencies they need to become high-performing team members. Review each team skill listed and rate your skill level for each, using the following classification:

S = strong (capable and comfortable with effectively implementing the skill)

M = moderate (demonstrated skill in the past)

B = basic (minimal ability in this area)

N = not applicable (not relevant to the type of work I do)

Communication skills	*Skill level (S, M, B, or N)*
Speak effectively	_____
Foster open communications	_____
Listen to others	_____
Deliver presentations	_____
Prepare written communication	_____

Self-management skills	
Act with integrity	_____
Demonstrate adaptability	_____
Engage in personal development	_____
Strive for results	_____
Display a commitment to work	_____

(Continued)

Thought-process skills

Find innovative solutions to problems   _____

Use sound judgment   _____

Analyze issues   _____

Think "outside the box"   _____

Organizational skills

Know the business   _____

Use technical/functional expertise   _____

Use financial/quantitative data   _____

Strategic (broad business perspective) skills

Recognize "big picture" impact   _____

Promote corporate citizenship   _____

Focus on customer needs   _____

Commit to quality   _____

Manage profitability   _____

Interpretation: We do not provide a scoring key for this questionnaire. Its purpose is simply to raise your awareness of the types of skills that are required to be a successful team member in business.

When members from different specialties work together, they can take into account each other's perspectives when making their contribution. To perform well on a cross-functional team a person would have to think in terms of the good of the larger organization, rather than in terms of his or her own specialty. For example, if the marketing representative knows that a web site requires certain features to attract a specific type of audience, his or her skills are critical for development if the site is to be successful. A major advantage of cross-functional teams for product development is that they improve communication across groups, thereby saving time.

In addition to product development and stress reduction, cross-functional teams are used for such purposes as improving quality, reducing costs, and running a company (in the form of a top management team).

VIRTUAL TEAMS

Some teams communicate more through electronic messages than face-to-face meetings. A **virtual team** is a small group of people that conducts almost all of its collaborative work by electronic communication rather than face-to-face meetings. Email, including IM (instant messaging), is the usual medium for sharing information and conducting meetings. *Groupware* is another widely used approach to conducting an electronic meeting. Using groupware, several people can edit a document at the same time, or in sequence. Desktop videoconferencing is another technological advance that makes the virtual team possible. Electronic brainstorming, described in Chapter 5, is well-suited to the virtual team.

Most high-tech companies make some use of virtual teams and electronic meetings. Strategic alliances in which geographically dispersed companies work with one another are well-suited to virtual teams. It is less expensive for the field technician in Iceland to hold a cybermeeting with her counterparts in South Africa, Mexico, and California than it is to bring them all together in one physical location. The computer manufacturer IBM makes use of virtual teams in selling information-technology systems, partially because so many IBM field personnel work from their homes and vehicles. Virtual teams are sometimes the answer to the challenge of hiring workers with essential skills who do not want to relocate.

With team members geographically dispersed, precise communications are all the more important for virtual teams. The virtual team members usually need a formal document outlining job responsibilities and team goals and objectives. A communication problem may arise when the virtual team is composed of both in-house workers and those in remote locations. The office-bound members become jealous of the seemingly cushy set-up enjoyed by the teleworkers. One solution to this problem is for every member of the team to be given a chance to prove he or she can work off-site.[7]

Despite the efficiency of virtual teams, there are times when face-to-face interaction is necessary to deal with complex and emotional issues. Negotiating a new contract between management and a labour union, for example, is not well-suited to an electronic meeting.

CREWS

We are all familiar with common usage of the term *crew* in relation to such groups as those who operate airplanes, boats, and firefighting equipment. The technical meaning of the term is virtually the same. A **crew** is a group of specialists, each with specific roles, who perform brief events that are closely synchronized with each other, and repeat these events under different environmental conditions. A crew is identified by the technology it handles, such as an aircraft crew, or a deep-sea salvage operation. The crew members rarely rotate specialties, such as the flight attendant taking over for the chief pilot. (Special training and licensing would be required.) The following are several criteria of a group qualifying as a crew:[8]

- Clear roles and responsibilities
- Workflow well established before anyone joins the team
- Careful coordination required with other members in order to perform the task
- Group needs to be in a specific environment to complete its task
- Different people can join the group without interfering with its operation or mission

Because of the specialized roles they play, and the essential tasks they perform, much is expected of crews. The future of crews is promising. For example, computer-virus-fighting crews would be a welcome addition to business and society. Mutual trust is especially important in a crew because good cooperation could save a member's life, such as in a firefighting crew.

ADVANTAGES AND DISADVANTAGES OF TEAMS AND TEAMWORK

Groups have always been the building blocks of organizations. Yet groups and teams have recently grown in importance as the basic unit for organizing work. In an attempt to cope with numerous changes in the outside world, many organizations have granted teams increased independence and flexibility. Further, teams are often required to work more closely with customers and suppliers. The increased acceptance of teams suggests that group work offers many advantages. Nevertheless, it is useful to specify several of these advantages and also examine the potential problems of groups. Being aware of these potential pitfalls can often help a person avoid them. These same advantages and disadvantages also apply to group decision-making, described in Chapter 5.

ADVANTAGES OF GROUP WORK AND TEAMWORK

Group work and group decision-making offer several advantages over individual effort. If several knowledgeable people are brought into the decision-making process, a number of worthwhile possibilities may be uncovered. It is also possible to gain **synergy**, whereby the group's total output exceeds the sum of individual contributions. For example, it would be a rare person working alone who could build a racing car. Dozens of case histories have been collected about successes with work teams; below is one such case:

> At Pratt & Whitney Canada, of Longueuil, Quebec, a concurrent engineering team (a type of cross-functional team that includes members from all areas responsible for the finished product, including design, manufacturing, marketing, and purchasing) designed the PW500 turbofan jet engine in less than 12 months. Using the company's traditional design approach, this process would have taken 18 to 24 months.[9]

Group decision-making also helps garner acceptance and commitment. The argument is that people who contribute to making a decision will feel some ownership of it during implementation. Team members often evaluate each other's thinking, so the team is likely to avoid major errors. An advertising specialist was developing a campaign to attract seniors to live in a retirement community. The proposed ads had photographs of senior citizens engaged in playing shuffleboard, visiting the pharmacy, and sleeping in a hammock. Another team member on the project pointed out that many seniors perceive themselves to be energetic and youthful. Ads emphasizing advanced age might therefore backfire. A successful advertising campaign was then developed that featured seniors in more youthful activities, such as jogging and dancing.

Working in teams and groups also increases the job satisfaction of members. Being a member of a work group makes it possible to satisfy more needs than can be met working alone. Among these needs are affiliation, security, self-esteem, and self-fulfillment. (See Chapter 9 for details about psychological needs.)

DISADVANTAGES OF GROUP WORK AND TEAMWORK

Group activity has some potential disadvantages for both individuals and the organization. Teams and other groups often waste time because they talk too much and act too little. Committees appear to suffer from more inaction than teams. Abigail

Johnson, a top executive at Fidelity Corp., the financial services giant, says that committees are not effective decision-makers. "They have tended to be slow and overly risk averse. Even worse, I believe, they can drain an organization of talent, because the group can only be as good as the average."[10]

One major problem is that members face pressures to conform to group standards of performance and conduct, as the above suggests. Some teams might shun a person who is much more productive than his or her co-workers. Shirking of individual responsibility is another problem frequently noted in groups. Unless work is carefully assigned to each team member, an undermotivated person can often squeeze by without contributing his or her fair share to a group effort.

Social loafing is the psychological term for shirking individual responsibility in a group setting. The social loafer risks being ostracized (shunned) by the group but may be willing to pay the price rather than work hard. Loafing of this type is sometimes found in groups such as committees and project teams. Have you ever encountered a social loafer on a group project at school?

At their worst, teams and other groups foster conflict on the job. People within the work group often bicker about such matters as doing a fair share of the undesirable tasks within the department. Cohesive work groups can also become xenophobic (fearful of outsiders). As a consequence, they may grow to dislike other groups and enter into conflict with them. For example, a customer service group might put considerable effort into showing up a sales group because the latter makes promises to customers that the customer service group cannot keep.

A well-publicized disadvantage of group decision-making is **groupthink**, a deterioration of mental efficiency, reality testing, and moral judgment in the interest of group solidarity. Simply put, groupthink is an extreme form of consensus—the group values getting along more than it values getting things done. The group thinks as a unit, believes it is impervious to outside criticism, and begins to have illusions about its own invincibility. As a consequence, it loses its powers of critical analysis.[11] Groupthink appears to have contributed to several of the major financial scandals of the previous decade. Members of top management got together to vote themselves huge bonuses just before filing bankruptcy for their company. Several of the executives, including a few from Enron Corporation, were later sent to prison for their outrageous decisions.

The Canadian Scene

A STRATEGIC GUIDE FOR BUILDING EFFECTIVE TEAMS

Two professors from Dalhousie University have developed a process for building effective teams. **Please refer to the article in its entirety if you would like more detail by using your Research Navigator (AN 17178126).** Many team-building efforts fail, according to these researchers, for three main reasons. First, team building often relies on an external consultant with little knowledge of the organization. Secondly, many of these activities take place off-site in an artificial environment. Lastly,

(Continued)

most processes fail to plan for, monitor, and assess the transfer of team-building activities to the actual work environment. These authors believe that the failure to use the most critical resource in team building, the manager, is what is missing in these activities. As well, team building needs to occur within the organization where the teams actually interact and work. One of the manager's primary responsibilities is to plan for, build, monitor, and assess teams and their success in the organization. The researchers provide a seven-step framework to guide activities for effective team building:

1. *Identify team characteristics considered predictive of team success.* The key to building effective teams is to balance the characteristics of team members and the resources required to meet goals. The thirteen characteristics associated with team performance are listed and include agreement on group goals, and abilities to manage group conflicts.

2. *Measure existing team climate characteristics to produce a team profile.* Managers need methods to measure the degree to which relevant team characteristics currently exist within the team environment. The authors include a sample of a questionnaire to assess the existing team climate of current work groups. Observation methods and interviews are other approaches listed.

3. *Identify deficient team characteristics.* Using a method such as those in step 2, the manager can identify weak areas in the group.

4. *Use pre-established decision criteria to select the appropriate intervention sequence to change deficient climate characteristics.* Managers need to consider what deficiencies are to be addressed first by using some sort of decision-making method to develop criteria that will help them to develop interventions. Criteria include such variables as likelihood of success and the organizational culture and history. A complete table is included in the paper. It should be noted that each team is different and each situation has its own set of unique characteristics.

5. *Identify team-building strategies capable of overcoming deficiencies in team characteristics.* Once the deficiencies have been identified and prioritized in order for intervention, managers should attempt to articulate team-building strategies for the team to use. Again, the authors have included a table of intervention strategies to assist in building a winning team.

6. *Use pre-established decision criteria to select the appropriate intervention strategies to improve deficient team characteristics.* Once strategies have been identified, the manager needs to select the appropriate strategy, paying close attention to the costs and benefits of the strategies. Another table is presented for assistance.

7. *Implement and assess improvements.* This last step is similar to the problem-solving model presented in Chapter 3. Here, the manager takes a variety of steps to implement the strategy (there are several steps to implementation) and then finally to assess the effect of the strategy on group performance.

While this process may seem complicated, reading the article it becomes clear. A good team requires members who can work cooperatively to achieve organizational goals while still maintaining their own professional goals. Team building is an ongoing effort that does not occur only once a year at a retreat or in another artificial setting.

Two conditions are important for overcoming the potential disadvantages of teams and groups. First, the members must strive to act like a team,[12] following some of the suggestions given in the pages ahead. Second, the task given to the group should be one that can be better accomplished through collective effort than by individuals.

For example, an international business specialist would probably learn to conjugate verbs in a foreign language better by working alone than in a team. What is your opinion on this issue?

Regardless of the disadvantages of teamwork, teams are here to stay in the workplace. In order to overcome these disadvantages, part of the solution may be ensuring a strategic way for organizations to build and maintain effective teams. Two Canadian researchers have developed a process for such effective team-building. The Canadian Scene on pages 76 and 77 briefly summarizes their seven-step model of strategic team-building.

Figure 4-1 presents more information about key factors associated with effective work teams and groups. The more of these factors that are present, the more likely it is that a given team or group will be productive.

- The team has clear-cut goals linked to organizational goals so that group members feel connected to the entire organization. Members learn to think for themselves rather than expecting a supervisor to solve all the difficult problems. At the same time, the group believes it has the authority to solve a variety of problems without first obtaining approval from management.
- Members are assigned work they perceive as challenging, exciting, and rewarding. As a consequence, the work is self-rewarding.
- Members depend on one another to accomplish tasks, and work toward a common goal.
- Members learn to think "outside of the box" (are creative).
- Members receive extensive training in technical knowledge, problem-solving skills, and interpersonal skills.
- Members inspect their own work for quality.
- Members receive part of their pay related to team or group incentives rather than strictly based on individual performance.
- Group size is generally about six people, rather than ten or more.
- Team members have good intelligence and personality factors, such as conscientiousness and pride, that contribute to good performance.
- There is honest and open communication among group members and with other groups in the organization.
- Members have the philosophy of working as a team—twenty-five brains, not just fifty hands.
- Members are familiar with their jobs, coworkers, and the work environment. This experience adds to their expertise. The beneficial effects of experience may diminish after a while because the team needs fresh ideas and approaches.
- The team has emotional intelligence in the sense that it builds relationships both inside and outside the team. Part of this emotional intelligence are norms that establish mutual trust among members, a feeling of group identity, and group efficacy.

Figure 4-1   Key Characteristics of Effective Teams and Work Groups

Sources: Ben Nagler, "Recasting Employees into Teams," *Workforce*, January 1998, p. 104; Dale E. Yeatts and Cloyd Hyten, *High-Performing Self-Managed Work Teams: A Comparison of Theory and Practice* (Thousand Oaks, Calif.: Sage, 1998); Gerben S. Van Der Vegt et al., "Patterns of Interdependence in Work Teams: A Two-Level Investigation of the Relations with Job and Team Satisfaction," *Personnel Psychology*, Spring 2001, pp. 51–69; Shawn L. Berman, Jonathan Down, and Charles W. L. Hill, "Tacit Knowledge as a Source of Competitive Advantage in the National Basketball Association," *The Academy of Management Journal*, February 2002, pp. 13–31; Vanessa Urch Druskat and Steven B. Wolff, "Building the Emotional Intelligence of Groups," *Harvard Business Review*, March 2001, pp. 80–90.

TEAM MEMBER ROLES

A major challenge in learning to become an effective team member is to choose the right roles to occupy. If you successfully carry out positive roles, you will be perceived as a contributor to team effort. If you do not, you will be perceived as a poor contributor. Self-Assessment Quiz 4-3 will help you evaluate your present inclinations toward

Self-Assessment Quiz 4-3

TEAM PLAYER ROLES

Directions: For each of the following statements about team activity, check "Mostly agree" or "Mostly disagree." If you have not experienced such a situation, imagine how you would act or think if placed in that situation. In responding to the statements, assume that you are filling out the questionnaire with the intent of learning something about yourself.

	Mostly agree	Mostly disagree
1. It is rare that I ever miss a team meeting.	_____	_____
2. I regularly compliment team members when they do something exceptional.	_____	_____
3. Whenever I can, I avoid being the note-taker at a team meeting.	_____	_____
4. From time to time, other team members come to me for advice on technical matters.	_____	_____
5. I like to hide some information from other team members so I can be in control.	_____	_____
6. I welcome new team members who come to me for advice and to learn the ropes.	_____	_____
7. My priorities come first, leaving me with very little time to help other team members.	_____	_____
8. During a team meeting, it is not unusual for several people at a time to look to me for my opinion.	_____	_____
9. If I think the team is moving in an unethical direction, I will say so explicitly.	_____	_____
10. Rarely will I criticize the progress of the team, even if I think such criticism is deserved.	_____	_____
11. It is not unusual for me to summarize the progress of the team in a team meeting, even if not asked.	_____	_____
12. To conserve time, I attempt to minimize contact with my teammates outside our meetings.	_____	_____
13. I intensely dislike going along with a consensus decision if the decision runs contrary to my thoughts on the issue.	_____	_____
14. I rarely remind teammates of our mission statement as we go about our work.	_____	_____

(Continued)

15. Once I have made up my mind on an issue facing the team, I am unlikely to be persuaded in another direction. _____ _____

16. I am willing to accept negative feedback from team members. _____ _____

17. Just to get a new member of the team involved, I will ask his or her opinion. _____ _____

18. Even if the team has decided on a course of action, I am not hesitant to bring in new information that supports another position. _____ _____

19. Quite often I talk negatively about one team member to another.

20. My teammates are almost a family to me because I am truly concerned about their welfare. _____ _____

21. When it seems appropriate, I joke and kid with teammates.

22. My contribution to team tasks is as important to me as my individual work. _____ _____

23. From time to time I have pointed out to the team how we can all improve in reaching our goals. _____ _____

24. I will keep fighting to get my way even when the team does not support my viewpoint and wants to move toward consensus. _____ _____

25. I will confront the team if I believe that the members are thinking too much alike. _____ _____

Total Score _____

Scoring and Interpretation: Give yourself one point (+1) for each time your responses agree with those given below.

Question Number	Positive Role Answer	Question Number	Positive Role Answer
1.	Mostly agree	14.	Mostly disagree
2.	Mostly agree	15.	Mostly disagree
3.	Mostly disagree	16.	Mostly agree
4.	Mostly agree	17.	Mostly agree
5.	Mostly disagree	18.	Mostly agree
6.	Mostly agree	19.	Mostly disagree
7.	Mostly disagree	20.	Mostly agree
8.	Mostly agree	21.	Mostly agree
9.	Mostly agree	22.	Mostly agree
10.	Mostly disagree	23.	Mostly agree
11.	Mostly agree	24.	Mostly disagree
12.	Mostly disagree	25.	Mostly agree
13.	Mostly disagree		

(Continued)

20–25   You carry out a well-above-average number of positive team roles. Behaviour of this type contributes substantially to effective teamwork. Study the information in this chapter to build upon your already laudable sensitivity in occupying various positive roles within the team.

10–19   You carry out an average number of positive team roles. Study carefully the roles described in this chapter to search for ways to carry out a greater number of positive roles.

0–9   You carry out a substantially below-average number of positive team roles. If becoming an effective team player is important to you, you will need to assiduously search for ways to play positive team roles. Study the information in this chapter carefully.

occupying effective roles as a team member. In this section we describe a number of the most frequently observed positive roles played by team members.[13] This is followed by an activity in which the roles can be practised.

According to the role theory developed by R. Meredith Belbin and his group of researchers, there are nine frequent roles occupied by team members. All of these roles are influenced to some extent by an individual's personality.

1. *Plant.* The plant is creative, imaginative, and unorthodox. Such a person solves difficult problems. A potential weakness of this role is that the person tends to ignore fine details and becomes too immersed in the problem to communicate effectively.

2. *Resource investigator.* The resource investigator is extroverted, enthusiastic, and communicates freely with other team members. He or she will explore opportunities and develop valuable contacts. A potential weakness of this role is that the person can be overly optimistic and may lose interest after the initial enthusiasm wanes.

3. *Coordinator.* The coordinator is mature, confident, and a natural team leader. He or she clarifies goals, promotes decision making, and delegates effectively. A downside to occupying this role is that the person might be seen as manipulative and controlling. Some coordinators delegate too much by asking others to do some of the work they (the coordinators) should be doing.

4. *Shaper.* The shaper is challenging, dynamic, and thrives under pressure. He or she will use determination and courage to overcome obstacles. A potential weakness of the shaper is that he or she can be easily provoked and may ignore the feelings of others.

5. *Monitor-evaluator.* The monitor-evaluator is even-tempered, engages in strategic (big picture and long-term) thinking, and makes accurate judgments. He or she sees all the options and judges accurately. A potential weakness of this role occupant is that he or she might lack drive and the ability to inspire others.

6. *Team worker.* The team worker is cooperative, focuses on relationships, and is sensitive and diplomatic. He or she is a good listener who builds relationships, dislikes confrontation, and averts friction. A potential weakness is that the team worker can be indecisive in a crunch situation or crisis.

7. *Implementer.* The implementer is disciplined, reliable, conservative, and efficient. He or she will act quickly on ideas, and convert them into practical

actions. A potential weakness is that the implementer can be inflexible and slow to see new opportunities.

8. *Completer-Finisher.* The completer-finisher is conscientious and eager to get the job done. He or she has a good eye for detail, and is effective at searching out errors. He or she can be counted on for finishing a project and delivering on time. A potential weakness is that the completer-finisher can be a worrier and reluctant to delegate.

9. *Specialist.* The specialist is a single-minded self-starter. He or she is dedicated and provides knowledge and skill in rare supply. A potential weakness of the specialist is that he or she can be stuck in a niche with little interest in other knowledge and may dwell on technicalities.

The weaknesses in the first nine roles point to problems the team leader or manager can expect to emerge, and therefore an allowance should be made. Belbin refers to these potential problems as *allowable weaknesses* because an allowance should be made for them. To illustrate, if a team worker has a tendency to be indecisive in a crisis, the team should not have high expectations of the team worker when faced with a crisis. Team workers will be the most satisfied if the crisis is predicted and decisions involving them are made before the pressure mounts.[14]

Another perspective on team roles is that team members will sometimes engage in *self-oriented roles.* Members will sometimes focus on their own needs rather than those of the group. The individual might be overly aggressive because of a personal need such as wanting a bigger budget for his or her project. The individual might hunger for recognition or power. Similarly, the person might attempt to dominate the meeting, block others from contributing, or serve as a distraction. One of the ploys used by distracters recently is to engage in cellphone conversations during a meeting, blaming it on "those people who keep calling me."

The many roles just presented overlap somewhat. For example, the implementer might engage in specialist activities. Do not be concerned about the overlap. Instead, pick and choose from the many roles as the situation dictates—whether or not overlap exists. Skill-Building Exercise 4-1 gives you an opportunity to observe these roles in action. The behaviour associated with the roles just described is more important than remembering the labels. For example, remembering to be creative and imaginative is more important than remembering the specific label *plant.*

Skill-Building Exercise 4-1

TEAM MEMBER ROLES

A team of approximately six people is formed to conduct a 20-minute meeting on a significant topic of their choosing. The possible scenarios follow:

Scenario A: Management Team. A group of managers are pondering whether to lay off one-third of the workforce in order to increase profits. The company has had a tradition of caring for employees and regarding them as the company's most precious asset. However, the CEO has said privately that times have changed in our

(Continued)

competitive world, and the company must do whatever possible to enhance profits. The group wants to think through the advisability of laying off one-third of the workforce, as well as explore other alternatives.

Scenario B: Group of Sports Fans. A group of fans have volunteered to find a new team name to replace "Redskins" for the local baseball team. One person among the group of volunteers believes that the name "Redskins" should be retained because it is a compliment, rather than an insult, to Native Canadians. The other members of the group believe that a name change is in order, but they lack any good ideas for replacing a team name that has endured for over 40 years.

Scenario C: Community Group. A community group is attempting to launch an initiative to help battered adults and children. Opinions differ strongly as to what initiative would be truly helpful to battered adults and children. Among the alternatives are establishing a shelter for battered people, giving workshops on preventing violence, and providing self-defence training. Each group member with an idea strongly believes that he or she has come up with a workable possibility for helping with the problem of battered people.

While the team members are conducting their heated discussion, other class members make notes on which team members carry out which roles. Students should watch for the different roles as developed by Belbin and his associates, as well as the self-oriented roles. For example, students in the first row might look for examples of the plant. Use the role worksheet that follows to help make your observations. Summarize the comment that is indicative of the role. An example would be noting in the shaper category: "Linda said naming the team the 'Canadian Rainbows' seems like too much of an attempt to be politically correct."

Plant: _____

_____

_____

Resource Investigator: _____

_____

_____

Coordinator: _____

_____

_____

Shaper: _____

_____

_____

Monitor-Evaluator: _____

_____

_____

Team Worker: _____

_____

_____

(Continued)

Implementer: _____
_____
_____

Completer-Finisher: _____
_____
_____

Specialist: _____
_____
_____

Self-Oriented Roles: _____
_____
_____

GUIDELINES FOR THE INTERPERSONAL ASPECTS OF TEAM PLAY

The purpose of this and the following section is to help you increase your effectiveness as a team player by describing the necessary skills, actions, and attitudes. You can regard these *behaviours* (the collective term for skills, actions, and attitudes) as goals for personal improvement. Identify the actions and attitudes for which you need the most improvement, and proceed accordingly with self-development. Apply the model for skill development presented in Chapter 1.

One convenient method of classifying team activities in pursuit of goals is to categorize them as people-related or task-related. Remember, however, that the categorization of people- versus task-related activities is not entirely accurate. For example, if you are challenging your teammates with a difficult goal, are you focusing more on the people (offering them a motivational challenge) or the task (achieving the goal)? We begin with people-related actions and attitudes, followed in the next section by task-related actions and attitudes.

TRUSTING TEAM MEMBERS

The cornerstone attitude of an outstanding team player is to trust team members, including the leader. Working on a team is akin to a small-business partnership. If you do not believe that the other team members have your best interests at heart, it will be difficult for you to share opinions and ideas. You will fear that others will make negative statements behind your back.

Trusting team members also includes believing that their ideas are technically sound and rational until proven otherwise. Another manifestation of trust is taking risks with other team members, for example, trying out one of their unproven ideas. You can also take a risk by submitting an unproven idea and not worrying about being ridiculed.

DISPLAYING A HIGH LEVEL OF COOPERATION AND COLLABORATION

Cooperation and collaboration are synonymous with teamwork. If you display a willingness to help others by working cooperatively with them, you will be regarded as a team player. If you do not cooperate with other team members, the team structure breaks down. Collaboration at the team level refers to working jointly with others to solve mutual problems. Although working with another person on a given problem may take longer than working through a problem yourself, the long-term payoff is important. You have established a climate favourable to working on joint problems where collective action is necessary.

Achieving a cooperative team spirit is often a question of making the first move. Instead of grumbling about poor teamwork, take the initiative and launch a cooperative spirit in your group. Target the most individualistic, least cooperative member of the group. Ask the person for his or her input on an idea you are formulating. Thank the person, then state that you would be privileged to return the favour.

Another way of attaining good cooperation is to minimize confrontations. If you disagree with the opinion of another team member, patiently explain the reasons for your differences and look for a workable way to integrate both your ideas. A teammate might suggest, for example, that the team stay until midnight to get a project completed today. You have plans for the evening and are angered by the suggestion. Instead of lashing out at your teammate, you might say, "I agree we need to put in extra time and effort to get the job done. But why can't we spread out this extra effort over a few days? In this way those of us who cannot work until midnight this evening can still contribute."

Skill-Building Exercise 4-2 is a widely used technique for demonstrating the importance of cooperation and collaboration.

RECOGNIZING THE INTERESTS AND ACHIEVEMENTS OF OTHERS

A fundamental tactic for establishing yourself as a solid team player is to actively recognize the interests and achievements of others. Let others know you care about their interests. After you make a suggestion during a team meeting, ask, "Would my suggestion create any problems for anybody else?" or "How do my ideas fit into what you have planned?"

Recognizing the achievements of others is more straightforward than recognizing interests. Be prepared to compliment any tangible achievement, in a realistic way that is commensurate with the achievement; to do otherwise is to compromise your sincerity. For example, do not call someone a genius just because he or she showed you how to compute an exchange rate from one currency to another. Instead, you might say, "Thank you. I'm very impressed by your knowledge of exchange rates."

A technique has been developed to enable the entire team to recognize the interests and achievements of others. Playing the *anonymous praise* game, each team member

Skill-Building Exercise 4-2

THE SCAVENGER HUNT

The purpose of this teamwork exercise is to demonstrate the importance of cooperation and collaboration in accomplishing a task under pressure. The class is divided into teams of about five students. How much time you can devote to the task depends upon your particular class schedule. The instructor will supply each team with a list of items to find within a prescribed period of time—usually about 35 minutes. Given the time constraints, the group will usually have to conduct the hunt on campus. Following is a representative list of items to find in an on-campus scavenger hunt:

- A fountain pen
- A tie
- A brick

- A cap from a beer bottle
- A pop can
- A flash drive

When the groups return within 30 minutes, you hold a public discussion about what you learned about teamwork, and what insights you acquired.

lists what he or she admires about a specific co-worker. The team leader collects the responses and sends each team member the comments made about him or her. Using this technique, team members see a compilation of praise based on how co-workers perceive them. The anonymous praise game helps overcome the hesitancy some people have to praise another person face to face.[15]

GIVING HELPFUL CRITICISM

The outstanding team player offers constructive criticism when needed but does so diplomatically. To do otherwise is to let the team down. A high-performance team demands sincere and tactful criticism among members. No matter how diplomatic you are, keep your ratio of criticism to praise small. Keep two time-tested principles in mind. First, attempt to criticize the person's work, not the person. It is better to say, "The conclusion is missing from your analysis" than "You left out the conclusion." (The latter statement hurts because it sounds like your teammate did something wrong.)

Another key guideline for criticism is to ask a question rather than make a declarative statement. By answering a question, the person being criticized is involved in improving his or her work. In the above example, it would be effective to ask, "Do you think your report would have a greater impact if it contained a conclusion?" In this way, the person being criticized contributes a judgment about the conclusion. The person has a chance to say, "Yes, I will prepare a conclusion."

SHARING THE GLORY

An effective team player shares praise and other rewards for accomplishment even if he or she is the most deserving. Shared praise is usually merited to some extent because teammates have probably made at least some contribution to the achievement that received praise. For example, if a team member comes up with a powerful suggestion for cutting costs, it is likely that somebody else in the group sparked his or her thinking. Effective examples of sharing glory are easy to find. Think back to watching athletes and other entertainers who win a title or an award. Many of them are gracious enough to share the glory. Shortly after he retired, hockey legend Wayne Gretzky told a television reporter, "I never would have accomplished what I did if I hadn't played with such a great group of guys."

TAKING CARE NOT TO RAIN ON ANOTHER PERSON'S PARADE

As teamwork specialist Pamela Lovel observes, we all have achievements and accomplishments that are sources of pride. Belittling the achievements of others for no legitimate reason provokes tension and anger. Suppress your feelings of petty jealousy.[16] An example would be saying to someone who is proudly describing an accomplishment, "Don't take too much credit. It looks to me like you were at the right place at the right time." If you support teammates by acknowledging their accomplishments, you are more likely to receive their support when you need it.

GUIDELINES FOR THE TASK ASPECTS OF TEAM PLAY

The task aspects of team play are also key to becoming an effective team player. Below we describe six major task-related tactics. As mentioned earlier, a task aspect usually has interpersonal consequences.

TECHNICAL EXPERTISE (OR KNOWLEDGE OF THE TASK)

Most people are selected for a work team primarily because of their technical expertise. *Technical* refers to the intimate details of any task, not just tasks in engineering, physical science, and information technology. The sales promotion specialist on a product development team has technical expertise about sales promotion, whether or not sales promotion requires knowledge of engineering or computers.

As team consultant Glenn Parker observes, to use your technical expertise to outstanding advantage you must be willing to share it.[17] Some experts perceive their esoteric knowledge as a source of power. As a consequence, they hesitate to let others share their knowledge for fear of relinquishing power. Technical experts must communicate effectively with team members in other disciplines who lack the same technical background. Those who cannot explain the potential value of their contributions may not receive much attention.

ASSUMING RESPONSIBILITY FOR PROBLEMS

The outstanding team player assumes responsibilities for problems. If the task of solving a problem has not been assigned, he or she says, "I'll do it." For instance, one team member might note that true progress on the team's effort is blocked until the team benchmarks (compares itself) with other successful teams. The effective team player might say, "You are right, we need to benchmark. If it's OK with everybody else, I'll get started on the benchmarking project tomorrow. It will be my responsibility."

Taking responsibility must be combined with dependability. The person who takes responsibility for a task must produce, time after time.

SEEING THE BIG PICTURE

Effective team players need to think conceptually, or see the big picture. Discussion can get bogged down in small details in team effort, and the team might lose sight of what it is trying to accomplish. The team player (possibly the team leader) who can help the group focus on its broader purpose plays a vital role. The following case history illustrates what it means to see the big picture.

> A sales process improvement team was asked to make it easier for customers to purchase office equipment when they visited the company's retail centre. Under the existing process, five different people handled the sales transaction. The customer was often kept waiting for up to an hour. During its second meeting, the team vented its hostility toward the warehouse specialists. As the conversation became more heated, several team members discussed documenting all the problems created by the warehouse personnel and reporting them to the vice-president of marketing. As emotions intensified, several team members ridiculed the warehouse workers.

> Semona, the store manager and one of the team members, helped the group step back and see the big picture. She challenged the group in these words: "Hold on. Why are we here? Is our purpose to improve the sales process or to attack the very people who keep items for sale in stock?" The team acknowledged her point and praised Semona for her contribution. The team then refocused its effort on reducing the paperwork required to complete a sales transaction.

BELIEVING IN CONSENSUS

A major task-related attitude for outstanding team play is to believe that consensus has merit. **Consensus** is general acceptance of a decision by the group. Some members may not be thrilled about the decision, yet all of them are willing to support it. Believing that consensus is valuable enables you to participate fully in team decisions without thinking that you have sacrificed your beliefs or the right to think independently. To believe in consensus is to believe that the democratic process has relevance for organizations and that ideal solutions are not always possible.

FOCUSING ON DEADLINES

A notable source of individual differences among work group members is how much importance they attach to deadlines. Some work group members may regard deadlines as moral contracts, to be broken only in emergencies. Others may view deadlines as arbitrary dates imposed by someone external to the group. Still others may perceive deadlines as moderately important. Differences in perception about the importance of deadlines influence the group's ability to meet deadlines.[18]

Keeping the group focused on deadlines is valuable task behaviour because meeting them is vital to team success. But on many teams, the existence of divergent attitudes toward deadlines makes discussing their importance all the more helpful.

HELPING TEAM MEMBERS DO THEIR JOBS BETTER

Your stature as a team player will increase if you take the initiative to help co-workers make needed work improvements. Helping other team members with their work assignments is a high-level form of cooperation. Make suggestions in a constructive spirit rather than displaying an air of superiority. Identify a problem that a co-worker is having, and then suggest alternatives he or she might be interested in exploring. Avoid saying to team members that they "should" do something, because many people become defensive when told what they should do. The term *should* is usually perceived as a moral judgment of one person by another, such as being told that you should save money, should learn a second language, or should improve your math skills.

Skill-Building Exercise 4-3

HABITAT FOR THE HOMELESS

Organize the class into teams of about six people. Each team takes on the assignment of formulating plans for building temporary shelters for the homeless. The task will take about one hour and can be done inside or outside the classroom. The dwellings you plan to build, for example, might be two-room cottages with electricity and indoor plumbing.

During the time allotted for the task, formulate plans for going ahead with Habitat for the Homeless. Consider dividing up work by assigning certain roles to each team member. Sketch out tentative answers to the following questions:

1. How will you obtain funding for your venture?
2. Which homeless people will you help?
3. Where will your shelters be located?
4. Who will do the actual construction?

After your plan is completed, evaluate the quality of the teamwork that took place within the group. Specify which teamwork skills were evident and which ones did not surface. Search the chapter for techniques you might use to improve teamwork. The skills used to accomplish the habitat task could relate to the team skills presented in Self-Assessment Quiz 4-2, the interpersonal aspects of team play, the task aspects of team play, or some team skill not mentioned in this chapter. Here is a sampling of the many different skills that might be relevant in this exercise:

- Speaks effectively
- Listens to others
- Innovates solutions to problems
- Thinks outside the box
- Displays a high level of cooperation and collaboration
- Provides knowledge of the task
- Sees the big picture
- Focuses on deadlines

BEING A GOOD ORGANIZATIONAL CITIZEN

A comprehensive way of carrying out the task aspects of team play (as well as relationship aspects) is to help out beyond the requirements of your job description. As discussed in Chapter 2, such extra-role activity is referred to as organizational citizenship behaviour—working for the good of the organization even without the promise of a specific reward. As a result of many workers being good organizational citizens, the organization functions more effectively in such ways as improved product quantity and quality.[19] Good citizenship on the job encompasses many specific behaviours, including helping a co-worker with a job task and refraining from complaints or petty grievances. A good organizational citizen would carry out such specific acts as picking up litter in the company parking lot. He or she would also bring a reference to the office that could help a co-worker solve a job problem. Most of the other team player tactics described here are related to organizational citizenship behaviour.

Skill-Building Exercise 4-3 on page 88 will help you integrate the many suggestions presented here for developing teamwork skills.

SUMMARY

To be successful in the modern organization, it is necessary to be an effective team player. Team members have complementary skills and are committed to a common purpose. All teams have some characteristics in common, but four key types of teams are self-managing work teams, cross-functional teams, virtual teams, and crews. (A virtual team does most of its work electronically, instead of in face-to-face meetings.)

Groups and teams offer such advantages as synergy, avoiding major errors, and increased acceptance of and commitment to decisions. Working in groups can also increase job satisfaction. Groups and teams can also have disadvantages, such as tendencies toward inactivity and conformity, tolerance of social loafing, and conflict creation. A serious potential problem is groupthink, whereby bad decisions arise from strong consensus. Key characteristics of effective work groups are outlined in Figure 4-1.

An important part of being an effective team player is choosing effective roles. The roles studied here are: plant, resource investigator, coordinator, shaper, monitor-evaluator, team worker, implementer, completer-finisher, and specialist. Self-oriented roles are less effective and detract from group productivity.

Guidelines for effectively contributing to the interpersonal aspects of team play include (a) trusting team members, (b) displaying a high level of cooperation and collaboration, (c) recognizing the interests and achievements of others, (d) giving helpful criticism, (e) sharing the glory, and (f) taking care not to rain on another person's parade.

Guidelines for effectively contributing to the task aspects of team play include (a) providing technical expertise, (b) assuming responsibility for problems, (c) seeing the big picture, (d) believing in consensus, (e) focusing on deadlines, and (f) helping team members do their jobs better.

An Interpersonal Relations Case Problem

SHOWBOAT BRENT

Mary Tarkington, CEO of a major online retailer, became concerned that too many employees at the company were stressed out and physically unhealthy. Tarkington said, "I've walked through our distribution centre at many different times of the day and night, and I see the same troublesome scene. The place is littered with soft-drink cans and fast-food wrappers. Loads of our workers have stomachs bulging out of their pants. You always see a few workers huddled outside the building smoking. The unhealthiness around the company is also reflected in high absenteeism rates, and health insurance costs that are continually rising.

"I want to see a big improvement in the health of our employees. It makes sense from the standpoint of being a socially responsible company, and from the standpoint of becoming more profitable. With this in mind, I am appointing a project team to study how we can best design and implement a company wellness program. Each member of the team will work about five hours per week on the project. I want to receive a full report in 45 days, and I expect to see progress reports along the way."

Five people were appointed to the wellness task force: Ankit, a programmer; Jennifer, a website designer; Brent, a systems analyst; Derek, a logistics technician; and Kristine, a human resource specialist. During the first meeting, the group appointed Kristine as the wellness task force head because of her professional specialty. Ankit, Jennifer, and Derek offered Kristine their congratulations.

Brent offered a comment with a slightly different tone: "I can see why the group chose you to head our task force. I voted for you also, but I think we should be starting with a blank tablet. We are making no assumptions that anybody's ideas carry more professional weight than anybody else's ideas."

The next time the group met, each member reported some preliminary findings about wellness programs they had researched. Ankit summarized a magazine article on the topic, Jennifer reported on a friend's experience with his company's wellness program, Derek presented some data on how wellness programs can boost productivity and morale, and Kristine reported on www.workforce.com, a human resource website that carries information about wellness programs. Each spent about six minutes on his or her presentation.

Brent then walked up to the front of the conference room and delivered a 25-minute PowerPoint presentation about what he thought the committee should be doing, along with industry data about wellness programs. At the end of Brent's presentation, Kristine commented with a quizzical look, "Thanks Brent, but I thought we agreed to around a five-minute presentation this first time around."

Brent replied, "Good point Kristine, but I'm only doing what I consider best for getting our mission accomplished."

Ten days later, CEO Tarkington visited the task force to discuss its progress. Kristine, as the task force head, began the progress report. She pointed out that the group had gathered substantial information about corporate wellness programs. Kristine also noted that, based on their initial research, establishing one at the company looked feasible and worthwhile. She also noted that the group was beginning to assemble data about the physical requirements of a wellness program and the cost of implementation.

With a frown Brent said, "Not so fast, Kristine. Since we last met, I've taken another look at the productivity figures for wellness centres. People who run wellness programs apparently supplied these figures, so the information could be tainted. I say that we are rushing too fast to reach a decision. Let's get some objective data before making a recommendation to the company."

Kristine groaned as she looked at Mary Tarkington and the task force members. She whispered to Jennifer to her right, "There goes Brent, showboating again."

Case Questions

1. Which team player roles is Brent attempting to play?
2. Which team player roles is Kristine attempting to play?
3. What actions, if any, should the other task force members take to make Brent a better team player?

QUESTIONS FOR DISCUSSION AND REVIEW

1. Part of being a good team player is helping other members. How can members of a workplace team help each other?

2. How do team members know when they have achieved synergy?

3. What should the other team members do when they uncover a social loafer?

4. What is the potential downside of heavily emphasizing the *specialist* role?

5. How can the *monitor-evaluator* role backfire for a person?

6. Assume that you are a team member. What percent of your pay would you be willing to have based on team effort? Explain your reasoning.

7. How effective do you think the scavenger hunt really is in building cooperation among team members?

8. What team roles do you feel are the most important for motivating other team members to achieve goals? Explain your reasoning.

9. How can the challenger role backfire for a person?

10. The "little picture" in studying this chapter is learning details about teamwork skills. What is the "big picture"?

11. How can a person achieve individual recognition yet remain a team player?

WEBLINKS

www.workteams.unt.edu
This is the site for the Center for Collaborative Organizations at the University of North Texas.

http://content.monster.com/tools/quizzes/teamplayer
This site has information on being a team player, including a self-test.

www.employeedevelopmentsolutions.com/freearticles/teambuilding.htm
A site with free downloadable articles on teams.

Group Problem-Solving and Decision-Making

Jim Graf has his sights set on a target 100 million miles away. Sometimes it's closer. Sometimes it's farther. Mars. The target is moving. So is he. Each morning he leads a team of several managers in a stand-up meeting in his office at NASA's Jet Propulsion Laboratory on the top floor of a sprawling four-story building tucked into the foothills above Pasadena, California. Sitting is not allowed. All the meeting's participants are constantly in motion, changing positions with respect to one another, even as their target changes position with respect to Earth.

"We have a daily stand-up so we can talk about things," said Graf. "We physically stand up here. I want everybody a little uncomfortable so they get right to the point." Usually these meetings last about 15 minutes. Some mornings, they go longer.

"It's important to communicate," said Graf. "You wouldn't think a team member working on one thing would need to know about another team working on another thing, until suddenly you hear someone say, 'Wow, that impacts me!' The stand-up meetings are essential to our success."[1]

Standup meetings are but one way in which groups solve many key problems. Part of having high-level interpersonal skills is the ability to work closely with others in solving problems and making decisions. Applying the concepts presented in this chapter will improve your group problem-solving and decision-making skills. You will receive guidelines for applying several major group problem-solving methods. As a starting point in studying these techniques, first think through your present level of receptiveness toward group problem-solving by doing Self-Assessment Quiz 5-1.

Self-Assessment Quiz 5-1

MY PROBLEM-SOLVING TENDENCIES

Directions: Describe how well you agree with the following statements. Use the following scale: Disagree strongly (DS); Disagree (D); Neutral (N); Agree (A); Agree strongly (AS).

	DS	D	N	A	AS
1. Before reaching a final decision on a matter of significance, I like to discuss it with one or more people.	1	2	3	4	5
2. If I'm facing a major decision, I like to get away from others to think it through.	5	4	3	2	1
3. I get lonely working by myself.	1	2	3	4	5
4. Two heads are better than one.	1	2	3	4	5
5. A wide range of people should be consulted before an executive makes a major decision.	1	2	3	4	5
6. To arrive at a creative solution to a problem, it is best to rely on a group.	1	2	3	4	5
7. From what I've seen so far, group decision-making is a waste of time.	5	4	3	2	1
8. Most great ideas stem from the solitary effort of great thinkers.	5	4	3	2	1
9. Important legal cases should be decided by a jury rather than a judge.	1	2	3	4	5
10. Individuals are better suited than groups to solving technical problems.	5	4	3	2	1

Total Score _____

Scoring and Interpretation: Add the numbers you circled to obtain your total score.

46–50   You have strong positive attitudes toward group problem-solving and decision-making. You will therefore adapt well to the decision-making techniques widely used in organizations. Be careful, however, not to neglect your individual problem-solving skills.

30–45   You have neutral attitudes toward group problem-solving and decision-making. You may need to remind yourself that group problem-solving is well accepted in business.

10–29   You much prefer individual to group decision-making. Retain your pride in your ability to think independently, but do not overlook the contribution of group problem-solving and decision-making. You may need to develop more patience for collaborative work.

RATIONAL VERSUS POLITICAL DECISION-MAKING IN GROUPS

Group decision-making is the process of reaching a judgment based on feedback from more than one individual. Most people involved in group problem-solving may share the same purpose in agreeing on a solution and making a decision. Nevertheless, they may have different agendas and use different methods. Two such different approaches to group decision-making are the rational model and the political model.

The *rational decision-making model* is the traditional, logical approach to decision-making, based on the scientific method. It is grounded in establishing goals and alternatives, examining consequences, and hoping for optimum results. The search for optimum results is based on an economic view of decision-making—the idea that people hope to maximize gain and minimize loss when making a decision. For example, a work team would choose the lowest-cost, highest-quality supplier even though the team leader was good friends with the sales representative of a competitor.

The rational model also assumes that each alternative is evaluated in terms of how well it contributes to reaching the goals involved in making the decision. For example, if one of the goals in relocating a factory was to reduce energy costs and taxes, each alternative would be carefully examined in terms of its tax and energy consequences. A team member might say, "Setting up a factory in the Thunder Bay area sounds great. It's true that taxes are low, the labour market is wonderful, and we can access many federal grants. But did you know that the energy costs are very high because of the amount of heating required?"

The *political decision-making model* assumes that people bring preconceived notions and biases into the decision-making situation. Because the decision-makers are politically motivated (focused on satisfying their own interests), the individuals often do not make the most rational choice. In the relocation example at hand, two of the members might give the thumbs-up to Thunder Bay for reasons that satisfy their own needs. One team member might be fascinated with the Canadian Aboriginal culture so prevalent in Northern Ontario and therefore want to move to Thunder Bay. Another member might have retired parents living in Thunder Bay and be interested in living near them.

People who use the political model may operate on the basis of incomplete information. Facts and figures that conflict with personal biases and preferences might get blocked out of memory or rationalized away. A team member might say, "Those heating costs are exaggerated. I've heard that if you use heat pumps sourced to water, heating costs go way down."

In practice, it is sometimes difficult to determine whether a decision-maker is being rational or political. Have you ever noticed that many hotels do not have a 13th floor? The reason is both rational and political. The hotel manager might say rationally, "Many people are superstitious about the number 13, so they will refuse to take a room on the 13th floor. If we want to maximize room use, the rational decision for us is to label the 13th floor as 14. In this way, we will avoid the irrational (political) thinking of guests."

GUIDELINES FOR USING GENERAL PROBLEM-SOLVING GROUPS

Solving problems effectively in groups requires skill. Here we examine three aspects of group problem-solving that are useful in reaching more effective decisions: group problem-solving steps, managing disagreement about the decision, and aiming for inquiry rather than advocacy.

THE GROUP PROBLEM-SOLVING STEPS

When team members get together to solve a problem, they typically hold a discussion rather than rely on formal problem-solving techniques. Several team members might attempt to clarify the true nature of the problem, and a search then begins for an acceptable solution. Although this technique can be effective, the probability of solving the problem well (and therefore making the right decision) increases when the team follows a systematic procedure. The following guidelines represent a time-tested way of solving problems and making decisions within a group.[2] You may recognize these steps as having much in common with the scientific method. The same steps are therefore ideal for following the rational decision-making model. Two other aspects of group decision-making will be described here: managing disagreement and inquiry versus advocacy.

Assume that you are a team member of a small business that distributes food supplies to hospitals, nursing homes, and schools. Your business volume is adequate, but you have a cash-flow problem because some of your customers take more than 30 days to pay their bills. Here is how problem-solving would proceed following the steps for effective group problem-solving and decision-making:

1. *Identify the problem.* Describe specifically what the problem is and how it manifests itself. The surface problem is that some customers are paying their bills late. Your company's ultimate problem is that it does not have enough cash on hand to pay expenses.

2. *Clarify the problem.* If group members do not see the problem the same way, they will offer divergent solutions to their individual perceptions of the problem. To some team members, late payments may simply mean the company has less cash in the bank. As a result, the company earns a few dollars less in interest. Someone else on the team might perceive the problem as mostly an annoyance and inconvenience. Another person may perceive late payers as being immoral and therefore want to penalize them. The various perceptions of these problem-solvers contribute to their exercising a political model of decision-making. It is important for the group to reach consensus that the ultimate problem is that there is not enough cash on hand to run the business, as explained in Step 1.

3. *Analyze the cause.* To convert the existing situation into the desired one, the group must understand the cause or causes of specific problems and find ways to overcome them. Late payment of bills (over 30 days) can be caused by several factors. Customers may have cash-flow problems of their own; they may have slow-moving, bureaucratic procedures; or they may be understaffed. Another possibility is that the slow-paying customers are dissatisfied with the service and are holding back on payments in retaliation. Research, including interviewing customers, may be needed to analyze the cause or causes of the problem.

4. *Search for alternative solutions.* Remember that there are usually many alternative solutions to a problem. The alternative solutions you choose to focus on will depend on your analysis of the causes. Assume that you have found that customers are satisfied with your service but were slow in paying bills for a variety of other reasons. Your team then gets creative and develops a number

of alternatives. Among them are offering bigger discounts for quick payment, dropping slow-paying customers, sending out your own bills more promptly, and using follow-up phone calls to bring in money. Another possibility would be to set up a line of credit that would enable your firm to take out short-term loans to cover expenses until your bills were paid.

5. *Select alternatives.* Identify the criteria that solutions should meet and then discuss the pros and cons of the proposed alternatives. No solution should be laughed at or scorned. Specifying the criteria that proposed solutions should meet requires you to think deeply about your goals. For example, your team might establish the following criteria for solutions: that they (a) improve cash flow, (b) do not lose customers, (c) do not cost much to implement, and (d) do not make the company appear desperate. The pros and cons of each proposed alternative can be placed on a flip chart, chalkboard, or computer screen.

6. *Plan for implementation.* Decide what action is necessary to carry out the chosen solution to the problem. Suppose your group decides that establishing a bank line of credit is the most feasible alternative. The company president or the chief financial officer might then meet with several local banks to apply for a line of credit at the most favourable rate. Your group also chooses to initiate a program of friendly follow-up telephone calls to encourage more rapid payment.

7. *Clarify the contract.* The contract is a restatement of what group members have agreed to do and deadlines for accomplishment. In your situation, several team members are involved in establishing a line of credit and initiating a system of follow-up phone calls.

8. *Develop an action plan.* Specify who does what and when to carry out the terms of the contract. Each person involved in implementing alternatives develops an action plan in detail that stems logically from the previous step.

9. *Provide for evaluation and accountability.* After the plan is implemented, reconvene to discuss progress and to hold people accountable for results that have not been achieved. In the current example, progress will be measured in at least two objective ways. You can use accounting measures to evaluate whether the cash-flow situation has improved and whether the average cycle time on accounts receivable has decreased.

The above steps for effective group problem-solving are best applied to complex problems. Straightforward problems of minor consequence (such as deciding on holiday decorations for the office) do not require all the steps. Nevertheless, remember that virtually every problem has more than one feasible alternative as a solution. For practice in using the steps just described, do Skill-Building Exercise 5-1.

MANAGING DISAGREEMENT ABOUT GROUP DECISION-MAKING

A major reason that group decision-making does not proceed mechanically is that disagreement may surface. Such disagreement is not necessarily harmful to the final outcome of the decision because those who disagree may have valid points, and may help prevent groupthink. The idea is to manage disagreement so the decision-making process

Skill-Building Exercise 5-1

A GENERAL PROBLEM-SOLVING GROUP

The class is divided into groups of about six people. Each group takes the same complicated problem through the nine steps for effective group decision-making. Several of the steps will be hypothetical, because this is a simulated experience. Pretend you are a task force composed of people from different departments in the company. Choose one of the following possibilities:

Scenario 1: Your company wants your task force to decide whether to purchase a corporate jet for members of senior management or require them to continue to fly on commercial airlines.

Scenario 2: A paper product manufacturing company employs you. Data supplied by the marketing research department indicates that consumers want to buy more recycled paper products, something your company does not manufacture. Your task is to examine the feasibility of changing your product lines, suppliers, and equipment, and to look at whether doing so would be beneficial in the long run and increase profits

does not break down and the dissenters are not squelched. In one study, conflicts about decisions were examined among 43 cross-functional teams engaged in new product development. Disagreements about major issues led to positive outcomes for team performance (as measured by managers' ratings) under two conditions.[3]

First, the researchers concluded, dissenters have to feel they have the freedom to express doubt. To measure such freedom, participants in the study responded to such statements as "I sometimes get the feeling that others are not speaking up although they harbour serious doubts about the direction being taken." (Strongly disagreeing with this statement would suggest that group members had the freedom to express doubt.)

Second, doubts must be expressed collaboratively (trying to work together) rather than contentiously (in a quarrelsome way). An example of collaborative communication would be having used the following statement during decision-making: "We will be working together for a while. It's important that we both [all] feel comfortable with a solution to this problem." An example of contentious communication would be high agreement with the statement, "You're being difficult and rigid."

Conflict-resolution techniques, as described in Chapter 7, are another potentially useful approach to managing disagreement about decision-making.

INQUIRY VERSUS ADVOCACY IN GROUP DECISION-MAKING

Another useful perspective on group decision-making is to compare the difference between group members involved in *inquiry* (looking for the best alternative) versus *advocacy* (fighting for one position). Inquiry is an open process designed to generate multiple alternatives, encourage the exchange of ideas, and produce a well-reasoned solution. Decision-makers who care more about the good of the firm than personal gain are the most likely to engage in inquiry. According to David A. Garvin and Michael A. Roberto, this open-minded approach doesn't come easily to most people.[4]

Instead, most groups charged with making a decision tend to slip into the opposite mode, called advocacy. The two approaches look similar because under either mode the group members are busily immersed in work and appear to be searching for the best alternative. Yet the results from the two modes are quite different. Using an advocacy approach, participants approach decision-making as a contest with the intent of selecting the winning alternative. One member of the group might be trying to gain the largest share of the budget and become so passionate about winning budget share that he loses objectivity. Advocates might even withhold important information from the group, such as not revealing that their budget is big enough considering their decreased activity.

With an advocacy approach, the disagreements that arise tend to separate the group into antagonistic camps. Personality conflicts come into play, and one person might accuse the other side of not being able to see the big picture. In contrast, an inquiry-focused group carefully considers a variety of alternatives and collaborates to discover the best solution.

Conflict-resolution methods can be useful in helping the decision-makers overcome the advocacy approach. As part of resolving the conflict, the group leader must make sure everyone knows that his or her viewpoint is being carefully considered.

GUIDELINES FOR BRAINSTORMING

In many work situations, groups are expected to produce creative and imaginative solutions to problems. When the organization is seeking a large number of alternatives for solving problems, **brainstorming** is often the technique of choice. Brainstorming is a group problem-solving technique that promotes creativity by encouraging idea generation through non-critical discussion. The basic technique is to encourage unrestrained and spontaneous participation by group members. The term *brainstorm* has become so widely known that it is often used as a synonym for a clever idea.

Brainstorming is used both as a method of finding alternatives to real-life problems and as a creativity-training program. In the usual form of brainstorming, group members spontaneously call out alternative solutions to a problem facing them. Any member is free to improve or "hitchhike" upon the contribution of another person. At the end of the session, somebody sorts out the ideas and edits those that are less refined.

Brainstorming is widely used to develop new ideas for products, find names for products, develop advertising slogans, and solve customer problems. Brainstorming has also been used to develop a new organizational structure in a government agency and is now widely used in developing software. Examine the Canadian Scene on page 99 to see how some businesses exercise creativity in their decision-making.

Adhering to a few simple rules or guidelines helps ensure that creative alternative solutions to problems will be forthcoming. The brainstorming process usually falls into place without frequent reminders about guidelines. Nevertheless, here are nine rules to improve the chances of having a good session. Unless many of these rules are followed, brainstorming becomes a free-for-all, and is not brainstorming in its original intent.

1. *Group size should be about five to seven people.* If there are too few people, not enough suggestions are generated; if there are too many, the session becomes uncontrolled. However, brainstorming can be conducted with as few as three people.

The Canadian Scene

THERE'S ROOM FOR CREATIVITY IN JUST ABOUT ANY BUSINESS

There's little doubt that it takes creativity to make it in many businesses. So to illustrate the use of creativity, here are two very different business people who have used creativity to get to "the top."

What about an Ottawa engineering technologist who makes perfume? Michel Germain is a former electronic engineering technologist who took up this challenge when his wife couldn't find a perfume that she liked. He calls his perfume "Sexual" and was surprised that he could do this—no one had registered this name. "That kind of brazen creativity enabled [him] to come out of nowhere and take on some of the biggest fragrance brands—names like Calvin Klein and Ralph Lauren—in a fiercely competitive business."[i] Today, the fragrances, now also available for men, are in the top 20 fragrances in Canada.

Then there's Harry Rosen, who has been outfitting men for over 50 years. He believes that men lack a holistic approach to dress, and this is where a good salesperson can help. Instead of the conservative and safe suit, he likes to emulate good fashion-change-agents. "Don't go by formulas alone. If you've bought constructively, you can look at what you've got and put some delightful combinations together you never expected. That's where there's a little bit of personality and creativity."[ii]

Whether marketing or retail, a little creativity can go a long way!

Sources:

i. Zena Olijnyk, "The Sweet Smell of Success," *Canadian Business*, October 28, 2002, p. 1, www.canadianbusiness.com/shared/print.jsp?content=49257 downloaded May 20, 2004.

ii. Luba Krekhovetsky, "Live and Learn: Harry Rosen," *Canadian Business*, February 16, 2004, p. 1, www.canadian business.com/shared/print.jsp?content=20040116_58613_58613 downloaded May 20, 2004.

2. *Everybody is given the chance to suggest alternative solutions.* Members spontaneously call out alternatives to the problem facing the group. (Another approach is for people to speak in sequence.)

3. *No criticism is allowed.* All suggestions should be welcome; it is particularly important not to use derisive laughter.

4. *Freewheeling is encouraged.* Outlandish ideas often prove quite useful. It is easier to tame a wild idea than to originate one.

5. *Quantity and variety are very important.* The greater the number of ideas put forth, the greater the likelihood of a breakthrough idea.

6. *Combinations and improvements are encouraged.* Building upon the ideas of others, including combining them, is very productive. "Hitchhiking" or "piggybacking" is an essential part of brainstorming.

7. *Notes must be taken during the session by a person who serves as the recording secretary.* The session can also be taped, but this requires substantial time to retrieve ideas.

8. *Invite outsiders to the brainstorming session.* Inviting an outsider to the brainstorming session can add a new perspective the "insiders" might not think of themselves.

9. *Do not become overly structured by following any of the above eight "rules" too rigidly.* Brainstorming is a spontaneous group process.

A recent perspective on brainstorming is that the most productive sessions take place in physically stimulating environments, as opposed to a drab conference room. Natural light may stimulate thinking, so work in a room with windows, or outside if weather permits. Changing from a seated position to walking around from time to time can be mentally stimulating. Food and drink also contribute to an enhanced environment for brainstorming.[5]

Brainstorming is an effective technique for finding a large number of alternatives to problems, particularly when the list of alternatives is subsequently refined and edited. Brainstorming in groups is also valuable because it contributes to job satisfaction for many people. Skill-Building Exercise 5-2 gives you an opportunity to practise a commercially useful application of brainstorming.

One curious feature of brainstorming is that individuals working alone typically produce more useful ideas than those placed in a group. Brainstorming by individuals working alone is referred to as **brainwriting**. When electronic brainstorming is described in the next section, we will analyze why some people generate fewer ideas in a group setting. Skill-Building Exercise 5-3 gives you a chance to compare brainstorming and brainwriting.

Skill-Building Exercise 5-2

1-800-INSIGHT

Using conventional brainstorming, huddle in small groups. Your task is to develop 800, 888, or 900 numbers for firms in various enterprises. Keep in mind that the best 800, 888, or 900 numbers are easy to memorize and have a logical connection to the goods or services provided. After each group makes up its list of telephone numbers (approximately five for each firm on the list), compare results with the other groups. Here is the list of nationwide enterprises:

- A chain of funeral homes
- A heating and air-conditioning firm
- A student loan company.
- A used-car chain
- A dial-a-laugh service (a 900 number)
- An introduction (dating) service (a 900 number)

Skill-Building Exercise 5-3

BRAINSTORMING VERSUS BRAINWRITING

One-half of the class is organized into brainstorming groups of about six people. The rest work by themselves. Groups and individuals then work on the same problems for 10 minutes. The brainstorming groups follow the aforementioned guidelines. Individuals jot down as many alternatives as come to mind without interacting with other people. After the problem-solving sessions are completed, compare the alternatives developed by the groups and individuals.

The class chooses one of the following problems so that solutions to the same problem can be compared:

1. How might we effectively utilize the senior citizens in our community?

2. How can we earn extra money, aside from holding a regular job?

3. How can we find new people to date?

4. How can we save money on food costs?

5. How can we save money on gasoline?

GUIDELINES FOR ELECTRONIC BRAINSTORMING

There has been a promising electronic procedure developed to overcome the limitations of conventional brainstorming in groups. Below, we examine problems with brainstorming more carefully and then describe electronic brainstorming.

LIMITATIONS TO VERBAL BRAINSTORMING

The full potential of brainstorming has been held back by three forces that block production of ideas: evaluation apprehension, free riding, and inhibiting procedures.[6] Being aware of these production-blocking mechanisms can help you improve your skill in brainstorming.

Evaluation apprehension occurs when people are unwilling to come forth with their ideas because they fear being critically evaluated. This fear may be intensified when people are told that the group is being observed and rated or that experts are in the group. (Did you notice any evaluation apprehension in the brainstorming exercise?) When people work by themselves and do not have to present their ideas to the larger group, they will experience less evaluation apprehension.

Free riding is similar to social loafing. Free riders do not work as hard in a group as they would if they worked alone. They are willing to let the next person do the heavy thinking. One explanation offered for free riding is that being an outstanding contributor in a group carries the same reward as being a non-contributor. A person generating ideas alone would not have the opportunity to free ride.

An *inhibiting procedure* in verbal brainstorming is that only one person can speak at a time. This limits the idea generation and production time available to group members. As a result, some people forget what they wanted to say because they were listening to others. They might also ignore the ideas of others because they are rehearsing what they want to say. Further, they will hold back on ideas that are redundant.

THE ELECTRONIC BRAINSTORMING PROCEDURE

A development designed to overcome the problem of production blocking in brainstorming is **electronic brainstorming**. Using this method, group members simultaneously enter their suggestions into a computer, and the ideas are distributed to the screens of other group members. Although the group members do not talk to each other, they are able to build on each other's ideas and combine ideas.

Electronic brainstorming allows members to enter their ideas whenever they want and submit them anonymously. These two features reduce the inhibitions caused by waiting for other people to contribute and by fear of negative evaluations.

During electronic brainstorming, individuals work in face-to-face groups, typically seated around a U-shaped table. Each group member has a computer terminal connected to the other terminals and a monitor. *Electronic Brainstorming* is the title of representative software designed for this activity. It enables individuals to enter their ideas anonymously as they occur to them. (Good keyboarding skills are essential to keep up with the group.)

Each time an individual enters an idea, a random set of the group's ideas appears on the individual's monitor. Individuals can access other random sets of ideas by pressing a specified function key. Accessing these ideas can stimulate the person's own generation of new ideas and also allows for piggybacking.

An experiment with electronic brainstorming indicated that, with large groups, the method produces more useful ideas than verbal brainstorming (the usual type). In the study, a four-person electronic brainstorming group produced more non-redundant ideas than did verbal groups (traditional brainstorming). The group also produced more ideas than did non-electronic brainstormers who did not interact with people.[7]

Electronic brainstorming researcher Keng L. Siau suggests that brainstorming via email can increase both the quantity and quality of ideas. When participants do not face each other directly, they can concentrate more on the task at hand and less on the interpersonal aspects of interaction.[8]

If your school or employer is equipped with an electronic brainstorming capability, you are encouraged to try the procedure. Setting up such a capability is costly, however. Next, we describe a low-cost manual (non-electronic) procedure that offers many of the advantages of electronic brainstorming. In addition, you will be able to test the procedure yourself.

GUIDELINES FOR THE NOMINAL GROUP TECHNIQUE

A team leader or other manager who must make a decision about an important issue sometimes needs to know what alternatives are available and how people would react to them. In such cases, group input may be helpful. Verbal brainstorming is not advisable, because the problem is still in the exploration phase and requires more than a list of alternative solutions.

Nominal group technique (NGT) is a problem-solving technique that has been developed to fit the situation. The NGT is a group problem-solving technique that calls people together in a structured meeting with limited interaction. The group is called *nominal* (i.e., in name only) because people first present their ideas without interacting with one another as they would in a *real* group. (This aspect of the nominal group technique is incorporated into electronic brainstorming.) However, group discussion does take place at a later stage in the process.

An appropriate topic for NGT would be a decision about which of a company's suppliers or vendors should be eliminated. Many companies are shrinking their number of suppliers because they believe that working with fewer can lead to higher-quality components. It is easier to train a small number of suppliers, and it is also possible to build better working relationships when fewer people are involved.

A decision of this type can lead to hurt feelings and rupture old friendships. Suppose Pedro Ortiz, the team leader, is empowered to make the decision about reducing the number of suppliers. The nominal group technique is followed to arrive at this decision, using a six-step decision process.

1. Work-team members are assembled because they will all participate in the decision to reduce the number of companies serving as suppliers to the team. All team members are told in advance of the meeting and the agenda. The meeting is called, and an office assistant is invited to help take care of the administrative details.

2. The team leader presents a specific question. Ortiz tells the group, "Top management says we have to reduce our number of suppliers by two-thirds. It's too difficult to keep track of all these different suppliers and train them to meet our quality specs. I dislike terminating a supplier as much as anybody, but I can understand the logic of top management. Right now our team is doing business with 12 suppliers, and we should shrink that number to four. Your assignment is to develop criteria for choosing which suppliers to eliminate. I also need to know how you feel about the decision you make on supplier reduction and how it might affect the operations of our team."

3. Using notepads, the five team members write down their ideas about reducing the number of suppliers by two-thirds, without speaking to other members.

4. Each team member in turn presents one idea to the group. The group does not discuss the ideas. The office assistant summarizes each idea by writing it on a flip chart. Here are the ideas submitted by each team member:

   Alternative A. We'll carefully study the prices offered by all 12 suppliers. The eight suppliers with the highest average prices for comparable goods are given the boot. I like this idea because our team will save the company a bundle of money.

Alternative B. Let's keep the four suppliers who have the best quality record. We'll ask each supplier if they have won a quality award. If a supplier has won a quality award, the company is put on the retained list. We'll include awards from their customers or outside standards such as ISO 9000. If we find more than four of the suppliers have won awards, we'll retain those with the most impressive awards.

Alternative C. I say we reward good service. We keep the four suppliers among the 12 who have been the most prompt with deliveries. We'll also take into account how good the suppliers have been about accepting returns of damaged or defective merchandise.

Alternative D. Here's an opportunity to get in good with top management. Stop kidding each other. We know that Jake [the plant's general manager] has his favourite suppliers. Some of them are his fishing and golfing buddies. The suppliers who are friends with Jake get our vote. In this way, Jake will think our team shows really good judgment.

Alternative E. Let's reward the suppliers who have served us best. We'll rate each supplier on a 1-to-10 scale on three dimensions: the quality of goods they have provided us, price, and service in terms of prompt delivery and returns policy. We could do the ratings in less than an hour.

5. After each team member has presented his or her idea, the group clarifies and evaluates the suggestions. The length of the discussion for each of the ideas varies substantially. For example, the idea about rating suppliers on three criteria might precipitate a 30-minute discussion. The discussion about retaining the plant manager's political connections might last only five minutes.

6. The meeting ends with a silent, independent rating of the alternatives. The final group decision is the pooled outcome of the individual votes. The team members are instructed to rate each alternative on a 1-to-10 scale, with 10 being the most favourable rating. The ratings that follow are the *pooled ratings* (the sum of the individual ratings) received for each alternative. The maximum score is 50 (10 points × 5 raters).

Alternative A, price alone: 35

Alternative B, quality-award record: 30

Alternative C, good service: 39

Alternative D, plant manager's favourites: 14

Alternative E, combination of quality, price, and service: 44

Team leader Ortiz agrees with the group's preference for choosing the four suppliers with the best combination of quality, price, and service. He schedules a meeting to decide which suppliers meet these standards. Ortiz brings the team's recommendations to the plant manager, and they are accepted. Although the team is empowered to make the decision, it is still brought to management for final approval. To practise the nominal group technique, do Skill-Building Exercise 5-4.

The Job-Oriented Interpersonal Skills in Action box describes how a medical practice made good use of the nominal group technique.

Skill-Building Exercise 5-4

THE NOMINAL GROUP TECHNIQUE

With a clear understanding of the mechanics of the NGT as described in the text, the technique can be demonstrated in about 30 minutes. The class is divided into groups of about seven. One person plays the role of team leader, who can also assume the responsibility of the office assistant (recording information on flip charts).

You are the key members of a motion picture and television film production company. You have a contract to produce a series of four action films. The problem you face is which North American (US, Canadian, or Mexican) city to choose as the filming location. The president has ruled out Hollywood because expenses are too high. Solve this problem using the NGT, and make a decision about which city to choose for your filming location.

Job-Oriented Interpersonal Skills in Action

FAMILY PRACTICE DOCTOR PRESCRIBES THE NOMINAL GROUP TECHNIQUE FOR HIS OFFICE

Each staff member of a family medical practice sees a different aspect of the practice, from scheduling to vital-signs taking. As a consequence each professional and staff support worker has unique insights into how to strengthen the practice to improve care. Our small group practice (two physicians, a physician assistant, and 8.5 full-time-equivalent support staff) recently used the nominal group technique to answer two important questions:

1. What are five ways we could improve our existing level of customer service?

2. What are five things we should be doing to make our practice superior?

The nominal group technique takes a reasonable amount of time, but we modified the process slightly to make it briefer. Rather than conducting the entire technique in one long meeting, we completed some steps by individuals working alone. We gave each staff member our two questions and asked them to submit their ideas the next business day. We combined their suggestions and ideas into a master list, which we distributed to all employees. The next step was for the group to discuss the ideas in a meeting. We met again to discuss our votes. Later, each person ranked the ideas again and gave the ranks to the physician manager. Finally, we met once again to discuss the result and our next steps.

Our group of 13 people, including full- and part-time employees, came up with 47 different ideas. The five top-ranking ideas for improving our current level of customer service were as follows:

1. *Work as a team.* Teamwork in our context includes helping in whatever way is needed. Examples include cross-training individuals and allowing each person to describe at a staff meeting some unknown details of his or her job so that others can gain understanding of his or her role.

2. *Reduce chart confusion and scatter.* This includes filing more quickly, decreasing the possible locations for charts, and computerizing patient records.

3. *Return phone calls to patients more quickly.* Nurses should set aside time to respond to voice mail within an agreed-upon time frame, such as 24 hours.

(Continued)

4. *Make patients feel more welcome in our office.* For example, we would like to spend more time with patients, and provide coffee and nutritious snacks for them in the lobby.

5. *Reduce paperwork.* We want to decrease the amount of paperwork patients need to complete, including the amount of information required of first-time patients.

The top five ideas for making our practice superior were as follows:

1. *Have health providers phone patients with their test results.* Patients should receive timely feedback from the person most able to give them the information they need.

2. *Enhance non-medical contact with patients.* We could easily send cards for birthdays and other special events in our patients' lives and make social phone calls to homebound patients.

3. *Improve the effectiveness of the referral process.* For example, we should send a copy of the medical chart note from the patient's last visit, including the problem list, with each referral. We should also note any precautions, such as allergic reactions to medication.

4. *Schedule longer appointments for new patients.* New patients require extra time from all of us, and their first impression is critical. We should emphasize relationship building during the first visit.

5. *Decorate the office for various seasons of the year, including holidays.* The patients will be more comfortable and staff members will feel better about their workplace. Our decorations will reflect the cultural diversity of our patient base.

In addition to generating these ideas, the nominal group technique has helped build commitment or buy-in by all workers in the practice. My observation is that group members have developed a sense of ownership as we have moved forward with each area of improvement. What in the past would have been considered "the doctors' ideas" by certain staff members are now *our ideas*, such as returning calls to patients promptly.

Questions

1. From your standpoint as a patient, or potential patient, do you think the NGT produced any useful results?

2. Was the NGT, as used here, any better than just getting the staff together for a 30-minute traditional brainstorming session?

Source: Reproduced with permission from "Finding Diamonds in the Trenches with the Nominal Group Process," May 1999, *Family Practice Management*. Copyright © 1999 American Academy of Family Physicians. All Rights Reserved.

USING STAND-UP MEETINGS TO FACILITATE PROBLEM-SOLVING

Problem-solving and decision-making can sometimes be improved by conducting meetings with the participants standing instead of sitting down. The general idea is that participants standing up in the problem-solving group are more likely to be alert and will come to a decision more quickly. Some people solve problems better when standing because they literally "think well on their feet." Few people are willing to stand for several hours, so they reach a decision quickly.

Many meeting leaders who use stand-up meetings are pleased with the results in terms of reaching high-quality decisions rapidly. A team of researchers decided to investigate the validity of this technique.[9] Study participants were 555 students in an introduction to management course who were offered extra credit for participating in the study. The students were randomly assigned to five-person groups, producing 111 groups. They were divided almost equally into stand-up and sit-down groups.

All groups were assigned the "Lost on the Moon" exercise, which presents a scenario involving a crash on the moon. Participants were asked to rank 15 pieces of equipment that survived the crash by their importance for survival. Correct answers to the problem were the ranking of the equipment given by NASA astronauts and scientists. The major findings of the experiment were as follows:

1. Sit-down meetings lasted about 34 percent longer than did stand-up meetings (788 seconds versus 589 seconds).

2. Sit-down and stand-up meetings arrived at decisions of equal quality.

3. More suggestions about task accomplishment were used by groups in the sit-down than in the stand-up meetings.

4. Participants in the sit-down meetings were more satisfied than participants in the stand-up meetings.

One implication for this study is that people make decisions more quickly when standing up, without sacrificing decision quality. However, people prefer to sit down. In general, if you think that a task can be performed in 30 minutes or less, a stand-up meeting is likely to be effective.

USING EMAIL AND GROUPWARE TO FACILITATE GROUP DECISION-MAKING

The presence of so many teams in the workplace means that people must work collectively and that they must make decisions together. An obvious requirement of group decision-making is that group members engage in collective effort. Collective effort usually translates into meetings. Without meetings, people are working primarily on their own and thus are not benefiting from working in teams. However, with too many meetings it is difficult to accomplish individual work, such as making telephone calls, analyzing information, and preparing reports.

Appropriate use of email and groupware can improve interaction among team members as well as group decision-making, while at the same time minimizing the number of meetings. (**Groupware** is technology designed to facilitate the work of groups.) Such use of email and other electronic tools makes possible the virtual teams described earlier in the chapter.

USING EMAIL TO FACILITATE MEETINGS

By using email, team members can feed important information to all other members of the team without the ritual of entering a meeting and passing around handouts.[10] The typical use of email is to send brief memos to people on a distribution list. Distribution lists can be formed so that only those involved in the decision are included in the emails. A more advanced use of email is to distribute word-processing documents as well as spreadsheets and graphics, including photographs, as attachments.

Think back to the decision reached by the team using the nominal group technique. As a follow-up to the meeting, the team was to get together to rate all 12 suppliers on quality, price, and service. Using email, the group could substantially cut down on the amount of time they would need to spend in a group meeting; they might even be able to eliminate it. Pedro Ortiz might instruct the team members to send their ratings and explanations to one another within 10 working days.

Each team member would rate all 12 suppliers on quality, service, and price. The ratings would then be sent to all other team members by email. Pedro could tally the results and email the final tally to each team member. Since all team members could have performed the same calculation themselves, there would be no claims of a biased decision. A team meeting could then be called to discuss the final results if Pedro or the other team members thought it was necessary.

Pushing the use of email too far can inhibit rather than improve group decision-making and teamwork. If people communicate with one another almost exclusively by email, the warmth of human interaction and perceiving facial expressions is lost. Piggybacking of ideas is possible by reading one another's ideas on a computer monitor. Nevertheless, the wink of an eye, the shared laughter, and the encouraging smiles that take place in a traditional meeting make an important contribution to team effort, including group problem-solving.

Also, people often receive so much email that their responses might not be timely, or might be too late for them to have input into the decision. It is not uncommon for workers to receive thirty or more emails in one business day. In the face of such overload, face-to-face meetings may be a welcome break from the bombardment of email.

USING GROUPWARE TO FACILITATE GROUP PROBLEM-SOLVING

The application of email just described can be considered part of groupware because email was used to streamline work in groups. Electronic brainstorming also relies on groupware because software is applied to improve group decision-making. At its best, groupware offers certain advantages over single-user systems. Some of the most common reasons people use groupware are as follows:[11]

- To improve communication by making it faster, clearer, and more persuasive
- To communicate when it would not otherwise be possible
- To enable telecommuting (working from home)
- To reduce travel costs
- To bring together multiple perspectives and diverse expertise
- To assemble groups with common interests where it would not be possible to gather a sufficient number of people face-to-face
- To improve group problem-solving

Another example of groupware is a shared whiteboard (similar to a whiteboard in a classroom, only this one is on your computer screen and the team can all write their ideas on it). The whiteboard allows two or more people to view and draw on a shared drawing surface even when they are at a distance. Depending on the nature of the business, drawing sketches and diagrams might be an important part of the decision-making process. An example would be a sales team suggesting ways of dividing up a geographic territory for selling.

A shared whiteboard can be used during a telephone call, with each person jotting down notes or several participants working together on a visual problem. Typical shared whiteboards are designed for informal conversation, but they can also service more technical applications such as collaborative graphic design and working out a manufacturing problem. The various drawings, or modifications of an existing drawing, submitted by group members are indicated by telepointers, colour-coded to identify each person.

Despite all these potential applications and benefits of groupware, the system will break down unless almost all the parties involved use the software successfully. For example, all members of the virtual team must be willing to get online at the same time to have a successful meeting.

SUMMARY

An important aspect of interpersonal relations in organizations is that groups solve many key problems. Group problem-solvers and decision-makers most often use either the rational or the political model. The rational decision-making model is the traditional, logical approach to decision-making, based on the scientific method. This model assumes that each alternative is evaluated in terms of how well it contributes to reaching the goals involved in making the overall decision.

The political decision-making model assumes that people bring preconceived notions and biases into the decision-making situation. Because the decision-makers are politically motivated, the individuals involved often do not make the most rational choice. Instead, the decision-makers attempt to satisfy their own needs.

General problem-solving groups are likely to arrive at better decisions when they follow standard guidelines for group problem-solving. The guidelines are as follows: (a) identify the problem; (b) clarify the problem; (c) analyze the cause; (d) search for alternative solutions; (e) select alternatives; (f) plan for implementation; (g) clarify the contract; (h) develop an action plan; and (i) provide for evaluation and accountability.

When the organization is seeking a large number of alternatives to problems, brainstorming is often the technique of choice. Brainstorming is used as a method of finding alternatives to real-life problems and as a creativity-training program. Using the technique, group members spontaneously call out alternative solutions to the problem. Members build on the ideas of one another, and ideas are not screened or evaluated until a later stage. Brainstorming by working alone, or brainwriting, is also effective in generating alternative solutions.

Electronic brainstorming is designed to overcome the problem of production blocking, such as free riding, in brainstorming. Using electronic brainstorming, group members simultaneously enter their suggestions into a computer, and the ideas are transmitted to the screens of other group members. Building on one another's ideas is allowed. Experiments with electronic brainstorming have shown favourable results.

The nominal group technique (NGT) is recommended for a situation in which a leader needs to know what alternatives are available and how people will react to them. In the NGT, a small group of people contribute written solutions to the problem. Other members respond to their ideas later. Members rate one another's ideas numerically, and the final group decision is the sum of the pooled individual votes.

Problem-solving and decision-making can sometimes be improved by conducting meetings with participants standing up instead of sitting down. The general idea is that participants who are standing up are more likely to be alert and come to a decision quickly. An experiment with management students indicated that stand-up groups made decisions more quickly, but that decision-makers who sat down were more satisfied.

Electronic mail can be used to improve group decision-making because members can feed information to one another without having to meet as a group. Memos, spreadsheet analyses, and graphics can be distributed through the network. Too much emphasis on email, however, results in losing the value of face-to-face human interaction.

Various types of groupware, including email and electronic brainstorming, can improve group decision-making. Also, a shared whiteboard allows two or more people to view and draw on a shared drawing surface, even when they are at a distance.

An Interpersonal Relations Case Problem

STRUGGLING TO MAKE A DECISION AT BMI

Building Maintenance Inc., a firm of 325 full- and part-time employees, is engaged in the cleaning and general maintenance of offices and shopping plazas. Bud Nyrod founded BMI as "one man and one van" 10 years ago. The four other members of the executive team also have a financial stake in the business.

BMI is headquartered in an old office building scheduled for demolition. The pending demolition has forced the firm to face a relocation decision. Bud called a 10 a.m. meeting of the executive team to address the problem. As he entered the conference room, Karen, Liz, Marty, and Marc were already seated.

Bud: Good to see the whole team here. I assume that you have already given some thought to our relocation decision. Let me review the alternatives I see. We can either relocate to some decent space in one of the newly refurbished downtown buildings, or we can get some slightly better space in a suburban park. Karen, as our financial officer, you must have some relevant facts and figures.

Karen: As you requested a few weeks ago, Bud, I have looked into a variety of possibilities. We can get some decent downtown space at about $35 per square foot. And, we can get first-rate accommodations in a suburban office park for about $38 per square foot. Relocation costs would be about the same.

Marty: Customers are influenced by image. So long as we have a good image, I think the customers will be satisfied. By the way, we are doing something that is negatively affecting our image. Our customer-service representatives are just too rude over the phone. I think these folks should have proper training before we turn them loose on the customer phone. Lots of other companies have good brooms, vacuum cleaners, and power-cleaning equipment. Our only edge is the good service we offer customers.

Bud: Liz, what is your position on this relocation decision?

Liz: As employment director, I have a lot to say about relocation. I agree with Marty that customer service

(Continued)

should receive top weight in any decision we make about relocation. Customer service, of course, is a direct result of having an efficient crew of maintenance employees. A suburban office park may sound glamorous, but it could be a disaster in terms of recruiting staff. Maintenance workers can afford to get downtown. The vast majority of them live in the city, and they are dependent on mass transit to get to work.

You typically need private transportation to get to an office park. The vast majority of our permanent and temporary employees do not own cars or trucks. And many of them that do own vehicles usually can't afford to keep them in good repair. Many of the temporary help can put gas in their cars only on payday.

So if we relocate to a suburban park, we'll have to rent a small employment office downtown anyway.

Bud: So you're telling us that maybe we should choose both alternatives. We should open an employment office downtown and move the executive office to a suburban office park.

Liz: Now we're introducing a third alternative. We could have two offices downtown: one for the executive and clerical staff and one for hiring maintenance workers.

Bud: Marc, what do you think? Which location would be best for you as director of maintenance operations?

Marc: I'm not in the office too much. I spend most of my time in the field overseeing our supervisors and their crews. Most of our help never see the office after they are hired unless they have a major problem. They report directly to the site. To them their place of work is the building or shopping plaza where they are assigned. Other things are more important than the location of company headquarters.

One of the most important things we should be considering is a big holiday party for this year. I think a year-end party is a real morale builder. It's cost effective in terms of how much turnover it reduces. Some of the maintenance staff will stay on an extra month just to attend the party.

Marty: It looks like you folks have got the major issues out on the table. I really don't care where we locate so long as the needs of our customers come first. I'm eager to know what you people decide. But right now I have to run. I have a luncheon appointment on the other side of town that could mean a big shopping-plaza contract for us.

Bud: Good luck with the sales call, Marty. However, I think you could have scheduled that luncheon for another day. This is a pretty important issue. I'd like you to stay for five more minutes.

Marc: It seems that it's premature for us to reach a decision on this important matter today. Maybe we should call in an office location consultant to help us decide what to do. In the meantime, let's talk some more about the office party. I kind of like that idea.

Case Questions

1. How effective is the BMI team as a problem-solving group?

2. What recommendations can you make to the BMI team to better solve the problem it is facing?

3. How might the team have used the nominal group technique to help solve the problem of office relocation?

An Interpersonal Relations Case Problem

THE GREAT WIPER BLADE MYSTERY

It was a mystery—a mystery with millions of dollars and hundreds of jobs riding on the answer. A huge 6.5 percent of the windshield wiper systems being manufactured at an ITT automotive plant in upstate New York for DaimlerChrysler's minivans were defective. Nobody could figure out why the defect existed. All the parts met specifications; they were assembled correctly, and engineers found no fault with the design. Yet, in a test run, many wipers failed to make a complete sweep across the windshield—a

(Continued)

potential disaster for Chrysler and for the 3800 automotive workers in the upstate plant.

Plant management assembled a six-person team including engineers, union members, and manufacturing experts to become a detective force to find the answers. The team felt a lot of pressure to resolve the problem because the livelihood of the plant was threatened. If its major product was defective, the plant might be shuttered.

Technical Aspects of the Problem

The new wiper system was the biggest and most complex ever assembled in the plant. Instead of just delivering wiper blades, the plant was given "black box responsibility" to deliver a perfectly functioning windshield system that Chrysler workers could just snap into place.

The blades, instead of moving right and left in tandem, came together in the centre of the windshield and spread apart again, making timing a crucial issue. "The number of things that could go wrong was exponentially greater than for anything we had ever done before," said Rob Price, manufacturing general supervisor. Just one thing did go wrong, but it was enough to threaten the project.

In 6.5 percent of the wipers, the blade's swing was up to 2.5 degrees short. That's equivalent to less than half a second on the face of a clock. But it was enough to make the blade fall short of sweeping the full area in front of the driver's face—an area that federal regulators insist be kept clear of rain and ice.

The Cross-Functional
Team Tackles the Problem

Responsibility for solving the problem fell to the Chrysler cross-functional team: the leader of the plant's Chrysler team, Craig Hysong; manufacturing general supervisor Rob Price; quality technician Rick Fisher; quality analyst Jeannine Marciano; engineer Mike Kinsky; and Ron Maor, an engineer from a sister plant in Ontario. Each new ITT automotive product has its cross-functional team, drawn from the different departments. The team's goal was to make sure the product was launched flawlessly.

The Chrysler team picked the best and worst of the wipers—called "Bob" and "Wow" for the best of the best and the worst of the worst. They thought that by comparing the best with the worst, they might somehow isolate and fix the problem.

The team felt intense pressure to perform because, unless they solved the mystery, Chrysler would have to find a new supplier for windshield wiper systems. Finally, Fisher, the technician, and Maor, the engineer from the plant that supplies the motors, found the answer. It was in the serrations (rough marks, like those on a serrated knife) on the motor's drive shaft that are meant to hold the crank in place.

Case Questions

1. Which approach to (or method of) group problem-solving did the plant team use?

2. To what extent did management make the right move in assigning the flawed windshield wiper problem to a team instead of to one engineer or technician?

3. If by chance you happen to have the right expertise, what would you guess was the problem with the windshield wiper system?

Source: Case excerpted and paraphrased from Phil Ebersole, "ITT Automotive Sleuths Solve a Design Mystery," Rochester, New York, *Democrat and Chronicle*, May 4, 1997, pp. 1E, 4E.

QUESTIONS FOR DISCUSSION AND REVIEW

1. Why are group decisions more likely to lead to commitment than decisions made by a manager acting alone?

2. Based on any experience you have had at school or at work, what process or method is usually followed in making group decisions?

3. Which personality characteristics described in Chapter 2 do you think would help a person be naturally effective in group problem solving?

4. Identify several job- or non-job-related problems for which you think brainstorming would be effective.

5. What is your opinion of the importance of the physical setting (such as sunlight and refreshments) for stimulating creative thinking during brainstorming?

6. What, if any, accommodations should be made in electronic brainstorming for group members who have poor keyboarding skills?

7. Identify two work-related problems for which the nominal group technique is particularly well-suited.

8. Companies have known about stand-up meetings for many years, and the results have been favourable in terms of productivity. Why, then, are stand-up meetings still not very popular?

9. Using the Research Navigator, find one study that uses the nominal group technique or evaluates its usefulness. Share the findings with the class. Were the results positive? What suggestions were offered in the study about the use of the nominal group technique? One good study (AN18386383) about the nominal group technique examines social loafing. Examine this article to understand social loafing and its impact on group techniques and project quality.

10. Which group decision-making technique described in this chapter do you think members of top management are the most likely to use? Why?

WEBLINKS

www.thinksmart.com
A site with information on creativity by the Innovation Network.

www.creativity.com
This site is devoted to creativity across many fields from business to artists.

www.nova-mind.com
Mind mapping for group and individual problem solving. See the demonstration.

www.enchantedmind.com
This site is devoted to the "mind" and includes a section on creativity, along with creativity tests.

Chapter 6

Cross-Cultural Relations and Diversity

Learning Outcomes

After reading and studying this chapter and doing the exercises, you should be able to

- Recognize who fits under the diversity umbrella.
- Describe the major values accounting for cultural differences.
- Specify some of the business implications of being sensitive to cultural differences.
- Overcome many cross-cultural communication barriers.
- Improve your cross-cultural relations.

Leanne was very excited when she was chosen to fly to China to discuss the details of a tender her company had succeeded in obtaining. The company she works for builds intricate measuring equipment used in mining and other geographic and geologic operations. As part of the marketing division, Leanne was to fly to China and meet with officials from the Chinese company for the final signing of all documentation and to familiarize herself with the company's operations.

Leanne had learned in similar dealings in Canada and the United States that the giving of a small gift when being treated to a meal is proper business etiquette. She had brought an elegant gift wrapped in beautiful white and black paper in the event such an occasion arose. As it happened, on her last evening in China—when all the business had been concluded—Leanne was invited out to dinner with Yen Lo, the owner, and his wife. Pleased with her gift of a carving done by a Canadian artist, Leanne was surprised by its stony reception. The rest of the evening was not very pleasant.

When Leanne returned home, she decided to approach an Asian friend of hers about the incident. When she told her about the gift, her friend suddenly interjected, "Oh my, you gave them a gift for mourning. We wrap gifts for those who have had a loved one die in black and white!"

Leanne made a mistake that is common when interacting with those from other cultures. She assumed that there were few differences between her North American cultural background and that of someone with an Asian upbringing. People often assume that, with technology, a global marketplace, and instant communication, differences between people are diminishing. While this may be true in some cultures, the assumption may hurt future business.

Cultures around the world still differ from each other in many ways and work to maintain their differences: their own set of beliefs, ideas, and ways of doing things, including how to do business. Being part of a global economy and global marketplace means that employees need to be more aware of cultural differences and other diversity issues. A competent employee would have researched Chinese customs before departing. With some prior knowledge of Chinese culture, Leanne would not have made such an embarrassing—and perhaps costly—mistake.

While many employees may have the opportunity to visit other countries, an extensive knowledge of cultural differences and diversity is also required for work within our own country. Canada is a diverse nation, and the workplace reflects this diversity. Not only is the workforce becoming more diverse, but business has also become increasingly international. Small- and medium-sized firms, as well as corporate giants, are increasingly dependent on trade with other countries. Furthermore, most manufactured goods contain components from abroad.

All this workplace diversity has an important implication for the career-minded individual. To succeed in today's workplace, you must be able to relate effectively to people from different cultural groups from within and outside this country. Being able to relate to a culturally diverse customer base is also necessary for success, as is working with others from different cultural or ethnic backgrounds. To become more familiar with the cultural diversity of Canada, examine the Canadian Scene below, which presents a statistical picture of Canadian diversity.

The Canadian Scene

A STATISTICAL PICTURE OF A CULTURALLY DIVERSE POPULATION

Immigration Statistics

Author's Note: *Below are the most up-to-date statistics at the time of writing. The census results from 2006 were not all available at this time.*

- Between 2001 and 2006, Canada's population increased 5.4 percent, the first time since 1991 that the census-to-census growth rate has accelerated. This acceleration is due to higher levels of immigration.
- As of May 15, 2001, 18.4 percent of Canadians were born outside the country.
- Of those who immigrated in the 1990s, 58 percent were born in Asia (including the Middle East), 20 percent in Europe, 11 percent in the Caribbean or Latin America, 8 percent in Africa, and 3 percent in the United States.
- The People's Republic of China was the leading country of birth among individuals who immigrated to Canada in the 1990s.

(Continued)

- In 2001, 13.4 percent of the population identified themselves as members of visible minorities. Visible minorities are defined as "persons, other than Aboriginal peoples, who are non-Caucasian in race or non-white in colour," according to the Employment Equity Act.

- The three largest visible minority groups in 2001 were Chinese, South Asian, and African Canadians, who together accounted for two-thirds of the visible minority population.

- People who identified themselves as Aboriginal in 2001 accounted for 3.3 percent of the nation's total population, up from 2.8 percent in the 1996 census.

- Of all immigrants to Canada, 73 percent live in three census metropolitan areas: Toronto, Vancouver, and Montreal.

- Calgary and Ottawa-Hull are emerging as centres of attraction for new immigrants. In both cities, immigrants now account for 3 percent of the labour force, similar to the percentage in Montreal.

- Canada is becoming more multilingual, with more than 100 mother tongues.

- Chinese is Canada's most common mother tongue after English and French.

- Between 1996 and 2001, language groups from the Middle East and Asia recorded the largest gains.

Languages

Along with this ethnic diversity, the number of mother tongues and home languages spoken within Canada is also growing, though English and French are still predominant. A mother tongue is the first language learned as a child. A home language is the language spoken by the individual at the time of the Canadian census. Here are the top mother tongues, in descending order of prevalence, from the 2001 census (excluding English and French):

1. Chinese

2. Italian

3. German

4. Punjabi

5. Spanish

6. Portuguese

7. Polish

8. Arabic

9. Tagalog

10. Dutch

Sources: Statistics Canada, *The Daily*, Catalogue 11–001, January 21, 2001; Statistics Canada, *The Daily*, March 13, 2007; Statistics Canada, "The Changing Profile of Canada's Labour Force," *2001 Census: Analysis Series*, Feb. 2003, Catalogue no. 96F0030XIE2001009; Statistics Canada, "The Census of Population: Language, Mobility, and Migration," *The Daily*, Tuesday, December 10, 2002, www.statcan.ca/Daily/English/021210/d021210a.html. Language breakdown from table by Statistics Canada, 2001 Census, "Population by Mother Tongue, Provinces and Territories," www.statcan.ca/english/Pgdb/demo18a.htm, last modified January 20, 2003.

This chapter presents concepts and techniques you can use to sharpen your ability to work effectively with people from diverse backgrounds. To get you started thinking about your readiness to work in a culturally diverse environment, take Self-Assessment Quiz 6-1.

Self-Assessment Quiz 6-1

CROSS-CULTURAL SKILLS AND ATTITUDES

Listed below are skills and attitudes that various employers and cross-cultural experts think are important for relating effectively to co-workers in a culturally diverse environment.

	Applies to Me Now	Not There Yet
1. I have spent some time in another country.		
2. At least one of my friends is deaf, blind, or uses a wheelchair.		
3. Currency from other countries is as real as the currency from my own country.		
4. I can read in a language other than my own.		
5. I can speak in a language other than my own.		
6. I can write in a language other than my own.		
7. I can understand people speaking in a language other than my own.		
8. I use my second language regularly.		
9. My friends include people of races different from my own.		
10. My friends include people of different ages.		
11. I feel (or would feel) comfortable having a friend with a sexual orientation different from mine.		
12. My attitude is that although another culture may be very different from mine, that culture is equally good.		
13. I would be willing to (or already do) hang art from different countries in my home.		
14. I would accept (or have already accepted) a work assignment of more than several months in another country.		
15. I have a valid passport.		

Interpretation: If you answered "Applies to me now" to 10 or more of the preceding questions, you most likely function well in a multicultural work environment. If you answered "Not there yet" to 10 or more of the questions, you need to develop more cross-cultural awareness and skills to work effectively in a multicultural work environment. You will notice that being bilingual gives you at least five points on this quiz.

Sources: Several ideas for statements on this quiz are derived from Ruthann Dirks and Janet Buzzard, "What CEOs Expect of Employees Hired for International Work," *Business Education Forum,* April 1997, pp. 3–7; and Gunnar Beeth, "Multicultural Managers Wanted," *Management Review,* May 1997, pp. 17–21.

THE DIVERSITY UMBRELLA

Improving cross-cultural relations includes understanding the true meaning of appreciating diversity. To appreciate diversity, a person must go beyond tolerating people from different racial and ethnic groups and treating them fairly. The true meaning of valuing diversity is to respect and enjoy a wide range of cultural and individual differences. Appreciating these differences is often referred to as *inclusion* to emphasize unity rather than diversity. To be diverse is to be different in some measurable way, even if what is measurable is not visible (such as religion or sexual orientation).

The diversity umbrella continues to include more people as the workforce encompasses a greater variety of people. The goal of a diverse organization is for persons of all cultural backgrounds to achieve their full potential, unrestrained by group identities such as sex, nationality, or race.[1] Another important goal is for these groups to work together harmoniously.

- Race
- Sex (or gender)
- Religion
- Age (young, middle-aged, and old)
- Ethnicity (country of origin)
- Education
- Abilities
- Mental disabilities (including attention deficit disorder)
- Physical disabilities (including hearing status, visual status, able-bodied, wheelchair user)
- Values and motivation
- Sexual orientation (heterosexual, homosexual, bisexual)
- Marital status (married, single, cohabitating, widow, widower)
- Family status (children, no children, two-parent family, single parent, grandparent)
- Personality traits
- Functional background (area of specialization)
- Technology interest (high-tech, low-tech, technophobe)
- Weight status (average, obese, underweight, anorexic)
- Hair status (full head of hair, bald, wild hair, tame hair, long hair, short hair)
- Tobacco status (smoker versus nonsmoker, chewer versus nonchewer)
- Styles of clothing and appearance (dress up, dress down, professional appearance, casual appearance)

Figure 6-1   The Diversity Umbrella

Figure 6-1 on the previous page presents a broad sampling of the ways in which workplace associates can differ from one another. Studying this list can help you anticipate the types of differences to understand and appreciate in a diverse workplace. The differences include cultural as well as individual factors. Individual factors are also important because people can be discriminated against for personal characteristics as well as group factors. Many people, for example, believe they are held back from promotion because of their weight-to-height ratio.

UNDERSTANDING CULTURAL DIFFERENCES

The groundwork for developing effective cross-cultural relations is to understand cultural differences. The information about different communication patterns between men and women presented in Chapter 3 is relevant here. Some researchers think that men and women represent different cultures! One cultural difference between the two groups is that women tend to speak indirectly and soften criticism. Men, in contrast, tend to be more direct in giving criticism. Here we discuss six aspects of understanding cultural differences: (1) cultural sensitivity, (2) cultural intelligence, (3) respect for all workers (4) cultural fluency (5) dimensions of differences in cultural values, and (6) avoidance of cultural bloopers. To work smoothly with people from other cultures, it is important to become competent in all six areas.

CULTURAL SENSITIVITY

To relate well to someone from a foreign country, a person must be alert to possible cultural differences. When working in another country, you must be willing to acquire knowledge about local customs and learn how to at least passably speak the native language. When working with people from different cultures, even fellow Canadians, you must be patient, adaptable, flexible, and willing to listen and learn. The characteristics just mentioned are part of **cultural sensitivity**, an awareness of and willingness to investigate the reasons why people of another culture act as they do.[2] A person with cultural sensitivity will recognize certain nuances in customs that will help him or her build better relationships with people from different cultural backgrounds.

CULTURAL INTELLIGENCE

An advanced aspect of cultural sensitivity is to be able to fit in comfortably with people of another culture by observing the subtle cues they give about how a person should act in their presence. **Cultural intelligence (CQ)** is an outsider's ability to interpret someone's unfamiliar and ambiguous behaviour the same way that person's compatriots would.[3] With high cultural intelligence a person would be able to figure out what behaviour would be true of all people and all groups, such as rapid shaking of a clenched fist to communicate anger. Also, the person with high cultural intelligence could figure out what is peculiar to this group, and those aspects of behaviour that are neither universal nor peculiar to the group. These ideas are so abstract, that an example will help clarify.

An English Canadian manager served on a design team that included two German engineers. As other team members floated their ideas, the engineers condemned them as incomplete or underdeveloped. The manager concluded that the Germans in general are rude and aggressive.

With average cultural intelligence the Canadian would have realized he was mistakenly equating the merit of an idea with the merit of the person presenting it. The Germans, however, were able to make a sharp distinction between the two. A manager with more advanced cultural intelligence might have tried to figure out how much of the two Germans' behaviour was typically German and how much was explained by the fact that they were engineers.

Similar to emotional intelligence, cultural intelligence encompasses several different aspects of behaviour. The three sources of cultural intelligence relate to the cognitive, emotional/motivational, and the physical, explained as follows:[4]

1. *Cognitive (the Head).* The cognitive part of CQ refers to what a person knows and how he or she can acquire new knowledge. Here you acquire facts about people from another culture such as their passion for football (soccer in North America), their business practices, and their promptness in paying bills. Another aspect of this source of cultural intelligence is figuring out how you can learn more about the other culture.

2. *Emotional/Motivational (the Heart).* The emotional/motivational aspect of CQ refers to energizing one's actions and building personal confidence. You need both confidence and motivation to adapt to another culture. A man on a business trip to Africa might say to himself, "When I greet a work associate in a restaurant, can I really pull off kissing him on both cheeks. What if he thinks I'm weird?" With strong motivation, the same person might say, "I'll give it a try. I kind of greet my grandfather the same way back in Quebec."

3. *Physical (The Body).* The body aspect of CQ is the action component. The body is the element for translating intentions into actions and desires. Kissing the same-sex African work associates on both cheeks is the *physical* aspect just mentioned. We often have an idea of what we should do, but implementation is not so easy. You might know, for example, that when entering an Asian person's home you should take off your shoes, yet you might not actually remove them—thereby offending your Asian work (or personal life) associate.

To practise high cultural intelligence, the mind, heart, and body have to work together. You need to figure out how to act with people from another culture; you need motivation and confidence to change; and you have to translate your knowledge and motivation into action. So when you are on a business trip to London, go ahead and hold your fork in your left hand!

RESPECT FOR ALL WORKERS AND CULTURES

An effective strategy for achieving cross-cultural understanding is to simply respect all others in the workplace, including their cultures. An important component of respect is to believe that although another person's culture is different from yours, it is equally good.

Respecting other people's customs can translate into specific attitudes, such as respecting one co-worker for wearing a yarmulke on Friday or another for wearing an

African costume to celebrate Kwanza. Another way of being respectful would be to listen carefully to the opinion of a senior worker who says the company should never have converted to voice mail from live phone assistance (even though you disagree).

Company policies that encourage respect for the rights of others are likely to create a positive influence on tolerance throughout the firm. An example is that many employers have taken steps to recognize and affirm the existence of gay and lesbian workers. Among these steps are the publication of formal statements of nondiscrimination and the inclusion of issues about sexual orientation in diversity training programs. A major policy change has been to grant same-sex couples the same benefits granted to opposite-sex couples.

A study of 537 gay and lesbian employees working for a variety of organizations demonstrated that the more prevalently a company's policies deal with respect, the more equitably sexual minorities are likely to be treated. More equitable treatment, in turn, was associated with gays and lesbians being more satisfied with their work and less likely to leave the firm.[5]

CULTURAL FLUENCY

A high-level goal in understanding cultural differences is to achieve **cultural fluency**, the ability to conduct business in a diverse, international environment.[6] Achieving cultural fluency includes a variety of skills, such as relating well to people from different cultures and knowing a second language. Cultural fluency also includes knowledge of the international business environment, such as how the exchange rate can affect profits.

Skill-Building Exercise 6-1 is a warm-up activity for achieving cultural sensitivity, and perhaps respect for all workers.

Skill-Building Exercise 6-1

DEVELOPING CULTURAL SENSITIVITY

Carefully observe how products and services such as tennis shoes, notebooks, bicycles, and banking services are marketed and sold in Canada, and then attempt to find out how they are marketed and sold in other countries. For a convenient reference source, interview foreign students and foreigners outside class about these products and services. Your digging for information might uncover such nuggets as the following:

- In India, cricket champions are celebrities comparable to American basketball stars, endorsing soft drinks like Coca-Cola and Pepsi.

- In Hungary, peanut butter is considered a luxury food item.

- In some countries in warm climates, meat is freshly killed and hung on hooks for sale—without refrigeration or freezing.

After conducting these product and service interviews, arrive at some kind of interpretation or conclusion. Share your insights with other class members.

Source: "Teaching International Business," *Keying In* (The Newsletter of the National Business Education Association), January 1999, p. 1.

DIMENSIONS OF DIFFERENCES IN CULTURAL VALUES

One way to understand how national cultures differ is to examine their values. Table 6-1 presents an introduction to the subject by comparing values in North America to collective values elsewhere. You can use this information as a general stereotype of how North Americans are likely to differ from people in many other countries.

We now focus our attention on a more detailed look at eight different values and how selected nationalities relate to them, based on the work of several researchers.[7]

1. *Individualism versus collectivism.* At one end of the continuum is **individualism**, a mental set in which people see themselves first as individuals and believe that their own interests take priority. In **collectivism**, at the other end of the continuum, the group and society receive top priority. Members of a society that values individualism tend to be more concerned with their careers than with the good of the firm. Members of a society that values collectivism, in contrast, are typically more concerned with the organization than they are with themselves.

   Highly individualistic cultures include Canada, the United States, Great Britain, Australia, and the Netherlands. Japan, Taiwan, Mexico, Greece, and Hong Kong are among the countries that strongly value collectivism.

2. *Acceptance of power and authority.* People from some cultures accept the idea that members of an organization have different levels of power and authority. In a culture that believes in concentration of power and authority, the boss makes many decisions simply because he or she is the boss. Group members readily comply because they have a positive orientation toward authority. In a culture with fewer acceptances of power and authority, employees do not readily recognize a power hierarchy. They accept directions only when they think the boss is right or when they feel threatened. Countries that readily accept power and authority include France, Spain, Japan, Mexico, and Brazil. Countries that have much less acceptance of power and authority are the United States, Canada and particularly the Scandinavian countries (e.g., Sweden).

Table 6-1   North American Values Versus Those in Many Other Countries

In North America	In many other countries
Time is to be controlled	Time is fluid, malleable
Emphasis on change	Tradition, continuity
Individualism	Group orientation
Personal privacy	Openness, accessibility
Informality	Formality
Individual competition	Cooperation
Equality/egalitarianism	Hierarchy/authority
Short-term emphasis	Long-term emphasis
Work emphasis ("One lives to work.")	Leisure + work emphasis ("One works to live.")
Task emphasis	People emphasis
Direct/explicit communication style	Indirect/implicit communication style
Action bias or emphasis	Planning and preparation emphasis

Source: Adaptation of chart prepared by International Orientation Resources.

3. *Materialism versus concern for others.* In this context, **materialism** refers to an emphasis on assertiveness and the acquisition of money and material objects; it also means less emphasis on caring for others. At the other end of the continuum is **concern for others**, an emphasis on personal relations and a concern for the welfare of others. Materialistic countries include Japan, Austria, and Italy. Canada is considered to be moderately materialistic. Scandinavian nations all emphasize caring as a national value. (At one time, this same dimension was referred to as *masculinity* versus *femininity.* Such terms are considered sexist today.)

4. *Formality versus informality.* A country that values **formality** attaches considerable importance to tradition, ceremony, social rules, and rank. At the other extreme, **informality** refers to a casual attitude toward tradition, ceremony, social rules, and rank. Workers in Latin American countries highly value formality, such as lavish public receptions and processions. Americans, Canadians, and Scandinavians are much more informal.

5. *Urgent time orientation versus casual time orientation.* Individuals and nations attach different importance to time. People with an **urgent time orientation** perceive time as a scarce resource and tend to be impatient. People with a **casual time orientation** view time as an unlimited and unending resource and tend to be patient. Americans are noted for their urgent time orientation. They frequently impose deadlines and are eager to get started doing business. Asians and Middle Easterners, in contrast, are patient negotiators.

6. *Work orientation versus leisure orientation.* A major cultural difference is the number of hours per week and weeks per year people expect to invest in work versus leisure, or other non-work activities. American corporate professionals typically work about 55 hours per week, take 45-minute lunch breaks, and two weeks of vacation. Japanese workers share similar values with respect to time invested in work. In contrast, many European countries have steadily reduced the work week in recent years, while lengthening vacations. In March 2005, France overturned its 35-hour work week and restored its 39-hour work week, illustrating that Europeans have a preference for a modest work week.

7. *High-context versus low-context cultures.* Cultures differ in how much importance they attach to the surrounding circumstances, or context, of an event. **High-context cultures** make more extensive use of body language. Some cultures, such as the Asian, Hispanic, and African-American cultures, are high context. In contrast, northern European cultures are low context and make less use of body language. The Anglo-American culture is considered to be medium-low context. People in low-context cultures seldom take time in business dealings to build relationships and establish trust.

How might a person use information about cultural differences to improve his or her interpersonal relations on the job? A starting point would be to recognize that a person's national values might influence his or her behaviour. Assume that you wanted to establish a good working relationship with a person from a high-context culture. An effective starting point would be to emphasize body language when communicating with that individual.

Attitudes toward hierarchy and status can make a difference in establishing working relationships. A worker who values deference to age, gender, or title might shy away from offering suggestions to an elder or manager to avoid appearing disrespectful. This worker would need considerable encouragement to collaborate in decision-making.[8] *Time-consciousness* may create a conflict if you are committed to making deadlines and a team member has a laid-back attitude toward time. You might explain that although you respect his attitudes toward time, the company insists on getting the project completed on time.

Self-Assessment Quiz 6-2 will help you think about how your values might be influencing your interpersonal relations in the workplace.

Self-Assessment Quiz 6-2

CHARTING YOUR CULTURAL-VALUE PROFILE

Directions: For each of the eight value dimensions, circle the number that most accurately fits your standing on the dimension. For example, if you perceive yourself to be "highly formal," circle 7 on the sixth dimension (item 6).

1. Individualism   Collectivism
        1   2   3   4   5   6   7

2. High acceptance of power and authority   Low acceptance of power and authority
        1   2   3   4   5   6   7

3. Materialism   Concern for others
        1   2   3   4   5   6   7

4. Formality   Informality
        1   2   3   4   5   6   7

5. Urgent time orientation   Casual time orientation
        1   2   3   4   5   6   7

6. Work orientation   Leisure orientation
        1   2   3   4   5   6   7

7. High-context culture   Low-context culture
        1   2   3   4   5   6   7

Scoring and Interpretation: After circling one number for each dimension, use a felt-tipped pen to connect the circles, thereby giving yourself a *profile of cultural values.* Do not be concerned if your marker cuts through the names of the dimensions. Compare your profile to others in the class. If time allows, develop a class profile by computing the class average for each of the eight points and then connecting the points.

CULTURAL BLOOPERS

An effective way of being culturally sensitive is to minimize actions that are likely to offend people from another culture, based on their values. Cultural bloopers are most likely to take place when you are visiting another country. The same bloopers, however, can also be committed when dealing with people from a different culture within your own country. To avoid these bloopers, you must carefully observe persons from another culture. Studying another culture through reading is also helpful.

E-commerce and other forms of internet communication have created new opportunities for creating cultural bloopers. Website developers and those responsible for adding content must have good cross-cultural literacy, including an awareness of how the information might be misinterpreted. Here are examples of two potential problems:

- Colours on websites must be chosen carefully. For example, in some cultures purple is the colour of royalty, whereas in Brazil purple is associated with death.

- Be careful of metaphors that may not make sense to a person for whom your language is a second language. Examples include "ethical meltdown" and "over the hill."

English has become the language of business and science throughout the world, yet communicating in a customer's native tongue has its advantages. International business specialist Rick Borelli suggests that being able to communicate your message directly in your customer's mother tongue provides a competitive advantage.[9] Furthermore, according to the research firm IDC, consumers are four times more likely to purchase a product online if the website is in their preferred language.[10] The translator, of course, must have good knowledge of the subtleties of the language to avoid committing a blooper. An English-to-French translator used the verb *baiser* instead of *baisser* to describe a program of lowering prices. *Baisser* is the French verb "to lower," but *baiser* means "kiss." Worse, in slang *baiser* is a verb that refers to intimate physical relations!

Keep two key facts in mind when attempting to avoid making cultural mistakes. One is that members of any cultural group show individual differences. What one member of the group might regard as an insensitive act, another might welcome. Recognize also that one or two cultural mistakes will not peg you permanently as a boor. Skill-Building Exercise 6-2 will help you minimize certain cultural bloopers.

Skill-Building Exercise 6-2

CULTURAL MISTAKES TO AVOID WITH SELECTED CULTURAL GROUPS

EUROPE

Great Britain
- Asking personal questions. The British protect their privacy.
- Thinking that a business person from England is unenthusiastic when he or she says "Not bad at all." English people understate positive emotion.
- Gossiping about royalty.

(Continued)

France	• Expecting to complete work during the French two-hour lunch.
	• Attempting to conduct significant business during August—*les vacances* (vacation time).
	• Greeting a French person for the first time and not using a title such as "sir" or "madam" (or "monsieur," "madame," or "mademoiselle").
Italy	• Eating too much pasta, as it is not the main course.
	• Handing out business cards freely. Italians use them infrequently.
Spain	• Expecting punctuality. Your appointments will usually arrive 20 to 30 minutes late.
	• Making the American sign for "OK" with your thumb and forefinger. In Spain (and many other countries) this is vulgar.
Scandinavia (Denmark, Sweden, Norway)	• Being overly conscious of rank. Scandinavians pay relatively little attention to a person's place in the hierarchy.

ASIA

All Asian countries	• Pressuring an Asian job applicant or employee to brag about his or her accomplishments. Asians feel self-conscious when boasting about individual accomplishments; they prefer to let the record speak for itself. In addition, they prefer to talk about group rather than individual accomplishment.
Japan	• Shaking hands or hugging Japanese people (as well as other Asians) in public. The Japanese consider these practices offensive.
	• Not interpreting "We'll consider it" as a "No" when spoken by a Japanese business person. Japanese negotiators mean "No" when they say "We'll consider it."
	• Not giving small gifts to Japanese people when conducting business. The Japanese are offended when they do not receive these gifts.
	• Giving your business card to a Japanese business person more than once. The Japanese prefer to give and receive business cards only once.
China	• Using black borders on stationery and business cards, because black is associated with death.
	• Giving small gifts to Chinese people when conducting business. The Chinese are offended by these gifts.
	• Making cold calls on Chinese business executives. An appropriate introduction is required for a first-time meeting with a Chinese official.
Korea	• Saying no. Koreans feel it is important to have visitors leave with good feelings.
India	• Telling Indians you prefer not to eat with your hands. If the Indians are not using cutlery when eating, they expect you to do likewise.

MEXICO AND LATIN AMERICA

Mexico	• Flying into a Mexican city in the morning and expecting to close a deal by lunch. Mexicans build business relationships slowly.
Brazil	• Attempting to impress Brazilians by speaking a few words of Spanish. Portuguese is the official language of Brazil.

(Continued)

| *Most Latin American countries* | • Wearing elegant and expensive jewellery during a business meeting. Most Latin Americans think people should appear more conservative in business settings. |

Note: A cultural mistake for Canadians and Americans to avoid when conducting business in most other countries is to insist on getting down to business quickly. North Americans in small towns also like to build a relationship before getting down to business. The preceding suggestions will lead to cross-cultural skills development if practised in the right setting. During the next 30 days, look for an opportunity to relate to a person from another culture in the way described in these suggestions. Observe the reaction of the other person for feedback on your cross-cultural effectiveness.

OVERCOMING CROSS-CULTURAL COMMUNICATION BARRIERS

We have already discussed the importance of overcoming communication barriers in Chapter 3. Cultural differences create additional barriers. The following guidelines will help you overcome cross-cultural communication barriers.

1. *Be sensitive to the fact that cross-cultural communication barriers exist. If you are aware of these potential barriers, you will be ready to deal with them.* When you are dealing with a person in the workplace with a different cultural background than your own, solicit feedback to minimize cross-cultural barriers to communication. Being aware of these potential barriers will help you develop cultural sensitivity.

2. *Show respect for all workers.* The same behaviour that promotes good cross-cultural relations in general helps overcome communication barriers. A widely used comment that implies disrespect is to say to a person from another culture, "You have a funny accent." Should you be transposed to that person's culture, you, too, might have a "funny accent."

3. *Use straightforward language and speak slowly and clearly.* When working with people who do not speak your language fluently, speak in an easy-to-understand manner. Minimize the use of idioms and analogies specific to your language. A computer analyst from Greece left confused after a discussion about a software problem with her manager. The manager said, "Let's talk about this another time because *I can't seem to get to first base with you.*" (The manager was referring to the fact that the conversation was headed nowhere because he couldn't come to an agreement with the analyst.) The computer analyst did not ask for clarification because she did not want to appear uninformed.

4. *Observe cultural differences in etiquette.* Violating rules of etiquette without explanation can erect immediate communication barriers. A major rule of etiquette in many countries is that people address each other by surname unless they have worked together for a long time. On the other hand, the superior might encourage your being on a first-name basis with him or her. Be aware that although an increasing number of cultures are moving toward the informal approach, it is best to err on the side of formality.

5. *Be sensitive to differences in nonverbal communication.* Stay alert to the possibility that your nonverbal signal may be misinterpreted by a person from another culture. For example, an engineer for a Manitoba company was asked a question by a German co-worker. He signalled OK by making a circle with his thumb and forefinger. The German worker stormed away because in his country the same gesture is a vulgar personal insult. One area of nonverbal communication that often is misinterpreted is the use of interpersonal space. Cultures vary in what is considered appropriate distances between people when speaking. The results from a study done at the University of Montreal demonstrated cultural differences. Anglo Saxons used the largest zone of personal space, followed by Asians, and Mediterraneans, and Latinos used the least amount of interpersonal distance.[11]

6. *Do not be diverted by style, accent, grammar, or personal appearance.* Although these superficial factors are all related to business success, they are difficult to interpret when judging a person from another culture. It is therefore better to judge the merits of the person's statement or behaviour.[12] A brilliant individual from another culture may still be learning your language and thus make basic mistakes in speaking it. Also, he or she might not yet have developed a sensitivity to the dress style of your culture.

7. *Be attentive to individual differences in appearance.* A major cross-cultural insult is to confuse the identity of people because they are members of the same race or ethnic group. An older economics professor reared in China and teaching in the US had difficulty communicating with students because he was unable to learn their names. The professor's defence was "So many of these Americans look alike to me." Recent research suggests that people have difficulty seeing individual differences among people of another race because they code race first, such as thinking, "He has the nose of an African-American." However, people can learn to search for more distinguishing features, such as a dimple or eye colour.[13] In this way, individual differences are recognized.

8. *Be aware of and understand that prejudice and discrimination still exist and that members of different cultures have experienced and continue to experience much prejudice and discrimination.* While human rights codes, labour laws and practices, and company policies may all aspire to equality for all, this has not always been the case for many minorities. Prejudice and discrimination can be very subtle and continue for many minorities in Canada. Recent articles continue to point out that racism against black Canadians is still prevalent.[14] Also, current news articles continue to underscore the many inequalities faced by Canadian Aboriginals. Many programs and services have been implemented to assist Aboriginals in developing skills to succeed in the business world and run their own businesses, such as *The Entrepreneurial Spirit: Introduction to Entrepreneurship, Business and Financial Management for Aboriginal Entrepreneurs,* launched by the Canadian Bankers Association. Also, with continued growth of the First Nations Bank, there will continue to be more employment and business

opportunities for Canadian Aboriginals.[15] The key point here is that while you may not be prejudiced or discriminatory, many people you encounter may have been the victims of such attitudes or treatment and we need to be sensitive to those experiences.

BUSINESS IMPLICATIONS OF UNDERSTANDING CULTURAL DIFFERENCES

Top-level management at many companies emphasize cross-cultural understanding, including overcoming communication barriers, because such activities improve profits. If you establish rapport with people from other cultures—and avoid antagonizing them—they will most likely become and remain your customers. Similarly, if you establish good rapport with valuable employees from other cultures, they are more likely to stay with the company.

A study conducted in the banking industry found that having a racially diverse workforce contributes to profitability primarily when the banks are growing and expanding.[16] It is possible that when a bank is growing, more opportunities are created for the culturally diverse members to make a contribution to profits. Establishing a culturally and demographically diverse organization has a proven record of enhancing hiring and retention (keeping employees).[17] The enhanced recruiting and retention takes place primarily among members of minority groups who feel more comfortable when a reasonable number of other people from their group are part of the workforce.

A woman who joined a printing firm as the only woman supervisor in the plant quit after six months. The problem was that she felt uncomfortable being singled out as the only female member of management. The woman joined a larger competitor where she was among five other women supervisors. She said she enjoyed being in her new work environment because her sex was not an issue.

Following are two examples of how cross-cultural understanding has improved profits or reduced costs:

- Xerox Corp. has a long-standing reputation of reaching out to minorities and appreciating the contributions of people from diverse cultures. As a result, Xerox has been able to recruit and retain talented people from many cultural groups. One of many examples is Ursula Burns, the head of worldwide manufacturing, who is helping the company find ways to cut per-unit manufacturing costs by 15 to 20 percent. Burns is the highest placed African-American woman in American manufacturing.

- Several large automobile dealerships across Canada and the US have deliberately cultivated a culturally diverse sales force. This type of cultural diversity often leads to much improved sales to the respective cultural groups. A Cadillac dealer in New York City reported that sales to Asiatic Indians have quadrupled since he hired a sales representative raised in India. The same dealer reports that more cultural diversity in the service end of the business has also boosted sales to diverse ethnic and racial groups.

TECHNIQUES FOR IMPROVING CROSS-CULTURAL RELATIONS AND VALUING DIFFERENCES

Depending on where you choose to work, your contact with various cultures and groups will vary. If you work in larger urban centres, the cultural and ethnic diversity will be more pronounced than in more rural settings. If you choose to work in the more northern regions of Canada, you will likely encounter more Aboriginal Canadians. However, all settings will have a large diversity of groups. It is in your best personal and professional interest, then, to learn skills that will help you succeed in this culturally diverse nation.

CULTURAL TRAINING

For many years, companies and government agencies have prepared their workers for overseas assignments. The method most frequently chosen is **cultural training**, a set of learning experiences designed to help employees understand the customs, traditions, and beliefs of another culture. In today's diverse business environment and international marketplace, learning about individuals raised in different cultural backgrounds has become more important. Many industries therefore train employees in cross-cultural relations.

Cultural training is also important for helping people of one culture understand their customers from another culture in particular, such as Chinese people learning to deal more effectively with their American customers. For example, in one training program Chinese businesspeople are taught how to sprinkle their email with English phrases like "How are you?" "It was great to hear from you" and "Can we work together?"[18]

The Job-Oriented Interpersonal Skills in Action box describes how cultural training can improve the effectiveness of establishing call centres overseas.

Many and varied types of training programs have been developed to improve cross-cultural relations and help employees learn to value diversity. All of the information presented so far in this chapter is likely to be included in such programs. Many college and university programs include courses about diversity as part of the curriculum, so that graduates will be knowledgeable about cultural differences. Proficiency in French and English is often required for federal government employment. The internet can also be a valuable tool for personal training. Consult the weblinks at the end of this chapter to locate some interesting cultural information.

To practise improving your cross-cultural relations, do Skill-Building Exercise 6-3.

CULTURAL INTELLIGENCE TRAINING

A new development in assisting people to work more effectively with workers from other cultures is *cultural intelligence training,* a program based on the principles of cultural intelligence described earlier in this chapter. A key part of the training is to learn the three contributors to CQ—head, heart, and body. Instead of learning a few simple guidelines for working effectively with people from another culture, the trainee is taught strategies for sizing up the environment to determine which course of action is best. The culturally intelligent overseas worker would learn how to determine how much humour to interject into meetings, what kind of handshake is most appropriate, and so forth. The following excerpt will give you a feel for what is involved in cultural intelligence training:

Skill-Building Exercise 6-3

CROSS-CULTURAL RELATIONS ROLE PLAY

One student plays the role of Ritu, a call centre representative in Bombay, India. Her specialty is helping customers with cellphone problems. Another student plays the role of Todd, an irate Canadian. His problem is that he cannot get his camera-equipped cellphone to transmit his photos over email. He is scheduled to attend a party in two hours, and wants to take loads of photos with his cellphone. Todd is impatient, and in the eyes of Ritu, somewhat overbearing. Ritu is good-natured and pleasant, but feels she must help Todd solve his problem without being bullied by him. Because Ritu is instructed to spend the minimum time necessary to resolve the problem, she spends about five minutes on this problem.

The observers should make note of how well Ritu has made the necessary cross-cultural adaptations.

Job-Oriented Interpersonal Skills in Action

INDIAN CALL CENTRE WORKERS LEARN TO THINK AND ACT LIKE AMERICANS

Author's Note: *Although this is an American case, many call centres that serve Canadian companies are also located in India. Thus this case is also relevant to Canadian readers.*

In a sleek new office building, two dozen young Indians are studying the customs of a place none of them have ever seen. One by one, the students present their conclusions about this fabled land. "Americans eat a lot of junk food. Table manners are very casual," says Ritu Khanna. "People are self-centred. The average American has 13 credit cards," says Nerissa Dcosata.

The Indians, who range in age from 20 to 27, have been hired to take calls from cranky or distraught Americans whose computers have gone haywire. To do this, they need to communicate in a language that is familiar but a culture that is foreign. "We're not saying India is better or America is better," says their trainer, Alefiya Rangsala. "We just want to be culturally sensitive so there's no disconnect when someone phones for tech support."

Call centres took root in India during the 2001 recession, when U.S. companies were struggling to reduce expenses. At first, training was simple. The centres gave employees names that were acceptable to American ears, with *Arjun* becoming *Aaron* and *Sangita* becoming *Susan*. The new hires were instructed to watch American television shows to get an idea of American folkways.

But whether Aaron and Susan were repairing computers, selling long-distance service, or fulfilling orders for diet tapes, problems immediately cropped up. The American callers often wanted a better deal or an impossibly swift resolution, and were aggressive and sometimes abrasive about saying so. The Indians responded according to their deepest natures: They were silent when they didn't understand, and they often committed to more than their employers could deliver. They would tell the Americans that someone would get back to them tomorrow to check on their problems, and no one would.

Customer satisfaction plummeted. The U.S. clients grew alarmed. Some even returned their business to U.S. call centres. Realizing that the multibillion-dollar industry with 150,000 employees was

(Continued)

at risk, Indian call centres have recently embarked on more comprehensive training. New hires are taught how to express empathy, strategies to successfully open and close conversations, and above all how to be assertive, however unnatural it might feel.

Khanna, Dcosata, and their new colleagues work for Sutherland Global Services, an upstate New York firm that is one of the larger outsourcing companies in India. They've been put through a three-week training session where they research hot-button issues, and pretend they are American anchors reporting the latest news, and imitate celebrities.

On the students' last day of cultural and voice training, Rangsala warns them that at least half a dozen are still speaking incomprehensibly and might wash out. As they slip away one by one to make a short recording that will test their pronunciation skills, K. S. Kumar, Sutherland's director of operations for India, gives a little graduation speech. "You're shortchanging yourself if you don't stick with this." (The shift work and difficult work goals contribute to high turnover.)

Originally, the ever-agreeable Indian agents had a hard time getting people to pay bills that were six months overdue. Too often, says trainer Deepa Nagraj, the calls would go like this:

"Hi," the Indian would say. "I'd like to set up a payment to get your account current. Can I help you do that?"

"No," the American responds.

"OK, let me know if you change your mind," the Indian says and hangs up.

Now, says Nagraj, the agents take no excuses.

Like Sutherland, Mphasis is basing a lot of its hopes on training. Indrandiel Ghosh, an Mphasis trainer, gives refresher courses to reps who handle customer-service accounts for a big credit-card company. One rep says he recently was helping a customer change his card data because his wife left him. When the rep expressed sympathy, the man cut him short, saying he hadn't really liked his wife.

"In case you empathize and then you see they don't want your empathy, move on," Ghosh advises. "This is someone from another culture. That increases the complexity tenfold."

Questions

1. What do you see as a major cultural difference between Indians and Americans that make the call centre job so challenging for Indians?

2. Some of the call centre representatives in India are instructed to identify themselves as students in Salt Lake City, in addition to giving them American first names. What is your take on the ethics of these disguises?

Source: From David Streitfeld, "A Crash Course on Irate Calls," August 2, 2004. *Los Angeles Times.* Reprinted with permission.

A Canadian manager is attempting to interpret a "Thai smile." First, she needs to observe the various cues provided in addition to the smile gesture itself (e.g., other facial or bodily gestures, significance of others who may be in proximity, source of the original smile gesture) and to assemble them into a meaningful whole and make sense of what is really experienced by the Thai employee. Second, she must have the requisite motivation (directed effort and self-confidence) to persist in the face of confusion, challenge, or apparently mixed signals. Third, she must choose, generate, and execute the right actions to respond appropriately. So what does this smile mean and does it have the same meaning as it does to us?

If any of these elements is deficient she is likely to be ineffective in dealing with the Thai employee. A high CQ manager has the capability to deal with all three facets as they act in unison.[19]

As the example illustrates, to be culturally intelligent you need to apply cognitive skills, have the right motivation, and then put your knowledge and confidence into action.

Armed with such skills you would know, for example, whether to greet a Mexican worker on a business trip to Texas with a handshake, a hug, or a kiss on both cheeks.

LANGUAGE TRAINING

Learning a foreign language is often part of cultural training, yet it can also be a separate activity. Knowledge of a second language is important because it builds better connections with people from other cultures than does relying on a translator. Building connections with people is still important even if English has become the international language of business. Many workers, aside from international business specialists, also choose to develop skills in a target language. Speaking another language can help build rapport with customers and employees who speak that language. As mentioned earlier, it is easier to sell to customers when using their native language.

Companies invest heavily in helping employees learn a target language because it facilitates conducting business in other countries. For this reason companies that offer language training and translation services are currently experiencing a boom. Medical specialists, police officers, and firefighters also find second language skills to be quite helpful because clients under stress, such as an injured person, are likely to revert to their native tongue. Learning a second language is particularly important when many of your customers and employees do not speak your country's official language.

As with any other skill training, investments in language training can pay off only if the trainee is willing to work hard at developing the new skill outside the training sessions. Allowing even 10 days to pass without practising your target language will result in a sharp decline in your ability to use that language.

Skill-Building Exercise 6-4 presents a low-cost, pleasant method of enhancing your foreign language and cross-cultural skills.

Skill-Building Exercise 6-4

USING THE INTERNET TO HELP DEVELOP FOREIGN-LANGUAGE SKILLS

A useful way of developing skills in another language, and learning more about another culture, is to create a "bookmark" or "favourite" written in your target language and designate it as your home page. In this way, each time you go to the internet on your own computer, your home page will contain fresh information in the language you want to develop.

To get started, use a search engine such as Yahoo! or Google that offers choices in several languages. Enter a search word such as "newspaper" or "current events" in the search probe. After you find a suitable choice, bookmark that newspaper as your home page. For example, imagine that French is your target language and culture. The Yahoo! France search engine might have brought you to www.france2.fr. This website, written in French, keeps you abreast of French and international news, sports, and cultural events. Now every time you access the internet, you can spend five minutes practising your second language. You can save a lot of travel costs and time using the internet to improve multicultural awareness.

ACTIVELY SEEK KNOWLEDGE AND INFORMATION

Often ignorance of different groups and their codes of conduct or other characteristics lies at the root of communication problems and barriers. We all have our views of the world and how it works, but we must remember that this view was taught to us within the confines of our mother culture. To understand other groups, you need to prepare yourself by acquiring knowledge about them.

There are a number of sources of relevant information, including books about different countries, travel brochures, art, geography books and maps, and the internet. You may travel as part of your career, and time spent researching may be better spent than time spent regretting a major breach of etiquette after it happens. The opening scenario about Leanne's trip to China was found on the internet. Before criticizing another or expressing our own ethnocentric views, we should take the time to research our differences. Such knowledge will often lead to better understanding.

BE OTHER-ORIENTED AND USE EMPATHY

When you meet or deal with an individual from a different background, try to put yourself in his or her place. Listen and respond actively, using the communication skills from Chapter 3 of this text. The person you are interacting with may have trouble with your language and you may have trouble with his or hers. Nonverbal communication may be more important than words, as you may have to rely on gesturing and pointing (just be careful how you gesture!). The key is to try to understand the person and his or her point of view. Understanding and empathy will not necessarily produce agreement, but they will create the groundwork for mutual respect.

Skill-Building Exercise 6-5 gives you an opportunity to simulate an empathy-building experience that may be used in some courses and training programs that emphasize valuing different cultures or groups.

DO NOT BE AFRAID TO ASK QUESTIONS

Sometimes we are afraid to ask questions. We engage in negative self-talk and say things to ourselves such as "I don't want to appear stupid," "This will be too embarrassing," or "What if I offend him or her?" If you have travelled, you may have found

Skill-Building Exercise 6-5

DEVELOPING EMPATHY FOR DIFFERENCES

Class members come up to the front of the room one by one and give a brief presentation (perhaps about three minutes) of any way in which they have been perceived as different, and how they felt about this perception. The difference can be of any kind, relating to characteristics such as ethnicity, race, choice of major, physical appearance, height, weight, hair colour, or body piercing. After each member of the class (perhaps even the instructor) has presented, class members discuss what they learned from the exercise. It is also important to discuss how this exercise can improve relationships on the job.

yourself in the uncomfortable position of not knowing what to do next in certain circumstances. So you tried to watch and copy (much like using chopsticks for the first time) and may have ended up feeling foolish. Few people are offended by being asked questions. For instance, a request such as "I'm not sure how I am supposed to do this; could you show me?" is rarely cause for alarm by the other party. In fact, many people are pleased and complimented by your desire to learn their traditions or ways of doing things.

SUMMARY

Today's workplace has become more culturally diverse, and business has become increasingly international. As a result, to succeed one must be able to relate effectively to people from different cultural groups from within and outside one's country. The true meaning of valuing diversity is to respect and enjoy a wide range of cultural and individual differences. The diversity umbrella continues to include more points of difference as the workforce encompasses a greater variety of people.

The groundwork for developing effective cross-cultural relations is to understand cultural differences. Six key aspects of understanding cultural differences are (1) cultural sensitivity, (2) cultural intelligence, (3) respect for all workers and all cultures, (4) cultural fluency—the ability to conduct business in a diverse, international environment, (5) differences in cultural values, and (6) avoidance of cultural bloopers. Cultural intelligence is based on cognitive, emotional/motivational, and physical (taking action) factors.

Countries differ in their national values, leading to differences in how most people from a given country will react to situations. The values studied here are (1) individualism versus collectivism, (2) acceptance of power and authority, (3) materialism versus concern for others, (4) formality versus informality, (5) urgent time orientation versus casual time orientation, and (7) high-context versus low-context cultures. An effective way of being culturally sensitive is to minimize actions that are likely to offend people from another culture, based on their values. Such cultural bloopers can take place when working in another country or when dealing with foreigners in one's own country. Studying potential cultural bloopers is helpful, but recognize also that individual differences may be of significance.

Communication barriers created by cultural differences can often be overcome by the following: (1) being sensitive to the fact that these barriers exist; (2) showing respect for all workers; (3) using straightforward language and speaking slowly and clearly; (4) observing cultural differences in etiquette; (5) being sensitive to differences in nonverbal communication; (6) not being diverted by style, accent, grammar, or personal appearance; (7) being aware of the continued existence of prejudice and discrimination; and (8) being attentive to individual differences in appearance.

To improve cross-cultural relations and to learn to value differences more, there are a variety of strategies that you may use to increase your intercultural competence. Engage in cultural training and take advantage of these training opportunities. In today's diverse business environment and international marketplace, learning about individuals raised in different cultural backgrounds has become more important.

Cultural intelligence training includes developing strategies for sizing up the environment to determine which course of action is best. Learning a foreign language is often part of cultural training, yet it can also be a separate activity. Actively seek knowledge and information about others different from you. Use empathy and be other-oriented and do not be afraid to ask questions.

An Interpersonal Relations Case Problem

RALPH LAUREN SEEKS RACIAL HARMONY

Author's Note: *Although this is the case of an American business and prominent designer, it is also a relevant experience for Canadians (especially those of us who wear this designer's clothes).*

Fashion magnate Ralph Lauren says he first became aware of racial tension within his company after an incident in 1997 at a Long Island sportswear boutique. A regional manager with Polo Ralph Lauren Corp. dropped by the new Polo Sport store in anticipation of an inspection by an important visitor: Jerome Lauren, Ralph's older brother and the executive overseeing Polo menswear. The mall where the boutique was located attracts a middle-class, racially integrated clientele. But the regional manager concluded that the store's ambiance was too "urban," meaning black, former Polo officials said.

The manager ordered two black and two Hispanic sales associates off the floor and back into the stock room, so they wouldn't be visible to Lauren. The sales associates followed orders, but they later hired a lawyer and threatened to sue Polo for discrimination. The company reached confidential settlements with the four.

Ralph Lauren says he learned about the incident several weeks after it happened and "was just sick" about it. The regional manager, Greg Ladley, was ordered to undergo racial-relations training but wasn't fired. A company spokesperson says that Ladley's recollection is that some sales associates working on inventory were asked to move to the stock room because they weren't "dressed appropriately."

After the episode, Ralph Lauren told subordinates, "We have to correct this. Let's make a change." But executives who worked at Polo at the time say their boss didn't make clear what changes he wanted.

Air of Exclusiveness

Polo, like some of its rivals, presents a multiracial face to the world, with black models in some of its ads, and a following of young black consumers wearing its familiar logo of a horse rider wielding a polo mallet. Yet internally, big fashion houses tend to exude an exclusiveness that is uninviting to many nonwhites. Few blacks or Hispanics have penetrated the upper ranks of major clothes manufacturers and retailers.

In response to complaints that have flared up at Polo, Lauren has met with lawyers, hired lieutenants to overhaul company personnel practices, and embraced diversity training. But he says he has left the details to others, as he is usually preoccupied with design work at his headquarters studio.

The Polo aura of Anglo-Saxon elitism is the elaborate creation of Polo's founder, Ralph Lauren, 62 years old, who remade himself as he rose from modest roots in the Bronx to become the chair and CEO of a fashion powerhouse. Polo retail supervisors routinely tell salespeople to think Hollywood. "Ralph is the director," the instruction goes, "and you are the actors, and we are here to make a movie." But some black and Hispanic employees say the movie seems to lack parts for them.

Colour-Blind?

Lauren says he is colour-blind when it comes to hiring talent. He frequently points out the wide visibility he has given Tyson Beckford, the striking shaven-headed black fashion model who has appeared in Polo ads since 1994. "Tyson is not just in jeans," Lauren says. "We put him in a pinstripe suit,

(Continued)

in our best Purple Label brand. Tyson is in the annual report, in our advertisements on TV."

Lauren says Polo "is a leader to do the right things to bring in the people who are the best in the industry." Some of his subordinates complain, however, that it is difficult to find black and Hispanic applicants with the credentials for design jobs coming out of the New York fashion schools where Polo usually recruits.

A Polo staffer recommended in 1998 that Lauren meet Lacey Moore, a 20-year-old African American from Brooklyn, who had taken some college-level communications courses and had aspirations to be in the music business. Since high school, Moore had worn Polo Oxford shirts and knit tops with flashy gold chains and a hip-hop attitude: precisely the sort of hybrid image Lauren hoped would draw younger customers. "Lacy is edgy—he gets it," Lauren recalls thinking, snapping his fingers for effect. He hired the young man as a design assistant.

The new recruit's rap-influenced personal style and lingo confounded his co-workers. Moore felt isolated. He says he understood that in any competitive workplace "there are people who don't like you." But in Polo's cliquish and overwhelmingly white Madison Avenue headquarters, he says co-workers made it clear he wasn't welcome. "I kept getting this bad vibe," he says. He quit in 2000.

Shocked, Lauren telephoned Moore at home. "Lacey, I want you to come back," he recalls saying. After listening to Moore's complaints, Lauren says he made it clear to the young man's white co-workers, "I want you all to work this out." A couple of weeks later, Moore returned, but warily.

Advice and Pressure

Polo has received advice and pressure on the race issue from a variety of outside counsellors and advocates. A civil rights authority advised Lauren that achieving a truly diverse workforce requires hiring more than a few black employees. A black activist minister met with Polo officials and helped some minority workers reach confidential settlements with the company.

Today Moore (the young design assistant) says his colleagues seem friendlier. The human resource vice president has given Moore reassurance. "You feel there is someone looking out for you," says the young assistant, who helps prepare for fashion shows and consults on clothing design.

Lauren says he is paying more attention to what he sees at work. For example, he recalls that at a company Christmas party in 2000, he was surprised that a group of blacks and Hispanics had congregated in a separate room. "Why is this happening?" he wondered. "What's not welcoming to those employees?"

According to Lauren he didn't approach his workers to ask them, however, and is still wondering about the answers to those questions.

Case Questions

1. What advice can you offer Lauren to achieve fuller workplace diversity at Polo?

2. Is the Christmas (holiday) party incident a symptom of an organizational problem? Or were the black and Hispanic employees just behaving as they chose?

3. Does Ralph Lauren "get it" as a leader with respect to cultural diversity in the workplace?

Source: Adapted from Teri Agins, "Color Line: A Fashion House with an Elite Aura Wrestles with Race," *The Wall Street Journal*, August 19, 2002, pp. A1, A9.

QUESTIONS FOR DISCUSSION AND REVIEW

1. Several well-known organizations conduct *awareness weeks* to celebrate certain diverse groups such as Aboriginals or homosexuals. What is your opinion of the effectiveness of such activities in bringing about workplace harmony?

2. How can a person demonstrate to others on the job that he or she is culturally fluent (gets along well with people from other cultures)?

3. Some companies, such as Singapore Airlines, make a deliberate effort for customer-contact personnel to be of the same ethnic group (Singapore natives). How justified is this practice in an era of cultural diversity and valuing differences?

4. A major purpose of diversity programs is to help people celebrate differences. Why should people celebrate a difference such as an attention deficit disorder?

5. Provide an example of cultural insensitivity of any kind that you have seen, read about, or can imagine.

6. How could you use the information presented in Table 6-1, comparing North American values to those of other countries, to help you succeed in business?

7. If you were a supervisor, how would you deal with a group member who had a very low acceptance of power and authority?

8. Many people speak loudly to deaf people, blind people, and those who speak a different language. Based on the information presented in this chapter, what mistakes are these people making?

9. The cultural bloopers presented in Skill-Building Exercise 6-2 all dealt with errors people make in regard to people who are not Canadian. Give an example of a cultural blooper a person from another country might make in Canada.

10. Using your Research Navigator, type in the search words "discrimination" and "Canada." In this search, you will find several articles and studies of the continued presence of discrimination and prejudice in Canada. This may be a good group mini presentation as students report their findings.

WEBLINKS

www.DiversityInc.com
This site has extensive information about cultural diversity in organizations.

www.inac.gc.ca
This is the site of Indian and Northern Affairs Canada.

www.afn.ca
The Assembly of First Nations website.

www.berlitz.com
Information about language training and cultural training in countries throughout the world. Investigate in your second language to enhance the cross-cultural experience.

Chapter 7

Resolving Conflicts with Others

Learning Outcomes

After reading and studying this chapter and doing the exercises, you should be able to
- Specify why so much interpersonal conflict exists in organizations.
- Recognize your typical method of resolving conflict.
- Identify the five modes of handling conflict.
- Develop effective techniques for resolving conflict and negotiating.
- Combat sexual harassment in the workplace.

A Canadian company upgraded its desktop computers, including the installation of the latest version of a widely used operating system. Users of the systems were informed that the new software had a "help" function that would answer practically all their technical questions. Many workers were confused by the help function, so they needed to rely on the information technology (IT) department for assistance. Yet, many workers said they felt "like an idiot" when they called the IT help desk for assistance with desktop computing problems. One of the non-IT workers surveyed described the problem this way: "I don't need to call someone on the phone to ask a question, then have him come in and go zoom, zoom, zoom, zip, zip, zip, with a mouse and he's lost me so I've never learned anything."[1]

The unfortunate situation between the worker from outside the IT department and the IT specialist illustrates two different meanings of **conflict.** A conflict is a situation in which two or more goals, values, or events are incompatible or mutually exclusive. The man with the problem wants his computer and software to run smoothly so he does not have to ask for help. Yet when he has to ask for help, he wants a deliberate, reassuring approach. The IT specialist is so busy that he wants to help people as quickly and efficiently as possible. Yet when he zips through the task, the person needing help is confused and has not learned much. A conflict is also a strife, quarrel, or battle. The worker needing help is angry that the help specialist moves so quickly through his process of giving assistance. In turn, the IT specialist wishes the person needing help were more computer savvy so he wouldn't receive an angry and confused look when he is trying to help.

This chapter will help you improve your ability to resolve conflicts with people at work. The same techniques are also useful in personal life. To improve your understanding of how to resolve conflict, we will present specific conflict-resolution techniques and also explain why so much conflict exists. To get you started relating the topic of conflict to yourself, take Self-Assessment Quiz 7-1.

Self-Assessment Quiz 7-1

STYLES OF CONFLICT MANAGEMENT

Directions: Check the alternative that best fits your typical reaction to the situation described.

Part I: The Quiz

1. When someone is overly hostile toward me, I usually
   - _____ A. respond in kind.
   - _____ B. persuade him or her to cool down.
   - _____ C. hear the person out.
   - _____ D. walk away.

2. When I walk in on a heated argument, I'm likely to
   - _____ A. jump in and take sides.
   - _____ B. mediate.
   - _____ C. keep quiet and observe.
   - _____ D. leave the scene.

3. When I suspect that another person is taking advantage of me, I
   - _____ A. try to get the person to stop.
   - _____ B. rely on persuasion and facts.
   - _____ C. change how I relate to the person.
   - _____ D. accept the situation.

4. When I don't see eye to eye with someone, I typically
   - _____ A. try to get him or her to see things my way.
   - _____ B. consider the problem logically.
   - _____ C. search for a workable compromise.
   - _____ D. let the problem work itself out.

5. After a run-in with someone I care about a great deal, I
   - _____ A. try to make him or her see it my way.
   - _____ B. try to work out our differences.
   - _____ C. wait before renewing contact.
   - _____ D. let it lie.

6. When I see conflict developing between two people I care about, I usually
   - _____ A. express disappointment.
   - _____ B. try to mediate.
   - _____ C. watch to see what develops.
   - _____ D. leave the scene.

(Continued)

7.   When I see conflict developing between two people who are relatively unimportant to me, I usually

_____   A. express disappointment.

_____   B. try to mediate.

_____   C. watch to see what develops.

_____   D. leave the scene.

8.   The feedback people give me indicates that I

_____   A. push hard to get what I want.

_____   B. try to work out differences.

_____   C. take a conciliatory stance.

_____   D. sidestep conflict.

9.   When having serious disagreements, I

_____   A. talk until I've made my point.

_____   B. talk a little more than I listen.

_____   C. listen and make sure I understand.

_____   D. listen passively.

10. When someone does something that angers me, I generally

_____   A. use strong, direct language.

_____   B. try to persuade him or her to stop.

_____   C. go easy, explaining how I feel.

_____   D. say and do nothing.

Part II: Score Analysis

When you've completed the questions, add all the As, Bs, Cs, and Ds to find where you collected the most responses. Then consider these profiles:

A. *Competitive.* If you picked mostly A responses, you feel best when you're able to direct and control others. Taken to extremes, you can be intimidating and judgmental. You are generally contemptuous of people who don't stand up for themselves, and you feel frustrated when you can't get through to someone.

B. *Collaborative.* If you scored high in this category, you may be from the "use your head to win" school of conflict management—strong-willed and ambitious, but not overbearing. You'll use persuasion, not intimidation, and are willing to compromise to end long-running conflicts.

C. *Sharing.* People who score high here don't get fired up. They listen to the opponent's point of view, analyze situations, and make a factual pitch for their case. But in the end, they will defer to opponents in the interest of harmony.

D. *Accommodative.* A high score suggests that you avoid conflict and confrontation at all costs and suppress your feelings—strong as they may be—to keep peace.

Observation: No one style of conflict management is better than another. Most people use all four, depending on the situation. But if you rely too much on one, start shifting your approach.

Source: Adapted with permission from *Executive Strategies,* National Institute of Business Management, February 20, 1990, p. 6.

SOURCES OF INTERPERSONAL CONFLICT IN ORGANIZATIONS

Conflict between and among people has many sources, or causes. In this section, we describe some of the leading sources. Understanding the cause of a particular conflict can help you resolve it and help prevent a recurrence. For example, if you learn that much conflict on the job is caused by a series of little hurts (*pinches*), you can apologize for these hurts. You can also be on guard to avoid such pinches in the future. Although specific sources of conflict can be identified, keep in mind an important fact: all conflict includes the underlying theme of incompatibility between your goals, values, or events and those of another person.

COMPETITION FOR LIMITED RESOURCES

An underlying source of job conflict is that few people can get all the resources they want. These resources include money, material, and human resources (or personnel). Conflict arises when two or more people squabble over who should get the resources. Even in a prosperous organization, resources have to be distributed in such a manner that not everybody gets what he or she wants.

Assume that you believe you need to have a desktop computer immediately accessible the full workday. The company, however, has decided that three people must share one computer. As a result, you are likely to enter into conflict with the two others sharing the computer. The conflict will be intense if your two co-workers also think they need full-time access to a desktop computer.

ROLE CONFLICT

A major source of conflict (and stress) on the job relates to being placed in a predicament. You are experiencing **role conflict** when you have to choose between competing demands or expectations. If you comply with one aspect of a role, compliance with the other is difficult or impossible. An important example would be receiving contradictory orders from two people above you in your company. If you comply with the wishes of one person, you will antagonize the other. Consider the following example:

> A high-performing sales representative received a job offer from a manager in another division in her company. Her present manager told her she was not allowed to transfer and made her a counter-offer. The sales representative found herself in conflict with the two managers. Distraught over the conflict, she found employment with a competitive firm in a comparable position to the internal job offer she had received.

Role conflict can take various forms. You might be asked to accomplish two objectives that are in apparent conflict. If your boss asked you to hurry up and finish your work but also make fewer mistakes, you would experience this type of conflict (plus perhaps a headache!). Another type of problem occurs when two or more people give you incompatible directions. Your immediate supervisor may want you to complete a crash project on time, but company policy temporarily prohibits authorizing overtime payments to clerical help or hiring office temporaries.

Role conflict also results when two different roles that you play are in conflict. Your company may expect you to travel 50 percent of the time, whereas your spouse threatens a divorce if you travel over 25 percent of the time. Finally, a form of role conflict takes place when the role(s) your organization expects you to occupy are in conflict with your basic values. Your company may ask you to fire substandard performers, but this could be in conflict with your humanistic values.

COMPETING WORK AND FAMILY DEMANDS

Balancing the demands of career and family life has become a major role conflict facing today's workforce. The challenge is particularly intense for employees who are part of a two-wage-earner family. **Work–family conflict** occurs when an individual's roles of worker and active participant in social and family life compete with one another. This type of conflict is frequent because the multiple roles are often incompatible. Imagine having planned to attend your child's solo recital and then being ordered at the last minute to be present at an after-hours meeting. Work–family conflict can lead to interpersonal conflict because your boss or co-workers might resent your asking them to cover for you while you attend to personal matters.

Work–family conflict can be a major stressor. An international survey found that Canadian workers feel the most stressed, with 41 percent stating that they "often" or "almost always" experience stress at work.[2] One of the major stressors was working long hours. Working long hours would certainly conflict with family time as workers try to work these longer hours and still participate in family life. The conflict over work versus family intensifies when the person is serious about both work and family responsibilities. The average professional employee works about 55 hours per week, including five hours on weekends. Adhering to such a schedule almost inevitably results in some incompatible demands. Conflict arises because the person wants to work sufficient hours to succeed on the job, yet still have enough time for a personal life.

Work–family conflict can also lead to emotional disorders, as revealed by a study of 2700 employed adults. Two types of work–family conflict were studied: family life creating problems at work, and work creating problems at home. Emotional problems were measured by diagnostic interviews. Both types of conflict were associated with having mood disorders, disturbing levels of anxiety, and substance abuse. Also, employees who reported work–family conflict were much more likely to have a clinically significant mental health problem.[3]

Work–family conflict takes place in different cultures, even if the gravity of the conflict might differ from one culture to another. A team of researchers compared work–family conflict between Chinese and American workers, many of whom were also studying for a master's degree in business. The major findings were that the Americans experienced greater family demands, with a greater impact on work–family conflict. Yet, the Chinese also experienced work–family conflict, especially in terms of time available for family and work responsibilities.[4]

Many companies offer flexible working hours to a majority of their employees. In this way, a worker might be able to meet family demands that take place during typical working hours. An example would be taking the morning off to care for an ill parent, then working later that same evening. People who are exceptionally good at organizing their time and efforts will often experience less work–family conflict, by such behaviour as staying on top of work to minimize periods of time when they are completely work-centered.[5]

PERSONALITY CLASHES

Many workplace disagreements arise because people simply dislike each other. A **personality clash** is an antagonistic relationship between two people based on differences in personal attributes, preferences, interests, values, and styles. A personality clash reflects negative chemistry between two people, while personal differences are based more specifically on a clash of values.

People involved in a personality clash often have difficulty specifying why they dislike each other. The end result, however, is that they cannot maintain an amiable work relationship. One peculiarity about personality clashes is that people who get along well may begin to clash after working together for a number of years. A contributing factor is that as both people change and the situation changes, the two people may no longer be compatible.

AGGRESSIVE PERSONALITIES, INCLUDING BULLIES

Co-workers naturally disagree about topics, issues, and ideas. Yet some people convert disagreement into an attack that puts down other people and damages their self-esteem. As a result, conflict surfaces. **Aggressive personalities** are people who frequently verbally, and sometimes physically, attack others. Verbal aggression takes the form of insults, teasing, ridicule, and profanity. Aggression may also be expressed as attacks on the victim's character, competence, background, and physical appearance.[6]

Aggressive personalities are also referred to as *workplace bullies.* Among the typical behaviours of workplace bullies are interrupting others, making humiliating comments and gestures, ranting in a loud voice, and making threats. One bullying manager would frequently ask people, "Are you going to be stupid the rest of your life?" Psychological harassment or workplace bullying costs Canadian companies millions of dollars in productivity.[7] Bullied workers complain of a range of psychological and physical ailments, including anxiety, sleeplessness, headache, irritable bowel syndrome, skin problems, panic attacks, and low self-esteem.[8]

Quebec, in 2004, implemented anti-bullying legislation for non-unionized workplaces and is the first jurisdiction in Canada to pass such legislation. Of 2200 complaints that were filed in the first two years of the legislation, over 1000 were considered to have merit.[9]

Aggression can also take the extreme form of the shooting or knifing of a former boss or colleague by a mentally unstable worker recently dismissed from the company. Much workplace violence is perpetuated by disgruntled workers or former employees harbouring unresolved conflicts. For example, on April 6, 1999, Pierre Lebrun shot and killed four of his colleagues at an Ottawa city bus garage. A 1994 survey by the Canadian Union of Public Employees showed that almost 70 percent of respondents believed that verbal aggression was the leading form of workplace violence, but physical violence in the workplace is more common in this country than you might think. A 1998 survey by the International Labour Organization found Canada to be among the top five nations in terms of workplace violence, including general and sexual assaults.[10] A 2004 Canadian study found that almost one in five violent incidents occurred in the victim's workplace. There were almost 356 000 violent incidents in Canadian workplaces.[11]

The workplace can also include colleges; recent campus shootings in Montreal and Virginia illustrate that extreme violence can erupt anywhere.

INCIVILITY AND RUDENESS

A milder form of aggression in the workplace is being rude or uncivil toward work associates. **Incivility** (or employees' lack of regard for one another) has gained attention as a cause of workplace conflict. What constitutes being uncivil or rude depends upon a person's perceptions and values.

Imagine two people having a business lunch together. One of them answers his cellphone during lunch, and while still eating engages the caller in conversation. To some people this everyday incident would be interpreted as double rudeness—interrupting lunch with a cellphone call and eating while talking. Another person might perceive the cellphone incident to be standard behaviour in a multitasking world. Rudeness also includes swearing at coworkers, a cubicle dweller shouting loudly on the phone while making a personal call, and performing other work at a meeting. Typical forms of "other work" are sorting through paper mail, texting on a cellphone or surfing the Internet on a notebook computer.

A study conducted by Lisa Penney found that 69 percent of 300 workers she surveyed reported experiencing condescending behaviour and put-downs in the workplace. Also, those who reported incivility on the job were more likely to engage in counterproductive behaviours including bad-mouthing their company, missing deadlines, and being rude to customers or clients. "Even though civility may not seem like a very serious thing," says Penney, "it is related to behaviours that have more serious consequences" that can affect profits.[12] An investigation using many forms of data collection with 2400 people found that being treated in an uncivil manner leads employees to decrease work effort, time on the job, and productivity. When incivility is not curtailed, job satisfaction and loyalty to the company also diminish.[13]

CONFLICT-MANAGEMENT STYLES

The information presented thus far is designed to help you understand the nature of conflict. Such background information is useful for resolving conflict because it helps you understand what is happening in a conflict situation. The next two sections offer more specific information about managing and resolving conflict. Before describing specific methods of resolving conflict, it is useful to present more detail about five general styles, or modes, of handling conflict. You received preliminary information on four of these five styles when you completed Self-Assessment Quiz 7-1.

As shown in Figure 7-1 on the next page, Kenneth Thomas has identified five major styles of conflict management. Each style is based on a combination of satisfying one's own concerns (assertiveness) and satisfying the concerns of others (cooperativeness).[14]

Competitive Style
The competitive style is marked by a desire to advance one's own concerns at the expense of the other party, or to dominate. A person with a competitive orientation is likely to engage in power struggles in which one side wins and the other loses (an approach

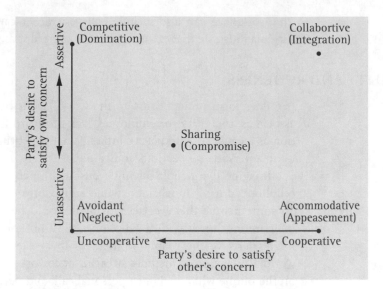

Figure 7-1   Conflict-Handling Styles According to Degree of Cooperation and Assertiveness

Source: Kenneth W. Thomas, "Organizational Conflict," in Steven Kerr, ed., *Organization Behavior* (Columbus, Ohio: Grid Publishing, 1979), p. 156.

referred to as *win–lose*). "My way or the highway" is a win–lose strategy. The competitive style works best when quick, decisive action is essential, such as in an emergency.

Accommodative Style

The accommodative style favours appeasement, or satisfying the other's concerns without taking care of one's own. People with this orientation may be generous or self-sacrificing just to maintain a relationship. Irate customers can be accommodated with full refunds, just to calm them down. The intent of such accommodation might also be to retain the customer's loyalty.

Accommodation sounds harmless, but according to Sidney Simon, when it runs unchecked at the expense of what somebody really wants it can lead to debilitating resentment, sickness, or even violence.[15] The problem is that the suppressed feelings create inner conflict and stress. Accommodation works best when you are wrong, or when the issues are more important to the other side. For example, an automobile sales associate might say yes to a last-minute demand for another $25 concession, rather than continuing to haggle.

Sharing Style

The sharing style lies halfway between domination and appeasement. Sharers prefer moderate but incomplete satisfaction for both parties, which results in a compromise. The term *splitting the difference* reflects this orientation, and is commonly used in such activities as purchasing a house or car. The sharing (or compromising) style is well suited to a situation in which both sides have equal power, yet are committed to mutually exclusive goals such as the buyer and seller of the house wanting to maximize financial gain.

Skill-Building Exercise 7-1

WIN–WIN CONFLICT RESOLUTION

The class breaks into small problem-solving groups. Each group spends about 10 minutes finding a win–win solution to one of the following conflict situations:

1. Two co-workers want you to go to lunch with them more regularly, but you believe you are too busy to go out to lunch regularly.

2. Deborah, a computer operator, wants workmates to call her Deborah. Yet several people in the office persist in calling her Deb or Debbie.

3. You are offered a transfer within your company to an exciting job that you want strongly. Your manager says he cannot let you go because you are too valuable.

Collaborative Style

In contrast to the other styles, the collaborative style reflects a desire to fully satisfy the desires of both parties. It is based on an underlying philosophy of **win–win**, the belief that after conflict has been resolved, both sides should gain something of value. The use of a win–win approach is genuinely aimed at arriving at a settlement that meets the needs of both parties, or at least does not badly damage the welfare of the other side. The option chosen results in a *mutual gain*. When collaborative approaches to resolving conflict are used, the relationships among the parties are built on and improved. The following example uses a win–win approach to resolve conflict.

> Karma is an office assistant in a company that supplies food to restaurants, hospitals, and nursing homes. According to her budget analysis, Karma needed a 5 percent salary increase to meet her monthly expenses. The company owner explained that there was no money in the budget for a salary increase. A cordial discussion about the issue led to an option for mutual gain. Karma would receive the 5 percent salary increase as long as she increased her productivity enough to cover the increase. Her target was to increase her productivity to the point that the company could decrease the hours worked by an office temporary. The amount of the decrease covered the 5 percent salary increase. Collaborating is particularly important when both sides must be committed to the solution. Divorcing parents also need collaboration in their division of assets because they need to work together long term for the good of the children.

Finding win–win solutions to problems (or options for mutual gain) is one of the most important conflict-resolution skills. To practise this skill, do Skill-Building Exercise 7-1.

Avoidant Style

The avoider is a combination of uncooperative and unassertive. He or she is indifferent to the concerns of either party. The person may actually be withdrawing from the conflict to rely upon fate. Avoiding works well when an issue is trivial, or there are more pressing issues to worry about. For example, a supervisor might not bother reprimanding workers who are a few minutes late because the supervisor is flooded with other work.

In the following description of specific techniques for resolving conflict, attempt to relate most of them to these five key styles. For example, you will observe that the confrontation and problem-solving technique reflects the collaborative style.

GUIDELINES AND TECHNIQUES FOR RESOLVING CONFLICTS

Interpersonal conflict in organizations is inevitable. Most jobs will involve various conflicts and afford you many opportunities to practise the guidelines and techniques outlined in this section. However, some jobs involve more conflict than others. Customer service careers, for example, often involve conflicts with clients and customers. This chapter's Canadian Scene box provides examples of three people with different and challenging careers.

The Canadian Scene

YOU THINK YOUR JOB HAS CONFLICT—TAKE A LOOK AT THESE JOBS

Some occupations are more conflict-prone than others. Any job where you spend your time dealing with dissatisfied customers is at the top of the list. Bruce Hood is the air travel complaints commissioner for the Canadian Transportation Agency. He spends a lot of his time dealing with disgruntled passengers, many of them complaining about Air Canada.[i]

Jobs that involve negotiating between potentially hostile groups may be suitable for those who thrive in conflict-prone positions. Buzz Hargrove, as head of the Canadian Auto Workers (CAW), has seen his share of battles, from negotiating with the "Big Three" automakers to conflicts with his own staff at CAW offices, who went on strike for six weeks in the summer of 2000.[ii] Hargrove is not always the public's idea of a negotiator, as he has been known to shout, name-call, and arrive at meetings with a baby spoon and a box of Pablum.[iii] Hargrove admits that he thrives on adversity.[iv]

Last but not least, what about jobs that involve leading a company with a bruised public image, investor skittishness, and a past leader facing insider-trading charges? Derek J. Burney has taken on this task as CEO of Corel Corporation.[v] He has many hurdles to overcome, including getting Corel back on track by cutting costs (limited-resource conflicts?), procuring more funds, and restoring the company's image.

While there are many other jobs that lend themselves to conflict, the real key is to be prepared and to manage conflict in such a way that both sides can still get along when the "war" is over.

i.   Deirdre McMurdy, "Jobs You Don't Want," *Maclean's*, August 28, 2000, pp. 27–28.

ii. McMurdy, "Jobs You Don't Want."

iii. Canadian Press, "Big Three Talks End with Ford Deal," *Canadian News Digest*, November 6, 1996, www.canoe.ca/NewsArchiveNov96/candigest_nov6.html.

iv. Deirdre McMurdy with Luke Fisher, "Big Bad Buzz," *Maclean's*, December 16, 1996, p. 22.

v.   McMurdy, "Jobs You Don't Want."

A career-minded person must learn effective ways of resolving conflict. In this section, we describe methods of conflict resolution that you can use on your own. All are based somewhat on the underlying model of win–win, or integrating the interests of both parties. Integrating the interests of others requires resolving the underlying concerns of the parties in conflict. In dealing with these concerns, it is understood that it is more worthwhile for both sides to resolve the conflict than it is to have no agreement.[16] Bear the following scenario in mind while reading about the specific conflict-resolution techniques outlined below:

> Suppose a man named Bill Molson wanted to open a brewery and name his beer Molson. The company lawyers from Molson Coors Brewing Company, who own the rights to the brand name Molson's, would attempt to block him from using the same brand name—even if his family name is Molson. Bill Molson would hire his own lawyer to fight back. Two key concerns must be addressed. Mr. Molson's underlying concern is that he feels his civil liberties have been violated because he cannot name a business after himself. And Molson's must deal with their concern about a smaller company capitalizing on its well-known name (brand equity).

Later in the chapter you will be asked to resolve the above conflict. First we will examine the following five conflict-resolution techniques:

1. Confrontation and problem-solving
2. Constructive handling of criticism
3. Cognitive restructuring
4. Negotiating and bargaining
5. Mediation

CONFRONTATION AND PROBLEM-SOLVING

The ideal approach to resolving any conflict is to confront the real issue and then solve the problem. Confrontation means taking a problem-solving approach to differences and identifying the underlying facts, logic, or emotions that account for them. When conflicts are resolved through confronting and understanding their causes, people feel responsible for finding the soundest answer.[17]

Confrontation can proceed gently, in a way that preserves a good working relationship, as shown by the following example. Assume that Mary, the person working at the desk next to you, loudly cracks chewing gum while she works. You find this behaviour both distracting and nauseating. If you do not bring the problem to Mary's attention, your annoyance will probably intensify with time. Yet you are hesitant to enter into an argument about something that a person might regard as a human right (the right to chew gum in public places).

A psychologically sound alternative is for you to approach her directly in this manner:

You: Mary, there is something bothering me that I would like to discuss with you.

She: Go ahead, I don't mind listening to other people's problems.

You: My problem concerns something you are doing that makes it difficult for me to concentrate on my work. When you chew gum you make loud cracking noises that grate on my nerves. It may be my problem, but the noise does bother me.

She: I guess I could stop chewing gum when you're working next to me. It's probably just a nervous habit.

CONSTRUCTIVE HANDLING OF CRITICISM

Learning to profit from criticism is an effective way of benefiting from conflict. People who benefit from criticism are able to stand outside themselves while being criticized. It is as if they are watching the criticism from a distance and looking for its possible merits. People who take criticism personally anguish when receiving negative feedback. Following are several specific suggestions for dealing with criticism, including two methods that will often get the other party on your side.[18]

1. *See yourself at a distance.* Place an imaginary Plexiglas shield between you and the person giving the criticism. Attempt to be a detached observer looking for useful information.

2. *Ask for clarification and specifics.* Ask politely for more details about the negative behaviour in question so you can change if change is warranted. If your boss is criticizing you for being rude to customers, you might respond: "I certainly do not want to be rude. Can you give me a couple of examples of how I was rude? I need your help in working on this problem." After asking questions, you can better determine whether the criticism is valid.

3. *Decide on a response.* An important part of learning from criticism is to respond appropriately to the critic. Let the criticizer know what aspects of the criticism you agree with. Apologize for the undesirable behaviour, such as saying, "I apologize for being rude to customers. I know what I can do differently now. I'll be more patient so as not to appear rude."

4. *Look for a pattern in terms of other criticism.* Is the criticism you are receiving something you have heard several times before from different people? The more times you have heard the same criticism, the more likely it is to be valid. If three different supervisors have told you that you do not follow through with your promises to get work done, the criticism is most likely valid.

5. *Disarm the opposition.* As an extension of the point just made, you will often decide to agree with the criticizer because the person has a legitimate complaint about you. If you deny the reality of that person's complaint, he or she will continue to harp on the point and the issue will remain unresolved. By agreeing with the criticism of you, you may set the stage for a true resolution of the problem.

Agreeing with criticism made by a person with formal authority over you is effective because by doing so you are then in a position to ask for his or her help in improving the situation. Rational managers realize that it is their responsibility to help subordinates overcome problems, not merely to criticize them. Imagine that you have been chronically

Skill-Building Exercise 7-2

DISARMING THE OPPOSITION

In each of these two scenarios, one person plays the role of the person with more power in the situation. The other person plays the role of the individual attempting to disarm the criticizer.

1. A representative from a credit organization telephones you at work to inform you that you are 60 days behind schedule on your car payment. The agent wants a settlement as soon as possible. Unfortunately, the credit agent is correct. Run this scenario for about five minutes.

2. Your manager calls you into the office to discuss the 10-page report you just submitted. The boss says in a harsh tone, "Your report is a piece of trash. I counted 25 word-use mistakes such as writing *whether* for *weather* and *seen* for *scene*. (Your spell checker couldn't catch these errors.) Besides that, I can't follow many of your sentences, and you left out the table of statistics. I'm wondering if you are qualified for this job."

late with reports during the last six months. It is time for a performance review, and you know that you will be reprimanded for your tardiness. You also hope that your manager will not downgrade all other aspects of your performance because of your tardy reports. Here is how disarming the opposition would work in this situation:

Your manager: Have a seat. It's time for your performance review, and we have a lot to talk about. I'm concerned about some things.

You: So am I. It appears that I'm having a difficult time getting my reports in on time. I wonder if I'm being a perfectionist. Do you have any suggestions?

Your manager: Well, I like your attitude. Maybe you are trying to make your reports too perfect before you turn them in. I think you can improve in getting your reports in on time. Try not to figure everything out to five decimal places. We need thoroughness around here, but we can't overdo it.

Disarming is effective because it takes the wind out of the other person's sails and has a calming effect. The other person is often waiting to clobber you if you deny guilt. If you admit guilt, you are more difficult to clobber. Skill-Building Exercise 7-2 gives you an opportunity to practise disarming the opposition.

COGNITIVE RESTRUCTURING

An indirect way of resolving interpersonal conflict is to lessen the conflicting elements in a situation by viewing them more positively. According to the technique of **cognitive restructuring**, you mentally convert negative aspects into positive ones by looking for the positive elements in a situation.[19] How you frame or choose your thoughts can determine the outcome of a conflict situation. Your thoughts influence your actions. If you search for the beneficial elements in the situation, there will be less area for dispute. Although this technique might sound like a *mind game* to you, it can work effectively.

Imagine that a co-worker of yours, Don, has been asking you repeated questions about how to carry out a work procedure. You are about ready to tell Don, "Go bother somebody else; I'm not paid to be a trainer." Instead, you look for the positive elements in the situation. You say to yourself, "Don has been asking me a lot of questions. This does take time, but answering these questions is valuable experience. If I want to become a manager, I will have to help group members with problems."

After having completed this cognitive restructuring, you can then deal with the conflict situation more positively. You might say to Don, "I welcome the opportunity to help you, but we need to find a mutually convenient time. In that way, I can concentrate better on my own work." To get started with cognitive restructuring, do Skill-Building Exercise 7-3.

NEGOTIATING AND BARGAINING

Conflicts can be considered situations calling for **negotiating**, or conferring with another person to resolve a problem. When you are negotiating a fair salary for yourself, you are trying to resolve a conflict. At first, the demands of the two parties

Skill-Building Exercise 7-3

COGNITIVE RESTRUCTURING

The following are examples of negative statements about co-workers. In the space provided, cognitively restructure (reframe) each comment in a positive way.

Negative: Nancy is getting on my nerves. It takes her two weeks longer than anyone else on the team to complete her input.

Positive: _____

_____

_____

_____

Negative: My boss is driving me crazy. He is forever telling me what I did wrong and making suggestions for improvement. He makes me feel like I'm in elementary school.

Positive: _____

_____

_____

_____

may seem incompatible, but through negotiation a salary figure may emerge that satisfies both.

Managers and staff specialists must negotiate both internally (e.g., with subordinates, managers, and team leaders) and externally (e.g., with suppliers and government agencies). Considerable negotiation also takes place among co-workers. Team members, for example, sometimes negotiate among themselves about work assignments. One might say to the other, "I'm willing to be note-taker this year if there is some way I can cut back on the number of plant visits I make this year." Six leading negotiating tactics are presented on the following pages. Before studying them, do Self-Assessment Quiz 7-2.

Self-Assessment Quiz 7-2

THE NEGOTIATOR QUIZ

Directions: The following quiz is designed to give you insight into your tendencies toward being an effective negotiator. Answer each statement "Mostly true" or "Mostly false" as it applies to you.

	Mostly true	Mostly false
1. Settling differences of opinion is a lot of fun.	_____	_____
2. I try to avoid conflict and confrontation with others as much as possible.	_____	_____
3. I am self-conscious asking people for favours they have not spontaneously offered me.	_____	_____
4. I am generally unwilling to compromise.	_____	_____
5. How the other side feels about the results of our negotiation is of little consequence to me.	_____	_____
6. I think very well under pressure.	_____	_____
7. People say that I am tactful and diplomatic.	_____	_____
8. I'm known for my ability to express my viewpoint clearly.	_____	_____
9. Very few things in life are not negotiable.	_____	_____
10. I always (or would always) accept whatever salary increase is offered to me.	_____	_____
11. A person's facial expression often reveals as much as what the person actually says.	_____	_____
12. I wouldn't mind taking a few short-range losses to win a long-range battle.	_____	_____
13. I'm willing to work long and hard to win a small advantage.	_____	_____
14. I'm usually too busy talking to do much listening.	_____	_____
15. It's fun to haggle over price when buying a car.	_____	_____
16. I almost always prepare in advance for a negotiating session.	_____	_____

(Continued)

17. When there is something I need from another person I usually get it. _____ _____

18. It would make me feel cheap if I offered somebody only two-thirds of his or her asking price. _____ _____

19. People are usually paid what they are worth, so there's no use haggling over starting salaries. _____ _____

20. I rarely take what people say at face value. _____ _____

21. It's easy for me to smile when involved in a serious discussion. _____ _____

22. For one side to win in negotiation, the other side has to lose. _____ _____

23. Once you start making concessions, the other side is bound to get more than you. _____ _____

24. A good negotiating session brings out my competitive urges. _____ _____

25. When negotiations are completed, both sides should walk away with something valuable. _____ _____

Total Score _____

Scoring and Interpretation: Score yourself +1 for each of your answers that agrees with the scoring key. The higher your score, the more likely it is that you currently have good negotiating skills, *providing your self-assessment is accurate.* It might prove useful to also have somebody who has observed you negotiate on several occasions answer the Negotiator Quiz for you. Scores of 7 or lower and 20 or higher are probably the most indicative of weak or strong negotiating potential. Here is the scoring key:

1. Mostly true	8. Mostly true	15. Mostly true	22. Mostly false
2. Mostly false	9. Mostly true	16. Mostly true	23. Mostly false
3. Mostly false	10. Mostly false	17. Mostly true	24. Mostly true
4. Mostly false	11. Mostly true	18. Mostly false	25. Mostly true
5. Mostly false	12. Mostly true	19. Mostly false	
6. Mostly true	13. Mostly true	20. Mostly true	
7. Mostly true	14. Mostly false	21. Mostly true	

Focus on Interests, Not Positions

Rather than clinging to specific negotiating points, keep your overall interests in mind and try to satisfy them. Remember that the true object of negotiation is to satisfy the underlying interests on both sides, as in the case of Bill Molson. Part of focusing on interests is to carefully study the other side's comments for clues to the type of agreement that will satisfy both of you.

Here is how this strategy works:

You are considering accepting a job offer that will enable you to work on the type of problems you prefer and also to develop your professional skills. You have a starting salary in mind that would make you very happy—15 percent higher than you are currently making. Your negotiating position is thus your present salary plus 15 percent. However, your true interests are probably to have more discretionary income than at present. (You want to make more purchases and invest more.) You will therefore be better off negotiating for a work situation that spreads your money further. You can now accept the offer by negotiating other points in addition to a 15 percent higher salary, including (1) work location in an area with a lower cost of living, (2) a better opportunity for earning a bonus, or (3) a generous expense account. During the negotiations you may discover that the other party is looking for a talented employee at a salary and benefits the company can afford.

Compromise

The most widely used negotiating tactic is **compromise**, settlement of differences by mutual concessions. One party agrees to do something if the other party agrees to do something else. Compromise is a realistic approach to resolving conflict. Most labour–management disputes are settled by compromise. For instance, labour may agree to accept a smaller salary increase if management will subcontract less work to other countries.

Some people argue that compromise is not a win–win tactic. The problem is that the two parties may wind up with a solution that pacifies both but does not solve the problem. One example would be purchasing for two department heads half the new equipment each one needs. As a result, neither department really shows a productivity gain. Nevertheless, compromise is both inevitable and useful.

Begin with a Plausible Demand or Offer, Yet Allow Room for Negotiation

The common-sense approach to negotiation suggests that you begin with an extreme, almost fanciful demand or offer. The final compromise will therefore be closer to your true demand or offer than if you opened the negotiations more realistically. However, a plausible demand is useful because it shows you are bargaining in good faith. Also, if a third party has to resolve a conflict, a plausible demand or offer will receive more sympathy than an implausible one will.

Consider the following case:

> A judge listened to the cases of two people who claimed they were the victims of age discrimination by the same employer. The lawyer for the first alleged victim asked for $10 million in damages; the lawyer for the second victim asked for $200 000. The first person was awarded $50 000 in damages and the second person $150 000. An inside source reported that the judge was so incensed by the first lawyer's demands that she decided to teach him a lesson.
>
> Although it is advisable to begin with a plausible demand, one must still allow room for negotiation. A basic strategy of negotiation is to begin with a demand that allows room for compromise and concession. If you think you need $5000 in new software for your department, you might begin negotiations by asking for a $7000 package. Your boss offers you $4000 as a starting point. After negotiation, you may wind up with the $5000 you need.

Make Small Concessions Gradually

Making steady concessions leads to more mutually satisfactory agreements in most situations. Gradually, you concede little things to the other side. The hard-line approach to bargaining is to make your concession early in the negotiation and then grant no further concession. The tactic of making small concessions is well-suited to purchasing a new car. To reach a price you consider acceptable, you might grant concessions such as agreeing to finance the car through the dealer or purchasing a service contract.

Know Your Best Alternative to a Negotiated Agreement (BATNA)

The reason you would probably negotiate would be to produce something better than the result obtainable without negotiating. The goal of negotiating is thus not just to agree, but to obtain more valuable results than would otherwise have occurred. When you are aware of your best alternative to a negotiated agreement (BATNA), it sets a floor to the agreement you are willing to accept. Your BATNA becomes the standard that can protect both parties from accepting terms that are too unfavourable. It also keeps you from walking away from terms that would be beneficial for you to accept.

What might a BATNA look like in practice? Suppose you are negotiating a starting salary for a full-time, professional position. The figure you have in mind is $40 000 per year. Your BATNA is $34 500, because this is the salary your future in-laws will pay you to enter the family business. You will therefore walk away from any offer of less than $35 000—just taking salary into account.

Knowing the other side's BATNA is also important, because it helps define the other participant's bargaining zone. Understanding one another's bargaining zones makes it possible to arrive at mutually profitable trade-offs. In the preceding salary negotiations, the company's BATNA might be to hire a less well-educated job candidate at $30 000 and then upgrade his or her knowledge on the job.

Use Anger to Your Advantage

Master negotiators make selective use of anger as a negotiating and bargaining tool. When a person becomes genuinely angry, the anger can energize him or her to be more resourceful and creative while bargaining. If you are angry with an issue or a negotiating point, the other side may be willing to submit to your demand rather than receive more of your anger. The director of a company wellness program might say with an angry look toward top management, "Why is there money in the budget for all kinds of frills like corporate jets, when a program that is preventing millions of dollars in lost productivity has to grovel for a decent budget?"

The downside of anger is that it can degenerate into incivility and personal insults. A touch of anger can be effective, but overdone it becomes self-defeating. You have to size up how far you can push people before damaging a work relationship—or being fired. To make effective use of anger during negotiation, it has to be used at the right time, with the right tone, and in the right amount.[20] A person who is always angry will often not be taken seriously.

Effective negotiation, as with any other form of conflict resolution, requires extensive practice and knowledge of basic principles and techniques. As a starting point you might take one of the negotiating tactics just described and practise it where the stakes are not so high. You might attempt to negotiate the price of a consumer electronics device, or negotiate for getting a particular Friday afternoon off from work.

MEDIATION

Some conflicts between two parties cannot be resolved, and a third party, or **mediator,** is required for successful resolution. For example, when two people refuse to listen to each other or refuse to see the "other side," chances are the conflict will not be resolved. **Mediation** is a formal method of conflict resolution that includes an objective third party. A mediator who has no vested interest in the resolution is more objective and will work to find a win–win outcome that will satisfy both parties. Mediation is similar to, but not the same as, negotiation. In a mediation situation, an independent third party assists the involved parties in resolving the dispute on their own. Negotiation, on the other hand, often occurs between the parties and does not always involve a third person. A mediator allows "the parties to clarify their choices, resources, and decisions by recognizing each others' perspectives.[21]

Growing in popularity, **alternative dispute resolution** involves a professional mediator hired to help people arrive at a mutually acceptable solution. The goal in alternative dispute resolution is to arrive at a solution that both parties can agree to and feel that their goals have been achieved. These professional mediators are often used in divorce situations as well as in business negotiations and other legal matters.

COMBATING SEXUAL HARASSMENT: A SPECIAL TYPE OF CONFLICT

Many employees face conflict because a supervisor, co-worker, or customer is sexually harassing them. The Canada Labour Code, the Canadian Human Rights Act, the Employment Equity Act, and provincial and territorial human rights codes prohibit all types of harassment, including sexual harassment. The Human Rights Code covers the federal public service and federally regulated industries such as banks, communications, and interprovincial transportation. Provincial human rights codes, such as that of Ontario, prohibit all types of harassment and make employers responsible for preventing and discouraging harassment. If an employer fails to do so, the employee may file a complaint with the Ontario Human Rights Commission. Thus, business and industries not covered by the various provincial and federal codes still must provide harassment-free workplaces for all employees. According to Labour Canada, 41 percent of workers covered by major collective agreements have some form of negotiated protection against harassment, including **sexual harassment**.[22]

The focus here will be on sexual harassment, but keep in mind that all types of harassment or discrimination are illegal and that many of the suggestions in this section can also be used to battle other harassment or discrimination-based workplace incidents. For example, if Sophie is a woman of colour and feels that she is being denied a promotion because of this, a grievance can be launched in the same manner as a sexual harassment grievance. Most workplace codes have a similar procedure for all types of harassment and other complaints.

Division XV.1 of Part III of the Canada Labour Code establishes that all employees have the right to be free of sexual harassment in the workplace and requires employers to take positive action to prevent it. The Canada Labour Code defines sexual harassment as "any conduct, comment, gesture, or contact of a sexual nature that is likely to cause offence or humiliation to any employee or that might, on reasonable grounds, be perceived by that employee as placing a condition of a sexual nature on employment or on any opportunity for training or promotion."[23] The Supreme Court of Canada defines sexual harassment as unwelcome behaviour of a sexual nature in the workplace that negatively affects the work environment or leads to adverse job-related consequences for the employee.

Sexual harassment can include something as violent as rape or as subtle as making a sexually oriented comment about another person's body or appearance. Decorating the work area with pictures of nude people or displaying pornographic pictures on a computer are examples of more subtle sexual harassment. A Canadian Human Rights Tribunal identified three characteristics of sexual harassment. The first is that the encounters must be unsolicited and unwelcome to the complainant. An example of this type of behaviour is unwelcome sexual remarks. The second characteristic is that the conduct continues despite the complainant's protests, or, if it does stop, that there are negative employment consequences to the complainant. For instance, the comments do not stop, or the comments stop and the complainant is denied a promised promotion. Third, any perceived cooperation by the complainant must be due to employment-related threats or promises.[24] However, there is still much "grey area" when interpreting what behaviour is to be considered sexual harassment.

Despite codes, acts, and employer policies, sexual harassment continues to be a serious problem in the workplace. In the past decade, sexual harassment has received increasing attention due to the growing ranks of women in nontraditional work environments and recent high-profile cases, such as alleged cover-ups of harassment in the Canadian Armed Forces and a murder-suicide at a Sears Canada store in Windsor, Ontario, that was related to sexual harassment. Increasing numbers of men and women are also reporting sexual harassment. Recent surveys indicate that about one-half of working women experience some form of sexual harassment in the workplace. The largest Canadian survey, the Survey on Sexual Harassment in Public Places and at Work (SSHPPW), reported that 56 percent of Canadian working women had experienced sexual harassment in the year prior to the survey.[25] The most common incidents were staring, jokes, or comments about women, and jokes about the respondents themselves. While most research is devoted to men harassing women, this does not mean that women do not harass men, or that harassment does not take place between individuals of the same sex. A poll conducted in British Columbia indicated that 14 percent of 400 men polled said they had experienced sexual harassment at work.[26]

THE ADVERSE EFFECTS OF SEXUAL HARASSMENT

Aside from being unethical, immoral, and illegal, sexual harassment has adverse consequences for both the individual and the organization. According to the SSHPPW, almost one-third of the women surveyed reported that their job was affected by harassment; stress was the most common effect. Other effects included being hindered in or unable to do their job, preoccupation, stress at home, and a diminished trust in men.[27] A related study of the long-term effects of sexual harassment indicated that the negative effects remained two years after the incident. For example, 24 months after an incident of sexual harassment, many women still experienced stress, a decrease in job satisfaction, and lowered productivity.[28]

GUIDELINES FOR PREVENTING AND DEALING WITH SEXUAL HARASSMENT

A starting point in dealing with sexual harassment is to develop an awareness of the types of behaviours that are considered sexual harassment. Often the difference is subtle. Suppose, for example, you placed copies of two nudes painted by Renoir, the French painter, on a co-worker's desk. Your co-worker might call that harassment. Yet if you took that co-worker to a museum to see the originals of the same nude prints, your behaviour usually would not be classified as harassment. One researcher and her colleagues have worked on a typology of sexual harassment that includes gender harassment (behaviours that indicate demeaning attitudes about women), unwanted sexual attention (both verbal and nonverbal), and sexual coercion (the use of threats or rewards to solicit sexual favours).[29] Following is a sampling of behaviours that will often be interpreted as sexual harassment.[30] If people refrain from these behaviours, many instances of sexual harassment will be avoided.

- *Inappropriate remarks and sexual implications.* Co-workers, subordinates, customers, and suppliers should not be referred to as sexual beings, and their appearance should not be referred to in a sexual manner. Telling a co-worker that she has gorgeous feet, or that he has fabulous biceps, is out of place at work.

- *Terms of endearment.* Refrain from calling others in the workplace by names such as "cutie," "sweetie pie," "honey," "dear," or "hunk." One might argue that these terms are simply *sexist* (different roles for men and women) and that using them is not sexual harassment. However, this argument is losing ground because from a legal perspective any behaviour that puts people down based on their gender can be interpreted as harassment. Keep in mind also that some people find terms of endearment to have a sexual connotation. If you felt no physical attraction toward another adult, would you call that person "cutie" or "hunk"?

- *Suggestive compliments.* It is acceptable to tell another person he or she looks nice, but avoid making sexually tinged comments such as mentioning that the person's clothing shows off his or her body to advantage.

- *Physical touching.* To avoid any appearance of sexual harassment, it is best to restrict physical touching to handshakes and an occasional sideways hug. Hugging a long-term work associate is much more acceptable than hugging a new hire. Minimize such behaviours as adjusting a co-worker's earring, touching hair, and tweaking a person's chin.

- *Work-related kissing.* It is best to avoid all kissing in a work context—except, perhaps, a light kiss at an office party. It is much more professional to greet a work associate with a warm, sincere handshake.

There is little doubt that implementing an effective organizational policy that prohibits all harassment, including sexual harassment, will have positive benefits for all employees. An effective harassment policy should state that the organization is committed to providing a harassment-free workplace, clearly define what constitutes harassment, outline the procedures for reporting and investigating harassment internally, and clearly stipulate the consequences of harassment, including discipline or termination.[31] Also, the policy should clearly outline all of the steps that a person can take if he or she is being harassed, including who the people are that the employee can turn to for help.

The policy should also be widely disseminated so that it is available to everyone within the organization; a policy does not do much good if employees are unaware of its existence. Copies of the policy should be distributed to all employees and given to all new employees upon hire. Many organizations with an internal website post the policy in a readable or downloadable format.

Brief company training programs covering the type of information presented in this chapter are also part of a serious program to prevent and deal with sexual harassment. However, a one-time presentation of a 15-minute videotape about sexual harassment is insufficient. Periodic discussion about the topic is recommended.

Once sexual harassment has taken place, the victim will usually want to resolve the conflict. Two key strategies are either to use a formal complaint procedure or to resolve the conflict on your own. If you choose the latter course, you will save yourself the time of going through a lengthy investigation procedure. Figure 7–2 presents details about the two key strategies for dealing with sexual harassment. Skill-Building Exercise 7-4 offers you an opportunity to simulate controlling sexual harassment.

The potential or actual victim of sexual harassment is advised to use the following methods and tactics to deal with the problem:

Formal Complaint Procedure. Whenever an employee believes that he or she has encountered sexual harassment, or if an employee is suspected to be the perpetrator of sexual harassment, the complainant should report the incident to his or her immediate supervisor (if that person is not the harasser) or to the next higher level of management if the supervisor is the harasser. The supervisor contacted is responsible for contacting a designated company official immediately regarding each complaint. The officer will explain the investigative procedures to the complainant and any supervisor involved. All matters will be kept strictly confidential, including private conversations with all parties.

Dealing with the Problem on Your Own. The easiest way to deal with sexual harassment is to speak up before it becomes serious. The first time it happens, respond with a statement such as: "I won't tolerate this kind of talk," or "I dislike sexually oriented jokes," or "Keep your hands off me."

Write the harasser a stern letter shortly after the first incident. Being confronted in writing dramatizes your seriousness of purpose in not wanting to be sexually harassed. Tell the actual or potential harasser: "You're practising sexual harassment. If you don't stop, I'm going to exercise my right to report you to management." Or: "I don't think I heard you right. Would you like to accompany me to the boss's office and repeat what you said to me?"

Figure 7-2   How to Deal with Sexual Harassment

Skill-Building Exercise 7-4

COMBATING SEXUAL HARASSMENT

The two role plays in this exercise provide practice in applying the recommended techniques for combating sexual harassment. The activities have an implied sexual content, and they are for educational purposes only. Any students offended by these role plays should exclude themselves from participating.

Scenario 1: The Offensive Jester. One student plays the role of Max, a man who delights in telling sexually oriented jokes and anecdotes in the office. He often brings a tabloid newspaper to the office to read sexually oriented passages to co-workers, both male and female. Another student assumes the role of Maxine, a woman in the office who takes offence to Max's sense of humour. She wants to convince Max that he is committing sexual harassment with his sexually oriented humour. Max does not see himself as committing sexual harassment.

Scenario 2: The Flirtatious Office Manager. One student assumes the role of Bertha, an office manager who is single. Another student plays the role of Bert, a married man who recently joined the company as an office assistant. Bert reports to Bertha, and she finds him physically attractive. Bertha visits Bert at his desk and makes such comments as "It looks like you have great quadriceps. I wonder what you look like in running shorts?" Bert wants to be on good terms with Bertha, but he feels uncomfortable with her advances. He also wants to behave professionally in the office.

Run both role plays in front of the class for about eight minutes. Other students in the class will observe the role plays and then provide feedback about how well Maxine and Bert were able to prevent or stop sexual harassment.

SUMMARY

A conflict is a situation in which two or more goals, values, or events are incompatible or mutually exclusive. Interpersonal conflicts have many sources or causes. An underlying source of job conflict is that people compete for limited resources. Another leading cause of incompatibility is role conflict, having to choose between two competing demands or expectations. Competing work and family demands represent a major role conflict. Other key sources of conflict are personality clashes; aggressive personalities, including bullies; and incivility and rudeness.

Five major styles of conflict management have been identified: competitive, accommodative, sharing, collaborative (win–win), and avoidant. Each style is based on a combination of satisfying one's own concerns (assertiveness) and satisfying the concerns of others (cooperativeness).

Confrontation and problem-solving is the ideal method for resolving conflict. Learning to benefit from criticism is an effective way of benefiting from conflict. People who benefit from criticism are able to stand outside themselves while being criticized. Another way to deal with criticism is to disarm the opposition by agreeing with his or her criticism. Cognitive restructuring lessens conflict by emphasizing the positive elements in a situation.

Negotiating is a major approach to resolving conflict. It includes focusing on interests rather than positions, compromise, beginning with a plausible demand or offer yet allowing room for negotiation, and making small concessions gradually. It is also important to know your BATNA (best alternative to a negotiated agreement). Some conflicts may require the use of a mediator for resolution. Using anger to your advantage can sometimes work. Alternative dispute resolution involves the use of a professional mediator to help the conflicting parties come to a mutually acceptable solution.

Sexual harassment is a form of interpersonal conflict with legal implications. Sexual harassment can be very overt, such as requesting sexual favours in exchange for a promotion, or it can be more subtle, such as making inappropriate jokes. Sexual harassment is widespread in the workplace, and while it affects more women than men, many men report harassment as well. Research has pinpointed adverse mental and physical consequences of sexual harassment.

A starting point in dealing with sexual harassment is to develop an awareness of the types of behaviours it encompasses. Company policies and complaint procedures about harassment are a major part of dealing with the problem. To deal directly with harassment, the harassed person can file a formal complaint or confront the harasser when the behaviour first begins.

An Interpersonal Relations Case Problem

A CONCERN ABOUT VIOLENCE

Vernon Bigsby is the CEO and owner of a large soft-drink bottling company in Guelph, Ontario. The company periodically invests money in training to help the management and supervisory staff remain abreast of important new trends in technology and managing human resources. Bigsby recently became concerned about workplace violence. Although the company had not yet experienced an outbreak of violence, Bigsby was intent on preventing violence in the future. To accomplish this goal, Bigsby hired a human resources consultant, Sara Toomey, to conduct a seminar on preventing workplace violence.

The seminar was given twice, with half the managers and supervisors attending each session. Chad Ditmar, a night-shift supervisor, made the first wisecrack during the seminar. He said, "What are we here for? To prevent workers from squirting 'pop' at each other?" Toomey responded, "My job would be easy if I were here only to prevent horseplay. Unfortunately the reality is that there are thousands of lethal weapons going past your workers every day.

Just think how much damage one angry worker could do to an innocent victim with one slash of a broken bottle." The laughter in the room quickly subsided.

About one hour into the seminar, Sara Toomey projected a PowerPoint slide outlining characteristics of a worker with potential for violence. She said, "Recognize that not every person who has many of these characteristics will become violent. However, they do constitute early warning signals. I would watch out for any worker with a large number of these traits and behaviours." (See Exhibit 1 for the computer slide in question.)

Ditmar supervises 45 workers directly involved in the bottling of three company brands of soft drinks. The workers in his department range in age from 18 to 57. The job usually can be learned within three days, so the workers are classified as semi-skilled. After his initial wisecrack, Ditmar took the seminar quite seriously. He made extensive notes on what the consultant said, and took back to his office a printed copy of the PowerPoint slide.

(Continued)

Exhibit 1

PROFILE OF THE VIOLENT EMPLOYEE

- Socially isolated (a loner) white male, between the ages of 30 and 40.
- Fascination with the military and weapons.
- Interest in recently published violent events.
- Temper control problem with history of threats.
- Alcohol and/or drug abuser.
- Increased mood swings.
- Makes unwanted sexual advances toward other employees.
- Accepts criticism poorly and holds a grudge against the criticizer.
- Shows paranoid thinking and believes that management is out to get him (or her).
- Blames others for his or her problems.
- Makes violent statements such as spoken threats about beating up other employees.
- Damage or destruction of company property.
- Decreased productivity or inconsistent work performance.

The morning following the seminar, Ditmar sent an email to Gary Bia, the vice-president of operations. Ditmar said, "I must see you today. I'm worried about a potentially explosive personnel problem." Bia made arrangements to see Ditmar at 5:45 in the afternoon, before Ditmar's shift began.

"What's up, Chad?" asked Bia.

"Here's what's up," said Ditmar. "After attending the seminar on violence, I think I've found our suspect. As you know, you do get some strange types working the night shift. Some of them don't have a normal life. I've got this one guy, Freddie Watkins. He's a loner. He wears his hair weird, with pink coloured spikes. He's got a tattoo and a huge gun collection that he brags about. I doubt the guy has any friends. He talks a lot about how he plays violent video games. Freddie told about how he once choked to death a dog that bit him.

"What really worries me is that Freddie once said he would punch out the next person who made a smart—s comment about his hair.

"Do you agree or not that we might have a candidate for workplace violence right here in my department? I'm talking to you first, Gary, but maybe I should be speaking to the antiviolence consultant or to our security officer. What should we do next?"

Bia said, "I'm happy that you are bringing this potential problem to my attention, but I need some more facts. First of all, have you had any discipline problems yet with Freddie?"

Ditmar responded, "Not yet Gary, but we're talking about a potential killer right here on my shift. I think we have to do something."

Bia said, "Chad, I'm taking your concerns seriously, but I don't want to jump too fast. Let me think over your problem for at least a day."

Case Questions

1. What actions, if any, should Gary Bia take?
2. What type of conflict is Chad Ditmar facing?
3. What career advice can you offer Freddie Watkins?

An Interpersonal Relations Case Problem

CAUGHT IN A SQUEEZE

Heather Crowe is a product development specialist at a telecommunications company. For the last seven months she has worked as a member of a product development team composed of people from five different departments within the company. Heather previously worked full-time in the marketing department. Her primary responsibilities were to research the market potential of an idea for a new product.

(Continued)

The product development team is now working on a product that will integrate a company's printers and copiers.

Heather's previous position in the marketing department was a satisfactory fit for her lifestyle. Heather thought that she was able to take care of her family responsibilities and her job without sacrificing one for the other. As Heather explains, "I worked about 45 predictable hours in my other job. My hours were essentially 8:30 to 4:30, with a little work at night and on Saturdays. But I could do the night and weekend work at home.

"Brad, my husband, and I had a smooth-working arrangement for sharing the responsibility for getting our son Christopher off to school and picking him up from the after-school childcare centre. Brad is a devoted accountant, so he understands the importance of giving high priority to a career while still being a good family person."

In her new position as a member of the product-development team, Heather is encountering some unanticipated demands. Three weeks ago, at 3:00 on a Tuesday, Tyler Watson, Heather's team leader, announced an emergency meeting to discuss a budget problem with the new product. The meeting would start at 4:00 and probably end at about 6:30. "Don't worry, folks," said the team leader. "If it looks like we're going past 6:30, we'll order in some Chinese food."

With a look of panic on her face, Heather responded to Tyler, "I can't make the meeting. Christopher will be expecting me at about 5:00 at the childcare centre. My husband is out of town, and the centre closes at 6:00 sharp. So count me out of today's meeting."

Tyler said, "I said that this is an emergency meeting, and that we need input from all the members. You need to organize your personal life better to be a contributing member to this team. But do what you have to do, at least this once."

Heather chose to leave the office at 4:30 so she could pick up Christopher. The next day, Tyler did not comment on her absence. However, he gave her a copy of the minutes and asked for her input. The budget problem surfaced again a week later. Top-level management asked the group to reduce the cost of the new product and its initial marketing costs by 15 percent.

Tyler said to the team on a Friday morning, "We have until Monday morning to arrive at a reduced cost structure on our product development. I am dividing up the project into segments. If we meet as a team Saturday morning at 8:00, we should get the job done by 6:00 at night. Get a good night's rest, so we can start fresh tomorrow morning. Breakfast and lunch will be on the company."

Heather could feel stress overwhelming her body, as she thought to herself, "Christopher is playing in the finals of his little league soccer match tomorrow morning at 10:00. Brad has made dinner reservations for 6:00, so we can make it to *The Phantom of the Opera* at 8:00. Should I tell Tyler he is being unreasonable? Should I quit? Should I tell Christopher and Brad that our special occasions together are less important than a Saturday business meeting?" (For a role play based on this conflict, see Skill-Building Exercise 7-5.)

Case Questions

1. What type of conflict is Heather facing?

2. What should Heather do to resolve her conflicts with respect to family and work responsibilities?

3. What should the company do to help deal with the type of conflict Heather is facing? Or should the company not consider Heather's dilemma to be their problem?

Skill-Building Exercise 7-5

CONFLICT RESOLUTION ROLE PLAY

Imagine that Heather, in the case just presented, decides that her job is taking too big a toll on her personal life. However, she still values her job and does not want to quit. She decides to discuss her problem with her team leader, Tyler. From Tyler's standpoint, a professional person must stand ready to meet unusual job demands and cannot expect an entirely predictable work schedule. One person plays the role of Heather, another the role of Tyler, as they attempt to resolve this conflict.

QUESTIONS FOR DISCUSSION AND REVIEW

1. How might conflict among students to obtain high grades be seen as competition for limited resources?

2. Why might it be useful for you to know a work associate's conflict style?

3. What are the disadvantages of having an accommodative style of handling conflict?

4. Remember the hypothetical conflict between Bill Molson and the Molson Coors Brewing Company? What solution do you propose to satisfy the underlying interests of both parties?

5. Have you ever attempted to disarm the opposition? How effective was the tactic?

6. How might a student use cognitive restructuring to get over the anger of having received a low grade in a course?

7. Visualize yourself buying a vehicle of your choice. Which negotiating technique (or techniques) would you be the most likely to use?

8. Studies have shown that women working in male-dominated positions, such as a female construction supervisor or bulldozer operator, are more likely to experience sexual harassment than women in other fields. What explanation can you offer for this finding?

9. Is inviting a co-worker to dinner a second time a form of sexual harassment if the co-worker refused the first invitation?

10. Violence also occurs in other settings with people who know each other, or even with strangers. Log onto your Research Navigator and access Article Number AN13257276 titled "Defense Mechanisms and Self-Reported Violence Toward Partners and Strangers." Although it has some limitations, this is an interesting study, with male college students as subjects. Do you think young people are more violent than older people? If so, what strategies would you propose to assist younger people in reducing violence after reading the results of this study?

Research
Navigator.com

WEBLINKS

www.canada.justice.gc.ca

This is the site for Justice Canada. From this site, you can access the *Canadian Human Rights Act* and articles about it.

www.hrdc-drhc.gc.ca

From the site of Human Resources Development Canada, you can access the Canada Labour Code.

www.mediate.com

This is a great site about mediation. You can sign up for a free newsletter that has many articles about mediation and other aspects of conflict resolution.

Chapter 8

Becoming an Effective Leader

Learning Outcomes

After reading and studying this chapter and doing the exercises, you should be able to
- Identify key leadership traits for personal development.
- Develop several attitudes and behaviours that will help you appear charismatic.
- Develop your team leadership skills.
- Develop your leadership potential.

The director of ecommerce of a children's furniture company invited Melissa Antonelli to her office. "Melissa, we're asking you to be the website team leader," said the director. "It's been obvious to us that you have good leadership potential, so we're giving you the opportunity."

Pleased, Melissa responded that she was flattered, but she wondered what she had done that suggested leadership potential. The manager answered, "You have a great work ethic, and you have expert knowledge of maintaining a website. Besides that, you get along fabulously with people. For those reasons, we know you will be an outstanding team leader."

Melissa's invitation to become a team leader illustrates two key points about developing leadership capability. You need the *right stuff* (effective personal characteristics) for leadership. You also need to carry out the *right actions* (such as getting along well with people). Leadership in the workplace involves influencing and persuading people to achieve worthwhile goals. It also involves helping to bring about constructive change, such as increasing sales or streamlining work.

There are many different definitions of leadership. In working toward improving your leadership ability, the following definition is a goal to strive for. **Leadership** is the ability to inspire support and confidence among the people who are needed to achieve organizational goals. Leadership can also be seen as a process that empowers followers and provides an environment where goals can be achieved.[1] Regardless of which definition you choose, leadership is about inspiring others to achieve goals. Leaders in organizations, therefore, have the task of inspiring and empowering workers to achieve organizational goals. A company president might have to inspire thousands of people, while a team leader such as Melissa is concerned with inspiring about six people. Both of these leaders play an important role.

Becoming a leader does not necessarily mean that the company has to put you in charge of others (or assign you a formal leadership position). You can also rise to leadership when people come to respect your opinion and personal characteristics and are thus influenced by you. Leadership is thought by many to exist at all levels with people anywhere in the organization being able to influence others if they have the right skills or know the right work procedures.[2] Your greatest opportunity for exerting leadership will come about from a combination of holding a formal position and exerting personal influence. An individual with appealing personal characteristics and expertise who is placed in a position of authority will find it relatively easy to exert leadership.

The purpose of this chapter is twofold: (1) to make you aware of the basic concepts you will need to become a leader and (2) to point you toward developing skills necessary for leadership effectiveness.

KEY LEADERSHIP TRAITS TO DEVELOP

An important part of being an effective leader is to have the *right stuff.* In this section and the following one about charisma, we describe personal attributes that help a person lead others in many situations. While this list does not include all the necessary traits for effective leadership, the items included have been well-documented in research.

Also, recognize that radically different situations require a different set of leadership characteristics. For example, a leader may need to be more assertive with group members performing distasteful work than with those whose work is enjoyable. The Canadian Scene on the next page offers some insight as to what one headhunter looks for in the candidates that he interviews.

Each of the nine leadership traits described next, and shown in Figure 8-1, can be developed. For such development to take place, you need to be aware of the importance

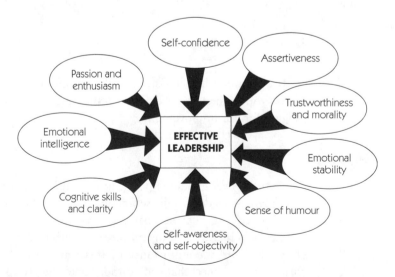

Figure 8-1   Nine Key Leadership Traits

The Canadian Scene

WHAT MAKES A LEADER, ACCORDING TO MICHAEL STERN

Michael Stern is the president and CEO of Michael Stern Associates, an executive search firm in Toronto. He is also a founding member of AEA International Search, with offices worldwide. As a professional "headhunter," he knows quite a bit about effective leadership. What does he look for in a leader? Here are a few of his "hallmarks of leadership."

Graciousness. "The best leaders come off as authoritative, but modest," according to Stern. They don't need to tell people how important they are. Instead their accomplishments speak for themselves.

Ability to Listen. In today's flatter organizational structures, you have to take people's feelings into account. Information flows from the bottom to the top, so the top needs to be able to listen.

Discipline. Stern looks for signs that candidates can execute a plan or strategy, especially a strategy in the face of uncertainty. He looks for "gumption, guts, and stick-to-it-ness."

Vision. The leader's mission is to help the entire organization move forward. In interviews, leaders set themselves apart by wanting to succeed on more than just their own departmental level. They also share this vision with others in the organization and keep people focused on inspirational and achievable goals.

Judgment. One of Stern's favourite interview questions is, "Tell me about a decision you made that turned out to be wrong, and what you did about it." Good judgment comes from experience and has to be learned. Leaders network widely, read up on a wide range of subjects, and prepare diligently for meetings and discussions. If a leader does not know something, he or she asks pertinent questions to be "brought up to speed."

Presence. Lastly, a candidate for leadership has to be impressively dressed and well-groomed. With only 60 minutes to interview and judge a candidate, appearance counts. Good leaders leave a lasting impression of "humanity, decency, and patience."

Do you have what it takes? According to Stern, if leaders were easy to find, few of his clients would need the services of professional search consultants for their senior positions. Talent and ambition are common enough, but what about these more elusive traits? Just some interesting ideas from a pro!

Source: Michael Stern, "The Right Stuff," *Canadian Business*, April 26, 2004, pp. 95–99. Used with permission of the author. For more information please refer to his website at www.michaelstern.com.

of the personal characteristic, and then monitor the progress of your own behaviour. To assist you with such development, the description of each trait is accompanied by a suggestion for improvement.

SELF-CONFIDENCE

In virtually every leadership setting, it is important for the leader to be realistically self-confident. A leader who is self-assured without being bombastic or overbearing instils confidence in group members. Self-confidence was among the first leadership traits researchers identified. Current research with leaders in many situations has continued to underscore the importance of this trait. In addition to being self-confident, the leader must project that self-confidence to the group.[3]

Self-confidence is not only a personality trait. It also refers to the behaviour a person exhibits in a number of situations. It is similar to being cool under pressure. We can conclude that a person is a self-confident leader when he or she retains composure during a crisis, such as flood damage during a busy season.

You can appear more self-confident to the group by using definitive wording, maintaining good posture, and making appropriate gestures such as counting off significant points of a speech with fingers for emphasis. Developing self-confidence is a lifelong process of performing well in a variety of situations. You need a series of easy victories to establish self-confidence. Further development of this trait requires performing well in challenging circumstances. Taking risks, such as volunteering to work on an unfamiliar project, contributes to self-confidence when the risk proves to be worthwhile.

ASSERTIVENESS

A widely recognized leadership trait is **assertiveness**, being forthright in expressing demands, opinions, feelings, and attitudes. If you are self-confident, it is easier to be assertive with people. An assertive team leader from the Ottawa area might say, "I know that the ice storm put us out of business for four days, but we can make up the time by working smart and pulling together. Within 30 days, we will have met or surpassed our goals for the quarter." This statement reflects self-confidence in the team leader's leadership capabilities and assertiveness in expressing exactly what this leader thinks. Assertiveness helps leaders perform many tasks and achieve goals. Among them are confronting group members about their mistakes, demanding higher performance, and setting high expectations. An assertive leader will also make legitimate demands on higher management, such as asking for equipment needed by the group.

Being assertive differs significantly from being aggressive or passive (or nonassertive). Aggressive people express their demands in an overly pushy, obnoxious, and abrasive manner. Passive people suppress their own ideas, attitudes, feelings, and thoughts as if they were likely to be perceived as controversial. Nonassertive people are also too accommodating.

Developing assertiveness is much like attempting to become less shy. You must force yourself to take the opportunity to express your feelings and demands. For example, if something a teammate does annoys you, make the statement, "I enjoy working with you in general, but what you are doing now annoys me." You can also practise expressing positive emotion, such as telling a co-worker, "I'm happy that you and I are working on this project together, because I like your approach to work."

Expressing demands is easier for most people to practise than expressing feelings. People who do start expressing their demands are often surprised at the result. For example, if you are contemplating the purchase of an item that is beyond your budget, try this statement: "I like this product very much. Yet all I have to spend is $45 below your asking price. Can we do business?"

For a reading on your own level of assertiveness, do Self-Assessment Quiz 8-1.

Self-Assessment Quiz 8-1

THE ASSERTIVENESS SCALE

Directions: Indicate whether each of the following statements is "Mostly true" or "Mostly false" as it applies to you. If in doubt about your reaction to a particular statement, think of how you would generally respond.

	Mostly true	Mostly false
1. It is extremely difficult for me to turn down a sales representative when that individual is a nice person.	_____	_____
2. I express criticism freely.	_____	_____
3. If another person is being very unfair, I bring it to his or her attention.	_____	_____
4. Work is no place to let your feelings show.	_____	_____
5. No use asking for favours; people get what they deserve.	_____	_____
6. Business is not the place for tact; say what you think.	_____	_____
7. In a supermarket line, if a person looks as if he or she is in a hurry, I let that person in front of me.	_____	_____
8. A weakness of mine is that I'm too nice a person.	_____	_____
9. I usually give other people what they want rather than do what I think is best, just to avoid an argument.	_____	_____
10. If the mood strikes me, I will laugh out loud in public.	_____	_____
11. People consider me too outspoken.	_____	_____
12. I am quite willing to return merchandise that I find has a minor blemish.	_____	_____
13. I dread having to express anger toward a co-worker.	_____	_____
14. People often say that I'm too reserved and emotionally controlled.	_____	_____
15. Nice guys and gals finish last in business.	_____	_____
16. I fight for my rights down to the last detail.	_____	_____
17. I have no misgivings about returning an overcoat to the store if it doesn't fit me right.	_____	_____
18. After I have an argument with a person, I try to avoid him or her.	_____	_____
19. I insist on my spouse (or roommate or partner) doing his or her fair share of undesirable chores.	_____	_____
20. It is difficult for me to look directly at another person when the two of us are in disagreement.	_____	_____
21. I have cried in front of friends more than once.	_____	_____
22. If someone near me at a movie keeps up a conversation with another person, I ask him or her to stop.	_____	_____

(Continued)

23. I am able to turn down social engagements with people I do not particularly care for. _____ _____

24. It is in poor taste to express what you really feel about another individual. _____ _____

25. I sometimes show my anger by swearing at or belittling another person. _____ _____

26. I am reluctant to speak up at meetings. _____ _____

27. I find it relatively easy to ask friends for small favours such as giving me a ride to work while my car is being repaired. _____ _____

28. If another person is talking very loudly in a restaurant and it bothers me, I tell that person. _____ _____

29. I often finish other people's sentences for them. _____ _____

30. It is relatively easy for me to express love and affection toward another person. _____ _____

Scoring Key

1. Mostly false	11. Mostly true	21. Mostly true
2. Mostly true	12. Mostly true	22. Mostly true
3. Mostly true	13. Mostly false	23. Mostly true
4. Mostly false	14. Mostly false	24. Mostly false
5. Mostly false	15. Mostly true	25. Mostly true
6. Mostly true	16. Mostly true	26. Mostly false
7. Mostly false	17. Mostly true	27. Mostly true
8. Mostly false	18. Mostly false	28. Mostly true
9. Mostly false	19. Mostly true	29. Mostly true
10. Mostly true	20. Mostly false	30. Mostly true

Interpretation: Score yourself one point (+1) for each of your answers that agrees with the scoring key. If your score is 15 or less, it is probable that you are currently nonassertive. A score of 16 through 24 suggests that you are assertive. A score of 25 or higher suggests that you are aggressive. Retake this quiz about 30 days from now to give yourself some indication of the stability of your answers. You might also discuss your answers with a close friend to determine whether that person has a similar perception of your assertiveness.

TRUSTWORTHINESS AND MORALITY

Group members consistently believe that leaders must display honesty, integrity, and credibility—and therefore trustworthiness. Leaders themselves believe that honesty makes a difference in their effectiveness. Being honest with team members helps to build trust, which in turn leads to good cooperation and team spirit. In recent years, trust in business leaders has been damaged by financial scandals in such name companies as the Enron Corporation. Executives enriched themselves by selling company stock just before the time they correctly forecast that the stock price would tumble. On the Canadian political scene, political incidents such as the "Sponsorship Scandal" have left many Canadians distrustful of political leaders.

Management authority Dale Zand regards trust, along with knowledge and power, as one of the three foundations of leadership.[4] In trusting group members, the leader has to be willing to give up some control over them, such as letting group members make more decisions and not challenging their expense accounts. The following anecdote told by Fred Smith, the founder of FedEx, illustrates what trust can mean in an organization:

> A blizzard shut down a radio relay located on top of a mountain, cutting phone service to several FedEx offices. The phone company said it would take five days to repair the problem. On his own, a FedEx telecommunications expert named Hal chartered a helicopter to get to the site. The pilot was unable to land, but he got close enough to the ground for Hal to jump safely. Hal slogged through the deep snow and fixed the problem.

According to Smith, Hal went to such great lengths to keep the organization going because there was mutual trust between employer and employee. Hal knew he would not be reprimanded for going to such expense to fix the telephone problem.[5]

Being moral is closely linked to trustworthiness because a moral leader is more likely to be trusted. A leader with high morality would perceive that he or she had an ethical responsibility to group members, as well as to outsiders.[6] The moral leader would therefore not give preferential treatment to workers with whom he had an outside-of-work friendship. At the same time the moral leader would not try to fool customers or make up false excuses for not paying bills on time to suppliers.

Chapter 13, about ethical behaviour, provides details concerning honesty on the job. Being honest is an effective way of getting others to trust you. A starting point in developing a strong sense of honesty is to follow a variation of the Golden Rule: Be as honest with others as you want them to be with you.

EMOTIONAL STABILITY

Anyone who has ever worked for an unstable supervisor will attest to the importance of emotional stability as a leadership trait. (As described in Chapter 2, emotional stability is equivalent to scoring low on neuroticism in the Five Factor Model.) Emotional stability is important for a leader because group members expect and need consistency in the way they are treated.

Kenneth Chenault, the chief executive officer of American Express—and the first African-American man to be the top executive of a Fortune 500 company—is known for his even temperament. Although an assertive and tough executive, he is calm and in control. A survey of Chenault's former and present colleagues found that his personality is free of the rough edges that usually accompany fierce ambition. Nobody questioned could recall Chenault losing his temper or even raising his voice. Chenault emphasizes that having the right values (such as caring for people) gives stability to a person's career.[7]

Emotional stability is difficult to develop, but people can learn to control many of their emotional outbursts. People who seek a leadership position but cannot control their emotions should seek assistance from a mental health professional.

SENSE OF HUMOUR

A sense of humour is borderline between being a trait and a behaviour. However you classify it, the effective use of humour is considered an important part of a leader's role.

Skill-Building Exercise 8-1

THE WITTY LEADER

Groups of about five students gather in problem-solving groups to invent humorous comments a leader might make in the following scenarios. After the problem-solving groups have formulated their witty comments, the comments can be shared and compared. Groups also have the option of deciding that a particular scenario is too grim for humour.

Scenario 1: A store manager wants to communicate to employees how bad business has been lately. Sales have declined about 20 percent for three consecutive weeks.

Scenario 2: A leader has to communicate to the group that salaries have been frozen for another year due to limited business. The leader knows that group members have been eagerly awaiting news about the salary increase.

Scenario 3: Due to an unprecedented surge in orders, all salaried personnel will be required to work about 65 hours per week for the next 10 weeks. Further, the office and factory must be staffed on Saturdays and Sundays.

Scenario 4: A consulting firm that specializes in helping companies downsize their workforce has seen the demand for their services decline substantially in recent months. The company must therefore downsize itself. The company founder has to announce the layoff decision to the company.

Humour serves such functions in the workplace as relieving tension and boredom and defusing hostility. Because humour helps the leader deal with tension and conflict in the workplace, it helps him or her exert power over the group. A study conducted in a large Canadian financial institution indicated that leaders who made frequent use of humour had higher-performing units. (Another interpretation is that it's easier to laugh when the group is performing well!) Among the forms of humour used by the managers were "[using] humour to take the edge off during stressful periods" and "[making] us laugh at ourselves when we are too serious."[8]

Self-effacing humour is the choice of comedians and organizational leaders alike. When you are self-effacing, nobody else is insulted or slighted; yet a point can be made. Creativity is required for humour. Just as creativity can be enhanced with practice, so can a sense of humour. To gather some experience in making humorous comments in the workplace, do Skill-Building Exercise 8-1.

SELF-AWARENESS AND SELF-OBJECTIVITY

Effective leaders are aware of their strengths and limitations. This awareness enables them to capitalize on their strengths and overcome their weaknesses. A leader, for example, might realize that he or she is naturally distrustful of others. Awareness of this problem cautions the leader to not distrust people without good evidence. Another leader might realize that he or she is adept at counselling team members. This leader might then emphasize that activity in an effort to improve performance. Self-objectivity refers to being detached or non-subjective about your perceived strengths and limitations.

You can enhance your self-awareness and self-objectivity by regularly asking for feedback from others. You then compare the feedback to your self-perception of your standing on the same factor. You might, for example, think that you communicate in colourful, interesting terms. In speaking to others about your communication style, you might discover that others agree. You can then conclude that your self-awareness about your communication skills is accurate.

Another technique for improving self-awareness and self-objectivity is to do a number of the type of self-examination exercises found in this text. Even if they do not describe you exactly, they stimulate you to reflect on your characteristics and behaviours.

COGNITIVE SKILLS AND CLARITY

Mental ability, as well as personality, is important for leadership success. To inspire people, bring about constructive changes, and solve problems creatively, leaders need to be mentally sharp. Problem-solving and intellectual skills are referred to collectively as **cognitive factors**. The term **cognition** refers to the mental process or faculty by which knowledge is gathered.

A major reason that cognitive skills have increased in importance for leadership is that they enable the leader to acquire knowledge, the processing of which is now considered to be the *core competence* (key ability) in organizations. The leader's role is to both originate useful ideas and collect them from smart people throughout the organization.[9]

Two cognitive skills were discussed in Chapter 2: mental ability and the personal factor of openness to experience. Another cognitive skill of major importance is *knowledge of the business,* or technical skill. An effective leader has to be technically or professionally competent in some discipline, particularly when leading a group of specialists. It is difficult for the leader to establish rapport with group members when he or she does not know what they are doing. A related damper on leadership effectiveness is when the group does not respect the leader's technical skill.

High intelligence is particularly important for leaders when they have the opportunity to make decisions by themselves and provide direction (such as giving technical instructions) to group members.[10] Problem-solving ability is less important when the leader delegates most of his or her responsibilities to others.

Closely related to cognitive skills is the leader's ability to be clear about what needs to be accomplished to build a better future, even if the future is next week. Based on his study of some of the world's most successful business leaders, Marcus Buckingham concludes that the leader should define the future in vivid terms so people can see where they are headed. The leader also has to be clear about such matters as who the group is trying to serve. For example, Denny Clements, the general manager of Toyota's Lexus Group, says that the only people Lexus is attempting to serve are those for whom time is a precious commodity. Both building and servicing the car are driven by considerations of saving customers time.[11] A beauty salon operator could provide clarity to her hair stylists with a statement such as, "Our real purpose here is to boost our customers' self-esteem. Every customer who leaves our salon should feel a little better about himself or herself."

Increasing one's mental ability, or raw intelligence, may not be easy to accomplish. Yet people can develop their cognitive skills through continuous study and by working on challenging problems. The mere act of keeping up with developments in your field can keep you mentally sharp. For a leader to provide clarity, the leader would have to think through clearly what it is that he or she is really attempting to accomplish.

EMOTIONAL INTELLIGENCE

Emotional intelligence, as described in Chapter 2, refers to the ability to recognize your emotions and those of people around you. Emotional intelligence also refers to being able to work effectively with the emotions of others to resolve problems, through listening and empathizing. Research conducted by Daniel Goleman in many different firms suggests that superb leaders all have one trait in common: superb emotional intelligence.[12] A specific example is that an effective manager or leader can often recognize the motives behind an employee's actions. In this regard, consider the following scenario:

> Visualize yourself as a team leader. Vanessa, one of the team members, says to you, "I'm worried about Rick. I think he needs help. He looks like he has a drinking problem." If you have good emotional intelligence, you might think to yourself, "I wonder why Vanessa is telling me this. Is she simply being helpful? Or is she out to stab Rick in the back?" So you would seek some tangible evidence about Rick's alleged problem before acting. You would also seek to spend more time with Vanessa so you can better understand her motives.
>
> "With much less emotional intelligence, you would immediately get in touch with Rick, accuse him of having a drinking problem, and tell him to get help or get fired."

Emotional intelligence is also reflected in a leader who incorporates the human touch into business activities, such as building personal relationships with employees and customers. Several years ago Robert A. Eckert was recruited from Kraft Foods to become chairman and CEO of toy maker Mattel. At the time Mattel was in deep financial trouble, and key Mattel managers were leaving the company. Eckert moved quickly to bring the famous toy manufacturer back to health. The first steps he took were to share meals with employees in the company cafeteria at every opportunity. During these lunches he engaged in candid dialogue with employees chosen at random. He reassured employees that their personal growth and development was a major part of his plans for rebuilding Mattel. Eckert notes, "In this case the emotional intelligence I'd developed over the years was even more important to my success than my traditional, analytical management skills were."[13]

Emotional intelligence can be developed through working on some of its components, as described in Chapter 2. It is also important to develop the habit of seeking to understand the feelings and emotions of people around you. Also, ask yourself, "How do I feel about what's going on here?" When you have a hunch about people's motives, look for feedback in the future to see if you were right. For example, investigation might indicate that indeed Vanessa and Rick are rivals and have a personality clash.

PASSION AND ENTHUSIASM

A prominent characteristic of effective leaders is the passion and enthusiasm they have for their work, much like the same quality in creative people. The passion reflects itself in such ways as an intense liking for the business, the customers, and employees.

Passion is also reflected in a relentless drive to get work accomplished and an obsession for achieving company goals. Passion for their work is especially evident in entrepreneurial leaders and small-business owners who are preoccupied with expanding their businesses. Many leaders use the term "love" to describe their passion for their work, business, and employees.

To display passion and enthusiasm for your work, you must first find work that creates an inner spark. The work that you choose should be at least as exciting as your favourite pastime. If not everything about your job excites you, search for its most satisfying or *intrinsically motivating* elements. For example, the Mattel executive described above is so excited about the interpersonal aspects of his work that his passion inspires employees.

SUGGESTIONS FOR DEVELOPING CHARISMA

The study of leadership in recent years has emphasized the importance of inspirational leaders who guide others toward great heights of achievement. Such leaders are said to possess **charisma**, a special quality of leaders whose purposes, powers, and extraordinary determination differentiate them from others.[14] An important fact about charisma is that it reflects a subjective perception on the part of the person being influenced. Past Prime Minister Pierre Elliott Trudeau, for instance, was described as having "indubitable leadership qualities" by one of his opponents, Quebec premier Lucien Bouchard. Yet he was also disliked by others such as Raymond Villeneuve, a former Front de Libération du Québec (FLQ) terrorist who described Trudeau as a "very good traitor."[15]

The term *charisma* is most frequently used in association with nationally and internationally known leaders. Yet first-level supervisors, team leaders, and minor sports coaches can also be charismatic. A naturally dynamic personality is a major component of charisma, but a person can engage in many tangible actions that also contribute to charisma. Following are a number of suggestions for behaving charismatically, all based on characteristics and behaviours often found in charismatic leaders. If you are not currently a leader, remember that being perceived as charismatic will help you become one.

1. *Communicate a vision.* A charismatic leader offers an exciting image of where the organization is headed and how to get there. A vision is more than a forecast because it describes an ideal version of the future of an entire organization or an organizational unit such as a department. Richard Branson, the colourful British entrepreneur, has inspired hundreds of employees with his vision of the Virgin brand's potential in dozens of fields. Among his accomplishments in realizing this vision have been the Virgin Atlantic airline, Virgin Megastores, and Virgin Cinema. A supervisor of paralegal services might communicate a vision such as "Our paralegal group will become known as the most professional and helpful paralegal group in British Columbia." Skill-Building Exercise 8-2 will give you a chance to develop your skills in visioning (a buzzword in business).

Skill-Building Exercise 8-2

CREATING A VISION

The class breaks into small problem-solving groups. Each group constructs a vision for a unit of an organization or for a total organization of its choosing. Students can choose an organization with which they are familiar or a well-known business firm or government agency. The vision should be approximately 25 words long and depict a glorious future. A vision is not simply a straightforward goal, such as "In 2005 our firm will gross $10 million in sales." Remember, the vision statement you draw up should inspire people throughout the organization.

2. *Make frequent use of metaphors and analogies.* To inspire people, the charismatic leader uses colourful language and exciting metaphors and analogies. Develop metaphors to inspire people around you. A commonly used one after a group has suffered a setback is, "Like the phoenix, we will rise from the ashes of defeat." To pick up the spirits of her maintenance group, a maintenance supervisor said, "We're a lot like the heating and cooling system in a house. A lot of people don't give us much thought, but without us their lives would be very uncomfortable."

3. *Inspire trust and confidence.* Make your deeds consistent with your promises. As mentioned earlier in this chapter, being trustworthy is a key leadership trait. Get people to believe in your competence by making your accomplishments known in a polite, tactful way.

4. *Be highly energetic and goal-oriented.* Impress others with your energy and resourcefulness. To increase your energy supply, exercise frequently, eat well, and get ample rest. Closely related to being goal-oriented is being optimistic about what you and the group can accomplish. People also associate optimism with energy. Being grumpy is often associated with being low on energy. You can also add to an image of energy by raising and lowering your voice frequently and avoiding a slow pace.

5. *Be emotionally expressive and warm.* A key characteristic of charismatic leaders is the ability to express feelings openly. Assertiveness is therefore an important component of charisma. In dealing with team members, refer to your feelings at the time, such as "I'm excited because I know we are going to hit our year-end target by mid-October." Nonverbal emotional expressiveness, such as warm gestures and frequent touching (nonsexual) of group members, also exhibits one's charisma. Remember, however, that many people resent being touched when at work. Frequent smiling is another way of being emotionally expressive. Also, a warm smile seems to indicate a confident, caring person, which contributes to a perception of charisma.

6. *Make ample use of true stories.* An excellent way of building rapport is to tell stories that deliver a message. People like to hear stories about how a department or company went through hard times when it started, such as

how Dell Computer began in a dormitory room at the University of Texas. Telling positive stories has become a widely accepted technique for building relationships with employees. Storytelling adds a touch of warmth to the teller and helps build connections among people who become familiar with the same story.

7. *Be candid and direct.* Practise saying what you want directly, rather than being indirect and evasive. If you want someone to help you, don't ask, "Are you busy?" Instead, ask, "Can you help me with a problem I'm having right now?"

8. *Make everybody you meet feel that he or she is important.* For example, at a company social gathering, shake the hand of every person you meet. Also, thank people frequently, both orally and by written notes.

9. *Increase the effectiveness of your handshake.* Shake firmly without creating pain, and make enough eye contact to notice the colour of the other person's eyes. When you take that much trouble, you project care and concern.[16]

10. *Stand up straight and use other nonverbal signals of self-confidence.* Practise having good posture. Minimize fidgeting, scratching, foot-tapping, and speaking in a monotone. Walk at a rapid pace, without appearing to be panicked. Dress fashionably, without going to the extreme that people notice your clothes more than they notice you.

11. *Be willing to take personal risks.* Charismatic leaders are typically risk-takers, and risk-taking adds to their charisma. Risks you might take would include extending additional credit to a start-up business, suggesting a bright but costly idea, and recommending that a former felon be given a chance in your firm.

12. *Be self-promotional.* Charismatic leaders are not shy. Instead, they toot their own horns and allow others to know how important they are. Without appearing self-absorbed, you, too, might let others know of your tangible accomplishments. Explain to others the key role that you played on your team or how you achieved a few tough goals.

Despite the importance of developing charisma, being excessively and flamboyantly charismatic can backfire because others may perceive you as self-serving. Therefore, the idea is to sprinkle your charisma with humility, such as admitting when you make a mistake.

DEVELOPING TEAM LEADERSHIP SKILLS

As organizations continue to increase their use of teams, some of the best opportunities for practising leadership occur as a team leader. A team leader typically reports to a higher-level manager. The team leader is not a boss in the old-fashioned sense but a facilitator or coach who shares decision-making with team members. (A facilitator is a person who helps make things happen without taking control.) A team leader practises **participative leadership**, or sharing authority with the group. Self-Assessment Quiz 8-2 gives you an opportunity to gauge your attitudes toward being a participative leader.

Self-Assessment Quiz 8-2

WHAT STYLE OF LEADER ARE YOU OR WOULD YOU BE?

Directions: Decide whether each of the following statements is "Mostly true" or "Mostly false."

	Mostly true	Mostly false
1. I am more likely to take care of a high-impact assignment myself than turn it over to a group member.	_____	_____
2. I would prefer the analytical aspects of a manager's job rather than working directly with group members.	_____	_____
3. An important part of my approach to managing a group is to keep the members informed almost daily of any information that could affect their work.	_____	_____
4. It's a good idea to give two people in the group the same problem and then choose what appears to be the best solution.	_____	_____
5. It makes good sense for the leader or manager to stay somewhat aloof from the group, so he or she can make a tough decision when necessary.	_____	_____
6. I look for opportunities to obtain group input before making a decision, even on straightforward issues.	_____	_____
7. I would reverse a decision if several of the group members presented evidence that I was wrong.	_____	_____
8. Differences of opinion in the work group are healthy.	_____	_____
9. I think that activities to build team spirit, like fixing up a poor family's house together on a Saturday, are an excellent investment of time.	_____	_____
10. If my group were hiring a new member, I would like the person to be interviewed by the entire group.	_____	_____
11. An effective team leader today uses email for about 98 percent of communication with team members.	_____	_____
12. Some of the best ideas are likely to come from the group members rather than the manager.	_____	_____
13. If our group were going to have a banquet, I would get input from each member on what type of food should be served.	_____	_____
14. I have never seen a statue of a committee in a museum or park, so why bother making decisions by a committee if you want to be recognized?	_____	_____
15. I dislike it intensely when a group member challenges my position on an issue.	_____	_____

(Continued)

16. I typically explain to group members what method they should use to accomplish an assigned task.   _____   _____

17. If I were out of the office for a week, most of the important work in the department would get accomplished anyway.   _____   _____

18. Delegation of important tasks is something that would be (or is) very difficult for me.   _____   _____

19. When a group member comes to me with a problem, I tend to jump right in with a proposed solution.   _____   _____

20. When a group member comes to me with a problem, I typically ask that person something like, "What alternative solutions have you thought of so far?"   _____   _____

Scoring and Interpretation: The answers in the participative/team-style leader direction are as follow

1. Mostly false	8. Mostly true	15. Mostly false
2. Mostly false	9. Mostly true	16. Mostly false
3. Mostly true	10. Mostly true	17. Mostly true
4. Mostly false	11. Mostly false	18. Mostly false
5. Mostly false	12. Mostly true	19. Mostly false
6. Mostly true	13. Mostly true	20. Mostly true
7. Mostly true	14. Mostly false	

If your score is 15 or higher, you are most likely (or would be) a participative or team-style leader. If your score is 5 or lower, you are most likely (or would be) an authoritarian leader.

Skill Development: The quiz you just completed is also an opportunity for skill development. Review the 20 questions and look for implied suggestions for engaging in participative leadership. For example, question 20 suggests that you encourage group members to work through their own solutions to problems. If your goal is to become an authoritarian (one who makes decisions primarily on his or her own), the questions can also serve as useful guidelines. For example, question 19 suggests that an authoritarian leader looks first to solve problems for group members.

On the pages that follow we describe nine techniques that would contribute to your effectiveness as a team leader, as outlined in Figure 8-2 (see page 181).

BUILD A MISSION STATEMENT

A starting point in developing teamwork is to specify the team's mission. The mission statement should contain a specific goal and purpose and should be optimistic and uplifting. Here is an example from a service team at a Cadillac dealership:

> To plan and implement a level of automobile service and repair of the highest quality, at a competitive price, that will delight customers and retain their loyalty.

The leader can help develop the mission statement when the team is first formed or at any other time. Developing a mission statement for a long-standing team breathes new life into its activities. Being committed to a mission improves teamwork,

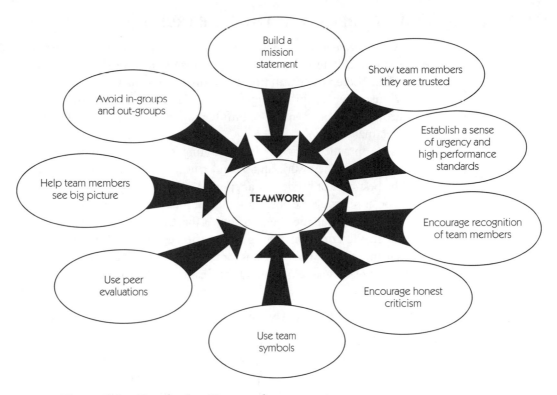

Figure 8-2   Developing Teamwork

as does the process of formulating a mission statement. A mission statement, however, needs to honestly represent the true goals and purpose of the team. An unrealistic mission statement that is not fully supported will do little for team morale or team development. Skill-Building Exercise 8-3 gives you practice in developing a mission statement for a team.

Skill-Building Exercise 8-3

DEVELOPING A TEAM MISSION STATEMENT

The class organizes into teams of about six people and appoints a team leader. Each team plays the role of a specific team within a company, government agency, or hospital; an example would be the customer service team at a gas and electric company. The task is to develop a mission statement approximating the type described in the text. The team leader might also take notes for the group.

Remember that a mission statement contains a goal and a purpose and is uplifting and optimistic. It should also differentiate your team from other teams within the organization (class). Allow about 20 minutes for preparing the mission statements. The groups then compare mission statements. One representative from each group presents the mission statements to the rest of the class.

SHOW YOUR TEAM MEMBERS THAT THEY ARE TRUSTED

An effective leader is perceived as honest and trustworthy, and he or she trusts team members. The leader should recognize and reward ethical behaviour, particularly when there is a temptation to be dishonest—as when reporting a quality defect to a customer or preparing tax returns. Raise expectations of honesty by telling group members you are confident they will act in ways that bring credit to the organization.[17]

A practical way of demonstrating trust in group members is to avoid closely monitoring their work, and second-guessing their decisions about minor matters such as the best type of border for a report. A **micromanager** is one who closely monitors most aspects of group members' activities, sometimes to the point of being a control freak. As a result, the group members do not feel that the leader or manager trusts them to make even the smallest decisions. One manager checked travel websites himself for the best deal after a team member booked plans for a business trip. As a result, team members felt that they were not trusted to care about the financial welfare of the company.

ESTABLISH A SENSE OF URGENCY AND HIGH PERFORMANCE STANDARDS

To build teamwork, members need to believe that the team has urgent, constructive purposes. A demanding performance challenge helps create and sustain the team. Team members also want to know exactly what is expected of them. The more urgent and relevant the rationale, the more likely it is that the team will perform well.[18] Based on this information, as a team leader you might project a sense of urgency and encourage setting high goals.

ENCOURAGE TEAM MEMBERS TO RECOGNIZE EACH OTHER'S ACCOMPLISHMENTS

Members of a high-spirited team look for ways to encourage and praise each other, including the traditional "high five" signifying an important contribution to the team. Encouragement and praise from the team leader is important, but team members also play an important role in giving positive reinforcement to each other. Team spirit develops as members receive frequent positive feedback from each other.[19]

ENCOURAGE HONEST CRITICISM

A superficial type of camaraderie develops when team members avoid honestly criticizing one another for the sake of group harmony. Avoiding criticism can result in groupthink. As a team leader, you should therefore explain that being a good team player includes offering honest feedback on mistakes and flawed ideas. The team benefits from mutual criticism. A stronger team spirit will develop because team members realize they are helping one another through honest feedback.

USE TEAM SYMBOLS

Teamwork on the athletic field is enhanced by team symbols such as uniforms and nicknames. Symbols can also be an effective team-builder in business. Trademarks, logos, mottoes, and other indicators of products both advertise the company and signify a joint effort. Company jackets, caps, T-shirts, mugs, ballpoint pens, and business cards can be modified to symbolize a work unit. As a team leader, you might therefore invest part of your team's budget in an appropriate symbol. Use the opportunity to practise participative leadership. Conduct a group problem-solving session to develop a team logo to place on a T-shirt or cap.

Caution: Screen team logo suggestions carefully. A member of a production team at a Harley-Davidson plant suggested that each team member tattoo his or her arm with a drawing of an armadillo!

USE PEER EVALUATIONS

In the traditional performance-evaluation system, the manager evaluates group members at regular intervals. With peer-evaluation systems, the team members contribute to the evaluation by submitting evaluations of one another. The evaluations might consist of filling out rating forms about one another's performance. Sometimes brief essays are written about other team members and then synthesized by the team leader.

Peer evaluations contribute to teamwork because team members realize that helping one another becomes as important as helping the boss. Similarly, team members recognize that pleasing one another counts as much as pleasing the boss.

As a team leader, you might not have the authority to initiate a peer-evaluation system without first checking with your manager. Making a recommendation for peer input into evaluations might demonstrate that you are committed to participative leadership.

HELP TEAM MEMBERS SEE THE BIG PICTURE

The team is likely to work together more smoothly when members have a clear understanding of how their work contributes to the company. Communicating the mission as described earlier is a good starting point. Showing the team its specific contribution to the overall organization is equally important. As the team leader you might create a flow chart that tracks an order from the time it is taken to when it is delivered. Show the team its role at each step. The team members may be aware of how they contribute to the team, but not how the team contributes to the success of the organization.[20] The team leader of a shipping department explains to his team regularly, "Let's keep this clearly in mind. A big factor in determining whether a customer stays with us is whether the goods arrive on time and in good shape."

MINIMIZE FORMATION OF IN-GROUPS AND OUT-GROUPS

An established leadership theory, the **leader-exchange model**, provides useful information for the aspiring team leader. According to this theory, leaders establish unique working relationships with group members. By so doing, they create in-groups and out-groups. The in-groups become part of a smoothly functioning team headed by the leader. Out-group members are less likely to experience good teamwork.[21] Figure 8-3, on page 184, depicts the major concept of the leader-exchange model.

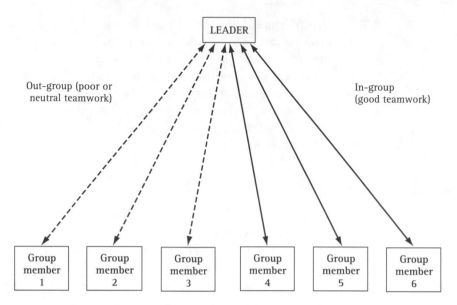

Figure 8-3   The Leader-Member Exchange Model

The in-group may develop because the leader prefers certain group members and therefore is motivated to form good working relationships with them. Conversely, the leader may neglect to form good relationships with people with whom he or she has limited rapport. First impressions count heavily when the leader decides on who is "in" and who is "out." A team leader should therefore guard against the formation of out-groups just because he or she is not fond of several team members or because a given team member gives a poor first impression.

The leader-exchange model does not mean that the team leader should avoid forming unique relationships with team members—what should be avoided is forming an out-group. One study investigated the relationships a group of female sales managers established with both male and female members of their sales groups. Treating members differently based on their needs contributed to leadership effectiveness, as evidenced in good team results.[22] An example of a unique relationship would be to give more recognition to a sales representative who craved recognition.

DEVELOPING YOUR LEADERSHIP POTENTIAL

Much of this book deals directly and indirectly with information that could improve your leadership effectiveness. Chapter 3, on communications, is a case in point. Improving your communications effectiveness would be one way to better your ability to lead people. Formal education and leadership development programs also contribute to increased leadership potential. (Many such programs include some of the activities found in this chapter.) Below we describe six additional strategies for developing your leadership potential. Also, see Skill-Building Exercise 8-4 about maintaining a personal leadership journal.

Skill-Building Exercise 8-4

MY PERSONAL LEADERSHIP JOURNAL

A potentially important aid in your development as a leader is to maintain a journal or diary of your leadership experiences. Make a journal entry within 24 hours after you carried out a leadership action of any kind, or failed to do so when the opportunity arose. You will therefore have entries dealing with leadership opportunities both capitalized upon and missed. An example, "A few of my neighbours were complaining about trash flying around the neighbourhood on trash pick-up days, particularly when the wind was strong. I took the initiative to send emails and flyers to neighbourhood residents discussing what could be done about the problem. I suggested that people pack their recycling boxes more tightly. I also suggested ever-so-politely that people should pick up their own flying trash. Soon the problem just about disappeared."

Also include in your journal such entries as feedback you receive on your leadership ability, leadership traits that you appear to be developing, and leadership ideas you learn about. Also, keep a list of leadership articles and books you intend to read. You might also want to record observations about significant acts of leadership or leadership blunders that you have observed in others, either firsthand or through the media.

Review your journal monthly, and make note of any progress you think you have made in developing your leadership skills. Also, consider preparing a graph of your progress in developing leadership skills. The vertical axis can represent skill level on a 1-to-100 scale, and the horizontal axis might be divided into time intervals, such as calendar quarters.

1. *Acquire broad experience.* Because leadership varies somewhat with the situation, a sound approach to improving leadership effectiveness is to attempt to gain supervisory experience in different settings. A person who wants to become an executive is well-advised to gain supervisory experience in at least two different organizational functions, such as marketing and operations.

   First-level supervisory jobs are an invaluable starting point for developing your leadership potential. It takes considerable skill to manage a fast-food restaurant or direct a public playground during the summer. First-level supervisors frequently face situations in which group members are poorly trained, poorly paid, and not well motivated to achieve company objectives. Motivating and inspiring entry-level workers is one of the major challenges facing organizations. One of the lessons learned from the US Marines is that if you want to fire up the front line, you must use discipline to develop pride. The point is that entry-level workers often take pride in being able to abide by tough rules.[23]

2. *Model effective leaders.* Another strategy for leadership development is to observe capable leaders in action and then model some of their approaches. You may not want to copy a particular leader entirely, but you can incorporate a few of the behaviour patterns into your own leadership style. For instance, most inexperienced leaders have difficulty confronting others. Observe how a skilled confronter handles the situation, and try that person's approach the next time you have unfavourable news to communicate to another person.

3. *Self-develop leadership traits and behaviours.* Study the leadership traits and behaviours described earlier in this chapter. As a starting point, identify several attributes you think you could strengthen within yourself, given some determination and perhaps combined with the right training program. For example, you might decide that with some effort you could improve your sense of humour. You might also believe that you could remember to encourage honest criticism within the team. It is also helpful to obtain feedback from valid sources (such as a trusted manager) about which traits and behaviours you particularly need to develop.

4. *Become an integrated human being.* A philosophical approach to leadership suggests that the model leader is first and foremost a fully functioning person. According to William D. Hitt, mastering the art of leadership comes with self-mastery. Leadership development is the process of self-development. As a result, the process of becoming a leader is similar to the process of becoming an integrated human being. For example, you need to develop values that guide your behaviour before you can adequately guide the behaviour of others.

   The model (or ideal) leader, according to Hitt, must possess six character traits: identity (know thyself), independence, authenticity, responsibility, courage, and integrity.[24] All of these traits have everyday meanings, but they can also have personal meanings. Part of becoming an integrated person is to answer such questions as "What do I mean when I say I have integrity?"

   Another approach to becoming an integrated human being, and therefore a more effective leader, is to figure out how you perceive the world. For example, if you perceive yourself as inferior to most people, you will forever be in competition with others to impress them. You will even compete rather than work collaboratively with team members.[25]

5. *Practise a little leadership.* An effective way of developing your leadership skills is to look for opportunities to exert a small amount of helpful leadership, in contrast to waiting for opportunities to accomplish extraordinary deeds. The "little leadership" might involve such behaviours as mentoring a struggling team member, coaching somebody about how to use a new high-tech device, or making a suggestion about improving a product. In the words of Michael E. McGill and John W. Slocum, Jr., "For those who want to stand atop the dugout, dance with the elephants, fly with the buffaloes, soar with eagles, or perform other mystical and heroic acts of large leadership, our little leadership may seem all too managerial, too modest, and too mundane."[26]

6. *Help your leader lead.* According to Michael Useem, leaders need your assistance so they can do a good job. "If people are afraid to help their leaders lead, their leaders will fail."[27] A group member is often closer to the market and closer to how the product is used. Therefore, he or she can provide useful information to the person in the formal leadership position. When you help the people above you avoid a mistake or capitalize upon an opportunity, you help the entire company. At the same time you are developing your ability to take the initiative and lead.

SUMMARY

Effective leadership depends on having the right personal characteristics and taking appropriate action. Leadership is the ability to inspire support and confidence among the people who are needed to achieve organizational goals. People can exercise leadership whether or not they occupy a formal leadership position.

Certain traits contribute heavily to leadership effectiveness. Among these are self-confidence, trustworthiness, assertiveness, emotional stability, a sense of humour, self-awareness and self-objectivity, cognitive skills and clarity, passion and enthusiasm, and emotional intelligence.

Although charisma depends heavily on personal characteristics, people can work toward being charismatic. Suggestions for behaving charismatically include the following:

1. Communicate a vision.

2. Make frequent use of metaphors and analogies.

3. Inspire trust and confidence.

4. Be highly energetic and oriented to goals and action.

5. Be emotionally expressive and warm.

6. Make ample use of true stories.

7. Smile frequently.

8. Be candid.

9. Make others feel important.

10. Shake hands effectively.

11. Appear self-confident through nonverbal signals.

12. Take personal risks.

13. Be self-promotional.

A team leader acts as a facilitator or coach who shares decision-making with team members, thus practising participative leadership. The following are some techniques to employ in becoming an effective team leader:

1. Build a mission statement.

2. Show team members that they are trusted.

3. Establish a sense of urgency and high performance standards.

4. Encourage team members to recognize each other's accomplishments.

5. Encourage honest criticism.

6. Use team symbols.

7. Use peer evaluations.

8. Help team members see the big picture.

9. Minimize the formation of in-groups and out-groups.

In addition to participating in formal leadership development programs, leadership potential can be developed through the following five strategies: (1) acquire broad experience; (2) model effective leaders; (3) self-develop leadership traits and behaviours; (4) become an integrated human being (a fully functioning person); (5) practise small leadership acts; and (6) help your leader lead.

An Interpersonal Relations Case Problem

LOW-KEY MARK HURD GETS THE TOP SPOT AT HP

Mark V. Hurd, an affable midwesterner who is almost entirely unknown in Silicon Valley, was chosen as the new CEO at Hewlett-Packard. He replaces Careleton S. ("Carly") Fiorina who was fired for not delivering on her promises of outstanding profits and an elevated stock price. Hurd, 48, is best known for his turnaround of NCR, the maker of automated teller machines and electronic cash registers. His supporters say he has developed a reputation for building trust within NCR.

Patricia C. Dunn, Hewlett's board chair, said the directors chose Hurd from a short list of candidates in part because of his "straightforward style" and his recognition of the importance of the corporate culture. "We are impressed by his emphasis on developing internal talent while reaching outside for new skills, his understanding of culture in a company's success and his personal integrity," Dunn said in a statement. "His straightforward style has won the respect of employees, customers, and investors." Hurd is also considered quiet and hardworking, but not particularly charismatic. In contrast, his predecessor Fiorina was considered by many to be flashy and charming.

Born in New York City, Hurd attended Baylor University in Waco, Texas, on a tennis scholarship. He received a degree in business administration in 1979, and went to work for NCR soon after that. He has spent the last 25 years at NCR in Dayton, Ohio, the last two years as its president and chief executive.

Despite his fairly low profile, Hurd is widely credited with rescuing NCR when its stock price was languishing and is profits were in decline. "When he took over as CEO of NCR, you had a company without a sense or urgency, a company that wasn't doing much of anything," said Reik Read, an outside analyst. "He had to undo the culture and bring back the sense of urgency." He was willing to lay off managers and other workers he did not believe were performing well.

Read described Hurd as a team builder who is "very likeable." But he is also "the kind of guy who is a change agent, a disruptive force," Read said. Hurd is considered to have a technical background and a willingness to share the spotlight. One of Hurd's first major decisions at HP was to lay off 14 000 workers in order to reduce costs.

Case Questions

1. Which leadership traits does Hurd appear to possess?
2. Which team leadership skills and behaviours does Hurd appear to possess?
3. How will Hurd succeed as CEO of HP if he rates so low on charisma?

Source: Laurie J. Flynn, "New Leader Is Called a Trust Builder," March 30, 2005; *The New York Times.* Reprinted with permission.

An Interpersonal Relations Case Problem

CHARISMATICALLY CHALLENGED COLLEEN

Twenty-seven-year-old Colleen McFerguson worked as a merchandising specialist for SmartMart, one of the largest international retail chains. Based in Canada, SmartMart also has a strong presence in the United States, Europe, Japan, and Hong Kong. Colleen began her employment with SmartMart as a cashier, and two years later she was invited into the training program for merchandising specialists.

Colleen performed well as a merchandising trainee in the soft-goods line. Her specialty areas included men's, women's, and children's clothing; linens and bedding; men's and women's jewellery; and home decorations. For several years in a row, Colleen received performance evaluation ratings of above average or outstanding. Among the write-in comments made by her supervisors were "diligent worker," "knows the tricks of merchandising," "good flair for buying the right products at the right price," and "fits right into the team."

Despite the positive performance appraisals supported with positive comments, Colleen had a gnawing discontent about her career at SmartMart. Despite five years of good performance, she was still not invited to become a member of the group called "SmartTrackers." The SmartTrackers are a group of merchandising and operations specialists who are regarded as being on the fast track to becoming future SmartMart leaders. The leaders hold high-level positions such as head merchandiser, regional vice-president, and store manager.

Several times when Colleen inquired as to why she was not invited to join the SmartTrackers, she was told something to the effect that she was not quite ready to be included in this elite group. She was also told not to be discouraged because the company still valued her contribution.

One day Colleen thought to herself, "I'm headed toward age 30, and I want a great future in the retail business now." So she convinced her boss, the merchandising supervisor (Evan Tyler), to set up a career conference between Colleen, Evan, and Evan's boss (Heather Bridges), the area merchandising manager. She let Evan know in advance that she wanted to talk about her potential for promotion.

Evan started the meeting by saying, "Colleen, perhaps you can tell Heather and me again why you requested this meeting."

Colleen responded, "Thanks for asking, Evan. As I mentioned before, I'm wondering what you think is wrong with me. I receive a lot of positive feedback about my performance, but I'm not a SmartTracker. Also, you seem to change the subject when I talk about wanting to become a merchandising supervisor and eventually a merchandising executive. What am I doing wrong?"

Heather responded, "Evan and I frequently talk about the performance and potential of all our merchandising specialists. You're a good performer, Colleen, but you lack that little spark that makes a person a leader. You go about your job efficiently and quietly, but that's not enough. We want future leaders of SmartMart to make an impact."

Evan added, "I go along with Heather's comments. Another point, Colleen, is that you rarely take the initiative to suggest ideas. I was a little shocked by your request for a three-way career interview because it's one of the few initiatives you've taken. You're generally pretty laid-back."

"Then what do I have to do to convince you two that I should be a SmartTracker?" asked Colleen.

Heather replied, "Start acting more like a leader. Be more charismatic." Evan nodded in agreement.

Case Questions

1. What career advice can you offer Colleen McFerguson?

2. What might Colleen do to develop more charisma?

3. What is your opinion of the fairness of the SmartTracker program?

QUESTIONS FOR DISCUSSION AND REVIEW

1. Informal observation suggests that people who were voted "most likely to succeed" in high school are frequently found in leadership positions later in life. What explanation can you offer for the frequent accuracy of these predictions of success?

2. How do you explain the fact that a person can be a leader even though he or she does not have a job that includes responsibility for others?

3. What does it mean to say that a person has the "right stuff" for being a leader?

4. Assertiveness is said to be important for leadership effectiveness. Can you give an example of an effective leader who is downright aggressive and obnoxious? (If necessary, give an example from sports leadership.)

5. A sense of humour is important for leadership effectiveness, yet telling rehearsed jokes is not considered effective. How do you account for this discrepancy?

6. What does the term *self-objectivity* mean to you, and why is it important for leadership?

7. What can you do this week to increase your charisma?

8. In what ways do the concepts of charismatic leadership and participative leadership differ substantially from one another?

9. Assume that a student obtains a part-time job as an assistant store manager. What can this person do to capitalize on the position to gain leadership experience?

10. Using your Research Navigator, locate article AN22232100. The article presents an interview with Karen Maidment, Chief Financial and Administrative Officer of BMO Financial Group and Canada's CFO of the year for 2006. Topics discussed include opportunities and challenges created for North American companies by globalization, the importance of the Asia-Pacific region in international trade, and her views on leadership. After reading this article, compare some of her views and ideas with those in this chapter. How are views similar and/or different from those in this chapter?

Research
Navigator.com

WEBLINKS

The following sites provide leadership assessments you can use to discern your leadership styles and traits as well as learn about leadership:

http://www.ccl.org
This is the site for the Centre for Creative Leadership.

http://www.dalecarnegie.com
This site has "Free Weekly Tips" for ideas about leadership development.

www.aimmconsult.com
Test your leading and influencing skills.

www.spacecolony.com
This is a problem-solving and leadership game that you can download for free (and it's fun!).

Chapter 9

Motivating Others

Learning Outcomes

After reading and studying this chapter and doing the exercises, you should be able to

- Motivate many people by responding to their self-interests.
- Apply positive reinforcement to motivate people in many situations.
- Make effective use of recognition to motivate others.
- Apply expectancy theory as a comprehensive way of motivating others.
- Diagnose many situations to analyze the strength of motivation present.

Motivation consultant Bob Nelson says on his website (www.nelson-motivation. com) that giving merchandise awards creates some problems. He notes that often the trinkets that employees are given to motivate them are perceived as a joke to many employees. "In other instances," he notes, "trinkets have become an outright insult. Sure, the first coffee mug you get for finishing a project is nice, but how many coffee mugs does one person need? Same with pen sets, t-shirts, and even certificates of appreciation. Just yesterday, I was reviewing the employee focus group comments on the topic of recognition from a large client. I noted employees were clear about what they did not want:

- *'No pens, pen sets, or watches'*
- *'No clocks, paperweights, or t-shirts'*
- *'Too many mugs'*

"Trophies, plaques, nominal gifts, and mementos fall into the same category from the employees' perspective. And printing your organization's logo on the merchandise doesn't magically transform it into something of value, especially if the object is something employees could have purchased themselves."[1]

The comments of Bob Nelson (the "guru of thank you") hint at the complexity of motivating people. Handing out trinkets alone may not be an effective motivational device. **Motivation** has two meanings: (1) an internal state that leads to effort expended toward objectives and (2) an activity performed by one person to get another to accomplish work.

We often think of a manager or leader attempting to motivate group members. Yet many people in the workplace have a need to motivate others. To accomplish their work, people must motivate individuals who report to them, co-workers, supervisors, or customers. Developing motivational skills will therefore help you accomplish more work than you would if you relied strictly on the good nature and team spirit of others.

This chapter describes how to develop motivational skills based on four related explanations of motivation. We progress from the simplest to the most complex explanation. To start thinking through how to motivate others, do Self-Assessment Quiz 9-1.

Self-Assessment Quiz 9-1

MY APPROACH TO MOTIVATING OTHERS

Instructions: Describe how often you act or think in the way indicated by the following statements when you are attempting to motivate another person. Circle the appropriate number for each statement. Scale: Very infrequently (VI); Infrequently (I); Sometimes (S); Frequently (F); Very frequently (VF).

	VI	I	S	F	VF
1. I ask the other person what he or she is hoping to achieve in the situation.	1	2	3	4	5
2. I attempt to figure out whether the person has the ability to do what I need done.	1	2	3	4	5
3. When another person is heel-dragging, it usually means he or she is lazy.	5	4	3	2	1
4. I explain exactly what I want to the person I'm trying to motivate.	1	2	3	4	5
5. I like to give the other person a reward up front so he or she will be motivated.	5	4	3	2	1
6. I give lots of feedback when another person is performing a task for me.	1	2	3	4	5
7. I like to belittle another person enough so that he or she will be intimidated into doing what I need done.	5	4	3	2	1
8. I make sure that the other person feels treated fairly.	1	2	3	4	5
9. I figure that if I smile nicely I can get the other person to work as hard as I need them to.	5	4	3	2	1
10. I attempt to get what I need done by instilling fear in the other person.	5	4	3	2	1
11. I specify exactly what needs to be accomplished.	1	2	3	4	5
12. I generously praise people who help me get my work accomplished.	1	2	3	4	5
13. A job well done is its own reward. I therefore keep praise to a minimum.	5	4	3	2	1
14. I make sure I let people know how well they have done in meeting my expectations on a task.	1	2	3	4	5
15. To be fair, I attempt to reward people similarly no matter how well they have performed.	5	4	3	2	1

(Continued)

16. When somebody doing work for me performs well, I recognize his or her accomplishments promptly.	1	2	3	4	5
17. Before giving somebody a reward, I attempt to find out what would appeal to that person.	1	2	3	4	5
18. I make it a policy not to thank somebody for doing a job he or she is paid to do.	5	4	3	2	1
19. If people do not know how to perform a task, motivation will suffer.	1	2	3	4	5
20. If properly laid out, many jobs can be self-rewarding.	1	2	3	4	5

Total Score _____

Scoring and Interpretation: Add the circled numbers to obtain your total score.

90–100   You have advanced knowledge and skill with respect to motivating others in a work environment. Continue to build on the solid base you have established.

50–89   You have average knowledge and skill with respect to motivating others. With additional study and experience, you will probably develop advanced motivational skills.

20–49   To effectively motivate others in a work environment, you will need to greatly expand your knowledge of motivation theory and techniques.

Source: The idea for this quiz and a few of its items are from David A. Whetton and Kim S. Cameron, *Developing Management Skills*, 2nd ed. (New York: HarperCollins, 1991), pp. 336–337.

MOTIVATION SKILL BASED ON THE PRINCIPLE OF "WHAT'S IN IT FOR ME?"

The most fundamental principle of human motivation is that people are motivated by self-interest. This principle is referred to as "What's in it for me?" or WIIFM (pronounced *wiff'em*). Reflect on your own experience. Before working hard to accomplish a task, you probably want to know how you will benefit. If your manager asks you to work extra hours to take care of an emergency, you will most likely oblige. Yet underneath you might be thinking, "If I work these extra hours, my boss will think highly of me. As a result, I will probably receive a good performance evaluation and maybe a better-than-average salary increase."

If your instructor asks you to prepare a lengthy research paper, you might be motivated to work to the best of your ability. But before getting down to the task, it is likely that questions will have raced through your mind, such as "Will this paper elevate my grade?" or "Will I pick up information that will help me in my career?"

A perplexing issue is how the WIIFM principle explains why people are motivated to help others. Why would a company president donate gift baskets of food to the homeless? Why hire a virtually unemployable person for a nonproductive job in the mail room? People who perform acts of social good receive the reward of feeling better about themselves. In psychological terms, they satisfy their needs to nurture (take care of) others. More cynically, helping the unfortunate leads to recognition for being a humanitarian.

According to Gerald Kushel, to use the WIIFM principle in motivating others, you have to be aware of the intensity of the person's desire.[2] A person can be highly motivated, mildly motivated, or only slightly motivated, depending on the intensity of his or her WIIFM principle. A company might offer outstanding performers the opportunity to work at home one day per week. Employees who are intensely motivated to work at home will work virtually up to capacity to achieve a rating of outstanding performer. A recent Canadian study by Hewitt Associates found that of 232 companies surveyed, 60 percent currently offer the option of working at home and 70 percent of the companies plan to have this option in place by 2009.[3] Having *flex-time* hours may motivate employees who have busy personal lives and find it difficult to be at work at set times. Employees must be present for certain core hours on the job but may choose when to come to work and when to leave depending upon personal needs. According to Human Resources Development Canada, flex-time is widespread and has been gaining in popularity.[4]

To use the WIIFM principle in motivating others, you must find out what needs, desires, or motives a person is attempting to satisfy. In general language, responding to the needs of people is referred to as *touching their hot buttons.* You find out what these needs are by asking people what they want or by observing what interests them. For instance, the way a manager might motivate a recognition-hungry group member is to tell that person, "If you perform 10 percent above quota for six consecutive months, we will have a luncheon to congratulate you."

Employee needs have been classified in many ways, yet most of these lists overlap. According to a representative classification, 99 percent of employees are motivated by one or more of the following seven needs:

1. *The need for achievement.* Employees with strong achievement needs seek the satisfaction of completing projects successfully. They want to apply their talents to attain success, and they find joy in accomplishment for its own sake.

2. *The need for power.* Employees with a strong power need derive satisfaction from influencing and controlling others, and they aspire to becoming executives. These employees like to lead and persuade and be in charge of resources such as budgets.

3. *The need for affiliation.* Employees with a strong need for affiliation derive satisfaction from interacting with others, being part of a work group, and forming friendships. The same employees are motivated to avoid working alone for long periods of time.

4. *The need for autonomy.* Employees with a strong need for autonomy seek freedom and independence, such as having almost complete responsibility for a project. The same employees are motivated to avoid working in a team effort for long periods of time. Many industrial sales representatives (those who sell to companies) have a strong need for autonomy.

5. *The need for esteem.* Employees with a strong need for esteem want to feel good about themselves, and they judge their worth to a large extent based on how much recognition and praise they receive.

Skill-Building Exercise 9-1

BACKGROUND WORK FOR THE WIIFM

The class divides into pairs of students. In each pair, one student plays the role of a team leader who is developing a plan to highly motivate the team member being interviewed. The other student plays the role of the team member being interviewed. The twist to this role play, however, is that the team member reflects on his or her actual motivators.

The team leader might ask several or all of the following questions while conducting an interview for approximately 15 minutes. In addition, when the team member reveals an important piece of information, the team leader will dig for more details. The team leader should use effective listening skills, as described in Chapter 3. Suggested interview questions are as follows:

1. Why are you working on this team?

2. What can the company do to make you really happy?

3. What would be a fair reward for performing up to your capacity? On a 1-to-10 scale, how badly do you want this reward?

4. What would you consider an outstanding reward for performing up to your capacity? On a 1-to-10 scale, how badly do you want this reward?

5. What would you consider a fantasy reward for performing up to your capacity? On a 1-to-10 scale, how badly do you want this reward?

6. What do you hope to get out of this job?

A brief class discussion might follow the completion of the interviews. A key issue to address in the discussion is the extent to which the interview would be helpful in motivating the team member.

6. *The need for safety and security.* Employees with strong needs for safety and security seek job security, steady income, ample medical and dental insurance, and a hazard-free work environment.

7. *The need for equity.* Employees with a strong need for equity seek fair treatment. They often compare working hours, job responsibilities, salary, and privileges with those of co-workers, and they will become discouraged if co-workers are receiving better treatment.[5]

Recognizing such needs, as well as other needs and interests, helps you apply the WIIFM principle. Skill-Building Exercise 9-1 gives you the opportunity to do the preliminary work needed for applying this principle.

USING POSITIVE REINFORCEMENT TO MOTIVATE OTHERS

The most widely used formal method of motivating people in the workplace is **behaviour modification**, an attempt to change behaviour by manipulating rewards and punishments. Behaviour modification is based on a fundamental principle of human behaviour: the **law of effect**. According to the law of effect, behaviour that leads to a positive consequence for the individual tends to be repeated, whereas behaviour that leads to a negative consequence tends not to be repeated.

The focus of behaviour modification on the job is to reward employees for behaving in ways that support what the organization is attempting to accomplish, such as improved productivity. Our approach to skill development in behaviour modification is to emphasize positive reinforcement, because this is the modification strategy most widely used in the workplace. **Positive reinforcement** means increasing the probability that behaviour will be repeated by rewarding people for making the desired response. The phrase *increasing the probability* means that positive reinforcement improves learning and motivation, but is not 100 percent effective. The phrase *making the desired response* is also noteworthy. To use positive reinforcement properly, a reward must be contingent upon doing something right. Simply paying somebody a compliment or giving the person something of value is not positive reinforcement. Behaviour modification involves linking consequences to what the person has or has not accomplished.

Positive reinforcement is easy to visualize with well-structured jobs such as data entry or producing parts. Yet positive reinforcement is also used to encourage desired behaviour in highly paid, complex jobs. An accountant who developed a new method for the company to get paid faster might be rewarded with two extra days of vacation. A survey of how companies are using rewards indicated that a growing number of firms are giving specific rewards to workers who reach targeted business results.[6] As an example, a web specialist might be rewarded for developing a new corporate website that attracted more visitors who stayed longer and led to achieving or exceeding a specified sales volume.

Negative reinforcement *(or avoidance motivation)* means rewarding people by taking away an uncomfortable consequence of their behaviour. It is the withdrawal or avoidance of a disliked consequence. You are subject to negative reinforcement when you are told your insurance rate will go down if you receive no traffic violations for 12 months. The uncomfortable consequence removed is a high insurance premium. Removing the undesirable consequence is contingent upon your making the right response—driving within the law.

Be careful not to make the common mistake of confusing negative reinforcement with punishment. Negative reinforcement is the opposite of punishment. It involves rewarding someone by removing a punishment or uncomfortable situation.

To use behaviour modification effectively, certain rules and procedures must be followed. Although using rewards and punishments to motivate people seems straightforward, behaviour modification requires a systematic approach. The rules are specified from the standpoint of the person trying to motivate another individual, such as a group member, co-worker, supervisor, or customer.

Rule 1: State Clearly What Behaviour Will Lead to a Reward

The nature of good performance, or the goals, must be agreed upon by the manager and group member. Clarification might take this form: "We need to decrease by 40 percent the number of new credit card customers who have delinquent accounts of 60 days or more." Workers also need to know specifically which types of behaviour will lead to punishment, such as being late for work three or more times in one month.

Rule 2: Choose an Appropriate Reward

An appropriate reward or punishment is both effective in motivating a given person and feasible from the standpoint of the individual or the company. If one reward does not motivate the person, try another. The importance of choosing the right reward underscores the fact that not all rewards are reinforcers. A reward is something perceived as valuable by the person giving the reward. However, if the reward does not lead to strengthening a desired response (such as wearing safety goggles), it is not a true reinforcer.[7]

Figure 9-1 provides a ranking of factors by employees as to what would satisfy them on the job. At the same time, these factors can be translated into potential

---

The 2004 Job Satisfaction Survey conducted by the Society for Human Resource Management and CNNfn found the factors listed below as "very important" by 600 employees at a variety of companies. The list shows the order of importance of job satisfaction factors among employees as a group.

Rank According to Employees	*Rank According to You*
1. Benefits	_____
2. Compensation/pay	_____
3. Feeling safe in the work environment	_____
4. Job security	_____
5. Flexibility to balance work/life issues	_____
6. Communication between employees and senior management	_____
7. Relationship with immediate supervisor	_____
8. Management recognition of employee job performance	_____
9. Opportunities to use skills/abilities	_____
10. The work itself	_____
11. Overall corporate culture	_____
12. Autonomy and independence	_____
13. Career development opportunities	_____
14. Meaningfulness of the job	_____
15. Variety of work	_____
16. Career advancement opportunities	_____
17. Contribution of work to organization's business goals	_____
18. Organization's commitment to professional development	_____
19. Job-specific training	_____
20. Relationship with co-workers	_____
21. Networking	_____

Question: Why do you think modern employees rank benefits (e.g., medical insurance and life insurance) the most important job satisfaction factor?

Suggestion: Make your own ranking of the 21 factors. What big differences do you see between your ranking and the national ranking?

Figure 9-1   Ranking of Job Satisfaction Factors by 600 Employees

Source: Reprinted with permission from Pamela Babcock, "Find What Workers Want," *HR Magazine*, April 2005, p. 53. Reprinted with permission.

rewards for employees. For example, if employees value job security (factor number 4), a high-performing employee might be given some assurance of stable employment. Because employees rank all of these factors as very important job factors, all of them are potentially appropriate rewards.

Rule 3: Supply Ample Feedback
Behaviour modification cannot work without frequent feedback to individuals. Feedback can take the form of simply telling people they have done something right or wrong. Brief email messages or handwritten notes are other forms of feedback. Many effective motivators, including Jack Welch, the long-time CEO of General Electric, make extensive use of handwritten thank-you notes. Negative feedback by email should be written tactfully to avoid resentment.

Rule 4: Schedule Rewards Intermittently
Rewards should not be given on every occasion of good performance. **Intermittent rewards** sustain desired behaviours longer and also slow down the process of behaviours fading away when they are not rewarded. If each correct performance results in a reward, the behaviour will stop shortly after a performance in which the reward is not received. Another problem is that a reward given continuously may lose its impact. A practical value of intermittent reinforcement is that it saves time. Few managers or team leaders have enough time to dispense rewards for every correct action by group members.

Rule 5: Make Sure the Rewards Follow the Observed Behaviour Closely in Time
For maximum effectiveness, people should be rewarded soon after doing something right. A built-in, or intrinsic, feedback system, such as a computer program's working or not working, capitalizes on this principle. If you are administering rewards and punishments, strive to administer them the same day they are earned.

Rule 6: Make the Reward Fit the Behaviour
People who are inexperienced in applying positive reinforcement often overdo the intensity of spoken rewards. When an employee does something of an ordinary nature correctly, a simple word of praise such as "Good job" is preferable to something like "Fantastic performance." A related idea is that the magnitude of the reward should vary with the magnitude of the accomplishment.

Rule 7: Make the Rewards Visible
Another important characteristic of an effective reward is the extent to which it is visible, or noticeable, to other employees. When other workers notice the reward, its impact multiplies because other people observe what kind of behaviour is rewarded.[8] Assume that you are informed about a co-worker's having received an exciting assignment because of high performance. You might strive to accomplish the same level of performance. Rewards should also be visible, or noticeable, to the employee. A reward of five dollars per week added to a person's paycheque might be hardly noticeable, after payroll deductions. However, a bonus cheque for $200 might be very noticeable.

Rule 8: Change the Reward Periodically

Rewards do not retain their effectiveness indefinitely. Employees and customers lose interest in striving for a reward they have received many times in the past. This is particularly true of a repetitive statement such as "Nice job" or "Congratulations." It is helpful for the person giving out the rewards to study the list of potential rewards and try different ones from time to time.

A general approach applying to the previous rules is to look for creative ways to apply behaviour modification. The creativity might be in the selection of the reward, or how the reward is administered. Here are a few ideas:

- *Applause*: Choose an especially effective employee, and at the end of the week or month have co-workers gather and clap for the person.

- *Giraffe award*: Give a certificate saying, "Thanks for sticking your neck out." The name of the reward and the certificate reward risk-taking.

- *Safety jackpot*: Managers give "lotto" cards to employees who follow safety practices. Workers scratch off the cards to learn how many points they have won. Points are then redeemed via a gift catalogue or website.[9]

Now do Skill-Building Exercise 9-2 to practise several of these rules for using behaviour modification.

Skill-Building Exercise 9-2

BEHAVIOUR MODIFICATION

In both of the following scenarios, one student plays the role of the person attempting to modify the behaviour of (motivate) the other individual. Another student plays the role of the person who is the recipient of these motivation attempts.

Scenario 1: Rewarding a Customer Service Representative. The customer service manager carefully reviews customer service reports to discover that one service rep has resolved the most complaints for four weeks in a row. Since this rep has been on the job only six months, the manager wants to make sure the rep feels amply rewarded and appreciated. The manager calls the rep into his or her office to discuss this outstanding performance and give an appropriate reward.

Scenario 2: Rewarding Your Boss. The group member has just received a wonderful assignment from the boss, offering the opportunity to spend a few days with key customers who are located out of town. This is the group member's first really exciting extra assignment. As a consequence, the worker wants to encourage the boss to keep him or her in mind for future assignments of this nature. The boss was not expecting to be rewarded for making an assignment that fit the company's needs.

Others in the class observe the two scenarios so they can provide feedback on how well behaviour modification principles were applied.

USING RECOGNITION TO MOTIVATE OTHERS

Motivating others by giving them recognition and praise can be considered a direct application of positive reinforcement. Nevertheless, recognition is such a potentially powerful motivator that it merits separate attention. Also, recognition programs to reward and motivate employees are a standard practice in business and nonprofit firms. Examples would be rewarding high-performing employees with a crystal vase (company logo inscribed) or designating them "employee of the month." One Sears Canada store gives "employees of the month" preferred parking spaces to reward top performance in various departments. In keeping with the theme of this book, our emphasis is on individual, rather than organizational, use of recognition to motivate.

Recognition is a strong motivator because the craving for recognition is a normal human need. At the same time, recognition is effective because most workers feel they do not receive enough of it. Several studies conducted over a 50-year time span have indicated that employees welcome praise for a job well done as much as a regular paycheque. This finding should not be interpreted to mean that praise is an adequate substitute for salary. Employees tend to regard compensation as an entitlement, whereas recognition is perceived as a gift.[10] Workers, including your co-workers, want to know that their output is useful to somebody.

To appeal to the recognition needs of others, identify a meritorious behaviour and then recognize that behaviour with an oral, written, or material reward. The rules for the use of behaviour modification are directly applicable. You will notice that many of the rewards listed in Figure 9-1 are recognition related. The category *status symbols* might also be interpreted as a form of recognition. Some specific examples of using recognition to sustain desired behaviour (a key aspect of motivation) follow:

- A co-worker shows you how to do an important internet-based task that you were struggling with. Three days later, you send her an email message with a copy to the boss: "Hi Jessica, your suggestion about copying company logos was dynamite. I've used it five times with success since you showed me what to do." (You are reinforcing Jessica's helpful and cooperative behaviour.)

- As the team leader, you receive a glowing letter from a customer about how Lin, one of your team members, solved the customer's problem. You have the letter laminated and present it as a gift to Lin. (The behaviour you are reinforcing is good customer service.)

- One member of your department, Ahmed, is a mechanical engineer. While at a department lunch taking place during National Engineers Week, you stand up and say, "I want to toast Ahmed in celebration of National Engineers Week. I certainly wouldn't want to be sitting in this office building today if a mechanical engineer hadn't assisted in its construction." (Here the only behaviour you are reinforcing is Ahmed's goodwill, so your motivational approach is general rather than specific.)

An outstanding advantage of recognition is that, although it is a powerful motivator, it costs little or nothing. Recognition thus provides an enormous return on investment in comparison to a cash bonus. A challenge in using recognition effectively is that not everyone responds well to the same form of recognition. A good example is that highly technical people tend not to like general praise such as "Great job" or "Awesome."

Instead, they prefer a laid-back, factual statement of how their output made a contribution. Furthermore, women are slightly more responsive to praise than are men, as revealed in a recent study of working adults.[11]

Giving recognition to others as a motivational tactic is more likely to be effective if a culture of recognition exists within the company. This is true because the person giving the recognition will feel that what he or she is doing fits what top management thinks is appropriate behaviour. At the same time the recipient of the recognition is likely to take it seriously. The Job-Oriented Interpersonal Skills in Action box illustrates the meaning of a culture of recognition.

Job-Oriented Interpersonal Skills in Action

A CULTURE OF RECOGNITION AT KEYSPAN

A few weeks ago, Elizabeth Kousidis found a message on her voice mail from Bob Cattell, the chair and CEO of KeySpan Corp., where she works as an administrative assistant in sales and marketing. "He told me I was one of the company's unsung heroes," she says. "He even called me Betty, which is what everybody around here calls me. I was so surprised and happy."

Kousidis isn't the first person at KeySpan to be singled out for such praise. In fact, Cattell has been delivering messages of appreciation nearly every week for the last four years to employees who have been recognized—anonymously—by their managers for a job well done. His personal thumbs-up is not the only way good work is acknowledged at the fifth-largest distributor of natural gas in the United States. However, it reflects a corporate culture that is finding new ways to say thank-you to those who probably don't hear it enough.

In the past, says Catell, KeySpan had used traditional recognition and compensation plans, relying mostly on salary and "some modest incentive programs." Those rewards were tied to output and budgets and customer retention.

Kenny Moore, human resources official at KeySpan, found that the attack on the World Trade Centre in 2001 was an epochal event that confirmed his belief that employee recognition should be broader and deeper than the quid-pro-quo approach that typifies most American businesses.

"9/11 made heroes of everyone," he recalls. "I wanted to start rewarding people for who they are, not what they do. I looked for ways to recognize the employees in good times and bad, for things seen and unseen. Everyone is deserving at some point."

One day Moore sent flowers to two unsuspecting employees, one of them a manager. Their delighted responses encouraged him to continue, as he does to this day, despite the doubts of a colleague who felt that the gesture "did not acknowledge a specific behaviour. 'Your flowers don't discriminate!'" Moore recalls her saying.

After answering the questions below, you may want to examine the Canadian Scene with a focus on two Canadian companies.

Questions

1. Why do "unsung heroes" deserve recognition at KeySpan (or any other workplace)?

2. What is your take on the criticism that flowers sent to employees not based on any particular good performance are of limited value?

Source: Matthew Gilbert, "A Culture That Recognizes the Contribution Made by Unsung Heroes," *Workforce*, November 2004, © Crain Communications, Inc. Reprinted with permission.

The Canadian Scene

HOW DO COMPANIES MOTIVATE EMPLOYEES?

If you look at all the companies and organizations around you, armed with the theories and ideas from this chapter, you have to wonder what companies really do to get their employees to rise to the challenge of achieving company goals. It must be more than paycheques, as we have all met people with high-paying jobs who despise what they do and often do it poorly. We have also met people with low-paying jobs who love what they do. Here, we look at two companies and some of the ideas of their staff and managers.

Debra Elliott was a troubleshooter for The Body Shop Canada. At one trouble-spot location in Vancouver, she believed she increased profits by helping employees become more well-rounded as human beings. She states, "You can get excited selling soap if you think you're part of a bigger mission or vision." The employees began to use their volunteer time (The Body Shop has a policy of donating 16 hours per month of staff time for volunteering in the community) to help organizations within the store's neighbourhood. In the following year, profits increased by 500 percent. As the staff became involved locally, their morale rose. Obviously, so did their motivation. As the stature of The Body Shop increased, staff felt valued and recognized for their contributions.

Another example of using motivation to improve a company's growth took place at Acro Aerospace, also in British Columbia. A few years ago, Michael Coughlin took over as president. Turnover was high, morale was low, and employees did not trust anyone and were "intimidated by management." What did he do to turn the tide? He had meetings where employees could vent their frustrations, he chatted casually to employees, he made coffee free for everyone (not just for managers anymore), and he let employees have a say in what they did. He also recognized employee efforts with barbecues and other "fun" things. The result? Double-digit growth and Acro's winning of a Quality Council of BC Award of Distinction for People Focus.

These are just two examples of companies that used rewards, recognition, and other motivators to turn operations around. Poor profits became outstanding profits and low morale became high morale. If employees are achieving and obtaining the personal goals and rewards they want, they are more satisfied and are motivated to achieve company goals.

Source: Roberta Staley, "Satisfaction Guaranteed," *BC Business*, August 2000, pp. 29–37. Used with permission of author.

The Canadian Scene above illustrates how two individuals used recognition as a powerful motivator to make their businesses more profitable and productive.

USING EXPECTANCY THEORY TO MOTIVATE OTHERS

So far we have described motivating others through applying the principle of "What's in it for me?" (WIIFM) and behaviour modification, including recognition. We now shift to expectancy theory, a more comprehensive explanation of motivation that includes elements of the two other approaches. Expectancy theory is given special attention here for three reasons. First, the theory is comprehensive because it incorporates many different aspects of motivating others. Second, expectancy theory can help you diagnose motivational problems. Third, it gives the person attempting to motivate others many guidelines for triggering and sustaining constructive effort from group members.

CAPSULE OVERVIEW OF EXPECTANCY THEORY

The **expectancy theory** of motivation is based on the premise that how much effort people expend depends on the reward they expect to receive in return. (Notice the similarity to WIIFM?) Expectancy theory assumes that people are rational and logical. In any given situation, they want to maximize gain and minimize loss. The theory assumes that people choose among alternatives by selecting the one they think they have the best chance of attaining. Further, they choose the alternative that appears to have the biggest personal payoff. How intensely they want that alternative is also an important consideration. Given a choice, people select an assignment they think they can handle, and that will benefit them the most.

An example will help clarify the central thesis of expectancy theory. Hector, a 27-year-old credit analyst at a machine tool company, recognizes that he needs to increase his income by about $400 per month to cover his expenses. After carefully reviewing his options, Hector narrows his alternatives to the following three choices:

1. Work as a dining-room server one night a week and on most weekends, with a variable income of somewhere between $500 and $700 per month.

2. Work for an income tax preparation service about four months per year for 20 hours per week, yielding an annual income of about $6000.

3. Work extra hard at his regular job, including taking a course in corporate finance, to improve his chances of receiving a promotion and a salary increase of $600 per month.

Hector rejects the first choice. Although he knows he can do the work, he anticipates several negative outcomes. He would much prefer to engage in extra work related to his field of expertise. The unpredictable income associated with being a dining-room server is also a concern. Hector sees merit in the second alternative because income tax preparation work relates to his accounting background. Further, the outcome (amount of pay) is relatively certain. But Hector also has some concerns that working so many extra hours for four months a year could hurt his performance on his day job.

Hector decides to take a chance with the third alternative of going all out to position himself for promotion. He is confident he can elevate his performance, but he is much less certain that hard work will lead to promotion. Yet Hector attaches such high value to being promoted and upgrading his professional credentials that he is willing to gamble.

BASIC COMPONENTS OF EXPECTANCY THEORY

All versions of expectancy theory have the following three major components: effort-to-performance expectancy, performance-to-outcome expectancy, and valence.[12] Figure 9-2 presents a glimpse of expectancy theory.

Effort-to-Performance Expectancy
Effort-to-performance expectancy is the probability assigned by the individual that effort will lead to performing the task correctly. An important question rational people ask

---

Person will
be motivated
under these
conditions
{
A. Effort-to-performance expectancy is high: Person believes he
or she can perform the task.
B. Performance-to-outcome expectancy is high: Person believes
that performance will lead to certain outcomes.
C. Valence is high: Person highly values the outcomes.

Figure 9-2   A Basic Version of Expectancy Theory

themselves before putting forth effort to accomplish a task is this: "If I put in all this work, will I really get the job done properly?" Each behaviour is associated in the individual's mind with a certain expectancy, or subjective hunch of the probability of success.

Expectancies range from 0 to 1.0. The expectancy would be 0 if the person thought that there was no chance of performing the task correctly. An expectancy of 1.0 would signify absolute faith in being able to perform the task properly. Expectancies thus influence whether you will even strive to earn a reward. Self-confident people have higher expectancies than do those with low self-confidence. Being well-trained will also increase your subjective hunch that you can perform the task.

The importance of having high expectancies for motivation meshes well with a thrust in work motivation that emphasizes the contribution of **self-efficacy**, your confidence in your ability to carry out a specific task. If you have high self-efficacy about the task, your motivation will be high. Low self-efficacy leads to low motivation. Some people are poorly motivated to skydive because they doubt they will be able to pull the rip cord while free-falling at 200 kilometres per hour. A more technical definition and explanation will help you appreciate self-efficacy's contribution to motivation:[13]

Self-efficacy refers to an individual's convictions (or confidence) about his or her abilities to mobilize the motivation, cognitive resources, and course of action needed to successfully execute a specific task within a given context.

In short, if you are confident about your task-related skills, you will get your act together to do the task. This is one reason motivators need to give people the skills and confidence they need for them to exert effort.

Performance-to-Outcome Expectancy
Performance-to-outcome expectancy is the probability assigned by the individual that performance will lead to certain outcomes or rewards. When people engage in a particular behaviour, they do so with the intention of achieving a desired outcome or reward. Performance-to-outcome expectancies also range from 0 to 1.0. If you believe there is no chance of receiving the desired reward, the assigned probability is 0. If you believe the reward is certain to follow from performing correctly, the assigned probability is 1.0. For example: "I know for sure that if I show up for work every day this month, I will receive my paycheque."

Valence
A **valence** is the value, worth, or attractiveness of an outcome. It signifies how intensely you want something (as described in WIIFM). In each work situation there are multiple

outcomes, each with a valence of its own. Remember Hector, the credit analyst? The potential outcomes of working part-time as an income tax preparer would include extra income, new experience, and interference with his day job.

In the version of expectancy theory presented here, valences range from −100 to +100. A valence of +100 means that you desire an outcome strongly. A valence of −100 means that you are strongly motivated to avoid an outcome, such as being fired. A valence of 0 means that you are indifferent toward an outcome, and it is therefore of no use as a motivator. An outcome with a probable valence of 0 would be as follows: To gain the cooperation of co-workers, you promise them gold stars as a reward (or outcome).

Skill-Building Exercise 9-3 will help sensitize you to the importance of estimating valences when attempting to motivate others. A major problem faced by managers and others who attempt to motivate others is that they have limited knowledge about the valences of their motivators (or rewards).

Skill-Building Exercise 9-3

ESTIMATING VALENCES FOR APPLYING EXPECTANCY THEORY

Directions: Listed here are rewards and punishments (outcomes) stemming from the information in Figures 9-1 and 9-2. Also included is a space for rating the reward or punishment on a scale of −100 to +100. Work with about six teammates, with each person rating all the rewards and punishments. Compute the mean (average) rating for each reward and punishment.

Potential Outcome	Rating (−100 to +100)
1. A 20 percent salary increase	_____
2. Profit-sharing plan in successful company	_____
3. Stock ownership in company	_____
4. Fully paid three-day leave	_____
5. $7000 performance bonus	_____
6. $300 gift certificate	_____
7. Outstanding performance review	_____
8. Above-average performance review	_____
9. One-step promotion	_____
10. Two-step promotion	_____
11. Flexible working hours	_____
12. Chance to work at home one day per week	_____
13. Chance to do more of preferred task	_____
14. Take over for supervisor when supervisor is away	_____
15. Fancy job title without change in pay	_____
16. Bigger work area	_____

(Continued)

Potential Outcome	Rating (−100 to +100)
17. Private office	_____
18. Company-paid cellphone	_____
19. Wall plaque indicating accomplishment	_____
20. Employee-of-the-month designation	_____
21. Warm smile and word of appreciation	_____
22. Compliment in front of others	_____
23. Threat of being suspended for one month	_____
24. One-month suspension without pay	_____
25. Demotion to undesirable job	_____
26. Being fired	_____
27. Being fired combined with promise of negative references	_____
28. Being placed on probation	_____
29. Being ridiculed in front of others	_____
30. A 30 percent pay reduction	_____

After completing the ratings, discuss the following topics:

1. Which outcomes received the most variable ratings?
2. Which outcomes received the most similar ratings?
3. Which are the three most desirable rewards?
4. Which are the three most undesirable punishments?

Another analytical approach would be to compute the class mean for all 30 outcomes. Each student could then compare his or her rating with the class average.

To apply this technique to the job, modify the preceding outcomes to fit the outcomes available in your work situation. Explain to team members that you are attempting to do a better job of rewarding and disciplining and that you need their input. The ratings made by team members will give strong clues to which rewards and punishments would be the most effective in motivating them.

HOW MOODS INFLUENCE EXPECTANCY THEORY

Expectancy theory emphasizes the rational side of people, yet emotions still play a key role in determining the impact of expectancies, instrumentalities, and valences. Moods are relatively long-lasting emotional states that do not appear to be tied to a clear source of the emotion. For example, a person might be in a good mood despite experiencing a negative situation such as an automobile breaking down. Also, people may feel glum despite good news such as having won a prize.

Several studies have shown that moods shape people's perceptions of expectancies and valence in expectancy theory. A positive mood increases the perceived connection between effort and performance (E→P expectancy), between performance and desired outcome (P→O expectancy) and in the valence attached to those outcomes. When we are in a good mood, we are more likely to believe that we can accomplish a task, so we have more of a "can do" attitude. We are also more optimistic about the outcomes (rewards) of our effort, and the outcomes look even better to us.[14] The opposite might also be true—when we are in a bad mood we feel less capable of task accomplishment; we are more pessimistic about getting the reward; and the reward appears less enticing.

DIAGNOSING MOTIVATION WITH EXPECTANCY THEORY

An important potential contribution of expectancy theory to interpersonal relations is that it helps a person diagnose whether motivation is present, and the intensity of the motivation. In performing your diagnosis, seek answers to the following questions:

1. Does the person I am attempting to motivate have the skills and self-efficacy to do the job? If the person feels ill-equipped to perform, he or she will be discouraged and show very little motivation.

2. What assurance does the person have that if he or she performs the work the promised reward will be forthcoming? Does the company have a decent reputation for following through on promises? What about me? Have I established my credibility as a person who follows through on promises? (If you and/or the company are not trusted, motivation could be reduced to zero.)

3. How badly does the person want the reward being offered in the situation? Am I offering a reward that will make it worthwhile for the person to do what I need done? If the sum of the valences of the outcomes in the situation is close to 0 (some positive, some negative), motivation will be absent.

4. Are there any 0s in response to the first three questions? If there are, motivation will be absent, because the expectancy theory equation is Motivation = (effort-to-performance expectancies) × (performance-to-outcome expectancies) × (the sum of the valences for all the outcomes). Remember what happens when you multiply by 0 in an equation.

5. Is the person in a reasonably good mood? Perhaps the person is poorly motivated today because of being in a bad mood.

GUIDELINES FOR APPLYING EXPECTANCY THEORY

The information about expectancy theory presented so far provides ideas for motivating others. Here we present several additional specific guidelines to improve your skill in motivating others.

1. *Train and encourage people.* If you are a manager, you should give employees the necessary training and encouragement to be confident that they can perform the required task. Some employees who appear to be poorly motivated might simply lack the right skills and self-efficacy.

2. *Make the link between rewards and performance explicit.* Employees should be reassured that if they perform the job up to standard, they will receive the promised reward. It is sometimes helpful for employees to ask co-workers whether they received promised rewards.

3. *Make sure the rewards are substantial enough.* Some rewards fail to motivate people because, although they are the right kind, they are not in the right amount. The promise of a large salary increase might be motivational, but a 1 percent increase will probably have little motivational thrust for most workers.

4. *Understand individual differences in valences.* To motivate others in the workplace effectively, you must discover individual differences in preferences for rewards. An attempt should be made to offer a worker rewards to which he or she attaches a high valence. For instance, one employee might value a high-adventure assignment; another might attach a high valence to a routine, tranquil assignment. Also keep individual differences in mind when attempting to motivate customers. One customer might attach a high valence to a volume discount, while another might favour follow-up service.

5. *Use the Pygmalion effect to increase effort-to-performance expectancies.* The **Pygmalion effect** refers to the phenomenon that people will rise (or fall) to the expectations another person has of them. Even if these expectations are not communicated explicitly, the other person will catch on to the nonverbal language. As the levels of expectation increase, so will performance. High expectations thus become a self-fulfilling prophecy.

Skill-Building Exercise 9-4

APPLYING EXPECTANCY THEORY

One student plays the role of the manager of telemarketing (selling over the telephone). Another student plays the role of Terry, a telemarketing specialist who has been with the company for three months. Terry is 40 percent below target in selling magazine renewals. The manager calls Terry into the office for a discussion of the problem.

Terry goes on at length to explain how confusing the job has become. Terry makes comments such as "I don't even know if I have the right kind of voice for this job. People I reach on the phone think I'm just a kid." Terry also wonders what kind of money he can make in this job and whether it is a dead-end job. (The student who plays the role of Terry can improvise about more of these kinds of problems.)

The manager will apply expectancy theory to motivate Terry to achieve satisfactory performance. Other class members should jot down statements the manager makes that indicate the use of expectancy theory. Also, observe whether it appears that Terry is being helped.

It is difficult to keep all the points made about expectancy theory in your head at the same time. Nevertheless, with practice and by referring to this book and your notes, you can apply many of the ideas. Skill-Building Exercise 9-4 will help you get started in applying expectancy theory.

SUMMARY

Motivation refers to an internal state that leads to effort being expended toward achieving objectives and to an activity performed by one person to get another person to work. Managers, as well as people working by themselves, often need to motivate others.

The most fundamental principle of human motivation is that people are motivated by self-interest, referred to as "What's in it for me?" (WIIFM). Even those who help others are simultaneously helping themselves, in that they feel good doing so. In using the WIIFM principle, be aware of the intensity of a person's desire for a reward.

Behaviour modification is an attempt to change behaviour by manipulating rewards and punishments. Its key principle is the law of effect—behaviour that leads to a positive effect tends to be repeated, while the opposite is also true. The basic behaviour modification strategies are positive reinforcement, negative reinforcement, punishment, and **extinction**. Extinction is eliminating problem behaviour by systematically ignoring it. For example, if you ignore a co-worker's complaints about the boss, the co-worker may stop this behaviour, as it no longer gets your attention.

Rules for the effective use of behaviour modification include the following:

1. State clearly what behaviour will lead to a reward.

2. Choose an appropriate reward.

3. Supply ample feedback.

4. Schedule rewards intermittently.

5. Give rewards shortly after the event.

6. Make the reward fit the behaviour.

7. Make the reward visible.

8. Change the reward periodically.

A general approach to applying the above rules is to look for creative ways to apply positive reinforcement.

Motivating others by giving them recognition and praise is a direct application of positive reinforcement. Recognition is a strong motivator because it is a normal human need to crave recognition, and most workers feel they do not get enough recognition.

The expectancy theory of motivation assumes that people are decision-makers who choose among alternatives by selecting the one that appears to have the biggest personal payoff at the time. Expectancy theory has three major components: expectancies about being able to perform, expectancies about performance leading to certain outcomes, and valence (the value attached to the reward). A positive mood state can enhance the components of expectancy theory.

Expectancy theory is useful in diagnosing whether motivation is present by examining the strength of the expectancies and the valences of the rewards. If any element is 0, motivation will not be present. Expectancy theory provides important ideas for motivating others, including the following:

1. Train and encourage people.
2. Show the link between rewards and performance.
3. Make the rewards substantial enough.
4. Observe individual differences.
5. Use the Pygmalion effect to increase effort-to-performance expectancies.

An Interpersonal Relations Case Problem

MOTIVATING THE KITCHEN STAFF AT THE BLUE GARDENIA

Jimmy Gomez aspires to someday be the manager of a large hotel. To help work toward that goal he is working part-time on a degree in hospitality administration. He attends classes at various times to fit his demanding full-time position as the kitchen staff supervisor at the Blue Gardenia, a well-established downtown hotel. Gomez supervises a staff of about 45 kitchen workers, including food preparers, butchers, bakers, and cooks. The highly paid chefs report to the restaurant manager, Sonya Rosato, who is also Gomez's manager.

The average wage is $9.00 per hour for the kitchen staff reporting to Gomez. Half of these workers work part-time and receive almost no benefits. Full-time staff members receive a few modest benefits, such as vacation, a $25 000 life insurance policy, and medical insurance. Blue Gardenia management believes strongly that the company pays competitive wages for kitchen staff and that paying them much more would eat into profits too much.

During a goal-setting conference with Rosato, Gomez agreed that an important area for improvement in his operation would be to reduce turnover and increase productivity among the kitchen staff. Rosato pointed out that although the turnover rate for Gomez's employees was about average for kitchen staff in the geographic area (75 percent per year), it was still too high. If the turnover rate could be trimmed down to about 45 percent, it would save the hotel thousands of dollars in hiring and training costs. Also, less food would be wasted because trainees make so many mistakes in food

preparation. Skilled workers also drop fewer dishes and glasses.

Rosato and Gomez also agreed that lower turnover would mean more kitchen staff would have good job skills and therefore would be able to produce more. For example, a skilled salad-maker can make twice as many salads as a beginner. Another concern Rosato expressed was that many of the kitchen staff seemed lazy.

During the week following the meeting with his boss, Gomez kept thinking about the problem. He decided tentatively that he was really dealing with a motivational issue. He reasoned that if the staff were better motivated, they would stay with the job longer and obviously should not appear lazy. As a starting point in attempting to better motivate the kitchen staff, Gomez conducted a few informal interviews with them during breaks and toward the end of the workday. He asked 12 of the kitchen workers what Blue Gardenia management could do to keep kitchen staff on the job longer and working harder. A few of the comments Gomez collected were as follows:

- "What do you expect for $9.00 an hour? Some kind of superman? I work as hard as a factory worker, but I don't get paid like a factory worker."
- "This is like a dead-end job. If I could find a job with a better future, I'd be out of here in no time."
- "I like this job fine. But just like a few of the other guys here, I've got a problem. My wife and I are expecting a child. If I stay in this job, I won't be

(Continued)

able to support my child. My wife wants to drop out of work for a year to care for the baby."

- "Not me, but I think some of the workers here think management doesn't care much about them. So if they can find another job that pays even 35 cents more per hour, they're gone."

- "I like this kind of work. I mean, we're really doing some good. People like nice entertainment, and eating good food is a form of entertainment. Also, we're keeping people healthy and helping them live longer. Our food is made with the best ingredients. Even the beef we prepare is lean and healthy."

- "My gripe is not with the work, but that we don't get enough respect. The chef gets the glory, but we do a lot of the real work. I think I'm doing important work, but nobody tells me I am. Sometimes I think I'm treated like just another piece of kitchen equipment. A few of the other guys and gals feel the same way about how they're treated."

After the interviews were completed, Gomez thought to himself that he had a lot of information. Yet he wondered how he could translate all this information into an action plan that would reduce turnover and keep the kitchen staff working harder.

Case Questions

1. How effective do you think it was for Jimmy Gomez to interview members of the kitchen staff to investigate possible motivational problems?

2. What does the information revealed by the kitchen staff tell you about their valences?

3. Which needs among the people interviewed are not being satisfied?

4. What recommendations can you make to Blue Gardenia management about decreasing the turnover and increasing the productivity of the kitchen staff?

An Interpersonal Relations Case Problem

REWARDS AND RECOGNITION AT TEL-SERVICE

Tel-Service is a fast-growing customer service and fulfillment firm, based in New Jersey. The company's core business is responding to customer questions, complaints, and comments that arrive via 800-telephone numbers. Companies such as Sony, Tetley, and PR Newswire outsource much of their customer-service activities to Tel-Service. Any time a customer of the client companies calls the 800-number listed on the packaging and literature, they are actually reaching Tel-Service.

At Tel-Service headquarters, 300 employees respond to customer phone calls. To maintain high levels of both direct-customer and end-customer satisfaction, Tel-Service employees are closely monitored. Workers are evaluated based on criteria such as courtesy, thoroughness, and calls answered per hour. A particular challenge is meeting performance standards when dealing with very annoyed customers.

Up until one year ago, employee turnover at Tel-Service was unacceptably high. Employees stayed

at the job for an average of only eight months. Considering that each new employee received two months of training, the eight-month average stay was particularly troublesome to management. Nathan Samuels, the Director of Operations at Tel-Service, knew that the high turnover had to be reduced. An increasing amount of money was being invested in training staff, and the company had to rely on increasingly less-experienced customer service representatives (CSRs) to respond to customer inquiries. If the CSRs were doing a poor job, customers might complain, which could lead to Tel-Service's losing a client. Samuels recognized that skilled CSRs were critical to the success of the firm.

Samuels decided that the first step in fixing the high turnover problem was to determine what was wrong in the first place. He decided to interview a sample of CSRs. Samuels thought that a good perspective on the problem could be reached by interviewing experienced employees as well as those

(Continued)

less experienced. The sample consisted of those who had been working for the company for three years, and others who were barely out of training.

The interview questions focused mostly on the working atmosphere. Among the questions were "What do you enjoy about your work?" and "What could make your work time better?" Interviewees were encouraged to be frank, and it was made clear that there would be no repercussions from making negative comments. Based on the interviews, Samuels observed several themes:

- The more experienced employees remained because they needed the job. Most of these employees were not thrilled with the work, but they stayed with it to pay for necessities. Samuels reasoned that the motivation of this group of employees was not high enough to result in superior performance.

- The new employees were excited about the work but nervous about the horror stories told by their peers.

- CSRs felt overworked and underappreciated by the rude and degrading customers they dealt with daily.

Based on these interview findings, Samuels believed he had a good grasp of the problems facing the CSRs. After reading a few leadership trade journals, Samuels decided that a reward and recognition program might be enough to motivate the reps and make them feel appreciated. He decided to give some sort of reward for those employees who maintained a superior level of customer service. The reward would serve a dual function. First, it would motivate the CSRs to work harder to achieve their reward. Second, it would help the CSRs feel better appreciated by management to help compensate for the lack of appreciation by customers.

The plan was to hold an office party during which rewards would be presented. In this way, other employees in addition to the winner would receive something of value. After receiving approval from the CEO, Samuels decided that every three months one employee would win a vacation to Disney World. Tel-Service would pay for the accommodations and airfare. Samuels and the CEO thought that a reward of this magnitude would be very motivational.

The CSRs were elated when they heard about the new program. Average performance based on the standards in use jumped 39 percent, including the number of telephone calls handled per hour. For the next three months not a single CSR left without giving notice. Several clients sent letters or email messages explaining how satisfied their customers were with the telephone support. During this same period, two large new accounts joined Tel-Service through recommendations from other firms.

When the first three months were completed, it was time to reward the winner and throw the party. Since not all representatives could leave the phones at the same time, coffee and cake were placed at a central location where the reps could serve themselves at breaks. During lunch hour, when the largest number of reps were off the phone, the winner was announced—Kristine Santora. Although the competition was fierce, all employees were very proud of Santora. Samuels made sure to remind them that the start of the next contest was immediate, and everyone else had a chance to win. The reward program was instantly refuelled with new fervour and motivation.

After giving the reward of the Disney trip three times, Samuels phased down the program and replaced it with smaller, more personalized rewards like watches and sporting equipment. The office parties to celebrate the rewards were retained.

One year after the start of the program, CSR turnover at Tel-Service is approximately 15 percent, and the representatives appear happier in their jobs. According to Samuels, "I doubt we would have ever gotten the customer service rep problem under control without having implemented the reward and recognition program."

Case Questions

1. Identify the motivational techniques used by Samuels to enhance the performance of the CSRs.

2. What can Samuels do to keep the customer service staff motivated in the future?

3. Use expectancy theory to analyze why the reward and recognition program is working.

Source: Case prepared by Brian Romanko, Rochester Institute of Technology, November 2000.

QUESTIONS FOR DISCUSSION AND REVIEW

1. For what purpose would someone need to motivate his or her supervisor?

2. Almost every major airline hires a baggage transport company that delivers lost luggage to owners. The van drivers and luggage-delivery persons are typically men in their late 60s and beyond, and these workers are quite dependable. What motivates men in their 60s and 70s to do this sort of job, and to perform well?

3. If people really live by the WIIFM principle, how can a leader still achieve teamwork?

4. What evidence can you suggest that demonstrates that people who do exciting and interesting work still expect exceptional financial rewards?

5. Explain whether the ability to motivate others is a soft skill or hard skill.

6. Identify several rewards in Figure 9-1 that you think would be particularly effective in motivating managers and professionals. Explain your reasoning.

7. Answer question 6 for entry-level service workers, such as supermarket cashiers.

8. How do individual differences show themselves in attempting to motivate others?

9. How might you use expectancy theory to improve your own level of work motivation?

10. There are many theories and applications of theories of motivation. Using your Research Navigator, find a study that illustrates the application of a theory. For example, find a study that shows how positive reinforcement is being used to change a specific workplace problem. Share your study with others in the class.

Research
Navigator.com

WEBLINKS

www.vlib.org/overview.html
This is a virtual library with access to thousands of articles on psychology and other social sciences, including articles on motivation.

www.leadersdirect.com/motive.html
This site is about motivating others. Several other areas you can explore include leading, managing, and self-management.

www.bbll.com/ch26.html
This chapter from the web "book" *Lessons in Lifemanship* is about motivating others.

www.awards.com
A one-stop super-site for rewards and recognition.

www.topachievement.com/goalsetting.html
Learn how to write powerful goals in seven easy steps!

Chapter 10

Helping Others Develop and Grow

Learning Outcomes

After reading and studying this chapter and doing the exercises, you should be able to

- Recognize your responsibility for helping others in your work environment to grow and develop.
- Demonstrate how being a nurturing, positive person can influence the development of co-workers.
- Specify the behaviours and skills that are helpful in being a mentor and role model.
- Acquire beginning skills in coaching and training.
- Deal with difficult people on the job.

Two months after being hired, Sing turned to her officemate. "I'm really stuck. I can't figure out how to track my days to submit my electronic attendance record for Human Resources. Every time I think I have the month done, it will not save when I try to submit it."

"Ah, a mentor moment!" replied her officemate, a professor with 18 years of experience. "This will just take a moment. Just pull your chair over here, and I'll show you as I do mine."

Fleming College recognizes the importance of mentors in the professional development of new faculty. New hires are paired with volunteer mentors who make themselves available for assistance in everything from using the classrooms' smart boards and managing student behaviour to dealing with pressing work–life issues. The mentoring becomes part of the mentor's weekly work hours and training is provided for those who would like to become mentors.[1]

This chapter describes the major ways in which employees help each other and lays the groundwork for skill development in these vital activities. Among the key helping roles are nurturing others, mentoring, coaching and training, and helping difficult people become more cooperative. A study of how new employees are developed, involving 378 recent graduates, underscored the importance of workers helping each other. Among the findings relevant here were that (1) buddying with a co-worker was the most helpful developmental method, and (2) the company in the study did not provide enough mentoring, despite its emphasis on mentorship.[2]

Do Self-Assessment Quiz 10-1 to gain preliminary insight into your attitudes toward helping others in the workplace.

Self-Assessment Quiz 10-1

ATTITUDES TOWARD HELPING OTHERS

Directions: Describe how well you agree with the following statements by circling the appropriate letter after each statement: Disagree (D); Neutral (N); Agree (A).

1. If I see a co-worker make a mistake, I do not inform him or her of the mistake.	D	N	A
2. It should be part of everybody's job to share skills and ideas with co-workers.	D	N	A
3. The manager should have exclusive responsibility for coaching people within the work unit.	D	N	A
4. I can think of many instances in my life when somebody thanked me for showing him or her how to do something.	D	N	A
5. I have very little patience with co-workers who do not give me their full cooperation.	D	N	A
6. To save time, I will do a task for another person rather than invest the time needed to show him or her how to do it.	D	N	A
7. I would take the initiative to take an inexperienced worker under my wing.	D	N	A
8. As a child, I often took the time to show younger children how to do things.	D	N	A
9. Rather than ask a co-worker for help, I will wait until the manager is available to help me.	D	N	A
10. It is best not to share key information with a co-worker because that person could then perform as well as or better than me.	D	N	A

Total Score: _____

Scoring and Interpretation: Use the following score key to obtain your score for each answer, and then calculate your total score.

1. D = 3, N = 2, A = 1	6. D = 3, N = 2, A = 1
2. D = 1, N = 2, A = 3	7. D = 1, N = 2, A = 3
3. D = 3, N = 2, A = 1	8. D = 1, N = 2, A = 3
4. D = 1, N = 2, A = 3	9. D = 3, N = 2, A = 1
5. D = 3, N = 2, A = 1	10. D = 3, N = 2, A = 1

25–30 Very positive attitudes toward helping, developing, and training others in the workplace. Such attitudes reflect strong teamwork and a compassion for the growth needs of others.

16–24 Mixed positive and negative attitudes toward helping, developing, and training others in the workplace. You may need to develop more sensitivity to the growth needs of others to be considered a strong team player.

10–15 Negative attitudes toward helping, developing, and training others in the workplace. Guard against being so self-centred that it will be held against you.

BEING A NURTURING, POSITIVE PERSON

A major strategy for helping others grow and develop is to be a nourishing, positive person. A **nurturing person** promotes the growth of others. Nurturing people are positive and supportive and typically look for the good qualities in others. A **toxic person** stands in contrast to a nourishing person because he or she dwells on the negative.[3] Visualize the following scenario to appreciate the differences between nurturing and toxic people:

> Randy, a purchasing specialist, enters the office, where two co-workers are talking. One is a nurturing person, the other toxic. With a look of panic, Randy says, "I'm sorry to barge in like this, but can anybody help me? I've been working for three hours preparing a file on the computer, and it seems to have vanished. Maybe one of you can help me retrieve it."
>
> Margot, the nourishing person, says, "I'm no computer expert, but since I'm not the one who lost the file, I can be calm enough to help. Let's go right now." Ralph, the toxic person, whispers to Margot: "Tell Randy to use his computer manual. If you help him now, you'll only find him on your doorstep every time he needs help."

If you listen to toxic people long enough, you are likely to feel listless, depressed, and drained. Toxic people have been described as *energy vampires* because they suck all the positive energy out of you.[4] Nurturing people, in contrast, are positive, enthusiastic, and supportive.

The guideline for skill development here is to engage in thoughts and actions every day that will be interpreted by others as nourishing. Following are three actions and attitudes that support being a nourishing person:

1. *Recognize that most people have growth needs.* Almost everybody has a need for self-fulfillment, although people vary widely in the extent of this need. If you recognize this need in others, it may propel you toward helping people satisfy their need. You might engage in interactions with co-workers such as sharing new skills with them, clipping relevant news articles, or telling them about an important new website you have discovered. You might also tell them about an exciting course you have taken that has increased your self-confidence.

2. *Team up with a co-worker in your department or another one so the two of you can form a buddy system.* Children in swimming programs and even soldiers in combat use the buddy system. The same system can be used by you and a friend to keep each other informed of decisions and events that could affect your careers. You might nurture your buddy by telling about growth opportunities in the company he or she might not have heard about. Your buddy would reciprocate. One person told her buddy about expanding opportunities for company employees who were fluent in both English and French. The two buddies, who already knew some French, worked together to become fluent.

3. *Be a role model for others.* An indirect way of being a nurturing, positive person is to conduct yourself in such a way that others will model your behaviour. By serving as a role model, you help another person develop. How to become a role model for co-workers is as comprehensive a topic as learning to be successful. Among the many factors that make you role-model material are

---

Skill-Building Exercise 10-1

THE NURTURING, POSITIVE PERSON

One student plays the role of Pat, a worker who is experiencing difficulty on the job and in her personal life. Pat approaches Leslie, a co-worker, during lunch in the company cafeteria and says: "What a day! I just received a rotten performance appraisal. If my work doesn't improve within a month, the company may let me go. To add to my woes, my fiancé has threatened to break off the engagement if I don't get a big raise or a promotion. I feel like my whole world is collapsing." The other person plays the role of Leslie, who attempts to be nurturing and positive in order to help get Pat out of the doldrums. Run the role play for about 10 minutes.

The rest of the class provides feedback on Leslie's skill in being nurturing and helpful. Jot down specific behaviours you think are most effective.

---

a strong work ethic, job expertise, personal warmth, good speaking ability, a professional appearance, and great ethics. Do you qualify yet, or do you need some more work?

Being a nurturing, positive person is a lifelong process rather than a tactic that can be used at will. Nevertheless, making a conscious attempt to be nurturing and positive can help you develop the right mindset. Skill-Building Exercise 10-1 provides an opportunity to practise being a positive person.

BEING A MENTOR TO CO-WORKERS

In Homer's tale *The Odyssey*, Mentor was a wise and trusted friend as well as a counsellor and adviser. The term *mentor* has become a buzzword in the workplace. A **mentor** is generally defined as an individual with advanced experience and knowledge who is committed to giving support and career advice to a less experienced person. The less experienced person is the **protégé** (from the French word for *protected*).

A mentor usually outranks the protégé and is older or more experienced. For present purposes, however, be aware that one co-worker can be a mentor to another. The Vancouver-based 1–800-GOTJUNK? purposefully hires employees over the age of 40. The people director of the company feels that the younger people can learn from their more-seasoned colleagues.[5] However, mentoring is not always just about age. As long as you are more experienced and wiser than a co-worker in some important aspect of the job, you can be a mentor. A person who is not a manager can also be a mentor in another important way. He or she can select an entry-level person in the firm and serve as the inexperienced person's coach and adviser. Even when a person has a high-ranking person as a mentor, you can also be his or her mentor. The reason is that having more than one mentor improves a person's chances for developing job and career skills.[6] Mentoring is more important than ever because it supports the modern, team-based organization. Also, after years of downsizing, many organizations have fewer managers available to mentor employees. Co-workers often have to fill this void. More people work together as equals, and they are expected to train and develop one another. Mentoring facilitates such learning and also supports the current emphasis on continuous learning.[7]

Mentoring often takes the form of the mentor and protégé communicating by email, referred to as *ementoring*. As the time of corporate professionals and managers has become more scarce, ementoring increases in practicality. Also, ementoring gives the protégé an opportunity to be mentored by someone who is geographically distant, even overseas. The person being mentored might send a quick email to the mentor explaining that he just received an outstanding performance review. The mentor might reply back with an email of encouragement. When asked about a problem facing the protégé, the mentor might reply with advice quickly. Answers by the mentor within 48 hours are recommended to communicate an attitude of concern.[8]

Serving as a mentor is an excellent way of helping others on the job. Mentoring is also gaining acceptance off the job. Many professors often continue mentoring relationships with past students as the student continues his or her education or begins a career. Many communities have developed programs whereby working adults volunteer to serve as mentors to youths. Mentoring in many of these programs is designed to help adolescents and teenagers succeed at school, avoid a life of crime and substance abuse, and gain early experiences in the workplace. To be a mentor, a person engages in a wide range of helping behaviours, all related to being a trusted friend, coach, and teacher. To prepare you for mentoring a less experienced person, a list of specific mentoring behaviours follows.[9] Mentoring is often not only a professional responsibility, it is often a highly satisfying personal one for both the mentor and the protégé.

- *Sponsoring.* A mentor actively nominates somebody else for promotions and desirable positions. In some situations, one person is asked to nominate a co-worker for a promotion to supervisor or team leader or for a special assignment.

- *Coaching.* A mentor gives on-the-spot advice to the protégé to help her or him improve skills. Coaching is such an important part of helping others that it receives separate mention in this chapter.

- *Protecting.* A mentor might shield a junior person from potentially harmful situations or from the boss. For example, the mentor might tell her protégé, "In your meeting today with the boss, make sure you are well-prepared and have all your facts at hand. He's in an ugly mood and will attack any weakness."

- *Sharing challenging assignments.* One member of the team does not ordinarily give assignments to another, yet in some situations you can request that your protégé help you with a difficult task. You would then offer feedback on your protégé's performance. The purpose of these high demands is to help the protégé develop more quickly than if he or she were not offered new challenges.

- *Acting as a referral agent.* The mentor sometimes refers the protégé to resources inside and outside the company to help with a particular problem. For example, the protégé might want to know how one goes about getting the employee benefits package modified.

- *Role modelling.* An important part of being a mentor is demonstrating to the protégé a pattern of values and behaviours to emulate. Several of the specific behaviours associated with being a role model were described earlier in connection with being a positive, nurturing person. In the opening example, mentors often attend a protégé's class and offer feedback and advice to improve teaching strategies and methodologies. The goal of such a visit is to help improve teaching ability in a supportive and non-threatening way.

- *Giving support and encouragement.* A mentor can be helpful just by giving support and encouragement. In turn, the protégé is supposed to support the mentor by offering compliments and defending the mentor's ideas. In a team meeting, for example, the protégé might make a statement such as "I think John's ideas will work wonders. We should give them a try."

- *Counselling.* A mentor listens to the protégé's problems and offers advice. Given that counselling plays such a central role in helping others, it, too, receives separate mention in this chapter.

- *Providing friendship.* A mentor is, above all, a trusted friend, and the friendship extends two ways. *Trusted* means that the mentor will not pass on confidential information or stab you in the back.

- *Encouraging problem-solving.* Mentors help their protégés solve problems by themselves and make their own discoveries. A comment frequently made to mentors is "I'm glad you made me think through the problem myself. You jogged my mind."

- *Explaining the ropes.* A general-purpose function of the mentor is to help the protégé learn the ropes, which translates into explaining the values and "dos and don'ts" of the organization.

- *Teaching the right skills.* The original role of the mentor in teaching skills (such as a master teaching an apprentice) is highly relevant today. Among the many skills a mentor can help the protégé develop are those dealing with information technology, customer service, corporate finance, and producing high-quality work.

- *Encouraging continuous learning.* A major role for the modern mentor is to encourage the protégé to keep learning. Part of encouraging lifelong learning is to emphasize that formal education and an occasional workshop are not sufficient for maintaining expertise in today's fast-changing workplace. The individual has to stay abreast of new developments through courses and self-study. A specific way in which the mentor can encourage continuous learning is to ask the protégé questions about new developments in the field.

As implied by the preceding list, mentoring is a complex activity that involves a variety of helping behaviours. To develop mentoring skills, you need to offer help to several people for at least six months. In preparation for becoming a mentor, it is helpful to think of the type of person you would prefer to have as a protégé. Skill-Building Exercise 10-2 is designed to help you think through this issue. Be prepared for a potential protégé seeking you out because many people serious about advancing their careers search for potential mentors with whom they have rapport. Similarly, if you are looking for a mentor, take the initiative to establish contact with someone you like and who you think could help you. A study conducted at York University recommends that companies using a mentoring system for training match mentor and protégé carefully and ensure that mentors are trained in mentoring skills.[10]

Mentoring is designed to help another individual grow and develop; yet mentoring can also help your employer at the same time. Workers who receive mentoring are likely to feel more satisfied about their jobs and stay with the organization longer. A study with over 1300 Army officers showed that officers who were mentored felt more emotionally committed to the Army than did their non-mentored counterparts. Furthermore, mentored officers felt more likely to stay in the Army, and were less likely to leave the military voluntarily.[11]

Mentoring has also been successful in promoting a more diverse workforce representation in a business or organization. The Bank of Montreal is notable for several of its mentoring initiatives and programs to increase the bank's employee diversity. The Canadian Scene box provides a brief overview of several of the bank's programs and initiatives.

The Canadian Scene

TRAINING INITIATIVES AT THE BANK OF MONTREAL

The Bank of Montreal (BMO) launched several workplace initiatives in the 1990s to make employment opportunities more equitable for several groups that had been disadvantaged in the past. The financial institution declared its commitment to having an equitable workplace by establishing a permanent working group, the Chairman's Council on the Equitable Workplace, which has launched several initiatives. Women were one group that was under-represented, at least in management. BMO Financial Group has placed a strong emphasis on eliminating the barriers (glass ceiling) for women in its own workforce. Mentoring and the active encouragement of women is a way for firms and other organizations to achieve their full potential. As of January 14, 2003, 35 percent of BMO bank executives were women, up from 9 percent only 13 years previously.[i]

Two groups of visible minorities, Aboriginal and black Canadians, were also under-represented as bank employees. Other visible minorities, while not under-represented, reported that they "felt excluded or underdeveloped at the bank." To combat the under-representation of the two groups and more fully develop other employees, the bank undertook several avenues for training. It networked with Aboriginal organizations, developed recruitment materials to attract more Aboriginal employees, and matched them with fellow Aboriginal employees (mentoring) once they had been hired. Upgrading programs were also offered to "jump-start" new Aboriginal employees, so that required employment skills were acquired for various bank positions.

Also, to assist minorities in the "hiring game," the bank partnered with the Board of Education for the City of York and the Black Business and Professional Association (BBPA) to create the program Leadership for Tomorrow Today. Through the program, junior and senior high school students work two full days at the bank per week and attend classes the other three days. The bank offers the students

(Continued)

job placements and workplace mentors. The BBPA provides community mentors with similar cultural backgrounds to those of the students.

Another minority, people with disabilities, was also under-represented. However, barriers to these individuals, like some of those for women, were "myth-driven" (such as the belief that those with disabilities take more sick days) rather than being attributable to the skill, opportunity, or knowledge gaps faced by other minorities. Accommodations such as Braille manuals (most purchased for under $500) were made and managers were trained to increase their understanding of applicants with disabilities.[ii]

While this box offers just a brief overview of several new training initiatives, it is clear that the Bank of Montreal values its workers, uses coaching and mentoring in a variety of ways, and is pursuing goals to make the bank a more equitable workplace for all employees.

Sources:

i. BMO Financial Group, "Business Leaders Should Spend More Time Mentoring Women," Speech by Rose M. Patten, Executive Vice-President, Human Resources and Head of Management, BMO Financial Group, given on January 14, 2003, at the Women in Capital Markets Mentoring Reception, Toronto, Ontario (retrieved from www2.bmo.com/bmo/files/news%20release/4/1/Jan1403_RosePattenWCM_EN.html).

ii. Gillian Flynn, "Bank of Montreal Invests in Its Workers," *Workforce*, December 1997, pp. 30–38.

Skill-Building Exercise 10-2

SELECTING A PROTÉGÉ

To be a successful mentor, it is necessary to select protégés who will respond well to your advice and coaching. Since the mentor–protégé relationship is personal, much like any friendship, one must choose protégés carefully. In about 50 words (in the space provided), describe the type of person you would like for a protégé. Include cognitive, personality, and demographic factors in your description (refer to Chapter 2 for ideas). Indicate why you think the characteristics you chose are important.

My Ideal Protégé

_____

_____

_____

_____

_____

_____

As many class members as time allows can present their descriptions to the rest of the class. Look for agreement on characteristics of an ideal protégé.

COACHING AND TRAINING OTHERS

Coaching and training are two direct approaches to helping others in the workplace. In the traditional organization, managers have most of the responsibility for coaching and training, with some assistance from the human resources department. In the new workplace, team members share responsibility for coaching and training. An example is the *Leaders in Learning* program at Rosenbluth International, a global travel firm. Front-line workers volunteer to be leaders in learning. Those selected for the position receive training for three days on how to coach and share information with co-workers to solve problems immediately. Workers post learning needs on a conference room flip chart. The leaders in learning put notes next to the needs they can address, such as "Sit with me as I work with international clients, and I'll show you how to monitor those accounts."[12]

Below we describe coaching and training separately, but recognize that the two processes are closely related.

COACHING SKILLS AND TECHNIQUES

Most readers probably have some experience in coaching, whether or not the activity was given a formal label. If you have helped somebody else improve his or her performance on the job, on the athletic field, in a musical band, or on the dance floor, you have some coaching experience. In the workplace, **coaching** is a method of helping workers grow and improve their job competence by providing suggestions and encouragement. According to Donald Brooks of KPMG Canada, coaching is providing a person with "alternative ways of acting or performing [a] task to produce better results."[13] The suggestions for coaching presented next are generally easier to implement if you have formal authority over the person being coached. Nevertheless, with a positive, helpful attitude on your part, co-workers are likely to accept your coaching.

Coaching other employees requires skill. One way of acquiring this skill is to study basic principles and then practise them on the job. Another way is to coach under simulated conditions, such as role-playing and modelling an effective coach. Below we provide nine suggestions for effective coaching. For the best results, combine them with the suggestions for effective listening presented in Chapter 3.

1. *Provide specific feedback.* Instead of stating generalities about an area of improvement for another person, pinpoint areas of concern. A generality might be, "You just don't seem as if you're into this job." A specific on the same problem might be, "You neglect to call in on days that you are off sick. When you do that, you're letting down the team." Sometimes it can be effective to make a generalization (such as not being "into the job") after you first produce several concrete examples. Closely related to minimizing generalizations is to avoid exaggerating, for example, saying such things as "You are always letting down the team." Specific feedback is sometimes referred to as **behavioural feedback** because it pinpoints behaviour rather than personal characteristics or attitudes. "Neglecting to call in" pinpoints behaviour, whereas "not into the job" focuses more on an attitude.

2. *Make criticism pain-free and positive.* To be an effective coach, you will inevitably have to point out something negative the person you coach has done, or is planning to do. It is helpful to come right to the point about your criticism, such as "In our department meeting this morning, you acted so angry and hostile that you alienated the rest of the group. I know that you are generally a positive person, so I was surprised. My recommendation is that you keep your bad days to yourself when in a meeting." The positive aspect is important because you want to maintain good communications with the person you coach, whether you are the person's supervisor or co-worker.[14]

3. *Encourage the person you are coaching to talk.* Part of being a good listener is encouraging the person being coached to talk. Ask the person you are coaching open-ended questions. Closed questions do not provide the same opportunity for self-expression, and they often elicit short, uninformative answers. Assume you are coaching a co-worker on how to use the company's instant messaging system properly. An effective, open-ended question might be, "Where are you having the biggest problems using the system?" A closed question covering the same topic might be, "Do you understand how to use instant messaging?" The latter question would not provide good clues to specific problem areas faced by your co-worker.

4. *Ask powerful questions.* A major role for the coach is to ask *powerful* or *tough* questions that help the protégé think through the strengths and weaknesses of what he or she is doing or thinking. The powerful question is confrontational in a helpful way. The person being coached might be thinking of using an application of digital storytelling to sell a product. Your powerful question might be, "How will you purchase the required software in order to design your project?"

5. *Provide emotional support.* By being helpful and constructive, you provide much-needed emotional support to the person who needs help in improving job performance. A coaching session should not be an interrogation. An effective way of providing emotional support is to use positive rather than negative motivators. For example, as a team leader you might say to a team member, "If you learn how to analyze manufacturing costs, you will be eligible for an outstanding performance review." A negative motivator on the same topic might be, "If you don't learn how to analyze manufacturing costs, you're going to get zapped on your performance appraisal."

   Workers who are performing well can also profit from praise and encouragement, often so they can perform even better. Also, even the best performers have flaws that might be preventing them from elevating their performance.[15] As a team leader or co-worker, you can therefore make a contribution by giving emotional support to a star performer.

6. *Give some constructive advice.* Giving too much advice interferes with two-way communication, yet some advice can lead to improved performance. Assist the person being coached to answer the question, "What can I do about this problem?" Advice in the form of a question or suppositional statement is often effective. One example is, "Could the root of your problem be that you haven't studied the user manual?"

7. *Coach with "could," not "should."* When helping somebody to improve, tell the person that he or she *could* do something, rather than that he or she *should* do it. *Should* implies the person is doing something morally wrong, as illustrated by the following statement: "You should recycle the used-up laser cartridges." *Could* leaves the person with a choice to make: to accept or reject your input and weigh the consequences.[16]

8. *Interpret what is happening.* An interpretation given by the person doing the coaching is an explanation of why the person being coached is acting in a particular manner. The interpretation is designed to give the person being coached insight into the nature of the problem. For instance, a food service manager might be listening to the problems of a cafeteria manager with regard to cafeteria cleanliness. After listening a while, the food service manager might say, "You're angry and upset with your employees because they don't keep a careful eye on cleanliness. So you avoid dealing with them, and it only makes problems worse." If the manager's diagnosis is correct, interpretation can be extremely helpful.

9. *Allow for modelling of desired performance and behaviour.* An effective coaching technique is to show the person being coached an example of what constitutes the desired behaviour. A customer service manager was harsh with customers when facing heavy pressure. One way the supervisor coached the service manager was by taking over the manager's desk during a busy period. The service manager then watched the supervisor deal tactfully with demanding customers.

Many people are concerned that if they offer too much coaching and feedback to others, they will be perceived as interfering with their work, or being a *micromanager.* In reality, the majority of workers believe that they do not receive enough coaching and guidance on the job. RainmakerThinking Inc. has conducted long-term research suggesting that the undermanaged worker struggles because his or her supervisor is not sufficiently engaged to provide the needed direction and support.[17]

One implication of the coaching suggestions just presented is that some people are more adept at coaching than others. Self-Assessment Quiz 10-2 provides insight into the *right stuff* required for being an effective coach. After doing the exercise and reading the suggestions, you will be prepared for Skill-Building Exercise 10-3 about coaching.

TRAINING OTHERS

One direct way of helping others in the workplace is to train them. **Training** is the process of helping others acquire a job-related skill. Supervisors and trainers are responsible for much of the training in organizations. Yet as organizations operate with fewer managers, co-workers have more responsibility to train one another. Vancouver City Savings Credit Union is one organization that successfully uses peer training to train new employees, with very good results.[18]

Self-Assessment Quiz 10-2

CHARACTERISTICS OF AN EFFECTIVE COACH

Directions: Following is a list of traits, attitudes, and behaviours of effective coaches. Indicate next to each of these whether you need to improve (for example, "need to become more patient"). Prepare an action plan for improving each one you need to develop.

Trait, attitude, or behaviour	Action plan for improvement
Empathy	*Sample:* Will listen until I understand other person's point of view.
	Your own: _____
	_____
Listening skill	*Sample:* Will concentrate extra hard to listen.
	Your own: _____
	_____
Ability to size up people	*Sample:* Will jot down observations about people upon first meeting, then verify in the future.
	Your own: _____
	_____
Diplomacy and tact	*Sample:* Will study book of etiquette.
	Your own: _____
	_____
Patience toward people	*Sample:* Will practise staying calm when someone makes a mistake.
	Your own: _____
	_____
Concern for welfare of others	*Sample:* When interacting with another person will ask self, "How can this person's interests best be served?"
	Your own: _____
	_____
Self-confidence	*Sample:* Will attempt to have at least one personal success each week.
	Your own: _____
	_____
Non-competitiveness with team members	*Sample:* Will keep reminding myself that all boats rise with the same tide.
	Your own: _____
	_____
Enthusiasm for people	*Sample:* Will search for the good in each person.
	Your own: _____
	_____

Skill-Building Exercise 10-3

COACHING A GOOD PERFORMER

Visualize a team of five people working at a Sir Speedy print shop. The shop provides such services as photo-copying, desktop publishing, and printing. One student plays the role of the team leader and owner of this Sir Speedy franchise. Another student plays the role of Chris, a team member who is a standout performer. A problem, however, is the impatience Chris displays toward teammates when taking care of a good customer. When Chris is taking care of a large job, he expects others on the team to drop everything to help with that customer. "When I'm serving a customer, that customer's needs come first," says Chris.

The team leader and Chris get together for a coaching session initiated by the team leader. Chris is convinced that he is right to place customer needs over those of team members. Students not actively participating in this role play will observe the two role players. Be alert for indicators of both good and poor coaching by the team leader.

While training others, keep in mind the following time-tested principles that aid learning—and therefore training. Applying these principles consistently will increase the chances that the people you are training will acquire new skills.

1. *Encourage concentration.* Not much learning takes place unless the trainee concentrates carefully on what is being learned. Concentration improves the ability to do both mental and physical tasks. In short, encourage the person you are training to concentrate.

2. *Motivate interest.* People learn best when they are interested in the problem facing them. Explain to the trainee how the skill being taught will increase his or her value as an employee, or relate the skill to the person's professional goals. Trainees can be encouraged to look for some relationship between the information at hand and their personal welfare. With this relationship in mind, the person will have a stronger intention to learn. This is an effective example of the WIIFM principle discussed in the previous chapter. For example, when training new professors to use more online learning activities, explaining how such activities save time (a valuable commodity) is often a motivator to learn new online techniques.

3. *Remind learners to intend to remember.* We often fail to remember something because we do not intend to commit it to memory. Many executives are particularly effective at remembering the names of employees and customers. When one executive was asked how she could commit so many names to memory, she replied, "I look at the person, listen to the name, and try hard to remember." An example of reminding a protégé to remember would be to advise him or her to memorize the company mission statement.

4. *Ensure the material is meaningful.* The material to be learned should be organized in a meaningful manner. Each successive experience should build on the ones before. In training another person how to process a customer order, you might teach the skill in terms of the flow of activities from customer inquiry to product delivery.

5. *Provide feedback on progress.* As a person's training progresses, motivation may be maintained and increased by providing feedback on progress. To measure progress, it may be necessary to ask the trainee questions or request a job sample. For example, you might ask the person being trained on invoices to prepare a sample invoice.

6. *Ask the trainee to reflect on what he or she has learned.* Research indicates that if you think carefully about what you have learned, your retention of the information increases. The idea is to step back from the experience to carefully and persistently ponder its meaning to you.[19] After participating in a team development exercise involving whitewater rafting, a person might reflect, "What did I really learn about being a better team player? How was I perceived by my teammates in the rubber raft? Did they even notice my contribution? Or did they think I was an important part of the team success?"

7. *Deal with trainee defensiveness.* Training is sometimes impeded because the person being trained is defensive about information or skills that clash with his or her beliefs and practices. The person might have so much emotional energy invested in the status quo that he or she resists the training. For example, a sales representative might resist learning how to use ecommerce because she believes that her warm smile and interpersonal skills have made her an excellent communicator. She is concerned that if she communicates with customers exclusively through email, her human touch will be lost. Sensing this defensiveness, the trainer is advised to talk about ecommerce as being a supplement to, but not a substitute for, in-person communication. (However, the sales rep might also be worried that her position will be eliminated.)

8. *Take into account learning style.* Another key factor that influences training is **learning style**, the way in which a person best learns new information. An example of a learning style is passive learning. People who learn best through passive learning quickly acquire information by studying texts, manuals, magazine articles, and websites. They can juggle images in their mind as they read about abstract concepts such as supply and demand, cultural diversity, or customer service. Others learn best by doing rather than studying—for example, learning about customer service by dealing with customers in many situations.

   Another key dimension of learning styles is whether a person learns best by working alone or cooperatively in a study group. Learning by oneself may allow for more intense concentration, and one can proceed at one's own pace. Learning in groups through classroom discussion allows people to exchange viewpoints and perspectives.

   Because of differences in learning styles, you may decide to design training to fit these differences. For example, if your trainees prefer cooperative learning you could combine learning from reading books, articles, and online information with discussions in a conference room.

To start applying these principles of learning to training, do Skill-Building Exercise 10-4.

Skill-Building Exercise 10-4

DESIGNING A TRAINING PROGRAM

The class organizes into training-design teams of approximately six people. Each team sketches the design of a training program to teach an interpersonal skill to employees, such as being polite to customers or interviewing job candidates. The teams are not responsible for selecting the exact content of the training program they choose. Instead, they are responsible for designing a training program based on the principles of learning.

The activity should take about 15 minutes and can therefore be done inside or outside class. After the teams have designed their programs, they can compare the various versions.

The Job-Oriented Interpersonal Skills in Action box describes a method of helping others that includes both coaching and training.

Job-Oriented Interpersonal Skills in Action

RICH LEVIN, REAL ESTATE COACH AND TRAINER

Rich Levin enjoyed a solid career as a real estate agent. He was a top producer for several firms and owned his own agency, ringing up large sales volumes wherever he went. In the early 1990s he decided to start passing those skills on to others by running his own training and consulting firm. His business, Rich Levin Training and Coaching, has been growing steadily, and Levin, working from his home, is now attempting to expand on a national scale. Levin has built a network of clients in states as far away as Alabama and Idaho. He plans to offer more training seminars and establish consulting relationships across the country.

Levin says he uses a blend of goal setting, skill building, and marketing to help his clients produce results. He develops a goal sheet for each agent, with sales targets and methods the client will use to reach those targets. Tasks are broken down into digestible chunks over days and weeks, Levin said.

"I'm a results coach, not a feel-good coach," Levin explains. "If a coach helps you reach the results you want, you'll feel better about yourself anyway." Levin uses computer aptitude tests to help analyze client strengths. He also helps clients come up with their own "brand"—ways of increasing their name recognition with customers.

The business has five employees right now and could add more trainers this year as the business grows. Real estate agents who use Levin's services praise his methods. Cathy McWilliams has been working with Levin since 1995. Over that nine-year period her sales volume grew from $2 million to $17 million. "I think what I like most about it is it keeps me on task," McWilliams said. "It becomes something you think about every week. When you set goals on paper, everything is right there for you to see." McWilliams started using the progress charts that Levin designed for her with her own buyers' agents.

Jeff Scofield, an agent with a division of Realty USA, said Levin taught him how to manage his business by hiring the right buyers' agents to help. "I keep track of where my clients are coming from and advertise appropriately," Scofield said. "I have more of a sharp-shooting approach."

Levin also helped Scofield improve the service he was giving his customers. "I went from selling 80 houses a year to 140, and I think those 140 families are getting better service now," Scofield commented.

(Continued)

Levin thinks his consulting methods can work in other fields. He's in the early stages of working with a financial planner and a medical research company.

"I feel like I can help people help themselves and other people," Levin said.

Questions

1. What principles of coaching is Levin using?
2. What principles of training is Levin using?
3. In what way might Levin be helping his clients boost their self-confidence?

Source: David Tyler, "Coaching Success: Levin Sees National Audience for Real Estate Service," Rochester, New York, *Democrat and Chronicle*, January 10, 2005, pp. 1D, 7D. Reprinted with permission.

HELPING DIFFICULT PEOPLE

A challenge we all face from time to time is dealing constructively with workers who appear intent on creating problems. For a variety of reasons, these difficult or counterproductive people perform poorly themselves or interfere with the job performance of others. A **difficult person** is an individual who creates problems for others yet has the skill and mental ability to be more productive. Below we briefly describe various types of difficult people and then emphasize methods for helping them behave more productively. To pretest your skill in dealing with and helping difficult people, do Self-Assessment Quiz 10-3.

Self-Assessment Quiz 10-3

HELPING DIFFICULT PEOPLE

Directions: For each of the following scenarios, choose the method of handling the situation you think would be the most effective. Make a choice, even though more than one method of handling the situation seems plausible.

1. A co-worker in the cubicle next to you is talking loudly on the telephone about the fabulous weekend she and a few friends enjoyed. You are attempting to handle a challenging work problem. To deal with this situation, you

   a. Get up from your chair, stand close to her, and say loudly, "Shut up, you jerk. I'm trying to do my work."

   b. Slip her a handwritten note that says, "I'm happy that you had a great weekend, but I have problems concentrating on my work when you are talking so loudly. Thanks for your help."

   c. Get the boss on the phone and ask that she please do something about the problem.

   d. Wait until lunch and then say to her, "I'm happy that you had a great weekend, but I have problems concentrating on my work when you are talking so loudly. Thanks for your help."

(Continued)

2. One of your co-workers, Olaf, rarely carries his fair load of the work. He forever has a good reason for not having the time to do an assignment. This morning he has approached you to load some new software onto his personal computer. You deal with this situation by

   a. Carefully explaining that you will help him, providing he will take over a certain specified task for you.

   b. Telling him that you absolutely refuse to help a person as lazy as he is.

   c. Counselling him about fair play and reciprocity.

   d. Reviewing with him a list of five times he has asked other people to help him out. You then ask if he thinks this is a good way to treat co-workers.

3. In your role as supervisor, you have noticed that Diane, one of the group members, spends far too much work time laughing and joking. You schedule a meeting with her. As the meeting opens, you

   a. Joke and laugh with her to establish rapport.

   b. Explain to Diane that you have called this meeting to discuss her too-frequent laughing and joking.

   c. Talk for a few moments about the good things Diane has done for the department, then confront the real issue.

   d. Explain to Diane that she is on the verge of losing her job if she doesn't act more maturely.

4. As a team member, you have become increasingly annoyed with Jerry's ethnic, racist, and sexist jokes. One day during a team meeting, he tells a joke you believe is particularly offensive. To deal with the situation, you

   a. Meet privately with the team leader to discuss Jerry's offensive behaviour.

   b. Catch up with Jerry later when he is alone, and tell him how uncomfortable his joke made you feel.

   c. Confront Jerry on the spot and say, "Hold on Jerry. I find your joke offensive."

   d. Tell the group an even more offensive joke to illustrate how Jerry's behaviour can get out of hand.

5. You have been placed on a task force to look for ways to save the company money, including making recommendations for eliminating jobs. You interview a supervisor about the efficiency of her department. She suddenly becomes rude and defensive. In response, you

   a. Politely point out how her behaviour is coming across to you.

   b. Get your revenge by recommending that three jobs be eliminated from her department.

   c. Explain that you have used up enough of her time for today and ask for another meeting later in the week.

   d. Tell her that unless she becomes more cooperative, the interview cannot continue.

Scoring and Interpretation: Use the following key to obtain your score:

1. a. 1	**2.** a. 4	**3.** a. 1	**4.** a. 2	**5.** a. 4
b. 4	b. 1	b. 4	b. 4	b. 1
c. 2	c. 3	c. 3	c. 3	c. 2
d. 3	d. 2	d. 2	d. 1	d. 3

18–20 You have good intuition about helping difficult people.
10–17 You have average intuition about helping difficult people.
 5–9   You need to improve your sensitivity about helping difficult people.

TYPES OF DIFFICULT PEOPLE

Dozens of types of difficult people have been identified, with considerable overlap among the types. For example, one method of classifying difficult people might identify the *dictator*, while another method might identify the same individual as the *bully*. Our purposes will be served by listing a sampling of the many types of difficult people found in the workplace and as customers. As you read the following list, look for familiar types:[20]

- *Know-it-alls* believe they are experts on everything. They have opinions on every issue, yet when they are wrong they pass the buck or become defensive.

- *Blamers* are workers who never solve their own problems. When faced with a challenge or hitch, they think the problem belongs to the supervisor or a group member.

- *Gossips* spread negative rumours about others and attempt to set people against each other.

- *Bullies* cajole and intimidate others. They are blunt to the point of being insulting, and will sometimes use harsh, vulgar language to attain their goals. Bullies constantly make demands on workmates.

- *Repulsives* are people whose poor personal hygiene, eating habits, appearance, or foul language disrupts the tranquility of others.

- *Yes-people* agree to any commitment and promise any deadline, yet rarely deliver. Although sorry about being late, they cannot be trusted to deliver as promised.

- *No-people* are negative and pessimistic and quick to point out why something will not work. They are also inflexible, resist change, and complain frequently.

- *Jekyll-and-Hydes* have a split personality. When dealing with supervisors, customers, or clients, they are pleasant, engaging people; yet when carrying out the role of supervisors they become tyrannical.

- *Whiners* gripe about people, processes, and company regulations. They complain about being overworked and underpaid, or not receiving assignments up to their true capabilities.

- *Backstabbers* pretend to befriend you and encourage you to talk freely about problems or personality clashes you face. Later, the backstabber reports the information—often in exaggerated form—to the person you mentioned in a negative light. Or the backstabber simply says negative things about you behind your back to discredit you to others.

- *High-maintenance types* require considerable attention from others in such forms as demanding much of the supervisor's time, making unusual requests to the human resources department, and taking the maximum number of sick days and personal days allowable. High-maintenance types are often a combination of several of the previous types described above.

TACTICS FOR DEALING WITH DIFFICULT PEOPLE

How one deals most effectively with a difficult person depends to some extent on the person's type. For example, you may need different tactics to deal with a co-worker who gets nothing done than you would need with a co-worker who makes too many mistakes but insists she knows it all. Bullies are another type of difficult person to deal with in the workplace. Figure 10-1, presents information about bullying by the Canada Safety Council. (You will recall that bullying was described in Chapter 7 as a source of workplace conflict.)

The following techniques are broadly applicable to helping difficult people change to a more constructive behaviour pattern. This general approach should prove more helpful than being concerned with specific tactics for each type of difficult person you encounter.

Provide Ample Feedback

The primary technique for dealing with counterproductive behaviour is to feed back to the difficult person how his or her behaviour affects you. Focus on the person's behaviour rather than on his or her characteristics or values. If a *repulsive type* is annoying you by constantly eating when you are working together, say something to this effect: "I have a hard time concentrating on the work when you're eating." Such a statement will engender less resentment than saying, "I find you repulsive, and it annoys me." As in coaching, it is better to avoid *should* statements because they often create defensiveness instead of triggering positive behaviour. Instead of saying "You shouldn't be eating when you are working," you might try, "Could you find another place to eat when we are working together?"

Criticize Constructively

Feedback sets the stage for criticism. It is best to criticize in private and to begin with mild criticism. Base your criticism on objective facts rather than subjective impressions. Point out, for example, that the yes-person's lack of follow-through resulted in $10 000 in lost sales. Express your criticism in terms of a common goal. For example,

According to the Canada Safety Council (CSC), bullying (general harassment) is far more prevalent than other destructive behaviours covered by legislation, such as sexual harassment and racial harassment. Over 80 percent of bullies are bosses, some are co-workers, and a minority are workers who bully higher-ups. Of interest, bullies are equally likely to be men or women. Also notable: according to the CSC, individuals who are the victims of bullies are not weaklings, oddballs, or loners. Instead, the victim is often a capable, dedicated, cooperative, and well-liked person who prefers a non-confrontational personal style. The CSC recommends that bullying be officially identified as unacceptable behaviour in staff handbooks and that organizations have proper systems for investigating bullying incidents along the same lines as other forms of harassment and discrimination. In other words, there is no place for bullies in organizations that are well-run and truly value workers and workers' rights.

Figure 10-1   Bullying in the Workplace

Source: Canada Safety Council, "Bullying in the Workplace," www.safety-council.org/info/OSH/bullies.html.

"*We* can get the report done quickly if *you'll* firm up the statistical data while I edit the text." When you criticize a co-worker, avoid acting as if you have formal authority over the person.

Help the Difficult Person Feel More Confident

Many counterproductive employees are simply low in self-confidence and self-efficacy. They use stalling and evasive tactics because they are afraid to fail. Working with your manager or team leader, you might be able to arrange a project or task in which you know the difficult person will succeed. With a small dose of self-confidence and self-efficacy, the person may begin to complain less. With additional successes, the person may soon become less difficult.[21] Self-confidence building takes time. However, self-efficacy can build more quickly as the person learns a new skill.

Use Tact and Diplomacy

Tactful actions on your part can sometimes take care of co-workers' annoying behaviour without confrontation. Close your door, for example, if noisy co-workers are gathered outside. When the subtle approach fails, it may be necessary to proceed to a more confronting type of feedback.

Tact and diplomacy can still be incorporated into confrontation. In addition to confronting the person, you might also point out a strength of the individual. In dealing with a know-it-all you might say, "I realize you are creative and filled with good ideas. However, I wish you would give me an opportunity to express my opinion."

Use Non-hostile Humour

Non-hostile humour can often be used to help a difficult person understand how his or her behaviour is blocking others. Also, the humour will help you defuse the conflict between you and that person. The humour should point to the person's unacceptable behaviour yet not belittle him or her. Assume that you and a co-worker are working jointly on a report. For each idea that you submit, your co-worker gets into the know-it-all mode and informs you of important facts you have neglected. Following is an example of non-hostile humour that might jolt the co-worker into realizing that his or her approach is annoying:

> If there is ever a contest to choose the human being with a brain that can compete against a Zip drive, I will nominate you. But even though my brain is limited to human capacity, I still think I can supply a few facts for our report.

Your humour may help the other person recognize that he or she is attempting to overwhelm you with facts at his or her disposal. You are being self-effacing and thereby drawing criticism away from your co-worker. Self-effacement is an effective humour tactic in such situations.

Work Out a Deal

A direct approach to dealing with problems created by a difficult person is to work out a deal or negotiated solution. Workers who do not carry their load are successful in getting others to do their work. The next time such a worker wants you to carry out a task, agree to it if he or she will reciprocate by performing a task that will benefit you. For working out a deal to be effective, you must be specific about the terms of the deal. The worker may at first complain about your demands for reciprocity, so it is important to be firm.

Skill-Building Exercise 10-5

DEALING WITH DIFFICULT PEOPLE

In both of the following scenarios, one person plays the role of a group member whose work and morale suffer because of a difficult person. The other person plays the role of the difficult person, who may lack insight into what he or she is doing wrong. It is important for the suffering person to put emotion into the role.

Scenario 1: The Bully. A bully is present at a meeting called to plan a company morale-boosting event. Several students play the roles of the group members. One student plays the role of a group member who suggests that the event centre on doing a social good such as refurbishing a poor family's house or conducting a neighbourhood cleanup. Another student plays the role of a bully who thinks the idea is "a bummer"—pointlessly unpleasant. The group member being intimidated decides to deal effectively with the bully.

Scenario 2: A No-Person. One student plays the role of a worker with a lot of creative energy whose manager is a no-person. The energetic worker has what he or she thinks is a wonderful way for the company to generate additional revenue: conducting a garage sale of surplus equipment and furnishings. The worker presents this idea to the no-person manager, played by another student. When the manager acts true to form, the worker will attempt to overcome his or her objections.

Reinforce Civil Behaviour and Good Moods

In the spirit of positive reinforcement, when a generally difficult person is behaving acceptably, recognize the behaviour in some way. Reinforcing statements would include, "It's fun working with you today" and "I appreciate your professional attitude."

Ask the Difficult Person to THINK Before Speaking

Human relations specialist John Maxwell suggests that you ask the difficult person to THINK before he or she speaks, with "THINK" referring to the acronym:[22]

T	Is it true?
H	Is it helpful?
I	Is it inspiring?
N	Is it necessary?
K	Is it kind?

Although Maxwell's suggestion is aimed at difficult people, is would be a helpful rule of thumb for building relationships with people in many situations.

Report Behaviour That Continues to Be Unacceptable or Inappropriate

If the behaviour is truly problematic, such as bullying or harassment, do not hesitate to report the behaviour to your manager (or his or her boss if the problem person is your manager). If you have exhausted all of your ideas and nothing has worked, to continue to have to deal with this person can become very disheartening and stressful. Most organizations do have policies and procedures in place (and in some cases it is law) to assist you when you are the victim of repeated hostility, bullying, or harassment of any kind.

The tactics for dealing with difficult people just described require practice to be effective. When you next encounter a difficult person, try one of the tactics that seems to fit the occasion. Role plays, such as those presented in Skill-Building Exercise 10-5 on page 234, are a good starting point for employing the appropriate tactic in dealing with difficult people.

SUMMARY

Workers have a responsibility to help one another learn, grow, and develop. An important strategy in helping others grow and develop is to be a nurturing, positive person. A toxic person stands in contrast to a nurturing person because he or she dwells on the negative. Nurturing people are positive, enthusiastic, and supportive. Three actions and attitudes that support being a nurturing person are (1) recognizing growth needs in others, (2) using the buddy system, and (3) being a role model.

Being a mentor is another way of helping others. To be a mentor, a person engages in a wide range of helping behaviours. Among them are sponsoring, coaching, protecting, sharing challenging assignments, and being a referral agent. Mentors also help protégés solve problems and learn the ropes of an organization. Mentoring has become recognized as an important vehicle for the advancement of minorities in the workplace.

Coaching and training are direct helping roles. Coaching is a method of helping workers grow and develop by providing them with suggestions and encouragement. Suggestions for effective coaching include the following:

1. Provide specific feedback.
2. Make criticism pain-free and positive.
3. Encourage the person you are coaching to talk.
4. Ask powerful questions.
5. Provide emotional support.
6. Give some constructive advice.
7. Coach with "could," not "should."
8. Interpret what is happening.
9. Allow for modelling of desired performance and behaviour.

Training involves helping people acquire job skills. To facilitate training, apply principles of learning such as the following: (1) encourage concentration, (2) use motivated interest, (3) remind learners to intend to remember, (4) ensure the meaningfulness of material, (5) give feedback on progress, (6) ask the trainee to reflect on what he or she has learned, (7) deal with trainee defensiveness, and (8) take into account learning style.

Dealing with difficult people is a major challenge in helping others. The many types of difficult people include know-it-alls, blamers, gossips, bullies, repulsives, yes-people, no-people, Jekyll and Hydes, whiners, backstabbers, and high-maintenance types. Tactics for dealing with them include (1) give ample feedback, (2) criticize constructively, (3) help the difficult person feel more confident, (4) use tact and diplomacy, (5) use humour, (6) work out a deal, (7) reinforce civil behaviour and good moods, and (8) ask the person to THINK before speaking. Report behaviour that continues to be unacceptable or inappropriate.

An Interpersonal Relations Case Problem

THE DEMANDING PROTÉGÉ

Dawn Albright is a sales representative for an office-supply company. She has five years of successful experience selling furnishings and interior designs to business firms in her area. Dawn worked her way up from taking telephone orders for small supplies such as computer paper, print cartridges, pencils, ballpoint pens, and pencils. By the fifth year of her employment, Dawn became the highest producer in the office. Later she was placed in charge of orders received on the company's website.

One day Dawn's manager, Jim Bastian, requested a favour: "Dawn, would you be willing to take Marilyn Lake under your wing? Marilyn is the newest member of the sales staff. I think she could benefit from the guidance of a real pro like you." Dawn enthusiastically agreed to assume responsibility for becoming Marilyn's mentor. She told Jim, "I sure could have used help myself when I was getting started."

Jim explained to Dawn that Marilyn might need a lot of help. He pointed out that the company was taking a chance on placing Marilyn in a sales position. Jim's reasoning was that although Marilyn had a professional appearance, she didn't appear to have much self-confidence. When Dawn asked Jim to give her a few specifics, he commented: "A lot of little things have given me the impression that Marilyn needs more self-confidence. When I interviewed her, Marilyn could not give me any examples of how she had ever been a leader in anything. Also, when I ask her opinion about almost anything, she says, 'I'm really not sure' or 'I don't have an informed opinion.'"

Dawn later met with Marilyn to explain that although she was not her boss she had volunteered to spend time showing her the ropes. Marilyn expressed appreciation and acknowledged that she had a lot to learn about the business.

Dawn began working with Marilyn by taking her along on visits to a few of her best accounts. Dawn even allowed Marilyn to receive credit for the sale of a few desks, chairs, and coffee tables because she assisted in the sales. Over the next several months, Dawn would discuss Marilyn's sales progress with her from time to time. The two would discuss Marilyn's tactics and the plans she formulated to develop each account. Marilyn listened attentively and followed Dawn's advice carefully.

Toward the end of the sixth month of their working relationship, Dawn received a telephone call from Marilyn late one night. Marilyn pleaded with Dawn to accompany her on a sales call to a potentially big account. "I know that if you are present at this meeting, between the two of us we will close the sale," said Marilyn.

Dawn's first thought was that Marilyn needed the experience of closing a big sale herself, yet she obliged. "Marilyn has a point," thought Dawn to herself. "Experience is a big factor in closing such a large account. And our firm could sure use the business."

As the months rolled by Marilyn made an increasing number of requests for Dawn's advice on sales tactics. Twice more she pressured Dawn into helping her close big sales. Dawn hinted that Marilyn should close the sale herself, but Marilyn insisted that she needed help just one more time.

Soon Marilyn began to seek Dawn's advice on matters outside work. One day Marilyn asked if Dawn would help her choose a dress for an engagement shower. Another time Marilyn sought Dawn's advice on how she should handle her parents' negative reaction to her latest boyfriend. Soon Marilyn

(Continued)

was telephoning Dawn at least twice a weekend, asking to discuss questions about both work and her personal life. Marilyn would also send regular email messages to Dawn, asking her opinion on many small matters such as, "How much should I thank a customer for a small order?"

One day Dawn thought to herself, "My being a mentor to Marilyn has gone too far. I'm her confidante, her big sister, and her sales consultant. At times I also feel I'm her mother. This relationship is draining me."

Case Questions

1. How effective is Dawn as Marilyn's mentor?

2. In what way might Dawn be hindering her protégée's development?

3. What should Dawn do about her relationship with Marilyn?

4. What underlying issue might Dawn be neglecting in dealing with Marilyn?

An Interpersonal Relations Case Problem

THE NIGHTMARE IN THE LOGISTICS DEPARTMENT

Larry Smits was happy to join the distribution department of his company as a logistics specialist. His position centred on keeping track of shipments to customers and from vendors. A distribution specialist works extensively with computers to track shipments, but part of the job description involves telephone and face-to-face contact with company insiders and outsiders.

Larry enthusiastically explained his new job to his girlfriend: "Here's a great opportunity for me. I'll be using a sophisticated software system, and I'll have lots of contact with a variety of people. I'll be talking to marketing executives, purchasing agents, truckers, package-delivery people, and office assistants. Equally good, I'll be learning about a very important part of the business. If the company doesn't ship goods to customers, we can't collect money. And if we don't receive shipments of supplies that we need, we can't produce anything ourselves."

During the first four months on the job, Larry's enthusiasm continued. The job proved to be as exciting as he anticipated. Larry got along well with all his co-workers and developed his closest friendship with Rudy Bianchi, a senior distribution specialist. Rudy said that since he had several more years of experience than Larry, he would be willing to help him with any job problem he encountered. One day Larry

took Rudy up on his offer. Larry was having a little difficulty understanding how to verify the accuracy of tariffs paid to several European countries. Part of Larry's job was to make sure the company was paying its fair share of tariffs, but no more than necessary. Larry sent Rudy an email message asking for clarification on three tariff questions. Rudy answered promptly and provided Larry with useful information.

When Larry next saw Rudy in person during lunch, he thanked him again for the technical assistance. "No problem," said Rudy. "I told you that I'm always willing to help a buddy. By sharing knowledge, we multiply our effectiveness." Larry detected a trace of insincerity in Rudy's message but later thought he might be overreacting to Rudy's colourful way of expressing himself.

Several days later Larry was reviewing a work assignment with his supervisor, Ellie Wentworth. She said to him, "How are you coming along with the problems you were having understanding how to verify tariffs? That's a key part of your job, you know."

Larry explained to Ellie that he wasn't having any real problems, but that he had asked for clarification on a couple of complicated rates. He also pointed out that he quickly obtained the clarification

(Continued)

he needed. Larry thought to himself, "Oh, I guess Ellie must have misinterpreted a comment by Rudy about my clarifying a few tariff rates with him. I doubt Rudy would have told our boss that I was having trouble. Why should I be paranoid?"

One week later Rudy stopped by Larry's cubicle. At the moment, Larry had the classified ad section of the *Globe and Mail* on his desk. "Are you job hunting, Larry? You're a rising star in our department. Why look elsewhere?"

"I'm not job hunting," said Larry. "I was just curious to see what kind of demand exists for logistics specialists. It's just part of my interest in the field. It's reassuring to know we're part of a growing profession."

"That's a great answer," said Rudy. "I was just pulling your chain a little anyway."

A week later Ellie was reviewing some work assignments with Larry. As the discussion about the work assignment was completed, Ellie said, "I think highly of how you're progressing in your job, Larry, but I want to make sure of one thing. Before we give you another major assignment, I want to know if you're happy in your job. If for any reason you are

planning to leave the company, please let us know now."

"What are you talking about?" said Larry with a puzzled expression. "I intend to be with the company for a long, long time. I can't imagine what gave you the impression that I am not happy here."

As Larry left the office, he was furious. He began to wonder if someone might be spreading malicious rumours about him. He muttered silently, "It couldn't be Rudy. He's supposed to be my friend, my mentor. But I have to get to the root of this problem. I feel like I'm being sabotaged."

Case Questions

1. What devious technique might Rudy, or another co-worker, be using against Larry?

2. What motivation might a co-worker have for raising questions about Larry's job knowledge and loyalty to the company?

3. How should Larry deal with his suspicions?

4. How effectively has Ellie dealt with her two concerns about Larry?

QUESTIONS FOR DISCUSSION AND REVIEW

1. Explain your position on whether workers have a responsibility to help one another grow and develop.

2. What is your opinion of the potential effectiveness of the buddy system in your career?

3. If you were to have a mentor (or do have one), what roles would you want (or do you want) that person to play?

4. Describe any constructive advice you have received from anybody who has coached you. What was the impact of this advice?

5. In what way does a coach in the workplace function much like an athletic coach?

6. Describe any barrier to good performance you have encountered. How might your supervisor have helped?

7. Do you think trainee defensiveness is a bigger problem in teaching technical or interpersonal skills? Explain.

8. How would you know if people perceive you as a *difficult person*?

9. How might humour help you deal with the repulsive type of difficult person? Supply an example of a witty comment you might use with him or her.

10. Using your Research Navigator, find article AN 22080195 on dealing with difficult people. This article lists several strategies to deal with a difficult boss or co-worker including managing your own emotions. Compare these strategies to the ones in this text.

WEBLINKS

www.coachingandmentoring.com
This site is devoted to coaching, from self-coaching to business coaching.

www.canadianbusiness.com/entrepreneur/quiz/article.jsp?content=20060804_134934_3180
Try this quiz about how good a mentor you are! From Canadian Business Online.

www.michelematt.com/difficultpeople.htm
This site has strategies for dealing with difficult people.

www.stressdoc.com/difficult.htm
Another site that provides tips for dealing with difficult people at work.

Chapter 11

Positive Political Skills

Learning Outcomes

After reading and studying this chapter and doing the exercises, you should be able to

- More effectively manage the impression you give, including developing an awareness of the rules of business etiquette.
- Identify political techniques for building relationships with managers.
- Identify political techniques for building relationships with co-workers and other worker associates.
- Avoid committing political blunders.

Todd Madison, age 26, was working successfully as a heating and air conditioning technician for a large firm in Atlanta, Georgia. With technicians in his field in high demand in Atlanta, Todd was earning more money than he had anticipated when he graduated from technical school several years earlier. Madison and his wife, a licensed practical nurse, were looking toward purchasing a condominium.

A close friend of Madison's, Jerry Weaver, age 27, was also in the heating and air conditioning field. Weaver, however, was a little more advanced in his career, working as a manager in the largest firm of its kind in Atlanta. Madison and Weaver were friends in a number of ways. Their families entertained each other at home occasionally, the two men fished and played golf together from time to time, and sometimes they watched Atlanta Falcons games together.

During one golf outing together, Weaver surprised Madison with an offer to become an area supervisor in his firm, reporting directly to Weaver. After careful reflection about the prospects of having a close buddy as a boss, Madison accepted the position as a heating and air conditioning supervisor, with 12 technicians reporting to him. As he settled into the job, Madison began to wonder how he was going to deal with any charges of favouritism, and how he would handle any disagreements with Weaver. At the same time, Weaver began to worry how he would discipline Madison if necessary, and how he should avoid any possible favouritism in terms of performance evaluations and recommended salary increases.

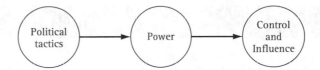

Figure 11-1   Relationships Among Politics, Power, and Influence
Political tactics, such as developing contacts with key people, lead to power, which enables one to control and influence others.

One implication of the anecdote about the two friends is that to prosper in the workplace you have to be aware of the political factors that could damage a working relationship. At the same time, the proper use of positive political tactics helps build good interpersonal relationships. In turn, these good relationships can facilitate achieving career goals. Recognize, however, that being competent in your job is still the most effective method of achieving career success. After skill come hard work and luck as important success factors. A fourth ingredient is also important for success—positive political skills.

Few people can achieve success for themselves or their group without having some awareness of the political forces around them and how to use them to advantage. It may be necessary for the career-minded person to take the offensive in using positive and ethical political tactics.

As used here, the term **organizational politics** refers to gaining power through any means other than merit or luck. (Luck, of course, is what happens when preparation meets opportunity.) Politics is such an important part of the job that it has been defined as "the art of trying to accomplish things in organizations."[1] People play politics to achieve power, either directly or indirectly. **Power** refers to the ability or potential to control anything of value and to influence decisions. The results of such power may take such diverse forms as being promoted, being transferred, receiving a salary increase, or avoiding an uncomfortable assignment. Figure 11-1 depicts the relationships among politics, power, and control and influence.

Political tactics, such as developing contacts with key people, lead to power, which enables one to control and influence others.

In this chapter, we approach skill development in organizational (or office) politics from several standpoints. Information is presented about such topics as managing the impression you make, using political tactics to improve interpersonal relationships, and avoiding hazardous political mistakes. In addition, you will have the opportunity to take two quizzes about political tactics and engage in skill-building exercises. To measure your current tendencies toward playing politics, do Self-Assessment Quiz 11-1.

IMPRESSION MANAGEMENT AND ETIQUETTE

Being an effective, responsible contributor is not always sufficient to gain you the attention you deserve. It may also be necessary to make others aware of your capabilities. **Impression management** is a set of behaviours directed at improving one's image by drawing attention to oneself. Often the attention is directed toward superficial aspects of the self, such as clothing and appearance. Impression management also includes telling people about your accomplishments and appearing self-confident. Our presentation of impression management includes a listing of specific tactics and a discussion of business etiquette.

Self-Assessment Quiz 11-1

ORGANIZATIONAL POLITICS QUESTIONNAIRE

Directions: Answer each question "Mostly agree" or "Mostly disagree," even if it is difficult for you to decide which alternative best describes your opinion.

	Mostly agree	Mostly disagree
1. The boss or team leader is always right.	_____	_____
2. It is wise to flatter important people.	_____	_____
3. If you do somebody a favour, remember to cash in on it.	_____	_____
4. Given the opportunity, I would cultivate friendships with powerful people.	_____	_____
5. I would be willing to say nice things about a rival to get that person transferred from my department.	_____	_____
6. If it would help me get ahead, I would take credit for someone else's work.	_____	_____
7. Given the chance, I would offer to help my boss build some shelves for his or her den.	_____	_____
8. I laugh heartily at my boss's humour, even if I do not think it is funny.	_____	_____
9. Dressing for success is silly. At work, wear clothing that you find to be the most comfortable.	_____	_____
10. Never waste lunchtime by eating with somebody who can't help you solve a problem or gain advantage.	_____	_____
11. I think using email to zap somebody for his or her mistakes, and sending copies to key people, is a good idea.	_____	_____
12. If somebody higher up in the organization offends you, look for ways to get even with him or her.	_____	_____
13. Honesty is the best policy, even if it means insulting somebody.	_____	_____
14. Power for its own sake is one of life's most precious commodities.	_____	_____
15. If I had a legitimate gripe against my employer, I would air my views publicly (for instance, distributing my comments over the internet).	_____	_____
16. I would invite my boss or team leader to a party at my home even if I didn't like him or her.	_____	_____
17. An effective way to impress people is to tell them what they want to hear.	_____	_____
18. Having a high school or skyscraper named after me would be an incredible thrill.	_____	_____
19. Hard work and good performance are usually sufficient for career success.	_____	_____
20. Even if I made only a minor contribution to a project, I would get my name listed as being associated with it.	_____	_____
21. I would never publicly correct mistakes made by my boss or team leader.	_____	_____
22. I would never use my personal contacts to gain a promotion.	_____	_____

(Continued)

23. If you happen to dislike a person who receives a big promotion in your firm, don't bother sending that person a congratulatory note.   _____   _____

24. I would never openly criticize a powerful executive in my organization.   _____   _____

25. I would stay late in the office just to impress my boss or team leader.   _____   _____

Scoring and Interpretation: Give yourself a + 1 for each answer you gave in agreement with the keyed answer. Note that we did not use the term *correct* answer. Whether or not an answer is correct is a question of personal values and ethics. Each question that receives a score of + 1 shows a tendency toward playing organizational politics. The scoring key is as follows:

1. Mostly agree
2. Mostly agree
3. Mostly agree
4. Mostly agree
5. Mostly agree
6. Mostly agree
7. Mostly agree
8. Mostly agree
9. Mostly disagree
10. Mostly agree
11. Mostly agree
12. Mostly disagree
13. Mostly disagree
14. Mostly agree
15. Mostly disagree
16. Mostly agree
17. Mostly agree
18. Mostly agree
19. Mostly disagree
20. Mostly agree
21. Mostly agree
22. Mostly disagree
23. Mostly disagree
24. Mostly agree
25. Mostly agree

In an earlier version of this test, based on a sample of 750 men and women managers, professionals, administrators, sales representatives, and business owners,[i] the mean score is 10. Scores of 1 through 7 suggest a below-average tendency to play politics. Scores between 8 and 12 suggest an average tendency to play office politics. Scores of 13 and above suggest an above-average tendency to play office politics and a strong need for power.

i. Andrew J. DuBrin, "Career Maturity, Organizational Rank, and Political Behavior Tendencies: A Correlational Analysis of Organizational Politics and Career Experience," *Psychological Reports,* vol. 63, 1988, pp. 531–37; DuBrin, "Sex Differences in Endorsement of Influence Tactics and Political Behavior Tendencies," *Journal of Business and Psychology,* Fall 1989, pp. 3–14.

TACTICS OF IMPRESSION MANAGEMENT

Managing the impression you create encompasses dozens of specific tactics, limited only by what you imagine will impress others. As you work through Self-Assessment Quiz 11-2 on the next page, you will become familiar with these tactics. The numbered items constitute a representative list of what higher-level workers can do to impress others—including doing an outstanding job.

When managing the impression you create, be mindful of the advice offered by William L. Gardner III. He urges that you be yourself. When selecting an image, do not attempt to be somebody you are not, because people will see through this facade. Gardner concludes, "Make every effort to put your best foot forward—but never at the cost of your identity or integrity!"[2] Gardner's comment helps emphasize the fact that impression management is geared toward looking good, but not creating a false impression. Another essential part of impression management is to avoid creating a negative

Self-Assessment Quiz 11-2

THE POSITIVE-IMPRESSION SURVEY

Directions: Please indicate how often you use the following ways of impressing work associates, including customers. Use the following ratings: 1 = Very infrequently (VI); 2 = Infrequently (I); 3 = Sometimes (S); 4 = Frequently (F); and 5 = Very frequently (VF). Circle the most accurate answer.

Tactic or Method	VI	I	S	F	VF
1. Dressing well	1	2	3	4	5
2. Making a favourable appearance other than through dress	1	2	3	4	5
3. Using colourful speech	1	2	3	4	5
4. Being cheerful	1	2	3	4	5
5. Appearing self-confident	1	2	3	4	5
6. Being neat and orderly	1	2	3	4	5
7. Pretending to others that I am in demand	1	2	3	4	5
8. Talking about quality as it relates to the job	1	2	3	4	5
9. Talking about own accomplishments	1	2	3	4	5
10. Being knowledgeable about the topic at hand	1	2	3	4	5
11. Achieving high job performance	1	2	3	4	5
12. Creating a problem and then solving it to look good	1	2	3	4	5
13. Talking about team play	1	2	3	4	5
14. Being diplomatic	1	2	3	4	5
15. Sharing expertise with others	1	2	3	4	5
16. Sharing credit with others	1	2	3	4	5
17. Giving warmth and support	1	2	3	4	5
18. Following through with promises	1	2	3	4	5
19. Exaggerating my accomplishments	1	2	3	4	5
20. Saying what the other person wants to hear	1	2	3	4	5
21. Listening carefully	1	2	3	4	5
22. Making small talk	1	2	3	4	5
23. Talking about work	1	2	3	4	5
24. Showing good ethics	1	2	3	4	5
25. Sending greeting cards to work associates	1	2	3	4	5
26. Avoiding a direct "No" in dealing with others	1	2	3	4	5
27. Being calm under pressure	1	2	3	4	5
28. Flattering others	1	2	3	4	5

(Continued)

Interpretation: This questionnaire is not designed to provide a score. Instead, compare your frequency ratings to those of a group of 300 men and women holding a variety of managerial, sales, and professional jobs. The following mean scores refer to ratings on the 1-to-5 scale.

1. Dressing well, 4.1
2. Favourable appearance, 4.3
3. Colourful speech, 3.6
4. Cheerfulness, 4.3
5. Self-confident appearance, 4.5
6. Neatness, 4.2
7. Pretending to be in demand, 2.0
8. Talk of quality, 4.2
9. Talk of accomplishments, 2.6
10. Knowledge of topic, 4.2
11. High performance, 4.7
12. Creating problems, 1.8
13. Team player talk, 3.6
14. Diplomacy, 4.0
15. Share expertise, 4.2
16. Share credit, 3.9
17. Warmth and support, 4.1
18. Following through, 4.4
19. Exaggeration, 2.0
20. Saying what people want to hear, 2.7
21. Listening, 4.1
22. Small talk, 3.0
23. Work talk, 3.3
24. Ethics display, 4.4
25. Greeting cards, 2.6
26. Avoid direct "No," 3.1
27. Pressure handling, 4.1
28. Flattery, 0.9

Your rating of the impression-management tactics may provide useful clues to skill development. If you use a given tactic much less frequently than others, you might consider evaluating whether you are using this tactic enough. For example, if you make very infrequent use of warmth and support to impress others, you might increase the frequency of such behaviour to the norm (4.1 = frequently). In other instances, you might decide that you are overusing a tactic (such as exaggerating).

Note: In the comparison groups, only one statistically significant difference was found between men and women in the use of these impression tactics. Women gave a mean frequency rating of 2.9 for the use of greeting cards, while men gave a frequency rating of 2.3.

Source: Andrew J. DuBrin, "Sex Differences in the Use and Effectiveness of Tactics of Impression Management," *Psychological Reports*, vol. 74, 1994, pp. 531–544.

impression through such behaviours as frequently being absent or late, speaking poorly, or talking in a meeting while the presenter is speaking. The discussion of etiquette may help guide you away from behaviours that could bring you negative attention.

BUSINESS ETIQUETTE

A major component of managing your impression is practising good etiquette. **Business etiquette** is a special code of behaviour required in work situations. The term *manners* has an equivalent meaning. Both manners and etiquette generally refer to behaving in a refined and acceptable manner. Jim Rucker and Anna Sellers explain that business etiquette is much more than knowing how to use the correct utensil or how to dress in a given situation. Business people today must know how to be at ease with strangers and with groups, be able to offer congratulations smoothly, know how to make introductions, and know how to conduct themselves at company social functions.[3] Studying etiquette is important because knowing and using proper business etiquette contributes to individual and business success.[4] People who are considerate of the feelings of others, and companies that are courteous toward customers, are more likely to succeed than are their rude counterparts.

Business etiquette includes many aspects of interpersonal relations in organizations, as described in the following discussion.[5] What is considered proper etiquette in the workplace changes over time and may vary with the situation. At one time, addressing one's superior by his or her first name was considered brash. Today it is commonplace behaviour, at least in North America. A sampling of etiquette guidelines is helpful. Nevertheless, a general principle of being considerate of the feelings of work associates is more important than any one act of etiquette or courtesy. Keep in mind also that you will find contradictory statements in writings about etiquette. Before reading ahead, you are invited to take Self-Assessment Quiz 11-3.

Self-Assessment Quiz 11-3

BUSINESS ETIQUETTE

1. How would you introduce a sales representative to your supervisor?
   a. Ms. Mint, this is Joe Majors, a sales rep from Power Office Machines.
   b. Joe Majors, I would like you to meet my boss, Ms. Alice Mint.
   c. Joe, this is the boss.
   d. Ms. Alice Mint, meet Joe.

2. Who should exit first on an elevator?
   a. all women
   b. the woman closest to the door
   c. the man or woman closest to the door
   d. the largest person in the elevator, male or female

3. When a woman conducts business in a foreign country, she should always
   a. explain clearly that she will not serve coffee or run errands.
   b. play a subjugated (inferior) role to male business companions.
   c. be sensitive to differences in culture.
   d. enjoy complete freedom.

4. At a business dinner, how should you signal a server that you are ready to order?
   a. Call the server in a loud but non-threatening voice.
   b. Close the menu.
   c. Say in a low but audible voice, "Where's our server?" when another server or bus person is nearby.
   d. Stand up and make the hand gesture that signals "Come over here."

(Continued)

5. In a restaurant, when is it proper to unfold a napkin and place it in your lap?

   a. as soon as you sit down

   b. when the first course arrives

   c. immediately after beverages have been ordered

   d. whenever you feel so inclined

6. When is it appropriate to put elbows on the table?

   a. only between courses

   b. always

   c. never

   d. whenever you are drinking a beverage

7. How much should the host tip a wine steward?

   a. $3 to $4 per bottle

   b. 15% of the price of the meal plus the wine

   c. 10% of the price of the wine

   d. nothing, because tipping is not necessary

8. At a cocktail party, even if no alcohol is consumed, which hand holds the drink glass?

   a. right

   b. left

   c. right for right-handers, left for left-handers

   d. left for right-handers, right for left-handers

9. If, by oversight, you are left out of the introduction in a group at the office, what is the best way to correct the error?

   a. ignore the oversight

   b. make a joke about how the other group members are jealous of you

   c. introduce yourself

   d. point out the oversight in a strong manner

10. Jennifer (age 26), a sales rep, invites Max (age 49), a vice-president of purchasing, to lunch. What should take place after the server brings the bill?

    a. Jennifer should pay because Max is the customer and she invited him.

    b. The person closest to where the bill was placed by the server should pay.

    c. Jennifer and Max should each pay one-half of the bill.

    d. Max should pay because he is male and older.

Answers: 1. a; 2. c; 3. c; 4. b; 5. a; 6. a; 7. a; 8. b; 9. c; 10. a.

The higher you scored, the more you know about business etiquette. A low score most likely means you need to study and observe more about business etiquette.

Source: Adapted and expanded from "A Business Etiquette Quiz," *Keying In*, January 1996, p. 7.

Etiquette for Work Behaviour, Including Clothing

General work etiquette includes all aspects of performing in the work environment, such as completing work on time, punctuality, being a good team player, listening to others, and following through. For instance, having the courtesy to complete a project when it is due demonstrates good manners and respect for the work of others.

Clothing might be considered part of general work behaviour. The casual standards in the information technology field, along with dress-down days, have created confusion about proper office attire. A general rule is that *casual* should not be interpreted as sloppy, such as torn jeans or a stained sweatshirt. Many companies have moved back toward emphasizing traditional business attire, such as suits for men and women. In many work situations, dressing more formally may constitute proper etiquette.

Introductions

The basic rule for introductions is to present the lower ranking person to the higher ranking person regardless of age or sex. "Ms. Barker (the CEO), I would like you to meet my new coworker, Pierre Lacome." (Observe that the higher ranking person's name is mentioned first.) If the two people being introduced are of equal rank, mention the older one first. Providing a little information about the person being introduced is considered good manners. When introducing one person to the group, present the group to the individual. "Sid Foster, this is our information systems team." When being introduced to a person, concentrate on the name and repeat it soon, thus enhancing learning. A fundamental display of good manners is to remember people's names and to pronounce them correctly. When dealing with people senior to you or of higher rank, call them by their last name and title until told otherwise. (Maybe Ms. Barker, above, will tell you, "Please call me Kathy.")

It is good manners and good etiquette to remember the names of work associates to whom you are introduced, even if you see them only occasionally. If you forget the name of a person, it is better to admit this than to guess and come up with the wrong name. Just say, "I apologize, but I've forgotten your name. Tell me once more, and I won't forget."

A major change in introducing people is that men and women are now both expected to extend their right hand when being introduced. Give a firm but not over-powering handshake, and establish eye contact with the person you are greeting.

Relationships Between Men and Women and Between People of Different Ages

Social etiquette is based on chivalry and the gender of the person, whereas business etiquette is based on generally equal treatment for all. Women should no longer be treated differently when approaching a door, riding in an elevator, or walking in the street. According to the new rules, the person in the lead (no matter the sex or age) should proceed first and hold the door for the others following. However, a man should still follow a woman when using an escalator. When using stairs, a man usually follows a woman going up and precedes her going down. Men no longer have to walk next to the street when walking with one or two women. Correct etiquette now states that men should always walk on either side, but not in the middle of two women. Elders should still be respected, but not in such ways as holding doors open for them, helping them off with their overcoats, or getting coffee for them.

Unless you are good friends who typically hug when meeting, it is best to avoid touching others of the same or opposite sex except for a handshake. Some people believe that nonsexual touching is part of being charming and warm, yet many workers are offended when touched by another worker. The subject is controversial because public figures often drape their arms around others, and physical touching is part of the ritual of offering congratulations in sports.

Telephone Use

Despite the prominence of voice mail and text messaging, most business communication over the telephone requires live interaction between people. Guidelines for proper telephone usage include the following:

- Answer the phone by the third ring.

- Identify your company, your department, and yourself.

- Say good morning, good afternoon, or good evening.

- Always end the call on a pleasant note and say goodbye. Never say bye-bye (except for social calls).

- If possible, avoid call waiting and other forms of putting people on hold. Putting people on hold after the conversation has begun is very rude. Cell telephones have created substantial challenges in etiquette, going beyond the points just mentioned. The general point is not to annoy or irritate others with your cellphone, particularly by being loud and rude. Among the cellphone behaviours likely to be interpreted as rude (at least by some people) are making personal calls while in your cubicle, using your cellphone in meetings or during luncheons, and talking loudly into your cellphone while in public space such as hallways, dining areas, and break rooms. Above all, do not answer the cellphone while talking to customers or your manager face-to-face.

Dining

Etiquette surrounding meals involves planning for the meeting, making seating arrangements, paying the bill, tipping, using proper table manners, and appropriate drinking of alcoholic beverages. We all know not to slurp spaghetti one strand at a time, pour ketchup over sauce, or leave a 50¢ tip. Less obvious are the following guidelines:

- Arrange seating for meal meetings in advance.

- Establish with the server who will be paying the cheque.

- You will be served from the right, so be prepared to lean slightly to the left to allow the server to place the food and beverages.

- Place your napkin on your lap immediately after being seated.

- Bread should not be used to push food onto a fork or spoon.

- Attempt to pace your eating speed to that of others at the table.

- The wait staff, not the diners, should be responsible for moving plates around the table. Circulate rolls and bread to the right, not the left.

- Order an alcoholic beverage only when invited to do so by the person sponsoring the meal, and then only if he or she does. Avoid drunkenness or feeling tipsy.

Etiquette for Hard Copy and Email Correspondence

Many people believe that formality and careful use of language can be neglected when sending messages by email. Remember, however, that the way in which any message is sent tells something about the sender. Email messages should be proofread, should be sent only when necessary, and generally should be no longer than one screen—not including attachments. Although many email users rely on a strikingly informal and casual writing style, such informality for business correspondence is poor etiquette. For example, avoid confirming a meeting with your CEO in these words: "C U later, 4 sure." Overloading the company system with attachments containing space-consuming graphics is often considered rude.

An email etiquette problem with legal implications is that company email messages are the property of the company, not the sender. So avoid sending through email insulting, vulgar, or inflammatory comments because even deleted email messages can be retrieved. Be careful not to forward an email message that has negative comments about the recipient. For example, a customer service representative sent an email to a customer attempting to resolve a complaint. However, instead of beginning with a fresh email, the representative included an email from her boss that said, "Give this idiot what she wants to get her off our back." The customer later sued the company, and then agreed to a small financial settlement.

Instant messaging has created new challenges for email etiquette. Because instant messaging allows you to intrude on co-workers at any time—and them to drop in on you—the opportunities to be rude multiply. Managers should not intrude upon workers through instant messaging unless it is urgent. Think before you send, and make sure the message has real value to the recipient. Suggest politely to "buddies" who are taking up too much of your time with messages that they contact you after work.[6]

Using Electronic Devices

Electronic devices such as internet access devices, personal digital assistants (PDAs), (now often included in cellphones) create opportunities for good and poor etiquette. Violations of etiquette surrounding the internet include receiving non-work-related material on your monitor in the presence of others and surfing the internet on company time. A growing etiquette problem is workers at meetings using their notebook computers to do other work. Yet in some companies such multitasking may be regarded as acceptable behaviour. Displaying pornographic or sports sites on an office computer is taboo. An open pornographic site might lead to charges of sexual harassment.

Key violations of photocopier etiquette include hogging the machine, jumping in ahead of others, and leaving the machine jammed or at a setting only you require. A generally accepted guideline is that if you are using the photocopying machine for a large job and somebody approaches with a small job, let that person go first.

Cross-Cultural Relations

What constitutes proper etiquette may differ from culture to culture. Be alert to differences in etiquette in areas such as gift giving, dining, drinking alcoholic beverages, and when and where to discuss business. Many of these differences in customs were described in Chapter 6.

Violating these customs is poor etiquette. For example, using the index finger to point is considered rude in most Asian and Middle Eastern countries. Also, people in

Middle Eastern countries tend to stand as close as two or three inches from the person with whom they are talking. To back away is interpreted as an insult. An American visitor to China nearly lost a major sale because after receiving a business card from the Chinese company representative, he stuffed it in his pocket without first carefully reading the card. Proper etiquette in China is to carefully read the giver's business card, and perhaps holding it with both hands out of respect.

Suppose you are in doubt about the proper etiquette for any situation, and you do not have a handbook of etiquette readily available. As a substitute, observe how your host or a successful person in the group behaves.

Interacting with People with Disabilities
Many able-bodied people are puzzled by what is proper etiquette in working with people with disabilities. Be as natural and open as you can. In addition, consider these guidelines for displaying good manners when dealing with a physical disability:

- Speak directly to a person with a disability, not to the person's companion.

- Don't assume that a person with a disability needs help. If someone is struggling, ask for permission to assist.

- When talking to a person in a wheelchair, place yourself at that person's eye level.

- When speaking to a person with impaired vision; identify yourself and anyone who may be with you. Do not shout when speaking to a blind person.

- To get the attention of a deaf person, tap the person's shoulder or wave your hand. The Canadian Scene below has more information on interacting with individuals with a hearing impairment who use an interpreter.

- Treat a person with a disability as you would anyone else except for the differences noted in this list.[7]

The Canadian Scene

COMMUNICATING WITH A DEAF PERSON WITH AN INTERPRETER

The Canadian Hearing Society offers advice (read etiquette) for communicating with a deaf person who is using sign language with an interpreter. While this advice is geared to deaf individuals with interpreters, you can most likely apply some of these suggestions to any situation where an interpreter is used. This could include a language interpreter when dealing with someone who does not speak your language.

Do I need to speak slowly?
Speak at your natural pace but be aware that the interpreter must hear and understand a complete thought before signing it. Taking turns in a conversation may be different from what you are used to, owing to the lag time necessary for the interpreting process.

(Continued)

Should I look at the interpreter?
Look and speak directly to the deaf person. Do not say "tell him/her." The deaf person will be watching the interpreter and glancing back and forth at you.

Where should I sit?
Usually it is best to position the interpreter next to you (the hearing person), opposite the deaf person. This makes it easy for the deaf person to see you and the interpreter in one line of vision.

What about a group situation?
Semicircular seating arrangements are best for discussion formats. For large group settings, such as conferences and performances, be sure to reserve a "deaf participants and friends" seating area near the front for clear visibility of the interpreter.

Do I need any special visual aids?
Visual aids such as handouts or writing on a chalkboard can be a tremendous help to both the interpreter and the deaf person, ensuring correct spelling of names or vocabulary.

Can I ask the interpreter about the deaf person or sign language?
The interpreter is present to facilitate communication. If you have questions about the deaf person or sign language, ask the deaf person directly and the interpreter will interpret (but not answer) your questions.

Source: *How to Use Sign Language Interpreters Effectively.* The Canadian Hearing Society, Toronto.

Skill-Building Exercise 11-1 gives you an opportunity to practise appropriate etiquette in several situations.

Skill-Building Exercise 11-1

BUSINESS ETIQUETTE

An effective way of improving business etiquette is to be disciplined enough to use one's best manners and courtesy in real-life situations. Role-playing etiquette scenarios can also contribute to helping you develop the right mindset for using good etiquette.

Scenario 1: Dining Etiquette. A small group of students plan to conduct a high-etiquette meal at a local fast-food restaurant during non-peak hours. Pretend the plastic eating utensils are fine silver and that the Styrofoam cups are crystal. Assume that your Big Mac is beef Wellington or that your submarine sandwich is a delicately prepared capon. Each class member uses his or her best etiquette. At the same time, each group member carefully observes the etiquette displayed by the other members.

At the conclusion of the meal, critique each other's etiquette. If you were courteous enough to invite your instructor to your high-etiquette meal, get his or her feedback.

Scenario 2: Telephone Etiquette. Two people using cellphones are separated by about six feet. Several pairs of students might conduct phone conversations covering such matters as a customer complaint, a job inquiry, or an inquiry about product availability. (*Note:* The students merely *pretend* they are using the phone, rather than waste phone minutes.) Students not making the calls will carefully observe the callers. Look for examples of good and poor telephone etiquette. Feedback will be provided after the telephone conversations are completed.

BUILDING RELATIONSHIPS WITH MANAGERS AND OTHER KEY PEOPLE

The political purpose of building good relationships with managers is to acquire power through such means as gaining a recommendation for promotion or a key assignment. A good relationship with the boss is also important for the basic purpose of receiving a good performance evaluation. Building these good relationships with managers is also important because it helps create a positive, supportive work environment. Good relationships can also be established with managers for the nonpolitical purpose of trying to get the job accomplished. The strategies and tactics described next are outlined in Figure 11-2 and should be used on a regular basis.

Network with Influential People

A basic strategy for success is developing contacts, or **networking**, among influential people. In addition to making contacts, networking involves gaining the trust and confidence of these influential people.[8] Networking also takes place with people both inside and outside the organization who are not your managers. Developing contacts with influential people is likely to pay big career dividends.

A standard procedure is to create a card or computer file of the people in your network and update it frequently. To keep your network effective, it is necessary to contact people on your list periodically. Sending greeting cards, as noted previously in Self-Assessment Quiz 11-2, is one small way of maintaining your network.

Developing a network of influential people requires alertness and planning. You need to identify influential people and then think of a sensible reason to contact them. Below are several possibilities.

- Send an email message to a high-ranking manager, offering a money-saving or revenue-producing suggestion. A related tactic is to inform the person of something of significance you have done in the past that might lie directly in his or her area of interest.

- Do a standout job as a member of a task force or committee that includes a high-ranking official.

1. Network with influential people.
2. Help your manager succeed.
3. Volunteer for assignments.
4. Flatter influential people sensibly.
5. Use information power.
6. Admit mistakes.
7. Appear cool under pressure.
8. Laugh at your manager's humour.
9. Express constructive disagreement.

Figure 11-2   Strategies and Tactics for Building Relationships with Managers and Other Key People

- Discuss your career plans with a neighbour who has an outstanding position.

- Take the initiative to develop a friendship with an influential person who is a member of your athletic club, other club, or place of worship.

Networking is so often used—and abused—that suggestions and guidelines for networking etiquette have emerged. A starting point is to be clear, concise, and specific when making requests of networking contacts.[9] Explain, for example, that you want to become an industry specialist and would like to acquire specific information. Be frank about the amount of time you would want from the network member, such as 15 minutes per month of email and telephone contact.

After making contact with a potential network member, explain the benefit this person is likely to derive from his or her association with you. Provide a *benefit statement* for interacting with you and helping you with you career.[10] Indicate specifically how this person might benefit from you being in his or her network. (If a person is in your network, you are also in that person's network.) If the potential network member is more powerful than you, it is still possible to think of what benefit you might be able to provide. Two examples follow:

- I would like to contact you a few times a year about career concerns. In return, I would be happy to help you prepare PowerPoint slides for any presentation you might be making.

- In return for my receiving career advice from you from time to time, I would be happy to collect information for you about how people in my area perceive one of your products. I have lots of useful contacts in my community.

Avoid being a pest. Many influential people are bombarded with requests to be part of someone's network, so ask for a modest amount of time and assistance. Good networking etiquette is to request a collaborative relationship in which you give as much as you get. The benefit statement just mentioned will place you in a collaborative relationship with the influential person.

Help Your Manager Succeed

The primary reason you are hired is to help your manager achieve the results necessary to succeed. Avoid an adversarial relationship with your manager. Determine both obvious and subtle ways of ensuring the manager's success. One subtle way of increasing your manager's chances for success is to help that person out when he or she is under attack from another department. One example of this would be to supply information to support your manager's position on a controversial issue. Also keep in mind the cornerstone tactic of performing your job superbly. Your manager will then share in your success.

Volunteer for Assignments

An easily implemented method of winning the approval of superiors is to become a "hand-raiser." By volunteering to take on assignments that do not fit neatly into your job description, you display the kind of initiative valued by employers. Among the many possible activities to volunteer for are fundraising campaigns assigned to your company, project membership, and working overtime when most people prefer not to (for example, on a Saturday in July). As noted under the discussion of networking, task-force assignments are also useful for being noticed by key people in the organization. As a team member, volunteer to assume any leadership responsibility you think you can handle. If your team offers rotating leadership assignments, express interest in taking your turn.

Flatter Influential People

One of the most effective relationship builders is to flatter people sensibly and credibly. Despite the risk of being called obsequious or a cheap office politician, the flatterer wins. A study on how to advance in big business pointed out that a company's top employees tend to be equal in performance. So advancing was based on image (30 percent) and contact time with the manager (50 percent). Flattery can play a big role in both.[11] A recent study indicates that even at the highest positions in business, flattery helps a person get ahead. Specifically, ingratiating oneself with the CEO, including flattery, was a major factor in receiving an appointment as a director on the board of major companies.[12]

Flattery is likely to be effective because most people want to receive accolades, even if they are not completely warranted. People who pay us compliments are likely to be treated kindly in turn.[13] Remember, however, the discussion about recognition in Chapter 9, suggesting that less technically oriented people are often the most receptive to praise and flattery. Flattery geared toward the more technically oriented person might have to be more concrete and tied to specific accomplishments.

An effective, general-purpose piece of flattery is to tell another person that you are impressed by something he or she has accomplished. The following anecdote illustrates this approach:

> A management trainee told the purchasing manager that she was impressed with his modern operation. "It's very similar to the ideal material management system described in my production and operations management course," said the trainee. Her flattery appeared to be instrumental in her being asked to become a permanent member of the purchasing department after her training period ended.

Another way of flattering somebody is to listen attentively. If you actively listen to the other person, he or she will feel flattered. The person might think, "What I have to say is valuable. This person really cares about what I have to offer." Flattery can also take the form of quoting another person, or referring to something he or she said to you earlier.

During the next two weeks, try out the flattery tactic with an influential person. In the interim, do Skill-Building Exercise 11-2.

Use Information Power

Power accrues to those who control vital information. At the same time, being a source of useful information will help you build constructive working relationships with managers. You will be relied on as an important contributor. Controlling vital information includes knowing how to gain access to useful information that others do not know how to retrieve. Many workers are aware of the mechanics of using the internet, but fewer have the skills to use it to retrieve commercially useful information. During a tight labour market, for example, human resource specialists can acquire power if they know how to use the internet to find talented people who might want to join the company.

Skill-Building Exercise 11-2

FLATTERING AN INFLUENTIAL PERSON

As a perceptive, intelligent reader, you have probably already guessed the nature of this role play. One student plays the role of a newcomer to the organization who is seeking to advance, or at least to secure, his or her position in the organization. Another person plays the role of a vice-president who is visiting the newcomer's department. The company holds this vice president in high esteem because he or she recently spearheaded the introduction of a highly successful product, a *smart mattress*. The mattress adjusts to the temperature and firmness requirements of its user. In some models the two sides of the mattress can have different settings to adapt to the heat and firmness preferences of two users sharing the same mattress.

The newcomer is asked to escort the vice-president to another part of the building. The walk should take about five minutes, giving the newcomer an opportunity to work in some flattery. Fortunately, the newcomer has read the sales literature about the smart mattress, and has even tried one out in the factory showroom. Although the vice-president is not naive, he or she is proud of his or her accomplishments. The two role players conduct the five-minute walk, perhaps circling the classroom.

Information power is closely related to *expert power*, which refers to having valuable expertise. If your expertise or skill is in high demand at the moment, power will flow in your direction. Currently, an important type of expert power stems from knowing how to operate enterprise software that links together several parts of an organization.

Admit Mistakes

Making a mistake is hardly an effective way to build relationships with key people. Yet admitting a mistake makes you appear much more honourable than covering it up or making naive excuses. According to consultant Ruth Sherman, being able to apologize for your mistakes can add to your being perceived as a go-to person. Admitting your mistakes suggests that you are an honest worker who takes responsibility when a negative event takes place.[14]

> A major air carrier recently displayed an internet ad citing a price of $10 for a round trip from anywhere in Canada to Vancouver. The company was flooded with requests for these tickets before the error was corrected. All requests for these tickets were honoured. The reservation agent who posted the wrong price on the website quickly volunteered that she made the mistake—an honest oversight. Instead of being fired, the worker was praised for her honesty. The manager in charge said with a smile that the publicity surrounding the blooper might help the airline in the long run.

Appear Cool Under Pressure

Showing signs of panic generally hurts your reputation with influential people. In contrast, appearing to be in control emotionally when things around you are falling apart helps convey the impression that you are worthy of additional responsibility.

Being cool under pressure is part of emotional stability, and it is a key leadership characteristic. An example of coolness under pressure follows.

> A snow-making machine technician was rushed to a British Columbia ski resort three days before the start of the holiday season. The problem was that the equipment wasn't spraying water with enough pressure for the water to convert to snow. When the technician arrived at the ski resort, a snarling owner said that if the equipment was not working within 24 hours, the technician's company would be sued for $5 million. Despite all the mental pressure, the technician fixed the water pressure problem within four hours. Several weeks later he was promoted to field maintenance supervisor.

Laugh at Your Manager's Humour

When you indicate by your laughter that you appreciate your manager's sense of humour, it helps establish rapport between the two of you. An indicator of good two-way communication between people is that the two parties comprehend each other's subtle points. Most humour in the workplace deals with subtle meanings about work-related topics. To implement the tactic of laughing at your manager's jokes, do not worry excessively about having heard the joke before.

Express Constructive Disagreement

At one time the office politician thought an effective way of pleasing the boss was to be a "yes-person." Whatever the supervisor thought was right, the yes-person agreed with. A more intelligent tactic in the modern business world is to be ready to disagree in a constructive manner when you sincerely believe the boss is wrong. In the long run you will probably earn more respect than if you agree with the boss just to please that person. Constructive disagreement is based on a careful analysis of the situation and is also tactful.

The right way to disagree means not putting your manager in a corner or embarrassing your manager by confronting him or her loudly or in public. If you disagree with your boss, use carefully worded, inoffensive statements. In this way you minimize the chances of a confrontation or hostile reaction. Remember the smart mattress mentioned in Skill-Building Exercise 11-2? Suppose the marketing vice president claims that the mattress is geared exclusively toward the senior citizen market, and you disagree. You might say, "I think that marketing our smart mattress to seniors is a breakthrough. Yet I also see some other possibilities. There are loads of cold-sensitive young people who wanted a heated mattress. Also, a lot of young people with athletic injuries or orthopaedic problems would welcome an adjustable mattress. Does my thinking make any sense?"

The reason constructive disagreement helps you build a good relationship with most managers is that the boss comes to respect your job knowledge and your integrity. However, if you are working with a very insecure boss, he or she may be taken aback by disagreement. In that case, you have to be extra tactful in expressing disagreement.

Before effectively using the tactics for developing a positive relationship with a boss, some people first need to overcome their inhibitions about performing well around a superior boss. The Job-Oriented Interpersonal Skills in Action box offers insight into overcoming this problem.

Job-Oriented Interpersonal Skills in Action

EXPERTS OFFER ADVICE ON OVERCOMING BOSSOPHOBIA

"I have this phobia in dealing with higher-ups," concedes an investment banker. One time while running through a client presentation in front of his boss, he realized midway through that he had flubbed some minor figures. In the end, "I bumbled so badly that it sounded 10 times worse," he says. "And because I started saying stupid things, he just went ballistic."

The banker says he doesn't have any trouble keeping his cool in front of peers, subordinates, or senior management at other firms. But around any current or even former boss, his mind goes blank and his heart races. He's convinced his most recent boss's dissatisfaction is one reason he lost his job. "I can't blame him," he says. "He doesn't know what I know."

Bossophobia is rarely discussed, but irrational fears of the supervisor are widespread and often prove debilitating for employees and costly for companies. The phobia is caused by people distorting the intentions of their manager or bringing some bad prior experience to the relationship. Even a single humiliating moment in the past, completely unrelated to a real-life boss, can feed a worker's fears.

John Weaver, a psychologist and coach in Waukesha, Wisconsin, estimates that perhaps a slim two percent or less of the population suffers from an extreme form of bossophobia, but estimates that 10 to 15 percent of people have moderate fears that hold them back from fully pursuing their careers. Dr. Weaver counsels them to expose themselves gradually to situations that provoke anxiety. "They have to put themselves in situations where they do have to perform in front of the boss," he says. "You can't get past an anxiety without confronting it."

You can approach your manager about a general case of bossophobia, but you need to assess how open you can be. It would be naive to think that all supervisors would respond positively to such openness, career coaches and psychologists say. Most workplaces contain a continuum of management personalities, with a dominant fear-based style at one end and a more open and compassionate style at the other.

"I'd like to think that in the modern era the more-enlightened boss wants to help people get comfortable and more productive," says Herb Rapport, a professor of psychology at Temple University.

Questions

1. How would a worker know if he or she were phobic about bosses?
2. How might relationships with instructors provide a clue as to whether a person was bossophobic?

Source: From Kris Maher, "The Jungle: Focus on Retirement, Pay and Getting Ahead," *The Wall Street Journal*, February 4, 2003, p. B4. Reprinted with permission.

BUILDING RELATIONSHIPS WITH CO-WORKERS AND OTHER WORK ASSOCIATES

Another strategy for increasing your power is to form alliances with co-workers and other work associates. You need the support of these people to get your work accomplished. Also, when you are being considered for promotion, co-workers and other work associates may be asked their opinion of you. Under a peer-evaluation system, the opinion of co-workers about your performance counts heavily. In this section, we describe eight representative strategies and techniques for developing good interpersonal relationships

1. Maintain honest and open relationships.
2. Make others feel important.
3. Be diplomatic.
4. Exchange favours.
5. Ask advice.
6. Share constructive gossip.
7. Minimize microinequities
8. Follow group norms.

Figure 11-3 Strategies and Tactics for Developing Relationships with Co-workers and Other Work Associates

at or below your level (see Figure 11-3). The information about developing teamwork skills presented in Chapter 4 is also relevant here. To examine your self-perception of your co-worker relations skills, do Self-Assessment Quiz 11-4. Expressing an interest in the work of others is an effective tactic because so many people are self-centred. They are eager to talk about their own work, but rarely pause to express a genuine interest in others. Expressing an interest in the work of others is also effective because it is a form of recognition. Self-Assessment Quiz 11-4 gives you an opportunity to think about your tendencies toward making others feel important.

Maintain Honest and Open Relationships

Although being honest may appear to contradict organizational politics, it is representative of the nature of positive politics. Giving co-workers frank but tactful answers to their requests for your opinion is one useful way of developing open relationships. Assume that a co-worker asks your opinion of an email he intends to send to his supervisor. As you read it, you find it somewhat incoherent and filled with spelling and grammatical errors. An honest response to this message might be: "I think your idea is a good one. But I think your email needs more work before that idea comes across clearly."

Accurately expressing your feelings, whether positive or negative, also leads to constructive relationships. If you have been singled out for good performance, let other team members know that you are happy and proud. If you arrive at work upset over a personal problem and appearing obviously fatigued, you can expect some reaction. A co-worker might say, "What seems to be the problem? Is everything all right?" A dishonest reply would be, "Everything is fine." In addition to making an obviously untrue statement, you would also be perceived as rejecting the person who asked the question. If you prefer not to discuss your problem, an honest response would be, "Thanks for your interest. I am facing some problems today. But I think things will work out."

Make Others Feel Important

A fundamental principle of fostering good relationships with co-workers and others is to make them feel important. Visualize that everyone in the workplace is wearing a small sign around the neck that says, "Please make me feel important."[15] Although the leader has the primary responsibility for satisfying this recognition need, co-workers also play a key role. One approach to making a co-worker feel important would be to bring a

Self-Assessment Quiz 11-4

HOW IMPORTANT DO I MAKE PEOPLE FEEL?

Directions: Indicate on a one-to-five scale how frequently you act (or would act if the situation presented itself) in the ways indicated below: very infrequently (VI); infrequently (I); sometimes (S); frequently (F); very frequently (VF). Circle the number underneath the column that best fits your answer.

	VI	I	S	F	VF
1. I do my best to correctly pronounce a co-worker's name.	1	2	3	4	5
2. I avoid letting other people's egos get too big.	5	4	3	2	1
3. I brag to others about the accomplishments of my co-workers.	1	2	3	4	5
4. I recognize the birthdays of friends in a tangible way.	1	2	3	4	5
5. It makes me anxious to listen to others brag about their accomplishments.	5	4	3	2	1
6. After hearing that a friend has done something outstanding, I shake his or her hand.	1	2	3	4	5
7. If a friend or co-worker recently received a degree or certificate, I would offer my congratulations.	1	2	3	4	5
8. If a friend or co-worker finished second in a contest, I would inquire why he or she did not finish first.	5	4	3	2	1
9. If a co-worker showed me how to do something, I would compliment that person's skill.	1	2	3	4	5
10. When a co-worker starts bragging about a family member's accomplishments, I do not respond.	5	4	3	2	1

Total Score _____

Scoring and Interpretation: Total the numbers corresponding to your answers. Scoring 40 to 50 points suggests that you typically make people feel important; 16 to 39 points suggests that you have a moderate tendency toward making others feel important; 10 to 15 points suggests that you need to develop skill in making others feel important. Study this chapter carefully.

notable accomplishment of his or hers to the attention of the group. Investing a small amount of time in recognizing a co-worker can pay large dividends in terms of cultivating an ally. Expressing an interest in the work of others helps them feel important. A basic way to accomplish this is to ask other employees questions such as the following:

- How is your work going?
- How does the company use output from your department?
- How did you establish all the contacts you did to be so successful in sales?
- How did you develop the skills to do your job?

Be Diplomatic

Despite all that has been said about the importance of openness and honesty in building relationships, most people fail to be convinced. Their egos are too tender to accept the raw truth when faced with disapproval of their thoughts or actions. Diplomacy is still an essential part of office politics. Translated into action, diplomacy often means finding the right phrase to convey disapproval, disagreement, or discontent. Below is an example of a delicate situation and a diplomatic response to it.

During a staff meeting, a co-worker suggests that the entire group schedule a weekend retreat to formulate a five-year plan for the department. The boss looks around the room to gauge the reactions of others to the proposal. You want to say: "What a stupid idea! Who needs to ruin an entire weekend to do something we could easily accomplish on a workday afternoon?" The diplomatic response is: "I've heard that retreats sometimes work. But would spending that much time on the five-year plan be cost-effective? Maybe we could work on the plan during one long meeting. If we don't get the planning accomplished in that time frame, we could then consider the retreat."

Exchange Favours

An important part of human interaction on and off the job is to reciprocate with others. Exchanging favours with others can make it easier for people to accomplish their work because they are able to call on assistance when needed. The adept political player performs a favour for another employee without asking a favour in return. The favour is then cashed in when a favour is needed. Here are three typical exchanges:

- A paralegal agrees to help another overburdened paralegal in the same law office, knowing that the other paralegal will reciprocate if needed in the future.

- A credit manager agrees to expedite a credit application for a sales representative. In reciprocation, the sales rep agrees to not commit the company to a delivery date on the next sale until the customer's credit has been evaluated.

- An assistant restaurant manager agrees to substitute for another assistant manager on New Year's Eve. One month later the first person asks the second to take over her shift, so she can get away for the weekend.

Ask Advice

Asking advice on technical and professional topics is a good way of building relationships with other employees. Asking for advice from another person—someone whose job does not require giving it—will usually be perceived as a compliment. Asking advice transmits the message, "I trust your judgment enough to ask your opinion on something important to me." You are also saying, "I trust you enough to think that the advice you give me will be in my best interest."

To avoid hard feelings, inform the person whose advice you are seeking that his or her opinion will not necessarily be binding. A request for advice might be prefaced with a comment such as, "I would like your opinion on a problem facing me. But I can't guarantee that I'll be in a position to act on it."

Share Constructive Gossip

An effective way of building workplace relationships is to share constructive gossip with others. Gossip serves as a socializing force because it is a mode of forging intimate relationships for many employees; workers get close to one another through the vehicle of gossip. It also serves as the lifeblood of personal relationships on the job. If you are the person supplying the gossip, people will develop positive attitudes toward you. **Positive gossip** is unofficial information that does not attack others, is based on truth, and does not leak confidential information. Given these restrictions, here is an example of positive gossip:

- "I heard that business is really picking up. If this week is any example, the company's profits for the quarter will far exceed expectations."

- "I heard yesterday that the director of public relations just got engaged to a cool guy she met on a cruise."

Minimize Microinequities

A potent way of alienating coworkers is to snub them, or put them down, in a small way without being aware of your behaviour. A **microinequity** is a small, semiconscious message we send with a powerful impact on the receiver. A microinequity might also be considered a subtle slight. The inequity might take the form of ignoring another person, a snub, or a sarcastic comment. Understanding microinequities can lead to changes in one-on-one relationships that may profoundly irritate others.[16]

Imagine that you are in line in the company cafeteria with three co-workers. You turn around and notice an old friend from school who is visiting the company. Next, you introduce your old friend to two of the co-workers with you, but not the third. That co-worker is likely to feel crushed and irritated, and it will take you awhile to patch your relationship. Looking at a microinequity from the standpoint of the receiver, a work associate might say to you, "Some computer illiterate sent me an email this morning without the attachment he said was there." You respond, "Excuse me, but that *computer illiterate* was me."

To overcome giving microinequities, it is important to think through the consequences of what you are doing and saying before taking action. In the cafeteria situation above, you might say to yourself, "Here comes time for an introduction, and this is not easy for me. I will remember to introduce everybody to my old friend."

Follow Group Norms

A summary principle to follow in getting along with other employees is to heed **group norms**, the unwritten set of expectations for group members. If you do not deviate too far from these norms, the group will accept much of your behaviour. Group norms also take the form of social cues about how to act, and therefore contribute to the organizational culture. Representative group norms include the following: (1) help co-workers with problems if you have the right expertise; (2) do not wear formal business attire on casual dress days; (3) have lunch with your co-workers at least once a week; (4) do not complain to the boss about a co-worker unless his or her negative behaviour is outrageously bad; (5) do not take a sick day unless you are really sick; (6) take your turn in bringing snacks to a meeting at least once a month; and

Skill-Building Exercise 11-3

GETTING ALONG WITH CO-WORKERS

An inventory auditor in a department store chain decides to take action aimed at getting along better with co-workers. In each of the following two scenarios, one person plays the role of the inventory auditor. Another person plays the role of an employee whom the auditor is attempting to cultivate.

Scenario 1: Exchanging Favours. The auditor decides to strike a bargain with a store associate. (The role player decides what this exchange of favours should be.) Unknown to the auditor, the store associate is concerned about an inventory audit because he is worried about being accused of stealing merchandise.

Scenario 2: Express an Interest in the Co-worker's Work. The auditor decides to express an interest in a tech fixer because he can be a valuable ally when conducting an inventory audit. The inventory audit is computerized, and the appropriate software is confusing and crashes frequently. The tech fixer has a heavy workload and is not much prone to small talk, but he does get excited talking about information technology.

(7) side with your co-workers rather than management when there is a dispute between the two groups.

If you do not deviate too far from these norms, the group will accept much of your behaviour. If you deviate too far, you will be subject to much rejection and therefore lose some of your power base. Yet if you conform too closely to group norms, higher-level management may perceive you as being unable to identify with management. Employees are sometimes blocked from moving up the ladder because they are regarded as "one of the gang."

Skill-Building Exercise 11-3 provides an opportunity to practise several techniques for building interpersonal relationships with co-workers and other work associates.

AVOIDING POLITICAL BLUNDERS

A strategy for not losing whatever power you have accumulated is to refrain from making power-eroding blunders. Committing these politically insensitive acts can also prevent you from attaining power. Self-Assessment Quiz 11-5 will get you started thinking about blunders. Several leading blunders are described in the following list.

1. *Criticizing your manager in a public forum.* The oldest saw in human relations is to "praise in public and criticize in private." Yet in the passion of the moment, you may still surrender to the irresistible impulse to criticize your manager publicly. As a result, the manager will harbour resentment toward you and perhaps block your chances for advancement.

2. *Bypassing the manager.* Many people believe that because most organizations are more democratic today, it is not important to respect the layers of authority (the chain of command). In reality, following etiquette is highly valued in most firms. Going around the manager to resolve a problem is therefore hazardous.

Self-Assessment Quiz 11-5

THE BLUNDER QUIZ

Indicate whether you agree or disagree with the following statements.

	Agree	Disagree
1. It's fine to criticize your manager in a meeting so long as the criticism is valid.	_____	_____
2. If I objected to a decision made by top management I would send a companywide email explaining my objection.	_____	_____
3. I am willing to insult any co-worker if the insult is deserved.	_____	_____
4. I see no problem in using competitors' products or services and letting my superiors know about it.	_____	_____
5. If I thought the CEO of my company were way overpaid, I would send him or her an email making my opinion known.	_____	_____
6. Never bother with company-sponsored social events, such as holiday parties, unless you are really interested.	_____	_____
7. I would not attend a company social function if I had the chance to attend another social activity of more interest to me.	_____	_____
8. I'm very open about passing along confidential information.	_____	_____
9. I openly criticize most new ventures my company or department is contemplating.	_____	_____
10. I avoid any deliberate attempt to please or impress coworkers.	_____	_____

Scoring and Interpretation: The greater the number of statements you agree with, the more prone you are to political blunders that can damage your interpersonal relationships and your career. You need to raise your awareness level of blunders on the job.

You might be able to accomplish the bypass, but your career could be damaged and your recourses limited. It is much better to work out differences with your manager using standard methods of resolving conflict.

3. *Overt displays of disloyalty.* Being disloyal to your organization is a basic political blunder. Making it known that you are looking for a position elsewhere is the best-known form of disloyalty. Criticizing your company in public settings, praising the high quality of competitors' products, and writing angry internal email messages about your company are others. You may not get fired, but overt signs of disloyalty may place you in permanent disfavour.

4. *Being a pest.* Common wisdom suggests that diligently pressing for one's demands is the path to success. This may be true up to a point, but when assertiveness is used too often it becomes annoying to many people. The unduly persistent person comes to be perceived as being a pest, which has

serious political consequences. An example of being a pest would be asking your manager every month when you are going to receive the raise you deserve.

5. *Being (or being perceived as) a poor team player.* An employee is expected to be a good team player in almost all organizations because cooperation makes collective effort possible. If you are a poor team player, or are perceived as such, your chances for promotion will diminish because you will be recognized as having poor interpersonal skills. Among the ways to be perceived as a poor team player are to engage in social loafing, miss numerous department meetings, take too much credit for group accomplishments, and minimizing your interactions with co-workers. In short, if you ignore all the advice about team play presented in Chapter 4, you will be committing a political blunder.

6. *Burning your bridges.* A potent political blunder is to create ill will among former employers or people who have helped you in the past. The most common form of bridge-burning occurs when a person departs from an organization. A person who leaves involuntarily is especially apt to express anger toward those responsible for the dismissal. Venting your anger may give a temporary boost to your mental health, but it can be detrimental in the long run.

If you want to overcome having committed a blunder, avoid defensiveness. Demonstrate that you are more interested in recovering from the blunder than in trying to share the blame for what happened. Focus on solutions to the problem rather than on fault-finding. Suppose you have been too critical of your team leader in a recent team meeting. Explain that your attempts to be constructively critical backfired and that you will choose your words more carefully in the future.

Another way to patch up a blunder is to stay poised. Admit that you made the mistake and apologize, but don't act or feel inferior. Mistakes are inevitable in a competitive work environment. Avoid looking sad and distraught. Instead, maintain eye contact with people when you describe your blunder.

SUMMARY

Positive political tactics help build good interpersonal relationships. Organizational politics refers to gaining power through any means other than merit or luck. Power refers to the ability or potential to control anything of value and influence decisions. Impression management is one aspect of organizational politics. Managing the impression you create encompasses a wide range of behaviours designed to create a positive influence on work associates.

A major component of managing the impression you create is business etiquette. The general principle of etiquette is to be considerate of the feelings of work associates. Areas of business etiquette include work behaviour and clothing, introducing people, relationships between people of different sexes and ages, telephone use, dining, email correspondence, use of electronic devices, cross-cultural relations, and interaction with people with disabilities.

Political strategies and tactics for building relationships with managers include the following: network with influential people; help your manager succeed; volunteer for assignments; flatter influential people sensibly; use information power; admit mistakes, appear cool under pressure; laugh at your manager's humour; and express constructive disagreement.

Political strategies and tactics for developing relationships with co-workers and other work associates include the following: maintain honest and open relationships; make others feel important; be diplomatic; exchange favours; ask for advice; share constructive gossip; minimize microinequities; and follow group norms.

A strategy for not losing whatever power you have accumulated is to refrain from making political blunders. Political blunders can also prevent you from attaining power. Representative blunders include criticizing your manager publicly, bypassing your manager, overt disloyalty, being a pest, being a poor team player, and burning your bridges. If you want to make up for a blunder, avoid defensiveness and stay poised.

An Interpersonal Relations Case Problem

WHAT DO MY TABLE MANNERS HAVE TO DO WITH THE JOB?

Suzanne Limeau was mentally set for a wonderful day. She was returning to AutoPay Inc. for her third job interview for a position as a human resources representative. As an HR rep Suzanne would have a variety of responsibilities including answering employee questions about benefits, organizing company parties and picnics, and conducting exit interviews with employees who quit the firm.

Suzanne reasoned that the third interview should be mostly to confirm the opinion of AutoPay managers that she was an excellent candidate for the position. Suzanne admired how AutoPay had grown into one of the largest payroll processing companies in the region, managing payroll and other human resource functions for hundreds of small employers. She also admired the professional appearance and behaviour of almost all the AutoPay workers she met.

Two hours before leaving for the job interview, Suzanne received an email message from her prospective boss, Steve Adams. The message indicated that there would be a slight change of schedule. Instead of her arriving at 10 a.m., Adams wanted Suzanne to arrive at 11:30 a.m. Adams and a few other company representatives decided they wanted to take her to lunch. The setting for the lunch would be Silo's, an upscale restaurant that emphasized Italian specialties.

On company premises, Suzanne met briefly with three company representatives and exchanged a few pleasantries. At this point, Suzanne knew that any heavy questions would be asked over lunch. The inevitable question about Suzanne's motives for entering human resources came up before the group even ordered: "Why do you want to work in human resources?" Suzanne knew to avoid the stereotypical answer, "Because I like people."

Instead, Suzanne explained that she enjoyed working with the complexity of people, and that she believed strongly that taking care of human resources translates directly into profits. Adams blurted out, "Great answer Suzanne."

The server came to the table and asked for drink orders. Two people ordered a glass of club soda, one person ordered tonic water, and Suzanne asked for a Blue Light "And, don't forget," she added, "I would like another one during the meal."

Suzanne ordered clams over linguini for an entrée. When the server asked if the diners wanted dessert, only Suzanne said yes. Her choice was Neapolitan ice cream.

(Continued)

Conversation flowed freely during the lunch, and Suzanne was feeling confident that she would receive a job offer. After lunch, Adams took her aside, thanked her for joining the group for lunch, and said that she would be hearing from them soon.

A week passed without hearing from Adams or another company representative. Suzanne sent an email thanking the company for the three interviews, and pointed out that she was still enthused about the prospects of working for AutoPay. Two days later a letter arrived in the mail explaining that the company had decided to offer the job to another candidate. A little bit shocked and disappointed, Suzanne telephoned Adams and asked if she could please be told exactly why she was turned down for a job, when she seemed so qualified, and the company seemed so interested.

"We all thought you were a strong candidate, Suzanne," answered Adams. "But my boss said we could not hire a person with such poor manners."

"Poor manners? What are you talking about?" inquired Suzanne.

"My boss and I noticed three faux pas. First, you were the only person to order an alcoholic beverage, and you ordered two. Second, you sucked in a strand of linguini more than once. Third, you were the only person to order dessert. I am very sorry."

Disappointed and angry, Suzanne asked, "What do my table manners have to do with the job? I didn't get drunk, and I wasn't a slob."

Case Questions

1. How justified were the company managers in turning down Suzanne based on their perception of her table manners?

2. Should Steve Adams have warned Suzanne Chavez that her table manners would be a factor in evaluating her job qualifications?

3. How might Suzanne benefit from the time she invested in her interviews with AutoPay?

An Interpersonal Relations Case Problem

THE UNNOTICED GROUP MEMBER

Troy Winston worked as a desktop publishing technician for a large printing firm, Tri-City Graphics. With five years of experience behind him, Troy was looking to be promoted into a supervisory position. His long-range goal was to become a printing company executive. Over the last three years, Troy received average or above-average ratings on his performance evaluation. During his most recent performance evaluation, Troy took the initiative to discuss his prospects for being promoted to team leader in his work group or supervisor in another department. Troy's boss, Penny Jacobin, shrugged her shoulders and said, "I wouldn't rule out your being promoted, but right now I don't see any openings. Bring up the issue again during next year's evaluation."

Troy was so concerned about Penny's lukewarm response to his interest in being promoted that he spoke to his mentor in the company, Sydney Marlin, a veteran production manager. Troy said to Sydney, "I don't seem to be getting anywhere in this company. I like being a desktop publishing specialist, but I also want to combine it with supervision or leadership."

Sydney said, "Your career plan sounds fine, as we've discussed in the past. Yet somehow your boss is kind of neutral about your potential for promotion. How can you explain Penny's lack of enthusiasm for your promotion potential?"

Troy thought for a moment and then answered, "Penny is a good manager and a fair manager. I have no major complaints about her. It's just that she doesn't notice me much. To her I'm just another professional worker who is getting the job done. The only tangible suggestion Penny has offered me is that I should strive to stay current with new technology in the field. You could say that about anybody. In desktop

(Continued)

publishing, some new development comes along every month."

Sydney told Troy, "Next time I talk with Penny, I'll ask how you are doing. Since I'm your mentor, that type of question would not be out of line."

Ten days later, Sydney met with Penny for another reason and asked about how Troy was coming along in his career. Penny commented, "He is a competent worker, but he kind of blends into the group. During a busy week, it's easy for me not to give Troy much thought. He's a nice guy, but I don't see anything remarkable about him. I see no reason for me or the other managers to look upon

him as being more deserving of promotion than lots of other good technical workers in the company."

"Thanks," said Sydney. "What you have told me could be useful in my advising Troy."

Case Questions

1. If you were Sydney, what advice would you give Troy?

2. Which techniques for getting along with one's manager might Troy be neglecting?

3. Is Penny being fair in her evaluation of Troy?

QUESTIONS FOR DISCUSSION AND REVIEW

1. To what extent are office-politics skills important for a person who is technically competent and hardworking?

2. Many people have said that a major reason for wanting to work out of their home is to avoid office politics. What type of behaviours are they really trying to avoid?

3. Identify three impression-management tactics presented in Self-Assessment Quiz 11-2 that would be acceptable to you. Explain your reasoning.

4. Identify three impression-management tactics presented in Self-Assessment Quiz 11-2 that would be unacceptable to you. Explain your reasoning.

5. Identify three job positions in which you think practising good business etiquette would be extremely important.

6. Etiquette training for people in high-level business positions is more popular than ever. How would you explain the popularity of such training in recent years?

7. A physically able man encounters his vice president, a frail woman, as they are both entering an airport. From an etiquette perspective, should the man ask to carry the woman's bags to the check-in counter? (The man does not have a suitcase with him.)

8. It has been said that although most business people can see through flattery, the technique still works. How would you explain this observation?

9. Describe how email can be used to play positive office politics, as well as used for unethical purposes.

10. Using Research Navigator, access article AN 7058356. This article, titled "Rude Awakening" is based on research in the United States about rude behaviours today. Read the article and in small groups, discuss if Canada is experiencing the same set of issues.

WEBLINKS

www.theproperthing.com
This site has tips and information on social etiquette and proper business protocol.

www.businessoftouch.com
Cartoon-illustrated ways of greeting people around the world.

http://lovequizzes.netfirms.com/boss.html
Quiz about your relationship with your boss.

www.fastcompany.com
This site is devoted to advice and information for business people. There are links to many interesting career development articles.

Chapter 12

Customer Satisfaction Skills

Learning Outcomes

After reading and studying this chapter and doing the exercises, you should be able to

- Satisfy customers better by using general principles of customer satisfaction.
- Create bonds with present or future customers.
- Have a plan for dealing effectively with customer dissatisfaction.
- Explain the contribution of customer service training.

As Tanya Polanski approached the receptionist counter at the hotel, she was tired, frustrated, and confused. "Everything has gone wrong for me the last two days," she explained to Kathy Chang, the receptionist. "My flight from Bejing arrived 10 hours late. I was delayed at customs for an hour. The man said they were doing a random inspection of passengers, even though I didn't look or act like a terrorist. When I tried to use my credit card at the airport, they told me the computer wasn't working so I had to come back a couple of hours later."

"You certainly have had a difficult couple of days, Ms. Polanski," said Chang. "After you are settled in your room, you will start to feel much better. Let me access your reservations." After checking her computer, Chang said, "There seems to be a little problem here. We do not have reservations for you."

In tears, Polanski said, "Has everything gone crazy in Canada? I made these reservations three months ago for the Holiday Inn right on this avenue."

"I understand why you are upset. Let's work out this problem together. Could it be that you made reservations at our other Holiday Inn, a little closer to downtown? It's on the same street. I will check into our worldwide reservation system right now."

"You're in luck, Ms. Polanski," said Chang after a few minutes at the terminal. "Your reservations are at our other Holiday Inn, just five blocks away.

I will have our van take you there right away, and I will phone ahead to make sure you get to the front of the line as soon as possible. Enjoy your stay in Canada, and we look forward to seeing you again."

"Thank you, thank you, you have saved my day," replied Polanski.

Maybe the hotel receptionist in question is naturally gifted in interpersonal skills, or maybe she combined the right personality traits with the right training to become a compassionate and helpful hotel receptionist. Either way she has a lesson for workers at all levels in many different types of jobs. Outstanding customer service enhances a company's reputation, and leads to repeat business. This chapter presents information and exercises that can enhance your ability to satisfy both external and internal customers at a high level.

External customers fit the traditional definition of customers, which includes clients, guests, and patients. External customers can be classified as retail or industrial. The latter would include one company buying from another, such as purchasing steel or a gross of printer cartridges. *Internal customers* are the people you serve within the organization or those who use the output from your job. Also, everyone you depend on is an internal customer. Much of this book deals with better serving internal customers, because improved interpersonal relationships increase the satisfaction of work associates. The emphasis in this chapter is on satisfying external customers.

Customer satisfaction skills are required by all workers who are in contact with external customers, such as sales representatives, customer service representatives (those who back up sales and take care of customer problems), and store associates. Various aspects of developing customer satisfaction skills are divided into three parts in this chapter: general principles, bonding with customers, and dealing with customer dissatisfaction. To reflect on your attitudes toward satisfying customers, do Self-Assessment Quiz 12-1.

Self-Assessment Quiz 12-1

THE CUSTOMER-ORIENTATION QUIZ

Directions: Answer each of the following statements about dealing with customers as "Mostly true" or "Mostly false." The statements relate to your attitudes, even if you lack direct experience in dealing with customers. Your experiences as a customer will also be helpful in responding to the statements.

	Mostly true	Mostly false
1. All work in a company should be geared to pleasing customers.		
2. The real boss in any business is the customer.		
3. Smiling at customers improves the chances of making a sale.		
4. I would rather find a new customer than attempt to satisfy one who is difficult to please.		
5. Dealing with customers is as rewarding as (or more rewarding than) dealing with co-workers.		
6. I enjoy (or would enjoy) helping a customer solve a problem related to the use of my product or service.		

(Continued)

7. The best way to get repeat business is to offer steep discounts.   _____   _____

8. In business, your customer is your partner.   _____   _____

9. Dealing directly with customers is (or would be) the most boring part of most jobs.   _____   _____

10. If you have the brand and model the customer wants, being nice to the customer is not so important.   _____   _____

11. A good customer is like a good friend.   _____   _____

12. If you are too friendly with a customer, he or she will take advantage of you.   _____   _____

13. Now that individual consumers and companies can shop online, the personal touch in business is losing importance.   _____   _____

14. Addressing a customer by his or her name helps build a relationship with that customer.   _____   _____

15. Satisfying a customer is fun whether or not it leads to a commission.   _____   _____

Scoring and Interpretation: Give yourself a +1 for each of the following statements receiving a response of "Mostly true": 1, 2, 3, 5, 6, 8, 11, 14, and 15. Give yourself a +1 for each of the following statements receiving a response of "Mostly false": 4, 7, 9, 10, 12, and 13.

13–15 points:	You have a strong orientation to providing excellent customer service.
8–12 points:	You have an average customer service orientation.
1–7 points:	You have a below-average orientation to providing excellent customer service.

GENERAL PRINCIPLES OF CUSTOMER SATISFACTION

Knowing how to satisfy customers is a subset of effective interpersonal relations in organizations. Nevertheless, there are certain general principles in this area that will sharpen your ability to satisfy customers and thereby improve customer retention. This section presents seven key principles for satisfying customers. Remember, however, that satisfaction is considered a minimum expectation. If you do an outstanding job of satisfying customers, they will experience delight.

Customer satisfaction is important for several reasons. Satisfied customers are likely to tell friends and acquaintances about their satisfactory experiences, helping a firm grow its business. In contrast, dissatisfied customers—especially those with an unresolved problem—are likely to tell many people about their dissatisfaction, thus dissuading a large number of people from becoming new customers. Studies indicate that an upset or angry customer tells an average of between 10 and 20 other people about an unhappy experience.[1] Customer satisfaction is also highly valued because it breeds customer loyalty, which in turn is very profitable. Repeat business is a success factor in both retail and industrial companies.

Another reason for satisfying customers is the humanitarian aspect. Satisfying people boosts their physical and mental health, whereas dissatisfaction creates negative stress. Have you ever been so angry as a result of poor service that you experienced stress?

SATISFY EMPLOYEES SO YOU CAN PROVIDE BETTER CUSTOMER SERVICE

Employees who are happy with their jobs are the most likely to satisfy customers. Treating employees well puts them in a better frame of mind to treat their customers well. For example, an extensive case history analysis of Sears found a strong relationship between employee and customer satisfaction. Employees who were satisfied influenced customers to be satisfied, resulting in more purchases and profits.[2] The first statement on the survey can be used to illustrate the basics of the process. The statement is "I like the kind of work I do."

> *Employee feels, "I like the kind of work I do."* → *Smiles at customer and is courteous.* → *Customer feels positive about Sears* → *buys a new lawnmower and two pairs of jeans* → *improves profits for Sears.*

Acting alone, you cannot improve company conditions that contribute to job satisfaction. What you can control to some extent, however, are your own related attitudes and beliefs. Following is a checklist of the ones over which you can exert some control:

- *Interest in the work itself.* Job satisfaction stems directly from being interested in what you are doing. People who love their work experience high job satisfaction and are therefore in the right frame of mind to satisfy customers.

- *A feeling of self-esteem.* If you have high self-esteem you are more likely to experience high job satisfaction. High-status occupations contribute more to self-esteem than do those of low status. Feelings of self-esteem also stem from doing work the individual sees as worthwhile. This perception is less influenced by external standards than is the status associated with a particular job or occupation.

- *Optimism and flexibility.* An optimistic and flexible person is predisposed to be a satisfied employee. A pessimistic and rigid person will most likely be a dissatisfied employee. Every company has its share of people who will always find something to complain about. Evidence suggests that a tendency toward optimism versus pessimism is inherited.[3] If you have a predisposition toward pessimism, it does not mean that you cannot become more optimistic with self-discipline. You can, for example, look for the positive aspects of a generally unpleasant situation.

- *Positive self-image.* People possessing a positive self-image are generally more satisfied with their jobs than are those possessing a negative self-image. One explanation is that the people who view themselves negatively tend to view most things negatively. You have to like yourself before you can like your job.

- *Positive expectations about the job.* People with positive expectations about their jobs are frequently more satisfied than are those with low expectations. These expectations illustrate a self-fulfilling prophecy. If you expect to like your job, you will behave in such a way that those expectations will be met. Similarly, if you expect your job not to satisfy your needs, you will do things to make your expectations come true. Assume that a worker expects to earn low commissions in a sales job. The person's negativity may come through to customers and prospective customers, thereby ensuring low customer satisfaction and low commissions.

- *Effective handling of abuse from customers.* Customer service workers are often verbally abused by customers over such matters as products not working, merchandise returns not being acceptable, and the customer having been charged a late fee. Automated telephone-answering systems often force callers to hack through a thicket of prompts before reaching a human being. By the time a live person is reached, the customer is angry and ready to lash out at the customer service representative.[4] To prevent these oral tirades from damaging one's job satisfaction, it is essential to use effective techniques of dealing with criticism and resolving conflict as described in Chapter 7. The section on dealing with dissatisfied customers presented later in this chapter is also important.

High job satisfaction contributes to good customer service in another important way. Employees who are satisfied with their jobs are more likely to engage in service-oriented organizational citizenship behaviour. As you will recall, *organizational citizenship behaviour* relates to going beyond your ordinary job description to help other workers and the company. A customer service worker with high organizational citizenship behaviour will go beyond ordinary expectations to find ways to solve a customer problem.[5] A member of the tech support staff in a consumer electronics store volunteered to drop by a customer's house to help him install a programmable DVD, even though such home visits were not required. As a result of the technician's kindness, the man purchased a $6000 plasma screen TV from the store.

RECEIVE EMOTIONAL SUPPORT FROM CO-WORKERS TO GIVE BETTER CUSTOMER SERVICE

Closely related to the idea that satisfied workers can better satisfy customers is the finding that the emotional support of co-workers often leads to providing better customer service. According to a research study, the support of co-workers is even more important than supervisory support. The participants in the study were 354 customer service workers employed in service-based facilities. Customer satisfaction surveys were collected from 269 customers. The major finding was that employees who perceived their co-workers to be supportive had a higher level of commitment to their customers.

The researchers concluded that it is important to have a supportive group of co-workers by your side to help you perform service-related duties. In this study, supervisory support was less important than co-worker support in terms of bringing about a strong customer orientation. (A *customer service orientation* includes a desire to help customers, and a willingness to act in ways that would satisfy a customer. The hotel receptionist portrayed in the chapter opener exemplifies a service worker with a strong customer orientation.) Another important conclusion drawn from the study was that customer satisfaction was positively associated with the strength of the service worker's customer orientation.[6]

UNDERSTAND CUSTOMER NEEDS AND PUT THEM FIRST

The most basic principle of selling is to identify and satisfy customer needs. One challenge is that many customers may not be able to express their needs clearly. To help identify customer needs, you may have to probe for information. For example, the associate in a camera and video store might ask, "What uses do you have in mind for a video camera?" Knowing such information will help the associate identify which camcorder will satisfy the customer's needs.

The basic idea of satisfying customer needs continues to be expressed in different ways. Recent thinking suggests that highly competitive markets and abundant information (such as price information available on the internet) have caused a shift in power from suppliers to customers. Instead of being product-centred, successful companies have become customer-centred. The idea is to identify profitable customers and then anticipate their priorities.[7] If you satisfy customer needs, you are adding value for them. A person might be willing to pay $10 more per ticket to watch an athletic event if the extra $10 brought a better view and a chair instead of a backless bench. (The better view and more comfortable back add value for the spectator.)

After customer needs have been identified, the focus must be on satisfying those needs rather than the needs of oneself or the company. Assume that the customer says, "The only convenient time for me to receive delivery this week would be Thursday or Friday afternoon." The sales associate should not respond, "On Thursday and Friday our truckers prefer to make morning deliveries." Instead, the associate should respond, "I'll do whatever is possible to accommodate your request."

A major contributor to identifying customer needs is to listen actively to customers. Listening can take place during conversations with customers, and "listening" can also mean absorbing information sent by email and written letters. A policy at Southwest Airlines is that if a customer (or employee) has an idea, a manager must respond instantaneously.[8] For example, Southwest followed a customer suggestion that more reservation agents be Spanish-speaking.

FOCUS ON SOLVING PROBLEMS, NOT JUST TAKING ORDERS

In effective selling, sales representatives solve problems as well as take orders. An example is the approach taken by sales representatives for Xerox Corp. Instead of focusing on the sale of photocopiers and related equipment, the sales reps look to help customers solve their information-flow problems. The solution could involve selling machines, but it might also involve selling consulting services.

The focus on problem-solving enables sales representatives to become partners in the success of their customers' businesses. By helping the customer solve problems, the sales representative increases the value of the supplier-customer relationship to the customer. The customer is receiving consulting services in addition to the merchandise or service being offered. In some situations, a store associate can capitalize on the same principle. If the customer appears unsure about a purchase, ask him or her what problem is being faced that the product will solve. The following scenario in a computer store illustrates this point:

Customer: I think I would like to buy this computer. I'm pretty sure it's the one I want. But I don't know too much about computers other than how to use them for word processing, email, and basic research.

Store Associate: I am happy you would like to purchase a computer. But could you tell me what problems you are facing that you want a computer to help you solve?

Customer: Right now I feel I'm not capitalizing on the internet revolution. I want to do more online, and get into digital photography so I can send cool photos to friends all over. I also want to purchase music online, so I can walk around with an iPod like my friends do.

Store Associate: To solve your problem, you will need a more powerful computer than the one you are looking at. I would like you to consider another model that is about the same price as the one you have chosen. The difference is that it has the memory you need to email photos and download music from a subscription service.

RESPOND POSITIVELY TO MOMENTS OF TRUTH

An effective customer contact person performs well during situations in which a customer comes in contact with the company and forms an impression of its service. Such situations are referred to as **moments of truth**. If the customer experiences satisfaction or delight during a moment of truth, he or she is likely to return when the need for service arises again. A person who is frustrated or angered during a moment of truth will often not be a repeat customer. A moment of truth is an important part of customer service because what really matters in a service encounter is the customer's perception of what occurred.[9] Visualize a couple who have just dined at an expensive restaurant as part of celebrating their anniversary. The food, wine, and music might have been magnificent, but the couple perceives the service as poor because one of them slipped on ice in the restaurant parking lot.

You can probably visualize many moments of truth in your experiences with service personnel. Reflect on how you were treated by a store associate when you asked for assistance; the instructions you received when an airplane flight was cancelled; or how you were treated when you inquired about financial aid. Each business transaction has its own moment of truth. Yet they all follow the theme of a key interaction between a customer and a company employee.

One way you can track moments of truth is to prepare a cycle-of-service chart, as shown in Figure 12-1. The **cycle-of-service chart** summarizes the moments of truth encountered by a customer during the delivery of a service.[10] To gain insight into these charts, do Skill-Building Exercise 12-1.

BE READY TO ACCEPT EMPOWERMENT

A major strategy for improving customer service is to empower customer contact employees to resolve problems. **Empowerment** refers to managers transferring, or sharing, power with lower-ranking employees. In terms of customer relations, it means pushing decision-making and complaint resolution downward to employees who are in direct contact with customers. The traditional method of dealing with all but the most routine customer problems is for the customer contact worker to refer them to the manager. Many manufacturing firms and service firms now authorize customer contact workers to take care of customer problems themselves, within limits. Employees at Ritz-Carlton hotels have the authority to spend up to $2000 to solve a customer problem. At less luxurious hotels, such as the Hampton Inn, any worker can offer a guest a free night of lodging to compensate for a service problem.

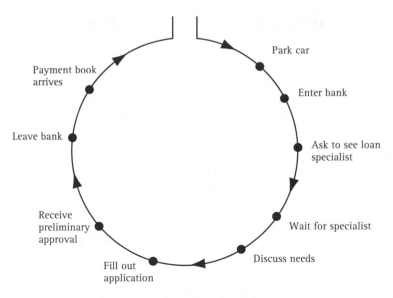

Figure 12-1   A Cycle-of-Service Chart for Obtaining a Car Loan at a Bank

Empowerment is not giving away the store, especially because limits are established to the customer contact worker's authority. Empowerment does involve taking a reasonable risk based on company principles to provide meaningful customer service. For empowerment to work, the company must grant decision-making latitude to employees. The employees, in turn, must be willing to accept empowerment (or decision-making authority).[11] Imagine yourself in a customer contact position. For empowerment to work effectively, you should be able to answer the following statements affirmatively:

- I am willing to arrive at a quick decision as to whether the company or the customer is right.
- I would be willing to admit to a customer that the company has made a mistake.
- I would be willing to take the risk that at times I will lose money for the company on a given transaction.
- I would be comfortable making an out-of-the-ordinary decision about a customer problem without consulting a manager.

Skill-Building Exercise 12-1

MOMENTS OF TRUTH

The class breaks into small groups to discuss what can go right versus what can go wrong during customer moments of truth. First refer to the cycle-of-service chart shown in Figure 12-1. Discuss what can go right or wrong at each moment of truth. The team then develops its own cycle-of-service chart for another service, using its own experiences and imagination.

After making the two analyses, discuss the usefulness of a cycle-of-service chart for improving customer satisfaction.

ENHANCE CUSTOMER SERVICE THROUGH INFORMATION TECHNOLOGY

Much has been said and written about how information technology has depersonalized customer service, such as having customers select from a long menu of choices on a touch-tone telephone. Information technology, however, also plays an important role in recording customer preferences and individualizing service. A major contribution of information technology to enhancing customer service is to develop individualized appeals to customers. With the right software in place, you can make a direct appeal to customer preferences based on past purchases, and the habits of customers with similar preferences. For example, the Fairmont chain of hotels keeps track of customer preferences such as what kinds of pillows you prefer and your preference of room location (near an elevator for example) when you join their free President's Club. If you have purchased online at a major etailer like Amazon.com, you may be familiar with this technology. Two examples follow:

1. Computerized information tells you immediately what the customer on the phone or online has bought in the past, so you may ask a question such as, "Two years ago you installed a centralized vacuum cleaning system. Do you need another set of bags by now?"

2. Speaking to the person, or sending an email message to the customer, you may say, "Last year you purchased a heated doghouse for your Yorkshire terrier. Our information suggests that people who own a heated doghouse are also interested in dog sweaters. Please take a moment to look at our new line of dog sweaters for canines who appreciate warmth." Developing individualized appeals to customers is likely to be included in customer relationship management (CRM) software. The complex software is used to implement a strategy of interacting with your customers to bring them more value, and more profits to your firm. One of its basic purposes is to make the company easier for customers to do business with, including facilitating placing orders over the internet.[12] As such, the individual customer service worker would not have the authority to install such a system. Yet the individual worker can always look for ways to apply the CRM system (such as that provided by Salesforce.com) in a way that best serves the customer.

A major challenge in providing good customer service when using information technology is preserving the human touch. Here are some hints for adding a personal touch into your electronic communications to help build customer loyalty.

Using Voice Mail

1. Vary your voice tone and inflection when leaving messages and in your greeting to avoid sounding bored or uninterested in your job and the company.

2. Smile while leaving your message—somehow a smile gets transmitted over the telephone wires or optic fibres!

3. Use voice mail to minimize "telephone tag" rather than to increase it. If your greeting specifies when you will return, callers can choose to call again or to leave a message. When you leave a message, suggest a good time to return your call. Another way to minimize telephone tag is to assure the person you are calling that you will keep trying.

4. Place an informative and friendly greeting (outgoing message) on your voice mail or answering machine. Used effectively, a voice-mail greeting will minimize the number of people irritated by not talking to a person.

5. When you are leaving a voice-mail message, include specific, relevant information. As mentioned above, be specific about why you are calling and what you want from the person called. The probability of receiving a return call increases when you leave honest and useful information. If you are selling something or asking for a favour, be honest about your intent.

6. When leaving your message, avoid the most common voice-mail error by stating your name and telephone number clearly enough to be understood. Most recipients of a message dislike intensely listening to it several times to pick up identifying information.

Using Email[13]

1. Use the customer's name. Begin with a personal greeting, e.g., "Hello, Lisa King." Many companies now greet customers by their first name only, but some customers consider this practice very rude. However, few people are likely to be offended when you use both their first and last names.

2. Choose a human email address. *Marysmith@hotmail.com* feels more personal than an odd sequence of numbers, letters, and dashes.

3. Be conversational. Mention events you have shared, such as "I enjoyed seeing you at the company meeting."

4. Sign your name. Don't neglect your signature. "Best regards, Jim Woods."

AVOID RUDENESS

We have reserved the most frequently violated principle of good customer service for last: avoid being rude to customers. Although rudeness to customers is obviously a poor business practice, the problem is widespread. Rudeness of customer contact personnel is a major problem from the employer's standpoint. Rude treatment loses more business than does poor product quality or high prices. To assess rudeness in retail business, one author surveyed a class of students who came from across Canada. The Canadian Scene below illustrates just a few examples of rude behaviour.

To elevate your awareness level about rudeness among customer-contact personnel, do Self-Assessment Quiz 12-2.

The Canadian Scene

SO HOW RUDE CAN AN EMPLOYEE BE?

When beginning work on this book, I went to a small electronics business to purchase a new battery for a cellphone. The clerk in the store was on the phone but realized I was there. She then proceeded to continue the conversation—a personal one—for several minutes. I recalled other incidents and started to wonder about such rudeness, and sometimes aggression, that I had encountered. Have others had these experiences? Are they common? Isn't Canada the most polite nation in the world (so I have heard)?

So I asked a class these questions and recorded the answers. While the incidents the students related were at times quite funny and there was much giggling, the cumulative effect was disturbing. Every student had at least one example to share. Obviously, this survey did not follow rigorous research principles, but it does illustrate how much rudeness there is in many businesses. The stories came from all across Canada and included customer experiences with small businesses, major chain stores, exclusive retail stores, and restaurants. Only a few are offered here.

- One student was at a popular chain restaurant and found a hair on her salad. When she complained, the server simply removed the hair with his fingers and walked away.

- Another student tried on a sweater at a very expensive store. When she noticed lipstick on the collar, she went to the clerk to ask if there was another in her size and to call attention to the lipstick smear. The clerk then accused her of putting the lipstick on the sweater to obtain a discount, even calling her a liar in front of other customers. Interestingly, this student does not wear lipstick or other makeup due to allergies. She also does not shop there anymore.

- Another student waited to pay for a purchase while the clerk at the counter talked on the phone. Not only did the clerk continue the conversation, but she turned her back and began talking more softly so that the conversation could not be heard. When the student then cleared her throat loudly, the clerk turned around and said "Shh!" before turning back to resume the phone conversation.

- When trying on jeans, a student heard one clerk remark to another clerk about her weight, followed by loud giggling. She was so embarrassed, she didn't want to leave the dressing room.

- On a long flight, one student ordered a drink. The flight attendant brought the drink without ice. When he then asked for ice, the attendant sarcastically said, "Do you want me to drink it for you too?" When questioned, the attendant said it was just a joke and that he should lighten up a bit.

Obviously, many employers are taking steps to combat such rudeness. I did call the retail store where I had purchased the cellphone battery and the owner was glad I did. With so much competition and so many options for consumers, businesses cannot afford to lose customers because of one rude employee.

Self-Assessment Quiz 12-2

AM I BEING RUDE?

Directions: Following is a list of behaviours of customer contact workers that many would interpret as rude. Indicate whether you have engaged in such behaviour in your dealings with customers, or whether you would be likely to do so if your job did involve customer contact.

	Yes	No
1. I talk to a co-worker while serving a customer.		
2. I conduct a telephone conversation with someone else while serving a customer.		
3. I address customers by their first names without having their permission.		
4. I address customers as "You guys."		
5. I chew gum or eat while dealing with a customer.		
6. I laugh when customers describe an agonizing problem they are having with one of our company's products or services.		
7. I minimize eye contact with customers.		
8. I say the same thing to every customer, such as "Have a nice day," in a monotone.		
9. I accuse customers of attempting to cheat the company before carefully investigating the situation.		
10. I hurry customers when my break time approaches.		
11. I comment on a customer's appearance in a flirtatious, sexually oriented way.		
12. I sometimes complain about or make fun of one customer when I am serving another.		
13. I sometimes use my cellphone to talk to another person while serving a customer.		

Interpretation: The more of these behaviours you have engaged in, the ruder you are and the more likely that you are losing potential business for your company. If you have not engaged in any of these behaviours, even when faced with a rude customer, you are an asset to your employer. You are also tolerant.

CREATING A BOND WITH YOUR CUSTOMER

Another key perspective on achieving customer satisfaction and delight is to create a bond—or emotional relationship—with customers. The rationale is that if you form warm, constructive relationships with your customers, they will keep buying from your company. Staying focused on the importance of customers will help provide the motivation for forming such a bond. The willingness to form a bond with the customer is part of having a strong customer orientation, defined as "a set of basic individual predispositions and an inclination to provide service, to be courteous and helpful in dealing with customers and associates."[14] You may recall Self-Assessment Quiz 12-1 about customer orientation at the outset of the chapter. Service-oriented organizational citizenship behaviour relates to the same idea of focusing on customer needs.

Creating a bond is aimed at increasing sales, but it also enhances service. If the customer relies on and trusts the sales representative, the customer will perceive the service to be of high quality. Similarly, people perceive medical and legal services to be of high quality if they trust the physician or lawyer. Virtually all of the principles and techniques presented in this chapter will help form a bond with customers. However, six key principles are as follows:

1. Create a welcoming attitude, including a smile.

2. Provide exceptional service.

3. Show care and concern.

4. Make the buyer feel good.

5. Build a personal relationship.

6. Invite the customer back.

Create a Welcoming Attitude, Including a Smile

An effective starting point in creating a customer bond is to use enthusiastic expressions, including a smile, when greeting customers. Attempt to show a sincere, positive attitude that conveys to customers and prospects "I'm here to make you happy."[15] In addition to being an effective greeting, smiling is also a natural relationship builder and can help you bond with your customer. Smile several times at each customer meeting, even if your customer is angry with your product or service. A camcorder is a useful device for getting feedback on the quality of your smile. Practising your smile in front of a mirror might feel a little less natural, but it is still helpful. Smiling at customers has a potential disadvantage, despite its general effectiveness. If your smile is too friendly and inviting, the customer might think that you want to get to know him or her outside the business relationship.

Provide Exceptional Service

The best-accepted axiom about keeping customers is to provide exceptional service. Many successful companies contend that good service is their competitive advantage. An excellent example is State Farm Insurance. When the ice storm hit eastern Ontario and Quebec in the winter of 1997, State Farm Insurance handled thousands of damage claims resulting from the storm. Thousands of households were without electricity and other services for up to three weeks. The company provided emergency relief services and had claims adjusters on-site within hours of many claimants' calls. State Farm capitalized on this service with subsequent advertisements outlining their outstanding services during and after the storm.

Exceptional service includes dozens of customer transactions, including prompt delivery, a fair returns policy, accurate billing, and prompt attention to a customer's presence. Exceptional service also includes giving customers good advice about using the product or service.

Show Care and Concern

During contacts with the customer, the sales representative should show concern for the customer's welfare. The representative should ask questions such as "How have you enjoyed the optical scanner you bought a while back?" and "How are you feeling today?" After asking the question, the sales representative should project a genuine interest in the answer.

Make the Buyer Feel Good

A fundamental way of keeping a relationship going is to make the buyer feel good about himself or herself. Also, the customer should be made to feel good because of having bought from the representative. Offer compliments about the customer's appearance or about a report he or she prepared that specified vendor requirements clearly. An effective feel-good line is, "I enjoy doing business with you."

Build a Personal Relationship

Building a good working relationship with a customer often leads to a positive personal relationship. A bold approach is to do the reverse—build a working relationship based on an authentic personal relationship. You gather personal facts about the interests of your customers and then appeal to those interests. A case history of a bank manager, Jack Foxboro, shows the potential effectiveness of this technique:

> Several years ago, Jack Foxboro was a commercial loan officer. He acquired a base of existing accounts from the previous officer and gradually increased his base. Jack invested considerable time telephoning and sending emails to existing loan holders. He collected facts about them, such as birthdays, names of family members, golf handicaps, hobbies, and favourite sports teams. Jack entered all this information into a database.
>
> Jack would send cards to customers in recognition of their birthdays and special accomplishments. When a customer visited the bank to talk about an existing loan or to apply for a new one, he would retrieve relevant personal facts from the database. Jack's clients were so impressed that he enlarged existing accounts and received substantial referral business. David Pace, Starbuck's executive vice president of partner resources said, "It's definitely a profitable strategy. When a customer comes in and the person behind the counter says hello, and maybe greets you by name, you feel a connection you don't find with most retailers anymore. It makes you feel welcome, and it makes you want to come back"[16]

A high-tech way of building relationships with large numbers of customers is to interact with them through company blogs, or web logs. The company representative is authorized to chat with hundreds of customers and potential customers by placing informal comments on the web log in a manner similar to a personal diary. The worker lets out tidbits of information to customers without betraying company confidences or making defamatory statements about the company. However, the blog entries are not usually as positive as advertisements, which helps form bonds with the customers. Many customers post replies and swap ideas with the company rep. Company-approved blogs are growing rapidly, as customers demand information presented in a more unvarnished way. A major advantage of blogs is that they humanize large organizations, such as the company representative mentioning a favourite recipe as well as chatting about a new product.[17]

Invite the Customer Back

The southern US expression "Y'all come back, now!" is well-suited to bonding with customers. Specific invitations to return may help increase repeat business. The more

Skill-Building Exercise 12-2

BONDING WITH CUSTOMERS

Role players in this exercise will demonstrate two related techniques for bonding with customers: showing care and concern and making the buyer feel good.

Scenario 1: Show Care and Concern. A sales representative meets with two company representatives to talk about installing a new information system for employee benefits. One of the company representatives is from the human resources department and the other from the telecommunications department. The sales representative will attempt to show care and concern for both company representatives during the same meeting.

Scenario 2: Make the Buyer Feel Good. A couple, played by two role players, enters a new-car showroom to examine a model they have seen advertised on television. Although they are not in urgent need of a new car, they are strongly interested. The sales representative is behind quota for the month and would like to close a sale today. The rep decides to use the tactic "make the buyer feel good" to help form a bond.

focused and individualized the invitation, the more likely its impact on customer behaviour. ("Y'all come back, now!" is sometimes used too indiscriminately to be effective.) Pointing out why you enjoyed doing business with the customer, and what future problems you could help with, is an effective technique. An industrial cleaning company supervisor might say, "Our crew enjoyed cleaning such a fancy office. Keep us in mind when you would like your windows to sparkle." Despite the importance of forming a bond with your customer, getting too personal can backfire. Most customers want a business relationship with the company, and are not looking for a personal relationship with a company representative. As Daniel Askt observes, "Most customers want value and service without contending with a salesman who insists that he wants to be like family to you. Chances are you've already got a family, and for most of us, one is enough."[18]

Skill-Building Exercise 12-2 gives you an opportunity to practise techniques for bonding with customers.

DEALING WITH CUSTOMER DISSATISFACTION

Most companies put honest effort into preventing customer dissatisfaction. In addition to employing many of the principles and techniques already cited, many companies routinely survey customers to detect problem areas that could lead to dissatisfaction. A representative survey is shown in Figure 12-2.

Despite all these efforts to achieve total customer satisfaction, some customer dissatisfaction is inevitable. One reason is that mistakes in serving customers are almost inevitable; for example, a piece of equipment may have a faulty component unknown to the seller. A second reason is that some customers have a predisposition to complain. They will find something to complain about with respect to any product or service.

Dealing openly with dissatisfaction and complaints can improve both customer retention and sales. One study found that 63 percent of dissatisfied customers who do not complain will not buy from the company again. Given a chance to complain and have their problem resolved, 90 percent will remain loyal customers.[19]

HOW ARE WE DOING?
DICK'S CLOTHING AND SPORTING GOODS

NAME (OPTIONAL)

PHONE NUMBER

DATE AND TIME OF VISIT

ADDRESS

CITY

NAME OF ASSOCIATE WHO HELPED YOU

	EXCELLENT	GOOD	AVERAGE	NEEDS IMPROVEMENT	POOR
PROMPT AND COURTEOUS GREETING	☐	☐	☐	☐	☐
KNOWLEDGEABLE SALESPEOPLE	☐	☐	☐	☐	☐
STORE CLEANLINESS	☐	☐	☐	☐	☐
STORE DISPLAYS	☐	☐	☐	☐	☐
PRICES	☐	☐	☐	☐	☐
SPEEDY CHECKOUTS	☐	☐	☐	☐	☐
HOW DO YOU RATE US OVERALL?	☐	☐	☐	☐	☐

	NEWSPAPER	TV	RADIO	OTHER
WHAT BROUGHT YOU TO DICK'S?	☐	☐	☐	☐

DID YOU MAKE A PURCHASE? _____

ITEMS YOU WANTED THAT WE DID NOT HAVE? _____

GENERAL COMMENTS: _____

Figure 12-2   A Retail Store Customer Satisfaction Survey

Source: Dick's Clothing & Sporting Goods, Corporate Park Drive, P.O. Box 206, Conklin, NY 13748-9984.

Below we describe three broad approaches to handling customer dissatisfaction: dealing with complaints and anger, involving the customer in resolving a problem, and handling unreasonable requests.

An important point to remember in dealing with dissatisfied customers is that the negative personality traits of customers can bring down your level of customer service. For example, a study conducted in two major fast-food chains in Singapore found that customers who scored high on the trait of agreeableness tended to bring out positive emotion by the service personnel. In contrast, customers who scored high on negative affectivity (being disagreeable) brought out negative emotion among customer service personnel.[20] A service worker cannot change the personality traits of customers, yet a little self-management of emotion is in order. The service worker might say to himself or herself, "I won't let this nasty customer get me down. I will do my best to do my job without overreacting." Be careful not to fake your emotion too frequently because it can create stress. Instead be assertive with a comment like, "I want to help you, but might you tell me what you want in a more positive way?"

The next subsections describe four approaches to handling customer dissatisfaction: dealing with complaints and anger, involving the customer in working out a problem, handling an unreasonable request, and maintaining a realistic customer retention attitude.

DEAL CONSTRUCTIVELY WITH CUSTOMER COMPLAINTS AND ANGER

In an era when customer satisfaction is so highly valued, both retail and industrial customers are likely to be vocal in their demands. When faced with an angry customer, use one or more of the following techniques recommended by customer satisfaction specialists.[21]

1. *Acknowledge the customer's point of view.* Make statements such as "I understand," "I agree," and "I'm sorry." Assume, for example, a customer says: "The accounts payable department made a $1000 overcharge on my account last month. I want this fixed right away." You might respond, "I understand how annoying this must be for you. I'll work on the problem right away."

2. *Avoid placing blame.* Suggesting that the customer is responsible for the problem intensifies the conflict. With the customer who claims to have been overcharged, refrain from saying, "Customers who keep careful accounts of their orders never have this problem."

3. *Use six magic words to defuse anger.* The magic words are *I understand* [that this is a problem], *I agree* [that it needs to be solved], and *I'm sorry* [that this happened to you].

4. *Apologize for the problems created by you or your company.* To recover from a breakdown in customer service, it is best to acknowledge an error immediately. Apologies are most effective when stated in the first person (such as "I created the problem"). The corporate "we're sorry" sounds less sincere than when one specific person accepts responsibility for what went wrong.

5. *Take responsibility, act fast, and be thorough.* This technique is essentially a simplified framework for managing customer dissatisfaction. Mark Delp, the manager of a fleet maintenance service, illustrates: "Suppose a customer calls about an oil leak after Fleet Response services a car. I have the car immediately picked up from the office and clean any oil spots that may have been left on the driveway. I make sure there are no further leaks. Furthermore, I apologize and accept full responsibility, even if the problem is not our fault, such as when a part fails."[22]

6. *Tell the difficult customers how much you value them.* Quite often customers with problems feel unappreciated. Just before resolving the problem of a difficult customer, explain how important he or she is to your firm. You might say, "We value your business, so I want to correct this for you quickly."[23]

(Of course, you would value the customer even more after he or she becomes less difficult.)

7. *Follow up on the resolution of the problem.* Following up to see whether the resolution to the problem is satisfactory brings closure to the incident. The follow-up also helps the service deliverer know that he or she can rebound from an episode of customer dissatisfaction. One useful form of follow-up is to telephone the customer whose problem was solved. For example, a representative from the service department of an automobile dealership might telephone a customer whose new car required substantial warranty repairs. "Hello, this is Jill Gordon from Oak Automotive. We replaced your original transmission last month. How is the new transmission working?"

A less personal, and usually less effective, form of follow-up is to send a customer satisfaction questionnaire to the person with the problem. The questionnaire will often be interpreted as a company procedure that does not reflect specific concern about the individual's problem.

INVOLVE THE CUSTOMER IN WORKING OUT THE PROBLEM

Mistakes and problems in serving customers are inevitable, however hard the customer contact worker strives for perfection. To minimize the perception of poor service, the customer should be involved in deciding what should be done about the problem. By being involved in the solution, the customer is more likely to accept a deviation from the service originally promised. The ideal situation is for the customer service representative and dissatisfied customer to work as partners in resolving the problem. The following case history illustrates the technique of customer involvement and partnering.

Seth Bradbury is a sales promotion specialist at an advertising agency. A furniture store hired the agency to prepare and mail 3000 postcards advertising a new line of furniture. One side of the postcard contained a photograph of the furniture, and the other side contained product details and space for addressing and stamping the card. After the cards were mailed, Seth received an urgent call from the client. "The photograph of the furniture is printed vertically. It looks horrible. We agreed on a horizontal shot. This means 3000 cards have been mailed with a mistake."

After allowing the client to finish his complaint, Seth responded, "You're right, it is a vertical shot. Perhaps we misinterpreted your directions. However, I think your furniture still looks beautiful. The extra white space the vertical shot provides creates an interesting effect. It's unfortunate that the cards have already been mailed. What would you like us to do? It's important that you are satisfied."

The client responded, "I guess there's nothing we can do to change the photograph. Would you be willing to give us a discount off the price we agreed on?"

ANTICIPATE HOW TO HANDLE AN UNREASONABLE REQUEST

No matter how hard the customer contact worker attempts to provide outstanding customer service, at some point a customer comes along with an unreasonable request. Or the customer may raise an unfair objection. Speak to any experienced store associate to obtain a case history of a "customer from hell." For example, a small-business owner demanded that a store associate grant him exchange credit for six printer ribbons. The ribbons were purchased four years previously and were now obsolete.

Recognize that the customer who makes an unreasonable demand is usually aware it is unreasonable. The customer may not expect to be fully granted the request. Instead, the customer is bargaining by beginning with an unreasonable demand. The small-business owner who brought in the printer ribbons was probably looking to salvage whatever he could.

Sales representatives and other customer contact workers who stand their ground with dignity and courtesy generally will not lose customers with unreasonable requests. The suggestions presented next will help you deal with unreasonable demands while retaining the customer's business.[24]

- Let your customers retain their dignity by stating your position politely and reasonably.

- Avoid arguing with an upset customer. As the adage says, "You never win an argument with a customer."

- Appeal to your customer's sense of fair play and integrity. Explain that your intention is to do what is right and fair.

- Be firm by repeating the facts of the situation, but keep your temper under control.

- Accept responsibility for your decision rather than blaming company policy or your manager. Making somebody else the villain may intensify the problem.

- Be willing to say no to a customer when it is justifiable. Saying yes to an outrageous demand opens the door for a series of outrageous demands.

MAINTAIN A REALISTIC CUSTOMER RETENTION ATTITUDE

Some customers are too unreasonable, and therefore may not be worth keeping.[25] A realistic goal is to retain as many profitable customers as possible. An extreme example of a customer not worth keeping is the airline passenger who engages in *air rage*. Symptoms of air rage include (1) insisting on being served more alcoholic beverages than permissible by airline regulations, (2) sexually harassing or physically attacking flight attendants or other passengers, (3) refusing to fasten seat belts, (4) using electronic gear such as cellphones and laptop computers when not allowed by regulations, (5) smoking in the lavatory, and (6) using the aisles for a lavatory.

It is best to set limits for unruly customers and see if their behaviour changes. If the customer insists on creating disturbances, it is best to suggest the customer never return. Another problem is that some customers require so much service, or demand such high discounts, that they are unprofitable to retain. Good service to these customers means there is less time available to respond to the needs of profitable customers.

Dealing diplomatically and effectively with difficult customers requires an awareness of tactics described in the previous several pages. Practice on the firing line is indispensable. The type of experience provided by Skill-Building Exercise 12-3 is also helpful.

Skill-Building Exercise 12-3

DEALING WITH DIFFICULT CUSTOMERS

The following scenarios require one person to play the role of the customer contact worker and another person to play the difficult customer. As usual, the role players project their feelings into the role play by imagining how they would behave in the situation.

Scenario 1: One person is a store associate in a high-fashion women's clothing store. A woman who bought a $1000 gown the previous week brings the gown back today. She claims that she is returning the gown because it doesn't fit comfortably. The store associate strongly suspects the woman bought the gown to wear to a special occasion the past weekend and is now returning it as she no longer needs it.

Scenario 2: One person plays the role of a customer service representative in a consumer-electronics store. Another person plays the role of a customer who purchased a $3500 giant-screen television receiver three months ago. He comes up to the service rep's counter ranting about the store's ineptitude. The customer claims that the TV has broken down three times.

After the first repair, the TV worked for two weeks and then broke down again. The second repair lasted two weeks, only for the TV to break down during a Super Bowl party at his house. The customer is red in the face and shouting loudly. The service rep wants to resolve the customer's problem and prevent him from bad-mouthing the store.

CUSTOMER SERVICE TRAINING AT A LUXURY HOTEL CHAIN

The information and exercises already presented in this chapter have provided you with an appreciation of the nature of customer service training. (Such training should result in the development of customer satisfaction skills.) To help reinforce this information, we present portions of an interview with Leonardo Inghilleri, the senior vice-president of human resources for the Ritz-Carlton Hotel Company.[26] The company attributes much of the success of its 35 hotels to rigorous customer service training. Observe also how the Ritz-Carlton takes into account individual and cultural differences in achieving excellent customer service.

Author: Why does Ritz-Carlton feel it's important that every one of its nearly 16 000 employees undergo rigorous customer service training?

Inghilleri: Customers who come to our hotel pay a premium for perfection. We have the tremendous challenge to meet and exceed customer expectations. That's why we discuss customer service every single day of our lives. It starts with how we select our employees. We use scientific interviews to understand if an individual has the necessary behavioural traits to make him or her successful in our company. Only one of every 10 applicants is hired.

Author: What sort of traits? And how do you "scientifically" determine if a prospective employee has these traits?

Inghilleri: A person who works for us has to be hospitable, quality oriented, attentive to details, and so on. We've identified the top performers by job (waiters, chefs, housekeepers, etc.), and with the help of a psychological test we're able to determine the ideal profile for each specific job. If you want to be a successful housekeeper, for example, you have to have certain talents; and if you don't have these traits, you're not going to be hired. There also has to be the desire to use your talents, which a lot of people don't have. We interview each one of our employees in a scientific way to understand if that person possesses specific talents.

Author: How are the 120 hours of customer service training actually divvied up?

Inghilleri: It depends. Our entire training system is a combination of two key elements: technical skills and the Ritz-Carlton customer service philosophy. By technical training I mean how to serve in a fine-dining restaurant or how to make a bed according to standards. There may be 19 steps to making a bed. Until you make those beds perfectly, you're not going to earn a certification.

Customer service training is a little more complicated. We train our people how to resolve guest challenges. After all, it's an imperfect business we're in, and a lot of things that can go wrong will go wrong. A television at a certain point might break down. You have to train your people to instantly pacify our guests.

Author: What sort of financial and time commitments are we talking about here?

Inghilleri: It's a huge investment on our side. Think about it: Every employee spends 15 minutes every day in a meeting. Some might see this as a 15-minute loss of productivity, but we believe these are the most valuable 15 minutes of the day. We use this time to recognize and celebrate people, and create a sense of belonging.

Author: What exactly do your employees come away with after 120 or more hours of customer service training?

Inghilleri: From the training, they become professionals in the hospitality industry. In this industry, you're either a professional or you're a servant.

Making beds and cleaning toilets and serving meals are professions if they are done with pride. We create professional employees who have the desire to provide exceptional customer service, and who want to be part of our company.

Author: Does the fact that you have 35 hotels all over the world cause any sort of cultural problems when hiring and training employees in a customer service industry?

Inghilleri: We had to focus a lot on the cultural aspects. Every single culture has its own sense of hospitality. In Bali, we will not ask our ladies and gentlemen to say good morning and good afternoon. Instead, they'll greet in the traditional way by joining hands and bowing. We try to identify what makes that specific country special from a hospitality point of view. And then we adapt to its citizens' way of being hospitable.

Every Ritz-Carlton worker learns to "own the problem." This translates into each worker being empowered to spend up to $2000 at any time to address any customer's complaint.

The type of customer service training just described is a vehicle for achieving customer satisfaction. Customer service training in other industries, such as retailing or telecommunications, might have different content, but the principles are similar.

SUMMARY

Many companies today emphasize total customer satisfaction because it leads to goodwill, repeat business, and referrals. Customer satisfaction skills are required by all workers in contact with customers. Eight key principles for satisfying and delighting customers are as follows:

1. Satisfied employees provide better customer service. (Some of your own attitudes, such as optimism and flexibility, influence your job satisfaction.)

2. Receive emotional support from co-workers so you can give better customer service.

3. Understand customer needs and put them first.

4. Focus on solving problems, not just taking orders.

5. Respond positively to moments of truth (points at which the customer forms an impression of company service).

6. Be ready to accept empowerment. (Being empowered enables you to solve customer problems.)

7. Improve customer service through information technology.

8. Avoid rudeness (rude treatment of customers loses business).

Another key element in achieving customer satisfaction and delight is to create a bond—or emotional relationship—with customers. Almost any act of good customer service helps create a bond, but six principles are highlighted here:

1. Show a welcoming attitude, including a smile.

2. Provide exceptional service.

3. Express care and concern.

4. Make the buyer feel good.

5. Build a personal relationship.

6. Invite the customer back.

Despite the best efforts on the company's part, some customer dissatisfaction is inevitable. One approach to dealing with customer dissatisfaction is to deal constructively with customer complaints and anger. Tactics for achieving this end include the following:

1. Acknowledge the customer's point of view.

2. Avoid placing blame on the customer.

3. Use six magic words to defuse anger.

4. Apologize for the problem created by you or your company.

5. Take responsibility, act fast, and be thorough.

6. Tell the difficult customers how much you value them.

7. Follow up on the problem resolution.

Another approach to dealing with customer dissatisfaction is to involve the customer in working out the problem. The customer contact worker must sometimes deal with an unreasonable request. Remember that the customer probably recognizes that he or she is being unreasonable. Do not argue with an unreasonable customer, but at times you must say no. Maintain a realistic customer retention attitude; as hard as you to try to please, some customers are not worth keeping.

Customer service training encompasses many of the ideas in this chapter. Providing a high level of customer service can be a competitive advantage for a company.

An Interpersonal Relations Case Problem

REPEAT BUSINESS AT WHOPPER WASH

Jim McNamara worked for 25 years in a variety of sales and marketing positions for a large company. In his last position he was the manager of direct marketing (selling products directly to customers rather than through stores or other intermediaries). As part of a company downsizing, McNamara's position was consolidated with another department's and he was laid off.

McNamara said he was disappointed to lose a good job, but he recognized that dealing with drastic changes in one's life is part of the modern world. He also recognized that at age 50, he was still young enough to pursue a new career and a new lifestyle. McNamara and his wife, Gwen, discussed the situation for many days, and decided to work as partners in a franchise business. Gwen worked part time as a home health aid, so she could find time to help with the business. Many of the best-known franchises seemed out of reach for the McNamaras because of start-up prices as high as $500 000.

After several weeks of research the McNamaras decided to purchase a power washing franchise, Whopper Wash, for a start-up fee of $10 000. The company provided the training, including advice on marketing the program. Typical services for power washing would include cleaning house siding, swim-

ming pools, and the sidewalks of small businesses. Jim and Gwen would do the work themselves, including climbing on high ladders to wash the second level of a house.

The McNamaras opened their business officially on June 1 one year later. They placed ads in local newspapers, and had a Web site of their own, *http://www.JimandGwenWhopperWash.com*. Their first 10 orders for power washes were from friends and relatives, with the average price of the wash being $300. The newspaper ads were the most effective in drawing new customers, with the website also attracting some customers.

The business grew slowly. In a typical scenario, the McNamaras would show up at the site, get the job done in about two hours, and then receive payment. When Gwen had a conflict in the schedule, Jim would do the job himself. The customer would typically thank them for the service, and then say goodbye. Given the opportunity, either Jim or Gwen would attempt to engage the customer in light conversation. Gwen developed a standard joke to suggest repeat business. If she noticed that a dog was on the premises, she asked, "Can we power wash your dog next?" Not all pet owners laughed at her comment.

(Continued)

As the McNamaras reviewed their business results after six months, they observed a shortcoming. After completing a job, they would typically recommend that the service be repeated in two years. However, two years is a long time between repeat calls to a customer, the couple thought.

Jim remarked, "We don't have any good way of getting repeat business. I could see that our business could dry up quickly after we take care of most people who want their home or small business power washed. What do you think we can say to customers to get more repeat business?"

Case Questions

1. In what way is this case about customer satisfaction?
2. How might the McNamaras form better bonds with their customers?
3. What can this Whopper Wash couple do to get more repeat business?

An Interpersonal Relations Case Problem

THE TROUBLESOME BIG SCREEN

The Chavez nuclear family consists of Maria, an office manager at a hospital; Tony, an ambulance medic; and their daughter Jennifer, a grade eight student. A happy family, they share many activities. Among their joint activities is watching MuchMusic (music television). The family regularly scrunch down to watch their favourite music shows on a 10-year-old, 13-inch colour television.

One Thursday evening, Jennifer said, "Mom and Dad, I have a great idea. Let's do something exciting with some of your money. Let's buy a giant TV so we can have more fun watching the rock channel."

Maria and Tony thought that Jennifer's idea had merit. However, they both agreed that a giant-screen TV was a luxury item they could ill afford right now. Just before they fell asleep, the issue surfaced again. Maria said to Tony, "Deep down, we both agree with Jennifer. For less than $1000 we could bring much joy into our home."

Friday night the Chavez family visited Appliance City to look at television sets. Maria spotted a 29-inch TV that seemed ideal. A store associate, however, convinced them that the model they were inspecting was of mediocre quality. Instead, he recommended a domestic brand with a 32-inch screen that he claimed was the highest-quality model in its class. Spearheaded by Jennifer's exuberance, the Chavez family was convinced. The cost, including a three-year complete service warranty, was $1157.

The television set was delivered Monday evening as scheduled. For several days, the Chavez family enjoyed watching MuchMusic and other favourite programs on their new big-screen set. Friday evening, however, Maria, Tony, and Jennifer were mystified by an image that appeared on their screen. Shortly after Jennifer punched the menu button, an advertisement appeared on the screen touting the features of the set. Among the messages was one indicating that if the owner of this set were in a noisy room, he or she could mute the audio and watch the video.

Tony laughed as he explained that the demonstration mode was somehow triggered, and that the solution would be to just punch a few buttons. Next, Maria and he punched every button on the receiver and the TV remote control. The demonstration mode remained. Tony then pulled the plug and reinserted it, only for the demonstration mode to reappear.

Maria, Tony, and Jennifer then searched the owner's manual but found no information about the problem. Maria telephoned the dealer and got through to the service department after being placed on hold for six minutes. The service department said they knew nothing about the problem, but that she should speak to the sales department. After Maria explained her problem to a sales associate, she was told to speak to the service department.

Maria called back the service department and explained the problem again. A customer service

(Continued)

specialist said that the store relied on an outside TV appliance repair firm to handle such problems. She said she would call the repair firm on Monday and that the firm would contact the Chavez family. By Tuesday morning the Chavez family still had not heard from the repair firm.

In desperation, Tony scanned a customer information booklet that came with the TV receiver. He found a list of 10 authorized service centres throughout North America that repaired his brand of television. Tony telephoned a service centre in Halifax. A cheerful woman answered the phone and listened to Tony's problem. With a sympathetic laugh, she said, "We get lots of calls like this. No problem. Just push the volume-up and volume-down buttons at the same time. The demo mode will disappear. The mode was activated when somebody pressed the menu up and down buttons at the same time." Tony raced into the living room and triumphantly restored the TV set to normal functioning.

The Friday after, a representative from the local television repair shop called. She said, "This is Modern TV and Appliance. Do you still need service on your set?" With anger in her voice, Maria explained how the problem was finally resolved.

Later that night, as the family gathered to watch MuchMusic, Maria said, "I guess we all love our new giant-screen TV, but I wouldn't go back to Appliance City to buy even an electric can opener."

Case Questions

1. What mistakes in customer satisfaction principles did Appliance City personnel make?

2. What mistakes in customer satisfaction principles did Modern TV and Appliance make?

3. What would you do if you experienced a similar problem with an expensive TV receiver?

4. Should the manufacturer of the giant-screen TV set have any responsibility for the problem faced by the Chavez family?

QUESTIONS FOR DISCUSSION AND REVIEW

1. For what reason is a satisfied employee more likely to provide better customer service?

2. Describe a situation in your life in which you experienced customer delight. What made the experience delightful?

3. A couple walks into an automobile showroom and say they want a big safe vehicle for them and their three children, yet they are unsure about what vehicle they should purchase. Describe how you might identify customer needs in this situation.

4. Visualize yourself as an executive at Zellers. Develop a policy to empower customer service desk associates to resolve customer problems, including the limits to their empowerment.

5. Identify several typical ways in which customers are rude to customer contact workers.

6. How ethical is it for some fast food restaurants to satisfy customers by selling them food items that contain so much bad cholesterol?

7. What is your opinion of the impact of information technology on customer service? Offer at least two specifics in your answer.

8. Can you identify any ways in which a customer contact worker has made you feel good? If so, please provide the details.

9. How effective is the principle "the customer is always right" when dealing with dissatisfied customers?

10. Culture differences impact upon the perception of customer service and quality. An interesting study was done using Canadian, American, and Japanese clients. Using your Research Navigator, the number is AN 13991408. What did the researchers find as being the major cultural differences? What implications does this have for businesses in Canada?

WEBLINKS

Check out these retail and business sites for details about their customer service:

www.sears.ca
Sears Canada.

www.nygard.com
Nygard International.

www.hbc.com/zellers
Zellers.www.csmassociation.org
Customer Satisfaction Measurement Association.

Chapter 13

Enhancing Ethical Behaviour

Learning Outcomes

After reading and studying this chapter and doing the exercises, you should be able to

- Recognize the importance of ethical behaviour for establishing good interpersonal relationships in organizations.
- Identify several character traits associated with being an ethical person.
- Identify job situations that often present ethical dilemmas.
- Use a systematic method for making ethical decisions and behaving ethically.

As owner of a Mr. Handyman franchise in Los Angeles, T. L. Tenenbaum has rigid guidelines for the best approach to difficult drywall and plumbing problems. He also has ground rules for other home hazards his workers might encounter—say a misplaced pair of racy underwear or, as once happened, a butcher knife found under a bed. "Avert your eyes and pretend it doesn't exist," Tenenbaum instructs his techs on day one. "Pretend everything you see is perfectly normal."

Another common land mine: feuding spouses who involve technicians in personal matters—such as asking whether a married man should be a friend with an ex-girlfriend.

"Agree with everyone, and don't take sides. We are doctors for their homes, and—people feel—for their relationships as well," Tenenbaum notes.

Trade professionals have long faced unique challenges when conducting business in the privacy of their customers' homes, but how they handled them was generally up to the individual. Now, a fast-growing industry of branded, home-maintenance franchises with such names as House Doctors and Mr. Handyman are trying to hone protocols for prickly on-the-job scenarios, from scantily clad customers to overeager kids who want to play with tools.[1]

The scenario just described illustrates that ethical issues in the workplace are not just about big business and corporate executives. People performing all types of work need a good sense of ethics (and etiquette) to be successful. **Ethics** refers to what is good and bad, right and wrong, just and unjust, and what people should do. Ethics is the vehicle for turning values into action. If you value fair play, you will do such things as give honest performance evaluations to members of your group.

We study ethics here because a person's ethical code has a significant impact on his or her interpersonal relationships. Our approach will emphasize the importance of ethics, common ethical problems, and guidelines for behaving ethically. Self-Assessment Quiz 13-1 gives you the opportunity to examine your ethical beliefs and attitudes.

Self-Assessment Quiz 13-1

THE ETHICAL REASONING INVENTORY

Directions: Describe how well you agree with each of the following statements. Use the following scale: Disagree strongly (DS); Disagree (D); Neutral (N); Agree (A); Agree strongly (AS).

	DS	D	N	A	AS
1. When applying for a job, I would cover up the fact that I had been fired from my most recent job.	5	4	3	2	1
2. Cheating just a few dollars in one's favour on an expense account is OK if a person needs the money.	5	4	3	2	1
3. Employees should inform on one another for wrongdoing.	1	2	3	4	5
4. It is acceptable to give approximate figures for expense account items when one does not have all the receipts.	5	4	3	2	1
5. I see no problem with conducting a little personal business on company time.	5	4	3	2	1
6. Just to make a sale, I would stretch the truth about a delivery date.	5	4	3	2	1
7. I would set up a customer with a date just to close a sale.	5	4	3	2	1
8. I would flirt with my boss just to get a bigger salary increase.	5	4	3	2	1
9. If I received $200 for doing some odd jobs, I would report it on my income tax return.	1	2	3	4	5
10. I see no harm in taking home a few office supplies.	5	4	3	2	1
11. It is acceptable to read the email messages and faxes of other workers, even when not invited to do so.	5	4	3	2	1
12. It is unacceptable to call in sick just to take a day off, even if one only does it once or twice a year.	1	2	3	4	5
13. I would accept a permanent, full-time job even if I knew I wanted the job for only six months.	5	4	3	2	1
14. I would first check company policy before accepting an expensive gift from a supplier.	1	2	3	4	5
15. To be successful in business, a person usually has to ignore ethics.	5	4	3	2	1
16. If I felt physically attracted toward a job candidate, I would hire that person over a more qualified candidate.	5	4	3	2	1

(Continued)

17. On the job, I tell the truth all the time.	1	2	3	4	5
18. If a student were very pressed for time, it would be acceptable to either have a friend write a paper or purchase one.	5	4	3	2	1
19. I would authorize accepting an office machine on a 30-day trial period, even if I knew we had no intention of buying it.	5	4	3	2	1
20. I would never accept credit for a co-worker's ideas.	1	2	3	4	5

Scoring and Interpretation: Add the numbers you have circled to obtain your total score.

90–100   You are a strongly ethical person who may take a little ribbing from co-workers for being too strait-laced.

60–89   You show an average degree of ethical awareness, and therefore should become more sensitive to ethical issues.

41–59   Your ethics are underdeveloped, but you at least have some awareness of ethical issues. You need to raise your level of awareness of ethical issues.

20–40   Your ethical values are far below contemporary standards in business. Begin a serious study of business ethics.

WHY BE CONCERNED ABOUT BUSINESS ETHICS?

When asked why ethics is important, most people would respond with a statement resembling this one: "Ethics is important because it's the right thing to do. You behave decently in the workplace because your family and religious values have taught you what is right and wrong." All true so far, but the justification for behaving ethically is more complex, as described below. A major justification for behaving ethically on the job is to recognize that people are motivated by both self-interest and moral commitments. Most people want to maximize gain for themselves (remember the expectancy theory of motivation?). At the same time, most people are motivated to do something morally right. As one of many examples, vast numbers of people donate money to charity, although keeping that amount of money for themselves would provide more personal gain.

Many business executives want employees to behave ethically because a good reputation can help business. A favourable corporate reputation may enable firms to charge premium prices and attract better job applicants. A favourable reputation also helps attract investors, such as mutual fund managers who purchase stock in companies. Certain mutual funds, for example, invest only in companies that are environmentally friendly. Managers want employees to behave ethically because unethical behaviour is costly—for example, employee theft, lost production time, and lawsuits.

Behaving ethically is also important because many unethical acts are also illegal, which can lead to financial loss and imprisonment. According to one estimate, US industry loses about $400 billion annually to unethical or criminal behaviour.[2] A company that knowingly allows workers to engage in unsafe practices might be fined and the executives held personally liable. Further, unsafe practices can kill people. In recent history, two employees burned to death in a chicken processing plant in a fire they could not escape. Management had blocked the back doors to prevent employees from sneaking chicken parts out of the plant. Low ethics have also resulted in financial hardship for employees as company executives raid pension funds of other companies they purchase, sharply reducing or eliminating the retirement funds of many workers.

A subtle reason for behaving ethically is that a high standard of ethics increases the quality of one's working life. Ethics provides a set of guidelines that specify what makes for acceptable behaviour. Being ethical will point you toward actions that make life more satisfying for work associates. A company code of ethics specifies what constitutes ethical versus unethical behaviour. When employees follow this code, the overall quality of working life improves. Here are several sample clauses from ethical codes:

- Demonstrate courtesy, respect, honesty, and fairness.
- Do not use abusive language.
- Do not bring knives or other weapons to work.
- Do not offer bribes.
- Maintain confidentiality of records.
- Do not harass (sexually, racially, ethnically, or physically) subordinates, superiors, co-workers, customers, or suppliers.

To the extent that all members of the organization abide by this ethical code, the quality of working life will improve. At the same time, interpersonal relations in organizations will be strengthened.

COMMON ETHICAL PROBLEMS

To become more skilled at behaving ethically, it is important to familiarize yourself with common ethical problems in organizations. Whether or not a given situation presents an ethical problem for a person depends to some extent on its **moral intensity**, or how deeply others might be affected.[3] A worker might face a strong ethical conflict about dumping mercury into a water supply but would be less concerned about dumping cleaning fluid. Yet both acts would be considered unethical and illegal. Here we first look at why being ethical is not as easy as it sounds. We then look at some data about the frequency of ethical problems and an analysis of predictable ethical temptations, and also examine the subtle ethical dilemma of choosing between rights.

WHY BEING ETHICAL ISN'T EASY

As analyzed by Linda Klebe Treviño and Michael E. Brown, behaving ethically in business is more complex than it seems on the surface for a variety of reasons.[4] To begin with, ethical decisions are complex. For example, someone might argue that hiring children for factory jobs in overseas countries is unethical. Yet if these children lose their jobs, many would starve or turn to crime to survive. Second, people do not always recognize the moral issues involved in a decision. The home-maintenance worker who found a butcher knife under the bed might not think that he has a role to play in perhaps preventing murder. Sometimes language hides the moral issue involved, such as when the term "file sharing" music replaces "stealing" music.

Another complexity in making ethical decisions is that people have different levels of moral development. At one end of the scale some people behaviour morally just to escape punishment. At the other end of the scale, some people are morally developed to the point that they are guided by principles of justice and want to help as many people as possible. The environment in which we work also influences whether we behave ethically. Suppose a restaurant owner encourages such practices as serving customers food that was accidentally dropped on the kitchen floor. An individual server is more likely to engage in such behaviour to obey the demands of the owner.

A SURVEY OF THE EXTENT OF ETHICAL PROBLEMS

A substantial number of managers and employees engage in unethical behaviour, often because they feel pressured into making a quick profit. There has been substantial publicity in recent years of these misdeeds as well as those of Canadian government officials. Feeling under pressure, in general, or not taking the time to think through the ethics of an issue, can lead to unethical behaviour in the name of saving time.

However, ethical violations are not limited to executives, but also occur among rank and file employees. A survey of 2390 working adults by KPMG, a consulting and advisory group, provides some illuminating facts for both management and non-management employees. According to two separate surveys, more than one-third of workers admit to having fabricated their need for sick days and taken sick days when well. More employees are stretching the reasons for taking time off. Job applicants reporting false or embellished academic credentials have hit a three-year high.[5] Some of the study highlights are as follows:

- Seventy-six percent of workers say they have witnessed unethical or illegal behaviour by co-workers in the past year. The misconduct included theft, harassment and discrimination, lying, mishandling of confidential information, and cutting corners.

- Of those who saw misconduct, 49 percent considered it serious enough to damage public trust in their company if it ever became public knowledge.

- Sixty-one percent suspect that higher-ups caught doing something unethical or illegal would be disciplined less severely than would lower-ranking workers.

- Fifty-three percent of the employers surveyed believe their managers would not protect them from retaliation if they turned in an ethical violator.[6]

Although these findings might suggest that unethical and illegal behaviour is on the increase, another explanation is possible. Workers today might be more observant of ethical problems, and more willing to note them on a survey.

FREQUENT ETHICAL DILEMMAS

Certain ethical mistakes, including illegal actions, recur frequently in the workplace. Familiarizing oneself with them can be helpful in monitoring one's own behaviour. Here we describe a number of common ethical problems faced by business executives as well as workers at lower job levels.

The Temptation to Illegally Copy Software

A rampant ethical problem is whether or not to illegally copy software. According to the Business Software Alliance, approximately 35 percent of applications used in business are illegal.[7] Figure 13-1 offers details about and insight into this widespread ethical dilemma.

Treating People Unfairly

Being fair to people means practising equity, reciprocity, and impartiality. Fairness revolves around the issue of giving people equal rewards for accomplishing equal amounts of work. The goal of human-resource legislation is to encourage making decisions about people based on their qualifications and performance—not on the basis of demographic factors such as sex, race, or age. A fair working environment is where performance is the only factor that counts (*equity*). Employer-employee expectations must be understood and met (*reciprocity*). Prejudice and bias must be eliminated (*impartiality*).

To treat people fairly—and therefore ethically—an overemphasis on political factors would be unethical. Yet this ethical doctrine is not always easy to implement. It is human nature to want to give bigger rewards (such as fatter raises or bigger orders) to people we like.

Sexual Harassment

In Chapter 7, we looked at sexual harassment as a source of conflict and an illegal act. Sexual harassment is also an ethical issue, because it is morally wrong and unfair. All acts of sexual harassment fail an ethics test. Before sexually harassing another person, the potential harasser should ask, "Would I want a loved one to be treated this way?"

Conflict of Interest

Part of being ethical is making business judgments only on the basis of the merits or facts in a situation. Imagine that you are a supervisor who is romantically involved with a worker within the group. When it comes time to assign raises, it will be difficult for you to be objective. A **conflict of interest** occurs when your judgment or objectivity is compromised. Conflicts of interest often take place in the sales end of business. If a company representative accepts a large gift from a sales representative, it may be difficult to make objective judgments about buying from the representative. Yet being taken to dinner by a vendor would not ordinarily cloud one's judgment. Another common example of a conflict of interest is making a hiring decision about a friend who badly needs a job but is not well-qualified for the position.

Conflicts of interest have been behind some of the major business scandals in recent times, such as Enron Corporation auditors giving the company a favourable rating. Many outsiders dealing with Enron—including auditors, bankers, and even regulators—were tempted by a piece of the equity action.[8] The conflict occurs when one party paid to make objective judgments about the financial health of a second party has a personal interest in how profitable the second party looks to the public. An auditor might be hesitant to give a negative evaluation of the financial condition of a company if the auditor's firm also provides consulting services to that company. Some financial research analysts give glowing public reports about the fiscal condition of a company when that company is a client of the analyst's own firm. The analyst's firm sells services for issuing new stock and assisting with corporate mergers and acquisitions.

A flagrant unethical and *illegal* job behaviour is unauthorized copying of software. When confronted with software pirating, people are quick to rationalize their actions. Here are the top 10 defences of software pirates. (None of them are likely to hold up if you are caught.)

1. *I'm allowed to make a backup disk in case something happens to the original, so it must be okay to use it on another machine.* A backup is strictly a backup to be used on the same computer. The original should be safely locked away, and the copy should be stored away only.

2. *I didn't copy it—a friend gave it to me.* Technically, you are right. You would not be guilty of illegally copying software in this case, although your friend would. However, since illegally copied software is regarded as stolen property, you are just as guilty as you would be for stealing it in the first place.

3. *My boss (or department head, or instructor) told me to. It's that person's problem.* The defence "I was just following orders" is a weak one. Complying with your boss's demands to commit an illegal act does not get you off the hook. You could be fired for obeying an order to commit a crime.

4. *I bought the software; shouldn't I be able to do what I want with it?* Software is seldom ever sold to individuals. What is sold is a licence to use the software, not full rights to do what you want. When you break open the package, the law assumes that you have agreed to abide by those terms.

5. *It's not like I'm robbing somebody.* Software is intellectual property just like a song, a book, an article, or a trademark. You are taking bread from the table of software engineers when you copy their work.

6. *It's OK if you're using the software for educational purposes.* If education were a justification for theft, driving instructors would be able to steal cars with impunity. There is a doctrine of fair use that allows some limited use of written materials in classrooms without permission from the copyright holder.

7. *I needed it, but the price was unreasonably high. If I had to actually pay for it, there is no way I could ever afford it.* Software prices are high for the same reason the price of houses is high: both require a lot of highly skilled labour to create. You cannot steal a VCR just because you cannot afford one.

8. *I didn't know it was illegal.* Unauthorized duplication of software is a felony in many states and provinces. State and federal laws provide for civil and criminal penalties if you are convicted. It would be difficult to convince a judge or jury that you had no idea that unauthorized copying was illegal.

9. *It's only illegal if you get caught.* Criminal behaviour is illegal whether or not you are caught. If you do get caught illegally copying software, you could face fines, imprisonment, and/or civil penalties. Some educational institutions take disciplinary action against software pirates, including suspension.

10. *Oh, come on, everyone is doing it.* This excuse has been used to justify everything from speeding to lynching. The popularity of a criminal act does not make it legal.

Figure 13-1   The Top 10 Reasons for Illegally Copying Software (and Why None of Them Are Good Enough)

Source: Adapted with permission from Vince Incardona, "The Top Ten Reasons for Illegally Copying Software (and Why None of Them Are Good Enough)," *ITS News* (Rochester Institute of Technology), October 1998, p. 3.

Dealing with Confidential Information

An ethical person can be trusted by others not to divulge confidential information unless the welfare of others is at stake. Suppose a co-worker tells you in confidence that she is upset with the company and is therefore looking for another job. Behaving ethically, you do not pass this information along to your supervisor even though it would help your supervisor plan for a replacement. Now suppose the scenario changes slightly. Your co-worker tells you she is looking for another job because she is upset. She tells you she is so upset that she plans to destroy company computer files on her last day. If your friend does find another job, you might warn the company about her contemplated activities.

The challenge of dealing with confidential information arises in many areas of business, many of which affect interpersonal relations. If you learned that a co-worker was indicted for a crime, charged with sexual harassment, or facing bankruptcy, there would be a temptation to gossip about the person. A highly ethical person would not pass along information about the personal difficulties of another person.

Presenting Employment History

As noted above, many people are tempted to distort in a positive direction information about their employment history on their résumé, job application form, and during the interview. Distortion, or lying, of this type is considered to be unethical and can lead to immediate dismissal if discovered. A well-known case in point is George O'Leary, who was dismissed after five days on the job as head coach of the Notre Dame football team. After his résumé distortions were uncovered, O'Leary resigned and admitted he falsified his academic and athletic credentials for decades. He had falsely claimed to have a master's degree in education and to have played college football for three years.[9] Shortly thereafter, O'Leary made good use of his network of professional contacts and was hired by the Minnesota Vikings professional football team in a coaching position. Despite being disgraced nationally, O'Leary's political skills provided him with a safety net.

Use of Corporate Resources

A corporate resource is anything the company owns, including its name and reputation. If Jake Petro worked for Ford Motor Company, for example, it would be unethical for him to establish a body shop and put on his letterhead "Jake Petro, Manufacturing Technician, Ford Motor Company." Other uses of corporate resources fall more into the grey area. It might be quite ethical to borrow a laptop computer for the weekend from your employer to do work at home. But it would be less ethical to borrow the laptop computer to prepare personal income taxes. In the latter case you might be accused of using corporate resources for personal purposes. Loading personal software on company computers so you can access your bank account and so forth also can be considered an ethical violation.

Ethical Violations with Computers and Information Technology

As computers dominate the workplace, many ethical issues have arisen in addition to pirating software. One ethical dilemma that surfaces frequently is the fairness of tracking the websites a person visits and those from which he or she makes purchases. Should it be allowable for this information to be sold? Another issue is the fairness of having an employee work at a keyboard for 60 hours in one week when such behaviour frequently leads to repetitive strain injury. Figure 13-2 lists some major ethical issues involved in computer use.

1. Do not use a computer to harm other people. Avoid all obscene, defamatory, threatening, or otherwise harassing messages. Take precautions against others developing repetitive motion disorders.

2. Do not interfere with other people's computer work. (This includes intentionally spreading computer viruses.)

3. Do not snoop around in other people's files.

4. Do not use a computer to steal.

5. Do not use a computer to bear false witness.

6. Do not use or copy software for which you have not paid (see Figure 13-1).

7. Do not use other people's resources without authorization.

8. Do not appropriate other people's intellectual output.

9. Do not use the employer's computer for the personal promotion of commercial goods or services, unless granted permission by the employer.

10. Do think about the social consequences of the program you write.

11. Do use a computer in ways that show consideration and respect.

Figure 13-2 The 11 Commandments of Computer Ethics

Source: Adapted and updated from Arlene H. Rinaldi and Florida Atlantic University, rinaldi@acc.fau.edu; "Code of Conduct for Computer and Network Use," www.rit.edu/computerconduct.

You may have observed that these common ethical directions are not always clear-cut. Aside from obvious matters such as prohibitions against stealing, lying, cheating, and intimidating, subjectivity enters into ethical decision-making. Skill-Building Exercise 13-1 provides an opportunity to try out your ethical reasoning.

Skill-Building Exercise 13-1

THE ETHICS GAME

Citicorp (now part of Citigroup) has developed an ethics game, *The Work Ethic*.[10] The game teaches ethics by asking small teams of employees to confront difficult scenarios, such as those that follow. Discuss these ethical problems in teams. As you discuss the scenarios, identify the ethical issues involved.

Scenario 1: One of your assignments is to find a contractor to conduct building maintenance for your company headquarters. You invite bids for the job. High-Performance Cleaners, a firm staffed largely by teenagers from troubled families who have criminal records, bids on the job. Many of these teenagers also have severe learning disabilities and cannot readily find employment. High-Performance Cleaners proves to be the second-highest bidder. You

a. advise High-Performance Cleaners that its bid is too high for consideration and that your company is not a social agency.

b. award the bid to High-Performance Cleaners and justify your actions with a letter to top management by talking about social responsibility.

(Continued)

c. falsify the other bids in your report to management, making High-Performance Cleaners the low bidder—and thus the contract winner.

d. explain to High-Performance Cleaners that it lost the bid, but that you will award the company a piece of the contract because of its sterling work with needy teenagers.

Scenario 2: You live in Toronto and your company sends you on a three-day trip to New York City. Your business dealings in the Big Apple will keep you there Wednesday, Thursday, and Friday morning. You have several friends and relatives in New York, so you decide to stay there until Sunday afternoon. Besides, you want to engage in tourist activities, such as taking a boat tour around Manhattan and visiting Radio City Music Hall. When preparing your expense report for your trip, you request payment for all your business-related costs up through Friday afternoon, *plus*

a. your return trip on Sunday.

b. the return trip and the room cost for Friday and Saturday nights.

c. the return trip and one-half of your weekend food expenses as well as two extra nights in the hotel.

d. the return trip and your food costs for the weekend (which you justify because you ate at fast-food restaurants on Wednesday, Thursday, and Friday).

Scenario 3: You are the leader of a self-managing work team in a financial services company. The work of your team has expanded to the point where you are authorized to hire another team member. The team busily interviews a number of candidates from inside and outside the company. The other team members agree that one of the candidates (Pat) has truly outstanding credentials. You agree that Pat is a strong candidate. Yet you don't want Pat on the team because you and Pat were emotionally involved with one another in the past for about one year. You think that working with Pat would disrupt your concentration and bring back hurtful memories. You decide to

a. tell the group that you have some negative information about Pat's past that would disqualify Pat for the job.

b. telephone Pat and beg that Pat find employment elsewhere.

c. tell the group that you agree Pat is qualified, but explain your concerns about the disruption in concentration and emotional hurt working with Pat would cause you.

d. tell the group that you agree Pat is right for the position and mention nothing about the past relationship.

Scoring and Observation:

Scenario 1, about High-Performance Cleaners, raises dozens of ethical questions, including whether humanitarian considerations can outweigh profit concerns. Teams that chose *a* receive 0 points; *b,* 20 points; *c,* −10 points; *d,* 10 points.

Scenario 2 raises ethical issues about using company resources. Teams that chose *a* receive 20 points; *b,* −10 points; *c,* −15 points; *d,* 0 points.

Scenario 3 raises issues about fairness in making selection decisions. Teams that chose *a* receive −20 points; *b,* −10 points; *c,* 15 points; *d,* 0 points.

CHOOSING BETWEEN TWO RIGHTS: DEALING WITH DEFINING MOMENTS

Ethical decision-making usually involves choosing between two options: one we perceive to be right and one we perceive to be wrong. A challenging twist to ethical decision-making is to sort through your values when you have to choose between two *rights*, or two morally sound choices. Joseph L. Badaracco, Jr., uses the term **defining moment** to describe choosing between two or more ideals in which we deeply believe.[11] If you can learn to work through defining moments, your ethical skills will be improved. Let's first take a non-work example to illustrate a defining moment.

Imagine yourself as a basketball referee in a league for boys 10 years old and younger. Luis, the smallest boy on the team, has a self-confidence problem in general, and he has not scored a goal yet this season. This is the final game of the season. The other team is ahead by 10 points, with one minute to go. Luis lets fly with a shot that goes into the basket, but his right heel is on the line. If the goal is allowed, Luis will experience one of the happiest moments in his life, and his self-confidence might increase.

You strongly believe in helping people grow and develop. Yet you also strongly believe in following the rules of sports. What to do?

You may have recognized that a defining moment is a role conflict in which you have to choose between competing values. A CEO might deeply believe that she has an obligation to the stockholders to make a profit, and also believe in being generous and fair toward employees. However, to make a profit this year she will be forced to lay off several good employees with long seniority. The CEO now faces a moment of truth. Badaracco suggests that the individual can work through a defining moment by discovering "Who am I?" You discover who you are by arriving at soul-searching answers to three questions:

1. What feelings and intuitions are coming into conflict in this situation?

2. Which of the values that are in conflict are the most deeply rooted in my life?

Skill-Building Exercise 13-2

DEALING WITH DEFINING MOMENTS

The toughest ethical choices for many people occur when they need to choose between two *rights*. The result is a defining moment, because we are challenged to think in a deeper way by choosing between two or more ideals. Working individually or in teams, deal with the two following defining moments. Explain why these scenarios could require choosing between two rights, and explain the reasoning behind your decisions.

Scenario 1: You are the manager of a department in a business firm that assigns each department a fixed amount of money for salary increases each year. An average-performing member of the department asks you in advance for an above-average increase. He explains that his mother has developed multiple sclerosis and requires the services of a paid helper from time to time. You are concerned that if you give this man an above-average increase, somebody else in the department will need to receive a below-average increase.

Scenario 2: You are the team leader of an ecommerce business group. In recent months, each team member has been working about 60 hours per week, with little prospect of the workload decreasing in the future. Since the project is still losing money, higher management insists that one person be dropped from the team. One member of the team, Mildred, is willing to work only about 45 hours per week because she spends considerable time volunteering to work with autistic children. Mildred's work is satisfactory, but her output is the lowest in the group because of her shorter number of working hours. You must make a decision about whether to recommend that Mildred be dismissed.

3. What combinations of expediency and shrewdness, coupled with imagination and boldness, will help me implement my personal understanding of what is right?

Skill-Building Exercise 13-2 gives you an opportunity to deal with defining moments. The three questions just asked could help you find answers, but do not be constrained by these questions.

GUIDELINES FOR BEHAVING ETHICALLY

Following guidelines for ethical behaviour is the heart of being ethical. Although many people behave ethically without studying ethical guidelines, they are usually following guidelines programmed into their minds early in life. The Golden Rule exemplifies a guideline taught by parents, grandparents, and kindergarten teachers. In this section, we approach ethical guidelines from four perspectives: (1) developing the right character traits; (2) using corporate programs on ethics; (3) following a guide for ethical decision-making; (4) developing close relationships with work associates; and (5) following an applicable professional code of conduct.

DEVELOPING THE RIGHT CHARACTER TRAITS

Character traits develop early in life, yet with determination and self-discipline many people can modify old traits or develop new ones. A **character trait** is an enduring characteristic of a person that is related to moral and ethical behaviour that shows up consistently. For example, if a person has the character trait of untruthfulness, he or she will lie in many situations. Conversely, the character trait of honesty leads to behaving honestly in most situations.

The Character Counts Coalition is an organization formed to encourage young people to develop fairness, respect, trustworthiness, responsibility, caring, and good citizenship. The Coalition has developed a list of 10 key guidelines as a foundation for character development.[12] If you have developed these traits, it will be easy for you to behave ethically in business. As you read the following list, evaluate your own standing on each character trait. Remember, however, that extra effort is required to evaluate one's own character traits because most people have an inflated view of their own honesty and integrity.

1. *Be honest.* Tell the truth; be sincere; do not mislead or withhold information in relationships of trust; do not steal.

2. *Demonstrate integrity.* Stand up for your beliefs about right and wrong; be your best self; resist social pressure to do wrong.

3. *Keep promises.* Keep your word and honour your commitments; pay your debts and return what you borrow.

4. *Be loyal.* Stand by family, friends, employers, community, and country; do not talk about people behind their backs.

5. *Be responsible.* Think before you act; consider consequences; be accountable and "take your medicine."

6. *Pursue excellence.* Do your best with what you have; do not give up easily.

7. *Be kind and caring.* Show you care through generosity and compassion; do not be selfish or mean.

8. *Treat all people with respect.* Be courteous and polite; judge all people on their merits; be tolerant, appreciative, and accepting of individual differences.

9. *Be fair.* Treat all people fairly; be open-minded; listen to others and try to understand what they are saying and feeling.

10. *Be a good citizen.* Obey the law and respect the authority of appointed or elected officials; vote in local and national elections; volunteer your efforts; protect the environment.

If you score high on all of the preceding character traits and behaviours, you are an outstanding member of your company, community, and school. Your ethical behaviour is superior.

USING CORPORATE ETHICS PROGRAMS

Many organizations have various programs and procedures for promoting ethical behaviour. Among them are mission statements and guidelines that promote and encourage ethical behaviour, committees that monitor ethical behaviour, training programs in ethics, and vehicles for reporting ethical violations. The presence of these programs is designed to create an atmosphere in which unethical behaviour is discouraged and reporting of unethical behaviour is encouraged. A national survey indicates that employees are more willing to report misconduct than they were just 10 years ago. In 1994, only 48 percent said they reported misconduct. In 2003, the number rose to 65%.[13]

The Canadian Scene box on the next page summarizes some of the findings of a recent ethics survey of Canadian businesses. While policies rarely ensure compliance for employees and employers to behave ethically, they do constitute a fundamental starting place. Without a company commitment to ethical behaviour, employees may not feel it necessary to behave ethically.

Ethics hotlines are one of the best-established programs to help individuals avoid unethical behaviour. Should a person be faced with an ethical dilemma, the person calls a toll-free line to speak to a counsellor about the dilemma. Sometimes employees ask for help interpreting a policy, for example, "Is it OK to ask my boss for a date?" or "Are we supposed to give senior citizen discounts to customers who qualify but do not ask for one?" At other times, a more pressing ethical issue might be addressed, such as "Is it ethical to lay off a worker just five months short of his qualifying for a full pension?"

Sears has an ethics hotline the company refers to as an "Assist Line" because very few of the 15 000 calls it receives per year represent crises. Often the six full-time ethics specialists who handle the calls just listen; at other times they intervene to help resolve the problem. The Assist Line is designed to help with these kinds of calls: guidance about company policy; company code of conduct issues; workplace harassment and discrimination; selling practices; theft; and human resource issues. Employees and managers are able to access information and guidance without feeling they are facing a crisis. So the Assist Line is kind of a cross between "911" and "411" calls. At times an ethical problem of such high moral intensity is presented that employee confidentiality cannot be maintained. However, the Ethics Office handles the inquiries in as confidential a manner as practical and assigns them case identification numbers for follow-up.[14]

The link between the programs such as hot lines and individual ethical skills is that these programs assist a worker's skill development. For example, if you become comfortable asking about ethical issues, or turning in ethical violators, you have become more ethically skilled.

The Canadian Scene

BUSINESS ETHICS

While it is your individual responsibility to behave ethically using the various guidelines and strategies in this chapter, another way to stay ethical is to work for an ethical company. There are many examples of ethical companies in Canada—companies that treat employees fairly, treat customers with dignity and respect, and offer products that are safe, reliable, fairly priced, and do what they are supposed to do. How do you identify an "ethical company"? A November 1996 survey by KPMG of Canada (KPMG LLP is the Canadian member firm of KPMG International, a global network of professional service firms) surveyed 1000 Canadian public and private companies to get an up-to-date picture of current ethics-related practices and issues in Canada. Companies surveyed included those involved in health care, hospitality and tourism, finance, retail and wholesale, and insurance, to name a few. Among the 251 responses, some interesting trends emerged:

- Several areas were identified from academic research, and respondents were asked to rate the importance of each as a source of ethical "risk." These areas included conflict of interest, external relationships, handling company assets, customer relations, relations with suppliers, relations with competitors, and employee and workplace issues. "Employee and Workplace Issues" and "Company Assets" were identified as the most important sources of risk.

- "Integrity of Books" ranked as the top individual issue, with 71 percent of respondents rating this issue as "Very Important."

- Eighty-three percent of the companies surveyed had a published mission statement.

- Sixty-six percent of the companies surveyed had a published code of ethics, practice, or conduct, but only twenty-one percent claimed any kind of training in connection with this code.

- Of companies with over $1 billion in revenues, 90 percent reported a published code of ethics.

- Slightly over 40 percent of respondents indicated that they had someone who was "in charge" or responsible for their ethics programs, who was most likely to have the title of "Human Resources Manager."

These are only some of the results from this survey. When being interviewed by a prospective employer, you may want to ask if the company has a published code of ethics, who oversees the implementation of

(Continued)

the code, what happens to employees who violate the code, and how violations are reported. Another way to find "ethical companies" is to do a web search. Many companies, such as Compaq Canada or QLT Inc., have extensive websites with mission statements and other policies posted for public viewing. Of interest, 78 percent of respondents to the above survey stated that their companies had no formal policy to protect employees who report ethical violations. Those that did (e.g., Sears) used a confidential hotline or the like. It appears that many companies desire to have ethical employees but have no real means for violations to be reported.

Sources: KPMG, 1997 KPMG *Business Ethics Survey Report,* www.itcilo.it/english/actrav/telearn/global/ilo/code/1997kpmg.htm; QLT Inc., www.qlt.com; Compaq Canada, www6.compaq.ca.

FOLLOWING A GUIDE TO ETHICAL DECISION-MAKING

A powerful strategy for behaving ethically is to follow a guide for ethical decision-making. Such a guide for making contemplated decisions includes testing the ethics of the decision. **Ethical screening** refers to running a contemplated decision or action through an ethics test. Such screening makes the most sense when the contemplated action or decision is not clearly ethical or unethical. If a sales representative were to take a favourite customer to McDonald's for lunch, an ethical screen would not be necessary. Nobody would interpret a Big Mac as a serious bribe. Assume, instead, that the sales rep offered to give the customer an under-the-table gift of $700 for placing a large offer with the rep's firm. The sales rep's behaviour would be so blatantly unethical that conducting an ethical screen would be unnecessary.

Several useful ethical screens, or guides to ethical decision-making, have been developed. A guide developed by Treviño and Nelson is presented here because it incorporates the basic ideas in other ethical tests.[15] After studying this guide, you will be asked to ethically screen two different scenarios. The eight steps to sound ethical decision-making identified in the guide are as follows:

1. *Gather the facts.* When making an important decision in business, it is necessary to gather relevant facts. Ask yourself the following questions: "Are there any legal issues involved here?" "Is there a precedent in our firm with respect to this type of decision?" "Do I have the authority to make this decision?" "Are there company rules and regulations governing such decisions?"

    The manager of a childcare centre needed to hire an additional childcare specialist. One of the applicants was a 55-year-old male with experience as a father and grandfather. The manager judged him to be qualified, yet she knew that many parents would not want their preschool children to be cared for by a middle-aged male. Many people perceive that a younger woman is better qualified for childcare than an older man. The manager therefore had to gather considerable facts about the situation, including facts about job discrimination and precedents in hiring males as childcare specialists.

2. *Define the ethical issues.* The ethical issues in a given decision are often more complicated than a first glance suggests. When faced with a complex decision, it may be helpful to talk over the ethical issues with another person. The ethical issues might involve character traits such as being kind and caring and treating

others with respect. Or the ethical issues might relate to some of the common ethical problems described earlier in the chapter. Among them are conflict of interest, dealing with confidential information, and use of corporate resources.

The manager of the childcare centre is facing such ethical issues as fairness, job discrimination, and meeting the demands of customers at the expense of job applicants. The manager is also facing a diversity issue: should the workforce in a childcare centre be culturally diverse, or should only young women be hired?

3. *Identify the affected parties.* When faced with a complex ethical decision, it is important to identify all the affected parties. Major corporate decisions can affect thousands of people. If a company decides to shut down a plant and move its manufacturing to a low-wage country, thousands of individuals and many different parties are affected. Workers lose their jobs, suppliers lose their customers, local governments lose out on tax revenues, and local merchants lose many of their customers. You may need to brainstorm with a few others to think of all the parties affected by a given decision.

The parties affected by the decision about hiring or not hiring the 55-year-old male include the applicant himself, the children, the parents, and the board of directors of the childcare centre. The government might also be involved if the man were rejected and filed charges of age and sex discrimination.

4. *Identify the consequences.* After you have identified the parties affected by a decision, the next step is to predict the consequences for each party. It may not be necessary to identify every consequence, yet it is important to identify the consequences with the highest probability of occurring and those with the most negative outcomes. The problem is that many people can be harmed by an unethical decision, such as a decision to avoid describing the full possible side effects of a diet program.

Both short-term and long-term consequences should be specified. The company's closing a plant might create considerable short-term turmoil, but in the long-term the company might be healthier. People participating in a diet program might achieve their short-term objective of losing weight. Yet in the long term, their health might be adversely affected because the diet is not nutritionally balanced.

The *symbolic* consequences of an action are important. Every action and decision sends a message (the decision is a symbol of something). If a company moves manufacturing out of a community to save on labour costs, it means that the short term welfare of domestic employees is less important than profit or perhaps the company surviving.

Let us return to the childcare manager and the job applicant. If the applicant does not get the job, his welfare will be adversely affected. He has been laid off by a large employer and cannot find work in his regular field. His family will also suffer because he will not be able to make a financial contribution. Yet if the man is hired, the childcare centre may suffer. Many parents will say, "Absolutely not. I do not want my child cared for by a middle-aged man. He could be a child molester." (It may be unethical for people to have vicious stereotypes, yet they still exist.) If the childcare centre does hire the man, the act will symbolize the fact that the owners of the centre value diversity.

5. *Identify the obligations.* Identify the obligations and the reasons for each obligation when making a complex decision. The manufacturer of automotive brakes has an obligation to produce and sell only brakes that meet high safety standards. The obligation is to the auto manufacturer who purchases the brakes and, more important, to the ultimate consumer whose safety depends on effective brakes. The reason for the obligation to make safe brakes is that lives are at stake.

The childcare manager has an obligation to provide for the safety and health of the children at the centre. She must also provide for the peace of mind of the parents and be a good citizen of the community in which the centre is located. The decision about hiring the candidate in question must be balanced against all these obligations.

6. *Consider your character and integrity.* A core consideration when faced with an ethical dilemma is to consider how relevant people would judge your character and integrity in the light of the decision you make. What would your family, friends, significant others, teachers, and co-workers think of your actions? To refine this thinking further, how would you feel if your actions were publicly disclosed in the local newspaper or by email? Would you want the world to know that you gave an under-the-table kickback or that you sexually harassed a frightened teenager working for you? If you would be proud for others to know what decision you made when faced with an ethical dilemma, you are probably making the right decision.

The childcare-centre manager might ponder how she would feel if the following information were released in the local newspaper:

The manager of Good Times Child Care recently rejected the application of a 55-year-old man for a childcare-specialist position. She said that although Mr. _____ was well qualified from an experience and personality standpoint, she couldn't hire him. She said that Good Times would lose too much business because many parents would fear that Mr. _____ was a child molester or pedophile.

7. *Think creatively about potential actions.* When faced with an ethical dilemma, put yourself into a creative-thinking mode. Stretch your imagination to invent several options rather than thinking you have only two choices—to do or not do something. Creative thinking may point toward a third, and even a fourth, alternative. Imagine this ethical dilemma: A purchasing agent is told that if her firm awards a contract to the sales representative's firm, she will find a leather jacket of her choice delivered to her door. The purchasing agent says to herself, "I think we should award the contract to the firm, but I cannot accept the gift. Yet if I turn down the gift, I will be forfeiting a valuable possession that the company simply regards as a cost of doing business."

The purchasing agent can search for another alternative. She can say to the sales rep, "We will give the contract to your firm because your product fits our requirements. I thank you for the offer of the leather jacket. But I would like you to give that jacket to the Salvation Army instead of to me."

A creative alternative for the childcare manager might be to offer the applicant the next position that opens for an office manager or maintenance person in the centre. In this way, she would be offering a qualified applicant a job but placing him in a position more acceptable to parents. Or do you feel that this is a cop-out?

8. *Check your intuition.* So far, we have emphasized the rational side of ethical decision-making. Another effective way of conducting an ethical screen is to rely on your intuition. How does the contemplated decision feel? Would you be proud of yourself or would you hate yourself if you made the decision? Imagine how you would feel if you took money from the handbag of a woman sleeping in the park. Would you feel the same way if you went ahead and took a kickback, sold somebody a defective product, or sold an 80-year-old man an insurance policy he did not need? How will the manager of the childcare centre feel if she turns down the man for the childcare specialist position?

You are encouraged to use the guide for ethical decision-making when you next face an ethical dilemma of consequence. Skill-Building Exercise 13-3 gives you an opportunity to practise using these eight steps.

Skill-Building Exercise 13-3

ETHICAL DECISION-MAKING

Working in small groups, take one or more of the following ethical dilemmas through the eight steps for screening contemplated decisions. If more than one group chooses the same scenario, compare your answers for the various steps.

Scenario 1: To Recycle or Not. Your group is the top management team at a large insurance company. Despite the movement toward computerization, your firm still generates tonnes of paper each month. Customer payments alone account for truckloads of envelopes each year. The paper recyclers in your area claim they can hardly find a market any longer for used paper, so they will be charging you just to accept your paper for recycling. Your group is wondering whether to recycle.

Scenario 2: The Job Applicant with a Past. Emily has been working for the family business as an office manager for five years. Because the family business is being sold, Emily has started a job hunt. She also welcomes the opportunity to work in a larger company so she can learn more about how a big company operates. As she begins preparing her résumé, she ponders how to classify the year of unemployment prior to working at the family business. During that year she worked a total of 10 weeks in entry-level jobs at three fast-food restaurants. Otherwise she filled her time with such activities as walking in the park, watching daytime television shows, surfing the Internet, playing video games, and pursuing her hobby of visiting graveyards. Emily finally decides to tack that year onto the five years in the family business. She indicates on her résumé that she has been working *six* years at the family business. As Emily says, "It's a tight job market for office managers, and I don't want to raise any red flags." Evaluate the ethics of Emily's decision to fill in the year off from work, and perhaps offer her some advice.

Scenario 3: The High-Profit Toy. You are a toy company executive starting to plan your holiday season line. You anticipate that the season's hottest item will be Robo-Woman, a battery-operated crime fighter and superhero. Robo-Woman should wholesale for $18.50 and retail for $38.00. Your company figures to earn $10 per unit. You receive a sales call from a manufacturing broker who says he can produce any toy you want for one-third of your present manufacturing cost. He admits that the manufacturer he represents uses prison labour in China but insists that his business arrangement violates no law. You estimate you can earn $14 per unit if you do business with the manufacturing broker. Your decision is whether to do business with him.

DEVELOPING CLOSER RELATIONSHIPS WITH WORK ASSOCIATES

A provocative explanation of the causes of unethical behaviour emphasizes the strength of relationships among people.[16] Assume that two people have close ties to one another, such as having worked together for a long time or knowing one another both on and off the job. As a consequence, they are likely to behave ethically toward one another on the job. In contrast, if a weak relationship exists between two people, either party is more likely to engage in unethical behaviour toward the other. The owner of an auto-service centre is more likely to behave unethically toward a stranger passing through town than toward a long-time customer. The opportunity for unethical behaviour between strangers is often minimized because individuals typically do not trust strangers with sensitive information or valuables.

Building closer relationships with people is likely to enhance ethical behaviour. If you build close relationships with work associates, you are likely to behave more ethically toward them. Similarly, your work associates are likely to behave more ethically toward you. The work associates we refer to are all your contacts, or internal and external customers.

Professional Organization	Samples of Ethical Guidelines, Conduct and Regulations
Sears Canada	1. Associates are required to conduct themselves with respect, cooperation, and dignity towards all those with whom they have dealings on behalf of Sears.
	2. It is vital that we be truthful in all our business dealings with each other and with third parties. At no time should misleading information be provided to anyone, either verbally or in writing. We must always act in good faith.
Canadian Pacific Railway	1. Employees must avoid all actual or perceived conflicts of interest between their personal interests and their duties to CPR.
	2. CPR and its employees shall comply with all legal requirements, both domestic and foreign, applicable to CPR's business.
Bank of Montreal	1. Everything we do and every decision we make will be guided by principles of honesty, integrity, fair dealing, respect and high ethical standards.
	2. We must be alert to and immediately report concerns that may point to a breach of any laws, regulations or this Code to the appropriate persons or departments within BMO. Retaliation against a BMO employee for raising legitimate concerns under this Code is prohibited.

Figure 13-3   Excerpts from Professional Codes of Conduct

Sources: Sears Canada: www.sears.ca; Canadian Pacific Railway: www8.cpr.ca/cms/English/Investors/Governance/Policies/Code+of+Business+Ethics.htm; Bank of Montreal: http://www2.bmo.com/content/0,1089,divId-7_langId-1_navCode-4138,00.html

FOLLOWING AN APPLICABLE PROFESSIONAL CODE OF CONDUCT

Professional codes of conduct are prescribed for many occupational groups including physicians, nurses, lawyers, paralegals, purchasing managers and agents, and real estate salespeople. A useful ethical guide for members of these groups is to follow the code of conduct for their profession. If the profession or trade is licensed by the province, a worker can be punished for deviating from the code of conduct specified. The code of conduct developed by the profession or trade is separate from the legal code, but usually supports the same principles and practices. Some of these codes of conduct developed by professional associations are 50 and 60 pages long, yet all are guided by the kind of ethical principles implied in the ethical-decision-making guide described earlier. Figure 13-3 presents a sampling of provisions from these codes of conduct. The Bank of Montreal has seven principles, two which are noted in Figure 13-3, that make up its Code of Business Conduct and Ethics. One of the websites at the end of this chapter lists hundreds of Canadian companies and a variety of codes of conduct, ethical practices, and regulations.

SUMMARY

Ethics refers to what is good and bad, right and wrong, just and unjust, and what people should do. A person's ethical code has a significant impact on his or her interpersonal relationships.

Understanding ethics is important for a variety of reasons. First, people are motivated by self-interest and a desire to be morally right. Second, practising good ethics can be good for business and help avoid illegalities. Third, a high standard of ethics improves the quality of working life.

Being ethical isn't always easy for several reasons, including the complexity of ethical decisions, lack of recognition of the moral issues, poor moral development, and pressures from the work environment. Ethical violations in the form of lying are widespread in the workplace.

Commonly faced ethical problems include the following: the temptation to illegally copy software; treating people unfairly; job discrimination; sexual harassment; conflict of interest; mistreating confidential information; misrepresenting employment history; misuse of corporate resources; and misuse of computers and information technology.

A challenging twist to ethical decision-making is to sort through your values when you have to choose between two morally sound choices. A defining moment is when you have to choose between two or more ideals in which you deeply believe.

One strategy for behaving ethically is to develop the right character traits. Among these traits are honesty, integrity, promise-keeping, loyalty, responsibility, kindness, respect for others, fairness, and good citizenship. At times, using a corporate program such as an ethics hotline can help a person resolve an ethical dilemma.

Another strategy for behaving ethically is to work through the following eight steps in making a contemplated decision:

1. Gather the facts.
2. Define the ethical issues.

3. Identify the affected parties.

4. Identify the consequences.

5. Identify the obligations (such as to customers and society).

6. Consider your character and integrity.

7. Think creatively about potential actions.

8. Check your intuition.

Another way to raise the level of ethical behaviour is to form close relationships with work associates. This is true because people tend to behave more ethically toward people they are close to. Following an applicable code of professional conduct, such as that for accountants, paralegals, and purchasing specialists, is another guide to behaving ethically.

An Interpersonal Relations Case Problem

"HELP, I'M A VICTIM OF CLICK FRAUD"

Nathan McKelvey began to worry about foul play when Yahoo! Inc. refunded him $69.28 early last year. He grew more suspicious when a $16.91 refund arrived from Google Inc. The refunds were for "unusual clicks" and "invalid click activity" and they suggested someone was sabotaging McKelvey's advertising strategy. He pitches his charter-jet brokerage the way companies increasingly do: contracting with Yahoo! and Google to serve up small text ads to anyone searching the Web using certain words, such as "private jet" or "air charter." He pays the companies a fee every time someone clicks on his ads.

But Yahoo! and Google determined someone was clicking on CharterAuction.com Inc.'s ads with no intention of doing business, thus unfairly driving up the company's advertising costs. McKelvey, turning detective, combed through lists of Internet Protocol (IP) addresses, the identifying codes supplied by computers when they access Web sites. He found several suspicious clicks from one address and about 100 more from one that was similar. They belonged to a New York-based rival, Blue Star Jets LLC, McKelvey says.

He had run into "click fraud," a term the industry uses to describe someone clicking on a search ad with ill intent. A fraudulent clicker can exploit the way web ads work to rack up fees for a business rival, boost the placement of his or her own ads, or make money for himself or herself. Some people even employ software that automatically clicks on ads multiple times.

Some people believe that about 20 percent of clicks are from people not necessarily interested in the product advertised, and are therefore in the industry's view, fraudulent; others say the problem is less severe. What's clear is that if left unchecked, click fraud could damage the credibility of Google, Yahoo!, and the search-ad industry that spurred their meteoric growth. Click fraud is "the biggest threat to the internet economy," Google's chief financial officer, George Reyes, said during an investor's conference.

During his sleuthing, McKelvey discovered that his industry was rife with click manipulation. He and others in the jet-charter brokerage fields say Yahoo! and Google have been slow to help and vague on how they're tackling the problem. Meanwhile, McKelvey has cut his search-ad spending to $1000 a month from $20 000. "I'm skeptical of the whole thing now," he says. He shifted the remaining $19 000 into other outlets, including magazines and events. "I feel like I've been snookered," he says. "Am I willing to take the risk

(Continued)

and stick my neck out there at maybe $15 or $20 a click? Not now."

From the start of his business, McKelvey, now 35 years old, advertised through search engines. When a consumer search used words related to the charter-jet industry, his ad would pop up, often first on the list. Business rushed in, McKelvey says, and he bid on about 200 phrases including "jet charter," "business jet," "executive jet," and "charter flights." The advertiser who wins the bid gets his or her company's ad placed high in the search lists.

McKelvey's web-hosting company traced dozens of clicks to an address belonging to an internet service provider called BridgeCom International Inc. The company had assigned the IP address in question to Blue Star Jets. That was a lucky break for McKelvey because internet service providers typically keep such information private.

Howard Moses, chief marketing office for Blue Star Jets, says some of Blue Star's staff and salespeople might have clicked on rivals' search ads looking for information. He denies the company engaged in

any widespread, malicious clicking. "It's a little bit amusing to think that our staff is concentrating on driving their search-advertising spending up by $100 or something like that," Moses says.

McKelvey thinks the problem costs him more than the refunds he received. He believes there are more bad clicks he hasn't discovered. He says Yahoo! and Google haven't helped. He contacted the Massachusetts attorney general's office, which he says decided not to take up the matter.

Case Questions

1. Is this case more about crime than ethics? Or is it more about ethics than crime? Explain your reasoning.

2. What would you recommend that McKelvey do about using the internet searches as a source of leads for his business?

3. How might a code of ethics for companies that advertise on the internet help resolve the issues raised in this case?

Source: Kevin J. Delaney, "Click Fraud: Web Outfits Have a Costly Problem," in *The Wall Street Journal,* April 6, 2005, pp. A1, A6. Reprinted with permission.

An Interpersonal Relations Case Problem

THE HIGHLY RATED, BUT EXPENDABLE MARSHA

Department manager Nicholas had thought for a long time that Marsha, one of his financial analysts, created too many problems. Although Marsha performed her job in a satisfactory manner, she required a lot of supervisory time and attention. She frequently asked for time off when her presence was needed the most because of a heavy workload in the department. Marsha sent Nicholas many long and complicated email messages that required substantial time to read and respond to. When Nicholas responded to Marsha's email message, she would typically send another email back asking for clarification.

Marsha's behaviour during department meetings irritated Nicholas. She would demand more time than any other participant to explain her point

of view on a variety of issues. At a recent meeting she took ten minutes explaining how the company should be doing more to help the homeless and invest in the development of inner cities.

Nicholas coached Marsha frequently about the problems she was creating, but Marsha strongly disagreed with his criticism and concerns. At one time, Nicholas told Marsha that she was a high-maintenance employee. Yet Marsha perceived herself as a major contributor to the department. She commented once, "Could it be, Nick, that you have a problem with an assertive woman working in your department?"

Nicholas developed a tactic to get Marsha out of the department. He would give her outstanding performance evaluations, emphasizing her creativity

(*Continued*)

and persistence. Marsha would then be entered into the company database as an outstanding employee, thereby making her a strong candidate for transfer or promotion. Within six months, a manager in a new division of the company took the bait. She requested that Marsha be recruited into her department as a senior financial analyst. Nicholas said to the recruiting manager, "I hate to lose a valuable contributor like Marsha, but I do not want to block her career progress."

Two months later, Marsha's new manager telephoned Nicholas, and asked, "What's the problem with Marsha? She's kind of a pill to have working with us. I thought she was an outstanding employee."

Nicholas responded, "Give Marsha some time. She may be having a few problems adjusting to a new environment. Just give her a little constructive feedback. You'll find out what a dynamo she can be."

Case Questions

1. How ethical was Nicholas in giving Marsha a high performance evaluation for the purposes of making her attractive to other departments?

2. What should the manager do who was hooked by Nicholas's bait of the high performance evaluation?

3. What might the company do to prevent more incidents of inflated performance evaluations for the purpose of transferring an unwanted employee?

Interpersonal Skills Role Play

Confronting the Ethical Deviant

One student plays the role of the manager who transferred Marsha into his or her department. The new manager has become suspicious that Nicholas might have manipulated Marsha's performance evaluations to make her appear like a strong candidate for transfer or promotion. In fact, the new manager thinks he may have caught an ethical deviant. Another student plays the role of Nicholas, who wants to defend his reputation as an ethical manager. During the role play, pay some attention to ethical issues. As usual, other students will provide feedback on the effectiveness of the interaction they observed.

QUESTIONS FOR DISCUSSION AND REVIEW

1. How can behaving ethically improve a person's interpersonal relationships on the job?

2. What would most likely be some of the specific behaviours of a manager who scored 20 points on the ethical reasoning inventory?

3. A widespread practice is for top management to outsource (or "offshore") work such as call centres to low-wage countries such as India, the Philippines, and lately, Africa. What ethical problems do you see with outsourcing of this type?

4. Major business scandals in recent years have involved financial manipulations such as executives profiting from selling company stock while encouraging employees to buy the stock. In what ways do these financial scandals affect people?

5. Give an example from your own experience or that you learned of through the media in which a business executive did something of significance that was morally right.

6. Provide an example of an action in business that might be unethical but not illegal.

7. Virtually all accountants have studied ethics as part of their education, yet many business scandals involve accountants. What's their problem?

8. What "commandment" about computer use would you like to add to the list in Figure 13-2?

9. What decision of ethical consequence have you made in the last year that you would not mind having publicly disclosed?

Research
Navigator.com

10. In recent years, many companies have been accused of violating ethics. Using your Research Navigator, find one article or research study that discusses at least one case of such a breach of ethics. Share your results with the class.

WEBLINKS

www.ethics.org
This is the site for the Ethics Resource Center. It features articles and information about business ethics.

www.cbsr.ca
This is the site for Canadian Business for Social Responsibility. Businesses join this group and promote the conducting of business in transparent and ethical ways. Among current members are Alcan and the Royal Bank of Canada, to name just a couple.

www.itcilo.it/english/actrav/telearn/global/ilo/code/1997kpmg.htm
From KPMG, read the results of a 1997 Business Ethics Survey here.

www.businessethics.ca
Articles and a survey about business ethics.

www.lib.uwo.ca/business/canadiancoethics.html
This website contains the codes of conduct, ethical principles and guidelines of hundreds of Canadian companies.

Chapter 14

Personal Productivity and Stress Management

Learning Outcomes

After reading and studying this chapter and doing the exercises, you should be able to

- Reduce any tendencies you might have toward procrastination.
- Identify attitudes and values that will increase your productivity.
- Identify skills and techniques that will increase your productivity.
- Pinpoint potential time-wasters that drain your productivity.
- Explain many of the symptoms and consequences of stress, including burnout.
- Describe personality factors and job factors that contribute to stress.
- Be prepared to manage your own stress effectively.

Forty-one-year-old Fethiya Ahmed couldn't stand the routine of her life any longer. Juggling a full-time job with raising three young children was beginning to take its toll. Her husband was frequently out of town, and although he helped when he was home, she was starting to feel very stressed. Making matters worse, the commute to work often took at least an hour in the morning and sometimes longer in the evening. She felt she was hardly seeing her children, since they were in the care of a babysitter before and after school.

Finally, in desperation she went to her manager. After stating her problem, she and her manager came up with a solution. She could work from home two days per week and use flex-time on the other days to alleviate the commuting problems. Her stress level immediately plummeted. Two days every week she saw the children off to school and then got down to work. After three months, her manager commented: "This arrangement is working well for both of us. You're getting more done, and the quality of your work has really improved. We should have thought of this a year ago!"

This story illustrates two major workplace themes: workers want to be productive, but at the same time they must find realistic ways of managing stress and avoiding burnout. Although this book is primarily about interpersonal skills, information about increasing personal productivity and managing stress is relevant. Being more productive and keeping stress under control enable you to focus better on interpersonal relationships.

The first half of this chapter describes various approaches to increasing personal productivity; the second half deals with the nature of stress and how it can be managed. The two topics are as closely related as nutrition and health. When your work is under control, you avoid the heavy stress of feeling overwhelmed. And when you effectively manage stress, you can be more productive.

INCREASING PERSONAL PRODUCTIVITY

Increasing personal productivity is more in vogue than ever. Companies strive to operate with smaller staffs than in the past by pushing workers to achieve higher productivity. At the same time, there is a movement toward simplifying personal life by reducing clutter and cutting back on tasks that do not add much to the quality of working life. **Personal productivity** refers to the amount of resources, including time, you consume to achieve a certain level of output.

We approach productivity improvement from four perspectives: (1) dealing with procrastination, (2) attitudes and values that increase personal productivity, (3) work habits and skills that increase personal productivity, and (4) overcoming time-wasters.

DEALING WITH PROCRASTINATION

The person who **procrastinates** delays action for no good reason. Procrastination lowers productivity because it wastes time and many important tasks never get done. Even productive people sometimes procrastinate. If these people did not procrastinate, they would be even more productive.

Many people regard procrastination as a laughable weakness, particularly because procrastinators themselves joke about it. Yet procrastination has been evaluated as a profound, debilitating problem, with about 20 percent of working adults identifying themselves as chronic procrastinators.[1] Approximately 70 percent of college students report problems with overdue papers and delayed studying.[2] The enormity of the problem makes it worthwhile to examine methods for bringing it under control. Do Self-Assessment Quiz 14-1 on page 322 to think through your own tendencies toward procrastination—and don't wait until tomorrow!

Choose from among the following suggestions for controlling procrastination, based on those that appear to best fit your type of procrastination. A combination of techniques is likely to be the most effective.

1. *Calculate the cost of procrastination.* You can reduce procrastination by calculating its cost. You might lose out on obtaining a high-paying job you really want by not having your résumé and cover letter ready on time. Your cost of procrastination would include the difference in compensation between the

Self-Assessment Quiz 14-1

PROCRASTINATION TENDENCIES

Directions: Circle Yes or No for each item:

1. I usually do my best work under the pressure of deadlines.	Yes	No
2. Before starting a project, I go through such rituals as sharpening every pencil, straightening up my desk more than once, and discarding bent paper clips.	Yes	No
3. I crave the excitement of the "last-minute rush."	Yes	No
4. I often think that if I delay something, it will go away, or the person who asked for it will forget about it.	Yes	No
5. I extensively research something before taking action, such as obtaining three different estimates before getting the brakes repaired on my car.	Yes	No
6. I have a great deal of difficulty getting started on most projects, even those I enjoy.	Yes	No
7. I keep waiting for the right time to do something, such as getting started on an important report.	Yes	No
8. I often underestimate the time needed to do a project and say to myself, "I can do this quickly, so I'll wait until next week."	Yes	No
9. It is difficult for me to finish most projects or activities.	Yes	No
10. I have several favourite diversions or distractions that I use to keep me from doing something unpleasant.	Yes	No

Total Yes Responses _____

Scoring and Interpretation: The greater the number of Yes responses, the more likely it is that you have a serious procrastination problem. A score of 8, 9, or 10 strongly suggests that procrastination is lowering your productivity.

job you do find and the one you really wanted. Another cost would be the loss of potential job satisfaction.

2. *Follow the "WIFO" principle, which stands for "worst in, first out."*[3] If you tackle the worst task on your list first, doing the other tasks may function like a small reward. You get to do what you dislike the least by doing first what you dislike the most. Following the WIFO principle is particularly effective when one is faced with several tasks simultaneously.

3. *Break up the task into manageable chunks.* To reduce procrastination, cut down a task that seems overwhelming into smaller projects that seem less formidable. If your job calls for preparing an enormous database, begin by assembling some readily available information. Then take the next step by assembling

another small segment of the database—perhaps all customers whose last names begin with Z. Think of your task as pulling together a series of small databases that will fit into a master database.

4. *Make a commitment to other people.* Try to make it imperative that you get something done on time by making it a commitment to one or more other people. You might announce to co-workers that you are going to get something accomplished by a certain date. If you fail to meet this date, you are likely to feel embarrassed.

5. *Remove some clutter from your mind.* Procrastination escalates when people have many unfinished projects in the back of their minds, draining their concentration. Having too much to do can freeze us in inaction. Just eliminating a few trivial items from your to-do list can give you enough mental energy to overcome procrastination on a few major tasks. Note carefully that this approach to overcoming procrastination requires that you be self-disciplined enough to take the first step.

6. *Satisfy your stimulation quota in constructive ways.* If you procrastinate because you enjoy the rush of scrambling to meet deadlines, find a more constructive way of using busyness to keep you humming. If you need a high level of stimulation, enrich your life with extra projects and learning new skills. The fullness of your schedule will give you the stimulation you had been deriving from squeezing yourself to meet deadlines and get to appointments on time.[4]

7. *Eliminate tangible rewards you are giving yourself for procrastinating.* If you are procrastinating through socializing with co-workers, taking a walk to obtain a beverage, surfing the internet, or any other pleasant experience—stop rewarding yourself. Just sit alone in your work area doing nothing while procrastinating. If you remove the pleasant activities from your stalling routine, you may be able to reduce procrastination.[5]

ATTITUDES AND VALUES THAT INCREASE PERSONAL PRODUCTIVITY

Developing good work habits and time-management practices is often a matter of developing the right attitudes toward your work and toward time. If, for example, you think that your schoolwork or job is important and that time is a precious resource, you will be on your way toward developing good work habits. In this section, we describe a group of attitudes, values, and beliefs that can help a person become more productive through better use of time and improved work habits.

Begin with a Mission and Goals

A mission, or general purpose, propels you toward being productive. Assume that a person says, "My mission is to be an outstanding professional in my field and a loving, constructive spouse and parent." The mission serves as a compass to direct your activities, such as being well-organized in order to accomplish more work and be highly valued by your employer. Goals are more specific than mission statements; they support the mission statement, but the effect is the same. Being committed to a goal also propels you toward good use of time. If you know that you

Skill-Building Exercise 14-1

USING A MISSION STATEMENT AND GOALS TO POWER WORK HABITS

People with a well-defined mission statement and supporting goals tend to have better work habits and time-management skills than those who do not. The following exercise is designed to help you establish a mission statement and goals that will energize you to be more productive.

A. Mission Statement: To help develop your mission statement, or general purpose in life, ask yourself, "What are my five biggest wishes in life?" These wishes give you a hint of your purpose because they point toward an ideal purpose in life. Feel free to think big, because mission statements tend toward idealism.

B. Long-Range Goals to Support Mission Statement: Now write down what long-range goals would support your mission statement. Suppose your mission statement related to "creating a better life for disadvantaged people." Your long-range goals might include establishing a foundation that would fund your efforts. You would also need to be successful enough in your career to get the foundation started.

C. Intermediate-Range Goals to Support Long-Range Goals: Write down the intermediate-range goals needed to support the long-range goals. You will probably need to complete your education, obtain broad experience, and identify a lucrative form of self-employment.

D. Weekly Goals to Support Intermediate-Range Goals: Write down what you have to do this week to help you complete your education, such as researching and writing a paper for a particular course, registering for courses for next term, and inquiring about career opportunities in your field.

E. Today's Goals to Support Weekly Goals (My To-Do List): Here's where your lofty purpose in life gets translated into reality. What do you have to do today to get that paper written? Do you need to get your car battery replaced so you can get to the library to write your paper, so you can graduate, so you can become rich, so you can ultimately help all those disadvantaged people? Get going!

can obtain the position in international business that you really want by mastering a second language, you are likely to work diligently on learning that language. Skill-Building Exercise 14-1 gives you the opportunity to develop a mission statement and supporting goals.

Play the Inner Game of Work

Psychologist and tennis coach Timothy Gallwey developed the *inner game of tennis* to help tennis players better focus on their game. Over time the inner game spread to skiing, other sports, life in general, and work. The key concept is that by removing inner obstacles such as self-criticism, you can dramatically improve your ability to focus, learn, and perform. According to Gallwey, two selves exist inside each person. Self 1 is the critical, fearful, self-doubting voice that sends out messages like, "You've almost solved this tough problem for the customer. Don't blow it now." Intimidating comments like these hinder Self 2 from getting the job done. Self 2 encompasses all the inner resources—both actual and potential—of the individual.

Self 1 must be suppressed so Self 2 can accomplish its task and learn effectively without being lectured. The process required to move Self 1 aside is to focus your attention on a critical variable related to performance, rather than on the performance you are attempting to achieve. An example would be for a customer service representative to focus on the amount of tension in a caller's voice.[6] Or, you might focus on the facial expressions of your manager as you attempt to sell him or her on an idea for improving productivity.

Work Smarter, Not Harder

People caught up in trying to accomplish a job often wind up working hard, but not in an imaginative way that leads to good results. Much time and energy are therefore wasted. A working-smart approach also requires that you spend a few minutes carefully planning how to implement your task. An example of working smarter, not harder, is to invest a few minutes of critical thinking before conducting a telemarketing campaign for home replacement windows. Develop a list of homeowners of houses that are at least 15 years old. People with relatively new homes are poor prospects for replacing their windows.

Value Orderliness and Cleanliness

An orderly desk, work area, briefcase, or hard drive does not inevitably indicate an orderly mind. Yet it does help most people become more productive because they can better focus their minds. Also, less time is wasted and less energy is expended if you do not have to hunt for information that you thought you had on hand. According to time-management consultant Barbara Hemphill, the average person spends 150 hours per year searching for misplaced information. Hemphill says, "Your ability to accomplish any task or goal is directly related to your ability to find the right information at the right time."[7] Knowing where information is and what information you have available is a way of being in control of your job. When your job gets out of control, you are probably working at less than peak efficiency. Valuing cleanliness improves productivity in several ways. According to traditional Japanese thinking, cleanliness is the bedrock of quality. Also, after you have thoroughly cleaned your work area, you will usually attain a fresh outlook.

Value Good Attendance and Punctuality

Good attendance and punctuality are expected of both experienced and inexperienced employees. You cannot be productive if you are not physically present in your work area. The same principle applies whether you work on company premises or at home. One exception is that some people can work through solutions to job problems while engaged in recreation. Keep in mind, too, that being late for or absent from meetings sends the silent message that you do not regard the meeting as being important.

The relationship of lateness to absenteeism and work performance has been researched. Thirty studies of over 9000 workers found that employees who were late also tended to have high absenteeism records. In addition, employees who were late tended to have poorer work performance than did workers who were prompt, but that relationship was not strong.[8] Despite this weak association, being late must still be regarded as a productivity drain.

Attain a Balance in Life and Avoid Being a Workaholic

A productive attitude to maintain is that overwork can lead to negative stress and burnout. Proper physical rest and relaxation can contribute to mental alertness and improved ability to cope with frustration. A strategy for preventing overwork is to strive for a balance in which you derive satisfaction from various spheres of life. Major spheres in addition to work include family life, romance, sports, the arts and music, faith, and intellectual growth.

A strongly recommended technique for attaining balance between work and other spheres of life is to learn how to say no diplomatically to your boss and family members.[9] For example, your boss might ask you to take on a project when you are already overloaded. It would be necessary to *occasionally* explain that you are so overloaded that you could not do a good job with the new assignment. And, you might have to *occasionally* turn down your family's or friend's request to take a weekend vacation when you face heavy work demands.

Neglecting the normal need for rest and relaxation can lead to **workaholism**, an addiction to work in which not working is an uncomfortable experience. Some types of workaholics are perfectionists who are never satisfied with their work and therefore find it difficult to leave it behind. In addition, the perfectionist-type workaholic may become heavily focused on control, leading to rigid behaviour and strained interpersonal relationships. However, some people who work long and hard are classified as achievement-oriented workaholics who thrive on hard work and are usually highly productive.[10] For example, a person with strong family values might nevertheless work 65 hours per week for one year while establishing a new business.

WORK HABITS AND SKILLS THAT INCREASE PERSONAL PRODUCTIVITY

Overcoming procrastination and developing the right attitudes contribute to personal productivity, but effective work habits and skills are also essential. Six key work habits and skills are described next. They represent a mixture of traditional productivity boosters and those geared to information technology.

Prepare a To-Do List and Set Priorities

At the heart of every time-management system is list-making, whether the list is placed on an index card, in a leather-bound planner, or in a palm-sized computer. As already mentioned, the to-do list is the basic tool for achieving your daily goals, which in turn help you achieve bigger goals and your mission. Almost every successful person in any field composes a list of important and less important tasks that need to be done. Before you compose a useful list, you need to set aside a few minutes of quiet time every day to sort out the tasks at hand. This is the most basic aspect of planning.

As is well known, it is helpful to set priorities for items on the to-do list. A typical system is to use A to signify critical or essential items, B to signify important items, and C for the least important ones. Although an item might be regarded as a C (for example, emptying the wood shavings from the electric pencil sharpener), it still makes a contribution to your management of time and sense of well-being. Accomplishing anything reduces some stress. Also, many people obtain satisfaction from crossing off an item on their list, however trivial. If you are at all conscientious, small, unaccomplished items will come back to interfere with your concentration.

Time-management consultant Harold Taylor warns that preparing to-do lists should not become an end in itself, with so much time devoted to list-making that accomplishing some of the tasks gets neglected.[11] Another danger is filling the to-do list with items you would accomplish anyway, such as "check email." The to-do list can become so long that it becomes overwhelming.

Streamline Your Work and Emphasize Important Tasks

As companies continue to operate with fewer workers than in the past, despite prosperity, more unproductive work must be eliminated. Getting rid of unproductive work is part of *business process improvement* or re-engineering, in which work processes are radically redesigned and simplified. Every employee is expected to get rid of work that does not contribute to productivity or help customers.

In general, to streamline or re-engineer your work, look for duplication of effort and waste. An example of duplication of effort would be to routinely send people email and fax messages covering the same topic. An example of waste would be to call a meeting for disseminating information that could easily be communicated by email.

Emphasizing important tasks means that you make sure to take care of A items on your to-do list. It also implies that you seek to accomplish a few work activities that, if done well, would make a big difference in your job performance. Although important tasks may take less time to accomplish than many routine tasks, they can represent the difference between success and failure. Five minutes of telephone conversation with a major customer might do more good for your company than three hours of arranging obsolete inventory in the warehouse.

Concentrate on One Important Task at a Time

While working on important tasks, concentrate on what you are doing. Effective executives and professionals have a well-developed capacity to concentrate on the problem or person facing them, however surrounded they are with other obligations. Intense concentration leads to crisper judgment and analysis and also minimizes major errors. Another useful by-product of concentration is that it helps reduce absent-mindedness. If you really concentrate on what you are doing, the chances diminish that you will forget what you intended to do.

While concentrating on an important task, such as performing analytical work or writing a report, avoid multitasking, or performing more than one activity simultaneously. Common forms of multitasking include surfing the internet or reading email while engaged in a phone conversation with a co-worker or customer. Both experimental evidence and opinion has accumulated that multitasking while performing important tasks leads to problems in concentration, along with significant errors—for most people. Multitasking on routine tasks has less negative consequences, and can sometimes be a legitimate time saver. A classic experiment on the topic demonstrated that switching back and forth between tasks actually results in more time required to complete a task.[12]

According to time-management guru Stephanie Winston, the biggest mistake most people make is multitasking. She observes that successful CEOs do not multitask. Instead they concentrate on one thing at a time. "What stops the rest of us from doing likewise, is a reluctance to set boundaries," she says. "People tell me that they feel guilty if they turn off their instant messaging, even if it drives them crazy." Constant distractions interfere with accomplishing good work, so it is better to say, "No, I'm busy right now."[13]

Stay in Control of Paperwork and Electronic Work

Although it is fashionable to complain about paperwork in responsible jobs, the effective career person does not neglect it. (Paperwork includes electronic work, such as responding to email and voice mail.) Paperwork involves taking care of administrative details, such as correspondence, invoices, human resource reports, and inventory forms. A considerable amount of electronic work results in paperwork because many email messages and attachments wind up being printed. Unless paperwork and electronic work are attended to, a job may get out of control. A small amount of time should be invested in paperwork every day. Non-prime time (when you are at less than your peak of efficiency but not over-fatigued) is the best time to take care of paperwork.

An effective technique is to respond quickly to high-priority email messages, and permanently delete those you will most likely not need to refer to again. Print and file only those email messages of high importance to avoid being overwhelmed with piles of old messages.

Work Productively from Your Home Office or Virtual Office

A growing segment of the workforce works full- or part-time from home or from a **virtual office**. Such an office is a place of work without a fixed physical location from which the worker communicates his or her output electronically. A virtual office might be in a car, in a hotel room, on a park bench, or wherever the worker happens to be at the time. Many people adapt well to working at home and from virtual offices because they are self-starters and self-disciplined. Many other workers lack the self-discipline and effective work habits necessary to be productive outside a traditional office. Following is a list of representative suggestions for being productive while working independently:[14]

- Act as if you work in a traditional office. Set specific working hours, get dressed, go outside the house for a few minutes, then return and get to work. Also, close your home or virtual office at some regular time. Otherwise, you are open for business all the time. If you work at home, establish a clear workspace and let your family and friends know when you cannot be disturbed.

- Stay in touch with teammates to improve your team-player skills and avoid missing out on important information that could lower your effectiveness (such as missing an appointment at the traditional office).

- Minimize conducting your personal life at the same time as working (for example, watching television, talking to neighbours, or shopping over the internet during working hours).

- Schedule regular times for meals and snacks; otherwise you will lose many minutes and likely gain weight taking food and beverage breaks.

The practice of working at home or from virtual offices is increasingly popular, so these suggestions merit careful consideration. Several of these productivity ideas are also suited to the conventional office.

Improve Your Internet Search Skills

An important job skill is searching the internet for a variety of information. It follows that if you develop your internet search skills you will become more productive by spending less time obtaining the results you need. First, it is important to rely on several search engines to seek needed information. Several meta-search engines claim to be so comprehensive that no other engine is required. Such claims are exaggerated, because the same search word entered into several different comprehensive engines will reveal a different list of sources.

Second, give careful thought to the search word or phrase you use. The more specific you are, the better. Assume that you want to find software to increase your productivity and that you enter the word "software" into a search engine. You will probably receive a message indicating that 3 500 000 entries have been located in response to your inquiry. You are better advised to use the search phrase "software for increasing personal productivity" (without the quotation marks).

Third, for many searches, framing the query as a phrase by enclosing it in quotation marks refines the number of hits (or sites) returned.[15] Simply place quotation marks before and after the search phrase, such as "software for improving work habits."

Fourth, if you do not find what you want in your initial search, reframe your question in another way or change the terms. How about "software for time-management" or "computer programs for increasing personal efficiency"? (Note that the quotation-mark system works frequently, but not always.)

Skill-Building Exercise 14-2 will help you make better use of the internet to increase your personal productivity.

OVERCOMING TIME-WASTERS

Another basic thrust in improving personal productivity is to minimize wasting time. Many of the techniques already described in this chapter help save time, such as eliminating nonessential work. Whether or not an activity is a time-waster depends on the purpose of the activity. Suppose you play computer solitaire for 10 minutes to reduce stress and then return to work refreshed. In contrast, another worker who spends 10 minutes playing solitaire just for fun is wasting time.

Figure 14-1, on the next page, presents a list of common time-wasters and ideas to overcome them. Being aware of time-wasters will help sensitize you to the importance of minimizing them. Even if you save just 10 minutes per work day, the productivity gain over a year could be enormous.

To analyze whether you might be wasting time, do Skill-Building Exercise 14-3. Self-Assessment Quiz 14-2 gives you an opportunity to think through your tendencies toward a subtle type of time-wasting.

Skill-Building Exercise 14-2

BOOSTING PRODUCTIVITY THROUGH WORK HABITS ON THE INTERNET

The chapter has already given you ideas about using work habits to increase productivity. Here is a chance to make some personal applications of your own. Gather into small teams or work individually to identify 10 ways in which good work habits, as well as using the internet, can increase personal productivity either on the job or at home. To supplement your own thinking, you might search the internet for ideas on how the internet is supposed to boost productivity.

1. Use a time log for two weeks to track time-wasters. (See Skill-Building Exercise 14-3)

2. Minimize daydreaming on the job by forcing yourself to concentrate.

3. Avoid the computer as a diversion from work, such as sending jokes back and forth to network members, playing video games, and checking out recreational websites during working hours.

4. Batch together tasks such as returning phone calls or responding to email messages. For example, in most jobs it is possible to be polite and productive by reserving two or three 15-minute periods per day for taking care of email correspondence.

5. Socialize on the job just enough to build your network. Chatting with co-workers is a major drain on productivity.

6. Be prepared for meetings by, for example, having a clear agenda and sorting through the documents you will be referring to. Make sure electronic equipment is in working order before attempting to use it during the meeting.

7. Keep track of important names, places, and things to avoid wasting time searching for them.

8. Set a time limit for tasks after you have done them once or twice.

9. Prepare a computer template for letters and computer documents that you send frequently. (The template is essentially a form letter, especially with respect to the salutation and return address.)

10. When you arrive at work, be ready to get started working immediately. Greet people quickly, avoid checking personal email, and shut off your cellphone.

11. Take care of as much email correspondence as you can after you have finished your other work. Unless a key part of your job involves dealing with email, it consumes substantial time.

12. Avoid perfectionism, which leads you to keep redoing a project. Let go and move on to another project.

13. Make use of bits of time—for instance, five minutes between appointments. Invest those five minutes in sending a work-related business email or revising your to do list.

14. Minimize procrastination, the number one time-waster for most people.

15. Avoid spreading yourself too thin by doing too many things at once, such as having one project too many to handle. When you are overloaded, time can be wasted because of too many errors.

16. Manage interruptions by letting co-workers know when you are available for consultation, and when you need to work independently—except for emergencies. Respond to instant messages only if your job requires responding immediately. Batch your instant messages just as you would other emails.

Figure 14-1 Ways to Prevent and Overcome Time-Wasting

Source: Suggestions 4, 5, and 6 are based on Stephen R. Covey with Hyrum Smith, "What If You Could Chop an Hour from Your Day for Things That Matter Most?" *USA Weekend*, January 22–24, 1999, pp. 4–5; suggestion 10 is from Anita Bruzzese, "Tips to Avoid Wasting Time," Gannet News Service, August 9, 2004. Data about the productivity drain of interruptions are analyzed in Quintus R. Jett and Jennifer M. George, "Work Interrupted: A Closer Look at the Role of Interruptions in Organizational Life," *Academy of Management Review*, July 2003, pp. 494–507.

Skill-Building Exercise 14-3

MAINTAINING A TIME LOG

An effective starting point to avoid wasting time is to identify how you spend the 168 hours you have each week (24 hours × 7 days). For two weeks catalog all the time you spend, down to as much detail as you can tolerate. Include the large obvious items, as well as the small items that are easy to forget. Keep track of any activity that requires at least five minutes. Major items would include working, attending class, studying, reading, watching television, sleeping, eating, going places, spending time with loved ones and friends (hanging out). Small items would include visiting the coffee shop or vending machine, purchasing gum, and clipping your nails. If you multitask, such as walking and listening to music, do not double-count the time.

When your time logs have been completed, search for complete wastes of time, or activities that could be shortened. You might find, for example, that you spend about 45 minutes per day in the pursuit and consumption of coffee. If you reduced that time to 30 minutes you would have an additional 15 minutes per day that you could invest in your career. However, if coffee time includes forming alliances with people or maintaining relationships, maybe the 45-minute-per-day investment is worthwhile.

Self-Assessment Quiz 14-2

TENDENCIES TOWARD PERFECTIONISM

Directions: Many perfectionists hold some of the behaviours and attitudes described below. To help understand your tendencies toward perfectionism, rate how strongly you agree with each of the statements below on a scale of 0 to 4 by circling the appropriate number. 0 means disagree, 4 means agree.

1. Many people have told me that I am a perfectionist.	0	1	2	3	4
2. I often correct the speech of others.	0	1	2	3	4
3. It takes me a long time to write an email because I keep checking and rechecking my writing.	0	1	2	3	4
4. I often criticize the colour combinations my friends are wearing.	0	1	2	3	4
5. When I purchase food at a supermarket, I usually look at the expiration date so I can purchase the freshest.	0	1	2	3	4
6. I can't stand when people use the term "remote" instead of "remote control."	0	1	2	3	4
7. If a company representative asked me "What is your *social*," I would reply something like, "Do you mean my *social insurance number?*"	0	1	2	3	4
8. I hate to see dust on furniture.	0	1	2	3	4
9. I like the Martha Stewart idea of having every decoration in the home just right.	0	1	2	3	4
10. I never put a map back in the glove compartment until it is folded just right.	0	1	2	3	4

(Continued)

11. Once an eraser on a pencil of mine becomes hard and useless, I throw away the pencil.	0	1	2	3	4
12. I adjust all my watches and clocks so they show exactly the same time.	0	1	2	3	4
13. It bothers me that clocks on personal computers are often wrong by a few minutes.	0	1	2	3	4
14. I clean the keyboard on my computer at least once a week.	0	1	2	3	4
15. I organize my email messages and computer documents into many different, clearly labeled files.	0	1	2	3	4
16. You won't find old coffee cups or soft-drink containers on my desk.	0	1	2	3	4
17. I rarely start a new project or assignment until I have completed my present project or assignment.	0	1	2	3	4
18. It is very difficult for me to concentrate when my work area is disorganized.	0	1	2	3	4
19. Cobwebs in chandeliers and other lighting fixtures bother me.	0	1	2	3	4
20. It takes me a long time to make a purchase such as a digital camera because I keep studying the features on various models.	0	1	2	3	4
21. When I balance my chequebook, it usually comes out right within a few dollars.	0	1	2	3	4
22. I carry enough small coins and dollar bills with me so when I shop I can pay the exact amount without requiring change.	0	1	2	3	4
23. I throw out any underwear or t-shirts that have even the smallest holes or tears.	0	1	2	3	4
24. I become upset with myself if I make a mistake.	0	1	2	3	4
25. When a fingernail of mine is broken or chipped, I fix it as soon as possible.	0	1	2	3	4
26. I am carefully groomed whenever I leave my home.	0	1	2	3	4
27. When I notice packaged goods or cans on the floor in a supermarket, I will often place them back on the shelf.	0	1	2	3	4
28. I think that carrying around antibacterial cleaner for the hands is an excellent idea.	0	1	2	3	4
29. If I am with a friend, and he or she has a loose hair on the shoulder, I will remove it without asking.	0	1	2	3	4
30. I am a perfectionist.	0	1	2	3	4

Total Score _____

Scoring and Interpretation: Add the numbers you circled to obtain your total score.

91 or over: You have strong perfectionist tendencies to the point that it could interfere with your taking quick action when necessary. Also, you may annoy many people with your perfectionism.

61–90:   You have a moderate degree of perfectionism that could lead you to produce high-quality work and be a dependable person.

31–60:   You have a mild degree of perfectionism. You might be a perfectionist in some situations quite important to you, but not in others.

0–30:   You are not a perfectionist. You might be too casual about getting things done right, meeting deadlines, and being aware of details.

UNDERSTANDING AND MANAGING STRESS

A major challenge facing any worker who wants to stay healthy and have good interpersonal relationships is to manage stress effectively. There is little doubt that many people at the present time are feeling the effects of stress. This chapter's Canadian Scene summarizes some of the results from recent health surveys that inquired into respondents' stress levels and causes of stress. Although *stress* is an everyday term, a scientific definition helps clarify its meaning. **Stress** is an adaptive response that is the consequence of any action, situation, or event that places special demands on a person. Note that stress refers to a reaction to the situation, not the situation or force itself. A **stressor** is the external or internal force that brings on stress.

The Canadian Scene

CANADIANS AND STRESS

No matter what you call it, many Canadians are feeling stressed in life and at work. Data from several surveys—including Health Canada's 2001 National Work–Life Conflict Study, Work–Life Compendium 2001, and Health Canada's Work–Life Conflict in Canada in the New Millennium and the latest of Health Canada's publications on the predictors of work–life conflict—as well as information from Statistics Canada's Statistical Report on the Health of Canadians, all indicate increasing trends in the stress of Canadian employees. According to the last survey mentioned, stress-related health problems are the second-highest reason for hospitalization in Canada. The survey reported that 26 percent of Canadians rated themselves as experiencing high chronic stress, with those in Manitoba and Ontario reporting the highest levels. Newfoundland reported the lowest amount of life stress. Women were more likely than men to report a high stress level in their lives, with the most stress being felt by women between the ages of 20 and 24 years. As people age, stress both in life and at work appears to decline. Also, people with higher levels of education were not as stressed as those with lower levels of education. Single parents also reported more stress than individuals who are unattached or couples with children.[i]

What about work-related stress? With more Canadian employees assuming more job responsibilities and labour market changes, work–life conflict is a major source of stress. According to the 2001 National Work–Life Conflict Study, the "labour market changes of the 1990s and technological changes have increased job insecurity, elevated work demands and blurred the boundary between work and family."[ii]

Role overload is also a major stressor. Newer research such as Work–Life Conflict in Canada in the New Millennium found that 58 percent in the 2001 survey were experiencing high role overload, with one out of four employees putting in more than 50 hours per week, compared with the one in ten respondents from the 1991 survey. Role overload was defined as having too much to do in a given amount of time. This role overload contributes to work–life conflict for many employees. With so much time being devoted to work activities, work–life conflict occurs when the total demands on time and energy for roles at work and home are incompatible. In other words, many employees are feeling "too stretched" with multiple roles. One in four Canadians report that work responsibilities interfere with responsibilities at home.[iii]

The 2001 National Work–Life Conflict Study sheds some light on this stretching of roles. Since the early 1990s more employees assumed greater responsibilities with more women working, more dual-earner and single parent families, and the newer category of sandwich generation employees. The sandwich generation is

(Continued)

the generation of employees who are not only are the primary caregivers of children but also responsible for elder-care, such as having parents living in the same home. Of the workers studied in this sample, 70 percent were parents, 60 percent provided elder-care, and 13 percent had the responsibility of both childcare and elder-care.[iii] Approximately one in four of the individuals in this sample experienced what can be considered to be high levels of caregiver strain: physical, financial, or mental stress that comes from looking after an elderly dependent. While most respondents to this survey (74 percent) rarely experience this form of work-life conflict, 26 percent report high levels of caregiver strain.[iv]

Interestingly, while work is interfering with home life, home life does not appear to be interfering greatly with work. Only 10 percent of the 2001 survey respondents reported family demands as interfering with work demands.[ii]

With such high levels of reported stress, learning stress management techniques becomes absolutely necessary. On the other hand, organizations also need to find ways to help employees manage stress. One finding is clear: employers need to address work–life balance by such solutions as reducing employee workloads, implementing alternative work arrangements, providing time for elder-care and childcare, and recognizing unpaid overtime.[iii]

Sources:

i.   The Federal, Provincial, and Territorial Advisory Committee on Population Health, Statistical Report on the Health of Canadians, prepared for the meeting of ministers of health, September 1999, Statistics Canada Catalogue No. 82–570-X1E.

ii. Dr. Linda Duxbury and Dr. Chris Higgins, Work–Life Conflict in Canada in the New Millennium, Final Report, October 2003, Health Canada, www.hc-sc.gc.ca/pphb-dgspsp/work-travail/report2/index.html.

iii. Dr. Chris Higgins and Dr. Linda Duxbury, The National Work–Life Conflict Study, Final Report, March 2002, Health Canada, www.hc-sc.ca/pphb-dgspsp/publicat/work-travail/index.html.

iv. Dr. Chris Higgins and Dr. Linda Duxbury, Who is at Risk? Predictors of Work-Life Conflict: Report Four, 2005, Public Health Agency of Canada http://www.phac-aspc.gc.ca/publicat/work-travail/report4/index.html

Individual differences play a key role in determining what events are stressful. Giving a presentation to management, for example, is stressful for some people but not for others. The term *special* demands is also critical, because minor hassles, such as a pencil point that breaks, are usually not perceived as stressful.[16] Yet a piling on of minor hassles, such as having 10 small things go wrong in one day, is stressful. This is true because stress is cumulative: a series of small doses of stress can create a major stress problem.

Our approach to understanding stress centres on its symptoms and consequences, personality and job factors that contribute to stress, and methods and techniques for stress management. Managing stress receives more emphasis because the same techniques can be used to combat a variety of stressors.

SYMPTOMS AND CONSEQUENCES OF STRESS

The physiological changes that take place within the body in response to stress are responsible for most stress symptoms. These physiological changes are almost identical for both positive and negative stressors. Snowboarding, romantic attraction, and being downsized can make you feel about the same physically. The experience of stress helps activate hormones that prepare the body to fight or run when faced with a challenge. This battle against the stressor is referred to as the **fight-or-flight response**. It helps you deal with emergencies.

Recent studies suggest the possibility that women, along with females of other species, react differently to major stressors. Instead of the fight-or-flight response typical of males, they tend and befriend. When stress levels mount, women are more likely to protect and nurture their children (tend) and turn to social networks of supportive females (befriend). Women use affiliation with others to relieve stress. The researchers speculate that the tend-and-befriend behaviour became prevalent over the centuries because women who tended and befriended were more likely to have their offspring survive and pass on the mother's traits. Men may tend and befriend also, but to a lesser extent. The tend-and-befriend response can be traced to a hormone, oxytocin, produced in the brain. Although this research may not be politically correct, it has stimulated the interest of many scientists.[17]

A modern explanation of the fight-or-flight response theory explains that, when faced with stress, the brain acts much like a thermostat. When outside conditions deviate from an ideal point, the thermostat sends a signal to the furnace to increase heat or air conditioning. The brain senses stress as damage to well-being and therefore sends out a signal to the body to cope. The purpose of coping is to modify the discrepancy between the ideal (low-stress) and actual (high-stress) conditions.[18] The brain is thus a self-regulating system that helps us cope with stressors.

Physiological Reactions

The activation of hormones when the body has to cope with a stressor produces a short-term physiological reaction. Among the most familiar symptoms are increases in heart rate, blood pressure, blood glucose, and blood clotting. To help yourself recognize these symptoms, try to recall your internal bodily sensations the last time you were almost in an automobile accident or heard some wonderful news. Less familiar changes are a redirection of the blood flow toward the brain and large muscle groups and a release of stored fluids from places throughout the body into the bloodstream.

If stress is continuous and accompanied by these short-term physiological changes, annoying and life-threatening conditions can occur. Damage occurs when stress levels rarely subside. A stressful life event usually leads to a high cholesterol level (of the unhealthy type) and high blood pressure. Other conditions associated with stress are cardiac disease, migraine headaches, ulcers, allergies, skin disorders, irritable bowel syndrome, and cancer. A study of 812 Swedish workers conducted over a 25-year period found that work stress doubles the risk of dying from a heart attack. Seventy-three of the workers died from cardiac disease during the study. The major type of stress studied was having high work demands with little control over the work, combined with being underpaid.[19]

To make matters worse, stress can hamper the immune system, thereby increasing the severity of many diseases and disorders. For example, people whose stress level is high recover more slowly from colds and injuries, and they are more susceptible to sexually transmitted diseases. Stress symptoms vary considerably from one person to another. A general behavioural symptom of intense stress is for people's weakest tendencies to be exaggerated. For instance, a person with a strong temper who usually keeps cool under pressure may throw a tantrum under extreme stress. Common stress symptoms are listed in Figure 14-2 on the next page.

Mostly Physical and Physiological

Shaking or trembling   Mouth dryness
Dizziness   Upper and lower back pain
Heart palpitations   Frequent headaches
Difficulty breathing   Low energy and stamina
Chronic fatigue   Stomach problems
Unexplained chest pains   Constant craving for sweets
Frequent teeth grinding   Increased alcohol or cigarette consumption
Frequent nausea   Frequent need to eliminate

Mostly Emotional and Behavioural

Difficulty concentrating   Anxiety or depression
Nervousness   Forgetfulness
Crying   Restlessness
Anorexia   Frequent arguments with others
Declining interest in sex   Feeling high-strung much of the time
Frequent nail biting or hair tugging

Figure 14-2   A Variety of Stress Symptoms

Job Performance Consequences

Despite all the problems just mentioned, stress also plays a positive role in our lives. The right amount of stress prepares us for meeting difficult challenges and spurs us on to peak intellectual and physical performance. An optimum level of stress exists for most people and most tasks.

In general, performance tends to be best under moderate amounts of stress. If the stress is too great, people become temporarily ineffective; they may freeze or choke. Experiencing too little stress, people may become lethargic and inattentive. Figure 14-3 depicts the relationship between stress and performance. An exception to this relationship is that certain negative forms of stress are likely to lower performance even if the stress is moderate. For example, the stress created by an intimidating supervisor or worrying about radiation poisoning—even in moderate amounts—will not improve performance.

Job stress can also lower job performance indirectly because distressed workers are more likely to be absent from the job, thereby not accomplishing as much work. A study of 323 health service workers in the United Kingdom found that job-related psychological distress, particularly depression, was associated with more days absent, and a greater number of times absent.[20]

The job performance impact of a stressor on the individual is influenced by a variety of personal and environmental factors. The research of Steve M. Jex indicates that decreases in performance are least likely when employees (1) understand clearly what to expect in their jobs, (2) have high self-esteem, (3) have high commitment to the organization, and (4) have low levels of Type A behaviour (explained below).[21]

The optimum amount of stress is a positive force that is the equivalent of finding excitement and challenge. Your ability to solve problems and deal with challenge is

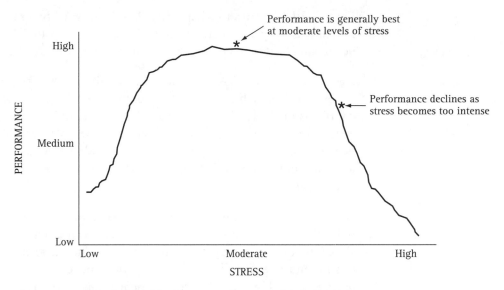

Figure 14-3   Relationship Between Stress and Job Performance

enhanced when the right amount of adrenalin flows in your blood to guide you toward peak performance. In fact, highly productive people are sometimes said to be hooked on adrenalin.

Burnout and Stress

One of the major problems of prolonged stress is that it may lead to **burnout**, a condition of emotional, mental, and physical exhaustion in response to long-term stressors. Burned-out people are often cynical. Burnout is a complex phenomenon, but it often occurs when people feel out of control. Other critical factors that contribute to burnout are insufficient recognition and reward, a lack of emotional support in the workplace, or an absence of fairness. Christina Maslach observes "When the workplace does not recognize the human side of work, then the risk of burnout grows, carrying with it a high price and hurting all the parties involved."[22]

The key feature of burnout is the distancing that occurs in response to work overload. Burnout sufferers shift into a mode of doing the minimum as a way of protecting themselves. They start leaving work early and dehumanizing their clients, patients, or customers. People experiencing burnout may do their job, but their heart is no longer in it.[23]

PERSONALITY AND JOB FACTORS CONTRIBUTING TO STRESS

Workers experience stress for many different reasons, including personal predispositions, factors stemming from the job, or the combined influence of both. If a person with an extreme negative predisposition has to deal with irate customers, he or she is most likely to experience substantial stress. Below we describe a sampling of important individual and organizational factors that contribute to job stress.

Personality Factors Predisposing People Toward Stress
Individuals vary considerably in their susceptibility to job stress, based on their personality traits and characteristics. Four such factors are described next.

Low Perceived Control. A key factor in determining whether workers experience stress is how much they believe they can control a given adverse circumstance. **Perceived control** is the belief that an individual has at his or her disposal a response that can control the negative aspects of an event. A survey of over 100 studies indicated that people with a high level of perceived control had low levels of physical and psychological symptoms of stress. Conversely, people with low perceived control are more likely to experience work stress.[24]

Low Self-Efficacy. Self-efficacy, like perceived control, is another personal factor that influences susceptibility to stress. (Note that because self-efficacy is tied to a specific situation, it is not strictly a personality trait.) When workers have both low perceived control and low self-efficacy the stress consequences may be much worse. However, having high self-efficacy (being confident in one's abilities) softens the stress consequences of demanding jobs.[25]

Two American studies of about 2300 soldiers each showed that respondents with strong self-efficacy were less stressed out mentally and physically by long work hours and work overload. A key conclusion of the studies is that high levels of self-efficacy may help employees cope more effectively with job stressors.[26] To illustrate, an active coping method would be to reorganize an overwhelming workload so it can be performed more efficiently.

Type A Behaviour. A person with **Type A behaviour** is demanding, impatient, and over-striving and is therefore prone to negative stress. Type A behaviour has two main components. One is the tendency to try to accomplish too many things in too little time. This causes the Type A individual to be impatient and demanding. The other component is free-floating hostility. Because of this sense of urgency and hostility, trivial things irritate these people. People with Type A behaviour are aggressive and hard-working.

Type A personalities frequently develop cardiac disease, including heart attacks and strokes, at an early age. However, only certain features of the Type A personality pattern may be related to coronary heart disease. The heart attack triggers are hostility, anger, cynicism, and suspiciousness—and not other Type A characteristics such as impatience, ambition, and being work-driven.[27] In fact, hostility is more strongly associated with coronary heart disease in men than smoking, drinking, overeating, or high levels of bad (LDL) cholesterol.[28] Note that the heart attack triggers also make for strained interpersonal relationships.

Negative Affectivity. A major contributor to being stress prone is **negative affectivity**, a tendency to experience aversive emotional states. Negative affectivity is a pervasive disposition to experience emotional stress, including feelings of nervousness, tension, and worry. The same disposition also includes such emotional states as anger, scorn, revulsion, guilt, self-dissatisfaction, and sadness.[29] Such negative personalities seem to search for important discrepancies between what they would like and what exists. Poor interpersonal relationships often result from the frequent complaining of people with negative affectivity.

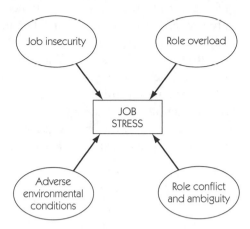

Figure 14-4   Four Significant Sources of Job Stress

Job Sources of Stress

Almost any job situation can act as a stressor for some employees but not others. As just described, certain personality factors make it more likely that a person with them will experience job stress. Further, other personal life stressors may spill over into the workplace, making it more likely that a person will experience job stress. Below we describe four frequently encountered job stressors, outlined in Figure 14-4.

Role Overload. Having too much work to do, or **role overload**, can create negative stress in two ways. First, the person may become fatigued and thus be less able to tolerate annoyances and irritations. Second, a person subject to unreasonable work demands may feel perpetually behind schedule, a situation that is itself a powerful stressor. Downsizing often creates overload because fewer people are left to handle the same workload as previously. (If work is carefully streamlined, role overload is minimized.) In a Canadian study, role overload was associated with both physical and emotional health problems. Of the sample, almost 60 percent of employees reported high levels of role overload. Employees who have high role overload are often less committed to their organization, report higher levels of job stress, and are less satisfied with their jobs. Also, employees with high role overload were more likely to have high rates of absenteeism and were more likely to report they intend to leave their jobs.[30] The Canadian Scene earlier in this chapter has more detail from Health Canada and other similar studies.

According to a recent study from Health Canada, work culture is the most powerful predictor of role overload. For both men and women, the single most important aspect of work culture with respect to the prediction of role overload was the extent to which the employee believed the organization promoted a culture that was supportive of work-life balance. Work cultures that emphasize over-commitment to work, such as expecting extra hours at the office or taking work home in the evenings contribute to overload.[31]

Role Conflict and Role Ambiguity. Role conflict, described in Chapter 7 as an important workplace conflict, is also a major workplace stressor. People experience stress when they have to choose between two sets of expectations. Suppose an accountant is asked by her manager to state company earnings in a way that conflicts with the professional norms of accountants. If she complies with her manager, she will feel that she is betraying her profession. If she insists on maintaining her professional norms, she will enter into dispute with the manager. The woman is likely to experience job stress.

Role ambiguity is a condition in which the jobholder is faced with confusing or poorly defined expectations. Workers in many organizations are placed in situations in which they are unsure of their true responsibilities. Some workers who are placed on a self-managing work team experience role ambiguity because they are asked to solve many problems by themselves. It is less ambiguous to have the manager tell you what to do. Many people experience stress symptoms when faced with role ambiguity.

Adverse Environmental Conditions. A variety of adverse organizational conditions are stressors, as identified by national and provincial occupational safety and health agencies and boards. Among these adverse organizational conditions are unpleasant or dangerous physical conditions, such as crowding, noise, air pollution, or ergonomic problems. Enough polluted air within an office building can create a sick building, in which a diverse range of airborne particles, vapours, moulds, and gases pollute the indoor environment. The result can be headaches, nausea, and respiratory infections, as well as the stress created by physical illness.[32]

Ergonomic problems refer to a poor fit between the physical and human requirements of a job. Working at a computer monitor for prolonged periods of time can lead to adverse physical and psychological reactions. The symptoms include headaches and fatigue, along with eye problems. Common visual problems are dry eyes and blurred or double vision. An estimated one out of five visits to vision-care professionals is for computer-related problems. Another vision-related problem is that people lean forward to scan the monitor, leading to physical problems such as back strain.

The repetitive-strain injury most frequently associated with keyboarding and the use of optical scanners is **carpal tunnel syndrome**. The syndrome occurs when repetitive flexing and extension of the wrist causes the tendons to swell, thus trapping and pinching the median nerve. Carpal tunnel syndrome creates stress because of the associated pain and misery. According to the Canadian Centre for Occupational Health and Safety, this disorder is fairly common. For example, 614 out of 982 supermarket checkers surveyed reported symptoms of carpal tunnel syndrome.[33] Thoughts of having to permanently leave a job requiring keyboarding constitute another potential stressor. If ergonomic principles, such as erect posture, are incorporated into computer usage, these stress symptoms diminish.

Job Insecurity. Worrying about losing your job is a major stressor. Even when jobs are plentiful, having to search for another job and facing the prospect of geographic relocation are stressors for many people. Downsizing and corporate mergers (which usually result in downsizing) have contributed to job insecurity. The anticipation of layoffs among employees can increase negative stress and lower job performance. In addition, the survivors of a downsizing often experience pressure from fear of future cuts, loss of friends, and worry about a sudden increase in workload.[34]

METHODS AND TECHNIQUES FOR MANAGING STRESS

Unless stress is managed properly, it may lead to harmful long-term consequences, including disabling physical illness and career impediment. Managing stress refers to controlling stress by making it a constructive force in your life. Managing stress thus involves both preventing and reducing stress. However, the distinction between methods of preventing and reducing stress is not clear-cut. For example, physical exercise not only reduces stress, it contributes to a relaxed lifestyle that helps you prevent stress.

Coping with, or managing, stress can be undertaken through hundreds of activities, with substantial personal differences in which technique is effective. Running is a case in point. For many people, running or jogging is an excellent method of stress reduction. Others find running creates new stressors, such as aching knees, shin splints, dizziness from breathing in vehicle exhaust, and worry about being hit by vehicles. In general, coping efforts involve cognitions and behaviours aimed at managing the stressor and its associated emotions. For example, you may need to decrease the troublesome elements in your job (such as role overload) and also deal with the tension generated by overwork. Below we describe eight representative methods for managing stress and include a list of everyday stress-busters.

Eliminate or Modify the Stressor. The most potent method of managing stress is to eliminate or modify the stressor giving you trouble. One value of relaxation techniques and tranquilizing medication is that they calm down a person enough so that he or she can deal constructively with the stressor. One helpful way to attack the cause of stress is to follow the steps in problem-solving and decision-making. You clarify the problem, identify the alternatives, weigh them, and select one. A difficulty, however, is that your evaluation of the real problem may be inaccurate. There is always a limit to self-analysis. For example, a person might think that work overload is the stressor when the true stressor is low self-efficacy.

Get Appropriate Physical Exercise. A moderate amount of physical exercise is a cornerstone of managing stress and achieving wellness. To manage stress it is important to select an exercise program that is physically challenging but does not lead to overexertion and muscle or bone injury. Competitive sports, if taken too seriously, can actually increase stress. Aerobic exercises are most beneficial because they make you breathe faster and raise your heart rate. A major mental and emotional benefit of physical exercise stems from endorphins produced in the thalamus portion of the brain when one exercises. The endorphins are associated with a state of euphoria referred to as a "runner's high." Endorphins also work like painkillers, adding to their stress-reduction value.

Millions of people seek to reduce and prevent stress through yoga, which is both physical exercise and a way of developing mental attitudes that calm the body and mind. One of yoga's many worthwhile goals is to solder a union between the mind and body, thereby achieving harmony and tranquility. Another benefit of yoga is that it helps people place aside negative thoughts that act as stressors.[35]

Get Sufficient Rest. Rest offers benefits similar to those of exercise, such as stress reduction, improved concentration, improved energy, and better tolerance for frustration. Achieving proper rest is closely linked to getting proper exercise. The current interest in adult napping reflects the awareness that proper rest makes a person less stress prone and increases productivity. A growing number of firms have napping facilities for workers, and many workers nap at their desks or in their parked vehicles during lunch breaks. Work-day power naps of about 15 minutes' duration serve as both energizers and stress-reducers.[36] Napping can help a worker become more productive and less stressed. A rested brain is a more effective brain. To keep the effectiveness of power-napping in perspective, workers who achieve sufficient rest during normal sleeping hours have less need for a nap during working hours.

Maintain a Healthy Diet. Another practical method of stress reduction and prevention is to maintain a well-balanced, and therefore healthy, diet. Nutritious food is valuable for physical and mental health, making it easier to cope with frustrations that are potential stressors. Some non-nutritious foods, such as those laden with caffeine or

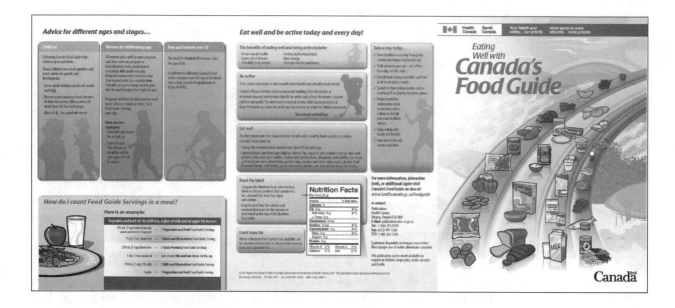

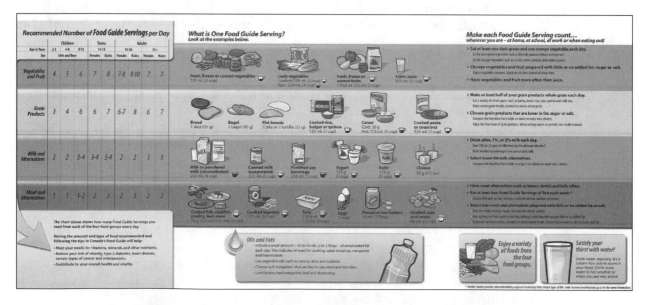

Figure 14-5   Canada's Food Guide

Source: Eating Well with Canada's Food Guide (2007), Health Canada. Reproduced with the permission of the Minister of Public Works and Government Services Canada, 2007.

sugar, tend to enhance a person's level of stress. According to Canada's Food Guide, from Health Canada, a healthy diet is one that

- Emphasizes fruits, vegetables, whole grains, and fat-free or low-fat milk and milk products.

- Includes lean meats, poultry, fish, beans, eggs, and nuts.

- Is low in saturated fats, *trans* fats, cholesterol, salt (sodium), and added sugars.

These recommendations are for the general public over two years of age. There is also additional information for specific age groups, pregnant women and First Nations peoples. Consult the complete guide shown in Figure 14-5 and visit Health Canada's website for more detailed information at www.hc-sc.gc.ca/fn-an/food-guide-aliment/index_e.html. The website for this guide provides more information about nutrition and healthy eating, including how to plan menus for healthy eating.

Build a Support Network. A **support network** is a group of people who can listen to your problems and provide emotional support. These people, or even one person, can help you through your difficult episodes. Members of your network can provide you with a sense of closeness, warmth, and acceptance that will reduce your stress. Also, the simple expedient of putting your feelings into words can be a healing experience. The way to develop this support network is to become a good listener yourself so that the other person will reciprocate. A support network is therefore a method of stress management based squarely on effective interpersonal skills.

Practise Visualization. Perhaps the most effortless and enjoyable relaxation technique for managing stress is to visualize a pleasant experience, as explained in Skill-Building Exercise 14-4. Like so many stress-reduction techniques, including meditation, visualization requires concentration. Concentrating helps slow down basic physiological processes, such as the heart rate, and dissipates stress. Forcing yourself to concentrate is also valuable, given that a key symptom of stress is difficulty in concentration.

Practise Everyday Methods of Stress Reduction. The simple expedient of learning how to relax is an important method of reducing the tension and anxiety brought about by both positive and negative stress. Visualization of a pleasant experience is one such method. Everyday suggestions for relaxation and other methods of stress reduction are presented in Figure 14-6. If you can accomplish these, you are less likely to need tranquilizing medication to keep you calm and in control. Your stress symptoms will ordinarily return, however, if you do not eliminate and modify the stressor. If the stress is from an emotional conflict you do not understand, assistance from a mental health professional is recommended.

Use the Freeze-Frame Technique. A scientifically based method of stress reduction that emphasizes reappraising a difficult event, along with some symptom management, is the **freeze-frame technique** developed by the HeartMath Institute. The method proceeds as follows:

Step 1. *Recognize the stressful feeling and freeze-frame it.* See your problem as a still photo, not a movie. Stop the inner conversation about it.

Step 2. Make a sincere effort to *shift your focus* away from the racing mind or disturbed emotions in the area around your heart. Pretend you are breathing through your heart to help focus energy in this area. Stay focused there for 10 seconds or more.

Skill-Building Exercise 14-4

VISUALIZATION FOR STRESS REDUCTION

A standard, easy-to-use method for reducing stress symptoms is to visualize a pleasant and calm experience. If you are experiencing stress right now, try the technique. Otherwise, wait until the next time you perceive your body to be experiencing stress. In this context, visualization means picturing yourself doing something that you would like to do. Whatever fantasy suits your fancy will work, according to the advocates of this relaxation technique. Visualizations that work for some people include smiling at a loved one, floating on a cloud, caressing a baby, petting a kitten or puppy, and walking in the woods. Notice that all of these scenes are relaxing rather than exciting. What visualization would work for you?

To implement the technique, close your eyes and bring the pleasant image into focus in your mind. Think of nothing else at the moment. Imagine that a videotape of the pleasant experience is playing on the television screen in your brain. Breathe softly and savour the experience. Slowly return to reality, refreshed, relaxed, and ready to tackle the challenges of the day.

- Give in to your emotions. If you are angry, disgusted, or confused, admit your feelings. Suppressing your emotions adds to stress.
- Take a brief break from the stressful situation and do something small and constructive, such as washing your car, emptying a wastebasket, or getting a haircut.
- Get a massage, because it can loosen tight muscles, improve your blood circulation, and calm you down.
- Get help with your stressful task from a co-worker, supervisor, or friend.
- Concentrate intensely on reading, surfing the internet, a sport, or a hobby. Contrary to common sense, concentration is at the heart of stress reduction.
- Have a quiet place at home and have a brief idle period there every day.
- Take a leisurely day off from your routine.
- Finish something you have started, however small. Accomplishing almost anything reduces some stress.
- Stop to smell the flowers, make friends with a young child or elderly person, or play with a kitten or puppy.
- Strive to do a good job, but not a perfect job.
- Work with your hands, doing a pleasant task.
- Find somebody or something that makes you laugh, and have a good laugh.
- Minimize drinking caffeinated or alcoholic beverages, and drink fruit juice or water instead. Take a piece of fruit out of the refrigerator rather than a can of beer.
- Help somebody less fortunate than yourself. The flood of good feelings will act like endorphins.

Figure 14-6   Stress-Busters

Step 3. *Recall a positive fun feeling or time* you've had in your life and visualize experiencing it again.

Step 4. Using your intuition, common sense, and sincerity, *ask your heart what would be a more efficient response* to the situation—one that will minimize future stress.

Step 5. *Listen to what your heart says* in answer to your question. Here you are using an in-house source of common sense solutions.

You may hear nothing, but at least you will feel calmer. You may receive confirmation of something you already know. Equally important, you may gain a perspective shift and see the problem in a different way. Although we may not have control over the event, we do have control over how we perceive it.[37]

SUMMARY

High personal productivity on the job is more in demand than ever. A starting point in improving productivity is to minimize procrastination, an enormous problem for many people that can be approached as follows: calculate the cost of procrastination; use the "worst in, first out" (WIFO) principle; break the task into manageable chunks; make a commitment to other people; remove some clutter from your mind; satisfy your stimulation quota in constructive ways; and eliminate rewards for procrastinating.

Developing good work habits and time-management practices is often a matter of developing the right attitudes toward your work and toward time, as follows: (1) begin with a mission statement and goals; (2) play the inner game of work; (3) work smarter, not harder; (4) value orderliness and cleanliness; (5) value good attendance and punctuality; and (6) attain a balance in life and avoid being a workaholic.

Effective work habits and skills are essential for high productivity, including the following: (1) prepare a to-do list and set priorities; (2) streamline your work and emphasize important tasks; (3) concentrate on one important task at a time; (4) stay in control of paperwork and electronic work; (5) work productively from your home office or virtual office; and (6) improve your internet search skills.

Another basic thrust in increasing personal productivity is to minimize time-wasting. Whether or not an activity is a time-waster depends on its purpose. Being aware of time-wasters such as those presented in Figure 14-1 will sensitize you to the importance of minimizing them.

A major challenge facing any worker who wants to stay healthy and have good interpersonal relationships is to manage stress effectively. Individual differences play a big role in determining whether an event will lead to stress. The physiological changes that take place within the body in response to stress are responsible for most of the stress symptoms. The fight-or-flight response prepares us for battle against the stressor. Updated information suggests that women are more likely to cope with a stressor through tend-and-befriend.

The activation of hormones when the body has to cope with a stressor produces short-term physiological reactions, including an increase in heart rate and blood pressure. When stress levels rarely subside, these physiological changes create damage. However, the right amount of stress prepares us to meet difficult challenges and improves performance. An optimum level of stress exists for most people and most tasks. In general, performance tends to be best under moderate amounts of stress. Performance decreases are less likely with certain worker characteristics such as high self-esteem.

One of the major problems of prolonged stress is that it may lead to burnout, a condition of emotional, mental, and physical exhaustion in response to long-term stressors. Burnout also leads to cynicism and a distancing from tasks and people.

Four personality factors predisposing people toward stress are low perceived control, low self-efficacy, Type A behaviour, and negative affectivity. The heart attack triggers associated with Type A behaviour are hostility, anger, cynicism, and suspiciousness. Four frequently encountered job stressors are role overload, role conflict and ambiguity, adverse environmental conditions, and job insecurity.

Managing stress involves controlling stress by making it a constructive force in your life. You can cope with, or manage, stress through hundreds of activities, with substantial personal differences in which technique is effective. Eight representative stress-management methods are to eliminate or modify the stressor, get appropriate physical exercise, rest sufficiently, maintain a healthy diet, build a support network, practise visualization, use everyday methods of stress reduction, and use the freeze-frame technique.

An Interpersonal Relations Case Problem

THE NEW MARKETING ASSISTANT

One year ago Jennie DaSilva returned enthusiastically to the workforce after 12 years of being a full-time homemaker and a part-time direct sales representative for beauty products. Jennie's major motive for finding a full-time professional job was to work toward her career goal of being a marketing manager in a medium-sized or large company. To help prepare for this career, DaSilva had completed a business degree over a five-year period.

Another compelling reason for returning to full-time employment was financial need. DaSilva's husband owned and operated an appliance and electronics store that was becoming less profitable each year. Several large appliance stores had moved into the area, resulting in fewer customers for Northside Appliances (the name of the family business). DaSilva and her husband, Fred, concluded that the family could not cover its bills unless Jennie earned the equivalent of a full-time income.

After three months of searching for full-time employment, Jennie responded to a newspaper ad for a marketing assistant position. The ad described the position as part of a management training program with an excellent future. Ten days after submitting her cover letter and résumé, Jennie was invited for an interview. The company proved to be a national provider of long-distance telephone service. The human resources interviewer and hiring manager both explained that Jennie's initial assignment would be as a telemarketer. Both people advised Jennie that large numbers of people were applying for these telemarketing positions.

Jennie would be required to telephone individual consumers and small-business owners, and make a sales pitch for them to transfer their long-distance telephone service to her company. The company supplied a computerized list with an almost inexhaustible list of names and telephone numbers across the country. In this way Jennie could take advantage of time-zone differences to telephone people during their dinnertime, as well as at other times. Jennie would receive a small commission for each customer who made the switch to her company. Her major responsibility, in addition to telephone soliciting, would be to enter the results of her conversations into a computer, as well as prepare summaries.

One week after the interview, Jennie was extended a job offer. She accepted the offer despite some concern that the position was a little too far

(Continued)

removed from the professional marketing position she sought. Jennie was assigned to a small cubicle in a large room with about 25 other telemarketers. She found the training program exciting, particularly with respect to techniques for overcoming customer resistance. Jennie reasoned that this experience, combined with her direct selling of beauty products, would give her excellent insights into how consumers think and behave. For the first two weeks Jennie found the calls to be uplifting. She experienced a surge of excitement when a customer agreed to switch to her company. As was the custom in the office, she shouted "Yes!" after concluding each customer conversion to her company.

As the weeks moved slowly on, Jennie became increasingly restless and concerned about the job. Her success ratio was falling below the company standard of a three percent success rate on the cold calls. A thought kept running through Jennie's mind, "Even if I'm doing well at this job, 97 percent of people I call will practically hang up on me. And I can't stand keyboarding all these worthless reports explaining what happened as a result of my calls. It's a horrible waste of time."

Jennie soon found it difficult to sleep peacefully, often pacing the apartment after Fred had fallen asleep. She also noticed that she was arguing much more with Fred and the two children. Jennie's stomach churned so much that she found eating uncomfortable. She often poked at her food but drank coffee and diet soft drinks much more than previously. After six months of working at the long-distance carrier, her weight had plunged from 135 pounds to 123 pounds.

Jennie's left thumb and wrists were constantly sore. One night when Fred asked her why she was rubbing the region below her thumb, Jennie said, "I keep pushing the mouse around so much during the day that my thumb feels like it's falling off."

During the next several months, Jennie spoke with her supervisor twice about her future in the company. Both times the supervisor explained that the best telemarketers become eligible for supervisory positions, providing they have proved themselves for at least three years. The supervisor also cautioned Jennie that her performance was adequate but not exceptional. Jennie thought to herself, "I'm banging my head against the wall, and I'm considered just average."

As Jennie approached a full year in her position; she and Fred reviewed the family finances. He said, "Sales at the store are getting worse and worse. I predict that this year your salary will be higher than profits from the store. It's great that we can count on at least one stable salary in the family. The kids and I really appreciate it."

Jennie thought to herself, "Now is the worst time to tell Fred how I really feel about my job. I'm falling apart inside, and the family needs my salary. What a mess!"

Case Questions

1. What aspects of work stress are revealed in this case?

2. What suggestions can you make to the company for decreasing the stressors in the position of telemarketer?

3. What advice can you offer Jennie to help her improve her productivity on the job?

An Interpersonal Relations Case Problem

GEOMANIA NAPS

Geomania is a telecommunications firm based in the information technology section of New York City. Some of the several hundred employees live in Manhattan, but many have commutes of up to two hours from other cities. Having survived the downturn in the telecommunications business during the late 1990s and early 2000s, Geomania is understaffed. Many staff members in professional, technical, support, and managerial jobs are doing work that was once performed by two people.

(Continued)

A case researcher asked human resources manager Stephanie Cohen what impact the heavy workload was having on employees. She replied, "We've got a bunch of great soldiers here, but the overload problem is taking its toll. Some staff members are having many more fights at home. More people are having serious medical problems like chest pains, migraine headaches, and stomach ulcers. I also think the error rate in work is going up. Manuel Gomez, the customer service manager, tells me Geomania is receiving more complaints about our systems not working."

The case researcher pointed out that Cohen's observations were to be expected when so many people are working so hard. She was asked if she noticed any other unusual behavior in the office in recent months. Cohen said that her assistant, Bonnie Boswell, had made some observations about unusual behavior, and that Boswell should be asked to participate in the interview.

Boswell got right to the heart of the matter, explaining that she has observed some behavior that could be helping productivity, hurting productivity, or a combination of both. "What I've noticed," said Boswell" is that our people are finding more and more creative ways to take naps on the job. The motto has become, 'You snooze you win,' instead of 'You snooze you lose.'

"There certainly is a positive side to napping. According to one NASA survey, 71 percent of corporate aviation pilots, 80 percent of regional pilots, and 60 percent of hospital workers said they took naps on the job. Another NASA study found that airline pilots who fell asleep on average for 26 minutes had a 34 percent improvement in performance and a 54 percent improvement in alertness. Of course, they were not sleeping while flying!

"But on the negative side, if you are sleeping you are not producing for the company. Besides that it looks so totally unprofessional to be sacked out in your cubicle, especially if you snore or scream because you are having a terrifying dream."

When asked where and how these workers were napping, both Boswell and Cohen had plenty of answers. Cohen said it has always been easy for executives to nap because they have private offices. Several keep their offices equipped with pillows, so they can nap comfortably on a couch, at their desk, or on the floor under the desk. Cohen said that she had walked in on napping executives by mistake, and an office assistant told her about the pillows.

Boswell said that cubicle dwellers have to be more creative about napping because other workers can readily see them. She explained, "Quite often they catch a nap during meetings. At some meetings half the audience is listing to one side or nap jerking (falling asleep, then quickly jerking the head to awake). One napper closes his eyes on his desk, and holds on to a bottle of eye drops to make it appear he is in the process of self-medication.

Many nappers sleep in their car during lunch break. "Some of the most stressed-out workers catch a few winks in the office supplies room by resting their head on a box."

Cohen said she was even wondering if Geomania should hire as a consultant psychologist, Bill Anthony, who founded The Napping Company, to promote productive naps in the workplace. He contends that companies do not have to set up special sleeping rooms. Instead, they can institutionalize nap breaks the way they have coffee breaks.

"My concern right now," concluded Cohen, "is what to recommend to top management. I think our CEO is opposed to napping on the job (except for his little 40 winks now and then), and napping does not look professional. Yet, a formal napping program could be a real productivity booster. Maybe we could even cut down on some medical problems."

Case Questions

1. If you worked for Geomania, and were stationed in a cubicle, explain why you would or would not nap on the job.

2. Would it be a good idea for management to just let workers decide for themselves whether to nap on the job? Explain your reasoning.

3. As the human resources director for Geomania, develop a written policy for napping on company time. (A policy is a general guideline to follow.) Include such aspects of napping as to when, where, under what circumstances, and for how long workers might nap. Mention whether or not Geomania should have a separate napping area.

4. How might a program of napping contribute to employee stress management at Geomania?

Source: Some of the facts in this case are from Jared Sandberg, "As Bosses Power Nap, Cubicle Dwellers Doze Under Clever Disguise," *The Wall Street Journal,* July 23, 2003, p. B1.

QUESTIONS FOR DISCUSSION AND REVIEW

1. Provide an example from your own or somebody else's life of how having a major goal in life can help a person be better organized.

2. Describe any way in which you have used information technology to make you more productive.

3. Many people who use a personal digital assistant (such as the type contained in a hand-held computer) find that they are no more organized or productive than before. What could be their problem?

4. Use information in this chapter to explain how a person might be well organized yet still not get very far in his or her career.

5. Ask an experienced high-level worker to identify his or her most effective method of time management.

6. Why might it be true that people who love their work live much longer than people who retire early because they dislike working?

7. A student told his instructor, "You have to give me a deadline for my paper. Otherwise, I can't handle it." What does this statement tell you about (1) the stressor he was facing and (2) how pressure influences his work performance?

8. Why might having your stress under control improve your interpersonal relationships?

9. Interview a person in a high-pressure job in any field. Find out whether the person experiences significant stress, and what method he or she uses to cope with it.

10. Using your Research Navigator, choose either procrastination or stress and find one study that provides some insights as to how to cope with or battle the problem. Find at least one method not included in this chapter to share with the class.

Research
Navigator.com

WEBLINKS

www.stress.org
This is the website of the American Institute of Stress.

www.ontario.cmha.ca
This is the site of the Ontario section of the Canadian Mental Health Association. Here you can access a wide variety of information on mental health.

http://stress.about.com
Considerable information about stress plus several self-quizzes.

www.theinnergame.com
The inner game of work, sports, and teambuilding.

Chapter 15

Job Search and Career Management Skills

Harold J. Mauer received a jolt of corporate culture shock when he joined a Chicago advertising agency a few years ago. The communication executive had spent most of his career in the traditional world of manufacturing. "Business casual" there meant pressed slacks, a button-down shirt, and a tie. But the ad agency was much more relaxed. His co-workers wore Hawaiian shirts, flip-flops, and shorts to work nearly every day in the summer. To fit in, Mauer dropped his ties and fished a Hawaiian shirt out of his closet. But he never felt at ease wearing super-casual clothes to work. "I'm much more comfortable in a more formal environment," the 57-year-old executive says.[1]

As the experience of the communication executive just described suggests, you are likely to be at your best when you perceive that you fit well into the climate of the firm. This final chapter of the book focuses on career success, including a description of strategies and tactics that will help you gain advantage.

Our approach to achieving career success is divided into three major segments: conducting a job campaign, understanding two major types of career paths, and using career advancement strategies and tactics. The previous 14 chapters also deal with topics and skills that are geared to success. However, the information presented in this chapter is more specifically about managing your career.

CONDUCTING A JOB SEARCH

The vast majority of workers need to conduct a job search at various times in their careers. Job searches are conducted to find employment in a firm the job hunter is not already working for or sometimes to find a new position within one's own firm. Some job hunters are attempting to switch careers or enter into growth areas. When job openings are in short supply, job search skills are especially important. This chapter's Canadian Scene below points out where the jobs are in Canada with good prospects. Even during the most prosperous of times, when jobs are in ample supply, learning more about conducting a job search is useful; it can help you land an excellent position. Important elements of the job search include job-hunting tactics and preparing a résumé and cover letter.

The Canadian Scene

WHERE ARE THE HOT JOBS

Where are the jobs in Canada and what are the prospects like for recent job seekers? According to a recent article in *Canadian Business Magazine* there is a desperate tug of war for workers across Canada, which has employers peddling sky-high pay and perks in the face of what many believe is a looming labour crisis as the boomer generation retires. For job seekers, though, there couldn't be a better time to find a new job. Just look at the unemployment rate—6.1% in February 2007. A quarter of Canadian employers are planning to increase their payrolls in the coming three months, says staffing firm Manpower Canada. Below is further information about some of the geographical zones in Canada and what jobs are "hot".

Yet for all that activity, output is lagging in this country. "In 2006, we saw labour productivity unfortunately only grow by 0.7%. It was quite weak," says Pedro Antunes, the director of national and provincial forecasting at the Conference Board of Canada, a think-tank in Ottawa. Statistics Canada blames this on a combination of disruptions in the mining sector, a warm winter and the economy's reliance on less-skilled labour. Productivity will rebound at the expense of hiring, says Antunes, as wages increase and it becomes more viable for companies to invest in capital equipment rather than new employees.

Topping the want-ad listings for now, though, are salespeople, according to staffing firm Manpower Canada, followed by health-care professionals (nurses, doctors and support staff), financial staff (such as accountants), information technology professionals, and construction workers.

The West

Alberta's employment rate hit a record high of 71.6% in February, making it Canada's biggest draw for jobs. The province has the highest population growth at 10.6% (double the national average) and strong gains in GDP. But the breakneck oil sands boom slightly distorts the job market. "Megaprojects in the energy sector have created great growth in employment, but that will peak, and when we look to 2008, 2009, and 2010 we actually see it easing," says Antunes. "You can't grow forever at seven percent." Still, anyone heading west today is almost guaranteed a job, "but finding somewhere to live is another thing," warns Cheri Tredree, manager of national recruitment at Manpower Canada.

Alberta currently relies heavily on younger workers, and even European tradespeople, to fill positions. Likewise, B.C. firms have been recruiting construction workers, welders, and labourers from Europe. And

(Continued)

the 2010 Olympics should only increase job openings—at least temporarily. "The Olympics are going to open up a lot of opportunity in service-related roles," says Tredree. Wholesale and retail trade and finance experts, specifically accountants, are the hot jobs in Vancouver.

The Centre

Oh, how the mighty have fallen. "Ontario used to be a province that attracted provincial migrants. Now, they are all going to Alberta and B.C.," says Antunes. Indeed, almost 60 000 people every year are leaving Ontario for other provinces, with the dismal decline in manufacturing only propelling this exodus. Since the manufacturing peak in 2002–03, 200 000 jobs have been lost in Canada—almost half of them in Ontario. Yet a rebound is looming, especially if the Big Three automakers ever finish restructuring. In the meantime, the manufacturing slump is cancelling job gains in other sectors, skewing the job picture, especially in Ontario and Quebec. Recent gains in Quebec have come from construction, finance, and services. Quebec also saw revived foreign interest in aerospace and telecommunication products in 2006.

Make no mistake. Toronto and Montreal are still major job markets, and thousands of jobs in finance, trade, and health care have been created in the past year. Nurses are in particular demand, as many continue to head to Alberta or the US for better pay. In the past year, the hottest jobs in Winnipeg have overwhelmingly been in trade, health care, and social assistance.

The East

For the coming quarter, 30 percent of employers are planning to hire in the eastern provinces to combat the mass migration of workers westward. The biggest demand is in the construction industry, where 70 percent of companies expect to be hiring. Other booming sectors in Atlantic Canada include transportation, public utilities, finance, insurance, and real estate. Manufacturing is expected to rebound in this region, with services and public administration also propelling growth.

Newfoundland and Labrador has the fastest-growing GDP in the country, at 5 percent, yet its unemployment rate still languishes in the double digits. The reason? Most of the gains have been in the resource sector, and they aren't expected to last past 2008. "The domestic economy in Newfoundland and Labrador is quite weak—the boom is really due to output," says Antunes. "The construction is over, so a lot of the jobs are gone."

The real hiring hotbed in the east is Moncton, N.B., where half of all employers plan to hire in the next three months. New Brunswick's unemployment rate hit a 31-year low in February, because of growth in natural gas exploration, making it a great place to look for work in the energy sector for now. The construction industry will lose jobs next year, however, as activities wind down at Irving Oil's natural gas plant.

The job market in Nova Scotia is also benefiting from a new extraction method for natural gas. Recent ads are calling professionals back to the province, especially for burgeoning life sciences and information technology jobs. With eastern prospects like these, it appears the west hasn't totally won.

Source: Marlene Rego, "Cool Jobs in Hot Markets," Joe Chidley, ed. *Canadian Business*, March 26, 2007. Adapted with permission.

JOB-HUNTING TACTICS

Most people already have usable knowledge about how to find a job. Some of the ideas discussed next will therefore be familiar; some will be unfamiliar. We recommend using this list of tactics as a checklist to ensure that you have not neglected something important. It is easy to overlook the obvious when job hunting, because your emotions may cloud your sense of logic.

Identify Your Job Objectives

An effective job search begins with a clear perception of what kind of position (or positions) you want. If you express indecision about the type of work you seek, the prospective employer will typically ask in a critical tone, "What kind of work are you looking for?" Your chances of finding suitable employment increase when several different types of positions will satisfy your job objectives. Assume that one person who majored in business administration is only willing to accept a position as an office manager in a corporation. Another person with the same major is seeking a position as (1) an office manager; (2) a management trainee in a corporation; (3) an assistant manager in a retail store, restaurant, or hotel; (4) a sales representative; (5) an assistant purchasing agent; or (6) a management analyst. The second person has a much better chance of finding a suitable position.

Be Aware of Qualifications Sought by Employers

What you are looking for in an employer must be matched against what an employer is looking for in an employee. If you are aware of what employers are seeking, you can emphasize those aspects of yourself when applying for a position. For example, applicants for almost any type of position should emphasize their computer skills. Job interviewers and hiring managers do not all agree on the qualifications they seek in employees. Nevertheless, a number of traits, characteristics, skills, and accomplishments are important to many employers.[2] In Chapter 1, the Employability Skills in the Canadian Scene on page 3 lists many of these skills and characteristics. Self-Assessment Quiz 15-1 summarizes some of these qualifications in a way that you can apply to yourself as you think about your job hunt.

Identify Your Skills and Potential Contribution

Today's job market is skill-based. Do you remember the Canadian Scene from Chapter 1 ("Skills for a Global Economy")? Employers are seeking all of these skills in greater or lesser degree. Employers typically seek out job candidates with tangible skills (including interpersonal skills) that can be put to immediate use in accomplishing work. These job-relevant skills included computer skills, written communication skills, oral communication skills, math skills, interpersonal skills, team skills, and listening skills. A successful candidate for a help-desk position at a telecommunications company told the interviewer: "I know I can help your customers with their software and hardware problems. I worked on the help desk at college, and my friends and family members are forever coming to me with their computer problems. I even get long-distance calls for help. Give me a chance to help your customers." (Notice that this candidate implied his or her listening skills.)

Develop a Comprehensive Marketing Strategy

A vital job-finding strategy is to use multiple approaches to reach the right prospective employer. This is particularly true when the position you seek is in short supply. Among the many approaches employers use to recruit candidates are employee referrals, newspaper ads, online recruiting, college and professional school recruitment, job fairs, temporary help firms, walk-ins, unsolicited résumés and phone calls, and government employment services. Some people looking for a highly specialized job place a position-wanted ad in a newspaper or on the internet. Such ads receive many inquiries from career agents who offer to help you find a suitable position.

Self-Assessment Quiz 15-1

QUALIFICATIONS SOUGHT BY EMPLOYERS

Following is a list of qualifications widely sought by prospective employers. After reading each qualification, rate yourself on a 1-to-5 scale on the particular dimension. 1 = very low; 2 = low; 3 = average; 4 = high; 5 = very high.

1. Appropriate education for the position under consideration and satisfactory grades — 1 2 3 4 5
2. Relevant work experience — 1 2 3 4 5
3. Communication and other interpersonal skills — 1 2 3 4 5
4. Motivation and energy — 1 2 3 4 5
5. Problem-solving ability (intelligence) and creativity — 1 2 3 4 5
6. Judgment and common sense — 1 2 3 4 5
7. Adaptability to change — 1 2 3 4 5
8. Emotional maturity (acting professionally and responsibly) — 1 2 3 4 5
9. Teamwork (ability and interest in working in a team effort) — 1 2 3 4 5
10. Positive attitude (enthusiasm about work and initiative) — 1 2 3 4 5
11. Emotional intelligence (ability to deal with own feelings and those of others) — 1 2 3 4 5
12. Customer service orientation (wanting to meet customer needs) — 1 2 3 4 5
13. Information technology skills — 1 2 3 4 5
14. Willingness to continue to study and learn about job, company, and industry — 1 2 3 4 5
15. Likableness and sense of humour — 1 2 3 4 5
16. Dependability, responsibility, and conscientiousness (including good work habits and time management) — 1 2 3 4 5
17. Willingness and ability to work well with co-workers and customers from different cultures — 1 2 3 4 5

Interpretation: Consider engaging in some serious self-development, training, and education for items on which you rated yourself 1 or 2. If you accurately rated yourself as 4 or 5 on all the dimensions, you are an exceptional job candidate.

Use Networking to Reach Company Insiders

The majority of successful job campaigns stem from personal contacts. Employers rely heavily on referrals from employees to fill positions. Positions that have not been filled by word of mouth are then publicly announced, for example, through internet listings or classified ads. In regard to job hunting, **networking** is contacting friends and acquaintances and building systematically on these relationships to create a still wider set of contacts who might lead to employment. Formal mechanisms to develop

- Co-workers and previous employers
- Friends and neighbours
- Faculty and staff
- Graduates of any schools you have attended
- Former employers
- Present employers (assuming you hold a temporary position)
- Professional workers such as bankers, brokers, and clergy
- Political leaders at the local level
- Members of your club or athletic team
- Community groups, churches, temples, and mosques
- Trade and professional associations
- Student professional associations
- Career fairs
- People met in airports and on airplanes
- People met in aerobics classes and health clubs
- People you get to know through internet chat rooms

Figure 15-1   Potential Sources of Network Contacts

network contacts have been introduced in recent years, such as bar parties in metropolitan areas devoted just to making job contacts. Figure 15-1 presents a list of potential network contacts.

The networking technique is so well-known today that it suffers from overuse. It is therefore important to use a tactful, low-key approach with a contact. For example, instead of asking a person in your network to furnish you with a job lead, ask that person how a person with qualifications similar to yours might find a job. And guard against taking up a large portion of a busy person's workday, for instance, by insisting on a luncheon meeting.

Another way of reaching company insiders is to write dozens of letters to potential employers. A surprisingly large number of people find jobs by contacting employers directly. Many company websites have a section allocated to inviting job inquiries as part of the employee recruitment program. Prepare a prospective employer list, including the names of executives to contact in each firm. The people who receive your letters and email messages become part of your network. A variation of this approach is to develop a 30-second telephone presentation of your background. After you have researched firms that may have opportunities for you, call them and make your pitch.

Use Job Boards and the Career Sections of Company Websites

The internet is a standard avenue for job hunting, even for middle-management and executive positions. For little or no cost, the job seeker can post a résumé or scroll through hundreds of job opportunities. A number of websites function as résumé database services because they give employers access to résumés submitted by job hunters.

Table 15-1   Popular Job Search Websites

Human Resources Development Canada (with access to Canada's Job Bank)	www.hrdc-drhc.gc.ca
Workopolis	www.workopolis.com
Career Builder	www.careerbuilder.com
Globe Careers	www.globecareers.com
Job Shark	www.jobshark.com
Hot Jobs	www.hotjobs.com
Monster Board	www.monster.com
PeopleSoft	www.peoplesoft.com
Employment Guide	www.employmentguide.com
NationJob Network	www.nationjob.com
Job Hunt: Online Job Search Guide	www.job-hunt.org

Many position announcements on the internet require the job seeker to send a résumé by attached file. A few position announcements still request that the résumé be sent by fax or paper mail. Table 15-1 lists some current popular job-hunting websites. Virtually all large employers have an employment section on their website (as already mentioned), and some of these employers prefer these sites over commercial job boards. Some websites even have job applications that can be filled out online. Hundreds of people every day land jobs they first learned about through a job board or company website, so this approach offers some promise.

Like searching the internet for information, searching these job boards requires some skill in navigation. Use specific job titles if possible or specific areas of job skill such as accounting or computer programming to narrow your search. Sites such as Workopolis and Human Resources Development Canada can also be searched by geographical region. If you are willing to relocate, you will have more job opportunities available across the country or internationally.

Job hunting on the internet can lead to a false sense of security. Using the internet, a résumé is cast over a wide net, and hundreds of job postings can be explored. As a consequence, the job seeker may think that he or she can sit back and wait for a job offer to come through email. In reality, the internet is just one source of leads that should be used in conjunction with other job-finding methods, especially personal contacts that might lead to an interview. Employers still extensively use print ads in newspapers to recruit employees. Remember also that thousands of other job seekers can access the same job opening, and many of the positions listed have already been filled.

Skill-Building Exercise 15-1 will give you an opportunity to learn first-hand about job hunting on the web.

Smile at Network Members and Interviewers and Be Enthusiastic

Assuming that you have the right qualifications, the simple act of smiling can be an effective job-hunting technique. One reason that smiling is effective at any stage of the job search is that it helps build a relationship, however brief. If by chance you use a webcam as part of your job search, smile on camera. Closely related to smiling is to display enthusiasm and excitement when speaking to people who can help you land

Skill-Building Exercise 15-1

JOB HUNTING ON THE INTERNET

Job hunting on the web can be a rewarding or frustrating experience, depending on your skill in navigating job search websites and the availability of positions for a person with your qualifications. Use several job search websites to locate a position opening for the following three persons:

Position 1: You. Find a position listed on the web that would appear to be an excellent fit for you at this point in your career.

Position 2: Sales representative, fluent in English and Japanese. Attempt to find an opening for an industrial sales representative or retail sales position that requires the applicant to be fluent in English and Japanese.

Position 3: Sports administrator. Attempt to find an opening for a sports administrator, typically a person who does administrative work for a professional sports team.

Set a time limit for your surfing, perhaps 60 minutes. If you are working in a team, each team member can search for one position. Share your approaches with one another, as well as the websites that appear to achieve the best results.

a position. Conducted properly, a job search should be exciting and invigorating, and you should express these emotions to your contacts.[3] The excitement and invigoration stem from each small step you take leading to your goal of finding suitable employment.

Smooth Out Rough Spots in Your Background

Many employers routinely conduct background investigations of prospective employees. A background investigation by a firm hired for the purpose could include speaking to neighbours and co-workers about your reputation. In addition, the investigator may delve into your driving record, check for criminal charges or convictions, survey your credit record, and find out whether you have had disputes with the government about taxes. Such information is used to supplement reference checks because so many employers are hesitant to say anything negative about past employees. The information uncovered through the background check is often compared to the information presented on your résumé. A discrepancy between the two sends up an immediate red flag.

Any job seeker who has severe negative factors in his or her background cannot readily change the past. Yet the job seeker can receive copies of a credit bureau report to make sure it is fair and accurate. If inaccuracies exist, or certain credit problems have been resolved, the credit report might be changed in the applicant's favour. Or, bring up the negative credit rating during an interview to present your side of the story. Perhaps you had co-signed a loan for a friend who fell behind on his or her payments or you have been a victim of identity theft. It might also be possible to obtain a more favourable reference from an employer by making a polite request. A third step can be to request a copy of the consumer report, which is a report of your reputation based on interviews with co-workers, neighbours, and others. A person might be able to negotiate a deletion of damaging information that is incorrect or exaggerated.[4]

Another way to learn about what public information exists about you is to place your own name into a couple of search engines. Sometimes another person with the same name as yours—particularly if many people have the same name as you—might have been involved in criminal activity, so be prepared to defend yourself!

What if you were fired from your last job? The best advice is to be honest about it, as your previous employer may be called. Monica Beauregard, president of Bridgepoint, a Toronto-based human-resources consulting and training firm, says the best advice is to come prepared to answer specific questions about your previous job and to talk about the strengths you can bring to the new one. For example, "If they were terminated because of management style, what management style was it that wasn't right? I like asking questions where there's no right or wrong answer, where you're actually getting at fit."[5]

THE RÉSUMÉ AND COVER LETTER

No matter what method of job hunting you choose, somebody will inevitably ask you for a résumé. Sometimes you will be asked to complete a job application form instead of, or in addition to, providing a résumé. Résumés are also important for job hunting within your own firm. You may need one to be considered for a transfer with a large firm, or to be assigned to a team or project. It is also potentially useful to present a résumé when your job performance is being evaluated, because it gives your manager a perspective of your career and your overall accomplishments.

Purpose of the Résumé

Regard your résumé as a marketing tool for selling your skills and your potential to handle new responsibilities. The most specific purpose of a résumé is to help you obtain an interview that can lead to a job. Your résumé must therefore attract enough attention for an employer to invite you for an interview. A poorly prepared résumé often leads to an immediate rejection of the candidate. Recognize that you are competing against many carefully prepared résumés, some of which have been prepared with professional assistance. If the demand for your skills is high enough, it is conceivable that you will be hired without an interview.

Résumé Length and Format

Opinions vary about the desirable length for a résumé. For a recent graduate with limited work experience, a one-page résumé may be acceptable. For more experienced people, it would seem too short. Employers today demand considerable detail in résumés, particularly about the candidate's skills, accomplishments, and teamwork and leadership experience. Nevertheless, a four-page or longer résumé may irritate an impatient reader. Two pages is therefore recommended for early stages in your career.

A general-purpose hard-copy résumé is presented in Figure 15-2. Recognize that hiring managers and human resource professionals have widely different perceptions of what constitutes an effective résumé. Check at least two résumé guides before preparing a final version of your résumé.

A study conducted with 64 business professionals provides some useful information about which résumé characteristics are perceived positively enough to result in

Scott Wayland
170 Glenview Drive
Toronto, Ontario M6P 2N5
Phone/Fax (416) 555-1000
swayland@frontiernet.net

Qualification Summary	Experience in selling industrial machinery. Education in business administration, combined with apprenticeship in tool-and-die making. In one year, sold $400 000 worth of excess machine inventory. Received letter of commendation from company president.
Job Objective	Industrial sales, handling large, complex machinery. Willing to work largely on commission basis.
Job Experience 2005–present	Industrial account representative, Bainbridge Corporation, Toronto. Sell line of tool-and-die equipment to companies in central Canada. Responsibilities include servicing established accounts and canvassing new ones. Served on team establishing e-commerce capability.
2003–2005	Inside sales representative, Bainbridge Corporation. Answered customer inquiries. Filled orders for replacement parts. Trained for outside sales position. Served as sales team representative on company quality-improvement team.
1999–2003	Tool-and-die-maker apprentice, Ontario Metals, Inc., Toronto. Assisted senior tool-and-die makers during four-year training program. Worked on milling machines, jigs, punch presses, computer-assisted manufacturing, computer-assisted design (CAD/CAM).
Formal Education 1999–2004	Ryerson Polytechnic University, Toronto, Ontario. Associate Degree in Business Administration; graduated with 82 percent average. Courses in marketing, sales techniques, human relations, accounting, and statistics. President of Commuter's Club.
1995–1999	East High, Toronto. Honours student; academic major with vocational elective. Played varsity football and basketball. Earned part of living by selling magazine subscriptions.
Job-Related Skills	Professional sales representative. Able to size up customer manufacturing problem and make recommendations for appropriate machinery. Precise in preparing call reports and expense accounts. Good skill in gathering input from the field for market research purposes.
Personal Interests and Hobbies	Information technology enthusiast (developed and installed own website), scuba diving, recreational golf player, read trade and business magazines. Auto enthusiast, including restoring a 1972 Corvette.
References	On file with placement office at Ryerson Polytechnic University.

Figure 15-2   A General-Purpose Résumé

inviting a job candidate for an interview. The business professionals reviewed résumés for new business graduates. The following résumé characteristics were more likely to lead to first choices for an interview: One page in contrast to two pages, a specific objective statement in comparison to a general objective statement, relevant coursework better than no coursework listed, GPAs of 3.0 in contrast to no GPA listed, GPAs of 3.50 in contrast to GPAs of 2.75, and accomplishment statements in contrast to no accomplishment statement.[6] In support of these findings, a résumé that does not list the candidate's skills and accomplishments is considered insufficient today.

In writing your résumé, keep in mind that certain keywords or references attract the attention of managers and specialists who scan job résumés. In today's market, these include: *languages, wireless, WiFi, achievement, hands-on, flexible, task-oriented, and ecommerce.*[7]

When submitting your résumé and cover letter electronically, make it easy for the employer to access, such as using an attached Word file. Many employers will refuse to open a Winzip compressed file, an Adobe Acrobat PDF, or a PowerPoint presentation. Furthermore, concerns about computer viruses have prompted some employers to refuse to open any attached file. So you might send an attached word processing file, plus insert your résumé in the email message. Make sure the formatting is not lost when cutting and pasting your document into email.

The Cover Letter

A résumé should be accompanied by a cover letter explaining who you are and why you are applying for the particular position. The cover letter customizes your approach to a particular employer, whereas the résumé is a more general approach. Sometimes it is helpful to prepare an attention-getting cover letter in which you make an assertive statement about how you intend to help the employer deal with an important problem. A person applying for a credit-manager position might state, "Let me help you improve your cash flow by using the latest methods for getting customers to pay on time, or even early."

Career advisor Jim Pawlak suggests that the cover letter should take no longer than one minute to read, and should focus on the skills and background you'll bring to the job. Follow this with a brief bullet-point list of your accomplishments. A useful alternative to the bulleted list is a two-column table that compares the requirements stated by the employer with your qualifications.[8] An example follows:

Your Requirements	My Qualifications
Sales experience	Four years of part-time selling, including working a newspaper subscription and renewal kiosk at a shopping mall.
Ability to resolve conflict	Worked three seasons as lifeguard, and frequently had to stop rule violators and people in fights. Worked as Little League baseball coach, and resolved many conflicts between parents and myself, or between parents and the umpires.

If possible, mention a company insider in your network, and then close the cover letter with appreciation for any consideration your qualifications might be given.

PERFORMING WELL IN A JOB INTERVIEW

After a prospective employer has reacted favourably to your cover letter and résumé, the next step may be a telephone screening interview or a more comprehensive job interview. The purpose of the telephone screening interview is generally to obtain some indication of the candidate's oral communication skills. Such an interview is most likely to occur when one applies for a customer contact position or a position that requires knowledge of a second language. Having passed the screening interview, the candidate is invited for an in-person job interview. In another type of screening interview, the candidate responds to computerized questions, including a sample job problem. His or her answers are printed for the interviewer to review. Candidates who get through the computer-assisted interview are then interviewed by a company representative.[9]

Typically, the applicant is interviewed by one person at a time; however, team interviews are becoming more commonplace. In this format, members of the team or department with whom you would be working take turns asking you questions. One justification for team interviews is to observe how the candidate fits in with the team.

A general guide for performing well in the job interview is to present a positive but accurate picture of yourself. Your chances of performing well in a job increase if you are suited to the job. Tricking a prospective employer into hiring you when you are not qualified is therefore self-defeating in terms of your career. As mentioned in Chapter 13, outright deception, such as falsifying one's educational or employment record, is widely practised during interviews, on résumés, and in cover letters. Based on a sample of 1.8 million background checks, it was found that one in four résumés contained a lie.[10] But if the person is hired and the deception is discovered later, he or she is subject to dismissal. Following is a list of some key points to keep in mind when being interviewed for a job you want:

1. *Be prepared, look relaxed, and make the interviewer feel comfortable.* Coming to the interview fully prepared to discuss yourself and your background and knowing key facts about the prospective employer will help you look relaxed. Many people today use company websites to gather background information about the prospective employer.

2. *Establish a link between you and the prospective employer.* A good way to build rapport between you and the prospective employer is to mention some plausible link you have with that firm. To illustrate, if being interviewed for a position at a Zellers, you might say, "It's interesting to visit the office part of Zellers. Our family has been shopping here for years. In fact, I bought a DVD player here last month, and it works great."

3. *Ask perceptive questions.* The best questions are sincere ones that reflect an interest in the content of the job (intrinsic motivators) and job performance, rather than benefits and social activities. A good question to ask is, "What would you consider to be an outstanding performance in this job?" If the issue of compensation is not introduced by the interviewer, ask about such matters after first discussing the job and your qualifications.

4. *Be prepared to discuss your strengths and developmental opportunities.* Most interviewers will ask you to discuss your strengths and developmental opportunities. (These and other frequently asked questions are presented in Figure 15-3.) Knowledge of strengths hints at how good your potential job performance will be. If you deny having areas for improvement, you will

An effective way of preparing for job interviews is to rehearse answers to the types of questions you will most likely be asked by the interviewer. The following questions are a sampling of the types found in most employment interviews. Rehearse answers to them prior to going out on job interviews. One good rehearsal method is to role-play the employment interview with a friend who asks these typical questions, or to videotape yourself.

1. Why did you apply for this job?
2. What are your career goals?
3. What salary are you worth?
4. What new job skills would you like to acquire in the next few years?
5. Give me an example of how you displayed good teamwork.
6. Describe how you have shown leadership on the job or off the job.
7. What are your strengths (or good points)?
8. What are your weaknesses (or areas for needed improvement)?
9. Why should we hire you instead of other candidates for this position?
10. How well do you work under pressure?
11. What positions with other companies are you applying for?
12. What makes you think you will be successful in business?
13. What do you know about our firm?
14. Here is a sample job problem. How would you handle it?
15. What questions do you have for me?

Figure 15-3   Questions Frequently Asked of Job Candidates

appear defensive or lacking in insight. Some candidates describe developmental opportunities that could be interpreted as strengths. A case in point: "I have been criticized for expecting too much from myself and others." Do you think this approach is unethical?

5. *Be prepared to respond to behavioural interview questions.* A *behavioural interview* asks questions directly about the candidate's behaviour in relation to an important job activity. The job candidate is expected to give samples of important job behaviours. The behavioural interview is therefore more applicable to candidates with substantial work experience. Two behavioural inquiries are "Tell me about a time in which your ability to work well on a team contributed to the success of a project" and "Give me an example of a creative suggestion you made that was actually implemented. In what way did it help the company?" To prepare for such questions, think of some examples of how you handled several difficult job challenges. The idea is to document specific actions you took or behaviours you engaged in that contributed to a favourable outcome.

6. *Show how you can help the employer.* A prospective employer wants to know whether you will be able to perform the job well. Direct much of your conversation toward how you intend to help the company solve problems and get

important work accomplished. Whatever the question, think about what details of your skills and experience will be useful to the employer.

7. *Use body language that projects confidence and decisiveness.* A job interviewer will often carefully observe the candidate's body language. Monitor your body language to appear confident and decisive. A case in point: An executive coach helped a manager hone his nonverbal communication skills. The manager was concerned because he came close to getting three job offers but did not get hired. The coach showed the manager how his relaxed posture and habit of picking up anything in reach made him appear indecisive. Therefore, the manager practised sitting upright and keeping his hands at his sides. Soon thereafter the manager was hired into a position he wanted.[11] Being carefully groomed, looking crisp and fresh, and having clean, unbroken nails also helps project self-confidence.

8. *Practise good etiquette during the interview, including during a meal.* Under the pressures of applying for a job, it is easy to let etiquette slip. To display poor etiquette and manners, however, could lead to a candidate being rejected from consideration. Most of the suggestions made about etiquette in Chapter 11 apply to the job interview, but be particularly sensitive to allowing company officials to talk without interrupting them, and practising good table manners. Even interviewers who are rude themselves, such as taking phone calls while interviewing you, expect *you* not to do the same.

9. *Send a follow-up letter.* Mail a courteous follow-up letter or send an email message several days after the interview, particularly if you want the job. A follow-up letter is a tip-off that you are truly interested in the position. You should state your attitudes toward the position, the team, and the company and summarize any conclusions reached about your discussion.

Now do Skill-Building Exercise 15-2 to practise the job interview.

Skill-Building Exercise 15-2

THE JOB INTERVIEW

As described in Figure 15-3, a good way to prepare for a job interview is to rehearse answers to frequently asked questions. In this role play, one student will be the interviewer and one the interviewee (job applicant). The job in question is that of property manager for a large apartment complex in Winnipeg, Manitoba. Assume that the applicant really wants the job. The interviewer, having taking a course in human resource management, will ask many of the questions in Figure 15-3. In addition, the interviewer will ask at least one behavioural question, perhaps about teamwork. The interviewer might also have other questions, such as "Why do you want to live in Winnipeg?"

Before proceeding with the role play, both people should review the information in this chapter about the job interview, and in Chapter 3 about listening.

VERTICAL AND HORIZONTAL CAREER PATHS

Career planning can begin at any point. Even a kindergarten child might say, "I want to be an astronaut." Many other people think about developing their career only after they have worked in a full-time professional position for several years. Planning and developing your career involves some form of goal-setting. If your goals are laid out systematically to lead to your ultimate career goal, you have established a **career path**, a sequence of positions necessary to achieve a goal. Here we look at the more traditional career path, with an emphasis on moving upward, along with the more contemporary path that emphasizes acquiring new skills and knowledge.

THE VERTICAL (TRADITIONAL) CAREER PATH

The vertical, or traditional, career path is based on the idea that a person continues to grow in responsibility with the aim of reaching a target position, such as becoming a top-level manager. The vertical career path is synonymous with "climbing the corporate ladder." The same path is based somewhat on the unwritten contract that a good performer will have the opportunity to work for one firm for a long time and receive many promotions in the process. However, a vertical career path can be spread out over several employers.

A career path should be related to the present and future demands of one firm or the industry. If you aspire toward a high-level manufacturing position, it would be vital to know the future of manufacturing in that firm and in the industry. Many Canadian firms, for example, are conducting more of their manufacturing in the Pacific Rim, Mexico, and the United States. If you were really determined, you might study the appropriate language and ready yourself for a foreign position.

While laying out a career path, it is also helpful to list your personal goals. They should mesh with your work plans to avoid major conflicts in your life. Some lifestyles, for example, are incompatible with some career paths. It would be difficult to develop a stable home life (spouse, children, friends, community activities, sports team, and garden) if a person aspired to hold field positions in international marketing. Contingency ("what if") plans should also be incorporated into a well-designed career path. For instance, "If I am not promoted within two years, I will pursue an advanced degree."

Mary Leclair, an ambitious 20-year-old, formulated the career path shown in Figure 15-4 on the next page prior to receiving an associate degree in business management. After she presented her tentative career path to her classmates, several accused Mary of aiming too high. Mary's career goals are high, but she has established contingency plans.

A career path laid out in chart form gives a person a clear perception of climbing steps toward his or her target position. As each position is attained, the corresponding step can be shaded in colour or cross-hatched. The steps, or goals, include a time element, which is helpful for sound career management even in work environments that are less predictable than they used to be. Your long-range goal might be clearly established in your mind (such as becoming regional manager of a hotel chain). At the same time, you must establish short-range (get any kind of job in a hotel) and intermediate-range (be manager of a hotel by age 27) goals. Goals set too far in the future that are not supported with more immediate goals may lose their motivational value.

Skill-Building Exercise 15-3 gives you the opportunity to practise your skills in setting goals for career and personal life. Such activity is the nucleus of career planning.

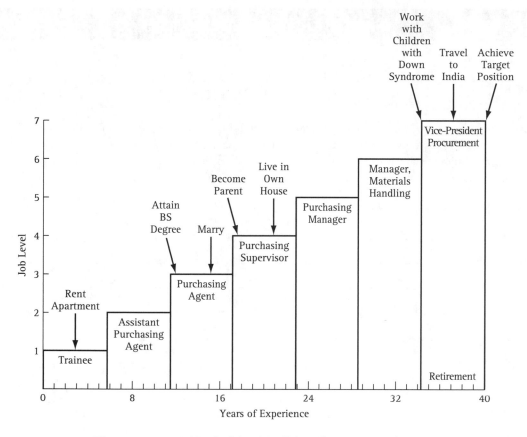

Figure 15-4   A Vertical (or Traditional) Career Path

THE HORIZONTAL CAREER PATH

In many organizations, the hope of staying for a long time and receiving a long series of promotions has vanished. Instead of climbing the ladder, the person is placed on a jungle gym in which he or she makes a series of moves in different directions, acquiring new skills and abilities to attain increased job satisfaction. Each position in the company represents a rung on the jungle gym. Managers and others make their careers by scrambling over the frame or moving between positions[12]

Typically, these moves in the modern organization are horizontal rather than vertical. A significant feature of the horizontal career path is that people are more likely to advance by moving sideways than up. Or at least people who get ahead will spend a considerable part of their career working in different positions at, or nearly at, the same level. In addition, they may occasionally move to a lower-level position to gain valuable experience. Thus with a horizontal career path, the major reward is no longer promotion, but the opportunity to gain more experience and increase job skills.

The horizontal career path is closely linked to the contemporary employment contract that offers shared responsibility for career growth. The old employment contract was lifetime employment in exchange for corporate loyalty. Instead, employees today get a chance to develop new technical and professional skills. Instead of being offered job security, they become more employable because of the diversity of skills they

Skill-Buiding Exercise 15-3

GOAL SETTING AND ACTION PLAN WORKSHEET

Here is an opportunity to apply the most fundamental skill in career planning, establishing goals. The action plan describes the steps you will take to attain the particular goal, such as saving money weekly and building a good credit rating by paying bills promptly so you can someday become a business owner. If you are not currently employed, set up hypothetical goals and action plans for a future job.

Long-Range Goals (beyond five years)

Work: _____

Action Plan: _____

Personal: _____

Action Plan: _____

Medium-Range Goals (two to five years)

Work: _____

Action Plan: _____

Personal: _____

Action Plan: _____

Short-Range Goals (within two years)

Work: _____

Action Plan: _____

Personal: _____

Action Plan: _____

Contingency Plans (What I will do if the above goals seem unattainable.)

Work: _____

Personal: _____

acquire. The company provides the environment for learning, and the employees are responsible for developing their skills. Despite this trend, many employers are reverting to the old promise of an opportunity to climb the organizational ladder. Further, it is not unusual for workers to aspire to higher-level, higher-paying positions.

A horizontal career path, as well as a traditional (or vertical) career path, does not necessarily mean the person stays with the same firm. For example, a worker might spend three years in one company as an electronics technician, three years in another as a sales representative, and then three years as a customer service specialist in a third

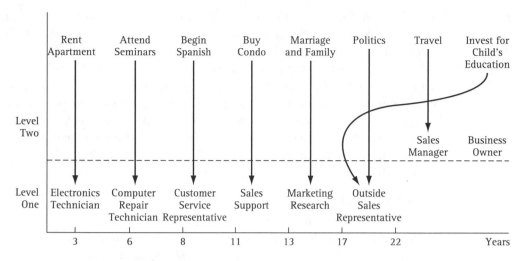

Figure 15-5   A Horizontal Career Path

company. All three positions would be approximately at the same level. The third company then promotes the individual to a much-deserved position as the marketing team leader. Figure 15-5 illustrates a horizontal career path for Larry Chang, a career school graduate who did attempt to make long-range predictions about his career. Notice that all the positions through year 17 are at the first level, and the positions for year 22 and beyond are at the second level. Chang's career contingency plans are as follows:

> (1) If cannot obtain experience as a market research analyst, customer service rep, or sales rep, will continue to develop as electronics technician. (2) If cannot find employment as a sales manager, will attempt to become supervisor of electronic technicians. (3) If do not raise sufficient funds for starting own business, will continue in corporate job until retirement.

CAREER ADVANCEMENT STRATEGIES AND TACTICS

The many ways of improving interpersonal relationships described in this book can also help advance and enhance a person's career. People who improve their relationships with others are laying a foundation for career advancement. Below we describe 14 other key strategies and tactics for career advancement, whether the advancement be vertical, horizontal, or a combination of the two. The first eight methods described deal more with controlling your own characteristics and behaviours, whereas the remaining six deal more with interacting with the environment.

Be Passionate About and Proud of Your Work

Successful people in all fields are passionate about their work. Without passion, you rely too heavily on external rewards to sustain effort. Passion contributes both to your career growth and company productivity.[13] Effective leaders and business owners are usually passionate about their work, and group members expect their leader to be passionate.[14] Being passionate is also important because it is linked to developing expertise and high job performance. Taking pride in your work stems naturally from passion. If you invest the emotional energy into having passion, you are likely to be proud of your work.

The surest path to career success is to identify your area of expertise and then build a career around it. The more passionate and proud you are about your area of expertise, the better. Becoming wealthy and achieving recognition are by-products of making effective use of your talents. Expertise combined with passion helps you attain consistently high job performance—the foundation upon which you build your career. Job competence is still the major success ingredient in all but the most political organizations (those where favouritism outweighs merit).

Develop a Code of Professional Ethics
Another solid foundation for developing a career is to establish a personal ethical code. An ethical code determines what behaviour is right or wrong, good or bad, based on values. Values stem from cultural upbringing, religious teachings, peer influences, and professional or industry standards. As implied in Chapter 13, a code of professional ethics helps a worker deal with such issues as bribes, backstabbing, and sexual harassment.

Develop a Proactive Personality
If you are an active agent in taking control of the forces around you, you stand a better chance of capitalizing on opportunities. Also, you will seek out opportunities, such as seeing problems that need fixing. A **proactive personality** is a person who is relatively unconstrained by situational forces and who brings about environmental change. The proactive personality has high perceived control over situations.

People who are highly proactive identify opportunities and act on them, show initiative, and keep trying until they bring about meaningful change. A health and safety specialist with a proactive personality, for example, might identify a health hazard others had missed. She would identify the nature of the problem and urge management to supply funding to control the problem. Ultimately, her efforts in preventing major health problems would be recognized. The proactive employee can also be regarded as displaying organizational citizenship behaviour because he or she is a good citizen who will step outside the job description to be helpful. For example, he or she might take the initiative to help a co-worker without being asked, or report a leaking faucet to the maintenance department.

Two studies conducted with close to 700 male and female workers in diverse occupations examined the relationship between career success and a proactive personality. Proactive personality, as measured by a test, was related to salary, promotions, taking the initiative in one's career, and career satisfaction.[15] Another reason that being proactive facilitates career success is that employees are expected to be more self-managing than in the past. The proactive employee will identify and resolve many problems without being directed to do so by the manager.

It may not be easy to develop a proactive personality, but a person can get started by taking more initiative to fix problems and attempt to be more self-starting.

Keep Growing Through Continuous Learning and Self-Development
Given that continuous learning is part of the new employment contract, engaging in regular learning can take many forms, including formal schooling, attending training

programs and seminars, and self-directed study, including using the internet. It is particularly important to engage in new learning in areas of interest to the company, such as developing proficiency in a second language if the company has customers and employees in other countries. Many companies support continuous learning because they perceive themselves to be *learning organizations*. It may therefore be easy for you to implement the tactic of growth through continuous learning.

Document Your Accomplishments

Keeping an accurate record of what you have accomplished in your career can pay off when you are being considered for reassignment or promotion, or applying for a position outside your company. The same log of accomplishments is useful for résumé preparation. Your ability to point to tangible, quantifiable accomplishments will make you less reliant on another person's subjective impression of your performance. Assume that a retail store manager reduced inventory shrinkage by 30 percent in one year. It would be better for the manager to state that fact than simply to record a statement from her boss saying, "Kelly shows outstanding ability to reduce inventory shrinkage."

Career coach Peggy Klaus recommends that you weave your accomplishments into an interesting story to tell other people.[16] The story approach has more appeal than a straightforward list of your accomplishments. Here is a fragment of a story that a man who worked for a food supplier to restaurants, schools, and hospitals used to document his accomplishments:

> Our area was hit with a vicious lightning storm last March 12. Our computer and telephone systems went haywire because of power outages. We had to be in touch with our customers. I rounded up 10 people in the company who had cellphones with them. Using all the battery power we had left in our phones, we were able to contact all our customers. My manager said my cellphone rescue effort saved the day.

Documenting your accomplishments in a business field is similar to preparing a portfolio of your work, the way a photographer, interior designer, or architect might do. When the person applies for a job or assignment, he or she carries along the portfolio of representative work. Documentation enables you to promote yourself in a dignified, tactful way. When discussing work with key people in the company, let them know of your good deeds without taking too much credit for team accomplishments. If you distinguish yourself in the community, for example, by fundraising for a shelter for the homeless, let your manager know of your activities. The rationale is that most companies want their workers to be responsible community members.

Project a Professional Image

If you are seeking career advancement, your clothing, desk and work area, speech, and general knowledge should project the image of a professional, responsible person. Good grammar and sentence structure can give you the edge, since so many people use highly informal patterns of speech. Being a knowledgeable person is important because today's professional business person is supposed to be aware of the external environment. Also, as noted by a human relations specialist, projecting a professional image hastens the development of trust and rapport in business relationships.[17]

A challenge in projecting a professional image is to figure out what constitutes a professional image in your particular environment. Less restrictive dress codes have made it more confusing to select clothing that will create a favourable appearance. Dominique Isbecque, an image consultant, says, "People are struggling over just what the new standard of appearance should be."[18] Since about 2004, business formal attire for both men and women has been making a strong comeback. Yet, the information technology field in Silicon Valley is still extremely informal. A programmer who wore a tank top and running shoes might be considered to project a professional image. Yet a marketing specialist for a health insurance provider behaving in the same way in Toronto would be perceived as unprofessional.

A general guideline is to dress somewhat like the successful people in your firm, or the customer's firm. It might pay to contact a company you plan to visit in advance and inquire about the dress standards for key people in the company. Skill-Building Exercise 15-4 is designed to sensitize you to what constitutes a professional image in a specific environment.

Perceive Yourself as a Provider of Services

A useful perspective for upgrading your professional self-image and increasing your feelings of job security is to perceive yourself as something other than a traditional employee. According to career specialist John A. Thomson, everyone should see himself or herself as a *personal service business entity.* Basically you are a business, offering the company (also your client from this perspective) a valuable service. You keep offering the service so long as the company keeps you on the payroll and you enjoy the work. Note the similarity to a high-level professional such as a dentist or information technology consultant. You are offering a service that many people need. Part of the same perception is that you own your skills, and that these are the service your business (you) offers to others.[19]

Another way of perceiving yourself as different from a traditional employee is to think of yourself as a professional-level temporary employee. Sometimes you will have a long stay with one employer, acting like a "perma-temp." At other times, you will quickly move on to another company where your skills are more in need.

Skill-Building Exercise 15-4

THE PROFESSIONAL IMAGE INVESTIGATION

Find out what constitutes a *professional image* in a specific job environment, either where you work or at another employer. Ask a handful of people, "What makes for a professional image here?" Speak to or correspond by email with a top-level manager, as well as a few workers without managerial responsibility. Another approach to this assignment is to make some observations directly in a retail establishment like Loblaws, Sears, Zellers, or Wal-Mart. How do your professors or teachers dress? And how does their dress differ from deans or chairs of the various departments in your college or school? How do the people in supervisory positions appear to dress, behave, and talk? Maybe you can conduct a one-minute interview with a service worker or two.

Share your observations with classmates, and see what conclusions can be drawn. For example, how does the type of company influence what constitutes a professional image? Are there different standards for men and women?

Apply the High-Performance Pyramid
High-performance specialists Jim Loehr and Tony Schwartz have developed a pyramidal framework to help people sustain a high level of energy and career performance. In the high-performance pyramid, the total person is involved, and you must train yourself as a "corporate athlete" to perform well at four levels: the body, the emotions, the mind, and the spirit. The four levels are described as follows.[20]

Level 1: Physical Capacity. Working on your physical capacity builds endurance and promotes mental and emotional recovery. Weight training is best for building physical capacity, particularly because the body oscillates between energy expenditure and recovery. Rituals, such as the tennis player staring at the racquet strings between points, help control the oscillation.

Level 2: Emotional Capacity. Building your emotional capacity creates the internal climate that drives the Ideal Performance State. Positive emotions such as feeling calm, challenged, and confident ignite the energy that drives high performance. Rituals to prevent negative emotions from interfering with emotional capacity include consciously relaxing your facial muscles and listening to music. The desired oscillation is to alternate between feeling emotionally charged and relaxed.

Level 3: Mental Capacity. Developing your mental capacity enables you to focus physical and emotional energy on the task at hand. Mental capacity includes cognitive skills such as focus, time management, and positive critical-thinking skills. Meditation is an effective ritual for quieting the mind, and shifting mental activity from the left brain (logical thinking) to the right brain (emotional and creative thinking). Alternating between stress and renewal brings about the oscillation needed to build mental capacity.

Level 4: Spiritual Capacity. Developing your spiritual capacity provides a powerful source of motivation, determination, and resilience. Spiritual capacity refers to the energy that is unleashed by tapping into your deepest values and pinpointing a strong sense of purpose. Connecting to an important value, such as caring for less fortunate people, can be a strong motivator. Examples of rituals that give a person a chance to pause and look within the self include meditation, keeping a diary, prayer, and service to others.

In short, you can facilitate career success by enhancing your physical, emotional, mental, and spiritual capacities that make up the high-performance pyramid. You need to develop routines and rituals to achieve success at each level.

Develop Depth and Breadth
A continuing concern about career management is whether to acquire substantial depth in a specialty or to obtain broader experience. Is it better to be a specialist or a generalist? In general, it pays to have good depth in one area of expertise yet also acquire broad experience. A distribution specialist who helped set up shipping systems in an automobile supply company, an office supply company, and a hospital supply company would have excellent credentials. Yet some career specialists would argue that knowing one industry well has its merits.

If your goal is to become an executive, broadening your experience is a career enhancer. A person who has held positions in sales and manufacturing would have broad experience. Breadth could also come about by experience in different industries, such as retailing and mining, or by holding positions in different companies. Being assigned to different teams, projects, and committees is another natural broadening experience. Conducting a job search within your company can often lead to a broadening experience, such as working with marketing people after having worked primarily with accountants. Another approach to broadening is to self-study different aspects of the business.

Rely on a Network of Successful People

Networking has already been described as a major assist in finding a job. Members of your network can also help you by advising you with difficult job problems, providing emotional support, buying your products or services, and offering you good prices on their products or services. The starting point in networking is to obtain an ample supply of business cards. You then give a card to any person you meet who might be able to help you now or in the future. As the recognition of the importance of networking for career advancement and career finding continues to grow, new suggestions emerge. One such suggestion is to hold brunch or dinner parties at your home, and invite an interesting cross section of guests.[21]

When first developing your network, be inclusive. Sandy Vilas says, "Remember the three-foot rule—anyone within three feet of you is someone you can network with."[22] Later, as your network develops, you can strive to include a greater number of influential and successful people. One reason that playing golf persists as a networking technique is that so many influential and successful people play golf.

Skill-Building Exercise 15-5 provides suggestions for systematically building your network.

Skill-Building Exercise 15-5

BUILDING YOUR NETWORK

From a career standpoint, networking involves developing a list of personal contacts who can help you achieve goals, and to whom you offer something of value in exchange.

Networking is a career-long process, but the time to begin is now. Quite often the people who have been in your network the longest become your most valuable contacts. To begin networking, or to systematize the networking you are now doing, implement the following steps:

Step 1: Write down the type of assistance you are seeking for the next several months. Perhaps you need leads for a job, advice about getting ahead in your industry, or help with a difficult computer problem.

Step 2: List all the people who might be able to provide you the assistance you need. Among them might be fellow students, former employers, neighbours, and faculty members. Prepare a contact card, or database entry, for each person on your list as if they were sales prospects. Include relevant details such as name, position, major, email address, phone numbers, postal address, and favourite pastimes. (Setting up a table with a word processor would work quite well for the list and entries.)

Step 3: Identify an action step for making contact with the potential network members. Quite often the initial contact will be by email. Gently mention that you would enjoy a telephone conversation or face-to-face meeting if it fits the contact's interest and schedule. You might also be able to think of creative ways to make the initial contact in person, such as attending professional meetings, or talking to a neighbour while he or she is washing a car or doing yard work.

(Continued)

Step 4: Identify how you might be able to help each person in your contact list, or how you can reciprocate. For example, if a marketing person gives you an idea for a job lead, you can become part of his or her company's *guerrilla marketing team* (you say nice things about the company product to friends and in public, or use the product in public). Sometimes the best approach is to ask the person who becomes part of your network what you can do to reciprocate.

Step 5: Maintain a log of all the contacts you make, and what took place, such as an agreed-upon face-to-face meeting, or specific assistance received. Indicate how you responded to the assistance, such as "I visited my contact's company website, went to the career section, and included her name as a person who is familiar with my work." Write down carefully your plans for reciprocity. Make a checklist as to whether you remembered to thank the person for any courtesy he or she extended to you.

Step 6: Update your log weekly, even if the activity requires only a few minutes of your attention. A network of helpers is a dynamic list, with people entering and exiting your network frequently. Each week ask yourself, "Whom can I add to my network this week?"

Work with a Mentor

In Chapter 10, mentoring was presented as a way of helping people grow and develop. Mention was also made that minority group members who advanced in their careers often attributed some of their success to mentors. We emphasize again here that having a mentor can facilitate career advancement. Ideally, a person should develop a small network of mentors who give advice and counsel on different topics, such as job advancement opportunities and how to solve a difficult problem.

Many people who receive exceptional promotions within their own firms, or excellent job offers from other companies, have in fact been chosen by their mentors. At the root of the successful protégé experience is the ability to attract and build a relationship with a person who is more experienced and talented than you.

The Job-Oriented Interpersonal Skills in Action box describes a successful business person who relies heavily on both networking and mentoring to advance his career.

Find a Good Person–Organization Fit

Assuming that you have the luxury of selecting among different prospective employers, it is best to work for a company where your personality and style fit the organizational culture. As implied at several places in the text, an **organization culture** is a system of shared values and beliefs that influence worker behaviour. You have to study the culture through observation and questioning to understand its nature. A good starting point is to ask, "In order to succeed, what is really expected of workers?" You might find out, for example, that pleasing customers and being honest is the path to success.

A **person–organization fit** is the degree of compatibility of the individual and the organization. Job interviews represent a good opportunity for evaluating a person–organization fit for both the applicant and the employer.[23] During a visit to the company to learn whether a culture tended to be formal or informal, you might observe the formality of the people and the emphasis on procedures such as a lengthy document to obtain a travel reimbursement.

The compatibility often centres on the extent to which a person's major work-related values and personality traits fit prominent elements of the organizational

Job-Oriented Interpersonal Skills in Action

HAMET WATT BUILDS RELATIONSHIPS TO STRENGTHEN HIS BUSINESS AND HELP OTHERS

Hamet Watt has always had a passion for entrepreneurship. He has held down a job since age 14 and has always pursued entrepreneurial activities. As an undergraduate at Florida A&M University in Tallahassee, Florida, Watt formed a company to move and store the furniture of other students over the summer. He also bought two single-family homes off campus and rented them to students.

A couple years after graduating, Watt became a partner in the North Carolina-based venture capital firm New Africa Opportunity Fund. There he helped many black- and minority-owned companies secure much-needed financing to start, grow, and sustain their businesses. Watt, age 32, makes it a point to support organizations that support black- and minority-owned businesses.

Watt says that a lack of capital and a lack of mentoring are two of the most challenging issues facing minority entrepreneurs who are trying to build successful companies. "It's surprisingly difficult to find mentors that have built successful businesses, especially technology-related businesses," says Watt. "I think mentorship is a key aspect of building a business."

Mentorship was important to Watt four years ago when he started NextMedium Inc., a company that provides information products and technology solutions to the entertainment and advertising industries and helps them respond to changes in the way people consume entertainment. The company helps those industries respond to the challenges brought on by personal recording devices and digital recording devices such as TIVO, which allows consumers to skip commercials. Watt knows he wouldn't have been able to help those industries had he not been diligent about creating relationships with people who have been valuable resources to his business. His goal is to help other business owners do the same thing.

As an entrepreneur, Watt joined the Marathon Club, an organization of minority entrepreneurs, investment professionals, executives, IT professionals, and support professionals (lawyers, accountants, consultants, etc.). Its members meet twice a year to discuss major issues tied to the creation of a strong, profitable, minority-owned business.

Through his entrepreneurial pursuits and having worked with professional organizations over the years, Watt has formed thousands of business relationships. "At the Marathon Club, the goal is to help entrepreneurs collaborate to build valuable businesses," explains Watt. "If you have people who are successful, they start other businesses and that breeds success in the community." Because he is well connected, Watt often helps businesses solve problems, or helps move them to the next level by simply picking up the phone.

Watt is excited about the future. The relationships he's built have helped him in the past and he knows they'll continue to be invaluable resources as he builds the company. NextMedium recently collaborated with Nielsen Media Research to launch the first product placement measurement service that tracks brand exposure in television shows. The collaboration was Watt's reaction to advertisers shifting away from passive advertising and moving toward more integrated messages in entertainment products, such as sending a brand's message during a television show or in a music video.

Questions

1. Why is networking so important for Watt's type of work?
2. What is your opinion of the ethics of embedding a product message into a television script or music video?

Source: Adaptation from Matthew S. Scott, "Connections for Business," November 2004, pp. 81–85. *Black Enterprise.* Reprinted with permission.

culture. Following this idea, a person who is adventuresome and a risk-taker would achieve highest performance and satisfaction in an organization in which adventurous behaviour and risk-taking are valued. Conversely, a methodical and conservative individual should join a slow-moving bureaucracy. How much an organization emphasizes individual effort versus teamwork is another important consideration in assessing person–organization fit. Workers who relish teamwork might fit better in a teamwork-oriented culture.

Person–organization fit can also include superficial aspects of behaviour such as physical appearance and dress. For example, a person who dresses like a Bay Street investment banker might not feel comfortable working in a high-tech firm where jeans and running shoes are standard work attire. As a consequence of not feeling comfortable in your work environment, you might not perform at your best. The consequences of a person fitting both the organization and the job have been systematically researched based on 25 studies. One of the conclusions reached was that commitment to the organization (a willingness to stay) was strongly associated with the person–organization fit. The study cautioned that it is not always easy for the job applicant to diagnose the fit in such areas as the conformance between the ethics of the individual and the company. When the topic arises, the hiring manager might be less than candid in explaining the company's true ethics.[24]

Take Sensible Risks

People who make it big in their careers usually take sensible risks on their journey to success. Among these risks might be working for a fledgling company that offers big promises but a modest starting salary, or taking an overseas assignment with no promise of a good position when you return. Purchasing stock in start-up companies is *sometimes* a sensible risk, if you do not absolutely need the funds for living expenses. Jorma Ollila, the top executive at cellphone and telecommunications giant Nokia, offers this perspective on risk-taking: "If you don't fail throughout your career at certain points, then you haven't stretched."[25]

Emphasize Relationships to Combat Being Outsourced

A major concern of many workers is that their job will be *outsourced* or *offshored* to a country where a competent worker will perform the same job at lower pay. As companies throughout the world struggle to stay competitive in a global economy, more and more jobs are outsourced. Call centre and information technology positions are the most frequently outsourced, but so are a variety of design work, some legal research, and medical diagnostic work. The positions least likely to be outsourced are those that require the physical presence of the worker, and that cannot easily be done remotely. Examples include nursing, real estate selling, teaching, funeral technician, massage therapist, and hair stylist. Managing people requires a physical presence, but not if your workers' positions have been outsourced.[26]

Another way to decrease the chance of your job being outsourced is to make relationship building a key part of your job, whether or not you are performing mostly technical work. A real estate agent with hundreds of personal contacts cannot be replaced by a website. And an information systems specialist who performs hands-on work with internal clients cannot be replaced by an IT specialist working 7000 miles away in another country.

In short, good interpersonal relationships will not only advance your career but also help you preserve your position through the turmoil of technological change.

SUMMARY

Recommended job-hunting tactics include the following:

1. Identify your job objectives.
2. Be aware of qualifications sought by employers.
3. Identify your skills and potential contribution.
4. Develop a comprehensive marketing strategy.
5. Use networking to reach company insiders.
6. Use job boards and the career sections of company websites.
7. Smile at network members and interviewers and be enthusiastic.
8. Smooth out the rough spots in your background.

Job hunting almost always requires a résumé, with two pages being the recommended length. A frequent requirement is to construct a résumé for an electronic database. Résumés should emphasize skills and accomplishments. A résumé should almost always be accompanied by a cover letter explaining how you can help the organization and why you are applying for this particular job.

Screening interviews, including computer-assisted ones, precede a full job interview. A general guide for performing well in an interview is to present a positive but accurate picture of yourself. More specific suggestions include the following:

1. Be prepared, look relaxed, and make the interviewer feel comfortable.
2. Establish a link between you and the employer.
3. Ask perceptive questions.
4. Be prepared to discuss your strengths and developmental opportunities.
5. Be prepared to respond to behavioural (examples of job behaviours) interview questions.
6. Show how you can help the employer.
7. Use body language that projects confidence and decisiveness.
8. Practise good etiquette during the interview, including during a meal.
9. Send a follow-up letter.

The vertical, or traditional, career path is based on the idea that a person continues to grow in responsibility, with the aim of reaching a target position, such as becoming a top-level manager. A vertical path is based on the traditional employment contract. A vertical career path should be related to the present and future demands of one firm or the industry. The horizontal career path is less predictable; it resembles a jungle gym rather than a ladder. A horizontal career path emphasizes lateral moves with an opportunity to gain more experience and increase job skills. A horizontal path is closely linked to the new employment contract that offers shared responsibility for career growth. Career paths should have contingency plans.

Improving interpersonal relationships assists career advancement. In addition, the following strategies and tactics are relevant:

1. Be passionate about your work.

2. Develop a code of professional ethics.

3. Develop a proactive personality.

4. Keep growing through continuous learning and self-development.

5. Document your accomplishments.

6. Project a professional image.

7. Perceive yourself as a provider of services.

8. Apply the high-performance pyramid (enhance your physical, emotional, mental, and spiritual capacities).

9. Develop depth and breadth.

10. Rely on a network of successful people.

11. Work with a mentor.

12. Find a good person–organization fit.

13. Take sensible risks.

14. Emphasize relationships to combat being outsourced.

An Interpersonal Relations Case Problem

WHY ISN'T MY RÉSUMÉ GETTING RESULTS?

Robbie Wentworth was working in the family business as a manufacturing technician while he attended career school. Although he got along well with his family members, Robbie wanted to find employment elsewhere so he could build a career on his own. Robbie's job objective was a position in industrial sales. He compiled a long list of prospective employers. He developed the list from personal contacts, classified ads in newspapers, and job openings posted on the internet. Robbie paper-clipped a business card with a brief handwritten note to each résumé. The note usually said something like, "Job sounds great. Let's schedule an interview at your convenience." The résumé is shown in the accompanying exhibit.

Six weeks after mailing out 200 résumés, Robbie still did not have an interview. He asked his uncle and mentor, the owner of the family business, "Why isn't my résumé getting results?"

Case Questions

1. What suggestions can you make to Robbie for improving his résumé? Or does it require improvement?

2. What is your evaluation of Robbie's approach to creating a cover letter?

(Continued)

Exhibit 1

RÉSUMÉ OF ROBBIE WENTWORTH

ROBBIE WENTWORTH
275 Birdwhistle Lane
Ottawa, Ontario K0B 2N2
(613) 555-7512 (Please call after 7 PM weekday nights)
Robbie@wentworth.com

Objective

Long-range goal is vice-president of sales of major corporation. For now, industrial sales representative paid by salary and commission.

Job Experience

Five years' experience in Wentworth Industries as manufacturing technician, tool-crib attendant, shipper, and floor sweeper. Voted "employee of the month" twice. Two years' experience in newspaper delivery business. Distributed newspapers door to door, responsible for accounts receivable and development of new business in my territory.

Education

Justin Peabody Career College, business administration major with manufacturing technology minor. Expect degree in June 2008. 65% average. Took courses in sales management and selling. Received a B+ in professional selling course.

Ottawa Heights High School, business and technology major, 2003–2007. Graduated 45th in class of 125. 82% average.

Skills and Talents

Good knowledge of manufacturing equipment; friends say I'm a born leader; have been offered supervisory position in Wentworth Industries; real go-getter.

References

OK to contact present employer except for my immediate supervisor Jill Baxter with whom I have a personality clash.

Interpersonal Skills Role Play

Helping Robbie with His Résumé

One student plays the role of a friend whom Robbie consults about his résumé. Robbie is quite proud of the résumé, and is looking for encouragement and support. The friend consulted, however, attempts to be objective and professional whenever he or she offers assistance. Run the role play for about eight minutes. Outsiders can judge if Robbie is on the road to being helped.

An Interpersonal Relations Case Problem

SAN DEEP WANTS THE FAST TRACK

At age 25, San Deep already had impressive leadership experience. She was the head of her Girl Guide pack at age 11, the president of the Asian Student Association in high school, and the captain of her soccer team both in high school and at university. She had also organized a food drive for homeless people in her hometown for three consecutive summers. So Deep believed these experiences, in addition to her formal education, were preparing her to be a corporate leader. At university, Deep majored in information systems and business administration.

Deep's first position in industry was a business analyst at a medium-sized consulting firm that helped clients implement large-scale systems such as enterprise software. She explained to her team leader at the outset that she wanted to be placed on a management track rather than a technical track, because she aspired to become a corporate executive. Deep's team leader explained, "San, I know you are in a hurry to get ahead. Lots of capable people are looking to climb the ladder. But you first have to build your career by proving that you are an outstanding analyst."

Deep thought, "It looks like the company may need a little convincing that I'm leadership material, so I'm going to dig in and perform like a star." And Deep did dig in, much to the pleasure of her clients, her team leader, and her co-workers. Her first few performance evaluations were outstanding, yet the company was still not ready to promote her to a team leader position. Deep's team leader explained, "Bob [the team leader's manager] and I both agree that you are doing an outstanding job, but promotions are hard to come by in our company these days. The company is shrinking more than expanding, so talks about promotion are a little futile right now."

Deep decided that it would take a long time to be promoted to team leader or manager in her present company, so she began to quietly look for a new position in her field. Her job hunt proceeded more swiftly than she anticipated. Through a sports club contact, Deep was granted a job interview with a partner in a larger consulting firm offering similar services. After a series of four interviews, Deep was hired as a senior business analyst, performing work on a system similar to the one she had been working with for two years. During her interviews, Deep emphasized her goals of occupying a leadership position as soon as the company believed that she was ready for such a role. Her first client assignment would be helping a team of consultants install a provincial sales tax call centre.

After a one-month-long orientation and training program, Deep was performing billable work for her new employer. At the outset, she reminded her new manager and team leader again that she preferred the managerial route to remaining in a technical position. After six months of hard work, Deep looked forward to her first formal performance evaluation. Deep's team leader informed her that her performance was better than average, but short of outstanding. Deep asked for an explanation of why her performance was not considered to be outstanding. She informed her team leader and manager, "I need an outstanding rating to help me achieve my goals of becoming a leader in our company."

The manager replied, "Our performance evaluations are based on your contribution to the company. We care much less about writing performance evaluations to help a senior business analyst reach her career goals. Besides, San, you've made your point enough about wanting to be a leader in our firm. Let your performance speak for itself."

That evening, Deep met with her fiancé Ryan to discuss her dilemma. "The problem, Ryan, is that they don't get it. I'm leadership material, and they don't see it yet. I'm performing well and letting my intentions be known, but my strategy isn't

(Continued)

working. The company is missing out on a golden opportunity by not putting me on a fast leadership track. I have to convince them of their error in judgment."

Ryan, a human resource specialist, replied, "I'm listening to you, and I want to give you good advice. Let me be objective here despite the fact that I love you. What have you done lately to prove to the company that you are leadership material?"

Case Questions

1. Who has the problem here? San Deep or the consulting firm in question?

2. What advice can you offer Deep to help her increase her chances of being promoted to a formal leadership position in the company?

3. What is your evaluation of the validity of the advice Ryan offered Deep?

QUESTIONS FOR DISCUSSION AND REVIEW

1. Identify four situations in a career in which conducting a job campaign would be necessary.

2. Why do many employers look for signs of emotional intelligence when hiring candidates for professional-level positions?

3. During a labour shortage (when there are more positions open than qualified applicants), why is it still important to have good job search skills?

4. What is your evaluation of the effectiveness of a job hunter using the internet as his or her only method of finding a job?

5. Why is a vertical career path still the dream of so many workers?

6. Give an example from your own life in which you behaved as if you were a proactive personality.

7. In what way do political tactics assist career advancement?

8. How might a person use a webcam to help build and sustain a network?

9. Log on to your Research Navigator and scroll down to the Link Library. Using "search by subject" scroll down to Mgt-HR Management and select "go." Choose "I" and click on "Interviewing". From the various interviewing topics, select a topic and then an article. Share your findings, comparing them to the information in this chapter. How might this information help you in preparing for a job interview?

10. What is the most useful idea you picked up from this chapter, either about conducting a job campaign or managing your career?

WEBLINKS

www.cacee.com
Run by the Canadian Association of Career Educators and Employers, this site is an online version of a campus career centre.

www.workopolis.com
A great website for jobs and job hunting tips, including writing résumés.

www.truecareers.com
Advice on a range of topics including employment interview preparation and following up on leads. While some material is free, many services require a fee.

www.jobhuntersbible.com
Career guru Dick Bolles guides career changers and suggests actions to take after they have exhausted internet job sites.

www.vault.com
Wealth of information about career advancement, job finding, and occupational profiles.

Glossary

action plan A series of steps designed to achieve a goal.

active listener A person who listens intently, with the goal of empathizing with the speaker.

aggressive personality A person who verbally, and sometimes physically, frequently attacks others.

alternative dispute resolution A formalized type of mediation, usually involving a hired professional who mediates a conflict between two or more parties.

assertiveness Forthrightness in expressing demands, opinions, feelings, and attitudes.

behaviour modification An attempt to change behaviour by manipulating rewards and punishments.

behavioural feedback Information given to another person that pinpoints behaviour rather than personal characteristics or attitudes.

bias A prejudgment about something, not usually based on fact.

brainstorming A group problem-solving technique that promotes creativity by encouraging idea generation through non-critical discussion.

brainwriting Brainstorming by individuals working alone.

burnout A condition of emotional, mental, and physical exhaustion in response to long-term stressors.

business etiquette A special code of behaviour required in work situations.

career path A sequence of positions necessary to achieve a goal.

carpal tunnel syndrome A condition that occurs when repetitive flexing and extending of the wrist cause the tendons to swell, thus trapping and pinching the median nerve.

casual time orientation A cultural characteristic in which people view time as an unlimited and unending resource and therefore tend to be patient.

character trait An enduring, consistently exhibited characteristic of a person that is related to moral and ethical behaviour.

charisma A special quality of leaders whose purposes, powers, and extraordinary determination differentiate them from others. (However, people other than leaders can be charismatic.)

coaching A method of helping workers grow and develop and improve their job competence by providing suggestions and encouragement.

cognition The mental process or faculty by which knowledge is gathered.

cognitive factors The collective term for problem-solving and intellectual skills.

cognitive restructuring Mentally converting negative aspects into positive ones by looking for the positive elements in a situation.

cognitive style Mental processes used to perceive and make judgments from situations.

collectivism A belief that the group and society should receive top priority, rather than the individual.

communication The sending, receiving, and understanding of messages.

compromise Settlement of differences by mutual concessions.

concern for others An emphasis on personal relationships and a concern for the welfare of others.

conflict A situation in which two or more goals, values, or events are incompatible or mutually exclusive.

conflict of interest A situation that occurs when a person's judgment or objectivity is compromised.

consensus General acceptance by the group of a decision.

crew A group of specialists, each of whom have specific roles, who perform brief events that are closely synchronized with each other, and repeat these events under different environmental conditions.

cross-functional team A work group composed of workers from different specialties.

cultural fluency The ability to conduct business in a diverse, international environment.

cultural intelligence (CQ) An outsider's ability to interpret someone's unfamiliar and ambiguous behaviour the same way that person's compatriots would.

cultural sensitivity An awareness of, and a willingness to investigate, the reasons why people of another culture act as they do.

cultural training A set of learning experiences designed to help employees understand the customs, traditions, and beliefs of another culture.

customer relationship management (CRM) Software packages that enhance customer relations for a business.

cycle-of-service chart A method of tracking the moments of truth with respect to customer service.

defensive communication The tendency to receive messages in such a way that self-esteem is protected.

defining moment A time when one must choose between two or more ideals in which one deeply believes.

denial The suppression of information a person finds uncomfortable.

developmental need A specific area in which a person needs to change or improve.

difficult person An individual who creates problems for others, even though he or she has the skill and mental ability to do otherwise.

disability A physical or mental condition that substantially limits an individual's major life activities.

effort-to-performance expectancy The probability assigned by the individual that effort will lead to performing the task correctly.

electronic brainstorming Method of generating ideas with the aid of a computer. Group members simultaneously and anonymously enter their suggestions into a computer, and the ideas are distributed to the monitors of other group members.

emotional intelligence Qualities such as understanding one's own feelings, empathy for others, and the regulation of emotion to one's own benefit.

empathy In communication, imagining oneself in the receiver's role, and assuming the viewpoints and emotions of that individual.

empowerment The process of managers transferring, or sharing, power with lower-ranking employees.

EQ Shortened term which refers to emotional intelligence, or emotional intelligence quotient, assessed by a variety of tests.

ethical screening Running a contemplated decision or action through an ethics test.

ethics The moral choices a person makes.

expectancy theory A motivation theory based on the premise that the effort people expend depends on the reward they expect to receive in return.

extinction Decreasing the frequency of undesirable behaviour by removing the desirable consequence of such behaviour.

feedback In communication, messages sent back from the receiver to the sender.

fight-or-flight response The body's physiological and chemical battle against a stressor, in which the person either tries to cope with the adversity head-on or tries to flee from the scene.

formality A cultural characteristic of attaching considerable importance to tradition, ceremony, social rules, and rank.

frame of reference A person's individual vantage point that causes him or her to perceive words and concepts differently.

freeze-frame technique A scientifically based method of stress reduction that emphasizes reappraising a difficult event, along with some symptom management.

g (general) factor A factor in intelligence that contributes to the ability to perform well in many tasks.

group decision-making The process of reaching a judgment based on feedback from more than one individual.

group norms The unwritten set of expectations for group members.

groupthink A deterioration of mental efficiency, reality testing, and moral judgment in the interest of group solidarity.

groupware Technology designed to facilitate the work of groups.

high-context culture A culture that makes extensive use of body language.

impression management A set of behaviours directed at improving one's image by drawing attention to oneself.

incivility In human relations, employees' lack of regard for each other.

individual differences Variations in how people respond to the same situation based on personal characteristics.

individualism A mental set in which people see themselves first as individuals and believe that their own interests take priority.

informal learning The acquisition of knowledge and skills that takes place naturally outside a structured learning environment.

informality A cultural characteristic of a casual attitude toward tradition, ceremony, social rules, and rank.

intelligence The capacity to acquire and apply knowledge, including solving problems.

intermittent reward A reward that is given for good performance occasionally, but not always.

internal customers The people within an individual's own company for whom the person performs a service in the course of doing his or her job.

interpersonal relations The technical term for relationships with people.

interpersonal skills training The teaching of skills in dealing with others.

intuition An experience-based way of knowing or reasoning in which the weighing and balancing of evidence are done automatically.

law of effect Behaviour that leads to a positive consequence for the individual tends to be repeated, whereas behaviour that leads to a negative consequence tends not to be repeated.

leadership The ability to inspire support and confidence among the people who are needed to achieve common goals.

learning style The way in which a person best learns new information.

materialism An emphasis on assertiveness and the acquisition of money and material objects.

mediation A type of conflict resolution whereby the two conflicting parties appeal to a third party to aid in arriving at a mutually satisfactory solution.

mediator A person who has usually received special training in helping two (or more) conflicting parties arrive at a resolution that satisfies the needs of both parties.

mentor An individual with advanced experience and knowledge who is committed to giving support and career advice to a less experienced person.

message A purpose or idea to be conveyed.

metacommunicate To communicate about your communication, to help overcome barriers or resolve a problem.

microinequity A small, semiconscious message we send with a powerful impact on the receiver.

micromanager One who closely monitors most aspects of group members' activities, sometimes to the point of being a control freak.

mirroring Subtly imitating someone.

moment of truth Situation in which a customer comes in contact with a company and forms an impression of its service.

moral intensity In ethical decision-making, how deeply others might be affected by the decision.

motivation An internal state that leads to effort expended toward objectives; an activity performed by one person to get another to accomplish work.

motivational state Any active needs and interests operating at a given time.

multiple intelligences A theory of intelligence contending that people know and understand the world in distinctly different ways and learn in different ways.

negative affectivity A tendency to experience aversive emotional states.

negative reinforcement (avoidance motivation) Rewarding people by taking away an uncomfortable consequence of their behaviour.

negotiating Conferring with another person to resolve a problem.

networking Developing contacts with influential people, including gaining their trust and confidence.

noise Anything that disrupts communication, including the attitudes and emotions of the receiver.

nominal group technique (NGT) A group problem-solving technique that calls people together in a structured meeting with limited interaction.

nonverbal communication The transmission of messages through means other than words.

nurturing person One who promotes the growth of others.

organization culture A system of shared values and beliefs that influence worker behaviour.

organizational citizenship behaviour The willingness to go beyond one's job description.

organizational politics Interpersonal relations in the workplace by which power is gained or held through any means other than merit or luck.

participative leadership Sharing authority with the group.

perceived control The belief that an individual has at his or her disposal a response that can control the negative aspects of an event.

performance-to-outcome expectancy The probability assigned by the individual that performance will lead to outcomes or rewards.

personal productivity A measure of a worker's output in relation to the resources, including time, that he or she consumes to achieve it.

personality Persistent and enduring behaviour patterns that tend to be expressed in a wide variety of situations.

personality clash An antagonistic relationship between two people based on differences in personal attributes, preferences, interests, values, and styles.

person–organization fit The compatibility of the individual and the organization.

person–role conflict The situation that occurs when the demands made by the organization clash with the basic values of the individual.

positive gossip Unofficial information that does not attack others, is based on truth, and does not leak confidential information.

positive reinforcement An attempt to increase the probability that behaviour will be repeated by rewarding people for making the desired response.

power The ability or potential to control anything of value and to influence decisions.

proactive personality A person who is relatively unconstrained by situational forces and who brings about environmental change.

procrastination Delaying action for no good reason.

protégé The less experienced person in a mentoring relationship who is helped by the mentor.

Pygmalion effect The phenomenon that people will rise (or fall) to the expectations that another person has of them.

role ambiguity A condition in which a job holder is faced with confusing or poorly defined expectations.

role conflict The situation that occurs when a person has to choose between two competing demands or expectations.

role overload Having too much work to do.

***s* (special) factors** Specific components of intelligence that contribute to problem-solving ability.

self-efficacy Confidence in one's ability to carry out a specific task.

self-managing work team A small group of employees responsible for managing and performing technical tasks to deliver a product or service to an external or internal customer.

sexual harassment Unwanted sexually oriented behaviour in the workplace that results in discomfort and/or interference with the job.

social loafing Shirking individual responsibility in a group setting.

stress An adaptive response that is the consequence of any action, situation, or event that places special demands on a person.

stressor The external or internal force that brings about stress.

summarization The process of summarizing, pulling together, condensing, and thereby clarifying the main points communicated by another person.

support network A group of people who can listen to your problems and provide emotional support.

synergy A situation in which the group's total output exceeds the sum of each individual's contribution.

team A small number of people with complementary skills who are committed to a common purpose, set of performance goals, and approach for which they hold themselves mutually accountable.

toxic person One who dwells exclusively on the failings of others and whose pessimistic behaviours undermine the group.

training The process of helping others acquire a job-related skill.

triarchic theory of intelligence An explanation of mental ability, holding that intelligence is composed of three different subtypes: analytical, creative, and practical.

Type A behaviour A behaviour pattern in which the individual is demanding, impatient, and over-striving, and therefore prone to negative stress.

universal training need An area for improvement common to most people.

urgent time orientation A cultural trait of perceiving time as a scarce resource, characterized by impatience.

valence The value, worth, or attractiveness of an outcome.

value The importance a person attaches to something.

virtual office A place of work without a fixed physical location, where the output is communicated electronically.

virtual team A small group of people that conducts almost all of its collaborative work by electronic communication rather than face-to-face meetings.

win–win The belief that after conflict has been resolved, both sides should gain something of value.

workaholism An addiction to work in which not working is an uncomfortable experience.

work–family conflict A state that occurs when an individual's role as a worker clashes with his or her role as an active participant in social and family life.

Notes

Chapter 1

1. *Dale Carnegie Training* brochure, Spring–Summer 2005, p. 12.

2. Joanne Lozar Glenn, "Lessons in Human Relations," *Business Education Forum,* October 2003, p. 10.

3. Research cited in Bob Wall, *Working Relationships: The Simple Truth About Getting Along with Friends and Foes at Work* (Palo Alto, CA: Davies-Black, 1999).

4. George B. Yancey, Chante P. Clarkson, Julie D. Baxa, and Rachel N. Clarkson, "Example of Good and Bad Interpersonal Skills at Work," *http://www.psichi.org/pubs/articles/article_368.asp*, p. 2, accessed February 2, 2004.

5. The model presented here is an extension of the one presented in Thomas V. Bonoma and Gerald Zaltman, *Psychology for Management* (Boston: Kent, 1981), pp. 88–92.

6. Gary P. Latham, "The Motivational Benefits of Goal-Setting," *Academy of Management Executive,* November 2004, pp. 126–127.

7. Roger B. Hill, "On-Line Instructional Resources—Lesson 3, Interpersonal Skills," *http://www.coe.uga.edu/~rhill/workethic/less3.htm*, p. 1, accessed March 17, 2005.

8. Nancy Day, "Informal Learning Gets Results," *Workforce,* June 1998, pp. 30–36; Marcia L. Conner, "Informal Learning," *Ageless Learner,* 1997–2005, *http://agelesslearner.com/intros/informal.html*, p. 2.

9. Morgan W. McCall, Jr., *High Flyers: Developing the Next Generation of Leaders* (Boston: Harvard Business School Press, 1998).

Chapter 2

1. Such is the theme of Kevin R. Murphy, *Individual Differences and Behavior in Organizations* (San Francisco: Jossey-Bass, 1996).

2. J. Madeline Nash, "The Personality Genes," *Time,* April 27, 1998, pp. 60–61; Dean Hamer, *Living with Our Genes* (New York: Doubleday, 1998).

3. Marvin Zuckerman, "Are You a Risk Taker?" *Psychology Today,* November/December 2000, p. 53.

4. Remus Ilies and Timothy A. Judge, "On the Heritability of Job Satisfaction: The Mediating Role of Personality," *Journal of Applied Psychology,* August 2003, pp. 750–759.

5. Robert R. McRae and Juri Allik, eds., *The Five-Factor Model of Personality Across Cultures.* New York: Kluwer, 2002.

6. Roger R. McRae and Paul T. Costa, Jr., "Personality Trait Structure as Human Universal," *American Psychologist,* May 1997, pp. 509–516.

7. Lawrence R. James and Michelle D. Mazerolle, *Personality in Work Organizations* (Thousand Oaks, CA: Sage, 2002).

8. "Which Traits Predict Job Performance?" *APA Help Center,* *http://www.apahelpcenter.org/articles/article.php?id533*, accessed March 22, 2005.

9. Gregory M. Hurtz and John J. Donovan, "Personality and Job Performance: The Big Five Revisited," *Journal of Applied Psychology,* December 2000, pp. 869–879.

10. David V. Day, Deidra J. Scheleicher, Amy L. Unckless, and Nathan J. Hiller, "Self-Monitoring Personality at Work: A Meta-Analytic Investigation of Construct Validity," *Journal of Applied Psychology,* April 2002, pp. 390–401.

11. Gerald L. Blakely, Martha C. Andrews, and Jack Fuller, "Are Chameleons Good Citizens? A Longitudinal Study of the Relationship Between Self-Monitoring and Organizational Citizenship Behavior," *Journal of Business and Psychology,* Winter 2003, pp. 131–144.

12. L. A. Witt, Lisa A. Burke, Murray R. Barrick, and Michael K. Mount, "The Interactive Effects of Conscientiousness and Agreeableness on Job Performance," *Journal of Applied Psychology,* February 2002, pp. 164–169;

13. Carl J. Thoresen, Jill C. Bradley, Paul D. Bliese, and Joseph D. Thoresen, "The Big Five Personality Traits and Individual Job Performance Growth Trajectories in Maintenance and Transitional Job Stages," *Journal of Applied Psychology,* October 2004, pp. 835–853.

14. L. A. Burke and L. A. Witt, "Personality and High-Maintenance Employee Behavior," *Journal of Business and Psychology,* Spring 2004, pp. 349–363.

15. Cited in David Stipp, "A Little Worry Is Good for Business," *Fortune,* November 24, 2003, p. 68.

16. The Myers-Briggs Type Indicator (MBTI) is published by Consulting Psychological Press Inc., Palo Alto, CA 94306. Much of the discussion here is based on Robert P. Vecchio, *Organizational Behavior: Core Concepts,* 4th ed. (Fort Worth,

TX: Dryden Press, 2000), pp. 44–45; Douglas P. Shuit, "Happy Birthday, Myers-Briggs," *Workforce Management,* December 2003, pp. 72–74.

17. An example of this research is John W. Slocum and Donald Hellriegel, "A Look at How Managers' Minds Work," *Business Horizons,* vol. 26, 1983, pp. 58–68.

18. Brian S. Young, Winfred Arthur, Jr., and John Finch, "Predictors of Managerial Performance: More than Cognitive Ability," *Journal of Business and Psychology,* Fall 2000, pp. 53–72.

19. Robert J. Sternberg, *Beyond IQ: A Triarchic Theory of Human Intelligence* (New York: Cambridge University Press, 1985); Bridget Murray, "Sparking Interest in Psychology Class," *APA Monitor,* October 1995, p. 51.

20. Howard Gardner, *Leading Minds: An Anatomy of Leadership* (New York: Basic Books, 1996); www.funderstanding.com/multipleint.htm.

21. Daniel Goleman, "What Makes a Leader?" *Harvard Business Review,* November–December 1998, p. 95; Bridget Murray, "Does 'Emotional Intelligence' Matter in the Workplace?" *APA Monitor,* July 1998, p. 21.

22. David C. McClelland, "How Motives, Skills, and Values Determine What People Do," *American Psychologist,* July 1985, p. 815.

23. John B. Miner, *Organizational Behavior: Performance and Productivity* (New York: Random House, 1988), p. 83.

Chapter 3

1. Ritch Sorenson, Grace DeBord, and Ida Ramirez, *Business and Management Communication: A Guide Book,* 4th ed. (Upper Saddle River, NJ: Prentice Hall, 2001), pp. 6–10.

2. Albert Mehrabian and M. Weiner, "Decoding of Inconsistent Communications," *Journal of Personality and Social Psychology,* 6, 1967, pp. 109–114.

3. Sue Morem, "Nonverbal Communication Help for Salespeople," *http://www.careerknowhow/com/ask_sue/nonverbal.htm.*

4. R. B. Zajonc and D. N. McIntosh, "Emotions Research: Some Promising Questions and Some Questionable Promises," *Psychological Science,* 3, 1992, pp. 70–74.

5. Jeffrey Jacobi, *The Vocal Advantage* (Upper Saddle River, N.J.: Prentice Hall, 1996).

6. Roberta H. Krapels and Vanessa D. Arnold, "Speaker Credibility in Persuasive Work Situations," *Business Education Forum,* December 1997, p. 25.

7. Amie Parnes, "Formal Business Dress Coming Back: Dot-com Casual Wears Off," *The New York Times* syndicated story, June 17, 2001.

8. Mark Henricks, "Can We Talk? Speaking Up About the Value of Dialogue," *Entrepreneur,* January 1998, p. 82.

9. Sharon Lund O'Neil, "An Empowered Attitude Can Enhance Communication Skills," *Business Education Forum,* April, 1998, pp. 28–30.

10. Jimmy Calano and Jeff Salzman, "Persuasiveness: Make It Your Power Booster," *Working Woman,* October 1988, pp. 124–125; Krapels and Arnold, "Speaker Credibility," pp. 24–26; Gayle Theiss, "Say It Smart," *Aspire,* November–December 1998, pp. 3–4.

11. Jean Mausehund and R. Neil Dortch, "Communications— Presentation Skills in the Digital Age," *Business Education Forum,* April 1999, pp. 30–32.

12. For more details, see Brian Fugere, Chelsea Hardaway, and Jon Warshawsky, *Why Business People Speak Like Idiots* (New York: Free Press, 2005).

13. The information in this section is from Holly Weeks, "Taking the Stress Out of Stressful Conversations," *Harvard Business Review,* July–August 2001, pp. 112–119. The quote is from page 117.

14. Deborah Tannen, *Talking from 9 to 5* (New York: William Morrow, 1994); Tannen, *You Just Don't Understand* (New York: Ballantine, 1990); John Gray, *Men Are from Mars, Women Are from Venus* (New York: HarperCollins, 1992).

15. Cited in Kris Maher, "The Jungle: Focus on Recruitment, Pay and Getting Ahead," *The Wall Street Journal,* October 19, 2004, p. B10.

16. Deborah S. Roberts, "Communication + Stress = Breakdown," *Dartnell's Communication at Work,* sample issue, undated.

Chapter 4

1. Michael Mercer, *Absolutely Fabulous Organizational Change* (Castlegate Publishers, 2000); Duncan Maxwell Anderson (ed.), "Hidden Forces," *Success,* April 1995, p. 1.

2. Conference Board report cited in "CEO Leadership Skips Teamwork, Article Says," Rochester, New York, *Democrat and Chronicle,* February 17, 2002, p. 1E.

3. Jon R. Katzenbach and Douglas K. Smith, "The Discipline of Teams," *Harvard Business Review,* March–April 1993, p. 112.

4. Deal E. Yeatts and Cloyd Hyten, *High Performing Self-Managed Work Teams: A Comparison of Theory and Practice* (Thousand Oaks, Calif.: Sage, 1998), p. xiii.

5. Rudy M. Yandrick, "A Team Effort," *HR Magazine,* June 2001, p. 138.

6. Claus W. Langfred, "Too Much Trust a Good Thing? Negative Effects of High Trust and Individual Autonomy

in Self-Managing Teams," *Academy of Management Journal,* June 2004, pp. 385–399.

7. "Shepherding Communications When the Flock Is Scattered," *Flexible Workplace Management,* sample issue, 2001.

8. Shelia Simsarian Webber and Richard J. Klimoski, "Crews: A Distinct Type of Work Team," *Journal of Business and Psychology,* Spring 2004, pp. 261–279.

9. K. Mark, "All in One Go," *Canadian Business* (Special Technology Issue), Spring 1994, pp. 39–43; Celine Bak, Lessons from the Veterans of TQM," *Canadian Business Review,* Winter 1992, pp. 17–20.

10. "When Committees Spell Trouble: Don't let Individuals Hide Within a Group," *WorkingSMART,* August 1998, p. 1.

11. Irving L. Janus, *Victims of Groupthink: A Psychological Study of Foreign Policy Decisions and Fiascos* (Boston: Houghton Mifflin, 1972); Glen Whyte, "Groupthink Reconsidered," *Academy of Management Review,* January 1989, pp. 40–56.

12. Martha A. Peak, "Treating Trauma in Teamland," *Management Review,* September 1997, p. 1.

13. "R. Meredith Belbin," in *Business: The Ultimate Resource* (Cambridge, MA: Perseus, 2002), pp. 966–967; Belbin, *Management Teams* (London: Elsevier Butterworth-Heinemann, 2003); Belbin® Team-Roles, *http://www.belbin.com/belbin-teamroles.htm.*

14. From a review of Meredith Belbin, *Management Teams,* by Colin Thomson appearing in *http:// www.accounting-web. co.uk.,* accessed April 14, 2004.

15. "Fly in Formation: Easy Ways to Build Team Spirit," *WorkingSMART,* March 2000, p. 6.

16. Pamela Lovell, "Healthy Teams Display Strong Vital Signs," *Teamwork,* sample issue, the Dartnell Corporation, 1997.

17. Glenn M. Parker, *Cross-Functional Teams: Working with Allies, Enemies, & Other Strangers* (San Francisco: Jossey-Bass, 1994), p. 170.

18. Mary J. Waller et al., "The Effect of Individual Perceptions of Deadlines on Team Performance," *Academy of Management Review,* October 2001, p. 597.

19. Mark G. Ehrhant and Stefanie E. Naumann, "Organizational Citizenship Behavior in Work Groups: A Group Norms Approach," *Journal of Applied Psychology,* December 2004, pp. 960–974.

Chapter 5

1. "Spacecraft Will Examine Mars in Greater Detail than Ever Before," *http://mars.jpl.nasa.gov/mro/spotlight/2004706.html,* accessed July 6, 2004.

2. Andrew E. Schwartz and Joy Levin, "Better Group Decision Making," *Supervisory Management,* June 1990, p. 4.

3. Kay Lovelace, Debra L. Shapiro, and Laurie R. Weingart, "Minimizing Cross-Functional New Product Teams' Innovativeness and Constraint Adherence: A Conflict Communications Perspective," *Academy of Management Journal,* August 2001, pp. 779–793.

4. David A. Garvin and Michael A. Roberto, "What You Don't Know About Making Decisions," *Harvard Business Review,* September 2001, pp. 110–111.

5. "Future Edisons of America: Turn Your Employees Into Inventors," *WorkingSMART,* June 2000, p. 2.

6. R. Brente Gallupe, William H. Cooper, Mary-Liz Grise, and Lana M. Bastianutti, "Blocking Electronic Brainstorms," *Journal of Applied Psychology,* February 1994, pp. 77–78.

7. R. Brent Gallupe and Associates, "Electronic Brainstorming and Group Size," *Academy of Management Journal,* June1992, p. 352; R. Brent Galuppe, Lana M. Bastianutti, and William H. Cooper, "Unblocking Brainstorms," *Journal of Applied Psychology,* February 1991, pp. 137–142.

8. Keng L. Siau, "Electronic Brainstorming," *Innovative Leader,* April 1997, p. 3.

9. Allen C. Bluedorn, Daniel B. Turban, and Mary Sue Love, "The Effects of Stand-Up and Sit-Down Meeting Formats on Meeting Outcomes," *Journal of Applied Psychology,* April 1999, pp. 277–285.

10. Howard Baker, "Promoting Interaction and Teamwork with Electronic Mail," *Business Education Forum,* October 1994, pp. 30–31.

11. "Introduction to Groupware," www.usabilityfirst.com/groupware/intro.html. Accessed June 3, 1999.

Chapter 6

1. Joan Crockett, "Winning Competitive Advantage Through a Diverse Workforce," *HRfocus,* May 1999, p. 9.

2. Arvind V. Phatak, *International Dimensions of Management* (Boston: Kent, 1983), p. 167.

3. P. Christopher Earley and Elaine Mosakowski, "Cultural Intelligence," *Harvard Business Review,* October 2004, p. 140. The example is from the same source, same page.

4. Earley and Mosakowski, "Toward Culture Intelligence: Turning Cultural Differences into a Workplace Advantage," *Academy of Management Executive,* August 2004, pp. 154–155.

5. Scott B. Button, "Organizational Efforts to Affirm Sexual Diversity: A Cross-Level Examination," *Journal of Applied Psychology,* February 2001, pp. 17–28.

6. Charlene Marmer Solomon, "Global Operations Demand That HR Rethink Diversity," *Personnel Journal,* July 1994, p. 50.

7. Geert Hofstede, *Culture's Consequences: International Differences in Work Related Values* (Beverly Hills, Calif.: Sage,

1980); updated and expanded in "A Conversation with Geert Hofstede," *Organizational Dynamics,* Spring 1993, pp. 53–61; Jim Kennedy and Anna Everest, "Put Diversity in Context," *Personnel Journal,* September 1991, pp. 50–54.

8. Lee Gardenswartz and Anita Rowe, "Cross-Cultural Awareness," *HR Magazine,* March 2001, p. 139.

9. Rick Borelli, "A Worldwide Language Trap," *Management Review,* October 1997, pp. 52–54.

10. Darren Fonda, "Selling in Tongues," *Time,* November 26, 2001, pp. B12–B13.

11. Catherine Beaulieu, "Intercultural Study of Personal Space," *Journal of Applied Social Psychology,* (34) 4, pp. 794–805.

12. Roger E. Axtell, *Gestures: The Do's and Taboos of Body Language Around the World* (New York: Wiley, 1990).

13. Siri Carpenter, "Why Do 'They All Look Alike'?" *Monitor on Psychology,* December 2000, p. 44.

14. "Let Down by the System," *Canada and the World Backgrounder,* April 1996, pp. 18–22.

15. Christopher Guly, "Banking on Aboriginal Entrepreneurs," *Canadian Banker,* November/December 1998, pp. 17–23.

16. Orlando C. Richard, "Racial Diversity: Business Strategy, and Firm Performance: A Resource-Based View," *Academy of Management Journal,* April 2000, pp. 164–177.

17. "Diversity: A `New' Tool for Retention," *HRfocus,* June 2000, pp. 1, 14–15.

18. Mei Fong, "Chinese Charm School," *The Wall Street Journal,* January 13, 2004, p. B1.

19. P. Christopher Earley and Randall S. Peterson, "The Elusive Cultural Chameleon: Cultural Intelligence as a New Approach to Intercultural Training for the Global Manager," *Academy of Management Learning and Education,* March 2004, p. 106.

Chapter 7

1. Based on facts in David Brown, "IT Culture Creates Discord," *Canadian HR Reporter,* May 3, 2004.

2. "Canadian Workers Most Stressed," *Worklife* (14), pp. 8–10, 2002.

3. Michael R. Frone, "Work–Family Conflict and Employee" Psychiatric Disorders: The National Comorbidity Survey, *Journal of Applied Psychology,* December 2000, pp. 888–895.

4. Nini Yang et al., "Sources of Work–Family Conflict: A Sino–U.S. Comparison of the Effects of Work and Family Demands," *Academy of Management Journal,* February 2000, pp. 113–123.

5. Anne Fisher, "How to Prevent Violence at Work," *Fortune,* February 21, 2005, p. 42.

6. Dominic A. Infante, *Arguing Constructively* (Prospect Heights, Illinois: Waveland Press, 1992).

7. Ross Marowits, "Anti-bullying Legislation Shows its Teeth," Montreal, Quebec, *The Gazette,* June 12, 2006 p. A.8.

8. Survey reported in Jessica Guynn, "Bullying Behavior Affects Morale as Well as the Bottom Line," Knight Ridder syndicated story, November 2, 1998.

9. Ross, June 12, 2006.

10. Press release of the International Labour Organization, *Violence on the Job—A Global Problem* (Geneva: ILO, July 20,1998), www.us.ilo.org/news/prsrls/violence.html.

11. Canadian Wire, "Workplace a Hotbed for Violent Incidents," Winnipeg, Manitoba, *Winnipeg Free Press,* February 17, 2007, p. A.3.

12. Deborah Smith, "I/O Conference Examines Army Special Forces, Workplace Incivility," *Monitor on Psychology,* June 2003, p. 11.

13. Christine M. Pearson and Christine L. Porath, "On the Nature, Consequences and Remedies of Workplace Incivility: No Time for 'Nice'? Think Again." *Academy of Management Executive,* February 2005, pp. 7–30. The definition of *incivility* is from the same source, p. 7.

14. Kenneth Thomas, "Conflict and Conflict Management," in Marvin D. Dunnette (ed.), *Handbook of Industrial and Organizational Psychology* (Chicago: Rand McNally College Publishing, 1976), pp. 900–902.

15. Simon, cited in Mark Liu, "You Can Learn to Be Less Accommodating—If You Want To," Rochester, New York, *Democrat and Chronicle,* April 25, 1999, p. 1C.

16. Catherine Tinsley, "Models of Conflict Resolution in Japanese, German, and American Cultures," *Journal of Applied Psychology,* April 1998, p. 317.

17. Robert R. Blake and Jane S. Mouton, *The Managerial Grid III* (Houston: Gulf Publishing, 1985), p. 101.

18. The first three suggestions are from Connirae Andreas and Steve Andreas, *Heart of the Mind* (Moab, Utah: Real People Press, 1991).

19. Kenneth Kaye, *Workplace Wars and How to End Them: Turning Personal Conflicts into Productive Teamwork* (New York: AMACOM, 1994).

20. Mark Diener, "Mad Skills," *Entrepreneur,* April 2003, p. 79.

21. Joseph P. Folger, Marshall Scott Poole, and Randall K. Stutman, *Working Through Conflict: Strategies for Relationships, Groups, and Organizations,* 4th ed. (Reading, Mass.: Addison Wesley Longman Inc., 2001).

22. "Sexual Harassment Clauses," *Worklife Report,* Vol. 8 (3), 1991, pp. 4–6.

23. Human Resources Development Canada, *Information on Labour Standards, 12, Sexual Harassment* [online], www.info.load-otea.hrdc-drhc.ca/-lsweb/harassment.htm.

24. H. F. Schwind, H. Das, W. Werther, and K. Davis, *Canadian Human Resource Management,* 4th ed. (Toronto: McGraw-Hill Ryerson Canada, 1995).

25. Diane Crocker and Valery Kalemba, "The Incidence and Impact of Women's Experiences of Sexual Harassment in Canadian Workplaces," *Canadian Review of Sociology & Anthropology,* November 1999, pp. 541–559.

26. M. Jinenez, "Sexual Harassment at Work Prevalent in B.C., Poll Shows," *Vancouver Sun,* May 4, 1998, pp. A1–A2.

27. Crocker and Kalemba, "The Incidence and Impact of Women's Experiences of Sexual Harassment in Canadian Workplaces."

28. Theresa M. Glomb, Liberty J. Munson, and Charles L. Hulin, "Structural Equation Models of Sexual Harassment: Longitudinal Explorations and Cross-Sectional Generalizations," *Journal of Applied Psychology,* February 1999, pp. 14–28.

29. Crocker and Kalemba, "The Incidence and Impact of Women's Experiences of Sexual Harassment in Canadian Workplaces."

30. Kathleen Neville, *Corporate Attractions: An Inside Account of Sexual Harassment with the New Sexual Roles for Men and Women on the Job* (Reston, Va.: Acropolis Books, 1992); Joanne Cole, "Sexual Harassment: New Rules, New Behavior," *HRfocus,* March 1999, pp. 1, 14–15.

31. Lauren M. Bernardi, "Maintaining a Harassment-Free Workplace," *Canadian Manager,* Spring 1998, pp. 13–16.

Chapter 8

1. Bill Bradley, "Whatever the Score—Bounce Back," *Parade Magazine,* October 18, 1998, p. 6.

2. Joseph A. Raelin, *Creating Leaderful Organizations: How to Bring Out Leadership in Everyone* (San Francisco: Berrett-Koehler, 2003).

3. Shelley A. Kirkpatrick and Edwin A. Locke, "Leadership: Do Traits Matter?" *The Executive,* May 1991, pp. 26–27; Nathaniel Brandon, *Self-Esteem at Work: How Confident People Make Powerful Companies* (San Francisco: Jossey-Bass, 1998).

4. Dale E. Zand, *The Leadership Triad: Knowledge, Trust, and Power* (New York: Oxford University Press, 1997).

5. Reported in "Developing Trust Pays Off," *Managers Edge,* April 1999, p. 9.

6. Douglas R. May, Adrian Y. L. Chan, Timothy D. Hodges, and Bruce J. Avolio, "Developing the Moral Component of Authentic Leadership," *Organizational Dynamics,* no. 3, 2003, pp. 247–260.

7. Anthony Bianco, "The Rise of a Star," *Business Week,* December 21, 1998, p. 63.

8. Bruce J. Avolio, Jane M. Howell, and John J. Sosik, "A Funny Thing Happened on the Way to the Bottom Line: Humor as a Moderator of Leadership Style Effects," *Academy of Management Journal,* April 1999, pp. 219–227.

9. Zand, *The Leadership Triad,* p. 8.

10. Studies on this topic are reviewed in Timothy A. Judge, Amy Colbert, and Remus Ilies, "Intelligence and Leadership: A Quantitative Review and Test of Theoretical Propositions," *Journal of Applied Psychology,* June 2004, p. 548.

11. Bill Breen, "The Clear Leader," *Fast Company,* March 2005, pp. 65–67.

12. Daniel Goleman, "What Makes a Leader?" *Harvard Business Review,* November–December 1998, p. 92.

13. Robert A. Eckert, "Where Leadership Starts," *Harvard Business Review,* November 2001, pp. 53–61. The quote is from page 54.

14. Jay A. Conger, *The Charismatic Leader: Behind the Mystique of Exceptional Leadership* (San Francisco: Jossey-Bass, 1989).

15. Nelson Wyatt, "Sovereigntist and Federalist Quebecers Acknowledge Trudeau's Legacy in His Home Province," *Canadian Press,* September 29, 2000, www.canoe.ca/CNEWSTrudeauNews/000929_trudeauque-cp.html.

16. Suggestions 7, 9, and 10 are from Roger Dawson, *Secrets of Power Persuasion* (Upper Saddle River, NJ: Prentice Hall, 1992), pp. 181–183.

17. "Bring Out the Leader in Everyone," *Managing People at Work,* sample issue, 2000p. 4.

18. Jon R. Katzenbach and Douglas K. Smith, "The Discipline of Teams," *Harvard Business Review,* March–April 1993, p. 118.

19. "Bring Out the Leader in Everyone," p. 4.

20. "What It Takes to Be an Effective Team Leader," *Manager's Edge,* March 2000, p. 6.

21. Terri A. Scandura and Chester A. Schrieisheim, "Leader-Member Exchange and Supervisor Career Mentoring as Complementary Constructs in Leadership Research," *Academy of Management Journal,* December 1994, pp. 1588–1602; George Graen and J. F. Cashman, "A Role Making Model of Leadership in Formal Organizations: A Developmental Approach," in J. G. Hunt and L. L. Larson (eds.), *Leadership Frontiers* (Kent, Ohio: Kent State University Press, 1975), pp. 143–165.

22. Francis J. Yammarino, Alan J. Dubinsky, Lucette B. Comer, and Marvin A. Jolson, "Women and Transformational and Contingent Reward Leadership: A Multiple-Levels-of-Analysis Perspective," *Academy of Management Journal,* February 1997, pp. 205–222.

23. Jon R. Katzenbach and Jason A. Santamaria, "Firing Up the Front Line," *Harvard Business Review,* May–June 1999, pp. 116–117.

24. William D. Hitt, *The Model Leader: A Fully Functioning Person* (Columbus, Ohio: Battelle Press, 1993).

25. Cheryl Dahle, "Natural Leader," *Fast Company*, December 2000, p. 270.

26. Michael E. McGill and John W. Slocum, Jr., "A *Little* Leadership Please?" *Organizational Dynamics*, Winter 1998, p. 48.

27. Bill Breen, "Trickle-Up Leadership," *Fast Company*, November 2001, pp. 70–72.

Chapter 9

1. Bob Nelson, "Why Formal Recognition Programs Don't Work," *www.nelson-motivation.com*. Reprinted with permission.

2. Gerald Kushel, *Reaching the Peak Performance Zone: How to Motivate Yourself and Others to Excel* (New York: AMACOM, 1994), p. 66.

3. Hewitt News and Information, "Canadian Employers Struggle to Attract and Retain Employees," *Canadian Manager*, Fall 2006, 12–13.

4. Dr. Linda Duxbury and Dr. Chris Higgins, *The 2001 National Work-Life Conflict Study: Report One*, Health Canada, March 2002; Human Resources Development Canada, *Report of the Advisory Group on Working Time and the Distribution of Work* (Ottawa: 1994).

5. Research summarized in "One of These Seven Things Will Motivate Any Employee in the Company," *The Motivational Manager*, sample issue, 1998 (Lawrence Ragan Communications, Inc.).

6. Jennifer J. Laabs, "Targeted Rewards Jump-start Motivation," *Workforce*, February 1998, p. 90.

7. Fred Luthans and Alexander D. Stajkovic, "Reinforce for Performance: The Need to Go Beyond Pay and Even Rewards," *Academy of Management Executive*, May 1999, p. 52.

8. Steven Kerr, *Ultimate Rewards: What Really Motivates People to Achieve* (Boston: Harvard Business School Publishing, 1997).

9. "Simple Rewards Are Powerful Motivators," *HRfocus*, August 2001, p. 10; Jennifer Laabs, "Satisfy Them with More Than Money," *Workforce*, November 1998, p. 43.

10. Jennifer Laabs, "Satisfy Them with More Than Money," *Workforce*, November 1998, p. 43.

11. Andrew J. DuBrin, "Self-Perceived Technical Orientation and Attitudes Toward Being Flattered," *Psychological Reports*, vol. 96, 2005, pp. 852–854.

12. The original version of expectancy theory applied to work motivation is Victor Vroom, *Work and Motivation* (New York: Wiley, 1964).

13. Alexander D. Stajkovic and Fred Luthans, "Social Cognitive Theory and Self-Efficacy: Going Beyond Traditional Motivational and Behavioral Approaches," *Organizational Dynamics*, Spring 1998, p. 66.

14. Steve McShane, "Getting Emotional about Employee Motivation," *Currents* (published by McGraw-Hill), September 2004, p. 1; Amir Erez and Alice M. Isen, "The Influence of Positive Affect on the Components of Expectancy Motivation," *Journal of Applied Psychology*, December 2002, pp. 1055–1067.

Chapter 10

1. This is a true experience provided by the author, October 2004. Only the name of the faculty member has been changed.

2. Elwood F. Holton III, "New Employee Development Tactics: Perceived Availability, Helpfulness, and Relationship with Job Attitudes," *Journal of Business and Psychology*, Fall 2001, pp. 73–85.

3. Jeffrey Keller, "Associate with Positive People," A Supplement to the *Pryor Report*, 1994.

4. Keller, "Associate with Positive People."

5. Erin Pooley, "Canada's Best Workplaces: Fairness First," *Canadian Business Magazine*, April 23, 2007

6. Monica C. Higgins and Kathy E. Kram, "Reconceptualizing Mentoring at Work: A Developmental Network Perspective," *Academy of Management Review*, April 2001, pp. 264–288.

7. Erik J. Van Slyke and Bud Van Slyke, "Mentoring: A Results-Oriented Approach," *HRfocus*, February 1998, p. 14.

8. Anne Field, "No Time to Mentor? Do It Online," *BusinessWeek*, March 3, 2003, p. 126; Stephenie Overman, "Mentors without Borders," *HR Magazine*, March 2004, pp. 3–85.

9. Based mostly on Kathy E. Kram, *Mentoring at Work: Developmental Relationships in Organizational Life* (Glenview, Ill.: Scott, Foresman, 1985), pp. 22–39; Van Slyke and Van Slyke, "Mentoring," 1998, p. 14.

10. J. Lorinc, "The Mentor Gap," *Canadian Business*, September 1990, pp. 93–95.

11. Stephanie C. Payne and Ann H. Huffman, "A Longitudinal Examination of the Influence of Mentoring on Organizational Commitment and Turnover," *Academy of Management Journal*, February 2005, pp. 158–168.

12. Hal Rosenbluth and Diane McFerrin Peters, *Good Company: Caring as Fiercely as You Compete* (Reading, Mass.: Addison Wesley, 1998).

13. Donald Brooks, "Vertical Team Building Releases an Organization's Pent-Up Energy," *Northern Ontario Business*, October 1994.

14. Editors of *Managers Edge, The Successful Manager's Guide to Giving and Receiving Feedback* (Alexander, VA: Briefings Publishing Group, 2004), p. 14.

15. "Coach Your Employees to Success with This Plan," *Manager's Edge,* May 2000, p. 1.

16. "Coach with 'Could,' not 'Should,'" *Executive Strategies,* April 1998, p. 1.

17. Bruce Tulgan, "The Under-Management Epidemic," *HR Magazine,* October 2004, p. 119.

18. Cy Charney, "Self-Directed Peer Training in Teams," *Journal for Quality & Participation,* October/November 1996, pp. 34–37.

19. Ian Cunningham and Linda Honald, "Everyone Can Be a Coach," *HRMagazine,* June 1998, pp. 63–66.

20. *Career Track* seminar, How to Deal with Difficult People, 1995; Kenneth Kaye, *Workplace Wars and How to End Them: Turning Personal Conflicts into Productive Teamwork* (New York: AMACOM, 1994); "Tame the Best Within You: How to Cope with Mood Swings in Yourself and Others," *WorkingSMART,* April 1999, p. 1. Joann S. Lublin, "Feeling Unappreciated? You May Find Griping Makes Things Worse," *The Wall Street Journal,* June 5, 2003, p. B1; Jared Sandberg, "Staff 'Handfuls' and the Bosses Who Coddle Them," *The Wall Street Journal,* October 8, 2003, p. B1.

21. "How to Deal with 'Problem' Workers," *Positive Leadership,* sample issue, distributed 2001; Martien Eerhart, "Top 7 Ideas for Dealing with Difficult Employees," http://top7business.com/archives/personnel/050499.html.

22. John C. Maxwell, *Winning with People: Discover the People Principles That Work for You Every Time* (Nashville, TN: Nelson Books, 2004), pp. 1428–1429.

Chapter 11

1. "New Kid in the Cubicle Has a Tough Job," Knight Ridder syndicated story, February 10, 2002.

2. William L. Gardner III, "Lessons in Organizational Dramaturgy: The Art of Impression Management," *Organizational Dynamics,* Summer 1992, p. 45.

3. Jim Rucker and Jean Anna Sellers, "Changes in Business Etiquette," *Business Education Forum,* February 1998, p. 45.

4. Rucker and Sellers, "Changes in Business Etiquette," p. 45.

5. This section of the chapter is based on Annette Vincent and Melanie Meche, "It's Time to Teach Business Etiquette," *Business Education Forum,* October 1993, pp. 39–41; "Business Etiquette: Teaching Students the Unwritten Rules," *Keying In,* January 1996, pp. 1–8; Rucker and Sellers, "Changes in Business Etiquette," pp. 43–45; Letitia Baldrige, *The Executive Advantage* (Washington, DC: Georgetown Publishing House, 1999); "Changes in Business Etiquette,"

pp. 43–45; "Culture Shock?" *Entrepreneur,* May 1998, p. 46; Ann Perry, "Finer Points of the Meet and Eat," *Toronto Star,* http://www.thestar.com, January 2, 2004; Blanca Torres, "Good Dining Manners Can Help Bet a Bigger Slice of the Job Pie," *Baltimore Sun* story, April 5, 2005; Erin White, "The Jungle: Focus on Recruitment, Pay and Getting Ahead," *The Wall Street Journal,* November 2, 2004, p. B8. The quotes are from the same sources.

6. Carrie Patton, "Mind Your Messages," *Working Woman,* May 2000, p. 81.

7. "Disability Etiquette," *Human Resources Forum* (a supplement to *Management Review*), June 1997, p. 3; "Helping Today's Blind Children Become the Winners of Tomorrow," American Blind Children's Council (flyer), 2002.

8. "Hardball Office Politics," *WorkingSMART,* September 1993, p. 5.

9. Deb Koen, "Jittery About Networking? Know the Etiquette," Rochester, New York, *Democrat and Chronicle,* April 14, 2002, p. 4E.

10. Brian Hilliard and James Palmer, *Networking Like a Pro* (Atlanta, GA: Agito Consulting, 2003) p. 52.

11. Research reported in Laura Lippman, "The Age of Obsequiousness: Flattering Your Way up the Corporate Ladder," Baltimore, Md., *The Sun,* October 24, 1994.

12. Research reported in Jennifer Reingold, "Suck Up and Move Up," *Fast Company,* January 2005, p. 34.

13. Marshall Goldsmith, "All of Us Are Stuck on Suck-Ups," *Fast Company,* December 2003, p. 117.

14. Cited in Joy Davia, "Make No Mistake: Come Clean When You Make One," Rochester, New York, *Democrat and Chronicle,* February 20, 2005, p. 1E.

15. Shelia Murray Bethel, *Making a Difference* (New York: G. P. Putnam's Sons, 1989).

16. Gary M. Stern, "Small Slights Bring Big Problems," *Workforce,* August 2002, p. 17; Joann S. Lublin, "How to Stop the Snubs That Demoralize You and Your Colleagues," *The Wall Street Journal,* December 7, 2004, p. B1.

Chapter 12

1. Paul R. Timm, *Customer Service: Career Success Through Customer Satisfaction,* 2nd ed. (Prentice Hall, 2001), p. 8.

2. Anthony J. Rucci, Steven P. Kirn, and Richard T. Quinn, "The Employee-Customer-Profit Chain at Sears," *Harvard Business Review,* January–February 1998, pp. 82–97.

3. Barry M. Stow and Jerry Ross, "Stability in the Midst of Change: A Dispositional Approach to Job Attitudes," *Journal of Applied Psychology,* August 1985, p. 471.

4. Sue Shellenbarger, "Domino Effect: The Unintended Results of Telling Off Customer-Service Staff," *The Wall Street Journal,* February 5, 2004, p. D1.

5. Lance A. Bettencourt, Kevin P. Gwinner, and Matthew L. Meuter, "A Comparison of Attitude, Personality, and Knowledge Predictors of Service-Oriented Organizational Citizenship Behavior," *Journal of Applied Psychology,* February 2001, pp. 29–41.

6. Alex M. Susskind, K. Michele Kacmar, and Carl P. Borchgrevink, "Customer Service Providers' Attitudes Relating to Customer Service and Customer Satisfaction in the Customer-Server Exchange," *Journal of Applied Psychology,* February 2003, pp. 179–187.

7. Adrian J. Slywotzky and David J. Morrison, "Forget the Product: Focus on the Customer," *Leadership* (Newsletter of the American Management Association International), February 1999, p. 2.

8. "The Chairman of the Board Looks Back," *Fortune,* May 28, 2001, p. 70.

9. Richard B. Chase and Sriram Dasu, "Want to Perfect Your Company's Service? Use Behavioral Science," *Harvard Business Review,* June 2001, pp. 78–84.

10. Karl Abrecht, *The Only Thing That Matters* (New York: HarperCollins, 1992).

11. Susan Okula, "Customer Service: New Tools for a Timeless Idea," *Business Education Forum,* December 1998, p. 7; Robert F. Gault, "Managing Customer Satisfaction for Profit," *Management Review,* April 1993, p. 23.

12. Amanda C. Kooser, "Crowd Control," *Entrepreneur,* August 2003, pp. 33–34.

13. Adapted from "For Extraordinary Service," *The Customer Service Professional,* October 1997, p. 3.

14. D. J. Cran, "Towards the Validation of the Service Orientation Construct," *The Service Industries Journal,* vol. 14, 1994, p. 36.

15. Dot Yandle, "Helping Your Employees Give Customers What They Want," *Success Workshop* (A supplement to *Managers Edge*), November 1998, p. 1.

16. Dave Pace, Starbucks executive vice president of partner resources, quoted in *Workforce Management,* February 2005, p. 30

17. Michelle Conlin and Andrew Park, "Blogging with the Boss's Blessing," *BusinessWeek,* June 28, 2004, p. 100–102.

18. Daniel Akst, book review of *Hug Your Customers* by Jack Mitchell (Hyperion, 2003), appearing in *The Wall Street Journal,* November 14, 2003, p. W9.

19. Research cited in "Service Facts," *Customer Service Professional,* October 1997, p. 1.

20. Hwee Hoon Tan, Maw Der Foo, and Min Hui Kwek, "The Effects of Customer Personality Traits on the Display of Positive Emotions," *Academy of Management Journal,* April 2004, pp. 287–296.

21. Donna Deeprose, "Helping Employees Handle Difficult Customers," *Supervisory Management,* September 1991,

p. 6; Chip R. Bell and Ron Zemke, "Service Breakdown— The Road to Recovery," in *Service Wisdom: Creating and Maintaining the Customer Service Edge* (Minneapolis, Minn.: Lakewood Books, 1992).

22. Jan Norman, "Caring About Clients Helps Companies Handle Crises," Knight Ridder story, December 3, 2000, p. 1G.

23. Hal Hardy, "Five Steps to Pleasing Difficult, Demanding Customers," *First-Rate Customer Service,* No. 1, 2005, p. 1.

24. "Customer Problem Clinics," in *Making . . . Serving . . . Keeping Customers,* (Chicago: Dartnell Corp.).

25. Timm, *Customer Service,* p. 43.

26. Excerpted and paraphrased from Scott Hays, "Exceptional Customer Service Takes the 'Ritz' Touch," *Workforce,* January 1999, pp. 99–102; Updated slightly from "How to Turn Your Customer Service Department into a Team of Superheroes," *Executive Focus,* January 2004, p. 12.

Chapter 13

1. Gwendolyn Bounds, "Handyman Etiquette: Stay Calm, Avert Eyes," *The Wall Street Journal,* May 10, 2005, pp. B1, B4.

2. Linda K. Treviño and Katherine A. Nelson, *Managing Business Ethics: Straight Talk About How to Do It Right* (New York: Wiley, 1995), pp. 24–35; "Why Have a Code of Ethics?" *The Fact Finder,* January 1995, p. 3; Ralph Estes, *Tyranny of the Bottom Line: Why Corporations Make Good People Do Bad Things* (San Francisco: Berrett-Koehler, 1996).

3. John S. McClenahen, "Your Employees Know Better," *Industry Week,* March 1, 1999, Vol. 248, Issue 5, pp 12–14; Thomas M. Jones, "Ethical Decision Making by Individuals in Organizations: An Issue Contingent Model," *Academy of Management Review,* April 1991, p. 391.

4. Linda Kelbe Treviño, "Managing to Be Ethical: Debunking Five Business Ethics Myths," *Academy of Management Executive,* May 2004, pp. 69–72.

5. Data from Ethics Resource Center and Kronos Inc., reported in Sue Shellenbarger, "How and Why We Lie at the Office: From Pilfered Pens to Padded Accounts," *The Wall Street Journal,* March 24, 2005, p. D1.

6. Brian Sharp, "Reports of Unethical Job Behavior on the Increase," Gannett News Service, June 12, 2000.

7. Data reported in "McAfee Anti-Piracy Information," *http://www.networkassociates.com/us/antipiracy_policy. htm,* accessed May 25, 2005.

8. Bruce Nussbaum, "Can You Trust Anybody Anymore?" *BusinessWeek,* January 28, 2002, p. 32.

9. "O'Leary Admits Lying, Quits," Associated Press, December 15, 2001.

10. The concept of the game is from Karen Ireland, "The Ethics Game," *Personnel Journal*, March 1991, p. 74. The scenarios are original.

11. Joseph L. Badaracco, Jr., "The Discipline of Building Character," *Harvard Business Review*, March–April 1998, pp. 114–124.

12. Michael S. Josephson, "Does Character Still Count?" *USA Weekend*, September 23–25, 1994, p. 20.

13. Matthew McClearn, "A Snitch in Time," *Canadian Business*," December 29, 2003, www.canadianbusiness.com/shared/print.jsp?content = 20031229_57946_57946.

14. "Extolling the Virtues of Hot Lines," *Workforce*, June 1998, pp. 125–126; Daryl Koehn, "An Interview with William Griffin," *http://www.stthom.edu/cbes/griffin. html* (Accessed May 27, 2005).

15. Treviño and Nelson, *Managing Business Ethics*, pp. 71–75.

16. Daniel J. Brass, Kenneth D. Butterfield, and Bruce C. Skaggs, "Relationships and Unethical Behavior: A Social Network Perspective," *Academy of Management Review*, January 1998, pp. 14–31.

Chapter 14

1. Robert Boice, *Procrastination and Blocking: A Novel, Practical Approach* (Westport, CT: Greenwood Publishing Group, 1996); Data reported in Jared Sandberg, "Fans of Procrastination Say It Boosts Control, Self-Esteem," *The Wall Street Journal*, February 9, 2005, p. B1.

2. Maia Szalavitz, "Stand & Deliver," *Psychology Today*, July/August 2003, p. 50.

3. The term *WIFO* has been contributed by Shale Paul, as cited in "Tips to Keep Procrastination Under Control," Gannett News Service syndicated story, November 9, 1998.

4. Dru Scott, *How to Put More Time in Your Life* (New York: New American Library, 1980), p. 1.

5. "Don't Procrastinate," *Practical Supervision*, undated sample issue, p. 7.

6. Cited in "The Voices in Your Head," *Entrepreneur*, July 2000, pp. 105–107.

7. Curtis Sittenfeld, "She's a Paper Tiger," *Fast Company*, August 2002, p. 34.

8. Meni Koslowsky and Abraham Sagie, "Correlates of Employee Lateness: Some Theoretical Considerations," *Journal of Applied Psychology*, February 1997, pp. 79–88.

9. Anne Fisher, "The Rebalancing Act," *Fortune*, October 6, 2003, p. 110; Andrea Kay, "Avoid 'Traps' to Gain the Free Time You Need," Gannet News Service, January 10, 2005.

10. Mildred L. Culp, "Working Productively with Workaholics While Minimizing Legal Risks," Passage Media syndicated story, 1997.

11. Cited in Jared Sandberg, "To-Do Lists Can Take More Time than Doing, But That Isn't the Point," *The Wall Street Journal*, September 8, 2004, p. B1.

12. Joshua S. Rubinstein, David E Meyer, and Jeffrey E. Evans, "Executive Control of Cognitive Processes in Task Switching," *Journal of Experimental Psychology—Human Perception and Performance*, Vol. 26, January 2000, No. 4, pp. 763–769.

13. Anne Fisher, "Get Organized at Work—Painlessly," *Fortune*, January 10, 2005, p. 30.

14. Amy Dunkin, "Saying 'Adios' to the Office," *Business Week*, October 12, 1998, p. 153; Heather Page, "Remote Control," *Entrepreneur*, October 1998, p. 148; Jenny C. McCune, "Telecommuting Revisited," *Management Review*, February 1998, p. 14; E. Jeffrey Hill, Brent C. Miller, Sara P. Weiner, and Joe Colihan, "Influences of the Virtual Office on Aspects of Work/Life Balance," *Personnel Psychology*, Autumn 1998, pp. 667–683.

15. John J. Fried, "Be a Sharp Web Detective," Knight Ridder syndicated story, June 27, 1999.

16. Richard S. DeFrank and John M. Ivancevich, "Stress on the Job: An Executive Update," *Academy of Management Executive*, August 1998, pp. 55–56.

17. Shelly E. Taylor et al., "Biobehavioral Responses to Stress in Females: Tend-and-Befriend, not Fight-or-Flight," *Psychological Review*, 107, 2000, pp. 411–429.

18. Jeffrey R. Edwards, "A Cybernetic Theory of Stress, Coping, and Well-Being in Organizations," *Academy of Management Review*, April 1992, p. 248.

19. *British Medical Journal* study reported in "Trop de Stress au Travail Double le Risque de Mourir d'une Crise de Coeur," *Journal de Montréal*, 18 octobre, 2002, p. 7.

20. Gillian E. Hardy, David Woods, and Toby D. Wall, "The Impact of Psychological Distress on Absence from Work," *Journal of Applied Psychology*, April 2003, pp. 306–314.

21. Steve M. Jex, *Stress and Job Performance: Theory, Research, and Implications for Managerial Practice* (Thousands Oaks, Calif.: Sage, 1998).

22. Quoted in "An Ounce of Prevention Beats Burnout," *HRfocus*, June 1999, p. 1.

23. Christina Maslach, *The Truth About Burnout* (San Francisco: Jossey-Bass, 1997). See also Dirk van Dierendonck, Wilmar B. Schaufeli, and Bram P. Buunk, "The Evaluation of an Individual Burnout Intervention Program: The Role of Equity and Social Support," Journal of Applied Psychology, June 1998, pp. 393–407.

24. M. Afalur Rahim, "Relationships of Stress, Locus of Control, and Social Support to Psychiatric Symptoms and Propensity to Leave a Job: A Field Study with Managers," *Journal of Business and Psychology*, Winter 1997, p. 159.

25. Steve M. Jex and Paul D. Bliese, "Efficacy Beliefs as a Moderator of the Impact of Work-Related Stressors: A Multilevel Study," *Journal of Applied Psychology*, June 1999, pp. 349–361; Steve M. Jex, Paul O. Bliese, Sheri Buzell, and Jessica Primeau, "The Impact of Self-Efficacy on Stressor-Strain Relations: Coping Style as an Explanatory Mechanism," *Journal of Applied Psychology*, June 2001, pp. 401–409.

26. John Schaubroeck and Deryl E. Merrit, "Divergent Effects of Job Control on Coping with Work Stressors: The Key Role of Self-Efficacy," *Academy of Management Journal*, June 1997, p. 750.

27. Jeffrey R. Edwards and A. J. Baglioni, Jr., "Relationships Between Type A Behavior Pattern and Mental and Physical Symptoms: A Comparison of Global and Component Measures," *Journal of Applied Psychology*, April 1991, p. 276.

28. Jeffrey R. Edwards and A. J. Baglioni, Jr., "Relationships between Type A Behavior Pattern and Mental and Physical Symptoms: A Comparison of Global and Component Measures," *Journal of Applied Psychology*, April 1991, p. 276; related research reported in Etienne Benson, "Hostility Is among Best Predictors of Heart Disease in Men," *Monitor on Psychology*, January 2003, p. 15.

29. Peter Y. Chen and Paul E. Spector, "Negative Affectivity as the Underlying Cause of Correlations Between Stressors and Strains," *Journal of Applied Psychology*, June 1991, p. 398.

30. Dr. Linda Druxbury and Dr. Chris Higgins, *Work–Life Conflict in Canada in the New Millennium: A Status Report*, Healthy Communities Division, Health Canada, October 2003.

31. Dr. Chris Higgins and Dr. Linda Duxbury, Who is at Risk? Predictors of Work-Life Conflict: Report Four, 2005, Public Health Agency of Canada http://www.phac-aspc.gc.ca/publicat/work-travail/report4/index.html.

32. William Atkinson, "Causes of Workplace Stress," *HR Magazine*, December 2000, p. 107; Michele Conlin, "Is Your Office Killing You?" *Business Week*, June 5, 2000, pp. 114–128.

33. Canadian Centre for Occupational Health and Safety, "OSH Answers: Carpal Tunnel Syndrome," www.ccohs.ca/oshanswers/diseases/carpal.html?print, downloaded May 6, 2004.

34. DeFrank and Ivancevich, "Stress on the Job," pp. 56–57.

35. Richard Corliss, "The Power of Yoga," *Time*, April 23, 2001, pp. 54–62; Stacy Forster, "Companies Say Yoga Isn't a Stretch," *The Wall Street Journal* October 14, 2003, p. D4.

36. Harriet Johnson Brackey, "Snoozing Studies Alarm Experts," Knight Ridder syndicated story, July 6, 1998; Donald J. McNerney, "Napping at Work: You Snooze, You Win!" *HRfocus*, March 1995, p. 3.

37. Bruce Cyer, Rolin McCraty, and Doc Childre, "Pulling the Plug On Stress," *Harvard Business Review*, July 2003, pp. 102–107; *http://www.HeartMath.com*, 2003.

Chapter 15

1. Joann S. Lublin, "Job-Hunt Workshops Can Boost Confidence of Grads Seeking Work," *The Wall Street Journal*, February 1, 2005. p. B1.

2. "CEOs Speak Out: What Is Needed to Work in Today's Ever-changing Business World," *Keying In*, November 1996, pp. 1–2; Brien N. Smith, Carolee Jones, and Judy Lane, "Employers' Perceptions of Work Skills," *Business Education Forum*, April 1997; Claudio Fernandez-Araoz, "Hiring Without Firing," *Harvard Business Review*, July–August 1999, p. 113.

3. "Kat & Dale Talk Jobs," King Features Syndicate, April 14, 2002.

4. Edward A. Robinson, "Beware—Job Seekers Have No Secrets," *Fortune*, December 29, 1997, p. 285.

5. Erin Pooley, "Careers: Life After Death," *Canadian Business Magazine*, March 13, 2006.

6. Peg Thomas et al., "Resume Characteristics as Predictors as an Invitation to Interview," *Journal of Business and Psychology*, Spring 1999, pp. 339–356.

7. Updated June 2005, from Carol Kleiman, "Key Words Bosses Seek When Scanning Résumés," *Chicago Tribune* syndicated story, October 27, 1997.

8. Jim Pawlak, "Keep Job Application Cover Letter Short," *detnews.com*, April 15, 2005.

9. Linda Thornburg, "Computer-Assisted Interviewing Shortens Hiring Cycle," *HRMagazine*, February 1998, pp. 73–79.

10. Louis Lavelle, "Résumés: Beware of Getting 'Creative,'" *BusinessWeek*, October 22, 2001, p. 134E6.

11. Anne Field, "Coach, Help Me Out with This Interview," *Business Week*, October 22, 2001, p. 134E2.

12. Hugh P. Gunz, R. Michael Jalland, and Martin G. Evans, "New Strategy, Wrong Managers? What You Need to Know About Career Streams," *Academy of Management Executive*, May 1998, p. 22.

13. Such is the theme of James R. Lucas, *The Passionate Organization: Igniting the Fire of Employee Commitment* (New York: AMACOM, 1999).

14. Richard Boyatzis, Annie McKee, and Daniel Goleman, "Reawakening Your Passion for Work," *Harvard Business Review*, April 2002, pp. 86–94.

15. Scott E. Seibert, Maria L. Kraimer, and J. Michael Crant, "What Do Proactive People Do? A Longitudinal Model Linking Proactive Personality and Career Success," *Personnel Psychology*, Winter 2001, pp. 845–874; Seibert,

Crant, and Kraimer, "Proactive Personality and Career Success," *Journal of Applied Psychology,* June 1999, pp. 416–427.

16. Cited in Cheryl Dahle, "Showing Your Worth Without Showing Off," *nytimes.com,* September 19, 2004; *http://www.bragbetter.com.*

17. Philip L. Hunsaker, "Projecting the Appropriate Image," *Supervisory Management,* May 1989, p. 26.

18. Quoted in Anne Field, "What Is Business Casual?" *BusinessWeek,* October 20, 2000, pp. 180–190.

19. "Taking Charge in a Temp World," *Fortune,* October 21, 1998, pp. 247–248.

20. Jim Loehr and Tony Schwartz, "The Making of the Corporate Athlete," *Harvard Business Review,* January 2001, pp. 120–128.

21. Anne Fisher, "How to Network—and Enjoy It," *Fortune,* April 4, 2005, p. 38.

22. Quoted in "Network Your Way Up," *WorkingSMART,* February 1997, p. 4.

23. Daniel L. Cable and Timothy A. Judge, "Interviewers' Perceptions of Person–Organization Fit and Organizational Selection Decisions," *Journal of Applied Psychology,* August 1997, pp. 546–561.

24. Amy L. Kristof-Brown, Ryan D. Zimmerman, and Erin C. Johnson, "Consequences of Individuals' Fit at Work: A Meta-Analysis of Person-Job, Person-Organization, Person-Group, and Person-Supervisor Fit," *Personnel Psychology,* Summer 2005, pp. 281–342.

25. From *Industry Week's* CEO of the year profile, as quoted in *Executive Leadership,* March 2001, p. 1.

26. David Wessel, "The Future of Jobs: New Ones Arise, Wage Gap Widens, "*The Wall Street Journal,*" April 2, 2004; Peter Svensson, "Hands-On Jobs May Be the Safest," Associated Press, July 9, 2004.

Index

Note: Entries for tables are followed by "*t*," entries for figures are followed by "*f*," and entries for notes are followed by an "*n*."